P9-DJV-898

Aviation Consumer Used Aircraft Guide

Expanded 3rd Edition

by Belvoir Publications, Inc.

TAB Books
Division of McGraw-Hill

New York San Francisco Washington, D.C. Auckland Bogotá
Caracas Lisbon London Madrid Mexico City Milan
Montreal New Delhi San Juan Singapore
Sydney Tokyo Toronto

© 1989 by **Belvoir Publications**.
Earlier editions © 1981, 1985, by Belvoir Publications.
TAB Books is a division of McGraw-Hill, Inc.

Printed in the United States of America. All rights reserved. The publisher takes no responsibility for the use of any of the materials or methods described in this book, nor for the products thereof.

pbk   9 10 11 12 13 14 15 16 KGP/KGP 9 9 8 7

Library of Congress Cataloging-in-Publication Data

Aviation consumer used aircraft guide / by Belvoir Publications.—
  Expanded 3rd ed.
      p.   cm.
    "Adapted from regular monthly issues of the Aviation consumer"-
-Introd.
    Includes index.
    ISBN 0-8306-2441-4 (pbk.)
    1. Used aircraft—Purchasing.   I. Belvoir Publications.
II. Aviation consumer.   III. Title: Used aircraft guide.
TL671.A95   1989
629.133'340422'029—dc19   89-4050
                                                     CIP

Contents

Twin-Engine Piston

Foreword

As you read this third edition of the Used Aircraft Guide, please remember this: The used aircraft sales market is in some ways identical to an actual aircraft. The market goes up and down, encounters turbulence and reacts to input from pilots; and like the weather, the market can be very unpredictable.

Please understand that every effort has been made to update crucial information, especially used aircraft prices. But the market cannot be controlled, nor can the aviation businesses that service the market be controlled. Both market and businesses respond to the environment and are inherently unpredictable. Therefore, prices, businesses, names, addresses and telephone numbers might have changed since published.

Also, aircraft are subject to continual review by the manufacturers, who issue service bulletins; the technicians, who submit service difficulty reports to the FAA; the NTSB, who investigates accidents; and the FAA, who issues airworthiness directives. Seek out these resources—especially service bulletins, service difficulty reports and airworthiness directives—to obtain up-to-date information when making a buying decision.

Introduction

This is the third edition of the Used Aircraft Guide. We published the first one in 1981 and a second one in 1985.

This time we have analyzed, in depth, squadrons of different models, and in some cases updated articles on popular aircraft included in the previous editions. Since we figure the safety record of each make and model is of such high concern among potential buyers, we have included an introductory section that analyzes the accident rates of two major classes of aircraft: the single-engine retractables and the light twins. And we have explored the always provocative topic—are twins or singles safer?

As before, in the tradition of *The Aviation Consumer*, we have let the facts fall as they may, and spared no model complete details about any nasty faults that may jeopardize either the flying safety of the readers or their pocketbooks, in their quest for the "perfect plane." We have gone to some effort to dig out the real-world strengths and weaknesses of each aircraft. To do this we have scoured National Transportation Safety Board accident records and Federal Aviation Administration Service Difficulty Reports. But perhaps most importantly, we have also secured the comments of owners who have been through good and bad with each aircraft.

We think the reader will find nuggets of information here that are in very short supply elsewhere. Along with the safety record and maintenance history of each aircraft, we have provided what we believe is a unique feature: graphs of their resale value. This allows the buyer to calculate whether his purchase is likely to shrink horribly in value through the years, or actually enhance his equity. For a court of last resort on information about the various models, we have listed the various owner associations. Note that the prices we have provided were the latest we could obtain, for the most part 1988 figures—but these change with the flux and flow of the economy and inflation. The articles in this volume are adapted from regular monthly issues of *The Aviation Consumer* and were written by its editors.

SAFETY ROUNDUPS

Single-Engine Retract-ables: Which are the Safest?

The strutted Cessna Skylane RG, a relative newcomer, leads the pack with the lowest fatal accident rate of them all.

When's the last time you heard a new plane buyer ask the salesman, "What are the accident and fatality rates of this Arrow compared to a Skylane RG?" Probably never. Human beings seem almost programmed not to think about nasty things like airplane accidents. Oh, sure, most pilots give lip service to safe piloting techniques, and some even practice them. But few ever stop to think that the design of the airplane they're flying may determine whether that day's flight ends safely.

Most pilots think about planes the way they think about cars: safety-wise, there's not much difference between a Ford and a Chevy, so there's probably not much difference between a Cessna and a Beech, either. But the accident rate of general aviation aircraft, on a passenger-mile basis, is at least ten times higher than that of passenger cars. And various types of aircraft have accident rates that differ widely—sometimes by as much as three or four hundred percent. In some cases, it turns out, there's a very big difference indeed between a Cessna and a Beechcraft.

There's much debate about the safety merits of various types of aircraft. Which is safer, a high-wing or a low-wing? Twins or singles? Does the low stall speed of a Cessna make it safer than say a Mooney? Aircraft manufacturers like to brag

make it safer than, say, a Mooney? Aircraft manufacturers like to brag about safety advances like simplified fuel systems, stronger structures, fool-proof stall traits and so forth, and the aviation press is quick to praise those features that theoretically improve safety.

The Bottom Line

But the bottom line of all this debate is one simple question: How often does each type of aircraft crash, and how likely are the occupants to be killed? Theoretical safety is born in the minds of industry engineers and FAA bureaucrats, but real safety is reflected only in cold, hard accident statistics.

Unfortunately, such statistics simply don't exist for the most part. Neither the FAA nor the NTSB assembles accident rate data on a regular basis. In 1979, the NTSB published a special study of accident rates by aircraft type covering the years 1972-76. (Ironically, *The Aviation Consumer* published its own study, based on essentially the same data, at about the same time). But except for that one-time study, the government simply does not have any accident rate data for individual aircraft types. The plane buyer who asks his salesman about accident rates will get a blank stare in return—not because the salesman is trying to

hide something, but because good numbers simply do not exist.

Filling the Vacuum

We have attempted to fill this statistical vacuum. Using raw data supplied by the NTSB and FAA (and in some cases estimated or projected, when no such data exists) we have calculated accident rates for seventeen popular aircraft types. The numbers show conclusively that not all airplanes are created equal—not by a long shot. If you fly the lowest-ranking aircraft on our list, you are nearly four times more likely to have a fatal accident than if you fly the highest.

To establish a *rate* of accidents, it's necessary to know two things; first, the number of accidents; and second, a measure of the exposure to accident risk in terms of flight hours, aircraft in the field, or some other measure. The standard industry measure of exposure is flight hours, with rates normally expressed in terms of accidents per 100,000 flight hours.

Digging out the number of accidents is no problem. The NTSB keeps careful records of all accidents, and its computer can sort them according to types. The NTSB also published for several years an annual document called "Listing of aircraft accidents/incidents by make and model." We culled through these lists for the years 1977-79, the last years the lists were published, and obtained individual computer printouts of accidents by type for 1980 and

1981. So our numbers for fatal accidents are virtually bulletproof, coming directly from NTSB files. Our figures of total accidents may have slight room for error, due to the grey area between what is classified as an accident and what's labeled an incident. We feel confident that our numbers for total accidents are accurate to within a percent or two, barring some NTSB computer sorting error in the printouts supplied to us.

Unfortunately, the hours-flown numbers we used to measure exposure are much less certain. Most of the numbers come from the FAA, which sends out questionnaires to a random sampling of aircraft owners, and from that projects a fleet total for various aircraft types. At best, the hours-flown numbers are estimates, albeit U.S. Government approved ones.

The Mooney 201 has only a fair to middling accident rate, but that is quite a bit better than the poor rate of the turbocharged 231 in total and fatal accidents.

Even more unfortunately, the FAA does a lousy job of sorting out the various aircraft types. Until 1977, the FAA hours-flown data was very detailed, and with enough hours spent hunched over squinting at computer printouts, it was possible to come up with some decent figures. (That's just what one of out bleary-eyed reporters did for the last study we did, covering the years 1972-1976).

Change in Procedures
But in 1977, the FAA changed its data-gathering procedures. Since then, hours-flown numbers are published only for very broad categories. For example, after 1976,

the FAA publishes only one annual hours-flown number for all Piper PA-28s. That grouping happens to include everything from a primary trainer (the Cherokee 140) to a retractable turbocharged T-tailed business aircraft (the Turbo Arrow). For our purposes, these numbers are essentially useless. Likewise, the latest FAA hours-flown numbers fail to distinguish between, for example, the 185-hp 1947 Model 35 Bonanza and the 285-hp 1982 V35B model built 35 years later; the Cessna Cardinal and Cardinal RG, not to mention the Skylane and Skylane RG or the 210 and the P210.

We complained to the FAA about these problems back in 1979, while researching our first accident-rate study, and were promised that things would improve shortly. They never did. As a result, we were forced to estimate hours flown for certain aircraft types in our listing. This was done mostly by analyzing fleet totals and projecting trends from the 1972-76 period, when good data was available.

For example, the FAA has hours-flown data for the Cessna 177 series, which includes both the retractable and straight-leg Cardinal. We determined that the RG made up 32 percent of the total 177 fleet. Therefore we assumed the

Accident Rate Summary 1972-1981

Aircraft	Hours Flown	Total Accidents	Total Rate	1972-1976 Total Rate	Fatal Accidents	Fatal Rate	1972-1976 Fatal Rate
Beech 24 Sierra	774,000	94	12.1	15.2	24	3.1	4.0
Beech 33 Debonair/Bonanza	2,567,000	118	4.6	4.6	35	1.4	1.0
Beech V-tail Bonanza (35-P35)	5,989,000*	638	10.7	11.8	199	3.3	3.6
Beech V-tail Bonanza (S35-V35B)	3,808,000*	221	5.8	7.0	66	1.7	2.0
Beech 36 Bonanza	1,905,000	98	5.1	4.7	28	1.5	1.7
Bellanca 17-30/31 Viking	1,413,000	156	11.0	16.8	39	2.8	4.2
Cessna 177 Cardinal RG	1,450,000*	128	7.8	8.2	21	1.5	1.6
Cessna R-182 Skylane RG	533,000*	37	6.9	—	4	0.8	—
Cessna 210	7,461,000	843	11.3	15.0	171	2.3	3.1
Cessna P210	255,000*	25	9.8	—	4	1.6	—
Mooney M-20B-G	6,266,000	599	9.6	11.3	137	2.2	2.4
Mooney M20J (201)	630,000*	41	6.5	—	15	2.4	—
Mooney M-20K (231)	189,000*	21	11.1	—	6	3.2	—
Piper PA-24 Comanche	4,660,000	698	15.0	16.8	133	2.9	2.9
Piper PA-28R Arrow series	6,984,000*	583	8.3	11.3	149	2.1	3.2
Piper PA-32R Lance/ Saratoga	1,191,000	127	10.7	14.1	39	3.3	5.9
Rockwell 112/114	1,413,000	156	11.0	—	39	2.8	—

* Hours-flown data based on projections from FAA data.

RG to have flown 32 percent of the total hours flown by the 177 fleet. Multiplying the FAA figure for the total 177 fleet by 0.32, we arrived at an estimate for RG hours flown.

We also double-checked our estimates by dividing them by the known fleet totals to get an average number of hours flown each year by each airplane. GAMA and FAA figures show that the average general-aviation aircraft flies between 150 and 200 hours per year. If our estimated number didn't yield a per-plane average in this range, we went back to the drawing board. In almost every case, the numbers agreed reasonably well.

How Accurate?

How accurate are our hours-flown numbers? We'd estimate they're within 20 percent. That means our final accident rates are also accurate to within about 20 percent. Readers should not panic and immediately trade in their old Mooney (fatal accident rate 2.2 per 100,000 flight hours) for an Arrow (2.1 per 100,000 hours) for the sake of the wife and kids. Comparing two planes, we wouldn't worry about a difference less than 50 percent or so. There's that much statistical ''slop'' in the numbers.

Because of this inherent imprecision, we have rounded off the accident rate numbers to the nearest tenth. Greater mathematical precision is possible from the raw data, but we feel that level of precision is not justified.

The Standings

Here's how the 17 most popular single-engine retractables stack up for the period 1972 through 1981. The numbers listed are accidents per 100,000 flight hours, the standard industry yardstick for measuring accident rates.

Cessna Skylane RG

The retractable version of Cessna's familiar Skylane didn't debut until 1978, too late for it to appear in our earlier study that covered the years 1972-1976. But the newcomer swept to the top of the chart with a

Fatal Accident Rates 1972-1981		Total Accident Rates 1972-1981	
Aircraft	Fatal Accident Rate*	Aircraft	Total Accident Rate*
1. Cessna Skylane RG	0.8	1. Beech 33 Bonanza/ Debonair	4.6
2. Beech 33 Bonanza/ Debonair	1.4	2. Beech 36 Bonanza	5.1
3. Cessna Cardinal RG	1.5	3. Beech V-tail Bonanza (S35-V35B)	5.8
4. Beech 36 Bonanza	1.5	4. Rockwell 112/114	6.5
5. Cessna P210	1.6	5. Mooney 201	6.5
6. Beech V-tail Bonanza (S35-V35B)	1.7	6. Cessna Skylane RG	6.9
7. Rockwell 112/114	1.8	7. Cessna Cardinal RG	7.8
8. Piper PA-28R Arrow	2.1	8. Piper PA-28R Arrow	8.3
9. Mooney M-20B-G	2.2	9. Mooney M-20B-G	9.6
10. Cessna 210	2.3	10. Cessna P210	9.8
11. Mooney 201	2.4	11. Beech V-tail Bonanza (35-P35)	10.7
12. Bellanca Viking	2.7	12. Piper PA-32R Lance/ Saratoga	10.7
13. Piper PA-24 Comanche	2.9	13. Bellanca Viking	11.0
14. Beech 24 Sierra	3.1	14. Mooney 231	11.1
15. Mooney 231	3.2	15. Cessna 210	11.3
16. Piper Lance/Saratoga	3.3	16. Beech 24 Sierra	12.1
17. Beech V-tail Bonanza (35-P35)	3.3	17. Piper PA-24 Comanche	15.0
*Fatal accidents per 100,000 hours		*Accidents per 100,000 hours	

sterling fatal accident rate of just 0.75 per 100,000 flight hours—nearly twice as good as the next best airplane. The Skylane RG's low fatal rate may be partly a statistical anomaly, since it has accumulated fewer hours than most of the other aircraft in the chart. But the undeniable fact is that NTSB records show only four fatal accidents in five years in a fleet of nearly 2,000 airplanes. That's a remarkable record.

The RG's total accident rate is not the best of the lot, but is still a low 6.9 per 100,000 hours. What's remarkable is the RG's low percentage of fatal accidents: four out of 37, or eleven percent. That's the lowest of any aircraft in the chart.

Our previous studies showed that, generally speaking, high-wing Cessnas have the best accident records, and the Skylane RG seems to carry on that trend. Apparently Cessna's design philosophy of low stall speed, docile stall characteristics, rock-solid handling qualities and strut-braced wings pays big safety dividends.

Cessna Cardinal RG

Cessna's retractable Cardinal also finished high in the pack with a fatal rate of 1.5 and an overall acci-

dent rating of 7.8. That's good for third place in fatals and seventh overall. Both numbers are slightly better than those for the 1972-76 period. (In fact, virtually every airplane on the list has improved its safety record substantially compared to our earlier 1972-76 study. This reflects the general trend of improving safety over the past decade; NTSB figures show a fatal accident rate for all of general aviation of 1.7 in 1983, compared to 2.7 in 1972).

Cessna 210

The big six-place 210 is the one Cessna that doesn't have an excellent safety record. In fact, the unpressurized C210 and T210 rank a dismal tenth out of 17 in fatal accidents and a mediocre 15th overall. Why the poor showing?

In an attempt to explain the 210's high accident rate, we closely examined all 210 accidents for the years 1975 and 1976 (about the middle of the 1972-1981 period for the entire study. Conclusion: Engine stoppage is the single most common cause of 210 accidents during those years (58 out of 181 accidents). About half the engine failures were mechanical problems—four crankshaft failures, for example—but the rest were fuel exhaustion or starvation. The notorious vapor lock syndrome likely played a role in the 210's high accident rate; a 1980 NTSB document cites 87 fuel starvation accidents in 200 series Cessnas through 1978, and suggests that many may be the result of vapor lock.

In-flight Breakups

Another factor may be in-flight breakups. Of the 171 fatal 210 accidents recorded during our sample period, 24 were in-flight breakups—about one in seven.

Surprisingly, the pressurized P210, widely known for numerous powerplant problems, has a good safety record in its first four years on the marketplace. Fatal rate was 1.6, number five in the rankings, and overall accident rate was 9.8, in the middle of the pack. Both are better than the standard 210's numbers.

Two cautions before we begin cheering, however: first, the P210 had only four years of exposure and 255,000 flight hours of exposure during the study period —among the lowest on our list. Therefore, the statistical validity of the number is also comparatively low. With only four fatal accidents, one more or less fatal P210 crash would have changed its rate by 20 percent. Secondly, we're aware of at least three P210 fatals in 1982 and 1983, just after the period of our study. As time goes on, it appears, the P210's fatal rate is rising from its initial very low level.

The V-tail Bonanzas

We divided the venerable Beech 35 into two categories, since it seems unwise to group a 37-year old 185-hp "straight 35" Bonanza with thin wing skins and an antiquated fuel system and instrument panel with a 3400-lb 285-hp 1982 V35B with radar and RNAV. A natural cutoff point seemed to lie between the 1963 P35 and the 1964 S35. With the S35 came the change to the 285-hp engine and a 175-pound gross weight increase, essentially identical to the last model V35B configuration in production.

How safe is the Bonanza? It all depends on which model you're talking about. Late models like the three shown here all show up well in our statistics, sweeping the top three positions for total accident rates and three of the top six places in fatality rates. Straight-tail 33 (rear) is best of the trio.

We were not surprised to find the huge difference in the accident rates of the 35-P35 and S35-V35B models, The answer to the question, "How safe is the V-tail?" immediately begs a second question: "Are you talking about an old one or a new one?"

Old is Awful

The old V-tails have the worst fatal accident rate of any of the 17 single-engine retractables we measured. At 3.3 fatal accidents per 100,000 hours, the 35-P35 series was statistically four times more likely to have a fatal crash than the top-ranked skylane RG, and nearly twice as likely as the newer V-tails. Overall accident rate was 11th out of the 17 planes, and still nearly twice as bad as the newer Bonanzas.

Why the terrible safety record of the old V-tails? Statistics don't tell why, of course, but the old Bonanzas have several safety problems that may contribute to their high accident rate. Among them:

• In-flight breakups. The well-known V-tail breakup syndrome applies mostly (although by no means exclusively) to the older aircraft. Of the 230-odd V-tail breakups, roughly 90 percent have involved the 35-P35 models. The original 1947 35 in particular has a horrendous breakup count—about 75 in all—due primarily to the very thin wing skin, absence of a shear web on the outer portion of the wing, and very light pitch forces in that model. Of the 199 fatal accidents accumulated by the "old" V-tails during our study period, we estimate that about 50 were in-flight breakups.

• Fuel sloshing. Most old Bonanzas were built without baffles in the fuel tanks to prevent sloshing in turbulence, uncoordinated flight or during turning takeoffs. By 1971, the FAA had identified 16 accidents caused by fuel sloshing, and an AD was issued. Baffles were made available for retrofit, but few of the old Bonanzas have them.

• Fuel mismanagement. A 1964 CAB report on fuel mismanagement showed that the Bonanza had the second highest rate of fuel mismanagement accidents of any light aircraft that year. A later

NTSB study covering the years 1965-69 rates the Bonanza as having the highest incidence of fuel starvation among lightplanes. This is probably the result of the poor placement of the fuel selector valve in the older Bonanzas (on the cockpit floor, out of sight), which encourages some pilots to switch tanks by feel. Selector detents are poorly defined in some old models, and the fuel gauging systems are not the best.

• Stall/spin accidents. According to an earlier *Aviation Consumer* study covering the years 1965-1973, the Bonanza had the highest stall/spin accident rate of any modern light aircraft still in production at that time. The Bonanza's stall/spin rate was triple that of the Cessna 210's in the NTSB study. (That study covered all Bonanzas, but in those days the vast majority of V-tails flying were 35-P35 models).

By contrast, the late-model 285-hp V-tails have an excellent safety record. Fatal accident rate was 1.6 per 100,000 hours, sixth best among the 17 planes in the survey, while overall accident rate was 5.8, third best of the group.

Straight-tail Bonanzas

The 33 and 36 model Bonanzas rank in the top four in terms of fatality rates, and first and second in the total accident standings. The late-model V-tail ranks third in overall accidents, making it a clean one-two-three sweep for Beech. The straight-tail airplanes virtually never break up in flight (about 24 times less often than the V-tails, according to an *Aviation Consumer* study) and most have improved fuel systems. The Straight-tail airplanes also have wider center-of-gravity envelopes than the V-tails, heavier pitch forces and improved yaw stability. All of these factors provide improved stability and handling qualities.

The Also-Rans

We studied three different types of Mooneys: the older M20B-G models (variously known as Super 21, Chaparral, Mark 21, Ranger,

The old V-tail Bonanzas have the worst fatal accident rate of all.

Statesman, etc.) and the new-generation 201 and 231, both currently in production. We should caution that the 201 and 231—particularly the latter—have a low exposure because of their newness and therefore their numbers are less certain, statistically. Also, in both cases, hours flown were estimated according to fleet ratios.

The older M-20s and the 201 showed up about average in both total and fatal accident rates. The 231,

however, ranked poorly: 15th out of 17 in fatal accidents, and 14th overall. This may well be a statistical aberration, but it might also reflect the lower reliability of the 231's Continental TSIO-360 engine compared to the four-cylinder Lycomings in the other Mooneys. The 201, incidentally, has a startlingly high ratio of fatal accidents to total. However, this may be due as much to an unexpectedly low number of non-fatal accidents as to an unusually high incidence of fatals.

The Piper Arrow, middle-of-the-roader that it is, has a nice middle-of-the-road accident rate: eighth out of 17 in both fatal and total-accidents.

The Lance's Poor Record

The other Pipers fare poorly. The PA-32R Lance and Saratoga have the second highest fatal accident rate of all, and the overall accident rate is sixth worst. The Lance

Fatality Ratio

We've also listed what we call the fatality ratio: the percentage of the total accidents that are fatal. We advise caution in the interpretation of this number, however. The fatality ratio almost certainly reflects both the severity of the typical crash and the crashworthiness of the aircraft (its ability to protect the occupants from impact and fire during the crash itself). The severity of the accident is affected by things like approach speed, (impact goes up by the square of the speed) and the way the aircraft is used. (An IFR weather crash is likely to be more serious than a primary training accident.)

But the fatality ratio may be deceptively low if one type of aircraft tends to have a lot of minor non-fatal accidents—gear-up landings, for example—which add to the accident totals but rarely hurt anybody. It's probably no coincidence that four of the top five airplanes (in terms of fatality ratio) are Cessnas that share the same basic landing gear system, a system that has had its share of problems, to put it mildly.

On the other hand, the Cardinal and Skylane RGs have lower stalling

Fatality Ratios 1972-1981
(Percentage of total accidents that are fatal)

Aircraft	Percentage Fatal
Cessna Skylane RG	11
Cessna P210	16
Cessna Cardinal RG	16
Piper Comanche	19
Cessna 210	20
Mooney M-20B-G	23
Bellanca Viking	25
Piper PA-28R Arrow	26
Beech 24 Sierra	26
Rockwell 112/114	28
Mooney 231	29
Beech 36 Bonanza	29
Beech 33 Bonanza/ Debonair	30
Beech V-Tail Bonanza (S35-V35B)	30
Piper PA-32R Lance/ Saratoga	31
Beech V-tail Bonanza (35-P35)	31
Mooney 201	37

speeds than the other airplanes on the chart, which lowers crash impact in certain types of accidents and could well generate a lower fatality ratio. And since neither of the two high-ranking Cessnas have a disproportionately large number of total accidents, we can infer no huge rash of "cheap" gear-up accidents.

showed up very bad in our earlier study for the years 1972-1976, but we dismissed the poor numbers because of low exposure. (The Lance had only been out one year at that point, and had just 85,000 hours of flight time.)

To see how the Lance/Saratoga SP measured up, we looked at NTSB accident records and FAA hours-flown estimates for the years 1977-1983. This time span encompasses every known PA-32R break-up (except for one that occurred early in 1984) and provides a reasonable statistical base for comparison with the 210 and Beech V-tail and conventional tail.

Worse than the Bonanza

Combining FAA hours-flown estimates and NTSB accident data, we figured the 32R's breakup rate to be 6.5 per million flight hours. Surprisingly, this is higher than the V-tail Bonanza's breakup rate (4.8) and more than twice as high as the 210's (3.3) during the same time span. The Lance/Saratoga is more than 10 times worse than the leader in this class, the straight-tailed Bonanza models 33 and 36. Only two straight-tails broke up in flight during our 1977-1983 sample period, for a rate of just 0.5.

We should point out that the total number of PA-32R breakups is not large—11 in our 1977-1983 sample period—and that the number of hours flown is small compared to that of the Bonanza and 210 (1.68

The Bellanca Viking, with the benefit of constant wing inspections and an improved fuel system design, has bettered its safety record in recent years.

million, compared to about seven million and six million for the 210 and Bonanza, respectively). Therefore, the rate figure is not as statistically significant as those for the Bonanza and 210.

The venerable Comanche ranks dead last—or worst—in total accidents and 13th out of 17 in fatals. The poor overall accident rate may be partly due to the antiquated landing gear system in the PA-24s, which result in a good number of gear-up landings. During the period 1971-1975, in fact, the Com-

In terms of total accident rate, the Piper Comanche has the most terrible record of all 17 aircraft. In fatal accidents it is merely worse than average.

anche led all single-engine aircraft with 114 gear-up accidents, according to an earlier *Aviation Consumer* study.

Beech's Sierra ranks a surprisingly bad 16th out of 17 in total accidents, and 14th in fatals. The Sierra has rather wicked porpoising tendencies and a high rate of overrun accidents, according to the 1972-76 NTSB study. *Aviation Consumer* figures also show the Sierra (along with its fixed-gear siblings, which are essentially identical aerodynamically) to have a high stall/spin accident rate.

The Bellanca Viking, while making a rather mediocre showing (12th and 13th in fatal and total rates, repectively) has at least made a big improvement from our earlier study, in which it ranked dead last in both categories. The Viking's fatal rate has improved from 4.2 to 2.7, and the total rate dropped from 16.8 to 11.0. Part of this may be due to the 1976 AD requiring inspection for wood rot in the aircraft's wing spar. Seven fatal in-flight airframe failures (most of them due to wood rot) occurred before the AD, but we're aware of only one Viking wing failure since then. (That occurred in 1983, too recently to be included in our study.)

One other factor may be the complex fuel system in older Viking; one out of four non-fatal Viking accidents is the result of fuel starvation. This is an extraordinarily high proportion. Perhaps the improved fuel systems in later Vikings is partly responsible for the lower accident rates.

Step-Up Decision: Heavy Single or Light Twin?

Analyzing the trade-offs in performance, cost and safety.

Airplane ownership is a step-up game. Start with a simple, cheap, easy-to-fly aircraft like a Cherokee or a Skyhawk. As cockpit experience and bank account grow, trade up to a faster, bigger plane that demands more piloting skill and money. If you're skilled enough and rich enough, you could end up owning a Learjet some day.

Not everybody climbs to the peak of the step-up pyramid, of course. But thousands of plane owners work their way up into the middle regions, the sphere of big, fast retractable singles and light twins. With prices currently running between $150,000 and $400,000, this class of aircraft—typified by the Bonanza, the Cessna 210, and the Piper Seneca—is the mainstay of the small business run by the hard-driving entrepreneur who likes to do the flying himself.

The step from heavy single to light twin is a perplexing one. Performance and load-carrying of the twins are usually a little better than that of the big singles. But the purchase price and operating costs are much higher. Is the bit of extra speed, range and load worth the megabucks it costs?

And then there's the question of safety. The second engine—along with the second vacuum pump and alternator—are a potent psychological crutch. But are twins really safer than singles?

And finally, there is the matter of style and status. Some pilots use their aircraft primarily to impress other people, and perhaps themselves. Ego plays a big role in aircraft sales, and there's little doubt that the twin is the better ego-massager and status symbol.

Guinea Pig Aircraft

For comparison, we've picked three single-vs.-twin matchups, one each from the Big Three manufacturers. Our task was made simpler by the parts-bin engineering philosophy of Beech and Piper, who "designed" their light twins by simply removing the engine from the nose of a well-proven

Beechcraft A36 Bonanza (top) is virtually identical to the 55 Baron (below), except for the number of engines. Price tag is half.

Baron does not hold its resale value nearly as well as the A36. A four-year-old 58 has lost more than $100,000 in value.

single-engine model and grafting a pair of motors onto the wings. In these cases, precise single-vs-twin comparisons are easy.

For Beech's pair, we selected the Bonanza A36 and 58 Baron, virtually identical airplanes except for the number of engines. Piper's Turbo Saratoga SP and Seneca III are also virtually identical except for the engine count.

Cessna has no such derivative twin, so we selected the Turbo 210 and the T-303 Crusader for comparison.

Purchase Price

Generally speaking, a light twin has a list price anywhere from half again to double that of a comparable single. For example, a 1985 Piper Seneca lists for about $270,000, compared to $190,500 for a Turbo Saratoga. That's a 42 percent difference.

A 1985 Beech A36 Bonanza goes for $246,000; a new 58 Baron lists for $446,000, a whopping 81 percent increase. A 1984 Cessna Turbo 210 went out the door at $182,000, while its stablemate light twin, the Crusader, would set you back $329,000. Difference: 81 percent.

In terms of dollars, the penalty of moving up to two engines in these examples ranges from $82,000 to $187,000, sums that would make most of us ponder.

Used Aircraft

For late-model used aircraft, the step-up penalty is less. For 1980 models of the same aircraft pairs, the cost of stepping up ranges from $10,000 to $52,000.

Oddly, the percentage step-up penalty is much smaller for the used airplanes, ranging from 23 to 66 percent in our sample pairs. (The new-plane figures ranged from 47 to 86 percent.) This suggests that the light twins tend to be overpriced when new, and depreciate more rapidly than the singles.

Take for example the Baron and the Bonanza. The 1980 Baron has retained 59 percent of its value, while the A36 has retained 82 percent. Both the Piper and Cessna singles in our comparison also beat their twin rivals handily in the resale value derby, 70 to 59 percent and 68 percent to 57, respectively. (Incidentally, we used the Cessna Turbo 310 rather than the Crusader in this example, since the Crusader didn't exist in 1980.)

These numbers foreshadow the answer to the central question of this article: is the extra cost of a twin worth it? In essence, the resale marketplace is saying no.

The depreciation numbers are telling us that the extra intrinsic value of a light twin doesn't justify the new-plane price difference—that the buyer of a new light twin, so hopeful and optimistic when he handed over the check to Cessna or Piper or Beech, is apparently sadder and wiser after using the airplane for a few years, and is willing to dump it at a significant loss.

On the other hand, the twin's faster loss of value can work in favor of the used-plane shopper. ''I bought a 1976 Turbo 310 because it was a lot of airplane for the money,'' one pilot told us. ''For my $60,000, I could have gotten a five-year old Mooney 201 or the 310. For me, it was no contest. The 310 can carry six people, it can fly 40 knots faster than the Mooney, and it's got radar, de-ice and dual systems. Sure, it costs more for gas

With nearly an identical cabin, Piper's Saratoga SP can fly nearly 200 nm farther than its Seneca counterpart.

and maintenance, but I fly less than 100 hours a year, so I can manage it. And all that stuff is tax deductible anyway.''

Performance

One buys an airplane, of course, to carry a load over a distance during a time. Generally speaking, a light twin climbs better, cruises quite a bit faster, hauls a bit more load, and can fly a little farther than a heavy retractable single. (See the comparison chart for details of our six example aircraft.)

Speed advantage of the twin ranges from 13 to 27 knots (we're comparing 65-percent cruise figures), and the extra engine helps get the twin up to cruising altitude sooner. On a typical 500-nm trip, the twin gets there quicker than its single-engine counterpart by anywhere from 17 to 36 minutes.

One would think that with nearly double the power, the twin would have a big advantage in load-carrying. Not necessarily so. Useful loads of our sample twins run 84 to 544 pounds higher than their single-engine counterparts. That averages out to an extra couple of people. But there's a catch.

Fuel consumption is nearly twice as high in the twin-engine airplanes, and extra fuel cuts into payload. For example, a Seneca has 345 pounds more useful load than a Turbo Saratoga SP. But to fly a 500-nm trip, the Seneca requires 128 pounds more fuel than the SP. Payload advantage is reduced to only 217 pounds—about one person and a travel kit.

The longer the trip, the smaller the payload advantage of the twin. For example, in the case of a 725-mile trip—the max for a Seneca III with tanks full—payload advantage over the Saratoga would be just 164 pounds.

The Turbo 210 can actually carry more payload than the Crusader on a longish trip. Useful load advantage of the Crusader is only 84 pounds, and on any trip longer than about 200 nm, the T210 has a *higher* payload than the gas-guzzling Crusader. On a long 750-mile trip, the T210 has a 180-pound payload advantage, enough for an extra passenger.

And of course the twin's appetite for fuel cuts into absolute range with full tanks. The Seneca, in fact, falls short of the Saratoga by nearly 200 miles. Only the Baron 58 has a significant range advantage over its single-engine counterpart.

In sum, the typical twin doesn't exactly overwhelm the heavy single in performance. On the average, if you fly a twin, you'll carry an extra passenger over the same distance and save 15 or 20 minutes.

Safety

All of these highfalutin performance numbers and economic analyses go up in smoke, however, when the pilot (or his wife) says, ''You know, I'd really feel safer with two engines.''

In the eyes of the general public, the simple fact that an airplane has two engines makes it safer. And most pilots agree. Yet there's been a growing debate in recent years about the safety of singles vs. twins.

It's beyond dispute that that the second engine has prevented many accidents and saved many lives when the first one quits. But what about the classic twin-engine Vmc stall/spin crash, which is virtually always fatal?

A growing school of thought believes that twins are actually more dangerous than singles if an engine quits—particularly on take-off—because of the airplane's roll/yaw tendency with an engine out. In a single, according to this line of reasoning, the pilot who suffers an engine failure will face up to the inevitable and bring the plane down to hit the ground level and under control, and perhaps walk away from it. The multi-engine pilot faced with an engine failure will make every attempt to keep flying. If he's not up to snuff, he may lose control entirely and hit the ground upside down—an event that nobody walks away from.

A 1980 NTSB study of engine-failure accidents in twins revealed that a person involved in an engine-failure crash in a twin is four times more likely to die than one who has an engine-failure crash in a single.

Crusader is only 13 knots faster than the T210. Useful load and maximum range are very close.

This debate will probably rage endlessly. But we can say one thing for sure: in terms of all accidents—not just engine-failure crashes—light twins have a better record than retractable singles. Past *Aviation Consumer* studies, based on NTSB accident records and FAA hours-flown data for the years 1972-1982, show that a representative sample of 18 popular twin-engine aircraft chalked up a combined fatal accident rate of 1.7 per 100,000 flight hours. The comparable figure for a group of 17 single-engine retractables is 2.3—about 35 percent higher.

In terms of total accidents, the rate is 6.5 for twins and 9.6 for retractable singles, an advantage for the twins of nearly 50 percent.

Single Vs. Twin Comparison

Aircraft	Equipped New Price	Equipped Used Price (1980 model)	65% Cruise Speed (kts)	500-nm Trip Time	Rate of Climb (fpm)	Equipped Useful Load (lbs)	Max Range (nm)
Beech 58 Baron	$446,000	$150,000	192	2:39	1,750	1,844	1,131
Beech A36 Bonanza	$246,000	$110,000	167	3:03	1,210	1,300	720
Piper PA-34 Seneca IV	$270,000	$84,000	175	2:55	1,400	1,708	725
Piper PA-32 Turbo Saratoga SP	$190,000	$78,000	148	3:26	1,120	1,363	895
Cessna 303 Crusader	$329,000	$160,000*	170	2:59	1,480	1,675	816
Cessna 210 Centurion	$182,000	$69,000	157	3:16	930	1,591	782

*1982 model

Cessna Turbo 210 has a useful load very close to that of the twin Crusader.

Our sample aircraft matchups followed the overall pattern. In each case, the twin has a better record than the single. The Baron 58 beat the A36 in fatal rate, 1.1 to 1.5, and in total rate, 4.5 to 5.1. The Seneca's numbers were 1.2/5.8, compared to 3.3/14.1 for the single-engine PA-32R series. And the Cessna 310 beat the 210 by a margin of 2.0/8.3 to 2.3./11.3.

These numbers may not be precise apples-to-apples comparisons, however. Keep in mind that the pilots of twins tend to be more experienced than those who fly retractable singles. And quite a few light twins are air taxi and charter aircraft flown by professional pilots. Pilot proficiency plays a big role in accidents, so the differences may not be all due to the airplanes themselves.

And keep in mind that twins are generally better equipped than heavy singles. Weather radar, for example, is almost exclusively the province of twins, and singles as a rule have only rudimentary de-ice equipment (with the exception of the Turbo 210 and P210, which are approved for flight into known icing conditions).

To pilots who habitually fly into heavy weather, the availablity of top-quality radar and de-ice equipment in a twin is often the deciding factor in the safety equation, quite

The old Piper Apache had the worst engine-failure accident rate in an NTSB study.

apart from the question of one engine vs. two.

Until a few years ago, a twin's dual vacuum pumps and alternators were a major plus. But the recent proliferation of standby vacuum systems and alternators for singles has mooted that advantage to some degree.

NTSB Report

The 1980 NTSB report on engine-failure crashes in twins sheds some unexpected light and skewers a few sacred cows. The report's most startling conclusion, as previously mentioned, is that engine-failure crashes are four times as likely to be fatal in twins than singles.

But notice that we said engine failure *crashes*, not engine failures. The multi-engine pilot who lost a motor and cruised uneventfully

home on the other one never appears in the NTSB statistics. No one knows what proportion of engine failures end up as crashes. Half? A third? Ten percent? There simply are no such statistics.

Likewise, no one knows what percentage of engine failures in singles result in accidents. Obviously, it's going to be much higher than in twins. But some fortunate and/or skillful pilots do manage to land successfully —either on an airport or off—when the only engine aboard gives out. What this proportion is, we have no idea. But we wouldn't be surprised if an engine failure resulted in a crash four times more often in a single than in a twin. But if the twin accident is four times as likely to be fatal, as the NTSB reported, then the whole thing might be a wash.

Crash From Cruise

The NTSB report does reveal some surprising facts about engine failures in twins. First of all, the engine failure in cruising flight is not the piece of cake that most pilots believe it to be. Theoretically, it shouldn't be so difficult to shut one down and bring it home when the failure occurs in cruise, with plenty of speed and altitude in the bank. But the NTSB found that a failure in cruise was more likely to result in an accident than in any other phase of flight—even takeoff.

Furthermore, the NTSB found a high correlation between engine-failure accident rate and power loading. The implication is that pilots may not be losing control of the airplane as much as they are simply unable to maintain altitude.

The twin with the worst engine-failure accident rate—by far—is the Piper Apache, which is notoriously underpowered and actually has a negative single-engine climb rate under some conditions.

Marginal Multis

But even the best single-engine climbers are very marginal. Unfortunately, this fact is almost mandated by the FAA certification regulations. The rules set down various performance standards, one of which is the ability to climb on a single engine at a certain minimum rate figured by a formula based on stall speed. (For a 75-knot stall speed, the minimum works out to about 150 fpm at 5,000 feet.) Manufacturers typically use this standard as a way to set gross weight. If a plane beats the climb requirement at a certain weight, the manufacturer usually responds by raising the weight until the requirement is just barely met.

As long as useful load numbers are deemed a better selling tool than single-engine climb numbers, it's likely that every light twin you can buy will, almost by definition, have marginal single-engine climb.

The only exceptions are the souped-up conversions like the Colemill Navajo Panther, Miller Twin Comanche and various Riley mods. These aircraft have bigger engines, but the small companies that produce them are usually unwilling or unable to go through all the testing and redesign of wing and landing gear that might be necessary to raise gross weight. The result is a big safety bonus for owners: the planes climb well on a single engine because gross weight remains the same as in the unmodified airplanes.

The Safety Equation

Summing up, there is no clear

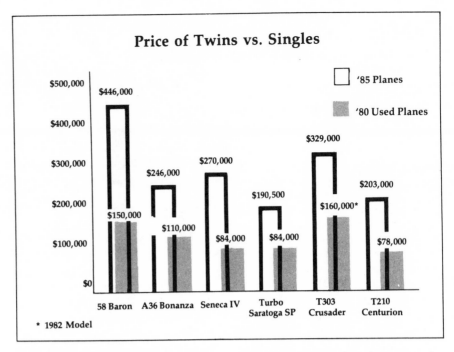

Price of Twins vs. Singles

□ '85 Planes
▨ '80 Used Planes

58 Baron: $446,000 / $150,000
A36 Bonanza: $246,000 / $110,000
Seneca IV: $270,000 / $84,000
Turbo Saratoga SP: $190,500 / $84,000
T303 Crusader: $329,000 / $160,000*
T210 Centurion: $203,000 / $78,000

* 1982 Model

answer to the safety question in the great debate of single vs. twin. Multis definitely have a better overall accident rate (both fatal and non-fatal), but this may be due as much to better pilots and equipment as the airplanes themselves.

If an engine quits, are you better off in a single or a twin? Nobody really knows. Clearly, you're less likely to crash in a twin, but if you do crash, you're more likely to die. Our feeling is that a twin is safer than a single in the hands of a cool, skillful, practiced pilot, and less safe in the hands of a mediocre pilot.

Operating Costs

While purchase price can be precisely nailed down, operating costs can't. Certain of the expenses of running an airplane—fuel, insurance and tiedown—are fairly predictable, but maintenance costs are a maelstrom of uncertainty. An owner knows the lower limit of his maintenance costs—the price of a flat rate annual or 100-hour inspection—but there is virtually no upper limit.

Fuel costs are quite predictable, and are usually about double for the twin-engine airplanes. A Baron, for example, will burn about 30 gallons an hour, the A36 about 15. (No surprise, the engines are the same.) But the Baron will

make the trip a bit faster and therefore beat the two-to-one ratio slightly.

Over a year, assuming 300 hours of flying, the typical light twin will use about $8,000 more fuel than a comparable single. If you plan to keep the airplane a while, it adds up at a frightening rate. At current fuel prices, a retractable single or light twin may well use up its new purchase price in fuel over a busy 20-year lifetime. That adds up to a $100,000-plus advantage for the single.

Insurance costs also run about double for a twin, since they are based on hull value. One insurance broker we talked to said that a new 36 Bonanza and a 58 Baron would have about the same percentage rate for hull insurance (two percent is a typical figure), assuming that both pilots were equally qualified for their type of aircraft. Liability insurance costs for each would be about $500 per year.

So total annual premium for a new Baron would run around $8,500 per year, compared to about $5,000 per year for the Bonanza.

Hangar costs would be fairly inconsequential compared to the vast amounts spent on fuel and insurance, but the single once again has the advantage. At one suburban airport we checked, fees were

$100 per month for a single and $185 for a light twin. That's a thousand-dollar-a-year advantage for the single.

Overall, assuming 300 hours a year of flying, the predictable operating costs of a twin run about $12,500 a year higher.

Maintenance

The monster that has shredded the checkbook of many a plane owner is maintenance. On the average, over the long haul, maintenance costs can be fairly well predicted. But try consoling the owner of a P210 who needs a top overhaul after 300 hours with Cessna's predicted hourly maintenance costs. It's sort of like telling a guy who just lost his job to cheer up because the unemployment rate dropped a half a percent last month.

Aviation Consumer owner surveys illustrate the unpredictability of maintenance costs. Owners of light twins reported hourly maintenance bills ranging from $30 to $50, while retractable single owners paid $20 to $35.

The manufacturer's figure estimated hourly maintenance costs for most of their aircraft. Piper and Beech did not respond to our requests for information, but Cessna estimates an hourly routine maintenance cost of $17.60 for the Turbo 210 and $20.48 for the Crusader. Assuming 300 hours per year, that's an $864-a-year advantage for the single.

We must also consider engine overhaul reserve. Naturally, this cost is about double for the twin—$15 per hour for the Baron, for example, compared to $7.50 for the A36. That's another plus for the single, this time to the tune of about $2,250 per year.

So, at the very least, the typical light twin will cost about $3,000 more per year to maintain than a heavy single. Almost certainly, the real cost penalty will be higher. And the potential for the stunning financial disaster in a twin is higher, too. A gear-up landing in a

Piper Seneca fatal accident rate is less than half of the PA-32R's. Is it due to the second engine, or perhaps better pilots?

twin, for example, will require two engine teardowns instead of just one, at a cost of $5,000 to $10,000 additional.

Summing Up

If you make your buying decision on the basis of coldly rational cost-effectiveness, it looks to us like the big single is the better deal in most cases. For a small sacrifice in performance, you'll save a hundred grand or better when you buy it, suffer less depreciation loss, and save at least $15,000 a year in operating expenses. The economic argument for the single is rather persuasive.

(Tax considerations blunt the single's economic advantage in many cases. Owners of this class of

Though twins are less likely than a single to crash when an engine fails, the chance of a fatal accident is more likely. Here NASA probes the crash characteristics of an Aztec.

aircraft usually find ways to make them tax deductible. And the investment tax credit can actually produce short-term positive cash flow. Some people make an up-front profit when they buy an airplane, and the more expensive the airplane, the bigger the profit. This generous arrangement has helped to sell a lot of twin-engine airplanes.)

For overall utility, a twin equipped with first-class radar and full de-ice equipment has the edge in heavy weather. There will be occasions when the twin flies and the single stays on the ground.

In terms of safety, there's no clear choice. Twins have lower accident rates, but this may be due to better pilots as much as the airplanes themselves. In case of an engine failure, the second engine can be a mixed blessing; a crash is less likely in a twin, but more likely to be fatal if it occurs.

On the other hand, the status and ego value of a twin are very persuasive. As much as GAMA and NBAA like to tout the practical utility of business aircraft, many airplanes are bought primarily as accoutrements of success and power. To the man on the street, a Piper Seminole is probably more impressive than a Malibu.

Our recommendations: If money matters a lot, buy the single. If it doesn't, and you are a cool, skilled and practiced pilot who wants to fly in virtually any weather, or over rough terrain at night, go with the twin.

Light Twin Accident Rates

A statistical look at the real-world safety records of the most popular twin-engine general aviation aircraft.

After poring over reams of NTSB accident printouts and FAA estimates of hours-flown data, we have figured the accident rates of light and medium twins in terms of accidents per 100,000 hours.

These numbers allow apples-to-apples comparisons of competitive aircraft. One can debate the merits of centerline thrust and counter-rotating props and good handling qualities and how they affect accident rates, but our hard numbers unequivocally answer the question, "How often does this type of plane crash, and how likely is the accident to be fatal?"

Our survey in most cases covers the most recent decade for which data is available, from 1972 through 1982. Several years ago, the NTSB published accident rate data for the years 1972-76. We have updated these numbers through 1982 in most cases, to give a full decade's worth of data.

In some cases, the NTSB made bad selections of aircraft in its 1972-76 study. For example, it groups the Cessna 401, 402, 411 and 414 together. As we discovered, this can be very misleading, for the 411 has a dramatically higher accident rate than the other Cessna twins

(and all other twins, for that matter) and distorts the composite accident rates.

Therefore, we have in some cases changed the groupings for our own study. As a result, we were unable to use the 1972-76 data in those cases, and our numbers will apply only to the years 1977-82.

We have also included newer aircraft like the Beech Duchess and Piper Seminole, which didn't exist at the time of the NTSB study. Obsolete aircraft like the Twin Bonanza, Queen Air and the Aero Commander 560 and 680 were eliminated. The FAA hours-flown estimates showed that these planes flew so little that any calculated accident rate would not be statistically significant.

Winners and Losers

No clear winner emerged from our figures. A trio of cabin-class Cessnas and the Piper Seneca all had less than one fatal accident per 100,000 hours to top the fatal accident rankings. But most of the rest of the light twins weren't too far behind. There seems to be a much narrower spread between the various twins than between the single-engine retractables, where the best were four times safer than the worst. Among the twins, the best seem to be only about twice as safe as the worst.

There's one glaring exception: the Cessna 411, a cabin-class twin built in the sixties. Astoundingly, the

Piper Seneca, a favorite of commercial air taxi operators, ranks among the safest in fatal accident rates.

411 had a fatal accident rate three times higher than the next-worst twin. This is most likely due to its atrocious single-engine handling qualities. A 1981 *Aviation Consumer* study showed that the 411 had a fatal engine-failure accident rate 10 times higher than the Cessna 401, a generally similar aircraft.

We did notice one pattern. Owner-flown "step-up" twins seemed to have higher accident rates than the big iron. The Cessna 337 Skymaster, touted as a "safety" twin for step-up pilots by virtue of its center-line thrust, and the Twin Comanche ranked poorly, while the big Cessnas, the Piper Navajo and the Baron 58 all looked good. Perhaps the type of pilot and the typical mission plays a larger role in an aircraft's accident rate than the inherent safety of the design.

Improvement

General aviation accident rates have improved steadily over the years. For example, the fatal accident rate in 1972, the first year of our study period, was 2.7. By 1982, the last year of the study, the fatal rate had improved to 1.8. Keep this in mind when evaluating the accident rates of certain types for which we had data only for the 1977-82 period. Even though an airplane's accident rate declines slightly from 1972 to 1982, it may actually be losing ground, since the rest of the field has improved even more.

The Barons

Beech's popular twins ranked about in the middle of the pack. From 1972-76, the entire Baron/Travel-Air series scored 2.8 and 8.3, respectively, for fatal and total accident rates. The same group improved to 1.4 and 5.3 in 1977-82, for overall scores of 2.0 and 6.5 for the entire decade.

We decided to separate the 58 and 55 models out of the group to see if there was a difference between the long-body 58s and their smaller forebears. The answer: not much. For the period 1977-82 only, the 58 had a low 1.1 fatal rate, while the 55 was a not-quite-so-low 1.4. The 58 also had a better overall accident rate, 4.5 to 6.4.

The Baron's accident rate might have been better without a bunch of stall/spin accidents. An earlier study commissioned by *Aviation Consumer* showed that for the years 1970-74, the Baron had a much higher stall/spin rate than other light twins. In fact, about a quarter of all fatal Baron accidents during that period were stall/spins. Eliminate those, and the Baron's accident rate would improve noticeably.

The Baron stall/spin rate has apparently declined in recent years, however, as more attention has been focused on the subject and Beech has mailed Baron owners handbook supplements warning of

Beech Baron 58 had a fairly good fatality rate, somewhat better than the short-body 55 Baron.

the problem. That may be a big part of the Baron's improved accident rate during the last half of the decade.

Beech Duke

The Baron's macho big brother also showed up in the middle of the safety standings, ranking ninth out of the 17 planes in both fatal and overall accidents. Note that the Duke figures cover only the years 1974-82, and that hours flown for the years 1974-76 were projected from FAA data for later years.

Some people may be surprised at the Duke's reasonably good showing. The rich, aggressive achiever-types who typically own and fly Dukes are often blamed for the high accident rates of planes like the Learjet and MU-2, but Duke pilots seem to hold their own among their supposedly more conservative fellow pilots.

Beech 76 Duchess

The Duchess light-light twin has flown too few hours to establish a good statistical base, but we have included it anyway out of curiosity. Over 151,000 flight hours (1978-81), the Duchess has had two fatal and five non-fatal accidents, for rates of 1.3 and 4.6.

Interestingly, the Duchess's chief marketplace rival, the Piper PA-44 Seminole, has virtually identical numbers: 1.2 and 4.8. The two

planes, quite similar in design and used for the same purpose (multi-engine training) have achieved virtually identical accident rates with only a few hundred thousand flying hours beteween them.

Cessna 310

Among the "big three" classic light twins—the Baron, 310 and Piper PA-23 Apache/Aztec—the 310 ranks best by a smidgin in fatal accidents, but worst of the three in total accident rates. Comparable fatal rates for all three aircraft is so close that it hardly matters: 1.95 for the 310, 2.02 for the Baron series, and 2.12 for the PA-23s. (These numbers have been rounded off to the nearest tenth in our tables.)

In overall accidents, the Baron/Travel-Air and Apache/Aztec, at 6.5 and 6.6 respectively, lead the 310, which registers 8.3.

All three of these popular aircraft started in the 50s as low-powered four-seaters, gradually evolving into high-performance six-seaters. About 3,500 of each of them are currently flying. And each flew more than six million hours during the last decade. It seems only appropriate that each has a virtually identical fatal accident rate.

The 310, like virtually all other twins in our study, improved its accident rate as time went on. The original 1972-76 study listed the 310 fatal and total rates as 2.2 and 9.8. Our figures for 1977-82 were 1.8 and 7.1. This is probably due to better avionics, systems, pilot training and perhaps more safety awareness among pilots.

Cessna 337

Cessna's unique "push-pull" Skymaster was designed as an easy-to-fly step-up twin for single-engine pilots. The centerline thrust eliminated the deadly engine-out roll/yaw reaction that has killed hundreds of pilots who couldn't cope with engine failures in conventional twins. If an engine quits, the Skymaster keeps flying straight by itself while the pilot identiifes and feathers the prop on the failed engine. The plane may not climb heroically on a single engine (though it does better than many other twins), but at least it will go down level and under control. Theoretically, that's a lot safer.

But the statistics show that theoretical safety features don't necessarily improve accident rates in the real world. The Skymaster's fatal rate of 2.5 and total accident rate of 9.5 are both among the worst of any light twin. The fatal rate is worse than any other twin except for the awful Cessna 411. (That's like saying that the Hindenburg was a lot safer than the Titanic. Ironically, both of those famed vehicles, like the Skymaster, were touted as major advances in safety.) The Skymaster's total accident rate was 15th out of 17 planes, better only than the 411 and the Twin Comanche.

Why does the Skymaster fare so poorly? Is centerline thrust actually more dangerous than the conventional arrangement? We think not. Admittedly, in the early days, some Skymasters crashed on takeoff when the rear engine quit and the pilot didn't notice—something that couldn't possibly occur in a 310. But better pilot awareness has apparently almost eliminated this type of accident. Still, the Skymasters keep crashing. Why?

Examining this question in 1979, we analyzed a five-year rundown of accident briefs on the aircraft. A close look at the causes of the fatal accidents—29 of them, amounting to 27 percent of the total number of crashes—showed that most were unrelated to the design of the aircraft, in our opinion. The largest single accident cause was weather-related, with seven fatals. None of the pilots involved could be described as an inexperienced pilot of the type who might be expected to select the Skymaster as a safe, easy stepup twin. All were commercial pilots with instrument ratings, and four were flight instructors.

Twelve of the other fatals were a mixed bag—like gyro failure, low flying, hit wires, pilot fatigue, nose-over—that could have occurred in any twin. In three accident categories, however, fatal crashes were obviously aircraft related. There were three fatal accidents caused by loss of power on takeoff and climbout. Two of those involved failure of the rear engine—the bugaboo that haunted the "push-pull" aircraft through the years. Also, there were two fatal accidents from engine failure because of fuel exhaustion and two attributed to stall/spins.

Most of the stall/spin or mush accidents appeared unrelated to any particular aircraft deficiency. Of the two fatals, one occurred during a buzzing incident, the other was attributed to pilot fatigue. We noticed however, that surprisingly often pilots who lost just one engine were unable to bring the aircraft back to a safe landing despite operating without the handicap of assymetrical thrust.

The Cabin-class Cessnas

If the bottom-of-the-line Cessna twins have less-than-sterling accident rates, the big machines make up for it. By our numbers, the Cessna 414, 340 and 401/402 have the best fatal accident rates on our list, and the 421 is not far behind.

Overall leader is the Cessna 414, the "small-engine" version of the pressurized 421. Its fatal and total accident rates of 0.8 and 3.2 both rank the best of the 17 aircraft we studied. One word of statistical caution, however: the 414 numbers cover only eight years (1974-82) and include three years of projected hours-flown data. Oddly, the 414 suffered half of its fatal accidents in just one year, 1974. If we consider only the 1977-82 period for which we have complete hours-flown data, the 414's fatal rate is a phenomenally low 0.5.

Close behind in the fatal accident rankings is the Cessna 340, a smaller "owner-flown" pressurized twin. Again, the 340's rate is based only on the years 1977-82, since the FAA did not include the 340 in its 1972-76 study.

Accident Rate Summary 1972-1982

Aircraft	Hours Flown	Fatal Accidents	Fatal Rate*	Total Accidents	Total Rate*
Aero Commander/Rockwell 500**	665,000	14	2.13	38	5.80
Beech 55 Baron	2,514,000	37	1.47	161	6.40
Beech 58 Baron**	1,886,000	20	1.11	84	4.45
Beech 55/56/58/95	8,149,000	165	2.02	528	6.47
Beech 60 Duke	659,000	9	1.36	37	5.61
Beech 76 Duchess**	151,000	2	1.32	6	4.63
Piper PA-23 Apache/Aztec	8,598,000	182	2.12	572	6.65
Piper PA-30/39 Twin Commanche	2,766,000	58	2.09	295	10.66
Piper PA-31 Navajo	6,155,000	69	1.12	227	3.69
Piper PA-34 Seneca	4,019,000	43	1.07	213	5.84
Piper PA-44 Seminole**	337,000	4	1.19	16	4.75
Cessna 310	6,664,000	130	1.95	555	8.33
Cessna 337 Skymaster	951,000	49	2.51	186	9.53
Cessna 340**	1,202,000	11	0.92	62	5.16
Cessna 401/402**	2,170,000	21	0.96	132	6.08
Cessna 411**	185,000	14	7.56	31	16.76
Cessna 414**	1,711,000	14	0.82	55	3.21
Cessna 421	3,018,000	36	1.19	164	5.43

*Accidents per 100,000.

**Data not available for full 1972-82 period.

The Cessna 401 and 402 rank third in fatality rates with an excellent 0.9 rate. (We combined the 401 and 402 into one category. Both are non-pressurized and use the same engine; the 402 is a slightly stretched ''commuter'' version.) In overall accidents, the 401/402 ranks 10th out of 17. We have some confidence in the 401/402 numbers; they are based on more than 2 million flight hours. However, they cover only the period 1977-82, since the NTSB unwisely lumped the 401 and 402 together with the 411 and 414 in its 1972-76 study.

The top-of-the-line pressurized 421 ranked seventh out of 17 in fatal accidents with a 1.2 rate, and eighth in total accidents with a 5.4. Why does the 421 rate less safe than the nearly identical 414? We don't know for sure, but virtually the only difference between the two aircraft is the engines. The 421's souped-up GTSIO-520 engines have had a spotty history, and engine problems may play a role in the 421's slightly higher accident rate. The difference may also be statistical; the 421 data starts in 1972, while the 414 numbers start in 1974. Also, the 421 was introduced before the 414, so the 421 fleet is, on the average, older than the 414 fleet.

The Deadly 411

Cessna's very first cabin-class 400-series twin holds the dark distinction of the worst accident rate of any twin—by far. The 411's 7.6 fatal rate is two times worse than any other twin, and the total accident rate is 50 percent worse. These numbers are so bad that, quite frankly, we would hesitate even to get into a 411.

To put things in perspective, the 411 has had 14 fatal accidents since 1977. That's double the number of fatal accidents of the 414 in the same period. Yet the 411 flew only 185,000 hours during those five years, compared to more than one million hours for the 414.

It's no big secret why: the 411 has truly awful single-engine handling qualities. Look at the size of the 411 tail and rudder in the picture

below. Compare it to the tail of the 421, which replaced the 411 after three years on the marketplace. Apparently, Cessna learned its lesson on the 411. Pilots should heed that lesson, too.

An earlier *Aviation Consumer* study showed the 411 to have a fatal engine-failure accident rate 10 times higher than the Cessna 402. In fact, nearly 10 percent of all 411s ever built have crashed after engine failures. The accidents began as soon as the 411 was introduced in 1965, and in 1969, the FAA, in cooperation with Cessna, supposedly did a complete certification review of the airplane, with special attention to single-engine handling. The FAA gave the airplane a clean bill of health, but it turns out that the FAA ''evaluation'' was, in our opinion, a sham, virtually made up out of thin air. Only one brief test flight was made, in gusty conditions.

Some years later, Cessna hired a test pilot to do single-engine tests in a 411. (The videotaped tests were to be used as evidence in a lawsuit against Cessna filed after the fatal engine-failure crash of a 411 in Minnesota.) The test pilot was Al White, former North American test pilot who flew the XB-70 and F-100, among other ex-

otic aircraft. White, in a carefully rehearsed intentional engine shutdown with cameras rolling, failed to feather in time and crashed ignominiously. (He was unhurt, but Cessna lost the case.)

Another test pilot hired by the plaintiff's lawyer in the same case found that rudder pressures required to keep the 411 straight at blue-line speeds were 270 pounds, nearly double the maximum allowed by FAA regulations.

The 411's engine-out problems are especially critical because the engines themselves were not very reliable. The 340-hp GTSIO-520-C Continentals were the first of the big geared engines, fearsomely complex, with a TBO of only 1,200 hours. After 20 years of refinement, the GTSIO-520s have become reasonably reliable in the current 421 models, but the 411 engine had its problems.

Complicating the picture even more are the current economics of the 411. The planes are very cheap on the used-plane market—as little as $30,000 in some cases—but the engines are horribly expensive to maintain. ($40,000 for a pair of remanufactured engines). As a result, 411s are often flown by shoestring operations that can't af-

Fatal Accident Rates 1972-1982

Aircraft	Fatal Accident Rate*
Cessna 414**	0.8
Cessna 340**	0.9
Cessna 401/402**	0.9
Piper PA-34 Seneca	1.1
Beech 58 Baron**	1.1
Piper PA-31 Navajo	1.1
Cessna 421	1.2
Piper PA-44 Seminole**	1.2
Beech 60 Duke	1.3
Beech 76 Duchess**	1.3
Beech 55 Baron**	1.5
Cessna 310	2.0
Piper PA-30/39 Twin Comanche	2.1
Piper Pa-23 Apache/ Aztec	2.1
Aero Commander/ Rockwell 500**	2.1
Cessna 337 Skymaster	2.5
Aerostar	3.8
Cessna 411**	7.6

*Accidents per 100,000 hours

**Data available for 1977-82 only

Total Accident Rates 1972-1982

Aircraft	Accident Rate*
Cessna 414**	3.2
Piper PA-31* Navajo	3.7
Beech 58 Baron**	4.5
Beech 76 Duchess**	4.6
Piper PA-44 Seminole**	4.8
Cessna 340**	5.2
Cessna 421	5.4
Beech 60 Duke	5.6
Aero Commander/ Rockwell 500**	5.8
Piper PA-34 Seneca	5.8
Cessna 401/402**	6.1
Beech 55 Baron**	6.4
Piper PA-23 Apache/ Aztec	6.6
Cessna 310	8.3
Cessna 337 Skymaster	9.5
Piper PA-30/39 Twin Comanche	10.7
Aerostar	11.1
Cessna 411**	16.7

*Accidents per 100,000 flight hours

**Data not available for entire 1972-82 period

ford to maintain the engines properly. It all adds up: a cheap old plane with expensive, unreliable engines and very poor engine-out handling qualities. Maybe it should come as no surprise that the 411, which probably should never have been certified in the first place, has the worst accident record of any twin.

Piper Seneca

The best of the Piper twins turns out to be the workhorse Seneca, which over the past decade has emerged as the runaway best-selling multi-engine aircraft. More than 2,000 are currently flying. The Seneca's 1.07 fatality rate (rounded to 1.1 in the table) is the best non-400 Cessna in the bunch, and its total rate of 5.8 ranks ninth best.

These good numbers come despite the fact that many Senecas are flown by relatively low-time pilots and multi-engine students—factors often blamed for the high accident rates of aircraft like the Cessna 337 and Piper Twin Comanche.

The Seneca's accident rates, like most other aircraft, improved over the years. For the first half of the decade, 1972-76, the PA-34 had fatal and total rates of 1.5 and 10.0. For the 1977-82 time span, the numbers were 1.1 and 5.8. Unfortunately, neither the NTSB nor the FAA distinguishes between the original Seneca and the improved Seneca II and III, which have better handling but less reliable turbocharged engines.

Piper Navajo

The venerable PA-3l Navajo series ranks just behind the Seneca in fatal accidents, with a fine 1.12 rate. The Navajo's total acccident rate is a superb 3.7, second only to the Cessna 414. The Navajo is one of the few aircraft that didn't improve its accident rate as the decade went on; first-half and second-half crash numbers were virtually identical.

The NTSB didn't sort out accidents for the pressurized PA-31P Navajo, a rather different airplane altogether. Nor did the FAA distinguish the P-Navajo in its hours-flown estimates, so were unable to come up with a separate number for the P-model.

Twin Comanche

The PA-30 and PA-39, still adored for their speed, efficiency and quiet, show up poorly in the accident statistics. The Twin Comanche's 2.1 fatal rate and 10.7 total rates rank 14th and 16th out of the 17 airplanes. The Twin-C is known for two safety problems: stall/spins and botched landings. The stall/spin accidents began occurring in the mid-60s when the Twin Comanche became popular for multi-engine training. Numerous fatal stall/spins occurred during Vmc and engine-out maneuvers. It turns out that Piper's Vmc number was hopelessly optimistic, and the FAA later raised it from 80 mph to 90. Piper also came out with an anti-spin retrofit mod, but few have been put into service.

The Twin Comanche's landing problems are well-known to anyone who flies the plane. A NASA team that evaluated the PA-30B (among other aircraft) in 1966 noted the Twin Comanche's nose-high attitude (with all three gear planted on the ground) caused pilots to land nosewheel first and to porpoise excessively. Takeoffs were also criticized for the same wheelbarrow tendency unless the aircraft was horsed off below Vmc. An old CAB report also noted that the Twin Comanche had a landing

Twin Comanche has superb reputation for speed and efficiency, but its accident record is discouraging.

The Cessna 411 has by far the worst accident rate of any twin. The main reason is extremely poor single-engine handling coupled with fairly unreliable engines.

overshoot rate triple that of the Bonanza, and suggested that the Piper's hopelessly optimistic handbook landing distances might have been to blame for giving Twin Comanche pilots a false sense of confidence.

Combine these factors with the Twin Comanche's rather crotchety landing gear system, and we have the formula for lots of non-fatal gear-up landings, hard landings and overshoots. This may account for this twin's unusually high number of non-fatal accidents —worse than any other airplane except the notorious Cessna 411.

Piper PA-23 Apache/Aztec

Piper's most popular twin ranks 15th out of 17 in fatal accident rates, but is only marginally worse than its historical rivals, the 310 and Baron. In total accidents, the PA-23 ranks 13th, just behind the Baron series, but well ahead of the Cessna 310.

Unfortunately, neither the FAA nor NTSB distinguished between the Apache and the Aztec versions of the PA-23. (The difference is considerable; early Apaches had 150 hp, while late Aztecs were equipped with turbocharged 250s.) The previously mentioned NASA study of handling qualities had harsh criticism for the Apache it tested. At aft c.g., the Apache was determined by NASA to have neutral stability in the approach configuration—a very dangerous state of affairs, particularly in IFR conditions. NASA called the trait "unacceptable."

An NTSB study a few years ago of engine-failure accidents in twins showed that the Apache had an engine-failure accident rate about twice as high as the other aircraft studied. (The 411, incidentally, was not individually analyzed in that study.) Since the Apache is known for benign engine-out handling qualities and marginal (if not negative) single-engine climb rates, the NTSB concluded that power loading was perhaps more important in avoiding engine-failure accidents than good handling qualities.

PA-44 Seminole

As in the case of the Duchess, the Seminole has flown too few hours to reach any grand conclusions about its safety record, but it's interesting to note that the Seminole's numbers are virtually identical to those of the Duchess. The little Piper ranks eighth out of 17 in fatal accident rates, and fifth in total accidents.

The Cessna Skymaster, touted as an easy-to-fly step-up twin, nevertheless has a high accident rate. Most surprising is poor record of landing safely with an engine out.

Aerostar

We were particularly curious about the accident rate of the sleek, unorthodox Ted Smith design that was taken over by Piper a few years back. The Aerostar has had more than its share of safety problems, most of them well-documented in these pages. Fuel system idiosyncracies caused nearly a dozen crashes before the FAA issued a series of ADs in 1978. Since then, the fuel-related accidents have died out. But we had noticed what seemed like an unusually high number of Aerostar accidents over the years, particularly engine-out stall/spins and engine fires. But we had nothing more to go on than a gut feel that the Aerostar was having a lot of accidents; without a full NTSB accident count combined with an FAA hours-flown esti-

Best fatal and total accident rates were chalked up by the Cessna 414.

mate, no assessment of the Aerostar's overall safety was possible.

Unfortunately, it looks like that assessment will have to wait. The FAA, for some reason, made hours-flown estimates only for the Aerostar 600 series, the original non-turbocharged version that appeared in 1969. The turbocharged 601 and the pressurized 601P and 602P, however, account for most of the Aerostar hours flown.

And, frankly, the FAA hours-flown numbers for the 600 look a little suspicious. For example, in 1977, the FAA estimates the Aerostar 600 flew 137,000 hours. The next year, the figure plummeted to 64,000. That doesn't make any sense. In 1978, the FAA had listings for both the "Smith 600" and the "Piper 600," with no explanation of the difference, if any, between the two.

Faced with these uncertainties, and with the prospect of energetic controversey between Aerostar critics and supporters, we decided it was simply impossible to give the Aerostar a fair shake with currently available data. However, we hope to pursue the Aerostar's mysterious hours-flown numbers through the bowels of the FAA bureacracy. If that doesn't work, we'll try to come up with an hours-flown estimate of our own, based on the number of Aerostars in service and FAA estimates of the average number of hours flown each year by each aircraft.

SINGLE-ENGINE
FIXED GEAR
TWO-PLACE

Citabria and Decathlon

When a line of airplanes goes out of production, the models become outcasts and their value drops. Right? Wrong—if you're talking about those venerable aerobatic performers called Citabria and Decathlon.

There are few airplanes that are as much fun to fly as the aerobatic Champions. The creature comfort is good, yet not so lavish as to overcomplicate what is basically a very simple design. Though aerobatically capable, they aren't limited to just that. The aircraft are great at short cross-country flights, where the visibility affords as good a view as you can get in a modern light-plane, without going the ultra-light route.

History

Did we say "modern?" Tube-and-fabric tail-draggers, with wooden spars? Well, they are. But they are also about the highest refinement of old-fashion technology as you can come by in aviation. This was exactly the tone of the marketing copy issued by Bellanca Aircraft (the last real producer of Champion aircraft) in the late seventies. Archaic things like bungee landing gear had been replaced with spring steel. The cowling became a two-piece fiberglass affair with an attractive, streamlined shape. And toe brakes and gas tanks in the wings made the plane less different from what was being produced in Wichita.

Similarly, the aerobatic Champions, produced from 1964 to 1980, should not be lumped together with what most people think of as "tail-draggers." You know—Cubs, Stinsons, Taylorcrafts and so on, which have been out of production for decades. While it is heartening to see these airplanes still flying,

The 1973 Citabria (airbatic backwards).

many of them meticulously restored and maintained by owners, most of them suffer from outdated attributes: Things like generators instead of alternators, two-piece windshields, old-style gauges and coffee-grinder radios (or no radios at all). In contrast, the Champions are modernized in all respects, save the wood, fabric and landing gear configuration. And it is arguable that these are still the best design for an airplane that does what the Citabria does.

In 1980 the Bellanca Aircraft Corp. filed for bankruptcy. The production line stopped, not only for the Champions, but the Vikings as well. The Champion assets of Bellanca were eventually sold to a company in Texas, which intended to restart production at their facility at Tomball Field. But after moving parts and tooling there from Osceola, Wisconsin, they were able to finish only a couple airplanes before having to file for Chapter 11 themselves.

The bank that now had security interest in the assets sold everything in turn to the present owner, Tetelestai, Inc., of Austin, Texas. These people have no interest in

building Champions again. Rather, their goal is entirely speculative. The Champion type certificates, STCs, tooling and remaining inventory are presently for sale to the highest bidder. Parts are not being individually sold. We talked to Tetelestai, and they indicated that there was moderate interest in the Champion line, especially from some foreign countries.

Alphabet Soup

The first Citabria came off the production line at Champion Aircraft in Osceola, Wis. in 1964. When the factory was finally shut down in 1980, over 4,000 Citabrias, and other models of its ilk, had been produced. The first Citabria, a direct outgrowth of the old Aeronca 7AC Champ, was the 7ECA model, which stayed in production to the end. Originally powered by a 100-hp Continental O-200, the 7ECA was soon converted to the 115 hp Lycoming O-235. All of the subsequent models of Citabrias, Decathlons and Scouts were derived from this airplane.

The Champion line is awash in a sea of alphanumerics. Though there must have been some rationale behind the resulting model designations like 7GCBC and 8KCAB, we shy from such an etymological treatise here. See the accompanying table of specifications for more details on the several Citabria (actually only four), and two Decathlon models.

The similarity in airframe appearance leads most pilots to infer that the various Champion models are just combinations and permutations of one fuselage design with different engines, wings, aerobatic oil systems, propellers and the like. In fact there is much more to it than meets the eye. You can't just hang a 150 hp engine, Decathlon wings and Christen inverted oil system on a 7ECA, for example, and have it automatically become an 8KCAB. Among other things, the 8KCAB has a beefed-up fuselage, different angle of incidence of its tail, battery in the rear (a bigger one, too), and a separate fuel header tank in the cockpit just above the pilot's shins.

The Decathlon was introduced in 1971 as a higher-performance "big brother" to the Citabria. The primary difference between the Citabria and Decathlon is the wing. The Decathlon has a semi-symmetrical airfoil and a shorter span. There is only one degree of dihedral in the Decathlon's wing, and a thicker windshield with a brace help raise redline airspeed to 180 versus the Citabria's 160. Redesigned ailerons mean that Decathlons can complete a roll in three seconds, while a Citabria takes nearly six. Designed to FAR Part 23 standards (The Citabria was built to the older CAR 3 regs.), the Decathlon wing has more ribs and internal bracing than a Citabria, so it is certified for +6 and −5 g-loading.

A constant-speed propeller was an option on the 150-hp Decathlon.

The empty weight of a Decathlon is over a hundred pounds more than a comparable Citabria (the 7KCAB). At sea level we have seen the little 115-horse "Standard" Citabria outclimb a Decathlon CS quite handily. As soon as you ask a Decathlon to go negative in a maneuver, however, the different wing shows its stuff. Slow rolls in a Decathlon aren't accompanied by the unnerving shaking and complaining that comes with the Citabria. A Decathlon is quite happy upside-down, but a Citabria wants desperately to right itself. We haven't checked the stall speed of a Citabria inverted, but it must be much higher than normal. That flat-bottomed wing really is designed to produce lift at positive, not negative, angles of attack.

The Decathlon is approved for all aerobatic maneuvers, except the lomcevak (which it can't do anyway) and tailslides. But we know of Pitts Special owners who don't allow tailslides in their airplanes (the forces are so tough on an airframe), so that isn't a real limitation. The Decathlon, therefore, can take a true aerobatic enthusiast well along in sanctioned competition, at least to the "Intermediate" and "Advanced" levels, but with some difficulty to the "Unlimited" category. Since it is more difficult to coax high-quality maneuvers out of a Citabria or Decathlon than a Pitts Special, there is talk in aerobatic circles about a handicapping scheme (like with sailboat racing) for the types of airplanes used in competition.

Adding a bigger engine to the original Decathlon was inevitable, and in 1977 the Super Decathlon was born, fitted with a 180 hp engine. The extra 30 horsepower provided sufficient excess power to make the airplane what it should have been from the start. Recognizing this, the used aircraft market now places a premium on Supers, and a clean low-time one commanded upwards of $30,000 in 1986, getting close to the price it could have sold for new in 1980.

Performance

The best all-around medal goes to the 7GCBC ("C" Package), with its longer wing and flaps. Stall speed is a low 46 mph with flaps at their

Citabria/Decathlon Resale Value Chart

The Decathlon wing has a shorter span and more ribs than the Citabria.

full 35-degree down position, and a landing ground roll of 310 feet is listed in the owner's manual. Take-off ground roll is 289 feet. The extra foot and a half or so of span drops cruise speed by two mph, however, to 127 at 75 percent.

The 7GCBC is the most popular of the Citabria models, and many see service as bush planes on skis, or with oversized tires, to say nothing of those enlisted to tow gliders and banners. Its simple carbureted engine burns between six and seven gph of 80/87 fuel. Tasked to doing prolonged full-power low-speed climbs, the cylinder head temperature can rise dramatically. An optional split door and window make the 7GCBC a good photo ship and general workhorse.

Nearly equal in numbers, the baby of the line 7ECA seems to have a very pleased following of owners indeed. The reliable O-235 gives it remarkably good cruise performance, just eight to ten mph slower than its 150-hp brethren. Climb

performance suffers, however, in comparison, particularly at a high density altitude. But still, there's a lot of wing out there for such a light bird, so performance is better than a Cessna 150's under similar conditions.

With 35 usable gallons of fuel the 7ECA "A" Package consumes less than five gph while still delivering 100 mph down at a 50-percent power setting. At 40 percent it can stay aloft fully 10 hours and cover a range of 880 miles, but unless you're a fish spotter, we can't imagine sitting in one of these that long. With an auto-fuel STC, you can cut the direct operating cost of a 7ECA to nearly pocket change, making the model that much more attractive. Because of its lighter engine up front, some think that the 7ECA is actually the best balanced of all the Citabrias when it comes to doing aerobatics.

The 7KCAB was dropped from production after 1977, indicating that inverted work ought really to be done in a Decathlon. We concur wholeheartedly, for though the engine can certainly hack limited

"outside" stuff, the flat-bottomed wing of the Citabria endures altogether too much stress for many hours of inverted aerobatics. Not to say that this plane doesn't have its market. Many were purchased by schools to cover both tailwheel transition and introductory aerobatic work, without having to purchase two airplanes to cover both bases.

The star performer is clearly the Decathlon, at least in the aerobatic realm. Cruise speed is a few mph faster than the Citabrias, but takeoff distance is twice that of a 7GCBC, owing to the different wing. Of course we're talking a whopping 575 feet here, which would still be STOL performance in comparison with other 150-hp airplanes. The performance difference with the constant-speed prop on the Decathlon appears minimal-to-none, according to the book, as well as our real-world experience. Unless you're concerned with accidentally over-revving the engine in aerobatics (something we don't think is a problem with this plane), the controllable prop only adds weight and expense at overhaul time.

On the 180 hp Super, however, it is nice and all Supers have the constant-speed propeller. Cruise speed does go up another five or so mph with the Super, but the real advantage is in a better rate of climb, up to 1,230 fpm. The ability to gain speed quickly in a dive in order to then translate that energy back into altitude is helped by the bigger engine. Vertical performance is better, and really only Supers can perform vertical rolls with any degree of consistency for the competition pilot. Vertical performance is still meager when compared with the Pitts, though there are some Decathlon owners who would disagree on this point.

Handling

These airplanes are unstable on the ground. Simple physics says that when the center of gravity is behind the main wheels (which it is—the plane rests on its tail doesn't it?), you have an unstable situation. Left to its own devices when in motion, the tail wants to swap ends on you, leading to directional-control problems for those used to just following along behind a nosewheel.

So why conventional gear, when we said this plane was otherwise quite modern? It's lighter, less complicated, has less drag, and is better-suited to rough-field operation. The only exception we might make to this generalization is the design of the nose gear on Cessna's Caravan I, the single-engine turbo-prop, which appears to be a stout solution for tricycle geared rough field operations.

Perhaps it is the added full-time attention to directional control on the ground in Champions, coupled with powerful rudder and pitch controls in the air that give pilots the feeling that they're really flying in these planes. There is no aileron-to-rudder interconnect. Tandem seating and control sticks keep the cockpit more of a cockpit and less of a living room environment. Overall, you feel more a part of the plane.

One clear problem, with the Citabrias at least, is the control force needed to work the ailerons at higher speeds. You can literally pull shoulder muscles doing rolls to the right. Some people even let go of the throttle and use two hands. Others turn their stick hand upside-down for better geometry. Most do rolls only to the left, where torque effects help a little, and human physiology allows pushing the stick more easily. Gap seals were an option on Citabrias, and they seem to help roll rate a bit. Other than some serious weight training at the club, the only solution to heavy aileron forces is to install a set of ''spades.'' These dramatically reduce the pressures needed, and

1976 Citabria 115

many Decathlons have them, even though forces are lower than in the Citabria to start with.

The only handling problem that pilots transitioning to the Champion taildraggers seem to have is one of pilot-induced pitching oscillation (PIO) that starts after a botched landing. Wheel landings in these planes must happen with a near-zero sink rate. Otherwise the spring-steel gear bounces the plane back into the air before the pilot can reduce angle of attack to keep the plane on the ground. But, of course, with the stick now forward (too late) and the plane airborne again, it heads for the runway for another touchdown at too high a sink rate, followed by another bounce and more of the same. Until you add power, climb back up and try it again.

Or else you risk catching a prop tip on the pavement. There is no trick to it, and any pilots that live by the misconceived gauge that forward stick will save a hard touchdown are looking for trouble in a Citabria. The solution is practice and honing the skill of bringing airplanes to the runway at nice shallow angles. Glider pilots have to cultivate this, for their planes have very little shock absorption capability in the landing gear (usually just the tire itself). Once accomplished by the

Citabria pilot, the skill has a noticeably beneficial effect on landing control in any airplane, and one often hears that ''if you can land a Citabria, you can land anything.''

Cabin Load and Comfort

Which Citabria can carry the most load? The one with the biggest engine and wing, right? Wrong. The little 115-horse 7ECA can, since it is the lightest of all the Champions, and all the models have the same maximum gross weight of 1,650 pounds. This means that with Citabrias, and Decathlons as well, if you put in full fuel, two 180-pound adults and parachutes, you are over-gross by a hundred or more pounds. The only thing you can do is to fly with reduced fuel. This is what most people do, though many feel that, since the airplane is strong enough for aerobatics, they can ignore the limitation. Not advisable.

The real problem isn't so much weight as it is center of gravity. The owner's manuals repeatedly caution not to exceed the aft limit when doing aerobatics. The problem is that spins can become unrecoverable. We experienced a touch of this first-hand when a spin took over one turn to recover.

Citabrias and Decathlons are usually delightful to spin, and just releasing back pressure immediately breaks the stall. What was different about our spin was the presence of a 30-pound video recorder in the baggage area. Needless to say, aerobatics aren't to be taken for granted when it comes to weight and balance. This holds true for any airplane certificated for same.

Cabin noise is more than in a Cessna 150, and a good deal more than in a Bonanza. Headsets are a must in Champions, and most people use the intercom capability of the factory-installed radio system. Many, however, go one better and install one of the popular voice-activated intercoms, a pair of David Clark headsets and a "pickle" switch on the stick to transmit. Convenience and comfort are well worth this installation, especially because of the tandem seating.

Ventilation is good, and many an instructor has been grateful for it when an aerobatic student has become queasy. Cabin heat is controlled by a simple air valve at the firewall, and the pilot's legs get blasted with very hot air. It's like the person with one hand on the stove and one in the freezer. On the average he's comfortable. You can open the vents to drop the heated air temperature for the pilot, but the rear-seat passenger won't get as much benefit. Citabria pilots get used to burning up in the front seat, in order to make things comfortable for their passenger in the back.

There is a rear-seat heater option that helps out, and it is probably worth trying to find one if you fly a lot in cold weather. Flying Champions in rain and snow requires dressing for it, for it is not unusual for water to drip from vents and the top edge of the windshield onto the pilot. There simply isn't any duct work in the airplane at all to trap moisture.

Citabria instrument panels, more often than not, don't have gyro systems, except for the required turn-and-bank. If you do much aerobatics, we advise putting a switch on it, so you can turn it off. Many don't even have a vertical-speed indicator. Further, the night-lighting of the panel may be nonexistent, or else consists of the old military-style bullet light mounted on the window frame. Since there are no courtesy lights whatsoever in the airplane, some owners have installed post lighting and a rheostat to control brightness. Night flying in Champions requires thinking ahead enough to plan some panel lighting and to bring along a flashlight. (You always have a flashlight for night flying anyway, don't you?)

Citabria seats are comfortable, and the controls are easily reachable for both occupants (except for the radio and mixture control, which you've got to get the guy in front to take care of). So-called "adjustable" seats became available in 1977. The adjustment range isn't that great, but it could be nicer for a very tall or short pilot. The seat belt system can be supplemented with a Pacific Scientific five-point harness system. With dual shoulder straps and a crotch-strap to prevent submarining in the event of a crash, this is without a doubt the best restraint system in any production light-plane.

The proper way to handle all the belts, since the regular seat belt system stays in the plane along with the acro harness, is to buckle into the harness and then hook the seat belt over that as well. This means that with a parachute on, you definitely can feel uncomfortable, especially since you have to pull the straps quite tight to do inverted work. In the words of a veteran aerobatic pilot and para-

chute jumper, "If it isn't uncomfortable, you haven't got it on right." We frequently fly Citabrias with everything hooked up, even on cross-country flights.

Safety Record

Examining the Champion accident records reveals that the airplanes aren't used like most tricycle-geared ships. The Citabrias have an unusually high percentage of off-field incidents; that is, arising out of operating from fields, wooded areas, lakes and snow; not from paved runways, in other words. These planes are subject to pilots who hit trees or swerve into ditches (or even cattle). There were also enough banner-towing accidents to make us wonder whether we'd ever allow ours to engage in such behavior.

Decathlons, on the other hand, are seldom so abused. They are simply offered the opportunity to defy the laws of nature by doing aerobatics at too low an altitude. The records showed lots of instances where show-offs were doing loops, rolls and spins down on the deck. There were only a handful of true stall-spin accidents, however, and these were mostly after takeoff from strips with obstacles, where the pilot let airspeed decay.

All of the Champions are afflicted with loss of control on the ground, mostly on landing. The vast majority of accidents are "ground loops," or (more accurately) loss of directional control, but mixed with these are hard landings, prop strikes and outright nose-overs. These accidents aren't as damaging to bodies as they are to egos. But they can be expensive. Replacing a spar and recovering a wing damaged in a ground loop can cost over $4,000 (1986 price).

Maintenance Considerations

These airplanes don't cost diddly to maintain—if you've got a good one to start with, and can keep it in a hangar. There just isn't that much to go wrong. Most of the hardware is standard AN or MS stuff. A misconception about the "modern" Champions is that the fabric is the weak link, and mechanics who don't know these planes are fond of poking holes in your fabric with the old testers used with cotton. The covering is lifetime Dacron and there is little reason to expect it to deteriorate, if it is treated properly. If you must "test" fabric strength, do it in a hidden spot—under a fairing or access cover.

Corrosion of the tubing is a far-more-serious thing to concern yourself with. Typically, the areas around the tailwheel and just aft of the baggage area are the ones to watch. Water collects here and rust gets started. A competent dope and fabric man can fix this without unsightly silver dope patching. With a little forethought the fabric can be cut in a strategic place, peeled back and replaced so that it doesn't require a complete repaint of the plane. Wing struts and screws can be kept free from rust by most owners.

The landing gear u-bolts are susceptible to cracking, and eventual failure, after hard landings, or rough-field operations. Make sure that you and your mechanic keep a good eye on these. Engine mounts wear through in only a couple-hundred hours, if you do a lot of aerobatics. An

external indication that this hasn't been kept up is that the 150-horse engines will sit low enough to blister the fiberglass cowling near the exhaust system.

The fuel cap washers need to be replaced from time to time, or else siphoning can cause loss of fuel (look for stains on the wing). An early sign is that fuel will burn unevenly from the tanks. The removable door, with its emergency hinge-pin release, is also nice when you need to load some outsized cargo through the door frame. If you haven't pulled the pin and taken the door off recently, do it. Corrosion and ridges can wear into the hinges. This is something frequently missed by mechanics on Champions, even though the FAA has issued bulletins that doors on all aerobatic airplanes be periodically checked.

One of the more dangerous things that can happen to these airplanes is that the back seat can flop forward and limit stick travel. There are restraint cables on the seats to prevent this; but we have seen Citabrias come out of annuals with the cables disconnected. Some people cut them so the seat back comes all the way down to aid in loading things into the baggage area. Not recommended. We're in the habit of looking for these on any Champions we fly, since it's

something the pilot can check easily.

Mecca for Champions

The best support for the entire Champion line is at Air Repair in Santa Paula, California. Air Repair was the preeminent warranty repair station when the factory was still going. Next door is Screaming Eagle Aircraft Sales, which sells more Citabrias and Decathlons than anyone. They were also the largest dealers of new Champions before production stopped. Owners have flown across the country just to have their planes worked on at Santa Paula.

Some parts are hard to come by, but Harrison Bemis of Air Repair seems to always get his hands on whatever it takes to get your Citabria or Decathlon airborne. There are always wings being rebuilt and planes being recovered at his shop. Harrison is fond of showing people through his facility, pointing out the differences in all the models as he walks them through the dope-filled atmosphere of a spray room.

Parts, service and owner's manuals are available through Air Repair. They will even copy all the service bulletins since time immemorial for you, if you must have them, but be prepared to pay for the copying. Air Repair says that the following

Models/Performance/Specifications _____

Model	Years Built	Number Built	Strength (G's)	Cruise Speed (kts)	Fuel Std/Opt (gals)	Useful Load (lbs)	Remarks	Engine	TBO (hrs)	Overhaul Cost
Citabria 7ECA Standard	1964-65	245	+5, −2	95	36	590	No Flaps, 100 hp	Cont O-200-A	1,800	$6,900
Citabria 7ECA Standard	1966-80	759	+5, −2	104	36	590	No Flaps, 115 hp	Lyc O-235-C1	2,000	$7,600
Citabria 7GCAA "A" Pkg.	1967-80	393	+5, −2	112	36	510	No Flaps, 150 hp	Lyc O-320-A2D	2,000	$8,000
Citabria 7KCAB "B" Pkg.	1969-77	619	+5, −2	112	36	510	No Flaps, Inverted	AEIO-320-E2A,B	2,000	$9,500
Citabria 7GCBC "C" Pkg.	967-80	1.177	+5, −2	110	36	500	Flaps, More Span	Lyc O-320-A2B,D	2,000	$8,000
Decathlon 8KCAB-150	1971-80		+6, −5	121	40	530	Inverted, 150 hp	AEIO-320-E1,2B	2,000	$9,900
Super Decathlon 8KCAB-180	1977-80	642*	+6, −5	131	40	530	Inverted, 180 hp	AEIO-360-H1A	2,000	$10,750

*All Decathlons—ratio of Supers to 150 hp's unknown

service bulletins are musts for all Citabrias and Decathlons: C-135, which covers the landing gear u-bolts. C-139A, on wing rib nails. C-141, regarding the fuel manifold in the aft fuselage. C-127, strut replacement. C-140, calling for belly fabric stringer supports.

Any airplane that has had its wing struck in any manner is covered by an FAA Airworthiness Alert (AC43-16). This is to detect possible spar damage. Airplanes that have been on their backs are highly suspect. Investigate closely the repairs to any Citabria or Decathlon that has flipped over. Air Repair is at P.O. Box 813, Santa Paula, Calif. 93060, (805)525-5553. Screaming Eagle is at 825 E. Santa Maria St., Santa Paula, Calif. 93060,(805) 525-7121.

Modifications

There is a plethora of STC'd modifications to the Citabrias, most of them involving the installation of various bush gear—floats, tundra tires and the like. The unleaded auto-fuel STCs are available from the EAA and Peterson Aviation for the carbureted models. And the Decathlon can be fitted with spades from either Marion Cole, 8906 Countryaire Drive, Shreveport, La. 71107, (318)929-2618; or Don Jackman, P.O. Box 3160, Riverside, Calif. 92519 (714)781-3121.

Air Repair says it takes two and a half mechanic-hours to install the spades, including a flight test. Performance of the two spade kits is said to be identical.

The Christen Inverted Oil System can be retrofitted to the pre-1974 models of the 7KCAB, and we'd consider this mandatory. You also avoid complying with a required inspection every 400 hours on the old system from Lycoming. The STC for the conversion to the Christen system is held by Lloyd Land, Star Route Box 65A, Hudson, Colo. 80642.

Resale Value

As we said earlier, the entire Champion line is holding its value very well. Because of the expense involved in recovering and re-painting an airplane, clean ones are especially sought-after. As a rule, the year of a particular model isn't as important as its condition. A mint 1977 Decathlon, with all the service bulletins complied with, is easily worth more than a 1980 that has been neglected or abused.

The premium is on the Super Decathlon. But the spry little 7ECA is becoming hard to find. The low cost of ownership and pleasant flying qualities must be endearing them to their present owners. One of our editors owns one, and values it highly. Of course, he'd like to see one of our more well-heeled readers buy the Champion line and keep it from going to Libya.

Owner Comments

I am the owner of a 1968 8GCAA, i.e., 150-hp, fixed-pitch Citabria—as in no flaps. As a 22-year USAF fighter pilot and eight-year FBO owner, the champ is my outlet for earthbound frustrations. Fifteen or 20 minutes of aerobatics is still the best therapy for the mind—and it's about as much fun as a fella can have with his trousers on.

A few years ago my bird went through a complete rebuild, including new ceconite, interior, new cables, electrics, etc. The 150-horse Lycoming is without doubt the best engine on the market and has per-formed flawlessly. With a thousand hours on an overhaul it still burns only a quart or so every 12 to 15 hours. In fact, the only problem I have with the bird is keeping the Escort 110 working—my "avionics" package.

Ground handling is a bit tricky due to the heel brakes, a true test of one's patience. There are tech-niques, such as keeping it rolling and using a little power on tight turns. Once rolling, it taxis smoothly, and forward visibility is actually pretty good.

The little bird is a dream to fly, trims up quite well and is a fine performer. Climb rate is about 1,000 fpm—it's hard to tell exactly since my spartan panel doesn't include a VSI. On the rare X-C I've flown (It is not a great bird to fly all day) I've gotten true airspeeds of 135 to 140 mph. One must recall this is the same engine the Warrior 151 has, at 500 pounds less weight.

Aerobatics are nice, a genuine treat. She goes over the top with the best of 'em and the various rolls, while requiring good technique to avoid "dishing out," are okay. Much better than anything else I've flown. As usual, landings are fun—taildraggers do make it interesting. I have found three-point, stall landings to be consistently a piece of cake. To taxi a taildragger is to learn never to get cocky until it's shut down and tied down!

I burn 9 to 10 gph doing aerobatics and 8.5 gph on trips (70–75%). Tires and brakes will last forever once you learn how to use them. Oh, there are a few minor glitches: the fuel gauges are hard to read, I think questionable in accuracy and, well, sort of a guide. I tend to keep it full, y'know? The heel brakes, well, what can you say about them? Once you get the hang of it, they're sort of okay, honest.

Why does the FAA insist on chutes in an aerobatic airplane? First of all, there's never enough time to get out, if indeed you could. Uncomfortable and unnecessary—also hot!

Maintenance cost is a good point. Just isn't much to break—or fix. Brakes occasionally, tires even less often, some plugs once in a while, and the usual 50-hour oil changes. Annuals will run $350-400. the radio, however, is a problem. I've tried Genave and Escort with poor reliability. Insurance isn't bad, particularly if you've got 10,000 hours, fighter experience and a couple of lunar landings. It helps if you can hangar the machine.

All in all, it's not really a very practical machine, but the thrill of looking back over your head through the greenhouse at the earth makes it all worthwhile. A fun airplane that every pilot should spend 5-10 hours in. It'll teach you more about flying than all the simulator/hood time in the world. I love it!

****

For some reason (possibly because it wasn't built in Wichita), the Champion line has received little, if any, press—and that's a shame, because I've enjoyed no other aircraft quite as much as my own Super Decathlon. I've owned two of the last Supers built, the first having been destroyed when another plane ran into mine on the ground. The second has 550 hours since new in 1980, and most of that was aerobatic training, tailwheel checkouts, chase flying for a friend's jet and an occasional cross-country for business or pleasure.

I truly love the wide range of activities that can be performed with the plane, and I wouldn't trade it for the world.

I've added a few things to make it a bit nicer, foremost of which was a pair of Marion Cole's spades for the ailerons. I figure these alone reduce full-deflection stick force by about 30%, and greatly reduce fatigue during a lesson. The factory hot mike intercom is adequate, but I added David Clark military headsets (lighter than the green ones), and a volume control. I also added the Holmsley smoke system, but have not been pleased with its construction, nor the mess it makes on the exterior of my plane, so I rarely use it.

The engine has been wonderful for aerobatics, and it's never even coughed in any attitude. The Scott tailwheel went back, because of a broken part, but they replaced it free. The factory-installed Edo radio is adequate, but has been in the shop more than once for various reasons. Several Decathlon owners I've met have gone to a King package, and at least three owners I know have full Loran and IFR panels installed.

My Super is a beauty in the air. I can roll rings around almost anything, shy of a Pitts. Inverted flying is a breeze, although the one-degree angle of incidence necessitates a two degree pitch change going negative. Aileron response is good and well-balanced. The elevator is very effective, and rudder is extremely authoritative. Flat turns are easily possible with rudder and outside aileron alone. The restraint system is very good and features a crotch strap.

As an aerobatic trainer it can't be beaten. But beware of the weight and balance envelope. When I first got my plane, and discovered that two adults and full fuel put us 145 pounds over gross, I was shocked.

Insurance costs are high, and are getting higher, especially if you instruct in aerobatics. I keep my plane in a hangar, as outside storage will rapidly fade the finish and age the plane before its time and drop its value significantly. The present value of my plane is equal to or better than when I bought it. I've had several offers for it, but won't part with it. It's simply the best of all the worlds I need, and very few compromises have to be made.

Dan Stroud
Oklahoma City, Okla.

I would like to put in my two cents regarding the Bellanca aircraft. I cannot offer much in the way of specifics as far as operation of the aircraft, but I can tell you that they are as much fun as you can have outside of bed. I have owned both a 7ECA and a 180-hp 8KCAB. These aircraft have been flown by my wife and myself and they are delightful both in the aerobatic mode, as well as the short-to-moderate length cross-country mode. Both aircraft have been extremely economical, with annuals running from $100 to $200. There have been a few minor problems with windshield molding screws backing out as well as fatigue cracks in the wheel pant mounting plates. Keeping them hangared is important in maintaining the paint and fabric.

William Steen
Shreveport, LA

Piper Tomahawk

Piper's PA-38 Tomahawk trainer is one of the very few "clean sheet of paper" designs of the last decade. Most Tomahawks are of course operated by flight schools, but the Tomahawk fleet is now beginning to age, and more and more of them are coming onto the used-plane market.

The 1981 model had some minor refinements, including larger tires.

It's an economical little two-place sport and traveling machine with a lot of good features and a distinct personality, but questions about quality control and stall/spin characteristics deserve close study by any potential buyer.

History

The Tomahawk first appeared in 1978, amid a great burst of Piper hoopla and carefully orchestrated "surprise." It was intended to be a replacement for the venerable Cherokee 140, which was a fine trainer, but too big, powerful and inefficient to do the job economically for Piper flight schools, who found their rental rates undercut several dollars per hour by the smaller, cheaper Cessna 150. Piper made much of the fact that it had surveyed hundreds of flight instructors to find out what they really wanted in a trainer. The Tomahawk was supposedly the answer to their prayers.

There have been very few major design changes over the years. Paint job aside, only an expert could tell a 1977 Tomahawk from a 1982 model. But there have been many important mechanical changes, virtually all of them the result of early problems. Because of this, a Tomahawk shopper should try to get the latest serial number he can.

The 1981 model year got the "Tomahawk II" name, as if to suggest a whole new generation of airplanes, but the improvements were mostly cosmetic and convenience changes. Perhaps the only significant change came in 1979, when a second set of stall strips was added to the wing in an attempt to tame the airplane's rather squirrelly stall. But the stall strips may be retrofitted, so there is no particular reason not to buy a two-strip airplane.

Resale Market

The Tomahawk had an unusual pattern of production. Because of pent-up demand by Piper dealers, a torrent of Tomahawks flowed out of Piper's Lock Haven plant during the 1978 and 1979 model years—nearly 2,000 aircraft in all. Then, in 1980, the torrent suddenly slowed to a trickle, and only a few hundred were built after 1979. So most Tomahawks on the used market will be '78 or '79 models.

Because of certain problems that we'll get into later—and of course because of the terrible market for single-engine planes in general—now is a buyer's market for the PA-38. "The Tomahawk market is lousy," according to one broker we talked to. "They're very difficult to sell." "Bluebook" retail value of a 1978-79 Tomahawk in 1985 is $9,000 with average equipment—about $2,000 less than a comparable Cessna 152. But a buyer should be able to do better than that.

Because the Tomahawk is a flight school airplane, some good deals may be had. A school may be renewing its fleet and put up half a dozen used Tomahawks for sale at once. Or you may find a flight school in financial distress that would be happy to unload a Tomahawk or two for some quick cash. But on the other hand, there are few things harder on an airplane than long-term flight-school duty. Thousands of student pilot landings and repeated pattern work take their toll on both airframe and engine.

Performance

The Tomahawk's performance is typical of most two-seaters. It'll cruise along at a modest 90 knots or so, burning about six gallons of fuel per hour. That's close to 17 nmpg, and about as good as the vaunted Mooney 201. Fuel capacity is 30 gallons, good for about four hours at moderate power, with reserves, so a range of up to 350 nm is possible. While this may seem piddling to pilots of bigger, faster airplanes, it is not bad for a production two-seater.

The Tomahawk has a good rate of climb, thanks to its efficient high-aspect-ratio wing. In side-by-side tests, *The Aviation Consumer* found that the Tomahawk smartly out-climbed both the Cessna 152 and Beech Skipper. Since two-place airplanes quite often take off at or near gross weight, climb performance can be critical. In this respect, the Tomahawk stacks up well—although on hot days at high altitudes, climb performance will be marginal.

Cockpit and Cabin

The Tomahawk is quite roomy for a two-seater. The cockpit is 42 inches wide, just as wide as the four-place Arrow series and five inches wider than the notoriously cramped Cessna 152.

Getting in and out of the Tomahawk is somewhat awkward, but still better than most two-placers. One must step over a rather high door sill. Each door has two latches, like the Cherokee. Because of poor quality control, door closing and sealing has been a problem.

The Tomahawk panel is excellent, although utilitarian. A huge three-position fuel selector lever dominates the panel, with the selector lever pointing directly to the gauge of the tank selected. This is a fine safety feature. Some pilots may find the throttle and mixture controls awkward because of the odd angle of travel.

Visibility is one of the best features of the airplane. The view is superb in all directions, but particularly over the nose. The cowling sits just on the horizon during a normal climbout, allowing full forward vision.

The interior appointments are in our opinion a bit chintzy, particularly in older aircraft. Compared to, say, the Beech Skipper, the Tomahawk seems crude and Spartan indeed.

Tomahawk (left) is virtually indistinguishable from its rival, the Beech Skipper.

Handling Qualities

We previously alluded to the Tomahawk's handling qualities by saying it had a "distinct personality." Either you like the way it flies or you don't. The Tomahawk's T-tail, a styling gimmick designed to fit Piper's grand plan for a full line of flashy T-tail airplanes, has some effect on the Tomahawk's handling qualities.

On the takeoff roll, the elevator is useless until about 30 knots because it is up out of the propeller blast. When the tail does take hold, it does so suddenly, and it's possible to overrotate on takeoff. Because the tail had to be big enough to rotate the plane at a reasonable speed without prop blast, it is very powerful—perhaps too powerful—at flying speed. Pitch control is very sensitive, and it's easy to overcontrol, particularly in the landing flare. However, most Tomahawk pilots like the powerful pitch control once they get used to it.

Rudder control is also very powerful and sensitive. On takeoff, very sure feet are required to roll absolutely true down the runway. In the air, the yaw stability is not very good. A bump of turbulence sets the tail wagging much like a V-tail Bonanza.

In contrast to the strong, sensitive pitch and roll control, the ailerons are rather slow and stiff. In this respect, the Tomahawk is not a well-harmonized airplane. (Compare the Grumman American

AA-1 series, which is light and sensitive in all three axes.)

Trim stability of the Tomahawk is excellent. If you trim it to 70 knots, and take your hands off, it will stay at 70 knots through all manner of power and flap adjustments. The trim system in the 1978 and 1979 models, however, is poorly set up. One pilot told us his Tomahawk could not be trimmed to approach speed—a rather startling drawback. Others complain that too much trim-wheel rolling is needed once the Tomahawk levels out in cruise flight. Another reported the trim system springs wore out, and that "even with the trim rolled all the way back, you couldn't fly hands off for even a moment without going into a nose dive."

The Tomahawk's flaps are not the big "barn-door" altitude-killers of

Read 'Em and Weep: Tomahawk ADs

The Piper Tomahawk has compiled an atrocious AD record. At one time or another, virtually all of the airplane's major systems and/or subassemblies have been targeted by Airworthiness Directives (some sweeping, some affecting only a limited run of serial numbers). In considering any prospective purchase, a Tomahawk buyer would do well to check the effectivity of the following ADs:

A.D.	Subject
78-22-1	rudder beefup
78-23-4	wing spar
78-23-9	control wheels
78-25-1	Slick mag coils
78-26-6	vertical fin spar
79-3-2	rudder hinge
79-8-2	stabilizer bolts
79-13-8	Airborne vacuum pumps
79-17-5	ground wire to instruments
79-18-5	ELT
80-06-5	mag impulse coupling
80-11-9	landing gear attach bolts
80-22-13	rudder hinge bracket
80-25-2	valve pushrods
80-25-7	Stewart-Warner oil cooler
81-16-5	mag coil
81-18-4	oil pump
81-23-7	engine mounts
82-2-1	aileron balance weights

the Cessna 150, but they allow a pretty good sink rate and lower approach speed by about eight knots. The flaps are manual, which allows quick, positive control and promises low maintenance costs. Maximum flap extension speed is only 80 knots, however.

The Tomahawk's rather sensitive "twitchy" handling springs partly from Piper's philosophy that a trainer should not be *too* forgiving and easy to fly, lest the student never learn from his mistakes. Later on, goes the teaching theory, the student will be more prepared to handle heavy high-performance aircraft that are not so forgiving as trainers like the Cessna 150 or Cherokee 140.

That philosophy may be fine for student pilots, but it makes little sense for the owner/pilot who simply wants to fly his Tomahawk as comfortably and smoothly as possible. Sensitivity to torque effect or adverse yaw has no saving graces for the non-student pilot.

Stall Spin

One of the Tomahawk's "distinct" traits is its stall and spin characteristics. The airplane has a sharp-breaking stall that can easily develop into a spin. Recovery from the spin demands quick, decisive and forceful pilot action. Once again, there are two schools of thought on the subject: one says a trainer *should* "bite" the student when he makes a mistake so that he will not make the same mistake in the future; the other camp says training airplanes should be forgiving and gentle because neophyte pilots are more likely to get into unintentional stalls and/or spins. But once again, the "let 'em learn the hard way" philosophy has no

Tomahawk panel is well laid out and features an easy-to-use fuel selector.

merit for the owner-pilot who wants to fly safely, not learn lessons for the future.

The Tomahawk stall/spin question took on new urgency after a rash of fatal stall/spin accidents, three in the state of Alabama alone during one four-month period several years ago.

We believe the Tomahawk's stall and spin characteristics are too unpredictable to justify the "scare the pants off the students so they'll make the mistake only once" philosophy. Instructors as well as students have been killed in Tomahawk stall/spin crashes.

The 1978 and 1979 models, which had a single stall strip on the outboard section of the wing, seem to have especially unpredictable stall traits. A former Piper engineering test pilot who flew Tomahawks to check their landing characteristics said he found no two that stalled alike. Some dropped the left wing sharply, others the right. Some dropped 30 degrees, some 60, some 90. (The maximum allowed

by certification regulations is 15 degrees.) Some rolled inverted.

After serial number 1400, a second set of stall strips was added in an attempt to moderate the Tomahawk stall. (This action by Piper reportedly came after a big Florida flight school refused to accept delivery of the fleet of Tomahawks it had ordered because the stall was too violent.) The new stall strips increased stall speed by about four knots and lengthened takeoff and landing distances. The new strips may be retrofitted to older Tomahawks at a cost of about $25, plus an additional $100 or so for a new airspeed indicator to reflect the higher stall speed. However, even the four-strip airplane is not exactly docile in the stall. We're aware of one flight school that will not teach stalls in the Tomahawk—even the four-strip models.

Spins

If a Tomahawk does accidentally get into a spin after a stall, the pilot is in for an interesting ride, to put it mildly. Piper made a big point of the fact that the Tomahawk was certified for spins, and flight instructors cheered when they first heard the news. But the Toma-

Cost/Performance/Specifications

Model	Year	Number Built	Average Retail Price*	Cruise Speed (kts)	Rate of Climb (fpm)	Gross Weight (lbs)	Useful Load (lbs)	Fuel (gals)	Engine	TBO (hrs)	Overhaul Cost
PA-38-112	1978	821	$ 9,000	108	718	1,670	540	30	112-hp Lyc. O-235-L2C	2,000	$7,500
PA-38-112	1979	1,179	$10,000	108	718	1,670	540	30	112-hp Lyc. O-235-L2C	2,000	$7,500
PA-38-112	1980	189	$11,500	108	718	1,670	540	30	112-hp Lyc. O-235-L2C	2,000	$7,500
PA-38-112	1981	173	$13,000	108	718	1,670	540	30	112-hp Lyc. O-235-L2C	2,000	$7,500
PA-38-112	1982	NA	$14,000	108	718	1,670	540	30	112-hp Lyc. O-235-L2C	2,000	$7,500

* Includes navcom, VOR, marker, transponder, gyros, lights, 900 hours on engine, all ADs complied. Wholesale prices approximately 20 percent less.

hawk is no Cub in a spin. It winds up quickly in a steep nose-down attitude. More importantly, quick and correct pilot action is required to recover from the spin. Full forward movement of the yoke—not just release of back pressure—and full anti-spin rudder is required for recovery. (Some other aircraft must be held *into* a spin, and will come out quickly if the controls are released. Not so with the PA-38.)

Once the pilot has reacted quickly and correctly to the spin, the Tomahawk will continue for one to two turns before it recovers. Altitude loss in a one-turn spin can be 1,000-1,500 feet, according to the Tomahawk manual. There is also what Piper calls a ''very steep, fast spin mode.'' If recovery procedure is incorrect or delayed, the spin winds up tighter. This can disorient the pilot, according to Piper. (Incidentally, the expanded handbook description of spins, including the info about the steep, fast spin mode, did not appear until April, 1981. Handbooks issued before that contained a much more cursory discussion of spins. We'd advise any potential Tomahawk buyer to get a copy of the updated manual.)

Production Problems

We could write a book about the Tomahawk's AD history and quality control problems, but we'll try to be mercifully brief. Several factors bear on the problem. Among them:

• Piper apparently believed price was a big factor in its sales battle with the Cessna 152. As a result, the Tomahawk was designed to be as economical to build as possible. (Uncharitable types might prefer the word ''cheap'' or ''chintzy.'')

• The Tomahawk prototype had been built and certified at Piper's Vero Beach, Fla. plant. But Piper decided to manufacture the plane in Lock Haven, Pa. Tools, jigs, and paperwork were transferred to Pennsylvania, but a good deal of Tomahawk expertise stayed in Florida. Also, the Southern Region FAA people who shepherded the airplane through certification couldn't afford to send anyone

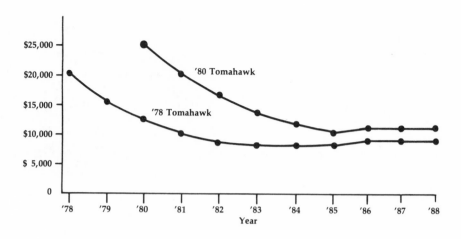

Tomahawk Resale Value Chart

'80 Tomahawk

'78 Tomahawk

north to watch over the Tomahawk production startup. In Lock Haven, both the Piper and FAA people charged with building the Tomahawk had to learn a lot very quickly.

• Piper built a whole bunch of Tomahawks very fast those first two years—about 2,000 aircraft in all. That's the most airplanes of one type Piper has built in such a short time since the great Cub-building spree of 1946. There was little time to work out the inevitable production-line bugs and get the production people on the front side of the learning curve.

• Piper had to hire hundreds of new production workers all at once, and in the great rush to churn out Tomahawks, we believe it's very likely that many of the rookie

In many early model Tomahawks, the doors are poorly sealed. The result can be difficult latching and a noisy cabin.

plane-builders did a lot of on-the-job learning.

• Piper's internal system of engineering-audit flight testing apparently broke down, and many Tomahawks went out the door without being checked carefully. (In some cases, horizontal tail bolts were found loose on brand-new aircraft.) The plan was for the engineering test pilots to fly the first five Tomahawks off the line, and a random sampling of aircraft thereafter. But the production people didn't deliver a Tomahawk to the engineering department for an audit flight until more than 100 airplanes had been shipped out, and only sparsely thereafter.

The Tomahawk seems to have been a classic case of an airplane that was designed to be cheap, rushed into production too fast, and not checked carefully enough before delivery. The results were predictable: a rash of ADs, service bulletins and quality control problems that have tainted the Tomahawk's reputation to this day.

The AD Parade

The first Tomahawks came off the line in February, 1978, and it didn't take long for the AD notes to start piling up. In four years, the PA-38 accumulated 19 ADs, a very high number. And 12 of the 19 concerned airframe problems resulting directly from poor design or quality control. (The other seven were engine and accessory ADs—oil pump, ELT, vacuum pump, oil cooler, etc.—that applied to many other airplanes as well.) Virtually every major piece of the airframe—fuselage, wing, ailerons, fin, rudder, stabilizer, landing gear and engine mount—were hit by ADs.

The fall of 1978 was a particularly bad time for Tomahawks (and their owners). Five major ADs came in a two-month period, including one that grounded the fleet for a month. At about the same time Piper issued a massive 20-page service letter (euphemistically labeled ''Tomahawk Product Refinement Program'') that listed 16 different service problems. Among them: loose carpeting in the cockpit and baggage compartment, backwards seatbelt bolts, leaky doors, loose spinner rivets, reversed oil cooler shroud clamps, cracked landing gear fairings, leaky fuselage, balky heater, etc. You get the picture. Obviously, before buying a PA-38, one should have a knowledgeable mechanic carefully check compliance with all ADs.

One AD in particular deserves mention. Directive 81-23-7 requires 50-hour inspections of the engine mount for cracks. (The mounts had begun cracking back in '78 and a

Piper service letter recommended reinforcing them. That didn't work.) But the mount must be replaced at 1,000 hours in any case. Flight schools have found the engine mount AD to be an expensive nuisance. ''You'd be surprised how many Tomahawks get put on the market with around 950 hours on them,'' one flight school operator told us.

Another potentially expensive service problem is the trim system. Updated trim wheel assemblies cost about $200 plus labor, according to Piper service letter 865. Other Tomahawk service bulletins that have not been turned into ADs deal with binding rudder fairings and jamming control wheels (S.B. 661).

If you get a Tomahawk with all ADs and service bulletins complied, maintenance costs should be reasonable. The plane is very simple, with excellent engine access and many interchangeable parts.

Like the rest of the late-model two-seat training fleet that uses the Lycoming O-235-L2C engine, the Tomahawk is very susceptible to lead fouling of the spark plugs. In extreme cases, this can cause engine failures; at best it will increase maintenance costs. Operat-

Low light in this photograph shows uneven wing skin—a possible contributor to the airplane's unpredictable stall characteristics.

ors should be careful to lean at all times below 75 percent power, particularly on the ground. The use of TCP anti-fouling additive also helps.

Safety

Overall, the Tomahawk seems to have a good safety record. According to statistics compiled by our sister publication, *Aviation Safety*, the Tomahawk had a lower accident rate than the Cessna 152 during the 28 months after the introduction of each airplane. The Tomahawk's fatal accident rate was about 16 percent lower than the Cessna 152, and its total accident rate about 38 percent lower.

One Owner's Maintenance Summary
1981 Tomahawk

Date	Descriptiion	A/C Time (hrs)	Labor Cost	Parts Cost	Amount Covered by Warranty	Running Total Cost
8/31/81	50 hr. #1 ignition lead	54	$ 36.92	$ 25.34	$ 86.95	$ 62.26
8/24/81	548-097 clock	73			$ 66.98	$ 62.26
8/26/81	77781-03 housing	77			$440.19	$ 62.26
9/8/81	100 hr.	105	$207.00	$ 38.67	$307.93	
9/28/81	50 hr.	148	$ 45.00	$ 25.60		$ 378.53
10/7/81	548-581 turn cord	160			$246.20	$ 378.53
10/14/81	61906-002 Ind.	164			$142.09	$ 378.53
11/4/81	100 hr.	200	$300.60	$ 71.16		$ 750.29
11/17/81	77519-02 guide	220	$ 18.00	$ 45.48		$ 813.77
1/14/82	100 hr.	299	$140.40	$ 32.52		$ 986.69
2/15/82	50 hr. linings	353	$ 54.00	$ 35.71		$1,076.40
3/8/82	100 hr.	405	$126.00	$ 47.14		$1,249.54
3/23/82	L&R tires	432	$ 48.60	$ 80.24		$1,378.38
4/5/82	50 hr.	450	$ 54.00	$ 21.75		$1,454.13
4/14/82	misc.	466	$ 48.60	$ 12.10		$1,514.83
4/23/82	492-022 valves	473	$ 9.00	$ 5.60		$1,529.43
5/10/82	100 hr.	493	$229.50	$ 30.95		$1,789.88
5/28/82	clean plugs	533	$ 25.20	$ 5.60		$1,820.68
6/11/82	landing light	550	$ 9.14			$1,829.82
6/28/82	annual	595	$107.92	$162.00		$2,099.74

As we mentioned, however, the Tomahawk has a special problem with stall/spin accidents. By mid-1982, the Tomahawk had a total of 19 fatal accidents, nine of which were stall/spins. That is an extraordinarily high percentage of fatal stall/spins. Mechanical problems have triggered several fatal Tomahawk crashes. Both the magneto coil and engine pushrod ADs were spurred by accidents, not by inspections or mechanics' reports.

Owner Comments

Concerning your Tomahawk survey, we have operated five PA-38s in our flight academy since they were first introduced. In fact, I believe we had the first "fleet" order of four aircraft placed with Piper Aircraft. Outside of the initial mag problems, the little machine has performed like a champ! Visibility, particularly in the pattern, is absolutely outstanding—a major flight safety issue when you fly thousands of hours a month as we do. The airplane is a fine "teaching aid," i.e., you must learn to use rudder, ailerons, and elevators to fly the machine well—you *cannot* flop around and get the job done as one can in some other trainers. It develops a better pilot.

Maintenance-wise, the PA-38 performs well, particularly the engine, gear and tires, and electronics. We can run a 100-hour inspection in about eight man-hours at an average cost of $250-$300.

There are a few glitches: the original carpeting was cheap and came unsecured rather quickly, the door latches were a bit "Mickey Mouse" and required replacing—otherwise, no problems.

All in all, I consider the airplane to be a major improvement over our previous trainers; i.e., the Cherokee 140 and Cessna 150/152. In fact, the Tomahawk blew the Cessnas right off our line. Once our students got a little PA-38 time, they would not fly the 150s, which soon departed. It is a comfortable, fun-to-fly machine, and certainly the safest trainer in our experience.

Jack Doub
H&D Aviation
Terre Haute, Ind.

The biggest problem I've found is the lack of a genuine trim tab system. They have a cheap, and less effective spring-load assist, and after a year or two the springs apparently weaken so that even with full aft trim one can't fly hands-off for even a moment without doing a nose dive. The plane isn't very stable in the lateral axis, either—perhaps a good thing for a student.

The noise level is awfully high, especially in view of the low performance level. It is so light and the elevator so responsive that one can delay a flare until the last moment; thus a student may not develop a proper respect for a high sink rate that might be more characteristic of a higher performance plane, such as the earlier Cherokees.

The abrupt pitch-down in stall-spin is a great "gut" test of a student's cool; however, for serious spin training perhaps it would have to be supplemented by a "flatter" type reaction plane. The nose steering is awfully sensitive.

On the positive side, first is the marvelous Piper mechanical flaps. The handle is right there beside either pilot, one can feel the clicks and never has to look down at an indicator. And you can control the rate up or down as desired, unlike electric flaps. I assume they are even more service-free than electrics. I love my '77 Mooney 201, but would pay extra to have the Piper flap system in it.

The visibility is great—much better than in the wider Cherokee, and better than in the 172, where the wing blocks the view everywhere except down and forward. The panel layout and fuel controls are excellent. I like the throttle quadrant; however a student transitioning to a more complex plane like my Mooney Ranger or an early Bonanza would have to discipline himself to look harder for items, especially in fuel management. Having full access to the engine with the removable cowling is excellent.

I'm a private pilot, 360 hours, and took my first lesson in a Tomahawk at San Diego Montgomery Field. I did most of my training in a Cherokee 140 since it was a bit more like a heavier "real" plane. I returned to the Tomahawk for spin training and have about 15 hours in it. While doing instrument training at Vero Beach (Flight Safety), I found most of the students liked the Tomahawk well enough, and the instructors felt it was a good teacher, though the older instructors preferred to ride in the 140s.

Bill Greenwood
Aspen, Colo.

I just finished training as a student pilot using a Tomahawk.

Pros: 1) It forced me to fly since it was very sensitive to changes in attitude.

2) Comfortable seating.

3) Good visibility.

Cons: 1) Sometimes the plane would not start even though the engine was well maintained. On two occasions, I had to cancel my lesson and once (for a X-C) we used a Warrior, because the Tomahawk would not start. The mechanic kept the plugs clean and checked and re-checked the engine. They never could figure out the cause of the starting failure.

2) The T-tail makes pre-flight check of the elevator very difficult.

3) Not very stable in up/down drafts.

Curt J. Firestone
Ukiah, Calif.

Cessna 152

Sleek and shiny, with good manners aloft, and designed to digest 100LL with ease, the Cessna 152 was to have been Cessna's ultimate improvement on the ultimate trainer—the venerable 150. But alas, a panoply of mechanical gremlins, plus high parts prices and high acquisition cost (not to mention one of the worst recessions ever to hit the U.S. aviation industry) sent new-152 sales into a screaming spiral dive just three years after the model's introduction. The used market, as a result, now draws from a vast reservoir of late-vintage Cessna 152s—many available at fire-sale prices.

Whether a used 152 represents a true bargain is another question. For the owner willing to live with 100-knot cruise speeds, frequent bouts with lead fouling, and relatively expensive (for a trainer) annual inspections, a several-year-old Cessna 152 can provide a reasonable modicum of performance and utility in the $7,000-$17,000 "sport plane" category. But the prospective 152 purchaser who thinks he's merely getting a modernized, "improved" Cessna 150 may need to think again. A fancy 150, the 152 is not.

History

"Operators of the 150 told us they wanted a training airplane that would burn 100-octane fuel, while producing lower noise levels, better fuel consumption and more payload," Cessna's Bob Lair remarked at the time of the 152's debut in spring of 1977. What operators got was an airplane that was—and is—subject to severe lead fouling, while delivering performance about equal to that of the Cessna 150—at a cost that made

some operators wince. The original 1978 Cessna 152 (introduced in May 1977) listed at $20,635 with Nav Pac.

In changing from the 150 to the 152, Cessna gave its trainer a 110-hp Lycoming engine (with 2,000-hr. TBO) to replace the previous 100-hp Continental (1,800-hr. TBO); a McCauley "gull wing" propeller; an oil cooler as standard equipment; a 28-volt electrical system; and flaps limited to 30 degrees (instead of the previous 40). For all these changes, the 152 owner got 40 pounds more useful load than was available in the original 1958 Cessna 150 (and about 60 pounds *less* than a 1948 Cessna 140 could carry).

After 1978, relatively few important model changes were made to the basic 152. Those that *were* made point to the original airplane's mechanical shortcomings, some of which were quite notable.

In the 1979 model year, for example, Cessna incorporated impulse couplings on both magnetos—rather than just the left one, as before—to improve the 152's conspicuously lousy starting characteristics. (Likewise, direct priming to all four cylinders was made standard.) In addition, a split cowl nose piece was conjured up (retrofittable under a service bulletin), to

Darling of the flight-school circuit, the 152 sold in prodigious numbers on its initial introduction in 1978. (A 1978 model is shown here.) Subsequent models have seen few outward changes, but many internal ones. The fleet now numbers in excess of 6,300. Production was halted for a while in 1985.

enable shops to remove the whole cowling without first taking off the plane's propeller. (If you intend to buy a '78 model, be sure it has this feature.) An improved brake master cylinder, with fewer parts, first made its appearance on 1979 models.

In 1980, again addressing the airplane's poor startability, Cessna went to a slower-turning starter (the applicable armature is retrofittable under Service Letter SE79-43), which allowed the impulse couplings to do their job better; and the plane's float carburetor got an accelerator pump as standard equipment. (Before, apparently, owners had been pumping the throttle to prime the engine, not realizing that without an accelerator pump, no fuel was coming from the carb.) Dual windshield defrosters were offered, and an even-more-expensive type of 24-volt battery (a "manifold" type) was made standard, eliminating the battery box.

In 1981, Cessna made the enlightened move of putting a spin-on oil filter on all 152s as standard—not optional—equipment. Larger battery contactors, with appropriate current capacity to eliminate contact welding, were instituted (to keep owners from having to replace so many $230 batteries after contactor fry-ups); and an avionics cooling fan became part of every avionics installation. Also in 1981, the 152's list price took a 25-percent jump, the largest single jump ever, to $30,175 equipped.

For 1982, Cessna added a quick-drain to the standpipe below the fuel selector (at the belly of the airplane), to allow drainage of sediment and water from the fuel system's true low point. This modification can be—and should be—retrofitted to all 150s and 152s (an STC'd kit is available for only $12.50 from Middle Tennessee Aircraft Components, P.O. Box 472, Smithville, TN 37166; Cessna wants $82.20 for its version of the kit), but has as yet been incorporated in relatively few applicable aircraft.

Finally, for 1983-model 152s, Cessna has gone to a 108-hp O-235-N2C engine that better tolerates the lead in 100-octane avgas; the avionics cooling fan is improved; a panel vacuum warning light is standard; and the gyro panel is redesigned to allow removal of gyro instruments from the front of the panel.

Investment Value

It generally takes four years for a new plane to bottom out on the depreciation curve—and that point was only recently reached in 1982 for the oldest 152s. However, trainers have been known to continue depreciating much longer than "normal" aircraft. Nonetheless, it is interesting to note that the 1978 models, after losing some 55 percent of their value in the first four years, had recouped six percent of their original value, or about $1,000 per airplane by mid-1984. As it turns out, this upswing in prices is not limited to 152s, but affects even 10- and 15-year-old 150s, which are also now commanding $1,000 more per

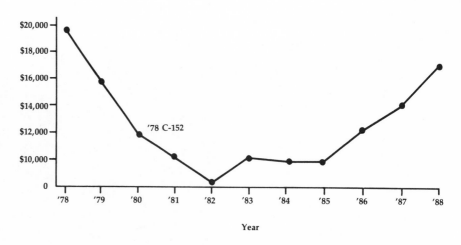

Cessna 152 Resale Value Chart

plane than they did a few years ago. (Piper Tomahawks have not done as well.) Evidently, buyer resistance to Cessna's latest new-152 prices has begun to put pressure on the used market. Several FBOs we talked to agreed. "I haven't got $36,000 to spend on a new 152 this year—or any year," one disgruntled flight school operator told us in 1983.

Sales of new 152s generally go to flight schools and/or school customers, who put the planes on leaseback. (In rental service, the plane becomes a source of revenue for lessor and lessee, while the owner realizes huge tax benefits. Or so the theory goes.) But leasebacks have been hard hit by the recession, and FBOs are struggling to maintain cash flow. Buyers for new 152s have suddenly disappeared. Recent sales figures confirm this: Cessna shipped 25 trainers in the first seven months of 1984 (compared to nearly 200 a month in 1978).

Still, training activity remains strong in many of the nation's flight schools, and replacement training aircraft have to come from somewhere. It will be interesting to see whether demand for used 152s at the FBO level will continue to increase, driving resale prices higher—or whether cost-conscious rental operators, realizing the potential of autogas, will opt for a return to the Continental-powered Cessna 150 (which can legally use

unleaded motor fuel, even in training use).

Performance and Handling

In terms of cruise performance and payload, the 152 enjoys no significant advantage over its Beech and Piper peers (the Skipper and Tomahawk), nor over the 150, for that matter. Top speed for the 152 is listed by Cessna as 109 knots, the same as for the Tomahawk and 150M (two knots more than the Skipper); likewise, the 152 Trainer's standard useful load of 528 pounds very nearly matches that of the Skipper (572 lbs.) and Tomahawk (542 lbs.). Some of the earlier 150s (E/F/G models) topped 600 pounds in load-carrying ability. But the useful-load issue is made moot by the 152's optional fuel capacity of 39 gallons—33 percent greater than the Skipper's 29 gallons or the Tomahawk's 30. In range and payload flexibility, the 152 thus enjoys a slight edge over its competitors—although you may well have to sacrifice a passenger (and/or baggage) to take full benefit of the 152's longer range.

Runway performance for the 152 is good. The Cessna simply gets off quicker—and stops shorter—than Brand B or Brand P trainers (a reflection of the 152's fortunate lack of a T tail). If short- or rough-field operations are being contemplated, the 152 wins hands down over its T-tail peers. Figure on an unstick distance of 725 feet for a fully grossed 152 at sea level (versus 780 and 820 feet for the Skipper and Tomahawk); and set aside a mere 475 feet for landing roll (vs. 670 or 707 ft. for the T-trainers). The 152, incidentally, lands about 10 percent longer than the 150—apparently due to the 152's 30-degree flap-travel restriction.

So where does the 152 really shine? Its confidence-inspiring slow-flight characteristics and straightforward Cessna-like handling provide the key. The plane stalls well and with plenty of warning. (Power on, you can get zero-knots indicated before approaching the burble.) Stability in all axes is outstanding. The barn-door flaps—electric, alas—are monstrously effective (but watch out for the pitch up on initial deployment). The 152's light wing loading makes it a bit uncomfortable in more than very light turbulence; otherwise, however, it flies very much like a miniature Skyhawk. Which is just what Cessna wanted, of course.

The 152, like the 150, also comes in an Aerobat version—which the Skipper and Tomahawk don't. (Only about one in 20 152s is an 'A' model, however.) If loops and hammerheads are your cup of pekoe, the A152 will grudgingly comply. But don't expect Pitts-like—or even Citabria-like—performance, and forget about sustained inverted flight (the engine dies).

Comfort

Although significantly better than, say, a Luscombe or Taylorcraft, the 152's cabin comfort is nothing to brag about (and in fact takes a back seat to that of either the Skipper or Tomahawk). Visibility is poor, noise level is high, and shoulder room is almost nonexistent. Thicker seat padding became standard with the 1979 models (the previous cushions taxed the endurance of even the most hardened CFIs), but even so, pillows are highly recommended for cross-country work.

Ventilation (via the wing-root pull tubes, and air leaks around the doors) has always been good in 150s and 152s, even, unfortunately, in the dead of winter. To add insult to misery, Cessna located cabin-heat and carb-heat pickoffs next to each other on the muffler shroud. (Even with carb heat turned off, the carb-heat plumbing provides a sizable plenum for the escape of desperately needed cabin BTUs.) In 1979, Cessna released a service letter, SE79-12, describing a kit to relocate the carb-heat source to the number-four exhaust riser. This allowed the muffler's total heat output to be utilized for cabin heat, resulting in a 30-percent increase in cabin heat flow. All 1980 and later 152s were delivered with this cabin-heat mod. The first 4,100 airplanes off the line, however, did not get the deluxe heater kit, and most remain unmodified. Check for compliance with Cessna Service Letter SEW79-12 before buying a '78 or '79 airplane.

Engine

In going from the 150 to the 152, Cessna switched from the venerable 80-octane Continental O-200-A to the somewhat more expensive (and powerful) Lycoming O-235-L2C. The rationale behind the engine change was threefold. First, with 80-octane avgas in increasingly short supply, more and more flight schools were reporting problems with lead buildup in their 150s' O-200 engines; Cessna wanted to give its dealers a trainer that could digest the higher-leaded 100-octane fuels. Second, the 150—which had seen empty-weight increases totalling nearly 150 pounds (or 15 percent) since 1958—was overdue for a horsepower boost. And third, Cessna—in accordance with proposed FAA and ICAO noise standards—wanted to see a reduction in the 150's internal and external sound levels. The high-compression Lycoming O-235-L2C, delivering 110 horsepower at 2,550 rpm instead of the O-200's 2,750, seemed a natural answer to all three requirements.

Many operators say that the switch to the Lycoming engine has been a mistake. Although it did rid the Cessna trainer of the O-200's starter-clutch woes (the small Continental uses a $600 starter adapter that can fail frequently and without warning), the Lycoming O-235 brought its own constellation of mechanical quirks. Parts prices were, in some cases, astoundingly high: The O-235-L2C's sodium-filled exhaust valves, for instance, listed for $213.08 each—versus only $64 for the O-200's solid-stemmed valves. (Likewise, a piston for the Lycoming engine cost about twice what the corresponding Continental piston cost.) What's more, the O-235's cylinders may not be ground over-size during a top overhaul (since it

Shoulder room is not great in a 152, and while the baggage area may look ample, useful load is not; Payload with full fuel (39 gals.) is 280 pounds—one pilot, plus enough left over to fill the copilot's seat or baggage area, but not both.

removes the nitride layer), whereas the O-200's jugs can be ground over. And if an owner elects to salvage run-out cylinders by chroming, extreme difficulty may be had in finding piston rings for final buildup. Unchromed rings must be used in chromed jugs—and no one, at present, supplies unchromed rings for 0-235s.

Other service quirks that have not endeared schools or their shops to the 152's powerplant:

• As originally delivered, the Cessna 152 came with Slick 4000-series "sealed" (i.e., unrepairable in the field) magnetos. A rash of unexplained capacitor problems led to engine failures in Tomahawks using the same engine/magneto combo, but the 152 was mysteriously unaffected. Nonetheless, operators soon tired of spending hundreds of dollars on new mags every time their "throw-away Slicks" needed points or bearings. A black market in bogus 152-mag "repair kits" sprang up, and Slick finally introduced a field-repairable version of the mags.

• The O-235 is one of few aircraft engines in current production that uses solid (not hydraulic) tappets. Valve lash in the O-235 thus varies with engine temperature, and O-235 valve-train clearances must be checked scrupulously every 100 hours, not unlike a motorcycle.

Lycoming, in an attempt to minimize lash problems, devised hollow-aluminum pushrods with steel ball ends (the idea being that the aluminum, which expands more than twice as much as steel on heating, would tend automatically to readjust lash at higher temperatures). Such construction calls for very critical ball-end fit tolerances, however, and—unfortunately—Lycoming's pushrod vendor failed, initially, to meet the necessary specs. As a result, pushrod "mushrooming" (pounding of the steel ball ends down into the pushrod) became common. After a fatal accident related to pushrod shortening in November 1980, FAA issued an AD on this subject. All defective rods should

Can you spot the maintenance design faux pas in this picture? Notice the one-piece nose cap, which presents total cowl removal with the propeller in place. (Late-model 152s have two-piece nose caps—a definite maintenance plus.)

by now have been taken out of circulation, but it bears mentioning that valve train clearances are critical and subject to frequent re-checking in the O-235.

• The O-235-L2C did not escape the inspection requirements of a 1981 AD (81-18-04) that called for replacement of iron oil pump impellers with late-configuration steel and aluminum ones. This caused many 2,000-hour engines to be summarily grounded.

Miscellaneous reports of low static rpm and uneven operation led Lycoming to issue a special bulletin for the O-235 (S.I. 1388C) outlining trouble-shooting procedures to restore full power. This service letter is now in its third revision.

Lead Fouling

Lead buildup—not only in spark plugs but in nooks and crannies in the combustion chamber, and on valves—has been a persistent problem in O-235 engines. So much so, in fact, that Champion designed a special spark plug just for this engine—the extended-electrode 'Y' series (e.g., REM37BY). The long-prong plugs do not scavenge lead any better than standard plugs; they merely have electrodes that sit far enough away from lead encrustations to constantly "burn clean." Once filled with lead, the 'Y' plugs continue to fire. (But they still must be replaced often.)

Most operators find that even with judicious leaning, spark plugs must be cleaned every 25 hours in a 152. "Otherwise," remarks one A&P, "at 100 hours, you can throw the plug away—it won't even be cleanable." Lead buildup on the inside of the cylinder affects spark plug life: Lycoming found that lead can be redeposited from the combustion chamber to clean spark plugs in as little as 25 hours. Accordingly, in Service Instruction 1418, Lycoming outlines a procedure whereby O-235 cylinders can be blast-cleaned with walnut shells without removal for top overhaul. (Prior to this, some operators were finding that early top overhauls were needed to prevent lead from reaching excessive levels in O-235 jugs.)

Safety

Safety statistics for the 150 and 152 are quite good. (In this regard, at least, trainers have come a long way since Piper Cub days.) An NTSB study found the Cessna 150 series with the lowest fatal accident rate—at 1.35 per 100,000 flight hours—of any two-seater, and one of the lowest fatal crash rates of *any* single-engine aircraft, period. The total accident rate, at 10.3 per 100,000 hours, is also quite respectable, again bettering most trainers *and* four-place aircraft.

If there's one fly in the safety ointment, it's the 152's relatively weak showing against the Piper Tomahawk. A special study by *Aviation Safety* (covering the period January 1978 through April 1980) found the 152 with a 38-percent higher total accident rate than the Tomahawk. (Fatal accident rates were about equal.) As a percentage of total accidents, the Cessna 152 is involved in disproportionately more groundloops, overshoots, undershoots, and fuel mismanagement accidents than the Tomahawk. The 152, on the other hand, fares much better than its Piper counterpart in the proportion of hard landing accidents and stall-spins.

Overall, the 152 has a sterling safety record, bolstered by the fact that there has never been an in-flight breakup of the airplane (despite a fair number of IFR-weather encounters by low-time pilots).

Maintenance

Many of the 152's early maintenance foibles (the most serious of which have been touched on above) have now been laid to rest and should not pose recurrent problems for used-trainer buyers. The 152's most serious ongoing maintenance problem involves lead fouling, which (according to some owners) can be severe even with proper leaning, the use of low-lead fuel, addition of TCP concentrate (a lead remover marketed by Alcor) to 100LL, correct adjustment of idle mixture, and switching to Champion long-prong plugs. All of these measures are unnecessary, of course, in a Cessna 150 operating on grade-80 avgas or unleaded automotive gasoline. But unfortunately, the 152's engine is restricted to 100-octane avgas for the foreseeable future. (In all fairness, private owners should experience fewer bouts of lead fouling than flight schools, since much of the 152's lead fouling is due to chronic overrich operation in the pattern.)

Prospective 152 buyers should check to see whether these important service bulletins have been complied with:
• E82-23 required a one-time inspection of 152 starter and battery contactors.
• SE81-38 outlined brake master cylinder modifications for 1979 through mid-'82 Cessna 152s (and post-1966 150s).
• SE81-24 puts a fuel quick-drain in the belly of pre-'82 Cessna 152 (and post-1966 150s).
• SE80-96 (Revision 1) calls for recurrent inspections of certain

The standard 152 panel features ARC radios, limited instrument space, and a generous amount of Royalite.

Stewart-Warner oil coolers on a variety of Cessnas, including the 152. This was also the subject of an AD.

• SE79-7 modifies the nose cap to allow removal of the cowl without first taking the prop off.
• SE79-11 and -43 concerned mods to improve the starting characteristics of pre-1980 152s.
• SE79-12 reroutes carb heat plumbing to improve cabin heat.
• SE79-16 outlines flap cable clamp mods that must be accomplished prior to 1,000 hours in service. This was also the subject of an AD (80-6-3); so make sure it has been complied with on any airplane you intend to buy.
• SE79-46 describes periodic inspection requirements for 152 carburetor airboxes. In 1982, Cessna came out with a service bulletin (SE82-12) describing an airscoop mod for the 152, compliance with which is also recommended.
• SE79-49 mandates vertical fin hardware attachment inspections every 100 hours. This now carries the force of law, under an AD (No. 80-11-04).
• SE79-57 describes a much-improved flap actuator mechanical stop for 1979 and earlier 152s.
• SE80-2: Another cabin heat mod.
• SE80-10 requires use of Loctite on certain starter screws, which have shown a tendency to back out.

We mentioned before the 152's bout with self-shortening pushrods (the subject of a late-1980 AD, and Lycoming S.B. 453). What we didn't mention is that compliance with this AD doesn't guarantee that you'll *never* see pushrod mushrooming in your 152's engine. There have been reports (not many, but a few), subsequent to the AD, of engines with the improved pushrods experiencing ball-hammering or mushrooming. Hence, along with a compression check, we'd recommend a check of valve clearances (or pushrod length) in any pre-purchase inspection of a 152.

Modifications

There are relatively few approved mods for the 152. Brackett Aircraft offers conversion kits for installation of wet-foam air filters on the 152 (replacement elements are only a few dollars for this type of filter, whereas Cessna gets about $25 for a new paper element). Brackett filters are available through any large FBO.

Avcon Industries holds STC No. SA1384CE for installation of a Lycoming O-320-E2D 150-hp engine in the A152 only. However, J&S Engineering, Inc., of San Antonio has an STC to install the 180-hp Lycoming O-360 in 150s as well as 152s, allowing a gross

Cost/Performance/Specifications

Model	Year	Number Built	Average Retail Price*	Cruise Speed (kts)	Engine	TBO (hrs)	Overhaul Cost
152	1978	2,625	$17,000	107	110-hp Lyc. O-235-L2C	2,000	$7,500
152	1979	1,559	$18,000	107	110-hp Lyc. O-235-L2C	2,000	$7,500
152	1980	949	$19,000	107	110-hp Lyc. O-235-L2C	2,000	$7,500
152	1981	619	$20,500	107	110-hp Lyc. O-235-L2C	2,000	$7,500
152	1982	432	$23,500	107	110-hp Lyc. O-235-L2C	2,000	$7,500
152	1983	245	$27,500**	106	108-hp Lyc. O-235-N2C	2,000	$7,500

Based on no damage history, six-month annual, all ADs complied, large tanks (39 vs. 26 gals.), 850 hours SMOH, full gyro panel, transponder with blind encoder, and 720-channel navcom. Add $500 if Aerobat. \
** *Deduct $47 per hour for every hour past 50 TTSN.*

weight increase of nearly 100 pounds to boot. Also, nose-wheel amputation is available through Custom Aircraft Conversions of San Antonio. The tailwheel conversion is claimed to boost speed by "8 to 10 mph," by eliminating drag and substituting prop thrust that would otherwise be blanked out by the nose gear. Details of the 180-hp engine conversion and the so-called Texas Taildragger mod can be obtained by calling Custom at 512-349-6347.

Organizations

The Cessna 150-152 Club has been around for several years and claims upwards of 1,000 members. The group's monthly newsletter (The Cessna 150-152 News), edited by Skip Carden, is an excellent clearinghouse of service-related information and info on new mods, discount parts sources, etc. Membership is $15/yr. domestic and Canada, $25/yr. foreign. Contact the club at 3557 Roxboro Rd., P.O. Box 15388, Durham, N.C. 27704, or phone 919-471-9492.

Owner Comments

We have operated four Cessna 152s for the past three and one half years here in our flight school. Our most popular one (a 1980 model) is doing about 700 hours per year. Hourly maintenance cost is about five dollars per hour. They burn six gallons per hour if properly leaned, lots more if run hard or full rich. All have had lousy compression since new, and even after tops or overhauls. 65/80 is typical throughout the 2,000 TBO span. Valve clearances must be checked each 100 hours. We go 100 hours without cleaning the plugs or changing the oil providing they are religiously leaned and run up to 1800 rpm for a minute before shut down. The 24-volt electrical system is a pain in the neck requiring $239 batteries at least once a year. The RT-385A radios are also expensive to repair when the lights (digits) burn out or they quit cold.

All in all it is a good trainer and rental but a few pet gripes of mine are:

Skylights on top provide a bit of extra visibility inside steep turns.

1) Who the hell needs a cruise prop (and therefore a 104 knot cruise speed) on a primary trainer used to build hours of training and proficiency? 2) It's a gas hog. 3) Cabin is four inches too narrow. 4) I miss the 40 degrees flap setting. 5) Too noisy (I *always* wear ear plugs). 6) Cessna Aircraft Co. overprices CPC supplies, parts, etc. 7) It's too damned expensive. In 1979 I bought two for $30,000. Now I can't get *one* for that price (new).

Despite the shortcomings, it is the best *new* airplane around for my purpose but honestly, I'd rather have a C-150 if I could find lots of clean low-time late models. Our answer to the problem is an Aeronca Champ. We have *one* but I hope it continues in popularity so we can buy another. In that Aeronca we can teach students how to really *fly* the airplane.

David B. O'Brien, Pres.
FBO Lakewood Airport
Bay Head, N.J.

My 1978 Cessna 152 is leased to a flying club, so perhaps all of my comments and data may not be comparable to aircraft operated by private owners. In addition, I am an A&P mechanic and do almost all of the maintenance myself, so labor cost is not included in maintenance cost, except for the annual inspection. But I am a pilot, so general comments are relevant.

Handling and performance are good, and the aircraft is certainly satisfactory for training purposes. However, on cross-country flights comfort is average to poor because

of lack of leg room for the taller pilot and skimpy seat padding. Seating width is poor for large people when both seats are in use. Power is adequate under all conditions (home field elevation is only 469 feet though).

Most complaints center around the rapid lead-fouling of the lower spark plugs which causes many flights to be cancelled after ground runup with a 200-300 rpm mag drop. Even using TCP and the newer Champion REM37BY plugs, the lower ones must be cleaned every 20-25 hours. Fuel availability is limited to 100 octane at the home field—no 100LL is available—so perhaps the plugs would stay clean longer with 100LL.

Nose wheel shimmy is a problem from time to time due to linkage wear and the pounding the nose gear takes from students and operation primarily from an unpaved runway.

I am not too happy with the 24-volt electrical system when it comes time to replace the battery. Last year the starter shorted internally and the parts cost for starter (rebuilt) and a Gill battery was $500. Parts availability is not a problem.

Cost of the last two annual inspections was $211 and $245. Annual **maintenance cost (without annual inspection or reserve) was $658 in 1981** (largely due to replacement of entire ignition system due to intermittent "misses") and $636 in 1982 (due mostly to the starter/battery failure).

The way the aircraft is used in flight training makes it difficult to accurately check fuel consumption (takeoffs and landings, forgetting to lean the mixture, etc.) but it appears to be close to the numbers published in Cessna's Pilot's Operating Handbook.

I hope your other readers will benefit from this information, and perhaps someone has a solution for the plug-fouling problem.

Norman J. Makowski
Fairport, N.Y.

Beech Skipper

The Beech Skipper was barely out of the starting blocks when the Great Aviation Depression set in. Beechcraft built only 312 of these two-place trainers, starting in 1979, and it abruptly halted production in 1981. The majority of Skippers are now in private hands, though a few still find duty on flight school lines and at Beech Aero Clubs across the country. How has the airplane fared, and what can a prospective owner expect from this two-placer? *Aviation Consumer* takes a look.

History

As a competitor to the Cessna 152, the Skipper actually stood a chance at creating a similar market niche for Beech. Though the design never reached maturation, the Model 77 (its numeric designation) represented a good training airplane. Despite its pleasant flying qualities (and barring a dramatic upswing in the training market), the Skipper has taken its spot on the endangered species list of general aviation, to dwindle through the years from the forces of attrition.

We first flew the Skipper in 1979, reporting on it in our January 1, 1980, issue. At that time we were mostly interested in comparing this newcomer with the Cessna 152 (the all-time training leader) and the Piper Tomahawk (another new design). Startlingly similar in outward appearance to the Tomahawk, the Skipper flew quite differently. It also represented a "major commitment" by Beechcraft to the bottom end of their product line.

Beech started up Beech Aero Centers (more on these follows), producing Jeppesen-Sanderson-style textbooks and course materials for flight training. It looked as though Beech was really getting its act together to compete with Cessna Pilot Centers, all the while furthering the brand-loyalty theory of future aircraft sales, their real motive. Then the bottom dropped out.

Light-aircraft deliveries entered the graveyard spiral from which they still have not recovered, and the Skipper was an early casualty. While the Beech Aero Center concept worked at some FBOs, only a few survive to this day. However, Beech still publishes a newsletter for Aero Centers, and active clubs have regular fly-ins around the country. We found just such an Aero Center at Hammonton Aviation in Hammonton, N.J.

Takes a Licking and Keeps On Ticking

We even found old serial number 39, the same Skipper we flew back in 1979, on their line. We were very interested to see how it had held

Beechcraft Skipper

up, after nearly 2,000 hours of training and rental time had been put on the tachometer.

Well, the engine had already been overhauled once, after a student taxied into a ditch and caught the prop, causing sudden stoppage.

And the tail skid had once been rammed up into the empennage after over-rotation on a soft-field takeoff. This required moderate repair, and the new lines of rivets sit in evidence. Other than that, the airframe had held up pretty well. Oh, there are places where fairings or inspection panels look a little ratty, but this is akin to the cracked plastic fairings one finds on Cessna landing gear and struts. Incidentally, the second Skipper on the line also hit its tail skid, but it didn't take as long to fix. As George Arslanian of Hammonton Aviation said, "We got pretty good at doing tail skid repairs, the second time around."

The tail on the Skipper is reasonably powerful, aerodynamically. But the cause of dinging the skid isn't the T-tail configuration, as

The NASA-developed GAW wing is fat, but attractive. It delivers alot of lift, but isn't really an improvement over the Cessna 152.

many might surmise. No, Beech did its homework with the tail aerodynamics on the Skipper. It delivers good control feel and response right down to taxi speeds, unlike the Tomahawk (and other Pipers with T-tails), which demonstrates an on-again-off-again behavior around rotation speed.

The Skipper's elevator control forces are light, but not so much so that overcontrol is a problem. Cessna 152s bang their tails on the ground from time to time, too, requiring sheet-metal repairs in the area of the tie-down ring. Minor accidents just come with the territory, when airplanes are relegated to the training environs.

Handling Qualities

Our evaluation pilot in 1979 characterized the Skipper "a de-

light to fly." Today we really can't argue with that appraisal. And our more recent flight was on a hot and gusty day with a strong crosswind—conditions that put not inconsiderable demands on the Model 77. Control forces in the airplane are well harmonized. Control response makes it easy for a student pilot to perceive the effects of his inputs. The Skipper is an "honest" airplane in that it is easy to see what the airplane is doing, versus what the pilot is doing.

Adverse yaw, for instance, is rather pronounced in the Skipper. There is no question about the rudder pressure and movement that the pilot has to employ to coordinate with aileron. However, there is a lack of good directional cues over the engine cowling, so instructors in Skippers have to guide their students' eyes to point out yaw. Pitch attitude is difficult for the beginning student to discern, as well, owing to the sloping nose as viewed from the

pilot's seat (kind of like a Porsche). But no trainer is perfect.

The ailerons on the Skipper are pleasantly light, and the roll rate is perhaps even a bit too high. (But after all, Wolfgang Langeweische does say in *Stick and Rudder*, that aileron design is the most difficult control for airplane builders to work out.) The odd thing about the Skipper's ailerons is that they rather rapidly lose effectiveness as the stall is approached—much more than other trainers. If the pilot continues into a full stall in the airplane, it is very easy to allow some yaw-induced roll to develop. Attempting to pick up the falling wing with aileron yields little result. As soon as the stall is broken, however, the ailerons are ample to right the little ship again.

To Spin or Not?

Adverse aileron at the stall is what will spin a Skipper, however. In fact, it won't spin *without* aggravated aileron at the entry. With no

The Skipper, Beech's Baby Bug-Smasher, is a roomy, noisy, fun little bird.

With no aileron input, you will get a steep spiral, which must be recognized for what it is and recovered from before overstressing the airplane. This leads to the classic dilemma about the use of ailerons in stalls. Should an airplane bite you when you use adverse aileron? Or should the ailerons keep flying right through the stall? Should trainers be spin-resistant, or spin-capable?

It's only our opinion, but we like a wing that gives up flying more definitively, without need for opposite aileron to induce a spin (if indeed a spin is what you wanted in the first place). The bottom line is that the Skipper is different from the Tomahawk or Cessna 152 in this regard. It is actually more like some of the pre-World War II trainers. So instructors in Skippers ought to be sure to discuss stalls and spins in depth with students.

As a two-seat airplane for the private pilot, the Skipper is very easy to trim. It holds trim speed tenaciously, in fact, regardless of power and flap extension. As a trainer, though, it might have been better to require the student to cope with trim a bit more. Skipper CFIs will have to be careful to make sure their students learn proper trimming. Elevator forces are light enough to allow pilots to just about ignore trim in the landing pattern—a bad habit. Incidentally, the trim indicator is an inaccurate and difficult-to-see affair below the throttle quadrant, so maybe it's good there isn't much need for it—except to make sure it is properly set for takeoff.

Landings and takeoffs in the Skipper are quite easy, even in a gusty crosswind. The airplane has sufficient controllability to do what you want it to do, despite its feeling kite-like (one pilot called it skittery), a trait it shares with the Cessna 152. It is rudder-limited in crosswind authority—more so than a lot of

airplanes. The nose is easy to hold off at flare, and there is no tendency toward PIO. The elevator, as we said, is powerful, even at slow speeds.

Performance

The Skipper is no homesick angel, that's for sure. Despite the fact that it is equipped with a Sensenich propeller that develops well over 2,500 rpm, the airplane takes forever to climb. And we flew it from a strip basically at sea level. We also had only one-third fuel on board. On one touch-and-go we didn't get organized and off again until nearly the end of the paved runway at Hammonton. We rose to about 50 feet and flew nearly level with the trees for another couple thousand feet. Consciously directing our attention to removing any side-slip that was remaining from our crosswind takeoff, we got the airplane to climb.

We'd like to fly the Skipper some more, but our impressions in the

Cost/Performance/Specifications _____

Model	Year	Number Built	Average Retail Price	Cruise Speed (kts)	Rate of Climb (fpm)	Useful Load (lbs)	Fuel Std/Opt (gals	Engine	TBO (hrs)	Overhaul Cost
77	1979	47	$13,000	97	720*	575	29	115-hp Lyc. O-235-L2C	2,000	$8,000
77	1980	140	$14,000	97	720*	575	29	115-hp Lyc. O-235-L2C	2,000	$8,000
77	1981	125	$15,500	97	720*	575	29	115-hp Lyc. O-235-L2C	2,000	$8,000

Value from Beechcraft Approved Flight Manual—actual performance may vary

pattern, and on extended climbs, is that the Skipper is unusually sensitive to sideslip. We did lean the mixture to best power and it got well over a hundred rpm more. (Referring to a Lycoming service bulletin about the O-235 engine led to the conclusion that the carburetor was definitely over-rich, and probably should be overhauled.) One thing is for sure—Beech's book figure for rate of climb is exaggerated at 720 feet per minute. The best climbing trainer around is the Cessna 152, with its advanced-design gull-wing propeller. Operating a Skipper from a high-density-altitude strip with obstacles is something to be considered with caution.

The day we flew the Skipper was hot, humid and turbulent. A speed check barely got us up to 85 knots indicated, and this was at 2,600 rpm. At 2,500 feet and full throttle we should have been showing upwards of 95 knots, according to the book. Our flight in 1979 came out closer to book figures, so we really couldn't get down to specifics from the later flight. From our previous flight with the Skipper and the similarly configured Piper Tomahawk we know that the Skipper is the slower. The Cessna handily beats both the T-tails.

Load Carrying

The load-carrying ability of the Skipper falls right in line with other two-place trainers. Full fuel (29 gallons) and two normal-size adults put you at gross weight, or even a tad over. The gross weight is 1,675 pounds, and our test plane had an empty weight of 1,177 pounds, owing to a dual-navcom full-IFR panel; thus, our useful load was just 498 pounds. The cavernous area behind the seats of the Skipper usually goes for naught, since you can't really use it unless you're solo.

Human Engineering

One of the Skipper's main claims to fame is its instrument panel, a wide

and substantial affair crafted of metal (there is no plastic in sight). Instruments, controls and gauges are logically and clearly laid out, except for the trim indicator we mentioned above, and the carb heat lever, which is located and configured like the propeller pitch control on a larger plane. The engine gauges are nicely positioned above the throttle quadrant, and normal scan includes them much more often than in a lot of presumably more "sophisticated" birds.

Creature Comfort

The other thing nice about the Skipper is its cabin width—fully five inches wider than the Cessna 152's. It may be even a bit *too* wide, in our opinion. We got the impression of being surrounded by the airplane, rather than a part of it. Of course, it takes a shoehorn to get some people into the Cessna, so that's the other end of the spectrum. Cabin noise is quite high, again indicative of an unrefined design. Sitting farther away from your cabinmate means you have to speak up that much more. The Skipper could use an intercom system, particularly for instruction.

Switches and circuit breakers are the typical beefy Beechcraft variety. We overheard a Skipper student say that she felt the metal panel and the kind of no-nonsense presentation were an indication of Beechcraft airplanes overall—solid and reliable. There's no doubt about it. The Skipper may fly differently than other Beechcraft, but it carries a Beechcraft motif throughout. That's okay—the Cessna 152 doesn't exactly fly like its big brother the 210 either, but it certainly *is* a Cessna in shape and form. Thus starts the brand-loyalty scheme of things.

Maintainability

The Skipper seems to be an easy airplane to maintain. We foresee two possible considerations, however, which could cause it to cost more than the ubiquitous Cessna 150/152 series. First, there aren't many Skippers out there. We called several Beech dealers who clearly stated that they had sold Skippers in their day, but that there weren't any around anymore—and certainly none on their flight lines. One dealer said he was a full-line Beech dealer, but when queried about the Skipper said, "Oh, no.

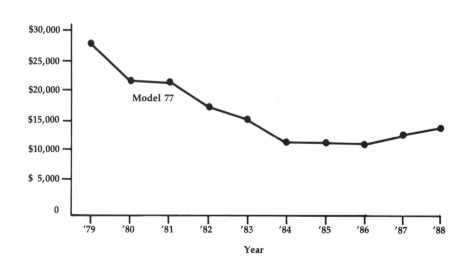

Skipper Resale Value Chart

We haven't trained or rented those for years; we use the Cessna 152.''

The small number in the Skipper fleet could make finding a mechanic who even recognizes one, much less has a maintenance manual, difficult. We'd recommend a new Skipper owner take his plane to a Beech dealer or Aero Center for his first inspection. The goal in this would be to learn as much as possible about the airplane, as well as to make sure everything is up to snuff (Beech service bulletins, etc.). This tactic would certainly cost a little more the first time around, but you would then be better equipped to direct a non-Skipper A&P at a future inspection.

The other problem is a source of parts, the only such being Beechcraft, of course. Beech's parts prices have historically been higher than the rest of the industry, so we'd expect the same for the Skipper. But the Skipper is such a simple airplane that, barring major airframe damage or the need for airframe parts, contributions to the Wichita economy should be minimized.

Powerplant

The engine in the Skipper is the Lycoming O-235-L2C, the same one in the Cessna 152 and Piper Tomahawk. This engine has had its problems with spark plug fouling, stuck valves and hard starting (among others), particularly in the Cessna, though its performance should be airframe-independent. Overhaul cost for the little Lycoming is listed as $6,000 in the *Aircraft Price Digest*, about $500 less than the O-320 series (1986 prices). Practical experience has shown that the O-235 can actually cost more to overhaul, since the likelihood of cylinder and/or valve problems is greater.

The most important maintenance item on the Skipper is the integrity of the exhaust system. When we first opened the door of our '79 test

ship, we immediately noticed the presence of a carbon monoxide test strip, an indication that leaky exhaust can spell trouble in this airplane. There was a rash of muffler problems with early Skippers, and the cabin design lends itself to sucking in stray exhaust and promptly turning a test strip black—perhaps because of the control cable channel on the underbelly of the plane. The muffler and stack design were changed early on, and all Skippers should have the newer system, but it would make sense always to pay particular attention to the exhaust on this bird.

A minor but annoying item has to do with the fuel tank vents, located near the wing root and leading edge of each wing. It is easy to bump one of the vents (a short piece of aluminum tubing facing into the airstream), and inadvertently cause an imbalance of fuel flow from the tanks. Apparently, if the vents aren't exactly symmetrical between the left and the right, a slight pressure differential results between fuel tanks. The Skipper's fuel system has positions for both or off, so in the both position the fuel can flow preferentially from one wing. Though the flow will proceed normally with quite divergent readings on the gauges, Skipper instructors tell us it's difficult to convince a student that things are okay when one tank reads empty and the other one is still quite full.

SDRs

A search of FAA Service Difficulty Reports filed by mechanics revealed no statistically significant trends concerning the Model 77. There *were* quite a number of reports filed on the shoulder harness attach brackets, but these were back in 1981. The bracket was promptly covered by an Airworthiness Directive late in that year, correcting the problem. It was the same situation with door hinges, save for the A.D. Make sure that

you check the door alignment and hinges on any Skipper you're eyeing, for (as with the Tomahawk) latching the doors can be a pain. And since it is common practice to leave the doors open on the ground to improve ventilation, fumbling around with the overhead latch comes at just the wrong time—right as you're cleared onto the active runway.

Accident History

We found four fatal accidents involving Skippers. One resulted from a student pilot taking a friend on an ''unauthorized'' night flight and losing control of the plane. He had no night experience. Another pilot had been known to skip his wheels on the surface of a lake. Nothing was found but a wheel floating in the water. The third Skipper struck trees on a VOR approach after the plane stalled due to excessive ice on the wings. And the last was a stall/spin after the engine failed because of a loose nut on an exhaust valve adjusting screw. The plane was on its test flight after top overhaul—the mechanic was in the left seat.

The other Skipper accidents were almost exclusively training-related: propeller strikes, smashed nose gears, veering off runways, landing short—that sort of thing. With the Skippers finding themselves into private hands in increasing ratio, these accidents should decline in frequency in the future.

Beech Aero Clubs

As we said above, Beechcraft positioned the Skipper at the bottom of its chain in the hopes that Beech-trained pilots would naturally upgrade into other Beech products. We think the ecological niche created for the Skipper made sense. It's too bad the baby Beechcraft wasn't born a few years earlier.

Summing Up

We still like the Skipper, though our editor on this assignment would have to disagree with the earlier assessment that the Skipper has more retail appeal than the 152. The Skipper flies as well as the Cessna, but it's a "fifty-footer" in comparison. Sure, it looks pert, cute and friendly from a distance. But closer than 50 feet and you notice the bluntness of the cowl, the rivet heads along the whole fuselage (Beech uses such big rivets), the unsculptured sheet metal construction of the whole plane. The Cessna, on the other hand,

benefits from years of evolution, so its lines are about as cleaned-up as can be cost-effectively accomplished on a two-seater.

Practically, the Skipper can be had for a little less money than a 152. The Cessnas are growing in value as flight schools snap up the good ones for their fleets. But the Beech might cost a little more to maintain in the long run, owing to its different-ness (there weren't

enough made) and the unknowns of parts prices. The Skipper is noisier and slower than the 152. Its lethargic rate of climb should be of concern where it matters, but otherwise could be lived with. The good visibility, roomy cabin and flighty controls make it fun to fly for both pilot and passenger. It would be nice to see a turnaround in general aviation include the resumption of Skipper production, but don't hold your breath.

Piper Super Cub

Piper's PA-18 Super Cub is an anachronism, an outdated airplane based on primitive 1930s technology—but for a flying job that requires hauling heavy loads out of short, rough fields, there's nothing better.

It's ironic that the only all-new lightplane to be certified in this country in the last few years, the Christen Husky, is essentially a polished-up Super Cub, and it came on the market only because Super Cub production stopped back in 1983.

There's still a big demand for the PA-18 in the used-plane marketplace, and resale prices have remained amazingly high over the years, holding a better percentage of their original value than even such blue-chippers as the Beech 33 and the Mooney 201. Although most Super Cubs were originally sold as hardworking bushplanes or cropdusters, used models make fine all-around STOL sportplanes—if you get one that hasn't been abused.

Genealogy

The Super Cub's family tree takes root in the legendary J-3 Cub, the model that personifies the phrase "small airplane" to three generations of the non-flying public. The J-3 was born in 1940, reached its production peak in 1946, and in 1948 was spruced up and renamed the PA-11. The first PA-18 Super Cub models appeared in 1950. One of them, called the PA-18-95, was simply an outgrowth of the PA-11 fitted with a 90-hp Continental. The other Super Cub model that year was the PA-18-105, which had a 115-hp Lycoming O-235, flaps, a counterbalanced elevator and other features that were to distinguish the Super Cub from its forebears. (Some purists, in fact, don't consider the PA-18-95 to be a "real" Super Cub, even though it was produced in small numbers until 1961.)

In 1951, the O-235 was replaced with a 125-hp O-290; in 1952, that engine got souped up to 135 hp. Finally, in 1955, the Super Cub got the engine that it really deserved: a 150-hp O-320, which remained the standard Super Cub engine until production stopped in 1983. The Super Cub remained essentially unchanged for those 28 years, a record of consistency matched by no other airplane we're aware of. (Bonanza boosters should note that the F33A's current 285-hp configuration is only 20 years old.)

Model Changes

Changes and options to the Super Cub were few over the years, and came, as in the old VW Beetle, only as necessary improvements. Here's a list of some of the more important functional changes:

• In 1961, an optional metal belly pan was made available on all Super Cubs. (Previously, it was supplied only on the crop-dusting

1978 Super Cub

versions.) The mod also includes a beefed-up lower rear fuselage. The option is a good one, but watch out: many of the airplanes ordered with it were used as chemical sprayers, and the structure may have suffered corrosion as a result.

• Vacuum pumps. In 1963, Piper switched from the old "wet" oil-lubricated pumps to the modern dry pump. Many pilots think it was a step backward; the wet pumps, although more expensive and messier, are the soul of reliability, and they can be overhauled at reasonable expense. The dry pumps, on the other hand, have a mediocre reliability record and cannot be overhauled. You pays your money and takes your choice.

• About 1965 (even Piper couldn't tell us the exact date), zinc chromate anti-corrosion treatment was added to the wings. If you're considering a mid-60s model, remove an inspection cover and check the color of the metal. Yellowish green is good, anything else is not so good. At the same time, Piper beefed up the fuselages with more 4130 steel and heli-arc welding.

- In 1971, Piper switched from the traditional Grade-A cotton fabric covering to long-lasting Ceconite. Although cotton shrinks less in very cold weather, it has a shorter lifespan, from three to a maximum of 10 years. Ceconite, by contrast, will last 10 years under most conditions, and can go much longer than that if pampered.

- In 1973, a tail-mounted strobe light was made available as an option.

- In 1976, the old visual float fuel gauges were replaced with panel-mounted electric gauges. Although they are neater looking, pilots tell us the old gauges are more accurate and reliable.

- In 1977, Piper switched from the old-style DC generator to a 60-amp alternator. The alternator is retro-fittable to older models, however, and is a desirable feature for Super Cubs equipped with multiple radios, strobes, etc.

- In 1978, the ailerons were changed from fabric to aluminum. Although cheaper to fabricate, the metal surfaces are not so easily repaired, a problem for bush operations. Like the alternator, the metal ailerons are retrofittable to older airplanes. The year 1978 also saw a switch to more powerful and reliable Cleveland brakes, a partial solution to the Super Cubs long-standing awkward and ineffective heel brakes. These are also retrofittable to older aircraft.

Like many other airplane models, the Super Cub died in the Big Slump that hit general aviation in the early 1980s. In 1981, Piper sold off the marketing of the Super Cub to a Texas company called Wes-Tex, for which Piper manufactured airplanes to order in lots of 50 or so. That arrangement lasted only two years, and production of the PA-18 line ceased altogether in 1983 after a total run of 33 years and 8,442 aircraft.

The Bear Market

The Super Cub, despite its antiquated appearance and dusty workhorse role, holds its value extremely well. Late-model PA-18s in good shape still fetch well over $30,000—nearly what they cost new, even in the inflated dollars of the period. A 1975 Super Cub has a "bluebook" value of $25,000—exactly what it cost to buy more than a decade ago. A 1968 model is worth 50 percent more than its new price, and a 1955 model is today worth double its new price tag.

The Super Cub's blue-chip status is nothing new; PA-18s were commanding top dollar on the used-plane market well before production ceased. A 1975 model, for example, sold new for $19,700, but dropped to only $16,500 the next year, a drop of 15 percent instead of the usual 20-25 percent for most aircraft. Instead of continuing to slide for another three or four years, as most used-plane resale values do, the value of that 1975 Super Cub rebounded to $17,250 the next year, and has held steady or appreciated every year since. Its current bluebook value is $22,000, a cool 112 percent of the original price.

By contrast, the supposedly much-in-demand Mooney 201 of similar vintage is worth about 77 percent, and a high-status Beech Baron 58 rings in at 51 percent of original value. If you're looking for a place to

A 1980 model like this can demand an average price of $38,000.

put your money after last October 19, you might try stockpiling Super Cubs.

Will the value of a Super Cub purchased today keep climbing indefinitely? Probably so. The last time we reported on Super Cubs, in 1980, we commented on the excellent resale value of the older models, but went on to predict, "It's not likely that the current production Super Cubs will do as well; the current new price of $30,000 is highly inflated, and it's doubtful that a 1980 Super Cub purchased today will ever fetch $30,000 again (assuming reasonable inflation rates)."

Well, guess what. Inflation has been very reasonable since then, but the current value of a 1980 Super Cub is $31,000. Lesson: don't underestimate the power of this bear market.

Performance

It's not hard to imagine what happens when you put a big engine and a big wing on a light two-place airplane: STOL (Short Take Off and Landing) performance to burn. Although other bigger, more complex and more expensive aircraft like the Helio Courier have established excellent reputations for STOL performance, if you ask the people who really use them—the bush pilots, the cropdusters, the outback charter pilots—the Super Cub is usually considered the ultimate STOL airplane. One grizzled Alaskan bush pilot sums it up this way: "I've been full circle from PA-12s to 170s, 180, 185s and a Helio Courier, but when you get right down to the dirty work, the Super Cub fits our needs better than any airplane ever built." Another Alaskan confirms, "Up here, the Super Cub is pretty much considered the ultimate airplane for bush flying and performance."

Here's what they mean: book takeoff roll at gross weight is 200 feet. Heavily overloaded, a Super Cub may grind along for 300 feet before becoming airborne, pilots tell us. According to one owner, he once won a short takeoff contest, defeating a Helio or two in the process, with a roll of precisely 19 feet. (There was a 20-knot wind down the runway.) He says one Super Cub or another has won the contest every year it's been held.

Rate of climb according to the book is 960 fpm, but coming at a speed of perhaps 50 mph, that's a preposterous climb gradient of about 22 percent, even at gross weight. "With just the pilot and a little bit of gas, the climbout angle approaches vertical," comments one owner. (We're talking here about the 150-hp model; earlier

Despite poor visibility, noisy cabin, and a general lack of comfort for pilot and passenger, the aircraft is revered by owners.

versions with less power will have proportionally less takeoff and climb performance.)

The Super Cub may be a vertical valedictorian, but it's a horizontal hog. Cruising speed is a modest 115 mph, and most pilots throttle back to 100 or less to save gas. We do have a report from one Super Cub owner who claims he once passed a Skyhawk, but he admits to using a cruise prop. Even then, we have our doubts. Whatever this fellow's claim, the fact remains, if you're looking for good cross-country performance, try a Skyhawk, or even a Tri-Pacer, for God's sake.

Payload-Range

Talking about the Super Cub's gross weight and useful load is an exercise in ivory-tower academics; the PA-18 is probably overloaded more consistently, by bigger margins, than any other airplane. Safety ninnies may shake their heads and tsk tsk at this flouting of the rules, but consider that a 150-hp Super Cub has the same engine as a Skyhawk, a bigger wing—but a gross weight 550 pounds less. "Overload" a Super Cub by 550 pounds, and you've still probably got more climb performance than a grossed-out Skyhawk. (But we don't advise it.)

For the academics, gross weight is 1,750, with typical empty weights around 1,000 pounds. That's a useful load of 750, enough for a 200-pound pilot, 200-pound pass-

enger, a full tank of 36 gallons, plus 134 pounds of luggage or cargo.

Stories abound of amazing Super Cub overloads; one bush pilot reports taking off with an entire moose aboard—plus the hunter who killed it. Another swears he once carried five people in a Super Cub floatplane: pilot in front, one passenger sitting on another's lap in the rear seat, and one more hanging for dear life onto each float. (Kids, dont' try this at home.)

Range is lousy by normal cross-country standards; typical cruise fuel consumption is about 8-9 gallons per hour, good for about 3.5 hours with a small reserve. At the modest cruise speeds of the Super Cub—say 100-110 in the real world—you're looking at a practical range of only about 350 miles, 400 max. But hey, moose hunters rarely need to fly more than 400 miles anyway. And who could hang onto a float more than four hours?

Handling Qualities

The Super Cub flies like . . . well, just like a Cub. It's generally stable, well-behaved, and rather ponderous on the controls. But this myth of the Cub being easy to fly needs some skewering; by modern standards, compared to nosewheel craft, the Super Cub is very unstable on the ground, hard to land or take off, especially in a crosswind, and it stalls sharply, with a full wing drop that might startle Cherokee-trained pilots.

But in the context of taildraggers—with the built-in assumptions of instability on the ground, bouncing tendencies, terrible visibility during landing, takeoff and especially taxi—the Super Cub is a cinch to handle, without the vicious crow-hopping tendency of the Cessna 180 or the erratic rudder control of the Luscombe. Any nosewheel pilot who knows how to use his feet should have little trouble transitioning to a Super Cub.

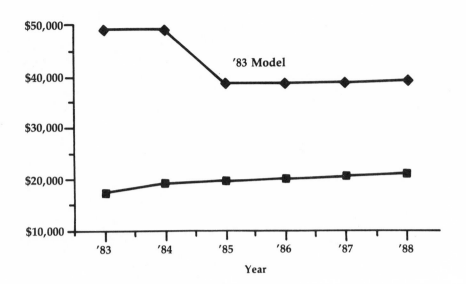

Super Cub Resale Value Chart

'83 Model

$50,000
$40,000
$30,000
$20,000
$10,000

'83   '84   '85   '86   '87   '88
Year

Limited aerobatics are permitted. It loops and spins nicely, but rolls are rather ponderous because of the sluggish ailerons.

Cabin Comfort

"Super Cub cabin comfort" is an oxymoron that ranks right up there with Army intelligence and jumbo shrimp. People must have been smaller back in the 1940s when the Cub was designed; anybody six feet or taller is going to have to perform some interesting gyrations to climb into a Super Cub. Actually, the PA-18 isn't as bad as the J-3, because the wing spar doesn't extend into the cabin, thereby allowing the seats to be raised and moved back slightly. This increases foot- and knee-room from nil to almost nil.

Baggage room is also very limited; there's only a small shoulder-wide compartment behind the rear seat. (To carry a moose, you've got to take the rear seat out.)

Visibility is lousy, and the noise level in the cabin is excruciating. E.A.R. plugs or good headsets should be standard equipment for any Super Cub pilot.

Safety

The Super Cub has a rotten accident record. This is partly due to its taildragger configuration (taildraggers as a group have accident rates double or triple that of comparable nosewheel aircraft); partly to the rugged high-risk type of flying that Super Cubs typically perform. (Hauling a moose off a sandbar is a bit more dangerous than doing touch and goes at Westchester County.)

The Super Cub's accident numbers are distressingly bad. Statistics from the early 1970s showed it had the worst accident record (both fatal and non-fatal) of any airplane in production as of 1980. Its fatality rate was three times higher than the Cessna 150's, for example. It had a particularly high incidence of stall accidents and mid-air collisions, according to National Transportation Safety Board figures. A study covering the years 1965-73 showed the PA-18 had a fatal stall/spin rate of 2.36 per 100,000 flight hours, second-worst of any plane then in production. By comparison, the Cessna 150 had a fatal stall/spin rate of 0.55, and the top-rated Cessna

182 scored 0.17—nearly 15 times better than the Super Cub's rate.

The very high rate of mid-air collisions can probably be blamed on two factors: first, the poor visibility, and second, the use of Super Cubs for fish-spotting, coyote-hunting and other low-level maneuvering flight involving pairs or teams of airplanes. The risk is obviously higher.

More recently, a printout of Super Cub accidents from 1982-87 (451 accidents in all, about 10 percent of them fatal) shows a similar pattern: stalls are by far the leading cause of fatal accidents. (We counted at least 16, more than a third of the total.) Moral for Super Cub pilots: although it has a reputation for "docile" handling, a Super Cub will stall readily, and if this occurs unexpectedly at low altitude, the result is often fatal.

Nearly half of all Super Cub fatal accidents during this period involved some sort of low-altitude maneuvering—crop-dusting, coyote-shooting, fish-spotting, or just plain old buzzing. Oddly, a lot of Super Cubs seem to go down

Cost/Performance/Specifications

Model	Year	Average Retail Price	Cruise Speed (kts)	Rate of Climb (fpm)	Useful Load (lbs)	Fuel Std/Opt (gals)	Engine	TBO (hrs)	Overhaul Cost
PA-18-95	1950-61	$9,000	85	710	700	18	90-hp Cont. C-90-12F	1,800	$4,500
PA-18-105	1950	$10,000	96	900	675	36	115-hp Lyc. O-235-C1	1,800	$7,000
PA-18-125	1951-52	$12,000	97	940	655	36	125-hp Lyc. O-290-D	2,000	$7,000
PA-18-135	1952-54	$13,000	95	870	872	36	135-hp Lyc. O-290-D2	1,500	$7,000
PA-18-150	1955-60	$15,000	100	960	804	36	150-hp Lyc. O-320-A2A	2,000	$7,000
PA-18-150	1961-65	$18,000	100	960	804	36	150-hp Lyc. O-320-A2A	2,000	$7,000
PA-18-150	1966-70	$19,750	100	960	804	36	150-hp Lyc. O-320-A2A	2,000	$7,000
PA-18-150	1971-73	$22,000	100	960	804	36	150-hp Lyc. O-320-A2A	2,000	$7,000
PA-18-150	1974-76	$26,000	100	960	804	36	150-hp Lyc. O-320-A2A	2,000	$7,000
PA-18-150	1977-79	$32,000	100	960	804	36	150-hp Lyc. O-320-A2A	2,000	$7,000
PA-18-150	1980-82	$38,000	100	960	804	36	150-hp Lyc. O-320-A2A	2,000	$7,000
PA-18-150	1983	$40,000	100	960	804	36	150-hp Lyc. O-320-A2A	2,000	$7,000

chasing animals of some sort. Accident reports mentioned cows, coyotes, bears, deer, wolverines and fish, among other fauna.

Nonfatal accidents accounted for the vast majority of Super Cub accidents, and often as not, the capsule description starts out with the phrase ''Pilot failed to maintain directional control . . .'' Another common thread of Super Cub non-fatal accidents seems to be the wide variety of off-field surfaces on which they occur. PA-18s have crashed while attempting to land or take off on, among other things, sand bars, gravel bars, beaches, dry lake beds, snow-covered lakes, dirt roads, prairies, tundra—and even a platform on a moving car. (That was an airshow act; the plane fell off the platform after touchdown.)

The Super Cub's huge excess of power and lift seems to encourage pilot zaniness that gets them into trouble. Several Super Cub accident reports mention that three or four people were aboard. And one fellow crashed when he lashed a boat to the right-hand float and tried to fly. To no one's surprise but the unfortunate pilot's, the plane entered an uncontrollable right turn shortly after takeoff and crashed.

The lesson for Super Cub pilots seems to be this: if you land on reasonable surfaces and don't maneuver at low altitude, you'll markedly improve your chances for survival. But of course, the Super Cub was essentially designed for rough-field operations and low-altitude maneuvering. Oh, well. Y'all be careful, now, hear?

Maintenance

Generally, the Super Cub is a rugged and robust airplane that's easy to fix in the field. (For example, a 1965 Super Cub has only 13 ADs against it—half the number of a Piper Cherokee of the same vintage.) Annual inspections typically run in the $300-$700 range, although some get by for next to nothing if the owner does a lot of the work himself. On the other hand, the fabric covering and steel tube fuselage means that the potential for catastrophic five-figure annuals is always just around the corner.

According to Super Cub mechanical mavens, here are some specific potential trouble spots to look for when considering any used PA-18 for purchase:

• Corrosion in the steel fuselage tubing. Particularly check the lower rear tubes, and be extra careful if the plane has done any spraying duty.

• Fatigue cracks in the threaded clevis bolts on the wing struts.

• Internal corrosion in the wing struts. (There's a big AD on this that should have been complied with, but check them again anyway.)

• Worn out landing gear hinge and shock strut bolts and bushings. The Super Cub gear is likely to have taken a frightful pounding over the years; inspect it closely.

• Worn top rudder hinge bushing, especially on aircraft with rudder-mounted beacons.

• Loose or worn out elevator trim jackscrew, especially in aircraft used for glider or banner towing.

• Check for ''metallization,'' which means that the steel tubes in the fuselage and tail have been coated with a corrosion-resistant layer of zinc (aluminum in the early models). This is a very desirable feature, since corrosion in the fuselage tubes is a big problem. The airplane's paperwork should indicate whether it's been metallized, and a stamp on the firewall is also an indicator.

Another item to consider: find out the airplane's service history, and inspect accordingly. Try to avoid airplanes used for glider or banner towing or cropdusting. If it served as a bushplane, check the landing gear carefully, and double-check the accident history and repair log. Pipeline patrol is easy on engines but tough on wings because of the constant turbulence at low levels. (Remember that the Cherokee wing crack brouhaha had its genesis in a pipeline-patrol aircraft.) And remember that taildraggers like the Super Cub are very likely to have a goundloop history, so check for hidden wingtip damage.

Service Difficulty Reports

A six-year FAA printout of Service Difficulty Reports shows only 143—barely two a month, and only a third of the number of accidents during the same period. This says two things to us: first, the Super Cub doesn't have a lot of mechanical problems; and second, that bush-pilots probably don't file many service difficulty reports.

We found no dominant patterns in the SDRs. Bad fabric cropped up on several reports, and the clevis on the tail bracket wire came under fire a few times. Several mentioned corrosion in the lift struts (not surprising, since an AD requires inspection for it), and there were several cases of sticking throttle butterflies. But overall, the Super Cub SDRs simply illustrate the wide variety of seeming random problems that can crop up on even a simple, well-proven aircraft.

Parts Support

The factory parts situation is, in the words of one dealer, "pretty iffy." On the other hand, the head of the Super Cub Pilots Assn. said there's no problem getting parts at all. Piper still manufactures some spare parts for the Super Cub, but in 1985 sold off the parts distribution business to Av-Pac, Box 81539, Lincoln, Neb. 68501, (402) 475-4125. An Av-Pac spokesman conceded some problems, particularly with wing ribs, but said Piper has promised to improve the Super Cub parts supply. At last word, however, Piper was reported preparing to resume production on the aircraft.

An alternative parts source is that old standby of rag-wing aircraft owners, Univair Aircraft Corp., Route 3, Box 59, Aurora, Colorado 80011, (303) 364-7661. Univair sells most Super Cub parts at very good prices.

Wag-Aero in Lyons, Wisc., (404) 763-9588 also sells some Super Cub parts.

Modifications

There is a raft of improvements and changes available for the estimated 4,100-plus Super Cubs active at last count. There are flaperons to lower stall speed, long-range fuel tanks, 180-hp engine upgrades with constant-speed prop, fish tubes in the fuselage, drooped tips and even left-side door arrangements.

Owner Group

There are two active groups supporting Super Cub pilots: the Super Cub Pilots Assn. in Yakima, Wash. and the Cub Club in Mt. Pleasant, Mich.

The Cub Club, formed in 1984, handles the entire cub line, from the E-2 on up through the PA-18, and issues a newsletter regularly. According to club chairperson John Bergeson, they have some 2,300 members. Dues are $10 a year for U.S. fliers, and $15 for Canadians.

Contact the Cub Club at P.O. Box 2002, Mt. Pleasant, MI 48858, (517) 561-2393.

Jim Richmond heads up the Super Cub Pilots Assn. (dues are $25 a year), and runs an organization named Cub Crafters, which provides a number of modifications.

One, called Top Cub, is a STOL kit installed at Yakima for $4,995, providing flaperons that reduce the stall by six mph.

Among the other STSs sold by Cub Crafters are one extending the baggage compartment ($225 for the kit), extended-range fuel tanks replacing the 36-gallon tanks for 61-gallon tanks (for $1,500) and a belly tank that adds 32 gallons, for the same price. More comfortable long-duration seats go for $350 a set, and big tundra tires and wheels go from about $2,500 new to around $1,000 used. Address of the Super Cub Assn. is P.O. Box 9823, Yakima, WA 98909, (509) 248-9491.

Owner Comments

We're a big aerial application operation, and we have two Super Cubs, a 150-hp and a 125-hp. We use them mostly for checking fields, shuttling personnel around, and low-level ag-pilot training. We also use them for aerial photography. We fly them each anywhere from 200 to 500 hours a year, depending on the year.

We've never had any problems with them. The lift struts have been okay. We figure our operating costs at around $22 an hour (assuming retail prices for gas). Annuals are cheap, less than $200. We figure about eight man-hours.

The major weak point is the difficulty of climbing in and out of them. The crosswind landings can be pretty squirrelly, especially with flaps down. My theory is that the flaps deflect a lot of air down away from the tail, which seems to reduce rudder authority. I also think the gear is a little stiff. I prefer the softer gear of an Aeronca Champ, for example.

The STOL performance is excellent. You can get one off the ground in 150 feet if you really push it. The 150-hp airplane cruises about 100 mph on 8.5 gph. It's a gas hog, but the 125 is a little better. Overall, we're satisfied with them. They do the job for us.

Jamestown Aviation
Jamestown, N.D.

We bought a 1976 Super Cub about 10 years ago for $17,000, as I recall. We've used it steadily since then, mostly for powerline patrol and wildlife surveys for the University of Georgia. During the winter months, we average 100-115 hours a month. It's a hell of a workhorse.

Most of our flying is low level and low power. For the line patrol, we throttle back to about 60 mph, with one notch of flaps. We get the fuel consumption down to five or six gph. Running that slow for seven or eight hours at a time, you'd expect lead-fouling problems, so we use TCP. It works well; we haven't had a lead problem. We don't use autogas, even though it would save us some money. We belong to the old school—you don't change horses in the middle of the stream.

The wildlife surveys are also low and slow, with a lot of maneuvering. We'll circle over a nest of wood storks, and then follow a pair wherever they go, radioing down to ground crews. The Super Cub is perfect for this sort of thing.

We do 50-hour oil and filter changes, and 100-hour inspections. The hundred-hours take two guys a day and a half or so, assuming there's nothing wrong. We occasionally have to pull a jug to replace a warped or burned valve, but the engine has been very reliable. We overhaul the engine every

couple of years, and we usually get the full 2,000 hours out of it. Occasionally we'll get more, up to 2,400 hours.

We've had no real airframe problems. The original fabric is still on the fuselage, although we had to replace the wing fabric after it ran into a flock of ducks. It's a good-performing airplane. It'll get in and out of anywhere there's a level place. Normal cruise is around 110 mph.

Overall, it's a hell of a workhorse, and a good money-maker for us. We rent it out with a pilot for $55 an hour, although of course the long-term contracts with Georgia Power and the University are less per hour. The Super Cub is a working airplane, not for pleasure. It's noisy and carries almost no baggage, but it does a good job at what it's supposed to do.

Forrest Boshears
Augusta Aviation
Augusta, GA.

I bought a 1976 Super Cub just for

fun. I paid $27,000, and it's been well worth the investment.

I fly it out of a very tough 1,200 foot strip down in a valley behind my house, with big obstacles at both ends. It's no problem at all. I've taken it into a 450-foot clearing with clear approaches. I suppose maybe a Helio or one of the new Huskies could get in and out of my strip, but not much else. We fly it just for fun, mostly just putting around at about 75 mph and a few hundred feet, looking at the scenery. My wife calls it a magic carpet. (Right now it's on skis.) We average about 75 hours a year.

Maintenance has been virtually nil. The two annuals have been about $300, and the total cost for unscheduled replacement parts was $8.50. Nothing at all has gone wrong with it.

A lot of people complain about comfort, but mine has a special interior with a lot of insulation, so it's much quieter.

Kenneth Hubble
Burlington, Conn.

Piper Cherokee 140

Thanks to a quirk of fate, Piper's Cherokee 140 at this stage in history has achieved a mildly special status. It's about as cheap and basic a knockabout flying machine as can be found this side of the old tail-dragger crowd that won't leave you feeling like a leaf pressed in a dictionary. That's because of its hybrid status—as a roomier-than-average two-placer that can carry four.

As for availability—there are zillions of them around at fields everywhere—6,300 is a ballpark figure from a recent census—and a great nesting ground of them in *Trade-A-Plane.* Furthermore it's an airplane every A&P can work on in his sleep—it's a known commodity in the maintenance shop. And it won't bite; it's as easy to fly as an airplane can be, and it has an excellent safety record, as well.

It's not, by the way, the cheapest transportation available. Among its contemporaries, the two-place Cessna 150 is a full $5,000 cheaper on the average for the same model year (1977, the last year the Cherokee 140 was built), and believe it or not a Piper Tomahawk of a year's later vintage can be had for even less than that ($8,500 or so). See the chart nearby.

History of the Line

It is perhaps fitting that the Cherokee 140, later to be given more genteel names like Flite Liner and Cruiser, began life as an improvisation. First came a four-place 160-hp Cherokee as a replacement to the rag-wing Tri-Pacer. For some unfathomable reason, a 150-hp version was brought out shortly after that.

Then it occurred to Piper to **retrogress** a bit further and make

the 150-horse version a 140-horse aircraft, throw out the two rear seats and make it an ad hoc trainer and a competitor to the Cessna 150, which was selling like hotcakes. Some convoluted marketing reasoning compelled the company to actually "derate" the engine to put out only 140 horses by using a restricted 2450 rpm on a climb prop.

When the silliness of this concept became apparent, in 1965 another prop was installed allowing the normal 2700 rpm, restoring the 10 horses temporarily lost. In the process the aircraft was given a 200-pound boost in gross weight (to 2,150 pounds) to restore it to full respectability. And the two-plus-two concept was introduced by slapping a couple of snap-on seats on top of the plywood plank that up till then had served as a luggage bin.

Following are other modest changes that came along through the years:

● In 1969 the B model came on the scene with a new instrument panel incorporating the famous "multi" throttle quadrant, introducing circuit breakers instead of fuses, and rocker switches for toggles. And it finally provided a decent, standard instrument layout in place of the scattergun arrangement used on Cherokees up till that point. The so-called deluxe Cruiser option

Starting in 1971 Piper brought out a stripped economy model of the 140 called the Flite Liner. This was a '73 version.

had wheel fairings and rear seats installed.

● With the 1970 C model came larger dynafocal (rubber) engine mounts to dampen engine vibration, along with overhead air vents and highly adjustable seats.

● The D model in 1971 brought a redesigned dorsal fin and inertial reel seat harnesses, with autopilots as an option. A stripped-down model was called the Flite Liner that year.

● In 1972 with the E model came the miracle of air conditioning—a great novelty in small aircraft, and a boon of no small dimensions for flight training in the blazing heat of the southlands in summer.

● In 1973 an entrance step was made standard.

● And in 1974 Piper put bungees on the rudders and increased the turn angle of the nosewheel for easier ground handling, and toe brakes became standard on the copilot's side.

● The last Cherokee 140 rolled off the line in 1977, eclipsed by the Tomahawk and overshadowed by the genuinely four-place Warrior.

Handling and Performance

The Cherokee 140 has come through the years with a deserved reputation as a benign trainer. In fact, its stall is so hard to induce that some instructors believe it insufficient to show the student a good, clean break. By the same token, some instructors say it's almost too easy to land.

Nevertheless, quite a few owners say it takes a bit of concentration to get a really nice greaser landing. Come in too fast and it floats; too slow, and it hits hard. One answer: come in slow with a little power in the flare.

The three-position manual flaps are quick and effective—so much so that many pilots say they rarely use over two notches. Watch that overhead trim—does it crank left or right? At least the nose pitches *down* with lowered flaps—a logical reaction if there has to be any. Some owners also complain of a high rate of sink at idle. The Hershey Bar wing is no sailplane airfoil.

When it comes to maneuverability, the 140 is no Pitts. Owners rate the control forces a bit heavy. The Warrior, by comparison, shows the beneficial effect of that plane's new wing geometry with lighter, more pleasant ailerons. The other side of the coin is stability, and instrument pilots characterize the 140 as a good, stable IFR platform.

As for performance, owners talk about cruise speeds of only 110 to 117 mph/96 to 102 knots TAS, though the book calls for 132 mph/115 knots at 75 percent power. Pilots count on burning about nine gph at 75 percent and seven to eight gph at 65 percent.

The 140 has 50-gallon capacity fuel tanks, with tab markings in the filler neck showing 36 gallons. In fact, the standard fuel was normally listed as 36 gallons, with 50 optional—presumably to discourage fliers from viewing the airplane as a true four-placer and overloading it.

Indeed, owners caution against ex-

The lowly 140 can really put on airs with air conditioning. Flight instructors and students need not "sweat it out" in southern summer climes.

pecting rocketship performance on takeoff and climbout in high-density altitude situations. Naturally, the temptation to load the aircraft too heavily when the rear seats are installed can lead to trouble.

Cabin Comfort

Since the 140 shares the same ample cabin width as other Cherokees, not counting the Lance, of course, it's a comfortable aircraft for two riders—much more so than the Cessna 150. This naturally makes the 140 a more sensible aircraft for cross-country flying. And if the rear compartment is used for baggage as originally intended, it's more than adequate. But there's no separate baggage bay when two passengers are in the back. Owners complain, incidentally, that there's no separate baggage door.

Comparison Buys

Except for its rather higher price, the Piper Warrior would be a much more sensible buy, since it has the same basic simplicity and durability of the 140, but nicer handling and standard seating for four plus space for baggage through a rear access door. On top of that it has another 90 pounds or so of useful load and better climb performance.

Unfortunately, the average price of the oldest, cheapest Warrior with

the 160-hp engine (the '77 model) is about $18,000, compared with $14,000 for the Cherokee 140. And older 140s can be bought for as low as $8,000.

Comparable Cessna 150s can be found for $6,000 to $9,000, and they'll yield better fuel economy; but this comes at the cost of shorter range, slightly lower cruise speed, a more cramped cockpit and lower payload. Cherokee 140 owners claim their aircraft gives a quieter cockpit as well.

Another even cheaper option is the Piper Tomahawk. Ironically, originally intended as a replacement for the 140, the T'hawk is selling for even less than the Cessna 150. Count on maybe $8,500 for a '78 model. Figure that one out. The used-plane market evidently has rated the Tomahawk a rather poor commodity.

Perhaps a dark horse in the two-place used-plane niche is the Beech Skipper, an "ultramodern" aircraft compared with the 140. The '79 model Skipper is going for an average of $12,000, though there aren't many of them out there, since only 312 were built.

Pilots with a fetish for aircraft with an abundance of *lebensraum* in their aircraft might also take a glance at the Beech Sport—which like the 140 is a kind of two-plus-two bird, but has an even more cavernous interior. The $12,500 average price tag (for a '77 model) afforded this aircraft, however, presumably reflects its even doggier performance.

Resale Value

Like most trainers, the Cherokee 140 does not exhibit the handsome rise in resale value of highly regarded aircraft with inflation—though that has now subsided. Instead, the typical resale value curve of a 140 is a dip to the bottom in three or four years, followed by a plateau for the rest of its history, perhaps with a modest rise in worth.

Tracking the history of a 1969 model, for example, we see that it dropped from an equipped list price of slightly over $15,000 to about $8,000 three years later. It then began an almost imperceptible rise in paper value through the years (hardly compensating for inflation) to where this year it has peaked at a bit over $10,000. A 140 produced in the last model year, 1977, started out at over $24,000 equipped and proceeded to plummet to a low of $11,300 or so six years later. This was less than half its original cost and close to the resale value of its much more ancient '69 hangarmate. In the last couple of years, however, the aircraft has taken a turn upward, perhaps reflecting the ever more exorbitant cost of new aircraft, and the drop in production of all the two-placers.

Maintenance

Owners describe the Cherokee 140 as a fairly easy, inexpensive aircraft to maintain, with widespread familiarity by mechanics in the field. However, they say parts are expensive out of proportion to the value of the aircraft. And during 1985 most Piper parts were extremely slow in coming for all classes of aircraft because of drastic company reorganization and relocation. The cost of an annual inspection ranged from $300 to $600 in reports from users to *The Aviation Consumer.*

Since the aircraft are often used as trainers, they've been put through the mill and experienced the toughest handling by students. Indeed, we noted a fair share of landing gear problems in the Service Difficulty Reports, suggesting lots of pounding on landings.

The right-side passenger door is the only access to the cabin. There is no separate baggage door—a distinct handicap when loading baggage.

Feedback by Cherokee 140 owners in 1981 warned of a series of problems we did not note in our current survey. These concerned matters like malfunctioning rotating beacon lamps and landing lights, landing gear struts sticking and shimmy dampers going on the fritz (though there were a few Service Difficulty Reports on this last item). Also, although in '81 we received complaints about fuel tank leakage, that pattern was not repeated this time around.

ADs and Service Bulletins

The Cherokee 140 has had a fairly demure AD history down through the years. Control balance weights came in for their share of attention in 1967 and 1970 as ADs called for inspections for possible corrosion or cracks in aileron balance weights, rudder horn assemblies and stabilator balance weight tubes.

In '69 mechanics were cautioned to peer beneath the Piper medallion on the control wheels to check for cracks to prevent possible failure of the wheel. This was to be a repetitive inspection unless the wheels were replaced by metal ram's horn types.

Other noteworthy ADs zeroed in on replacing the fuel selector valve cover to prevent possible binding of the handle, and installation of new oil hose assemblies to prevent possible rupture.

Fuel gauges on the Cherokee 140s have also come in for their share of attention, once for erratic indications, because of possible internal wire failures; and in 1977 for possibly showing as much as two and a half gallons of fuel remained when the tanks were actually empty. A placard warning pilots of this situation was mandated, until the gauges were correctly calibrated.

Nonmandatory Piper Service Bulletins worthy of note included ones calling for: baggage floor brace (in case none had been originally installed), replacement of the carburetor heat cable and rerouting away from the exhaust stack, inspection of stabilator hinge attach bolts, aft spar wing attach bolts and tailpipe replacement to

Cost/Performance/Specifications

Model	Year	Number Built	Average Retail Price	Cruise Speed (mph)	Rate of Climb (fpm)	Useful Load (lbs)	Fuel Std/Opt (gals)	Engine	TBO (hrs)	Overhaul Cost
PA-28-140	1964-65	1,386	$11,605	115	660	770	50	150-hp Lyc. O-320-E2A	2,000	$8,300
PA-28-140	1966-67	2,725	$11,605	115	660	970	50	150-hp Lyc. O-320-E2A	2,000	$8,300
PA-28-140B	1968-69	2,287	$13,000	115	660	970	50	150-hp Lyc. O-320-E2A	2,000	$8,300
PA-28-140C, D	1970-71	1,186	$14,250	115	660	970	50	150-hp Lyc. O-320-E2A	2,000	$8,300
PA-28-140E	1972-73	1,276	$15,000	115	660	970	50	150-hp Lyc. O-320-E3D	2,000	$8,300
PA-28-140	1974-75	784	$16,000	115	660	970	50	150-hp Lyc. O-320-E3D	2,000	$8,300
PA-28-140	1976-77	565	$17,000	115	660	970	50	150-hp Lyc. O-320-E3D	2,000	$8,300

prevent the restriction that could be caused from separation of the muffler inner baffle.

In December 1982 Piper also issued a SB (No. 753) giving elaborate instructions on how to spin the aircraft safely. Spinning is permitted when the aircraft is loaded in the utility category, which imposes certain gross weight and cg limitations. In this context the SB notes that even seat positions should be carefully calculated to prevent exceeding the aft limits. Placards were issued with the SBs.

The latest significant Service Bulletin, issued in May 1985 urged Cherokee 140 owners to install a special access panel to permit inspection of the aft wing spar. This was done because of reports from the field that the aft wing spars were inaccessible for corrosion inspection. If corrosion is found, Piper provides a spar modification kit. As we mentioned in our SDR survey, several reports described serious wing spar corrosion problems.

Service Difficulties

A survey of Service Difficulty Reports filed on the Cherokee 140 showed a broad range of airframe and engine problems that a buyer might be on the lookout for. One area that received more notice than others involved cracked aileron bellcrank brackets. Some users reported they suspected wind damage. There were 12 cases in this category.

Perhaps testimony to hard training use of the aircraft and extra strain on the landing gear system was a clutch of reports of broken or loose main landing gear attach bolts. There were cases of main landing gear torque link cracks, as well. In addition, some users reported cracks in the rudder pedal assembly, bar and support brackets, while there were half a dozen reports of loose attach bracket bolts for the vertical stabilizer.

A handful of pilots reported cracks in the control wheel, with a couple breaking off, one in flight. Luckily

The Hershey Bar wings hold 50 gallons of fuel, which gives the aircraft a generous five hours-plus of range.

the aircraft usually has another wheel to grab onto.

Pilots looking at older 140s might pay close attention to the integrity of the wing spars. There were several reports of heavy corrosion and delamination of spars, requiring wing replacement. As we mentioned earlier, Piper has brought out a kit to provide access to aft wing spars at the attach fittings to aid in inspecting for corrosion.

When it comes to engine longevity, broken exhaust valves apparently represent a big problem. There were 22 reports in this category. In eight instances there were problems with cracked or broken cylinders. Magneto failures took their toll in Cherokee 140s, as well, with no less than 39 reports, almost evenly divided between Slick and Bendix mags. Problems were reported with bearings, coils and gear teeth on the magnetos.

Worried about vacuum pump failure? Only five cases were reported for the 140—three EdoAire and two Airborne with driveshafts shearing.

There also was a handful of exhaust stack failures—something common to many aircraft, and muffler baffle problems. We noted seven cases of oil cooler hoses failing, deteriorating or chafing, and see that in 1977 Piper issued a Service Bulletin calling for replacement of engine oil hoses.

Incidentally, these trouble areas pretty well jibed with the results of an SDR search we performed in

1981, so things haven't changed much.

Modifications

There is a sizable catalog of Supplemental Type Certificate mods on the Cherokee 140—most designed, naturally, to coax greater performance from it. There are upgraded engines of both 160- and 180-hp. Among those offering 180-hp conversions are Avcon Conversions, Udall, Kans. One of those offering 160-hp upgrades is RAM Aircraft Corp. in Waco Tex.

R/STOL Systems, Inc., which took over Robertson's full dossier of mods, can equip the Cherokee 140 with everything from aileron gap seals to leading edge cuffs, stall fences and drooping flaperons. The full treatment goes for $7,995. They're at Snohomish County Airport, Bldg. C-72, Everett, Wash. 98204, (206) 355-2736.

Jim Bradshaw's Knots 2 U can provide speed mods for Cherokee 140s, including aileron and flap seals that are supposed to boost the cruise speed by about four to seven knots and lower the stall speed some and give crisper aileron control. The address is 1941 Highland Ave., Wilmette, Ill. 60091, (312) 256-4807.

Laminar Flow Systems has devoted a lot of its attention to sprucing up the Cherokee 140. With streamlined wheelpants, flap and aileron gap seals along flap track fairings, this company claims to coax as much as another 17 knots from the old bird. They're located in St. Thomas, the U.S. Virgin Islands, Box 8557, zip 00801, (809) 775-5515.

Met-Co-Aire in Fullerton, Calif. provides new wingtips, and Bob Fields Aerocessories in Santa Paula, Calif. will give you door seal.

A Lakeland, Fla. outfit, Globe Aero, will put a one-piece windshield on your Cherokee 140 for $775. Tinted glass is only slightly extra.

Safety Record

A survey of two years of Cherokee

140 accidents suggests the aircraft is no killer. Out of 451 accidents in 1980 and 1981 there were only 14 fatals, and five of those, or nearly 36 percent, involved pilots flying under the influence of alcohol. The others show a bizarre mix of causes that had little bearing on the inherent safety of the aircraft—such as flying inadvertently into IFR conditions, making low passes, a suicide. There was, however, one fatal when a 140 was climbing out and hit some trees. This may represent the tip of an iceberg, however, since there were quite a few similar nonfatal accidents of this category.

There were no instances in the two-year period of Cherokee 140s breaking up in flight. Since all the PA-28s are generally lumped together in breakup surveys, it is hard to isolate the 140, but the two-and four-place Cherokees in general are about in the middle of the pack, or average, in this category, statistically.

Among the nonfatal accidents, engine failure accidents took the heaviest toll—as is commonly the case with other aircraft. There were 24 of these. About half are shrouded in mystery, with no cause for the engine failure determined. The greatest number of engine stoppages—six—involved some kind of fuel interruption not of the pilot's doing. In one case it was noted that the engine-driven fuel pump failed. In three other cases there were cylinder problems and in one instance an oil problem. On two occasions carburetor ice was blamed.

Despite its reputation as a ''starter'' aircraft often used by low-time pilots and in flight instruction, there was only one instance of a pilot inadvertently shutting off the fuel—or fuel mismanagement. But on nine other occasions Cherokee 140 pilots simply ran out of fuel, which suggests inattention to the gauges, or pushing to make the last few miles—or perhaps poor-reading fuel instruments.

Although pilots like to rave about the wide-gear stance of the aircraft

The deluxe, so-called 2 + 2 Cruiser had full rear seats rather than snap-on pads. A split flexible cowling—the snaps may be barely visible in the photo—makes the engine eminently accessible from either side.

and, therefore, its adept handling in tricky crosswind situations, the 140 logged a hefty share of ground-loops and swerve accidents —19 in all. A total of 12 of these were on the landing; the other seven occurred during takeoff.

Since the number of undershoots (18) and overshoots (13) is so close, this appears to be evidence more of the inexperience of pilots rather than to some intrinsic shortcoming of the aircraft.

There were quite a few accidents (15) from Cherokee 140 pilots hitting obstacles on climbout after takeoff. And we mentioned there was one fatal. The aircraft is obviously no rocketship in climb, and it might be a temptation to overload what is basically a two-place aircraft.

Among the so-called miscellaneous accidents were quite a few involving reckless pilots making low passes.

The Association

Cherokee 140 owners can get in touch with the Cherokee Pilot's Assn., P.O. Box 20817, St. Petersburg, Fla. 33742, (813) 576-4992. Terry Lee Rogers is editor of the newsletter.

Owner Comments

I bought my Cherokee 140 in 1984 for $8,500, then sunk another $2,000 upgrading the avionics for IFR flight. Since then I've put over 200 hours on the plane, which I use primarily in my book packaging business. I make primarily short hops under an hour. Many planes aren't practical or economical for this sort of puddle-jumping, but this one does just fine.

The Cherokee 140 is a slow plane. I average about 100 knots ground-speed on my trips. But it's simple and easy to fly. A thorough pre-flight takes just 15 minutes. She handles well in turbulence and crosswinds, although there are times when I feel the response to the controls is a little sluggish.

Landings are sometimes a bit tricky. My Cherokee has the old constant-chord Hershey Bar wing. If you let the airspeed drop below 74 knots on approach, the plane loses altitude quickly, and you find yourself jockeying the throttle to make it to the runway. She also gets wing-heavy as she flies. As you use the gas from one wing tank, the other wing gets heavy. The handbook says to switch tanks every hour, but I find if I let it go much past a half hour, it gets hard to hold the heavy wing up, and the plane wants to wander off course. A crossfeed fuel system would have been a nice addition.

Still, I have very few complaints with the overall design. The cabin is roomy, and not as loud as many lightplanes I've been in. The engine compartment is easily accessible, since both sides of the cowling lift up. Brake shoes can be checked without removing the wheel pants.

The plane has an O-320 low-compression Lycoming, and I've got an STC for autogas from Petersen Aviation. I find there's absolutely no difference in performance from avgas. You have to change throttle settings a little more slowly to avoid backfiring, but this is no problem. The handbook advertises 7.2 gph, but with all the short hops I make, I find the plane drinks about eight gph. That's still plenty economical for me.

Maintenance has also been economical. The plane sat for almost eight years without being flown before I bought it. In that time, a lot of hoses, seals and gaskets dried up. For the first few months after I bought it, I was constantly cleaning or replacing some minor part. I began to think that I had a real lemon on my hands. But after a while, the plane straightened up and flew right.

For the last 150 hours, I've missed only one flight because of mechanical problems, and that was nothing more than a burned-out landing light.

Even with the host of minor mechanical problems in the first months, maintenance has run me about $1,200 since I bought the plane, and that includes a thorough annual. So far, it's costing me about $27 an hour in the air, including maintenance, gas, oil, insurance, loan payments and hangar fees. Mile for mile, that's about the same as it would cost to drive a new mid-size car.

Nick Engler
West Milton, Ohio

I purchased my '74 140 in 1984 from an owner that claimed to be an A&P mechanic. It had 1,600 hours on the tach and about 60 hours

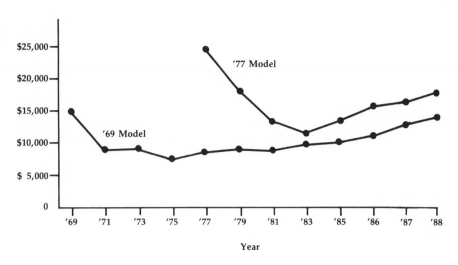

Cherokee 140 Resale Value Chart

since a total engine overhaul, according to the log. I thought I was getting a great deal. Only later did I wish I never purchased the aircraft.

On my first annual my mechanic found No. 2 cylinder with only 40 pounds of compression. He pulled the jug and found the cylinder was blued from overheating, the rocker arms were reversed so the oil holes did not line up, the rings were the wrong size and type, the exhaust valve was severely pitted. I had a bad feeling about the other cylinders so had them pulled. Sure enough, the others had the wrong rings and were severely worn and had other problems.

I ended up with a complete top overhaul. Now, everything on the engine is right.

As far as operating costs, my annual cost is $280. Cost per hour averages $25 to $30. A complete top overhaul cost $1,090. I replaced the right wheel fairing for $90 from Windy's. Piper wanted $350 for one.

Parts availability is poor. Ask the local Piper dealer for a part and you end up waiting three to six weeks for it. Some parts can't be had from Piper.

James L. Carl
Pikesville, Ind.

Among the Cherokee 140's good points is the low wing. It makes anybody's landings look good. The manual flaps are nice. There's less to go wrong. On long flights the plane is fairly comfortable and has ample legroom in front. The back seat is cramped for adults. The handling qualities are good, as is visibility.

There are only a couple of bad points. First, it's a dog climbing above 5,000 feet. Second, it has just one door, making loading of cargo very inconvenient.

We have found Piper parts extremely expensive for this price-class of airplane. Ours did not come with the hatshelf/baggage compartment bulkhead. Piper wanted an arm and a leg for a fiberglass factory model. We found a company in Kirkland, Wash. making a more attractive design out of a molded ABS material for half the price of Piper's. The company is Pegasus Northwest, (206) 822-0217. Another superb source of information is the Cherokee Pilots Assn.

Overall, we have enjoyed the Cherokee. I wish it had a bit more room in the back seat, and a bit more horsepower. But as it is, it's good, cheap, reliable flying.

Randall Schatz
Bothell, Wash.

Piper Cherokee 140

SINGLE-ENGINE
FIXED GEAR
FOUR-PLACE

Beech Musketeers

As the parade of aircraft cancelled for lack of interest—or overwhelming price shock—grows longer, the Beech Sundowner and Sport vie for attention as affordable, if unexciting basic transportation with wings.

In a world where performance and looks have always been boasting points, prosaic matters like cabin room and ease of access, instead, are the most often quoted selling points for these two models. "You may get there faster, in another airplane" their owners frequently concede, "but we'll arrive in greater comfort."

Alas, they won't arrive with the elegance of the rest of the Beech models, since the Sundowners and Sports were the curious legacy of a Musketeer line that sacrificed panache for utilitarianism. They used sensible construction materials like sandwich foam, and employed assembly line economies like constant-chord wings and skin bonding. Though they were designed with admirable qualities like fine, massive one-piece windshields, mile-wide landing gear and tough-enough construction to permit a utility category rating at full gross, they've rarely dazzled the beholder with good looks.

History

The Musketeers come in two basic models: the 19 and the 23. The Model 19 is powered by a 150-hp Lycoming and normally seats two. The Model 23 will seat four and most often comes with a 180-hp Lycoming. (We won't consider the retractable-gear Sierra Model 24 in this report.)

As with the Piper Cherokee, the Musketeer went through a series of engine changes before settling down. The first Musketeer in 1963 appeared with a 160-hp Lycoming. (The first 160-hp Cherokee had led the way two years earlier.) In 1964 Beech switched engines, putting in an oddball 165-hp Continental IO-346-A. Basically an IO-520 with two cylinders lopped off, it tended to run hot in the Musketeer.

This A23 model lasted until 1968, when it was succeeded by the 180-hp B23. Meanwhile, in 1966, Beech had brought out its Model 19 Sport, a 150-hp trainer that seated two and weighed in at a gross 150 pounds less than that of the A23. In 1970, the two models became the B19 and C23, respectively.

The Sport went through some strange weight machinations as the FAA discovered that the 2,250-pound-gross B19 could not meet minimum certifications standards for climb performance at that weight. So AD 73-25-4 was issued, limiting the gross weight of all B19s built up to then to 2,000 pounds. That included serial numbers MB-481 through -616. When a special Beech kit was installed, the gross could be raised back up to 2,150 pounds. All the Sports built after 1973 incorporated the mods and had gross weights of 2,150 pounds.

1969 Musketeer Sport. The Sport has a cavernous cabin, but fill it to gross on a warm day and the climb rate and service ceiling will be dismal.

The B19 continued in production until 1979, when the two-place Beech Skipper made its bow (and itself experienced an ephemeral existence until production was halted in 1981). The Beech 23 Sundowner held on until 1983, when it also bit the dust.

Performance

Lackluster is perhaps a flattering description for both models. Owners talk about getting a TAS of from 105 to 115 mph in the Sport, and 115 to 135 mph in the Sundowner. These speeds are easily eclipsed by all their competitors.

Climb performance, especially in the Sport, can be downright dismal, especially on a hot day. Said one owner, "On a hot day at full gross count on 300 to 400 fpm climb *max*." Another wrote, "I have noticed at or near gross weight, my Musketeer falls off in performance in hot weather much more than the book shows." To be fair, however, several owners claimed the handbook figures

1969 Musketeer Custom

claimed by Beech were quite realistic. One said he was able to climb to 9,500 feet at an average of 500 fpm with a cruise climb of 81 knots. Said another, ''The speed, rate-of-climb, etc. figures published by Beechcraft are reasonable and not exaggerated.''

Indeed, for the Sundowner, Beech listed the 75-percent cruise at 8,500 feet at only 136 mph, and claimed only a 792-fpm rate of climb at sea level with full throttle, loaded to gross weight.

Payload and Range
Except for certain models of the series, both the 19 and 23 carry 57 gallons of usable fuel. With the Sport, that translates to a range with reserve at high cruise of about 620 nm. With the Sundowner, the figure is about 530 nm. Competitors of the Sundowner with the same 180 hp—like the Piper Cherokee, Gulfstream American Tiger and Cessna Cardinal—all carry about seven gallons less fuel. But their greater speed allows them to cover about the same amount of territory.

Naturally, if you load the cabins of any of these airplanes with people and baggage, to stay within the weight limitations, you normally have to take off with a lot less fuel than the tanks will hold. Since the Sundowners can be expected to

have an equipped useful load of about 900 pounds, that means hauling three people and a bit less than 50 pounds of baggage with full fuel. With the Sport, figure on two people and full fuel—but watch the climb.

In summary, the useful load of the Musketeers compares quite closely with the others in their class.

Cabin Comfort
Here is where all the Musketeers shine. The cabins are big and roomy, with space to spare. And all but some of the earlier models have entry doors on both sides of the cabin—a nice feature to look for—though some owners complained of leaking doors.

Handling Qualities
Owners talk in flattering terms about Musketeer handling characteristics—*in the air*. They report smooth and responsive controls, and stability in rough air. But one owner complained of a ''severe'' pitchup when flaps were lowered anywhere in the white arc.

The great handling shortcoming of the Musketeers is generally acknowledged to be wicked landing habits—corroborated by accident tallies on the birds. They have a distinctly unpleasant porpoising tendency, and many a student—and even quite a few fully rated pilots—have put on a memorable

display of kangaroo leaps down the runway—often ending in calamity with a collapsed nose gear and damaged prop—and therefore an engine that is a candidate for a teardown.

The trailing beam landing gear has rather stiff rubber shock absorbers instead of air-oil oleos, as on most lightplanes. And pilots ruefully note how an inadvertent three-point touchdown on this gear can result in a series of jolting crow hops down the runway before the pilot is aware of what's happening.

Musketeer owners who responded to our call for comments reported awareness of this unhappy reputation. But they figured they had mastered the idiosyncrasy and were happy with their machines. Observed one matter-of-factly: ''Precise speed control is important because there is a tendency to porpoise.'' As with the Mooney, you carry a higher-than needed airspeed into the flare at your own risk.

Once safely slowed down on the ground, the landing gear is praised, at least for its turning alacrity. Using just nosewheel steering alone without brakes, the Musketeers will pivot in their own wing length—great for maneuvering around the ramp, and parking.

Aerobatic Bonus
Both aircraft, incidentally, are certified for aerobatics (with only two aboard, of course) when equipped with features like quick-release doors, G-meters and inertial reel shoulder harnesses. Pilots may be reassured to know the aircraft is strong enough to handle this rating without extra strengthening measures.

Strength notwithstanding, with hard landings a fact of life for many Musketeers, it pays to check landing gear, engine mounts and wing attach fittings with special care.

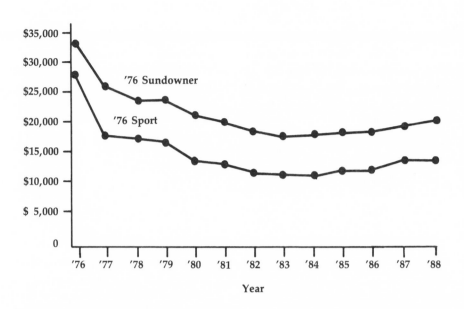

Musketeer Resale Value Chart

$35,000 —

$30,000 —

$25,000 —

$20,000 —

$15,000 —

$10,000 —

$ 5,000 —

0 —

'76 Sundowner

'76 Sport

'76 '77 '78 '79 '80 '81 '82 '83 '84 '85 '86 '87 '88

Year

Safety Record

As we mentioned earlier, Musketeer owners who commented to us for the 1986 report wrote that they were aware of the reputation of their aircraft for landing problems but were able to compensate. Unfortunately the safety statistics suggest that a frightening number of other Musketeer pilots were not able to do so. A search of the accident records for Model 19s and 23s for 1980 through 1985 discloses by far the greatest proportion of accidents stems from botched landings—ballooning, porpoising, bouncing, loss of directional control, hard landings—you name it.

Though seldom fatal, these accidents exacted a high toll in machinery, with a sizable number of nosegears being lopped off and props (and presumably therefore engines) damaged. On one occasion the pilot actually bashed off the nosegear but took the aircraft around, only to come around to the inevitable crunch on a final landing with only two main landing wheels.

Has the metal carnage diminished over the years? Hardly at all, as far as we could tell. For the five years overall, we estimated that about 46 percent of all Musketeer accidents involved landing mishaps. For the Model 19 Sport, 55 percent of the accidents were botched landings of one kind or another. For the Model 23 the figure was slightly lower—41 percent.

Student Calamities?

Are students perpetrating most of the damage on the landing accidents? Our tally suggests that about 64 percent of the landing problems on the Sports involved student pilots—which would seem appropriate for a trainer. And on the Sundowner, 39 percent of the landing prangs were perpetrated by students.

In a special study of accident patterns among 33 aircraft over the five-year span from 1972 through 1976, the NTSB ranked the Model 23 Sundowner worst in the hard landing category—and nearly five times as bad as both the Cherokee and Skyhawk.

In terms of overall safety rating, the Model 23 came out in the same study with a rather mediocre record—once again, not as good as aircraft like the Cherokee and Skyhawk. The Sundowner came up with a fatal accident rate of 2.5 per 100,000 flying hours, vs. 1.97 for the Cherokee PA-28 series and 1.47 for the Cessna 172. It bested the Grumman American Traveler, however, at 2.94.

Another accident category in which the Model 23 fared poorly was in overshoots. The Sundowner was third worst among the 33 compared, following only the Grumman Traveler and the Cessna 195.

Our study of accidents over the past five years showed no other particular pattern, though in three instances carburetor ice was suspected of causing engine failure accidents, and in 16 instances Musketeer pilots either exhausted their fuel totally or ran a tank dry.

Landing Strategies

Some experienced Musketeer flight instructors we talked with said they felt the aircraft was unjustly maligned for its landing characteristics. They stressed that the key element behind most of the landing (and takeoff) problems is proper speed control. The villain in almost every instance, they said, is too much speed on final and in the flare. If the pilot tries to plant the aircraft on the runway too soon, it will bite. The greater springback reaction from the rubber shock on the nosegear (than from a conventional oleo strut) can be expected to generate a healthy bounce, and the chain of awkward events has begun, unless the pilot knows how to make a proper recovery.

One instructor said he told students to aim for an approach speed of 1.3 Vso (flaps-down stall speed), subtracting a knot or so for each hundred pounds under gross. He

Cost/Performance/Specifications

Model	Year	Number Built	Average Retail Price	Cruise Speed (kts)	Rate of Climb (fpm)	Useful Load (lbs)	Fuel Std/Opt (gals)	Engine	TBO (hrs)	Overhaul Cost
19	1966-67	288	$10,750	108	680	875	57	150-hp Lyc. O-320-E2C	2,000	$8,300
19A	1968-69	192	$11,250	108	680	875	57	150-hp O-320-E2C	2,000	$8,300
B19	1970-73	139	$12,750	108	680	875	57	150-hp Lyc. O-320-E2C	2,000	$8,300
B19	1974-77	87	$14,000	108	680	875	57	150-hp Lyc. O-320-E2C	2,000	$8,300
B19	1978	40	$14,500	108	680	875	57	150-hp Lyc. O-320-E2C	2,000	$8,300
23	1963	554	$10,500	111	720	1,000	57	160-hp Lyc. O-320-D2B	2,000	$8,500
A23	1964-66	345	$11,500	119	728	1,025	57	165-hp Cont. IO-346-A	1,500	$9,800
A23	1967-68	26	$12,500	119	728	1,025	57	165-hp Cont. IO-346-A	1,500	$9,800
B23	1968-69	190	$13,750	119	792	975	57	180-hp Lyc. O-360-A2G	2,000	$9,000
C23	1970-73	205	$16,000	119	792	975	57	180-hp Lyc. O-360-A4G	2,000	$9,000
C23	1974-76	388	$20,000	119	792	975	57	180-hp Lyc. O-360-A4J	2,000	$9,000
C23	1977-79	359	$25,500	119	792	975	57	180-hp Lyc. O-360-A4K	2,000	$9,000
C23	1980-81	106	$34,000	119	792	975	57	180-hp Lyc. O-360-A4K	2,000	$9,000
C23	1982-83	50	$46,000	119	792	975	57	180-hp Lyc. O-360-A4K	2,000	$9,000

said that actually the wide landing gear stance on the Musketeers allowed them to handle greater crosswind components than many other aircraft. But the brakes seem more effective than normal, and an inadvertent over-strenuous stab on the rollout could lock a brake, rip a tire and cause bedlam.

At one Beech dealership they reported they were surprised by better landing characteristics that resulted from putting on the operational spin kit, which added strakes to the nose and stabilator along with a ventral fin to the rear fuselage. Other Musketeer instructors we talked with said they did not see any benefit from this strategy.

Maintenance

Owners who responded to our survey reported they were for the most part happy with the low maintenance demands of the Musketeers. Said one, "It is by far the best mechanical device I have owned." The reliability of the 180-hp Lycoming in the Sundowners received high marks as well. What few complaints there were centered around leaky windshields and doors, and water getting into the vacuum pump or air filter, shutting down the gyros. Service Difficulty Reports show

some evidence of gear stress from landing problems. There were a half dozen instances of gear housing cracks and breaks on the Model 23 and several cases of broken engine mounts, and severe shimmy on landing from broken nosegear components.

On the Model 19 there were 11 cases of aileron push-pull tubes and rod ends failed. Identical reports were made out on 11 cases where fuel cells had delaminated at the top skin between the skin and ribs near the filler opening. Another 11 reports told of cracks in the right inboard side of the keel assembly under the rudder pedal support. And 19 identical reports were filed on finding heavy corrosion at station 68 were the firewall pad contacts the aluminum structure. Beech issued mandatory service instructions (No. 1245) calling for inspection of this area for corrosion.

There were 14 cases of cracked elevator spars during inspections made according to Beech Service Instructions No. 1167. Another AD on the Musketeer stabilators (78-16-06) called for inspection of the trim tab actuator rod.

Among the key ADs affecting the Musketeers is the repetitive one (73-20-07) calling for inspection of

the forward wing attach frames and brackets for possible cracks.

A recent AD on these aircraft (85-05-02) ordered a fuel selector stop to be installed (along with a decal) on the fuel selector valve guard to reduce the chance of accidentally turning the fuel selector valve to the off position.

Modifications

There is a paucity of mods for the Musketeer series, except for the usual autopilot and strobe and carb ice detector accessories. There is, however, an STC for installation of an adjustable trim tab on the left aileron, issued to Aero-Trim, Inc. in Bay Harbor, Fla.

As far as we know, there is no owner organization serving the Musketeers.

Recapitulation

As the great shakeout of the mid-80's continues, the chief virtue of the Musketeers is their low price. They have to be considered the bargain buys of their respective classes. (Check the nearby comparison chart.) And here we are talking about the Sundowner in particular. We believe the Sport is, frankly, too doggy to consider even in these dog days.

Though both aircraft are followed by a cloud of suspicion because of their horrible landing accident record, a careful checkout by a knowledgeable Musketeer instructor may remove much of the onus for aficionados of (1) low prices, (2) abundantly roomy cabins, (3) low maintenance and (4) easy two-door access. Buyers willing to sacrifice five to 10 knots of cruise speed and who-knows-how-much climb rate will find the Sundowner a surprising bargain.

Owner Comments

As for performance, our 1980 Sundowner isn't fast, but it's solid, docile, forgiving and as friendly as an old glove. We cruise at 9,500 feet at about 2250 rpm indicating 113 knots and burning 9.8 gph. Our average climb rate from sea level to altitude with a full load is about 500 fpm at a cruise climb of 81 knots. It takes us about 18 to 20 minutes to get up there.

There are no handling problems or idiosyncrasies that I know of. The plane handles turbulence very nicely, and control pressures are always very light and responsive. It's not likely that a power-on stall would come without the plane talking to the pilot for several seconds before it tipped. Stalls under slow flight or approach to landing are more subtle, but still with considerable warning, both from the buzzer and from buffeting. It's almost as if the plane really doesn't want to stall.

As for maintenance, since new, the plane has had only one Airworthiness Directive (the oil cooler). The maintenance on this plane has been very minor. It has required no major work at all yet, at 1,400 hours TT. The vacuum pump has been replaced and the starter gear shaft went through a bearing.

Annual inspections have cost from $250 to $750, with me participating as much as I'm allowed. The higher-cost annual occurred when we had to fix the starter and vacuum pump. My total maintenance cost for 1985 was $1,380, with close to 100 hours flown. The two years before that the Sundowner required significantly less maintenance for the same amount of flying. My average maintenance cost since new has been very close to $9 per tach hour.

In terms of comfort, the Sundowner is very roomy and comfortable. We have taken some five-hour non-stop flights with no discomfort. The noise level seems very tolerable; we can carry on an almost normal conversation in flight. Heating, ventilation, defrost and control layout are quite adequate and well done. The seats are comfortable, and the large windows and high seating position makes for very good visibility. The two doors are commonplace to us, but much appreciated when we see other folks crawling across their planes to get to the pilot's seat.

Weaknesses: When it rains, it leaks—getting the floor carpeting wet. The paint job is of questionable quality. It has developed lots of pimples or very small bumps on the top surfaces.

Overall, the important thing to us is reliability, comfort, friendliness and troublefree operation. We are not enamored by great speed or high performance or the added maintenance that comes with retractable gear or variable pitch props. The Sundowner has probably hit our specs as close to anything we know.

Ray Bell
Los Gatos, Calif.

I have owned my 1975 Sundowner over nine and a half years, and have many good things to say

about it. It is by far the best mechanical device I have owned. It has been very reliable and is consistently available whenever I need it. It is very good on maintenance. The Lycoming 180 is a very reliable workhorse and goes extremely well on 100LL. The aircraft is very solid, well built and stable in rough air.

There are some drawbacks, however. The plane is now out of production, and parts are getting hard to come by; consequently, the price of an annual inspection has gone up more than a little. During the first seven years of ownership the average price of an annual ranged from $600 to $1,000. For the last two years, however, it was $1,400 and $1,800 respectively. Although I did use the Beechcraft East maintenance facility the last two years, this year I'm going back to the original, a former Aero Center dealer versed in dealing with the smaller aircraft. The established Beechcraft maintenance facilities are fine for the larger Beechcraft, but I don't recommend them for the Aero Club line.

Secondly, I did get hit with that infamous surprise of which all Sundowner owners must be aware. I keep my aircraft outside in harsh New England weather and for nine years the plane weathered well until the seals on the instrument vacuum pump filter eventually deteriorated.

All Sundowners leak around the doors and windshield and must be dried out after a heavy rain. One fine August day after one such rain, I innocently flipped on my master switch only to have an aging, tired vacuum pump proceed to dump about a cup and a half of pure rain water directly into the innards of my directional gyro and artificial horizon. It was (expensive) overhaul time for these!

Beechcraft East subsequently relocated the filter mount in

accordance with a previously issued service bulletin, but why wasn't this done ahead of time? Even at the factory? My insurance company disowned me.

However, in spite of these conditions, I still love my Sundowner. I know I could not afford to replace it with any comparable still-in-production model. It is indeed unfortunate that the Aero Club line never sold very well. Often this line was shadowed by the stigma that they were slow and expensive to buy, and the fact is that they are roomy and very comfortable. Any slowness is noticed only on paper next to the competitors' figures. The speed, rate-of-climb, etc. figures published by Beechcraft are reasonable and not exaggerated. After arriving from a long cross-country, one feels comfortable and relaxed.

The Beechcraft Sundowner is a very good value for the money. I would suggest to those looking for a used model to first check that all Beechcraft Service Bulletins have been complied with (especially the one described above). The Beech factory often pro-rates the parts and labor for compliance, and in some cases have paid for the entire job. Once this is done, any owner can expect to get very good enjoyment and practical transportation for his investment.

Lowell G. Powers, Jr.
Newport, R.I.

We have a '74 Sundowner. Performance is excellent. Usually flown 200 pounds under max gross, it will climb at 90 mph at 800 fpm at density altitudes over 3,000 feet. At cruise the numbers are close to the POH.

Handling is excellent, smooth and very responsive. There is moderate pitch-up, pitch-down with power changes, and a severe pitch-up when lowering flaps at any speed in the white arc.

Maintenance has not been a problem. In 200 hours, one set of brake pads, my request; one leaky spark plug wire, replaced complete set, my request. Added oil filter and adapter. Replaced battery.

Comfort is fantastic. You get out without being tired because you are not fighting the airplane. Noise level with the air vents open measured 73 dBA at 2500 rpm.

Parts availability: Stock at the parts houses in the Los Angeles area or at Beech FBOs locally.

Costs: fuel consumption the last 200 hours has averaged 8.2 gph; oil consumption, one quart every seven to eight hours; annual inspection, $350.

The Sundowner, I believe, is a much neglected aircraft. Flying one will make you a believer.

David Lipsky
La Mirada, Calif.

We just bought a '77 Sundowner, so our information is limited. We looked for about a year, starting with C-172s (we learned on C-152s), then switching the search to Piper Archers and Warrior IIs. We definitely preferred the low-wing visibility and liked the handling better. The problem was that any good Archer cost over $30,000.

Your safety report eliminated the Grummans. The landing accident record of Sundowners scared us, too, at first, but we talked to two or three Sundowner owner/pilots and flew one ourselves until we were sufficiently assured that flying and landing was no problem for us. We liked its handling as well.

We bought a 682TTSN creampuff for one-half the price of a similar Archer. So we go 10 mph slower, maybe roll a little longer. The plane is stronger, rated +6 and −3, was aerobatic with certain modifications, has two doors, which we

felt were a safety as well as convenience feature, and has had remarkably few ADs since new.

It's quite stable and comfortable, with the largest cabin dimensions of its class. I understand the higher wing loading is responsible for most of its good—and bad, traits.

Dr. Sheldon Dobkin
Coral Gables, Fla.

Maintenance costs have varied with the number of ADs and where the annual was performed. Expensive ADs have included main gear remounting and one-half valves to the cylinders. Anyone considering purchasing an older Musketeer should verify that the engine has the one-half-inch valve stems instead of the original three-eighth-inch stems.

A potentially costly AD requires removal of the wing tips to check for corrosion inside the wings. Also, a recurring AD requires checking wing attach bolts and spars annually for cracking, etc.

Older Musketeers had a free swivel on the nose gear, and braking was required while taxiing. On an icy ramp, braking just doesn't cut it. The Beech nose wheel steering kit is a necessity for winter flying "up north."

Another kit, no longer available, I wish I had installed is the split nosebowl. This allows removal of the bottom engine cowling without having to pull the prop spinner and prop off first. A simple adjustment such as tightening the generator belt requires removing both the top and bottom cowlings with the nosebowl attached to the bottom cowling. The split nosebowl kit should result in much cheaper annual labor costs.

Maintenance headaches include multiple problems with the

Goodyear brakes. There is a series of brake system improvements available, primarily to fix air lock problems with a shuttle valve which controls the four master cylinders. Going to a firewall-mounted master reservoir and Cleveland brakes (originally certified in 1963 but not factory installed until the early 70's) should solve all brake problems.

Douglas E. Mulloy
Seattle, Wash.

Until recently I owned a 1968 Beech Musketeer B23 with the 180-hp engine.

Performance: Cruise 135 mph at 5,000 feet with 75 percent power at 10.5 gph.

Handling: Cruise aileron response much like a Cherokee 140, not particularly crisp. Landing: precise speed control is important because there is a tendency to porpoise.

Maintenance: Typical Beechcraft with good documentation and adequate accessibility. Very high quality support from Beech with continuing service letters and high-level support. The Lycoming 180-hp is obviously reliable and Beech even has the larger plugs, harness and high-altitude mags fitted. I fixed the brakes, DG, voltage regulator, and our Musketeer did evidence cylinder cracks, requiring a top overhaul at 1,100 hours. This was likely due to a previous owner flying the aircraft in unapproved aerobatics with sudden engine cooling in climbs.

Comfort: There is excellent front and rear seat room.

Parts availability: Very good.

Cost of operation: Insurance $600 a year, maintenance $1,000 a year (due to top overhaul), $20 hourly in gas. Average annual is $400.

In summary, this is a much maligned plane which actually is a real bargain to fly and own, if not very exciting in airwork or appearance. It is very well built and quite strong, but slightly slow and can tend to porpoise if not landed properly. It really would be an excellent first plane for a careful pilot and can be bought for next to nothing with careful shopping.

Dr. Andrew Reiland
Leominster, Mass.

Cessna 172

Even today the Cessna 172 continues to be the airplane most commonly associated with general aviation. It's been built in such numbers that the word ubiquitous seems hardly sufficient when describing this commonest of commonplace singles. The 172's characteristic high-wing shape, docile, dependable performance and pleasant handling have introduced thousands to flying.

History

The 172 and its little brother, the 150, both appeared on the market in 1956. The new 172 spelled the end of the line for its taildragging older cousin, the venerable Cessna 170. It did this by outselling the 170 by a 10-to-one (1,170 to 174) margin in that first production year. Flightline planespotters can easily identify those first-edition 172s by the straight tail and "fastback" cabin. A peek under the cowl will reveal a 145-hp Continental engine, standard on the 172 line until 1968.

Changes in the 172 line have been slow in coming. The year 1960 saw the introduction of a sweptback tail in the "A" model; the 1963 "D" model featured "Omni-vision" rear windows. The 172E boasted electric flaps, to the chagrin of many pilots who considered them more a handicap than an improvement. Since that year, the 172 airframe has been virtually cut in stone with no changes to speak of.

What is probably the most important single improvement made to the 172 line came in 1968, when the 150-hp Lycoming replaced the old Continental engine as standard equipment. The following year's model was available with a 52-gallon fuel tank option, and by

1973 Cessna had re-designed the wing leading edge for supposedly better stall characteristics.

By 1974, Grumman American's Traveler was cutting deeply into the 172's market. Cessna countered with modifications to the wheelpants and cooling airflow, picking up some seven miles per hour in cruise speed.

As the ancient adage says, "If it ain't broke, don't fix it." Cessna ignored that advice in 1977 when the company shot itself in the foot by introducing the infamous 160-hp Lycoming O-320-H camshaft-and-valve-train-eating engine to the 172. The O-320-H episode lasted four years, and is remembered by both Cessna and Lycoming as a major embarrassment. (More on that in the "Engines" section to follow.)

Again, not content to leave well enough alone, Cessna opted for a 28-volt electrical system in the 172, a change that has meant problems for landing lights and rotating beacons.

Even these troubles have not done much to damage the 172s "generic airplane" image, although aircraft from the troubled '76-'81 period

Benign handling characteristics go with a superb safety record.

must be viewed with a jaundiced eye.

Used Skyhawks

With over 24,000 172s out there, the used market in Skyhawks is one of the busiest. A recent issue of *Trade-a-Plane* contained 220 ads for more than that number of 172s, since some ads offered more than one aircraft. With this much give-and-take in the market, prices tend to be rather steady, without much variation. An aircraft that's a true "steal" is unlikely because demand is so high. On the other hand, the supply is so great that no seller can get away with an exorbitant asking price.

However, used Skyhawk shoppers shouldn't waste too much time trying pinch the penultimate penny; their time would be better spent thoroughly checking out the mechanical condition of the aircraft, hopefully with the help of an experienced A&P.

Resale Value

In 1981, when *The Aviation Consumer* last reviewed the Cessna 172 line, we predicted that the older pre-1968, O-300-powered C-172s would not be able to hold onto their value due to the fact that replacement engines and parts would become more and more expensive and harder to find. According to the *Aircraft Price Digest*, this is just what happened.

A C-172D Skyhawk sold for $14,751 new in 1963, and is listed in the 1985 spring *Digest* at $10,750, a decrease of $4,001. This doesn't seem at first glance like that much of a decline after 22 years, but when the effects of inflation (the Consumer Price Index has more than tripled since then) are figured in, the weakness of this investment becomes readily apparent. The fact that prices are as high as they are reflects the relatively scarce supply of good condition 1963-model 172Ds, of which 1,027 were built.

While the cost of buying a 172D hasn't risen, the cost of overhauling its O-300-D powerplant has, rising to an average of $7,500 (TBO 1,800 hours), $1,500 more than the 150-hp O-320-E2D. While unusually low resale values for post-1977 model 172s have yet to appear, the listing in the *Aircraft Price Digest* bears an ominous asterisk, followed by the words, ''Price assume engine fixed—see notes below.'' The notes continue to say the stated price is for a 172 in compliance with ADs 77-20-7 (tappets) 78-12-9 (replace crankshaft) and 78-12-9 (replace oil pump impellers). More about pertinent ADs later.

Performance

The Skyhawk's performance is not exactly spectacular. Loaded up to

The 1983 Skyhawks placed landing lights up in the left wing leading edge, where they are less prey to vibration problems than in the nose.

gross weight, the 172 is lethargic, and we wouldn't want to try any hot-day, high-field takeoffs in a heavy airplane. The 1977 and later models, with their 160-hp engines, are, however, noticeably more energetic, with a book-climb rate about 20 percent higher than the 145- and 150-hp versions.

Cruise speed at 75 percent power is a modest 104 to 113 knots under most conditions, with a fuel burn of about eight gph. The post-'73 models are faster by four knots or so because of generally cleaner aero-dynamics. The 38-gallon standard usable fuel supply provides about four hours of flying with a small reserve, enough for about 435 nm or so if you really want to stretch it.

Optional 52-gallon tanks (48 usable) extend endurance to over five hours, enough for 522 nm or so. Of course, payload is reduced when 52 gallons of fuel are hoisted aloft; count on three medium-sized adults and no baggage, at best.

Handling Characteristics

In a word, the Skyhawk's handling is stable, even positively benign. Rather heavy controls inhibit pilots with Luke Skywalker fantasies, but these same steady controls make instrument work a pleasure. Elevator forces are very heavy, meaning that stalling is extremely difficult. The Skyhawk's handling characteristics are spectacularly average—for the simple reason that the airplane's universal popularity

has helped make it the standard against which other aircraft are judged. Almost by definition, the Skyhawk is the average airplane.

If all this makes the 'hawk seem a little lackluster, there is one flight regime in which the 172 positively excels: short-field performance. A skillful pilot can plunk a Skyhawk down in not much more runway than a so-called STOL specialty machine like a Rallye or Maule. At light weights, takeoffs can be nearly as short. The Skyhawk's huge flaps allow it to make steep, Space Shuttle-style approaches, and we wouldn't hesitate to pit a 'hawk against either a Rallye or Maule in a slow-flying contest.

Safety

A big part of the Skyhawk story is its superb safety record, pure and simple. In an NTSB study of accidents involving 48 different aircraft types between the years 1972 and 1976, the C-172 posted the best overall accident record of any four-place fixed-gear single. Its fatal accident rate also was excellent. In fact, out of the 32 most popular single-engine airplanes, the C-172 ranked in the top, or safest, 10 in eight out of 10 accident categories. It had the lowest engine failure rate and in-flight airframe failure rate of any lightplane.

The areas in which the Skyhawk is only average are mid-air collisions, presumably a result of the aircraft's poor visibility, and overshoot accidents.

A search of NTSB accident reports involving 172s in 1982, the latest year available, turned up total of 98, of which nine resulted in fatalities, with 20 deaths. Six of these deaths occurred in five VFR flights that continued into IFR conditions. A total 177 people came away with minor injuries or none at all. Seven people were killed in two midair collisions (there were five people in one of the airplanes involved).

The 172's good safety record is likely due to a variety of factors shared by all Cessna high-wing aircraft. High elevator forces and low stall speeds discourage killer stalls. Stalls accounted for just six of the 1982 mishaps and one of the fatalities.

The Skyhawk's fuel system is simplicity itself, with a well-placed selector that has only left, right, off and both positions. It takes a perverse form of determination to foul up the 172 fuel system, especially if pilots simply leave the selector on ''both,'' as most do. Even more simply, the high-wing gravity-feed system requires no fuel pumps.

Debates have raged for years among high-wing vs. low-wing fans, with claims made on both sides for visibility, handling qualities, aesthetics, and the like. And while the 'hawk's big, strut-braced wing may look old-fashioned, a fatal in-flight airframe failure in a Skyhawk is a great rarity.

The durability of that wing was evidenced by a June 1982 mishap in which a 172 struck and severed a number of powerlines, each a half inch in diameter. Afterwards, the airplane managed to return to its home field. Damage inspection revealed that three of the four left wing strut attach rivets were sheared, the entire engine cowling torn loose from the firewall attach points, and prop tips bent *forward* about three inches.

Engines

While the basic 172 airframe has changed little over the years, the 'hawk has been powered by three basic powerplant designs. Which one of these three engines lurks under the cowl of the used 172 you buy will play a starring role in how happy you'll be with the airplane. Our advice on engine choice can be summed up as follows: 1968-76 'hawks, terrific; 1956-67 models, fair; 1977-80 models, awful; 1981 through present models, again, fair.

The Lycoming O-320-D2J engine which replaced the troubled H2AD has had a fairly ordinary maintenance history, marred only by a service letter dealing with stuck valves. The problem seems to center on a buildup of gunk in the valve guides. This gunk inhibits valve movement when the engine is cold, causing rough running on startup. As the engine heats up, it smooths out. This so-called ''morning sickness'' in the D2J is a symptom that valve guides need to be checked.

For 12 years, new 172s trundled down runways and into the skies propelled by six-cylinder 145-hp Continental O-300s, an engine little more than a four-banger O-200 (used in the C-150) with an extra pair of cylinders tacked on. The O-300 has an adequate reliability record, but the combination of comparatively low 1,800-hour TBO and $7,500 overhaul cost make it a costly antique. ''The problem is you've got six of everything to replace instead of four,'' one overhauler told us. ''An old engine like this can be a real can of worms.''

Parts for the O-300 are available factory-direct, although their price adds to a total upkeep cost for the engine that is, in the words of one overhaul firm, ''not commensurate with the cost of the aircraft. It's just not worth it to put $7,500 worth of work into an aircraft with a value of only $11,000, which is about what one of those early '60s Skyhawks costs today.''

The Lycoming O-320-E2D engine climbed aboard the 172 in 1968, giving the airplane an extra five horsepower. That same engine costs $6,000 at its 2,000-hour TBO time, $1,500 less than the O-300 with a TBO that's 200 hours shorter.

Cost/Performance/Specifications

Model	Year	Number Built	Average Retail Price	Cruise Speed (Kts)	Rate of Climb (fpm)	Useful Load (lbs)	Fuel Std/Opt (gals)	Engine	TBO (hrs)	Overhaul Cost
172	1956-59	4,022	$12,000	108	660	940	37	Cont. O-300A	1,800	$9,500
172A	1960	991	$12,500	108	660	940	37	Cont. O-300C	1,800	$9,500
172B	1961	987	$13,000	114	730	875	42	Cont. O-300D	1,800	$9,500
172C	1962	809	$13,500	114	675	920	42	Cont. O-300D	1,800	$9,500
172D	1963	1,027	$14,000	114	645	970	42	Cont. O-300D	1,800	$9,500
172E	1964	1,249	$14,750	114	645	970	42	Cont. O-300D	1,800	$9,500
172F	1965	1,569	$15,500	114	645	970	42	Cont. O-300D	1,800	$9,500
172G	1966	1,499	$15,750	114	645	970	42	Cont. O-300D	1,800	$9,500
172H	1967	1,619	$16,000	114	645	970	42	Cont. O-300D	1,800	$9,500
172I	1968	630	$16,500	115	645	1,000	42	Lyc. O-320-E2D	2,000	$8,000
172K	1969-70	2,420	$17,500	115	645	985	42/52	Lyc. O-320-E2D	2,000	$8,000
172L	1971-72	1,533	$19,000	115	645	985	42/52	Lyc. O-320-E2D	2,000	$8,000
172M	1973	1,139	$20,000	115	645	965	42/52	Lyc. O-320-E2D	2,000	$8,000
172M	1974	1,559	$21,000	120	645	965	42/52	Lyc. O-320-E2D	2,000	$8,000
172M	1975	2,225	$24,500	120	645	965	42/52	Lyc. O-320-E2D	2,000	$8,000
172M	1976	1,899	$25,500	120	645	965	42/52	Lyc. O-320-E2D	2,000	$8,000
172N	1977	1,724	$25,000	120	770	876	43/54	Lyc. O-320-H2AD	2,000	$8,500
172N	1978	1,724	$27,500	122	770	876	43/54	Lyc. O-320-H2AD	2,000	$8,500
172N	1979	1,849	$29,500	122	770	876	43/54	Lyc. O-320-H2AD	2,000	$8,500
172	1980	1,124	$33,000	122	770	876	43/54	Lyc. O-320-H2AD	2,000	$8,500
172P	1981	1,024	$37,500	122	770	876	43/54	Lyc. O-320-D2J	2,000	$8,500
172P	1982	724	$42,000	122	770	876	43/54	Lyc. O-320-D2J	2,000	$8,500
172P	1983	319	$47,000	120	680	1,078	54/68	Lyc. O-320-A4N	2,000	$8,500
172P	1984	N/A	$51,500	120	680	1,078	54/68	Lyc. O-320-A4N	2,000	$8,500

This four-cylinder engine carries a reputation for going well beyond TBO with careful maintenance. Flight schools who put 100 hours a month on their airplanes and pay attention to maintenance regularly get 3,000 hours. "There's no better engine," one mechanic told us. The O-320 seems to handle 100LL with ease, as well as autogas, although careful leaning is recommended.

Messing with Perfection

As 80-octane avgas went the way of the nickel newspaper, Cessna ordered a redesigned O-320 from Lycoming. Dubbed the O-320-H2AD, it was a hard-luck powerplant, a disaster and major embarrassment for both Cessna and Lycoming and the first major engineering blunder to mar the 'hawk's record. Hundreds of 1977 Skyhawks suffered serious camshaft and valve train damage, at a cost of thousands of dollars borne by their owners. What's more, there were a dozen or so abrupt engine failures caused by sheared oil pumps and accessory drive gears. Admitting its error in April of 1978, Cessna recalled all 1977 and 1978 Skyhawks for major engine repairs.

Oil pump and drive gear problems were fixed at that time, but camshaft/tappet problems continued unsolved through the 1980 model. Lycoming tried three different camshaft/tappet mods. None of them worked. Cessna finally admitted defeat in 1981 and changed to the O-320-D2J.

After Cessna switched engines, Lycoming belatedly came up with a fourth major mod, featuring an enlarged crankcase, which it hoped would solve the problem once and for all. The modified engines have slowly worked their way into the fleet through attrition, replacing the original faulty equipment. This mod will be found on engines with serial numbers 7976 and above. Barring evidence to the contrary, it seems that this fix, while not cheap, has held. Trouble is, if a 172 owner is willing to spend the roughly $1,500 extra at TBO time for the so-called O-320-

H2ADT mod, opting for one of the extra-horsepower engine conversions may prove more cost-effective over the long run. More on them in the STC section of this article.

Our Opinion

We would not advise the purchase of a Skyhawk with an O-320 engine serial number below 7976, except at an extremely low price, low enough to allow for possible premature engine replacement. After 7976, the odds improve, but the engine is still far from a sure thing, in our opinion.

In 1981 Cessna had a special 2,000-hour, pro-rata warranty period. Under this, if a Skyhawk was purchased with 900 hours and the engine failed 100 hours later, Cessna would provide a new or remanufactured engine at half price. Four years after this offer, however, most 'hawks have flown enough to make the pro-rata discount percentage insignificant.

There is a Way Out

For 172 owners who would prefer to avoid the maintenance headaches of both the O-300 and -320-H, there are alternatives. Unfortunately, they're quite expensive, with costs approaching the value of the airplane itself in

Skyhawks with the Lycoming O-320-H engines suffered serious valve train problems of a sort that tested the patience of the most ardent C-172 fans.

many cases. RAM Aircraft Modifications, Inc., based at Madison Cooper Airport, Waco. Tex. 76708, (817) 752-8381 can put in a 160-hp O-320-D2G for between $10,000-12,000, depending on the model. That's 100 percent of the book value of a 172 built from 1956 to 1968.

A couple of firms offer upgrades that would make for a peppy Skyhawk with the addition of a 180-hp Lycoming O-360 engine, but again, it's an expensive improvement. Cost for an Avcon Industries installation complete with constant-speed prop comes to $17,260 for C-172s built before 1967, with the mod on 'hawks built after that date amounting to $16,935. If owners prefer to cut their own deal on a O-360 engine, installation kits (less prop governor and engine) for pre- and post-1967 'hawks are available for $2,875 and $2,750 respectively. Avcon Industries is at 1006 West 53rd North, Wichita, Kan. 67204. Phone: (316) 782-3317.

Mike Kelley Aircraft is marketing its own O-360 installation, this time with a fixed-pitch prop the company touts as lighter and cheaper. The Kelley mod used to be the property of Horton STOLcraft. Although the exact price varies by aircraft model year, the Kelley kit costs between $1,500 to $1,600. Add to that the approximately $7,500 cost for a used overhauled O-360, and cushion the shock of what this will cost with Kelley's claims of cruise speeds 13 knots over book. Mike Kelley Aircraft is at Wellington Municipal Airport; Wellington, Kan., (316) 326-8581.

If you want rocket-propelled performance and have a very large wad of cash burning a hole in your pocket, go for the 250-hp six-cylinder turbocharged Franklin 6AFAS350A conversion offered by Seaplane Flying Inc., Box 21586, Vancouver, Wash. 98666. Phone: (206) 694-6287. The engine transforms a stock 172 into "a little hot rod," in the words of a woman we know who has flown one. It should, considering the cost is $6,595 for the kit, with the engine itself another $11,995. The company also markets a 220-hp

Franklin conversion costing $4,695 for the kit, another $10,495 for the 6A350C Franklin.

A Very Special Problem

Thousands of 172s built between 1977 and 1982 have a good chance of developing an insidious illness that in extreme cases could lead to making the airplane unairworthy. We're talking about filiform corrosion, and it may affect the majority of the 25,000 airplanes built at Cessna's Pawnee Division plant in the years 1977-1982, including over 8,000 Skyhawks.

Filiform corrosion is almost impossible to spot in its early stages. It occurs principally on airplanes covered with polyurethane paint, since polyurethane is flexible and semipermeable and can allow water and contaminants to get next to the metal. The best defense against filiform is careful preparation of the bare metal surface prior to painting. DuPont, makers of Imron, a popular polyurethane paint, recommended a combination of Alodyne and epoxy primer surface treatment to Cessna, which evidently disregarded this advice, perhaps because Alodyne treatments require a 16- to 24- hour drying time. By opting for wash primer, a cheap surface prep requiring just a few hours' drying time, Cessna saved many man-hours of labor and plant space.

Careful inspection of any used 172 is therefore important before the decision is made to buy. Look around rivets and seams, where corrosion usually begins. Unfortunately, inspection won't always reveal filiform corrosion. It spreads subtly under the aircraft's finish, often without producing surface blistering and peeling, like ordinary corrosion. Like cancer, treatment often takes desperate forms. As a DuPont pamphlet says, ''If any trace of corrosion is found, it is quite likely to be widespread... as drastic as it sounds, the only reasonable action is to strip all the finish from the airplane and remove every spot of corrosion.''

So far the filiform problem is a localized one, cropping up in areas

Fuel gauges are on the pilot's side for better visibility than on some other Cessnas. Electric flap lever has pre-set notches for convenience.

of warm, humid coastal areas, such as Florida and the Gulf states. That is no guarantee that it won't happen in other areas as the 172 fleet ages. The best advice we can offer is to carefully check the history of any 1977-82 Cessna considered for purchase. If it was ever based in Florida, or any other hot, humid, seaside area, we suggest you be cautious about buying it. Perform a meticulous inspection (use a magnifying glass) in search of corrosion traces. Be suspicious if the 172 was recently painted. Even with a fresh paint job, filiform corrosion will likely return in a few months.

Today, new 172s come off the Wichita line wearing Alodyne underwear, but inexplicably Cessna still refuses to use epoxy primer.

ADs, SDRs

The 172 line has enjoyed a comparatively quiet AD history, aside from the O-320-H2AD episode. Some of the more recent Directives cover the 172M, N, and P models, requiring modification of the right-hand control yoke to prevent possible elevator control jamming (AD #83-10-3). The two most recent ADs (83-17-6 and 84-26-2, respectively) applied to 172 equipped with Robertson STOL mods, some of which had reported problems with aileron flutter, and with elderly induction air filters shedding bits of filter material into the intakes they're supposed to keep clean. Since the filter is an inexpensive

component, why not make it SOP to replace it at the annual?

A look at Service Difficulty Reports compiled from 1984 through April 15, 1985 (omitting engine SDRs) revealed the old familiar problems with stuck valves, including 19 reports on bent pushrods and bad guides on the older O-320-E2D powerplants. Other reports covered problems with brakes, chiefly cracked wheel hubs and brake housings; leaking, chafing and worn fuel lines on M,N, and P models; and the infamous Slick magnetos.

Maintenance

Economy and low maintenance costs have always been the Skyhawk's strong suits. With the post-1968 four-cylinder engine, fixed-pitch prop, fixed gear and no cowl flaps, the average Skyhawk owner should survive an annual for $400 or so.

Not that the 'hawks are without their weak points. Late model '77 and '78 Skyhawks with 28-volt electrical systems burn out their landing lights at a fantastic rate. Comments from one owner claimed an expenditure of $323 for landing light bulbs over the last 212 hours of flight, working out to $1.52 per flight hour, just for landing lights.

Cessna 172 Resale Value Chart

'78 C-172

'70 C-172

Year

Cessna has a "landing light improvement kit."

Cessna owners have reported similar problems with beacon bulbs, claiming they last a mere 100 hours and cost $40 a pop to replace. A remedy to this costly bother is offered by Aeroflash Signal Corp., 3900 West Palmer St., Chicago, Ill. 60647 Phone: (312) 342-4815. Aeroflash sells beacon bulbs carrying a 750-hour warranty.

Older Skyhawks tend towards problems with the nosewheel, particularly those flown by students and novice pilots who land fast and hard. Nosewheel problems can produce damage to the firewall where the nosewheel strut joins it. This should be checked before purchase. Mechanics tell us that Cessna nosewheels are notoriously chintzy and soon succumb to minor punishment. Nose gear shimmy can also be troublesome. Flap actuator jack screws have a dicey history, and are subject to an AD in pre-1973 models.

Operating Costs

Operating costs can vary widely depending on the aircraft's age, how much it is flown and what it is used for. Readers have reported average annual bills ranging from $100 to as high as $600. One meticulous reader reported operating costs of $29.75 per hour, including reserves, insurance, debt service, and taxes based on some hard flying: 1,240 hours in 15 months (the aircraft is used for IFR training).

Avionics

We usually don't talk about avionics in a used-plane article but in Cessna's case, we really must make an exception. The reason is the poor reliability of the ARC avionics inflicted on virtually all 172s since 1974. ARC had serious management, production, and quality control problems in the late 70s, and the result was a plethora of customer problems. The years 1977 and 1978 seemed to be especially bad.

If your search for a used 172 turns up a '74 or later model with Collins, Narco, or King equipment, you may save yourself future avionics headaches by buying it instead of an ARC-equipped airplane. If you must accept ARC avionics with your 'hawk, demand documentation of repairs and past problems. Particularly check the synthesizers in series 300 navcoms. If the Skyhawk you're looking at has a long history of avionics squawks, don't buy it. There are plenty more Skyhawks where that one came from, and you owe it to yourself to find one with reliable avionics.

Modifications

Everybody and his brother have come up with a mod for the 172 at one time or another. Many of the more popular STCs have changed hands repeatedly over the years, and tracking down some of the more esoteric can be frustrating. If you get stuck, we suggest contacting the Cessna Pilots Association at P.O. Box 12948, Wichita, Kan. 67277. Phone: (316) 721-4313. Executive Director John Frank edits the CPA newsletter and can be quite helpful.

Among the more popular mods:

• Robertson STOL has been bought out and reborn as RSTOL Systems, Inc, though the new company still resides in the same building at Everett, Wash.'s Snohomish County Airport. Cessna 172 STOL mods for the pre-1973 'hawks come with a recontoured leading edge and full-span flaps as well as drooped ailerons. Newer post-1973 Skyhawks already come with a leading edge cuff, so their STOL mods cost less. At a price of $6,200 for 1973-79 models and $7,200 (both factory-installed prices) for 1956-72 airplanes, we wonder if they're worth the money.

The Skyhawk already had very good short-field performance, and the aircraft's limited power means that, barring the use of JATO bottles, takeoffs will never be spectacular, no matter what is done to the wing. RSTOL Systems, Inc., Snohomish County Airport, Building C-72, Everett, Wash. 98274. Phone: (206) 355-2736

• Horton STOLcraft offers a much less expensive STOL kit in the $400 neighborhood. Horton will install the kit at their Wellington, Kan. plant for another $1,000. Owners report a 20-mph reduction in stall speed with resultant reduction in takeoff and landing rolls. A more "solid" feel in Vmc flight was also reported. Phone: (316) 326-2241.

• Flint long-range fuel tanks add 24 gallons capacity for $2,450 plus installation. The tanks are mounted internally and do not change the contour or size of the wing. Flint Aero, 8665 Mission Gorge, Building D-1, Santee, Calif. 92071. Phone: (619) 448-1551.

Owner Comments

The wing struts may look draggy, but they contribute to a nearly flawless record of avoiding in-flight airframe failures.

I'd have to say the Skyhawk is the greatest of the all-time greats and is already a legend in its own time. In time to come it will be in the same league as the DC-3 and other bigger-than-life aircraft.

I'm a part owner of a C-172 in a club where we also have a C-152 and a Comanche 260B. All three are popular, but the 'hawk outshines them all and not only pays for itself, but sometimes has to support the other two.

Pilots love it, and it's a joy to instruct in. You can park it alongside any other comparable aircraft and pilots will fly it two to one. It's easy to fly, is not a greenhouse in the summertime, and its high wings act as a shelter in the rain. The high wing eliminates problems getting in and out.

The aircraft is so stable you don't need automatic pilots, and since most students train in a C-150/152, a C-172 is a natural step-up. It's no wonder it's the world's most popular airplane.

As for performance, handling, maintenance, comfort and part availability, I would have to rate it excellent in every category. One fly in the ointment is that ordering a small part, like a knob or something similar, from Cessna is impossible. And trying to get a dealer (if you can find one) to order it is an even bigger impossibility.

Just how Cessna can build the world's greatest airplane, then do such a sorry job on small parts is unforgivable.

E. R. Ritch
Huntsville, Ala.

The plane (a 1981 model 172 P II) has, in general, been good to us. It now has 1,800 hours on it with no major engine problems or work to date. We've gone through more Slick mags than seems reasonable, including one that died shortly after being installed. I was so mad about that (it happened over mountainous terrain) that I demanded an explanation. Slick wrote back saying they don't normally explain themselves, but it was a quality control problem and they were upping their vigilance.

We were very fortunate to have purchased an '81, the year they went back to the O-320-D2J engine. My partners and I were unlicensed, unititiated, blind, dumb, and lucky when we bought the plane. It could just as easily been the valve-eater engine.

The radios are, of course, ARC. Never again. We had more than a bit of trouble with them at first, though they've been stable in the last two years. We installed a used 400 series DME. Two visits to the factory and about $1,500 in repairs later, it began working right. It should. They replaced every circuit board in it. Not exactly a bargain by the time we got done.

What can you say about Skyhawks? Reliable, easy to deal with, dependable, friendly, gentle. Not fast, not great load haulers. Ours has taken us to the tip of Baja, to Santa Fe, New Mexico, and to lots of places great and small. It has done so without causing missed heartbeats, and without the need to fly 50 hours a month in order to stay competent to cope.

The Skyhawk is a good, honest three-person airplane if you're really traveling somewhere far enough away to require baggage. As equipped, ours will haul 620 pounds, and full fuel. Four at 150 pounds plus the pilot's flight case just about gets you there. Three of us plus baggage sufficient for a one-week journey through Baja almost read tilt.

It's disappointing to see that on a $50,000 piece of equipment, the best we can get for air vents is two tubes that push in and out about the pilot and co-pilot's head and can never be tightly closed. This contributes a continuous source of both noise and cold air. The noise is never welcome, and cold air may or may not be, depending on the season. This arrangement makes the description "Mickey Mouse" seem like an improvement.

We're suffering filiform corrosion, for which I do not expect Cessna to run forward and claim responsibility. I'm certain they'll tell us it's absurd to expect to have an airplane parked within five miles of the ocean and not have it convert to aluminim dust by corrosion. I just wonder why they don't mention that possibility (necessity? inevitability?) *before* you buy?

I took my private and instrument instruction in the plane, and am glad I did. Life was a lot more comfortable there than it would have been in a 152, and I think it made getting through a lot easier and a lot more fun.

The plane isn't perfect, but it performs pretty much as advertised. For a first plane, I don't see how anyone can go too wrong with a Skyhawk, though I'm also not too certain how anyone can afford one anymore. I can only afford the payments on an '81 with the help of two partners and a leaseback, and then just barely.

Brian Weiss
Santa Monica, Calif.

Cessna 177 Cardinal

Cessna's 177 Cardinal is one of the few cult airplanes that lives up to its followers' hosannas. It's an airplane with an intriguing history: launched with great expectations but not much engineering, an early flop in the marketplace, its problems quickly fixed, but an initial bad rep that never went away.

After a troubled 11-year career, it was finally replaced in Cessna's lineup by the Hawk XP, an airplane inferior to the Cardinal in virtually every way.

A used Cardinal today is one of the best used-plane deals around. The later models are fine all-around airplanes, but the bad reputation earned by the quirky early models keeps the price of all Cardinals down. A 1977 Cardinal, for example, can be had for about $5,000 less than a comparable Piper Archer, which has similar performance but a lot less cabin room.

Genealogy

The Cardinal was first introduced in 1968. It was designed to be the Skyhawk of the future, building on the Skyhawk's classic traits as a reliable easy-to-fly 150-hp basic four-seater, but with snazzy good looks, more cabin room, better visibility and the latest in aerodynamic trendiness, a one-piece stabilator. Cessna was so confident that the Cardinal would be a winner that it shut down the Skyhawk production line in anticipation.

Unfortunately, the hardware didn't meet the expectations. That first 150-hp 1968 Cardinal, although good-looking and roomy was an

1969 Cardinal looks good, okay performance, lots of room, and a moderate price.

odd-handling, underpowered dog. Cessna had sold the Cardinal as a Skyhawk replacement, but it lacked the forgiving, safe, easy-flying qualities that have been the Skyhawk hallmark. Such flying qualities may have been acceptable in a bigger aircraft, but Cardinal buyers expected the Cardinal to fly like a Skyhawk. It didn't, and the plane's poor reputation was born.

In its optimism, Cessna cranked out 1,164 1968 Cardinals (nearly double Skyhawk production for the year), and the dealer organization managed to sell most of them before the word got out.

Reputation Justified

Most of the 1968 Cardinal's bad reputation was justified. The wing was a "high-performance" NACA 6400 series airfoil, the same one used in the Aerostar and Learjet. But that airfoil tends to build up drag quickly at high angle of attack and low speeds, which is not a good trait in a plane flown by low-time step-up pilots. Stall speed was higher than the Skyhawk's too. Although the book numbers for stall and rate of climb didn't look too bad, they turned out to be wildly optimistic. The 1968 Cardinal climbed very poorly under the best of conditions, and if the pilot got the nose up a little too high, drag built up quickly and climb rate sagged even more.

To make matters worse, the Cardinal had 50 pounds less useful load and bigger fuel tanks, so it was very easy to overload.

1975 Cardinal II - In 1975, the Cardinal got aerodynamic refinements, such as wheel pant fairing, that helped boost cruise speed to 150 mph.

The 1968 Cardinal was quite sensitive on the controls, particularly in the pitch mode. The stabilator could stall in the landing flare, resulting in a sudden loss of tailpower and a sudden whomp of the nosewheel onto the runway. Porpoising and bounced landings were commonplace. Overall, its tricky landing traits, overloading tendency and doggy rate of climb made it a real handful for the Skyhawk-type pilot for which it had been designed and marketed.

Correcting the Problem

Cessna quickly realized it had made a major gaffe with the Cardinal. It restarted the Skyhawk production line and set to work fixing the Cardinal's problems. Under the so-called "Cardinal Rule" program, it retrofitted stabilator slots to Cardinals already in the field. This reduced the stabilator-stalling problem. Cessna also revamped the 1969 model calling it the 177A. Major change was the move to a 180-hp engine and a 150-pound

increase in gross weight. The stabilator slots were incorporated, and the stabilator-to-wheel control linkage was changed to improve the pitch characteristics.

Despite the improvements, 1969 sales nosedived to about 200, while Skyhawk sales rebounded to their former league-leading levels.

A New Airfoil

In 1970, Cessna made more major improvements and called the Cardinal the 177B. The 6400 series airfoil was changed to a more conventional 2400 series similar to the Skyhawk's, and a constant-speed propeller was added for better takeoff and climb performance. More stabilator changes were made as well.

At last, the Cardinal had all the makings of a good airplane.

From 1971 on, the Cardinal got only minor changes. In 1973, a 61-gallon fuel tank became optional, and cowling improvements boosted cruise speed from 139 to 143 mph. In 1978, a 28-volt electrical system was added. In 1975, speed went up again, but this was merely a bit of

paperwork legerdemain by Cessna. Cruise rpm limit was increased so that 75 percent power could be obtained at 10,000 feet instead of 8,000 as before. At most altitudes, side by side under the same conditions, a 1975 Cardinal is no faster than a 1974 model. In 1976, the Cardinal got a new instrument panel.

Despite Cessna's successful efforts to fix the original Cardinal's quirks, the plane continued to be a slow seller. It was the only Cessna single that didn't lead its category in sales. (Piper's Cherokee 180 beat it handily, as did the upstart Grumman Tiger.)

In 1977, Cessna finally gave up on the Cardinal. While jacking up the Cardinal's price dramatically, it introduced at the Cardinal's old price the Hawk XP (same performance, uglier, worse handling, noisier, more cramped, much higher fuel consumption and engine maintenance, lower engine reliability and TBO). Customers preferred the Hawk XP by a four-to-one margin.

In 1978 Cessna made one last-ditch effort to save the Cardinal. It spruced it up with some fancy

1971 Cardinal

interior appointments and radio packages (along with an absurdly high price tag) and called it the Cardinal Classic. Buyers weren't fooled, however, and the Cardinal Classic went over about as well as New Coke.

Used Plane Marketplace

Cardinal owners prize their craft, but the general public apparently doesn't. Prices generally run several thousand dollars less than a comparable 180-hp Cherokee. (For example, 1986 "bluebook" retail price of a 1977 Cardinal is $25,000, compared to $29,000 for a 1977 Archer.) The Cardinal does command more than the Grumman Tiger or Beech Sundowner, however.

(Remember that "bluebook" retail prices are like automobile sticker prices; the actual selling price is usually somewhat lower.)

Cardinal 177B prices go as low as $15,000 (less with high-time engines or poor equipment.) An average 1969 177A will change hands for perhaps $12,000 to $13,000, while an unmodified 1968 177 will typically sell in the $11,000 to $12,000 range in average condition (1986 prices).

Many 1968 Cardinals have been converted to 180-hp engines and constant-speed propellers. This mod essentially turns the 177 into a 177A (except for the airfoil and different stabilator linkage), and commands a premium of several thousand dollars over a straight 177. In effect, a modified 1968 177 should be priced like a 1970 177B.

Performance

The Cardinal's performance is middle-of-the-road for 180-hp airplanes. Book cruise speeds range from 139 to 150 mph, while the 150-hp 177 is listed at 134 mph.

Those numbers are nowhere near as good as the Grumman Tiger (160 mph), about comparable with the Cherokee 180/Archer, and better than the pathetic Beech Sundowner.

Owners report real-world performance reasonably close to book figures, except for the 1968 model. Typical figures: 140 to 145 mph on 9 to 10 gph. The 1968 model, judging from owner reports, is fortunate to cruise 120 mph.

Climb rate is about average for this class of aircraft—again, with the exception of the 1968 airplane, whose owners universally complain about its lethargic climb performance.

Payload-Range

Owners typically report useful loads in the 850-950-pound range, depending on installed equipment. That's slightly less than the Cherokee 180 or Grumman Tiger, and not enough to excuse the owner from careful consideration of weight and balance.

Assuming a fairly typical 900-pound useful load and 49-gallon tanks, the Cardinal has about 600 pounds for people and bags once the tanks are filled. That's three FAA-standard people and 90 pounds of luggage. If you want to carry four full-size people and 100 pounds of luggage, you'll be limited to perhaps 20 gallons of fuel—barely enough to fly anywhere safely. Weight limitations make the Cardinal essentially a three-passenger airplane, or at best a two-plus-two (adults and kids).

With full tanks, the Cardinal has good range. The 49 gallons usable and typical 10-gph fuel flow allow the Cardinal to fly four hours with reserve, and cover more than 500 miles. The 60-gallon tanks available on post-1973 models boost endurance by an hour and range by 150 miles—but at the expense of 66 pounds payload. A typical 60-gallon Cardinal with tanks full can carry just 540 pounds of cabin load.

The 1968 150-hp Cardinal (2,350 pounds) has a gross weight 150 pounds lower than the 177A and 177B (2,500 pounds). Empty weight is only a bit less, so the 177's equipped useful load may be as low as 750 pounds. Put in four 170-pounders and 70 pounds of luggage, and there's zero—that's right, *zero*—left for fuel. (You could ride around behind a tow tug, though. Wouldn't that be fun?)

Legally speaking, the 177s converted to the 180-hp/constant-speed setup are even worse, since useful load may not be legally increased while the new engine/prop. are about 50 pounds heavier. But most pilots of the 180-hp 177s fly as if they have 177As or Bs. From the

performance point of view, they're perfectly safe doing that. (As far as the landing gear and wing spar go, we're not so sure.)

Creature Comforts

A major design goal of the Cardinal was interior comfort, and the goal was achieved. The cabin is fully six inches wider than a Cherokee, and puts its sibling Skyhawk to shame. Baggage compartment is huge. From the pilot's point of view, the Cardinal feels very spacious as well, since the wing sits higher and farther back, allowing excellent visibility out of the panoramic windshield. Unlike the Skyhawk and other high-wing Cessnas, the pilot's vision up and to the side is not blocked by the wing.

One Cardinal owner reports, "It's enormous in there...I often take the rear seats out and stand up a couple of ten-speed bicycles..the legroom in back is worth boasting about ...the general spaciousness makes you feel like you're riding in the back of a limousine." Overall, the Cardinal is probably the roomiest four-place airplane made (not

counting semi-six-seaters like the Bonanza).

It's also probably the easiest plane ever built to get in and out of. The doors are as wide as a soccer pitch, and there's no wing strut to get in the way. The floor sits lower to the ground than other high-wing Cessnas, so the step up is a small one. Tall people, however, will have to duck a bit to get under the low-slung wing.

Handling Qualities

The Cardinal generally wins praise from owners for its handling qualities. Even the odd pitch characteristics of the early models are typically excused by owners in a macho sort of way ("It may porpoise in the hands of the typical wimpy pilot, but hey, a superstud like me has no problem at all. Just a mater of technique, babe.")

In truth, the pitch sensitivity and porpoising tendencies of the Cardinal have never really been completely tamed. Pitch control forces are light (particularly compared to the notoriously nose-

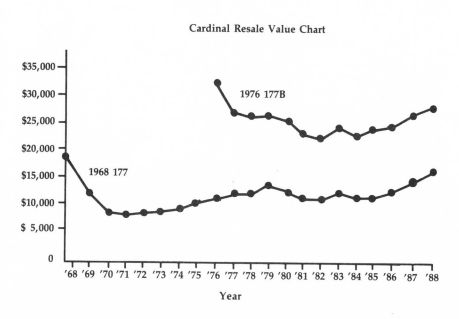

Cardinal Resale Value Chart

1976 177B

1968 177

Year

Cost/Performance/Specifications

Model	Year	Number Built	Average Retail Price	Cruise Speed (kts)	Rate of Climb (fpm)	Useful Load (lbs)	Fuel Std/Opt (gals)	Engine	TBO (hrs)	Overhaul Cost
177	1968	1,164	$15,250	113	670	935	49	150-hp Lyc. O-320-E2D	2,000	$8,250
177A	1969	206	$17,000	118	760	1,060	49	180-hp Lyc. O-360-A2F	2,000	$8,850
177B	1970	160	$18,000	119	840	1,025	49	180-hp Lyc. O-360-A2F	2,000	$8,850
177B	1971	103	$19,500	119	840	1,020	49	180-hp Lyc. O-360-A2F	2,000	$8,500
177B	1972	104	$21,000	119	840	1,015	49	180-hp Lyc. O-360-A2F	2,000	$8,850
177B	1973	200	$22,500	124	840	1,005	49/60	180-hp Lyc. O-360-A2F	2,000	$8,850
177B	1974	150	$24,000	130	840	995	49/60	180-hp Lyc. O-360-A2F	2,000	$8,850
177B	1975	190	$25,500	130	840	995	49/60	180-hp Lyc. O-360-A2F	2,000	$8,850
177B	1976	209	$27,500	130	840	967	49/60	180-hp Lyc. O-360-A2F	2,000	$8,850
177B	1977	150	$30,000	130	840	967	49/60	180-hp Lyc. O-360-A2F	2,000	$8,850
177B Classic	1978	80	$32,000	130	840	857	49/60	180-hp Lyc. O-360-A2F	2,000	$8,850

heavy Skyhawk and Skylane), and Skyhawk pilots are sometimes surprised by the responsiveness and pitch authority.

As one forthright Cardinal owner put it, "My own flying techniques and the Cardinal's characteristics on landing don't coincide very well. I feel like I run out of elevator effectiveness at recommended approach speeds, and thus land faster than I would like to. The very compliant landing gear saves my face a lot of times." Another owner writes, "It will porpoise for the inexperienced pilot. No problem for the owner-operator, but for this reason it is not a good aircraft for rental."

In flight tests by *Aviation Consumer* pilots, however, we've never had any problems, and frankly prefer the Cardinal's handling qualities overall to those of the Skyhawk. (Technique, babe.)

On takeoff, the Cardinal must be rotated for takeoff with firm wheel pressure, at least with two people in front and flaps up. (The pilot sits well ahead of the wing.) Dropping 15 degrees of flap for takeoff, however, will fly the Cardinal right off the runway without major yanks on the wheel.

In cruise flight, the Cardinal is a good steady IFR airplane—if you can get it trimmed out laterally and keep the fuel balanced. Several owners reported gross fuel-flow discrepancies when the fuel selector is on "both," with all fuel flowing from the left wing. Left-right switching every half hour may be necessary to maintain lateral trim.

Maintenance

Owner reports and service difficulty files suggest the Cardinal is a fairly simple, low-maintenance airplane. (Ironically, the retractable-gear 200-hp Cardinal RG is a real maintenance bear, with almost four times the rate of service difficulty reports on file as the fixed-gear airplane.) Annual inspections typically run $350-500 for the basic once-over. The engine and airframe have no major flaws that we're aware of. (The 180-hp Lycoming engine, in fact, is one of the most reliable of all.)

But there are some things to watch out for:

• McCauley prop inspection. It must be overhauled every five years or 1,500 hours. Check compliance on any airplane considered for purchase.

• Oil pump gears. Pre-1976 Cardinals should be checked for compliance with AD 75-08-09 on the oil pump gears. The Cardinal's engine model was not specifically called out in the vaguely-worded AD, and some mechanics may not be aware that the AD applies. Semantic hair-splitting aside, make sure this AD has been done.

• Other generic ADs that apply to many aircraft (Stewart oil coolers, Cessna fuel caps, vacuum pumps, ELT batteries, etc. etc.).

• Water leaks through the windshield and door. Many owners reported being plagued with leaks. Check the sealant and any water damage.

• "That #*&# Bendix mag," as one owner put it. The 1975-78 Cardinal unfortunately came with the notorious Bendix dual magneto.

• Some Cardinals, particularly those in humid coastal areas, have been afflicted with corrosion. See service bulletin SE 80-02 for details. Also, Cardinals built in 1977 and 1978 have slick polyurethane paint jobs. A nice idea, but unfortunately Cessna failed to alodyne and prime the metal properly, and there's been a rash of filiform corrosion on painted surfaces.

• Engine and fuel gauges. These are proving troublesome, and unfortunately the instrument manufacturer has gone out of business. Cessna's replacement gauges (hideously expensive, of course) are not internally lighted and therefore almost useless for night flying.

• Clunking nosewheels. These can be cured with shims and/or new O-rings. Find a mechanic who knows Cardinals to do the job. The nosewheel is like no other Cessna nosewheel.

• High engine temperatures. Owners sometimes report their CHTs run near redline in warm weather. (One says the number three cylinder runs especially hot.) This can be cured with an after-market exhaust pipe fairing that improves cooling air flow and reportedly drops temps by 75 degrees. (See the Mods section.)

Owners gripe that the cowling is hard to take off and needlessly runs up their annual and repair labor bills.

One other major maintenance factor: ARC radios. Virtually all Cardinals have avionics manufactured by Cessna's onetime captive ARC company. Starting in the mid-1970's, quality of ARC radios began to fall, reaching a nadir about 1977 or 1978, the last two years of Cardinal production. ARC gear, virtually across the board, rated dead last in our avionics owner surveys during that period, and there were big shakeups at the ARC factory at the time. An ARC panel is a major liability in any 1974-78 Cardinal, in our opinion. Check reliability and repair records carefully in any aircraft considered for purchase.

Safety

The Cardinal has an average accident rate—not great, not terrible. We have no recent statistics, but an NTSB study for the years 1972-76 shows the Cardinal to have a fatal accident rate of 2.4 per 100,000 flight hours. This is about average for four-place fixed-gear aircraft. (By comparison, the Skyhawk had a superb 1.5 fatal rate over the same period.)

In the various categories of accidents studied by the NTSB, the Cardinal showed only two unusual traits. It ranked very poorly (29th out of the 33 aircraft tabulated) in landing accidents, and very high (best of the 33 airplanes, in fact) in landing undershoot accidents. The hard landing rate is almost certainly related to the Cardinal's pitch sensitivity and unusual control feel in the flare.

According to the NTSB, the Cardinal ranked slightly worse than average in stall accidents. An *Aviation Consumer* study also ranked the Cardinal a bit below average, and well below the leaders in the four-place class, the Skyhawk and Cherokee.

Checking more recent accidents, we confirmed the patterns of the NTSB study. In 1979 alone, for example, there were seven Cardinal hard landing crashes, five involving 1968 models. There were also a bunch of takeoff accidents involving stall/mushes or impact with rising terrain—both a reflection of the aircraft's poor climbing ability. Again, most involved the 150-hp airplane with the 6400-series airfoil.

The lessons to be learned from the accident files: be very careful about overloaded takeoffs on short runways, at high density altitudes or with rising terrain (or heaven forbid, all three). And practice those landings. (Both warnings go double for the 1968 model.)

Modifications

The most important modification for Cardinal fans is the 180-hp constant-speed engine conversion for the 1968 model, which essentially converts it to the 177B configuration. Hundreds of 177s have been converted this way.

The conversion is quick and easy, basically a bolt-on job. Two different STCs are available from Avcon (316) 782-3317 and Bush (316) 782-3851. The two are very similar; both cost in the neigh-

borhood of $17,000 (less a trade-in allowance on the old engine) for the complete job. Both sell STC paperwork and kit parts if you want to buy an engine and prop elsewhere and do the labor yourself.

Avcon also has an STC to convert the fixed-pitch 177A to a constant-speed prop.

Horton Industries in Wichita, KS (316) 326-2241 offers a STOL kit for the Cardinal consisting of a leading-edge cuff, drooped wing tips and vortex generators on the vertical fin. According to Horton, the STOL mod is quite effective on the 1968-69 models. The above-mentioned Bush also offers a STOL mod for the 1968-69 Cardinal.

There's a burgeoning business in Cardinal speed mods. A Canadian named Roy Sobchuck came up with most of them, but they are now marketed in this country by C2 Enterprises, 3707 Pinehill Rd., Omaha, NB 68123 (402) 292-9327.

The mods include a nose strut fairing (a claimed speed gain of 8 mph), tailcone fairing (177B only, 7 mph) exhaust stack fairing (2 mph, 75 degree drop in engine temperature). The company also sells landing light covers, cowl cheek fairings, fuel drain fairings, ADF loop covers and mainwheel pants for which minor speed increases are claimed.

The C2 mods are not STCed, but may usually be signed off on a Form 337. (Check with your AI and FAA man before installation.) The company quotes no installation times due to wide variations in skill and experience in working with fiberglass.

Owner Clubs

Cardinal owners have a choice of two clubs. The Cessna Pilots Assn., Wichita Mid-Continent Airport, 2120 Airport Rd., P.O. Box 12948, Wichita, KS 67277, (316) 946-4777, is the biggest, and publishes much useful technical info. However, most of it applies to other single-engine Cessnas, so the Cardinal owner may feel lost in the crowd of Skyhawk and Skylane buffs. For the true Cardinal fan, there is the Cardinal Club, 1701 St. Andrew's Dr., Lawrence, KS 66046, (913) 842-7016. It tends to be more of a rah-rah social cub, with newsletters focused more on fly-ins than technical problems and solutions. We'd consider both worthwhile for any Cardinal owner.

Owner Comments

We have generally found the Cardinal to be a very reliable airplane. This is particularly true after Cessna made modifications to the early Cardinals under the Cardinal Rule program. In many respects, the original Cardinal, the 1968 177, is a different airplane, in both handling characteristics and performance, from the later 177A and 177B. This was primarily due to the different horsepower and airfoils.

We are beginning to see some parts difficulties. Parts take many, many months to arrive from Cessna, and will certainly cost many, many dollars. Because fewer than 3,000 fixed-gear Cardinals were built, salvage yards generally don't have a ready supply of Cardinal parts.

One thing that has really been a thorn in the side of Cardinal owners is the instrument cluster. These gauges, which include fuel quantity, oil pressure, oil temperature, cylinder head temperature, etc., were manufactured by Leigh Corp. Leigh went out of business, however, and Cessna's solution to the gauge problem was to recommend replacement with individual Stewart-Warner gauges. This is very expensive; the parts alone cost $800. Also, the S-W gauges are not internally lighted and require post lighting. (The Leigh gauges were internally lighted.)

The Cardinal was built differently than other Cessnas, and for this reason it's important to find a mechanic who understands the airplane. For example, Cardinal nose gears are known to develop a clunking sound. This can be cured by the use of an O-ring or by installing a shim at a certain location. This is not generally known by Cessna mechanics because the Cardinal's nose gear is not like other Cessna nosegears.

One of the more popular subjects among Cardinal owners these days is speed-up kits. The most popular one is marketed by C2 Enterprises, 3707 Pine Hill Rd., Omaha, NB 68123, (402) 292-9327. This modification, which includes a nosewheel pant, and various fairings, is claimed to give a 15-20-mph speed increase, and some users back up this claim. C2 also sells an exhaust pipe fairing, and we have received many positive comments about its ability to reduce engine and oil temperatures. Most people are able to install these mods under a Form 337 approval, although other FAA offices to refuse to allow this.

The Cardinal was not overwhelmingly popular during its production run, despite having reasonable performance numbers, good interior space and very attractive appearance. However, since production has ceased, it seems to be gaining in popularity. In fact, Cardinal owners seem to be so fanatical about their aircraft that they could almost be considered a cult.

Due to lower horsepower, the 1968 177 sells for less than the later models. Owning a Cardinal can be a real pleasure if one is willing to put up with the minor inconveniences of an aircraft built in small numbers and out of production for eight years.

John Frank
Executive Director
Cessna Pilots Assn.
Wichita, Kan.

Climb Shortcomings

In 1972 in California, a 1968 Cardinal with four people aboard crashed into a mountain ridge shortly after takeoff from a field with a density altitude of 5,000 feet. The pilot's survivors filed suit against Cessna, claiming the airplane did not meet the performance claimed in the handbook. The plaintiff's attorney in the case hired a professional test pilot, Mike Antoniou, to precisely measure the Cardinal's performance under carefully controlled conditions.

More than 100 hours of flight-testing was done, using sophisticated performance-measuring equipment. Says Antoniou, "It's very probable that the instrumentation used in these tests was more extensive than what Cessna used when it certified the airplane." The airplane was carefully rigged to Cessna specifications, and all radio antennas were removed to cut drag. After consultation with Lycoming, it was confirmed that the engine was putting out its full rated power.

The tests showed the Cardinal failed to meet its claimed performance in almost all areas—and in fact failed to meet minimum FAA certification standards in some cases. For example, rate of climb (gross weight, sea level) was found to be an anemic 560 fpm, compared to the book claim of 670 fpm. Flaps-up stall speed was discovered to be as high as 69 mph (at forward c.g.) compared to the handbook claim of 64 mph. FAA rules require rate of climb (in fpm) to be 10 times higher than the stall speed (in mph) in the takeoff configuration.

Thus, based on the Cardinal's true numbers, it should have had a climb rate of at least 690 fpm to be certified. It fell short of that requirement by nearly 20 percent. Airspeed errors also exceeded FAA limits.

Antoniou also discovered that the actual takeoff distance over a 50-foot obstacle at 7,500 feet density altitude and gross weight was 6,500 feet, not 4,680 feet as the book claimed. Cruise speed was about seven mph below book, max speed about 10 mph short.

I own a 1974 C-177B with 1,300 hours on it. It's IFR-equipped and has speed mods. Fuel burn is 37 liters/hr (that's 9.8 gph.—Ed.). Average speed with mods is 155 mph.

I fly 100-150 hours per year and do my own maintenance. Average maintenance cost (not counting my own labor) comes to about $450 Canadian per year.

Very stable airplane, lots of room. Excellent cross-country machine. Up here in Canada, it gets cold in the back seat during the winter. I have fixed that with a heating modification—now people complain that it's too hot.

Lots of water leaks around the doors and windshield. They have been repaired with new sealant under the wing root fairings, and new door seals. It's now quieter, and no more leaks.

Roy Sobchuck
Brandon, Manitoba

We've owned a 1968 Cardinal for the last 12 years. It has been modified with the Avcon 180-hp conversion and cuffed leading edge STOL kit.

Comfort is excellent. With 45 inches of shoulder room, it is significantly more comfortable than almost anything else. Two adults can sit in a Cardinal without rubbing elbows with each other or the vibrating airframe. You can slam the door without hitting yourself. The large doors open fully, unimpeded by a wing strut. Because the Cardinal sits low enough to back into (and then swing your feet up into the plane), I sawed off the entry step. The doors have to be the largest in the industry, with the back seat more accessible than any other single-engine plane.

As for visibility, unlike most other single-engine designs, the wing is located rearward so that a pilot can lean forward for complete visibility. The ability to see the leading edge is a great comfort when the plane starts icing up.

We've found maintenance to be stone simple. Annuals run $150 for the AI fee and $30-$60 for consumables like oil, filters, gaskets, etc. We open and close up the plane for inspection and do all the cleaning, lubrication and other maintenance that the owner is allowed to do. The Hartzell AD cost $605 in 1983. Brake pad wear from rusting discs and rain leaks past the fuel caps ended when I got into a T-hangar seven years ago.

The avionics shop gets $200 to $500 a year, regardless of hours flown. We do some of the avionics troubleshooting ourselves, with my partner's oscilloscope and $40 worth of manuals and test harnesses. In one case, we found a failed potentiometer. Cessna wanted $125 for the part, but we replaced it with a superior part with a more stringent mil-spec from a local electronics supply house for $3. Autopilot removal from the wing is a fine example of perverse service engineering—a difficult and frustrating task for a contortionist in a good mood.

Performance is right on book for a 1974 177B, which is essentially what you get with the Avcon 180-hp conversion. I have flown the same plane hundreds of hours with both the 150-hp and 180-hp engines, and frankly I didn't notice anything different in the way it handles other than rate of climb and a modest improvement in speed. The ability to get quickly to the smoother, cooler air at altitude is an important factor in passenger comfort.

Overgrossing is easily accomplished because the Avcon 180-hp

STC did not increase the gross weight as the factory did when they put in the larger engine. Our useful load is 815 pounds with all the avionics.

I have never experienced the lengendary porpoising problem on bounced landings that embarrassed so many 172ers and others accustomed to a fixed stabilizer.

I believe that the Cardinal is one of the great undiscovered treasures in the used aircraft fleet. It is very underpriced relative to more recently built planes of older design. The 172 and to some extent the Piper singles have adopted some of the features that can be bolted on an old design—larger fuel tanks, tubular landing gear, courtesy lights, etc.—but they will forever lack space and comfortable accommodations of a design dominated by these considerations.

Timothy J. Kramer
West Bloomfield, Mich.

I bought my 1973 C-177B in 1984 for $15,000. It had not been well maintained, and my initial maintenance figures are misleading. The McCauley prop had not been overhauled in seven years (five years of 1,500 hours is the TBO time), and I had to replace the hub as well as pay for the overhaul, for a total cost of $1,500. The carb heat box fell off into the bottom of the cowling. New muffler was $220. One of the fuel filler necks was badly rusted and had to be replaced for $325. The interior Royalite is doing what old Royalite does—falling apart after drying out and getting brittle. The plastic wingtips, stabilator tips and rudder tips are also cracking.

My biggest problem is the weird C-177 fuel-feed system. I have a real problem with drainage out the overflow vents on the wingtips. I have lost as much as 12 gallons of gas in a week due to siphoning overboard. The plane sits level, and this occurs regardless of the fuel selector position. It is absolutely imperative to check fuel level before every flight if the plane has been sitting—even overnight.

I also do not get any fuel feed from the right tank when the selector is on both. I have landed after a two-hour flight with the selector on ''both'' and found the right tank still completely full. No wonder it flew right-wing-heavy. When the selector is on ''right,'' however, the tank feeds fine.

Lest one think from the foregoing that the Cardinal is a dog, nothing would be further from the truth. The wide doors and spacious cabin will allow a lady to enter while wearing a dress and still be a lady. The cabin has more room than most twins.

Cruise speed at 5,500 feet is usually about 122 knots, according to the DME (in still air). Fuel consumption varies from about 8.5 to 11 gph depending on throttle and mixture. I normally set it up for about 10.2 gph, which allows the engine to run cool at about 72 percent power. I normally operate at 23 inches and 2300 rpm at about 5,000 feet.

The Cardinal has a yellow band on the tachometer between 1,700 and 1,900 rpm. This caution range must be adhered to religiously. My plane's logbooks show that it once threw 10 inches of one prop blade off in flight. According to my mechanic, it had been operated in the yellow arc range, and appar-ently there is a harmonic vibration with anode about 10 inches from the tip.

Cardinal handling is solid. The big stabilator is powerful and likes to stay right where you trim it. Cardinals have a bad reputation for nasty landing traits, but this has not been my experience. It sits lower on the ground, and because of the low landing position there is a tendency to flare high. The Cardinal's nastiest landing bugaboo is the porpoising you'll get into if you land too fast and don't flare enough.

Parked by a Skyhawk or a Cherokee, it looks like a Corvette next to a sedan. My wife likes that!

C.S. Stanley
Jackson, Miss.

Piper Archer/Cherokee 180

Guess which airplane is now the hottest item on the used-plane marketplace? The Piper PA-28-181 Archer—the late-model reincarnation of the good old reliable Cherokee 180—currently sells for a higher percentage of original value than any other propeller-driven airplane.

Although the Archer is a fine aircraft—an almost perfect compromise between cost and per-formance—it seems to have taken on a cachet that has driven prices out of proportion.

Take, for example, a 1979 Archer. The 1986 "bluebook" retail price of a seven-year old Archer was $35,000—up drastically from two years before, when a seven-year old Archer went for just $26,000. (Actual selling prices generally are less.) The three other 1979 180-hp fixed-gear planes available went for substantially less in 1986: $25,000 for a Beech Sundowner, $27,000 for a Grumman Tiger, and $29,500 for a Cessna Cardinal.

Vs. the Warrior

Or compare the Archer to its 160-hp stablemate, the Warrior. The two aircraft are essentially identical except for the Archer's extra 20 hp. The difference in manufacturing cost was no more than a few hundred dollars. (For marketing reasons, the Warrior originally sold for $5,000 less than the Archer.) Book cruise speed of the Archer is only four mph faster; climb rate a miniscule 35 fpm faster.

But a 1979 Warrior was worth a piddling $23,500 on the used-plane marketplace in 1986—not even two-thirds of the value of a 1979 Archer. For the $12,500 price difference be-

1982 Archer II

tween the two aircraft, you could buy gas for the Warrior for 1,000 hours of flying.

In terms of percentage resale value maintained, the 1979 Archer is worth an astonishing 84 percent of its new price—well above such traditional blue-chippers like the A36 Bonanza (78 percent), Mooney 201 (69 percent) and the recently much-in-demand Cessna 182 (77 percent). The nearly identical Warrior has held 68 percent of its original value. Let's face it, the Archer is hot.

Looking for Answers

Why the sudden Archer-mania? Certainly not high technology; the airframe and engine have been around for a quarter century now. Certainly not performance; the Archer rates about average for 180-hp aircraft, and well below the Grumman Tiger, for example. Not roominess; the Cardinal and Sundowner are just as good or better. Not looks; the Archer is about as average-looking as you can get. Not reliability or ease of maintenance; the Cessna Cutlass is just as reliable and easy to maintain, but is worth $9,000 less than an equivalent Archer.

So what's going on here?

To be quite honest, we haven't the foggiest notion. One factor may be that the Archer is the only 180-hp airplane still being sold new today. (The Tiger, Sundowner and Cardinal all expired years ago.) Perhaps used-plane buyers find an older version of a current model more desirable. As a current model, the Archer also has a 1986 price tag as a bench mark for used-Archer prices. (Typically, used-plane prices respond to sticker-price changes in new planes.) When a prospective Archer buyer sees a $90,000 price tag on a 1986 model, he begins to think that $35,000 for a virtually identical 1979 model is not so bad after all.

But then the Warrior is also a current model with a stratospheric sticker price—and a used Warrior sells for a third less than a used Archer. Any more theories?

The Yuppie Factor

Used-plane broker Mark Graubart offered one. "You've got more yuppie types these days who can pay for what they want in a personal airplane. They won't compromise on a Warrior just because it's cheaper. And the Archer really is a better airplane. The Warrior is a little marginal as a four-placer.''

Okay, Mark, so how come the yuppies aren't stepping up to Arrows? (A 1979 Arrow IV, with a sexy T-tail, 200 hp, constant-speed prop and retractable gear—and much better performance than an Archer—was listed in the bluebook for $36,500 in 1986—just a buck-fifty more than an Archer.) No, there's got to be another explanation for Archer mania.

We still haven't the foggiest. Any reader who has recently purchased an Archer at the going rate is urged to write *The Aviation Consumer* and tell us why he/she paid $10,000 more for an Archer than he/she could have paid for a Warrior of the same age and condition.

Genealogy

Like almost every single-engine Piper built in the last quarter-century, the Archer traces its lineage back to the very first PA-28 Cherokee, which appeared in both 150-hp and 160-hp models in 1962. The next year, a 180-hp model was added, and the same basic airplane has been in production ever since. Nearly 10,000 180-hp Cherokees have been built.

Major changes have been few. In 1967, the Lycoming O-360-A3A got larger exhaust valves, and engine TBO increased from 1,200 hours to 2,000. (This change, however, is not critical for used-plane shoppers; most small-valve airplanes have been overhauled or retrofitted by now with the bigger valves. But check it out on any 1963-67 considered for purchase.) In 1968 came a new instrument panel and a third window on either side. In 1973, Piper made its first major changes: the fuselage was stretched by five inches, and the wings extended by

two feet—both major improvements. A bigger stabilator was added as well. Gross weight increased by 50 pounds. At the same time, the door and cabin window were enlarged. The '73 model (called the Challenger that year) also had a new instrument panel and crashworthiness improvements in the seats.

But the big change that turned the Cherokee 180 into the Archer and made the airplane into the ultradesirable machine that it has become today, was the 1976 wing switcheroo. The venerable old ''Hershey Bar wing,'' the constant-chord slab that had become the Piper trademark, was replaced by a semi-tapered wing of three feet broader span. The difference was considered significant enough that the aircraft designator was changed from PA-28-180 to PA-28-181.

As a result of the new wing, the 1976 Archer picked up a few knots cruise speed, reduced the stall by five mph, increased gross weight by 100 pounds and increased rate of climb. Aileron response also improved.

Since then, the Archer has remained virtually unchanged. In 1977, the interior was spiffed up and Collins Microline avionics became available. Low-drag wheel pants became an option in 1978, which added 5-7 mph to cruise speeds.

The Archer got new low-drag mainwheel pants in 1978 that increased speed by 5 to 7 mph. But the pants had severe cracking problems in the beginning.

Performance

Archer performance is middle-of-the-road for 180-hp fixed-gears. It's worse than the Tiger, better than the Sundowner, comparable to the Cardinal. But it seems to be just good enough for a four-place IFR airplane, a notch above the 150/160-hp airplanes, which just don't quite have the oomph to haul around four people in a reasonable manner.

Owners report cruise speeds in the 135 to 140 mph range with the slick wheel pants. That's okay, but not great. (A Grumman Tiger will hit 160 mph on the same engine.) Climb performance is also average; the book says 740 fpm at sea level and gross weight, and owners say that's about right. The Archer really doesn't have enough power for four-passenger flying in the west; owners tell us that high-elevation takeoffs are sweaty-palms affairs and that if the MEA gets much above 7,000 or 8,000 feet, there's very little climb capability left. With one or two people aboard, the situation improves somewhat, of course.

The older aircraft with the shorter wings are not as sprightly. As one

The Archer has a good useful load and a 200-lb. baggage capacity, but the single right-hand door makes boarding awkward for the pilot.

owner puts it, "Rate of climb is marginal. At full gross, you'll get only 600 to 700 fpm at sea level, and you'll be down to 200 fpm at 7,000 feet. You have to assure the controllers you're still climbing if they've sent you high on an IFR flight."

Payload-Range

Here's where the Archer does run at the front of the pack. A typical IFR-equipped Archer will have a useful load of 900-950 pounds. That's almost 100 pounds better than the speedy Tiger. With the fuel tanks full, that's enough for four adults (but no baggage). Owners report that they are rarely weight-limited in the amount of people and paraphernalia they haul around in their Archers. Baggage compartment limitation is 200 pounds.

Fuel capacity is 50 gallons (48 usable), enough for more than four hours of moderate cruising with a decent reserve. (Typical fuel burn is about nine gallons per hour.) Practical range is about 600 miles.

Older Cherokee 180s with the Hershey Bar wing have gross weights 100 or 150 pounds less than

the Archer (the old wing was that much less efficient), but the airframes were lighter, and useful load is only a smidgen less. But speed, without the fancy fairings, is a good 10 mph lower on the older airplanes.

Handling Qualities

The Archer has good, solid, unremarkable handling qualities. As one owner put it, "The airplane refuses to do anything weird." Overall, the Archer has handling

qualities that make it perfect for the step-up pilot who may have learned in a Cherokee 140.

Pitch forces are fairly heavy; roll response, while better in the Archer than in its Cherokee 180 forebears, is not as light or as quick as the Tiger's. We have found in test-flying the Cherokees over the years, that it's hard to hold altitude; the nose seems to slowly wander up and down.

The Archer stall is benign in the Cherokee tradition. It never really breaks at all, but rather shudders and bobs with the wheel held full back. Stall speed is a modest 57 mph. On the ground, the Archer is a bit ponderous. A mushy nosewheel steering bungee can make maneuvering a bit awkward.

Engine

Under the cowling lies one of the Archer's secrets of success: the engine. The 180-hp Lycoming O-360-A4M is one of general aviation's best—smooth, easy-starting, reliable, with a 2,000-hour

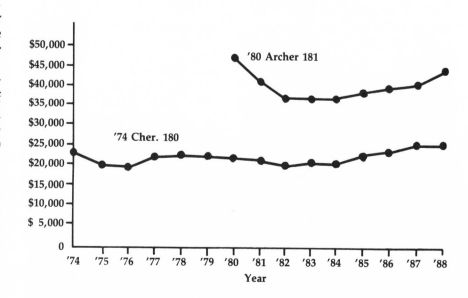

Cherokee/Archer Resale Value Chart

Cost/Performance/Specifications _____

Model	Year	Number Built	Average Retail Price	Cruise Speed (kts)	Rate of Climb (fpm)	Useful Load (lbs)	Fuel Std/Opt (gals)	Engine	TBO (hrs)	Overhaul Cost
PA-28-180B	1963-64	1,090	$15,500	124	750	1,170	48	180-hp Lyc. O-360-A3A	2,000	$9,000
PA-28-180B	1965-66	1,975	$16,500	124	750	1,170	48	180-hp Lyc. O-360-A3A	2,000	$9,000
PA-28-180C	1967	642	$17,000	124	750	1,170	48	180-hp Lyc. O-360-A3A	2,000	$9,000
PA-28-180D	1968-69	1,233	$18,500	124	750	1,250	48	180-hp Lyc. O-360-A3A	2,000	$9,000
PA-28-180E, F	1970-71	493	$20,250	124	750	1,250	48	180-hp Lyc. O-360-A3A	2,000	$9,000
PA-28-180G	1972	318	$21,500	124	750	1,250	48	180-hp Lyc. O-360-A3A	2,000	$9,000
Challenger	1973-74	880	$25,000	124	750	1,035	48	180-hp Lyc. O-360-A4A	2,000	$9,000
PA-28-181 Archer	1975-76	726	$29,500	122	725	1,060	48	180-hp Lyc. O-360-A4M	2,000	$9,000
PA-28-181 Archer	1977-78	1,159	$33,500	122	725	1,060	48	180-hp Lyc. O-360-A4M	2,000	$9,000
PA-28-181 Archer II	1979-80	961	$44,500	125	740	1,160	48	180-hp Lyc. O-360-A4M	2,000	$9,000
PA-28-181 Archer II	1981-82	491	$55,000	125	740	1,160	48	180-hp Lyc. O-360-A4M	2,000	$9,000
PA-28-181	1983-84	203	$65,500	125	740	1,160	48	180-hp Lyc. O-360-A4M	2,000	$9,000
PA-28-181	1985-86	92	$74,500	125	740	1,160	48	180-hp Lyc. O-360-A4M	2,000	$9,000

TBO that some operators have stretched to 3,000 hours and beyond. It's a match made in heaven: one of the world's most reliable, proven airframes and one of the world's most reliable, proven engines.

Virtually the only engine change made in the 24-year history of the PA-28-180/181 line was the switch from Bendix mags to Slicks in 1976. The purpose of the switch was not to improve the mags, but rather to cut costs; the predictable result is that FAA service difficulty reports show far more problems with the Slicks than the Bendixes.

Other than the usual Slick mag problems, the O-360's main problem seems to be the valve-sticking that has plagued all the small Lycoming engines over the past five or six years. The O-360 does not suffer the terrible lead problems of the smaller O-235.

Creature Comforts

Interior room is nothing in particular to brag about, particularly in the 1964-72 models. The rear seats could almost be considered kiddies-only. But the five-inch stretch in 1973 made the back seat livable for grownups. Still, the Archer lacks the interior room of the Cardinal or the Sundowner, and the good visibility of the Tiger. Cabin width is 42 inches, a bit on the tight side for four-place aircraft.

The Cherokees are notorious for having just one door, on the passenger's side. This means the pilot has to clamber in first. It also makes emergency escape more difficult in case of an accident, particularly if the plane flips or rolls over.

Later models are quieter, but the improvement is only relative. Like virtually any lightplane, the Archer is fearsomely noisy and can cause permanent hearing loss over a period of years.

Safety

The Cherokees over the years have had a low accident rate—although not as low as the ultra-safe high-wing Cessnas. We have no accurate accident-rate numbers for the 180/Archer in particular, but the PA-28 series as a whole, during the years 1972-76, had an accident rate of 10.5 per 100,000 flight hours, and a fatal accident rate of 2.0. Only the Cessna Skyhawk had a lower overall rate among the 11 fixed-gear four/six-placers we measured, and the Cherokee's fatal rate was fourth best.

Our sister publication *Aviation Safety* calculated accident rates for the 180/181 series for the years 1980 and 1981. (Two cautions: Because the FAA does not publish hours-flown data for the 180/181—it lumps all PA-28 hours flown into one big number—the hours-flown data had to be guesstimated by pro-rating fleet size. Also, two years is a brief period for statistical measurements, and figures based thereon will have more room for error.) Within these statistical limitations, the 180/181 had a total accident rate of 6.2—the best of any fixed-gear four-place aircraft—and a fatal rate of 1.6, about in the middle of the pack.

Statistically, the 180 and Archer seem to rank high (or well) in terms of all accidents, and about average in terms of fatal accidents.

Leading Causes

The leading cause of accidents was weather. That's usually a good sign; it means that pilot blunders rather than aircraft quirks cause most accidents. (The Grumman Tiger, by contrast, has a very low rate of weather accidents, but the plane's lethargic climb rate under marginal conditions and poor stall traits get some pilots in trouble.) Fuel exhaustion was the only other obvious 180/181 accident pattern.

This may be due partly to the wildly optimistic handbooks of the older 180s. Listed fuel capacity included unusable fuel, and fuel consumption figures were too low. In addition, the range figure was apparently calculated with no reserve for taxi, takeoff, climb or descent. No wonder pilots who flew "by the book" ran into trouble.

The Cherokee fuel selector is hardly a paragon of safety. It has no "both" position, and this requires the pilot to change tanks regularly. (The Skyhawk's set-it-and-forget-it "both" position is far safer.) It's also poorly located on the lower left cockpit sidewall, out of the pilot's direct line of view.

Maintenance

Archer owners tell us it's hard to spend less money on maintenance for a four-place airplane. The Archer is simple, rugged, reliable and familiar to virtually every aircraft mechanic. The systems are simple as pie: fixed gear, fixed pitch prop, carbureted engine. After 25 years and 10,000 copies, Piper has gotten most of the bugs out.

A typical annual inspection (no discrepancies) runs in the $300 to $500 range. One owner reports his total bill, including repairs, has averaged $684 over the four years from 1982 to 1986. Low figure was $250 for an inspection in which the owner helped out. A second owner reports an average of $647 for the five years from 1981 to 1986.

A typical figure for unscheduled maintenance is $5 per hour. One owner reports a total maintenance cost over five years of $11.63 per hour, and that seems typical for the 180 breed.

ADs and Trouble Spots

A long-time Cherokee trouble spot has been the fuel tank sealant. A 1967 AD required an inspection for peeling sealant, and the problem continued to crop up for years with the advent of low-lead fuel. (In fact, resealing Cherokee tanks was big business for years.) On any older 180 considered for purchase, check the history of the fuel tanks and their present condition.

Other old-timer ADs that should be checked: inspection for muffler cracks (1970), piston pin inspection (1973), oil pump shaft and impeller (1975), and Bendix magneto impulse coupling (1978).

The Archer had a spate of ADs in the late 70s and early 80s (some were catch-all ADs that applied to batteries, vacuum pumps, ELTs, magnetos and oil pumps found in a wide variety of aircraft; others were specific to the Cherokee or Archer line and included ammeters, throttle linkages, and fuel tank vents). Since 1981, the Archer has been relatively clean of ADs. The only Directives applied to widely used components (altimeters, air filters and the King autopilots) that were found on many aircraft.

FAA service difficulty reports show, in addition to AD-related problems, a pattern of troubles with shimmy dampeners, battery box covers, broken exhaust valves and broken alternator brackets.

Older 180s with the Hershey Bar wing were also subject to a Piper service bulletin calling for an inspection of the rear wing spar attach fitting for corrosion. A few cases were uncovered in humid coastal areas, but it has not been a widespread problem. If you buy a plane from a tropical area like Florida or the Gulf Coast, however, we'd recommend the inspection, which requires about two hours of labor, according to Piper.

A recent service bulletin calls for the replacement of aluminum battery cables and wiring with copper, which is less susceptible to corrosion. (Corrosion reduced battery power and made for wheezy cranking.) The bulletin, incidentally, applies to all Pipers, not just the Archers.

Modifications

Because the Cherokee line is so popular, there's a raft of aftermarket mods available for the aircraft. Among the more useful:

• Laminar Flow Systems speed mod. The full mod includes wing smoothing, gap seals, flap track fairings, mainwheel fairings and an entirely new nosewheel fairing.

The whole package can boost cruise speeds an impressive 15 to 20 mph and increase climb rate as well. Stall speed is also lowered.

The mods can be bought as a package or separately. Laminar Flow Systems, Box 8557, St. Thomas, USVI 00801, (809) 775-5515.

• Knots 2 U speed mod. Includes gap seals and various fairings. Speed increase: 7 to 10 mph. Price: $900 for the gap seals installed (7 mph), $150 for the flap hinge fairing installed and $400 for the wing root fairing installed (3 mph for both together). Knots 2 U, 1941 Highland Ave., Wilmette, Ill. 60091, (312) 256-4807.

• Horton STOL mod. Includes leading edge cuff, stall fences, dorsal fin fairing and vortex generators. Decreases stall speed, improves control at low speeds. Price: $799 for the 180 kit or $1,449 installed at Horton. Also flap and aileron seals are available for $395 or $615 installed. Horton STOLcraft, Wellington Municipal Airport, Wellington, Kans. 67152. Phone (316) 326-2241.

Owner Comments

I have owned a 1975 fat-winged Archer since 1981. I have kept complete records for the 575 hours I've flown it since then. Unscheduled repairs have amounted to about $2,400, or $4.23 per hour. (This figure doesn't count repairs during annual inspections or radio repairs.) There is no pattern of failure or recurring defect, except for the repeated annoyance of the red nav light burning out.

Four annual inspections averaged $685. This is weighted to the high side by my philosophy of ''when in doubt, fix it.'' My cheapest annual was 1984's $247, in which I helped out. This was a very good experience, hosted by Arnold Peterson of Navajo Aviation, Concord, Calif.

My average point-to-point ground speed for 440 cross-country hours has been 106 knots. This is takeoff to touchdown, including time in the pattern, holding, etc. Average fuel economy has been 12.3 nmpg, including taxi fuel burn. Fuel consumption on cross-country flights averages 8.6 gph.

About 50 hours have been spent in actual IMC. Except for a brief, unpleasant encounter with a thunderstorm west of Chattanooga and a load of ice over Fresno, the Archer has been very stable and easy to handle in cloud. The icing encounter was an interesting experience. The Archer, I am convinced, will pick up ice at any opportunity and does not shed it well. And the windshield defroster is virtually useless.

I flew the aircraft out of the San Francisco Bay Area. Flights into the Sierra at the 13,000-foot range were common. But while the Archer climbs fairly well, best performance is achieved at about 7,000 ft. When lightly loaded, it will land under 60 knots and get into a 2,000-foot downhill Colorado strip.

We have been very pleased with this reliable, simple airplane.

Gene Cutin
Wheaton, Ill.

I own a 1968 Cherokee 180, which I bought three years ago when it had only 800 hours total time—a real tiedown queen. I had all new instruments put in, repaired the upholstery, painted it and put on a set of drooped wingtips. I also replaced most of the hydraulic hoses, O-rings and put on new brake discs. I've also made various radio updates, including Mark 12Ds, DME 190, and a digital VOR.

The only problems I've encountered have been due to someone else's stupidity. For example, I got a service bulletin to replace the baggage door lock because somebody somewhere put his kid in back and he kicked open the door. Then some fool turned off the gas and I had to put in a new selector valve with a ''foolproof'' selector switch. There was also a replacement for the aluminum wiring (which had never caused a problem) with copper, a shunt for the ammeter and a check for spar corrosion (none).

Annuals run around $700, but only because my local FBO is charging about twice what everyone else does, not because of any problems with the airplane. The plane has been loyal, trustworthy, faithful, easy to fly and land, and fun to play around with.

It refuses to stall or do anything weird. It never did care much for stalls, particularly power off. It just sort of hangs there, and if you insist, dips its nose. With the droop tips, it doesn't even dip its nose, just sort of mushes along while you try to hold the yoke in your chest. At full power, it will slowly nose over, but definitely not ''break'' like a Tomahawk, which scared the hell out of me once.

Lightly loaded at sea level, the Cherokee will blast out at 1,500 fpm

up to about 2,000 feet, then climb out steadily at 1,000 fpm up to 3,500 feet, and then continue at 750 fpm up to 6,000 feet. It'll safely carry just about anything I can stuff in it.

It took some time to learn to land it properly. The Cherokee is a bit nose-heavy and needs some power on final approach, especially if you don't have any weight in the rear. My instructor recommended 50 pounds of ballast in the luggage compartment.

Routine maintenance is so low as to be almost non-existent. It does tend to foul one bank of plugs if you don't taxi with the mixture lean, but the runup cleans it out every time.

Wayman C. Dunlap
Vista, Calif.

I have a 1971 Cherokee 180 F. It is hard to beat this aircraft. It is fun to fly, forgiving, reasonably fast, easy to maintain and economical. There are plenty of them around, and with the aircraft market the way it is today, I doubt there has ever been a better time to buy one.

My aircraft has 5,100 hours on it. The engine has 475 hours since a Penn Yan overhaul with nitride jugs. The engine is a Lycoming O-360-A4A, and it is as reliable as the sunrise in the east. I have owned it five years, and my maintenance has averaged $11.63.

Major items have been brake discs, airspeed indicator, control cables, oil pump impeller, door latch, pitot heat, alternator, and tires. Total unscheduled maintenance came to $2,188 in five years.

Since 1982, annual inspections have cost about $700, $875, $400, $700 and $550. Average: $647.

The maintenance may look high, but much of it was incurred to make a high-time day-VFR trainer   into a   well-maintained   reliable   IFR aircraft. Once you get it in shape, the ongoing maintenance is minimal. In fact, the more I fly it, the better the reliability.

Fuel consumption averages 8.5 to 9 gph. Insurance, including hull, runs about $650 a year. Including tiedown, my total cost per hour is $44.58.

As far as performance goes, you get pretty much what the book says. Count on 130-135 mph. It flies well on instruments and is a very nice cross-country machine.

This is an airplane you want to keep the sun and heat out of. A good sunscreen will keep the radios in good health. The other secret on the radios is to make sure the windshield seal is tight. I check mine annually and recalk it every two years.

If you are shopping for a 180, be sure the service kit is installed for the rear wing spar inspection. Also,

you should consider looking at the spar behind the fuel tanks and checking the need for a new vent kit while you're in there. Older vent tubes crack and are prone to leak.

Daniel J. Baier
Honeoye Falls, N.Y.

I bought a '81 Archer II in late 1985. It had approximately 1,200 tach hours on the engine and was used as an IFR trainer. After I bought it, I put on a red belly strobe for collision avoidance. It did not have inertia belts, and they were a must since the shoulder harnesses in the plane kept coming off and unbuckled. That cost $323. I put in an alternate electric vacuum backup ($1,900), also a four-probe EGT for $750.

I have had a real problem with water leaks on the floor. They have sealed the windows, etc., and still can't find the cause. The wind has caught the door and snapped the pin five times.

At 75 percent power I burn 11 gph consistently. If you pull 65 percent, you cut the burn rate to about 8.5 gph; 55 percent is about 7.5 gph.

It is a very docile, forgiving airplane.

Take a look at my August '86 annual. The next 10 years better be low, huh?

John Carlson
McHenry, Ill.

(His annual cost $6,806, including a new carpet for $277 and an Alcor kit for $742, both installed. On top of the flat annual inspection cost of $335, he was charged $3,152 for 98.5 hours of labor—not counting labor for the carpet and Alcor kit. Cost of parts totaled $1,944, again not counting the carpet and Alcor kit. Most expensive items were $654 for magnetos. The invoice said: ''We appreciate your business.''—Ed.)

Grumman Tiger/Cheetah

The Grumman American Cheetah and Tiger have always been popular among pilots who prized speed, efficiency, and sportiness. "The best plane on three wheels," is a typical owner comment.

But one big knock against them has been their orphan status—out of production, with expensive, hard-to-get parts from a company that only grudgingly supports them.

But recently, that competitive disadvantage has disappeared—not because the Cheetah/Tiger situation has gotten any better, but because everybody else has gotten worse. Now virtually every single-engine plane is out of production, and the parts situation is stinko throughout the industry. So the Cheetah and Tiger suddenly have a new allure: if you're going to be buying an out-of-production model with a shaky factory support system anyway, hey, why not get one that's fast, good-handling and sporty-looking in the bargain?

Used-Plane Market

Both Tiger and Cheetah are quite modestly priced on today's market—from a top of about $30,000 down to about $15,000 for a raggedy old Tiger (1987 prices). The range for a Cheetah is about $12,000 to $20,000. Dare we say it, they might even be considered a bargain.

In the four-place fixed-gear arena, the Cheetah and Tiger rank about in the middle, well behind Piper and Cessna, in terms of buyer esteem. Leader in the 180-hp class is the Piper Cherokee Archer; in 1987 a 1979 model had a retail price of about $36,000. The Cessna

The Tiger, left, with 20 more horses, has a surprising margin of performance and price - over the Cheetah (right).

Cardinal ran a close second at $30,000 for 1978 model (there was no 1979 Cardinal), followed by the Tiger at $28,000 for a '79. Bringing up the rear was the woeful Beech Sundowner at $24,000.

In the Cheetah's 150/160-hp class, the price story is the same: Warrior, Skyhawk, Cheetah, Sport, in that order. What's remarkable is the huge price difference between the Cheetah and the Tiger, which are essentially identical except for the extra 30 hp of the Tiger. Although the difference between the Lycoming list price of the two engines was only a couple of hundred dollars back in 1979, and the original price difference of the two airplanes was $6,500 (about 20 percent), the difference in value of the two models was $8,000 in 1987—or better than 40 percent of the Cheetah's value.

Genealogy

The AA-5 series was born in 1972 as the Traveler, a 150-hp stretched version of the AA-1 Yankee two-seater. The Traveler was an okay airplane, but Grumman-American's chief engineer Roy Lopresti (later of Mooney and Beech fame) put in a new engine, redesigned the

cowling and cooling baffles, enlarged the elevator and did a detail drag cleanup program. The result, in 1975, was the Tiger.

The next year came the Cheetah, which was essentially a Tiger with the Traveler's old 150-hp engine. The two planes were in production only until 1979, when Allen Paulsen bought Grumman American and killed the Cheetah and Tiger to concentrate on the Gulfstream II bizjet. About 200 tigers were sitting at the factory when production stopped, and it took more than two years to sell them all off. (Paulsen, in retrospect, looks like a genius; he stopped production just before the aviation industry began its eight-year slide toward extinction.)

A total of about 1,300 Tigers and 800 Cheetahs were built. There were no major changes during the production runs, but some refinement occurred: in 1977, soundproofing was improved and windshield thickness doubled to a quarter-inch. Other changes: minor aerodynamic refinements, includ-

The 1978 Cheetah

Performance

including rubber fairings on the landing gear, improved windshield sealing and the addition of nose-strut shock absorber. In 1978, the seats were improved, and U-strips were added to the trailing edges of the control surfaces to prevent delamination of the bonds.

Performance

Both Cheetah and Tiger are at the head of the class in terms of speed. The Tiger has a book cruise speed of 160 mph, and *Aviation Consumer* editors have flown side-by-side with a Piper Arrow (200-hp, retractable gear) and pulled away in the Tiger. We've also watched a Piper Archer retreat outside the Tiger's window at about 15 knots. Running side-by-side, a Tiger will burn 20 percent less fuel and loaf along at about 60 percent power while the Archer is flat out. Owners report that real-world Tigers come pretty close to the book numbers. "At 2,600 rpm and 8,000 feet, I get 155 mph," is a typical comment. Another reports, "I flight-plan 130 knots and almost always beat that number from takeoff to touch-down." The Cheetah is about 15 mph slower, but still plenty faster than 150-hp competition like the Skyhawk and Warrior. Later 160-hp versions of the Warrior with speed pants can almost keep up with the Cheetah, however.

Climb performance is another story. At sea level and standard temperatures, the Tiger does reasonably well—850 fpm, about on par with the competition. But under tougher conditions—hot day, high altitude, heavy load—the Tiger's climb performance falls off very rapidly. Service ceiling is 13,800 feet, less than the Archer and Cardinal. Even the president of the American Yankee Assn., the hyperenthusiastic Tiger-Cheetah owner's club, admits that service ceiling is inadequate.

The Cheetah, with 30 less horsepower, is even more susceptible to this rapid decay of climb performance when hot, high or heavy. Book numbers are comparable to the 150-hp Skyhawk and Warrior, but our experience and reader reports suggest these are optimistic. One Cheetah owner reports a sickly 250-fpm climb at gross weight in hot weather. Another says that, 150 pounds below gross, he only manages about 500 fpm. "I always get outclimbed by a friend who has an old Skyhawk." This lack of climb power has resulted in a lot of accidents. (Details in the Safety section.)

Oddly, takeoff and climb performance can be enhanced by ignoring book procedures, which call for flaps up. Some experienced Tiger/Cheetah pilots put down about one-third flaps when takeoff

performance is critical. Says Tiger guru Ken Blackman, "The Tiger is a great short-field performer if flown properly. The manual recommends zero degrees flaps, but one-third to one-half flaps will make all the difference in the world. For grass fields, keep stick full back, the nose will lift off at about 20 knots and the airplane will lift off at about 45 knots in ground effect, then settling slightly before making like an elevator at 55 knots. For short hard-surface takeoffs, leave the nose flat and flaps up till 45 knots, then pull back and hit one-third flaps at the same time." Says another owner, "It is a lousy climber if you do it by the book, but with one-third flaps and an initial climb speed of 60-70 mph, it does very well."

Payload/Range

Gross weight of the Tiger is 2,400 pounds, and typical IFR aircraft run 1,450-1,500 pounds. That leaves a useful load of about 900 pounds, typical for the 180-hp four-placers. That's enough for full fuel (51 gallons) and three adults, plus a smidgin of baggage.

The Cheetah, with an empty weight only slightly less and a gross of 2,200 pounds, typically has a useful load around 750 pounds. That's good for full fuel (38 gallons) and not quite three 170-pound adults. (Some Cheetahs have optional 51-gallon tanks, but these can be filled only in the two-place mode.) The marginal useful load is all the more unfortunate because of the Cheetah's rapid loss of climb performance when overloaded. However tempted, one shouldn't mess with the Cheetah's weight limits.

The rather small baggage door helps out in this regard. Called a "mail slot" by one owner, it discourages the loading of large, heavy items into the baggage department. If you insist, you'll

The 1977 Tiger

have to lug them into the cockpit and over the back seat. Center of gravity is normally not a problem in either Cheetah or Tiger.

The Tiger's 51-gallon fuel capacity is just about right: good for more than four hours at max cruise power (about 10 gph) with a comfortable reserve. If you throttle back a bit, endurance shoots up to near six hours. A reasonable range figure with full tanks is 500-plus nm. One owner describes how he often flies non-stop from Los Angeles to Gunnison, Colo. (more than 600 nm) and lands with 50 minutes of fuel.

The standard-tank Cheetah, by comparison, has shorter legs. The 38-gallon supply is good for a bit less than four hours, with reserves. Call it 450 nm. As a two-placer with the optional 51-gallon tanks full, the Cheetah will fly a lot longer than you'd want to sit in a small plane.

Handling Qualities

Another big selling point of the Tiger and Cheetah is the superb handling qualities. These were inherited from its "sports car" AA-1 forebears, but the twitchiness, instability and violent stall characteristics of the AA-1 have been eliminated. In sum, the Tiger is an almost ideal blend of light, responsive handling and reasonable stability and docility. "I have never flown anything as nice as the Tiger," crows one owner. Cessna and Piper pilots will marvel.

The other side of the sports-car handling coin is less-than-ideal IFR stability. "It's adequate, but not a rock-steady machine,"says one owner. "It's easy to wobble your way down the glideslope," confirms another. An autopilot is a valuable helper on an IFR Tiger or Cheetah.

Landings are no particular problem; unlike the AA-1, the AA-5s don't sink like a brick and skitter around

on the ground. If anything, the AA-5s are floaters. The small flaps don't really make much difference. Comments one Tiger pilot who's spent hundreds of hours checking out transition pilots, "Because of the reputation of the AA-1 and the Tiger's high cruise speeds, people tend to bring it in way too fast. Seventy-five mph is the maximum approach speed under any conceivable condition, 70 is fine and 65 is great."

Comments another owner, "The Tiger is a candidate for speed brakes. I've made more go-arounds because of being high in the Tiger than any other airplane." The Tiger's floating tendencies—and the pilot's tendencies to bring it in too fast—make landing overshoots the number one cause of AA-5 accidents.

On the ground, the Tiger has an oddball swiveling nosewheel that requires steering by brakes. Once adjusted to, however, this procedure allows adroit maneuvering in tight spaces. On the other hand, the pilot does have to ride the brake during the first part of the takeoff roll, before the rudder is effective, and while taxiing in crosswinds. Old Tiger pros often start their takeoffs cocked well to the right. By the time the nose swings around straight, the rudder starts to work and no brake-riding is required at all.

Cockpit/Cabin

The first thing everybody notices is the Tiger/Cheetah's sliding canopy. If you're young and agile and wearing pants, no problem, but others may not like it. Also, everything gets wet if it's raining. The canopy provides superb visibility, but can be deadly in a crash. If the fuselage is warped by the impact, the canopy may jam, preventing escape in case of a fire. We're aware of one grisly accident in which a Tiger overran the runway— a minor accident, really —but caught fire. The canopy would open only a few inches, and the otherwise unhurt occupants burned to death. This is a rarity, however. (And of course doors in standard airplanes sometimes jam, too.)

The panel is well laid out, with plunger-type engine controls. The AA-5's fuel selector is a good one. Although it doesn't have a "both tanks" position and therefore requires tank-switching, the selec-tor/gauge system is just about idiot-proof: a prominent lever, right under the throttle, with the lever pointing directly at the gauge for the selected tank. In the last nine years, only two pilots have managed to crash from fuel starvation—a very good record, six times better than the AA-1 with its awful fuel system.

The Tiger/Cheetah interior is comfortable, if not cavernous—although the panoramic visibility makes it feel roomier than it really is. Some owners complain about lack of shoulder room. The seats are very basic, with no height or seatback adjustment. The interior appointments are Spartan ("Downright ugly" is how one owner puts it), and the original fabric faded quickly.

A unique feature is the fold-down rear seats, which provide a six-foot long cargo compartment that will hold a couple of ten-speed bicycles—or even two snoozing occupants in sleeping bags. One Florida water-ski distributor has a Tiger for shipping skis around the state.

Safety Record

The AA-5 series has an uncomfortably high accident rate considerably worse than competitors like the Skyhawk and Cherokee. During the period 1976 to 1984, the AA-5 series had a total accident rate of 11.9 per 100,000 hours, and a fatal rate of 2.3. These are much worse than the Cessna Skyhawk, which scored 7.5 total and 1.0 fatal—more than twice as good as the AA-5—during the years 1978 to 1979.

An exhaustive computer analysis of AA-5 accidents (see the July 1, 1986, *Aviation Consumer* for details) revealed several patterns.

• Pilots with low time in type had an astoundingly high proportion of AA-5 crashes. Median time in type for the 315 AA-5 accident pilots we studied was only 20 hours. More than a quarter of AA-5 accident pilots had 10 hours or less in type.

Moral: Newcomers have a great deal of trouble adjusting to the AA-5. The transition period is critical. Get a thorough checkout and be ultra-cautious for the first 50 hours.

• Obstacle crashes were a big problem. We counted 37 accidents—12 percent of the total—in which an AA-5 failed to get out of ground effect or clear an obstacle. (For comparison, a sample of Cessna Skyhawk accidents showed just one-percent obstacle accidents.)

Circumstances like grassy or snowy runways, high density altitude, overloads or snow on the wings played a big role in these accidents.

Moral: Leave big margins for error in takeoff and climb performance,

Cost/Performance/Specifications

Model	Year	Number Built	Average Retail Price	Cruise Speed (kts)	Rate of Climb (fpm)	Useful Load (lbs)	Fuel Std/Opt (gals)	Engine	TBO (hrs)	Overhaul Cost
AA-5A	1976	282	$18,000	128	660	800	38/51	150-hp Lyc. O-320-E2G	2,000	$8,800
AA-5A	1977	240	$19,000	128	660	800	38/51	150-hp Lyc. O-320-E2G	2,000	$8,800
AA-5A	1978	147	$20,000	128	660	800	38/51	150-hp Lyc. O-320-E2G	2,000	$8,800
AA-5A	1979	147	$22,000	128	660	800	38/51	150-hp Lyc. O-320-E2G	2,000	$8,800
AA-5B	1975	111	$22,250	139	850	950	51	180-hp Lyc. O-360-A4K	2,000	$9,500
AA-5B	1976	288	$24,250	139	850	950	51	180-hp Lyc. O-360-A4K	2,000	$9,500
AA-5B	1977	292	$26,250	139	850	950	51	180-hp Lyc. O-360-A4K	2,000	$9,500
AA-5B	1978	212	$29,500	139	850	950	51	180-hp Lyc. O-360-A4K	2,000	$9,500
AA-5B	1979	417	$31,250	139	850	950	51	180-hp Lyc. O-360-A4K	2,000	$9,500

particularly under the conditions cited above. Be especially careful with the Cheetah. Don't count on book performance. Don't overload. Ignore the POH; instead use partial flaps for takeoff and max climb performance.

• Landings—particularly overshoots—are a problem, accounting for 42 percent of all AA-5 accidents. The AA-5 ranked first of 33 aircraft measured in a 1976 NTSB study of landing overshoot accidents. The light pitch control and springy nosegear also accounted for an unusually high proportion of porpoising crashes—often the result of the pilot attempting to fly the plane onto the runway too fast. If you do porpoise badly, there's a good chance you'll hit the prop; ground clearance is minimal.

Moral: Carefully control airspeed on approach: 75 to 80 is the absolute fastest approach speed you should ever see (heavy weight, gusty wind). Normally, 70 to 75 is about right, and 65 is fine at light weights in still air. If you're too fast, go around.

Maintenance

The Tiger generally has proven to be a simple, reliable airplane. "Nothing ever seems to break," says one owner. Compared to other 160-mph airplanes, maintenance costs are low. (No retractable gear or constant-speed prop like the others.) Compared to other 180-hp fixed-gear aircraft of lesser performance, maintenance costs are similar.

Owners report typical annual inspection costs in the $500 to $700 range, although one fellow who helped out his mechanic paid only $125, and another who bought a long-neglected airplane spent close to $3,000 on his first annual.

Here's a checklist of the most common maintenance problems:

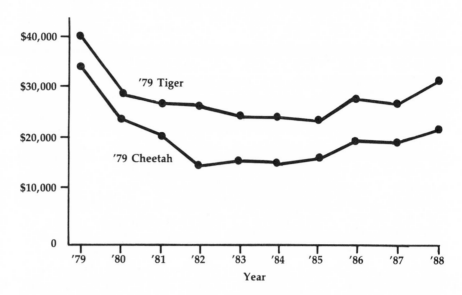

Tiger/Cheetah Resale Value Chart

• Cylinder problems. The 180-hp Lycoming O-360 and 150-hp O-320 are two of aviation's most enduring and reliable powerplants. Unfortunately, the installation in the AA-5s is not the best; in an attempt to wring every last knot out of the airplane, Grumman cut the cooling airflow margins very close, and some Tigers and Cheetahs tend to overheat. This shortens engine life, wears out rings and valves, and can cause high oil consumption. "The cylinder barrels run very hot," one mechanic told us, "and the walls get glazed and they start to pump oil." It's not unusual to see top overhauls in Tigers well before the 2,000-hour TBO.

The problem is exacerbated by thin, flimsy engine baffling and poor baffle sealing. If the baffles aren't in tip-top shape, cooling suffers even more. Closely inspect the baffling of any Tiger or Cheetah considered for purchase, and be sure to do careful compression checks and a borescope cylinder inspection to check for heat-related problems. We'd also recommend installing a four-probe cylinder-head temp gauge to more closely monitor the

engine. One owner who did reports seeing temperatures as high as 450 degrees. Another uses his to carefully monitor his leaning and keep CHTs below 400 degrees.

• Bond-line separation in the early models. The culprit turned out to be an improper bonding sealant, American Cyanimide FM-123, known as "purple passion" among production employees. The FM-123 was used in all Grumman-American aircraft built between April 1974 and December 1975—including Tigers up through about serial number 125.

At least one severe delamination occured in flight in a 1975 Tiger, but no accident resulted. At least two Tigers, serial numbers 15 and 19, were virtually rebuilt from scratch because of severe bonding problems. According to a former Grumman American production employee, 30 or 40 honeycomb fuselage test panels somehow found their way into production aircraft, possibly affecting Tigers with serial numbers below about 30.

A 1976 AD required rivets along bondlines, and the problem has receded in recent years. But any buyer of a 1975 or early 1976 Tiger should be aware of the potential for problems. As for the Cheetah, since it came along a year later, only a tiny handful of the earliest Cheetahs used the purple stuff. (Incidentally, you can check for the defective glue by pulling off the wingtip and inspecting the bonded seam at the spar-to-rib or rib-to-skin joint. If there's a purple line, you may have a problem.

• Nosewheel shimmy. The Tiger/Cheetah nosewheel not only looks like a shopping cart wheel, sometimes it acts like one, too. The shimmy problem is caused by a variety of factors: improper tension in the spring washers (they may be worn out, or the shop may have adjusted them too loose by improperly interpreting the 18 to 22-pound side-pull requirement as a torque requirement); loose axle nuts, bad tire, or loose torque tube strut. The nosegear demands a lot of maintenance, and must be lubricated and adjusted strictly by the book. (Not many shops even have the book.) In particular, the strut inside the torque tube should be free of corrosion and well lubricated.

The 1977 and later models have a shock absorber in the nosewheel, which helps to some degree, but they make removal of the nose gear rather tricky. If you have persistent shimmy problems, see a good mechanic who specializes in Grumman American aircraft.

• Cracking prop spinner. Pre-1979 Tigers (s/n 1047 and below) had problems with cracking spinners, possibly related to propeller vibration. Virtually all Tigers in the field have been retrofitted with improved spinners, but check to make sure.

• Magneto problems. The Slick mags in the AA-5s just don't seem to last. We have numerous reports of failures in 500 hours or less. Reports one Tiger owner, ''The

most expensive and annoying items have been the Slick magnetos. My airplane has needed five mags in 1,000 hours. Slick mags belong on garden tractors, not airplanes.'' Another owner referred to them as ''those throwaway Slick mags.''

• Leaky fuel tanks. Several owners reported leaks, and blamed it on the aromatics in low-lead fuel. The Cheetah, incidentally, may legally use leaded autogas, which should save a lot of many in addition to cutting down fuel tank sealant problems.

• High brake wear. Because of the steer-by-brakes system, pads wear out quickly. Clever AA-5 pilots manage to minimize brake use, however. Good brake maintenance is important; if there's a failure, the plane cannot be taxied.

• Fragile rudder return springs. Several owners reported repeated breaking of the rudder springs. One fellow took to always carrying a spare, just in case.

Airworthiness Directives

Tiger owners face two major repetitive AD annoyances. The first is the 200-hour inspection of the McCauley prop hub for cracks. Second is the 100-hour inspection of the ailerons.

In addition to the usual shotgun ADs that apply to many aircraft—Lycoming oil pumps, Airborne vacuum pumps, oil coolers, ELTs, air filters, altimeters, Bendix and Slick mags, etc.—the Tiger and/or Cheetah have had one-time ADs on the rudder bar, cowl hinge, mixture control, bonded skin, alternate static source, carb air box and carb heat valve. All of these should have been complied with, of course, on any aircraft considered for purchase.

Parts Supplies

Although Grumman American/ Gulfstream has historically done a

good job supporting the airplanes, parts are getting more and more expensive, with longer lead times for shipment. Some parts are now on a build-to-order basis, at astronomical prices. A good source of parts is Fletcher Aviation at Hobby Airport in Houston. (7786 Braniff St., Houston, Tex. 77061 (713)641-2023.) In addition to being a factory distributor with a big stock, Fletcher also sells aftermarket parts. One owner described how he got a quote from Gulfstream of $487 for a nosegear boot. Fletcher supplied the part for $75. Owner David Fletcher is a Grumman fanatic who can provide expert technical info (the Grumman factory reps call him for advice.

Modifications

We'd recommend three modifications for the Tiger. First, a Sensenich propeller in place of the AD-plagued McCauley. In addition to eliminating the AD inspection, the new prop also does away with an annoying rpm restriction between 1850 and 2250 rpm in descending flight. This yellow arc, due to vibration problems of the particular engine/prop combination, sits unfortunately right at the usual ILS approach speed. In addition, the Sensenich is claimed to increase speed two to four mph. It's available form Aeromod Corp., Bldg C-3, Paine Field, Everett, Wash. 98204 (206)353-3559. Cost is $1,855.

Aeromod, which specializes in AA-1 and AA-5 mods, also offers an oil cooler and baffle modification that is claimed to reduce oil temps by 25 to 40 degrees. Considering the Tiger/Cheetah's tendency to run hot, that's a good idea. Cost of the kit, which takes about four hours to install, is $375 (1987 price).

The third nice-to-have mod is modified cooling exit and baffle reseal/fixup by a fellow named Bill Heard (213)641-1729. The mod is basically an enlarged cooling outflow with a small fixed cowl flap. Heard claims a CHT drop of 50-75 degrees and no loss of performance. There's no STC, so the work must be done by Heard under a field approval.

Other mods are available to boost performance and cut maintenance costs. Aeromod offers three engine conversions for the AA-5:

• The Sabre-tooth Tiger, a 260-hp Lycoming installation with constant-speed prop. Claimed speed is 180 mph, with a 1,800-fpm climb rate, but the useful load penalty is about 100 pounds. And watch that fuel consumption! Cost in 1987 was $20,000 for a low-time used engine, more for a new one.

• A more practical conversion is Aeromod's upgrade to a 200-hp Lycoming and constant-speed prop. Cruise speed is up 10 mph to 170, and climb rate soars to 1,300 fpm. Useful load penalty on a Tiger is about 70 pounds. Cost in 1987 was about $16,000 for a low-time used engine.

• Aeromod can also turn a Cheetah into a Tiger with a 180-hp conversion. Total cost in 1987 was about $11,000 (for a mid-time engine). If a Cheetah owner wants to have the work done locally, the STC paperwork alone is $500. This mod might be a good way to take advantage of the big price difference between the Cheetah and Tiger. If you can't find a good Tiger, get a run-out Cheetah and modify it. You've got a nice mid-time Tiger that will return the full value of the conversion.

• Aeromod also offers an improved air box that lets the engine breathe easier and is cheaper to maintain. Aeromod also can offer advice on antenna locations that improve reception and add a couple of knots speed. Fletcher Aviation also offers hints for aerodynamic cleanups, and operates what it claims to be a perfectly stock 180-mph Tiger.

Owner Group

We also throw our full support behind the American Yankee Assn., the owners group for the Tiger and Cheetah (as well as all other Grumman American light aircraft). In addition to the usual newsletter and fly-in activities, the AYA is a useful source of technical and maintenance information. Such specialized expertise is almost a necessity to own and fly an oddball airplane like the AA-5 that may not be familiar to every local mechanic. The AYA also has a special group insurance plan that may save you some bucks, and can put you in touch with approved pilots for a proper AA-5 checkout. American Yankee Assn., P.O. Box 11757, Fresno, Calif.

Owner Comments

As an obvious supporter of the Grumman line of aircraft, let me turn the tables and contribute what I find to be the drawbacks of owning a Tiger. I have had a 1976 model for 10 years, and have some 1,500 hours on the airplane.

My major complaint is that the service ceiling is only 13,800 feet. While this is adequate for many, those of us who fly across the Sierras and Rockies find it occasionally restrictive. A second drawback is that without cooling modifications, the engine tends to run hot, necessitating cylinder work before TBO on most planes. My aircraft has a modification designed by Bill Heard (213)641-1729 (evenings) and I highly recommend it.

And that's it. I consider the Tiger to be the best bargain in aviation today. The aircraft provides an honest 130-knot cruise. Typical owner-assisted annuals run about $350, and aside from the usual maintenance items (tires, brakes, etc.) nothing much goes wrong.

Incidentally, we have a group insurance program and a pilot familiarization program to inform our new members about flight characteristics. Airspeed control is of great importance on final approach. but properly taught, this presents no problem.

William M. Marvel
President, American Yankee Assn.
Fresno, Calif.

My partner and I owned both a Tiger and a Mooney 231. The Tiger is a much easier airplane to operate than the Mooney, especially on the ground. I fly the Tiger long distances, with quite a bit of IFR. I flight plan for 130 knots, and almost always beat that number from lift-off to touchdown. Out west, most of the flying is at 9,000 feet or higher. At lower altitude, the 139-knot book cruise speed is easily bettered. Fuel burn is 10.5 gph down low, declining to 10.0 up high. I almost always fly at full throttle and/or 2,700 rpm.

The Tiger is considerably more difficult to fly on instrument approaches than the Mooney. The controls on the Grumman are sensitive, so a little goes a long way. Speed control on approaches is also more difficult. The Tiger is very clean in approach configuration, so very little power is required to hold 100 knots. The fixed-pitch prop also makes it harder to establish a stable power setting.

There are a couple of ADs that help keep maintenance costs up. Every 100 hours the ailerons have to be checked, and every 200 hours the prop has to be pulled and checked for cracks. That costs $100, including profiling and repaint. Annual inspections run about $600 when I don't do anything, and about $200 when I do the grunt work. The direct operating costs have worked out to $24 per hour, including a reserve for overhaul.

The interior is pretty noisy at cruise speed. Earplugs or a headset are a necessity. After 11 years use, everything in the interior is warped, faded, cracked or all three. The new replacements don't look much better. Parts are no problem at all. Fletcher Aviation in Houston seems to have everything required, and the parts are generally inexpensive.

William Barton
Encinitas, Calif.

I have been flying Grumman Tigers since 1981 and have owned a 1978 model for three years. I consider the Tiger a most economical aircraft that allows me to justify it for leisure-time purposes.

Initial investment is reasonable, maintenance minimal, fuel consumption averages about 9.6 gallons per tach-hour, insurance about $1,000 per year, annuals average about 16 hours' labor.

In IFR conditions, it bounces and rolls with turbulence, but is comfortable if you go with the flow. There is some learning curve in the transition from a Piper or Cessna. The Tiger has lots of fuel capacity. With full tanks, I carry 675 pounds payload, and consider it a good ''three people and gear'' plane for weekending. I recently replaced the McCauley prop with a Sensenich, and it eliminates the yellow arc from 1,850 to 2,250 rpm. It is also smoother, quieter and quicker on the climbout.

Ronald Esau
Edina, Minn.

I bought my 1976 Cheetah, serial number 60, in 1986 and have flown it 260 hours in 18 months. I cruise at 125 mph true at around 2475 rpm, and it uses about eight gph. My only performance complaint is its climb capability. At my usual weight of about 150 pounds under gross, I can only get about 500 fpm at best rate at sea level. I have long-range tanks, which come in very handy, but contribute to poor climb performance.

The airplane handles very crisply, but is a tailwagger in turbulence, and isn't as stable as a Cardinal or 172 on instrument approaches.

Insurance the first year was $1,174, declining to $1,074 the second year because I had gotten an instrument rating.

It's a bit tough getting passengers in through the canopy and over the front seats into the back. But otherwise it's a comfortable airplane. Visibility is great. In spite of it being the most accident-prone airplane in its class, it seems fairly docile. It mushes rather than breaks in the stall. Landings are smooth, but it's squirrelly on rollout because of the lack of nosewheel steering. Backing into a tiedown spot requires a towbar.

Gary Keck
San Diego, Calif.

Cessna 182

Even if the Cessna 182 hasn't been around as long as the Old Testament, it sometimes seems like it has. The third most popular lightplane in history, the Cessna 182 has long been the keystone of Cessna's step-up marketing philosophy, bridging the gulf between Cessna's low-profit 150/172 entry-level airplanes and the higher-profit, higher-performance 210 and light twin aircraft.

Back in the days of JFK and the New Frontier, the 182 got a cleaned-up look. Performance, however, remained basically the same.

Today, almost 30 years after the 182's introduction in 1956, the aircraft is still *the* basic medium-performance aircraft, an economical flying machine capable of hauling four people, bag and baggage, a reasonable distance, in comfort, and at a reasonable speed.

The first Skylanes rolled off the production line the same year as the first 172s. Together, the duo marked the beginning of Cessna's 20-year dominance of the single-engine market.

The basic 182 design was cut in stone in those days and both airframe and powerplant have remained fundamentally unchanged ever since. The overall effect is generous, with a fuselage of ample size, topped by a big slab of a wing.

In 1958, Cessna introduced the "Skylane," a 182 fitted with enough amenities and creature comforts to raise the empty weight approximately 100 pounds, and therefore decrease useful load by roughly the same amount. Those 1958 Skylanes included rudder trim and a ratchet click elevator trim device, along with optional autopilot. Later Cessna bestowed the Skylane name on the 182, and made the marginally upscale version of the same plane the "Skylane II."

The 230-hp Continental O-470 has proved a dependable performer through the years, despite some break-in problems reported in the later O-470-S model. Those first 182s used the O-470-L engine, which featured larger cast shell cylinder heads, thinner and more numerous cooling fins, and an engine mount improved over the early O-470-K installation in the Cessna 180 design.

Cars with enormous swept tail "fins" were all the rage in the late 1950's. Eventually this vogue found its way into airplane styling, with Cessna sweeping back the tail on the 180 in 1960. Basic fuel capacity was increased in 1960, from 55 gallons to 65, with long-range 84-gallon tanks introduced as an option. Later Skylanes would boast a 92-gallon capacity.

Two years later the airplane got a rear window and electric flaps. The year 1971 witnessed an alteration to the 182 in the form of its so-called camber lift wing. The wing was given a constant radius droop—a downward curl. The aim of the droop was to provide better low speed handling and stall reaction. Combined with the aircraft's washout, the result is good lateral control even while deep in the stall zone.

Gross weight has grown steadily over the years, from the original 2,550 pounds to 2,650 in 1957 to 3,100 today. Empty weight has also increased, although not quite as fast as gross, so that useful load numbers for the 182 have not increased dramatically, starting at 1,010 pounds in '57, and topping off at 1,377 today.

Overall, however, the 182 design has gone through remarkably few changes over the years.

Built for Comfort, Not for Speed

Book speeds have remained in the 139- to 143-knot range through the years with evolutionary aerodynamic refinements making up for the speed penalty of higher gross weights. Most owners report such speeds are possible in the 182, but prefer to drone along at lower power settings to save fuel, with 130 knots a commonly mentioned figure. One owner reported burning 12.5 gph to get 140 knots at 75 percent power. Another said his 182, burdened with a "full load" cruised at 135 knots at 75 percent between 6,500 and 8,500 feet, while consuming a quart of oil every four hours. Performance like this may seem pokey for an airplane driven by a 230-hp engine, and it is. The Mooney 201, albeit a retractable, slips through the air 30 knots faster than a 182, while using less horsepower.

While no one ever said the 182 was a racer, the airplane does climb, with 1,000 fpm easily obtainable at heavy weights, and 1,500 fpm at lighter weights (both from sea level, of course).

If the 182 doesn't get you there particularly fast, it treats you kindly along the way, thanks to a spacious interior. It's a real four-seater, the kind that allows the back seat mob to abandon the fetal position and stretch out. Two wide doors ease entry and exit. On the negative side, cabin noise levels approach brain-damage thresholds, and can make long flights fatiguing without a good pair of earplugs.

Handling

In a word, the 182 is stable. Most pilots praise it both as an IFR platform and as a reasonably comfortable aircraft in turbulence. Nonetheless, in the air, as on the ground, there ain't no free lunch, and this stability is paid for with rather heavy control forces.

To use another word, the 182 is ponderous, especially in pitch. With full flaps and two people aboard, flaring to land takes maximum muscle and maximum back trim. This heaviness of control is the price paid for the 182's vast CG envelope.

Trying to stall the 182 with power on is probably the nearest anyone will come to aerobatic maneuvering in this staid aircraft. It will buck and shake like a bronco until the pilot either relaxes back pressure to lower the nose or settles for a pronounced wing drop.

Such performance will never come as a surprise, however, because the 182's humungous elevator forces

make the airplane virtually impossible to stall by accident. Slow-speed maneuvering in a Skylane builds confidence; there's no feeling of flying right on the edge. On the other hand, aileron control at low speeds is relatively clumsy, and gusty crosswinds can prove challenging.

Loading

Unless you're transporting ingots of solid neutronium, the 182's load limits are pretty tough to bust. It's acknowledged as one of the few airplanes you can almost always fill all the seats, all the tanks, stuff the baggage compartment to capacity, and still be legal (and safe). Admittedly a well-equipped 182 with long-range tanks might require a degree of fuel/passenger tradeoff, but on the whole, Skylane pilots don't fuss much with weight and balance. If it fits, it's probably legal.

CG balance is also generous. One Skylane owner reports he can put himself up front, load a pair of 200-pounders in the back, fill the baggage compartment to the max, and still be within CG limits.

Safety

The Skylane has a good safety record—well above average as measured against the GA fleet overall. Both accident and fatality rates come in below the norm. FAA records from 1980-81 list 41 fatal accidents for the 182 fleet, with over 3 million hours flown during that period.

The Skylane has among the best stall/spin accident rates of any aircraft. In both a 1972 stall/spin study from the NTSB, and a 1984 study conducted by our sister publication *Aviation Safety*, the 182 scored

among the lowest in both accidents and fatalities attributed to stalls or spins.

Thanks in part to the airplane's megalithic pitch performance, in-flight structural failures are virtually unheard of. It's nearly impossible to pull hard enough on a 182 to overstress the airplane. That high-drag fuselage and fixed gear also limit speed buildup in an unintentional dive. When measured overall, Cessna designs featuring wing strut braces have an excellent record of holding together when the going gets tough.

The Skylane also excels in the area of fuel management. Its no-frills fuel system consists of a high-wing, gravity-feed system, and an idiot-proof left-right-both fuel selector.

Deadly Fuel Cells

One of the more disturbing ADs to emerge from the FAA's regulatory woods, AD 84-10-1 has caused thousands of Cessna owners to delve deep into the innards of their fuel-bladder equipped wings for potentially deadly water-trapping wrinkles. For years the problem eluded detection during the traditional sump-draining preflight because the water trapped by wrinkles could also be kept isolated from the quick-drain openings. Such a tank could be sumped and no water would show in the sample.

A simple attitude change, such as that encountered in takeoff, would spill the water out of its wrinkle containment area, through the intake, and into the engine. Too often, this water was more than the three ounces that can be stopped by the gascolator. Result: engine stoppage at the worst possible time, just seconds after takeoff. AD 84-10-1 affected all 182 models built between 1956 to 1978, the year Cessna changed over to a wet-wing design.

A worthwhile discussion of this AD requires some background. In an *Aviation Safety* examination of accidents from 1975 through 1981, 396 accidents in various types of aircraft were found in which water-contaminated fuel was cited as a cause or factor. A total of 155 (about 39 percent) of these accidents involved Cessna aircraft and 39 of those mishaps involved Cessna 182s.

What's more, 25 of the 39 C-182 accidents involved the P-model, the 182 model in production from 1972 through 1974. In those days, the rubber fuel bladders installed at the plant were made of Goodyear BTC-39. The passage of time revealed that BTC-39 bladders deteriorated rapidly, becoming brittle, "cheesy," and eventually leaking copiously. An AD mandated their replacement with bladders made of stiffer BTC-67, a urethane material.

The extra stiffness of BTC-67 seems to be the contributing factor to the wrinkle problems that were to be discovered later. As Bob Stevens, then FAA manager of Standards and Evaluations, put it, "There's two ways to install a tank like this. If the tank is put in on the assembly line as the airplane is built, that's fairly easy. The tank just fits in before the butt rib. It's installing the tank in the field as a replacement where the trouble starts. As delivered in the field, these tanks aren't too wrinkled. The procedure to install is to soften the BTC-67 tanks in warm water, and then wad

Skylane engines seem to suffer less from 100 LL than other 80-octane airplanes. They also can use autogas.

them up and stuff them into the wing. That's where I think the wrinkles come from."

"Smoothing and Blending"

The AD required an inspection of the bladders, "smoothing and blending" of any wrinkles found, and installation of new quick drains on aircraft in which the "smoothing and blending" process requirement involved movement of the drains. The chief target of the inspection is a water-trapping wrinkle that commonly extended at a 45-degree angle across the inboard rear corner of the fuel tank floor. Such a large wrinkle can trap quite a bit of water. More than a few 182 owners reported discovering their tanks harbored as much as a quart, sometimes more.

The entire "smoothing and blending" process is something akin to

eliminating the wrinkles in a carpet. Stomping on one wrinkle can make it vanish, only to reappear somewhere else on the carpet. Often what's needed is to take up the whole carpet and lay it again. In the fuel bladder case, this move required relocation of the drains. Cessna has provided a quick-drain kit for $89 (part number SK-206-24 and 25).

Rock n' Roll!

Another move mandated by AD 84-10-1 is the famed "rock n' roll preflight." The aircraft is sumped normally, on level ground. Then the tail is lowered to within five inches of the ground while rocking the wings 10 inches up and down at least 12 times. Then the sumps are drained again, checking for any water that may have been shaken out.

After the main wrinkle has been eliminated, the AD specifies that the amount of fluid trapped by any other wrinkles must be determined. If this trapped fluid measures more than three ounces, the aircraft is placarded with the "rock n' roll preflight" procedure, making those moves mandatory before flight.

The wording of AD 84-10-1 has been criticized as vague. For example, it's unclear whether these "rocking and rolling" moves have to be done simultaneously, something clearly beyond the ability of just one person. Plus, pilots of petite stature would probably find

Cost/Performance/Specifications

Model	Year	Number Built	Average Retail Price	Cruise Speed (Kts)	Rate of Climb (fpm)	Useful Load (lbs)	Fuel Std/Opt (gals)	Engine	TBO (hrs)	Overhaul Cost
182-A	1956-57	1,753	$16,000	117	1,210	1,010	55	230-hp Cont. O-470-L	1,500	$9,250
182-A&	1958-59	1,648	$18,000	120	1,030	1,090	55	230-hp Cont. O-470-L	1,500	$9,250
182-C&D	1960-61	1,239	$19,500	123	1,030	1,090	65/84	230-hp Cont. O-470-L	1,500	$9,250
182-E&F	1962-63	1,459	$20,500	123	980	1,190	65/84	230-hp Cont. O-470-R	1,500	$9,250
182-G&H	1964-65	1,175	$21,500	123	980	1,190	65/84	230-hp Cont. O-470-R	1,500	$9,250
182-J&K	1966-67	1,820	$22,500	123	980	1,175	65/84	230-hp Cont. O-470-R	1,500	$9,250
182-L&M	1968-69	1,549	$24,000	123	980	1,175	65/84	230-hp Cont. O-470-R	1,500	$9,250
182-N	1970-71	769	$26,000	121	850	1,310	65/84	230-hp Cont. O-470-R	1,500	$9,250
182-P	1972-74	1,009	$30,500	125	1,010	1,169	61/80	230-hp Cont. O-470-R	1,500	$9,250
182-P II	1975-76	1,699	$37,000	125	1,010	1,169	61/80	230-hp Cont. O-470-S	1,500	$9,250
182-Q II	1977-80	2,559	$51,000	121	1,010	1,169	61/80	230-hp Cont. O-470-U	1,500	$9,250
182-R II	1981	339	$59,500	124	865	1,390	92	230-hp Cont. O-470-U	1,500	$9,250
182-R II	1982	237	$65,500	124	865	1,373	92	230-hp Cont. O-470-U	1,500	$9,250
182R II	1983	74	$71,500	124	865	1,373	92	230-hp Cont. O-470-U	2,000	$9,250
182R II	1984	65	$80,000	124	865	1,373	92	230-hp Cont. O-470-U	2,000	$9,250

the tail-lowering maneuver impossible. And it's unclear as to just how owners of float-equipped aircraft are supposed to perform these moves.

As more and more 182s come into compliance with this AD, some evidence is emerging that it has been effective. Life-threatening wrinkles have been detected and corrected. However, there have also been reports of heavy labor costs for airplanes with particularly convoluted wrinkles.

What Else Can You Do About Water?

Two devices intended to prevent undrainable water from reaching the engine seem to us worthwhile. The Silver-Wells water separator is a well-known product by now. Basically an enlarged gascolator, the separator is so commodious it increases the maximum permissible amount of water trapped by wrinkles from three ounces to a full quart under provisions of the AD. As of this writing, it is the only approved alternate form of compliance for this portion of the AD.

The Silver-Wells separator costs $500. When added to the cost of compliance with the rest of the AD, the total tab can run upwards of $1,000. The separator is available from TurboPlus, 1520 26th Avenue NW, Gig Harbor, Wash. 98335, (800) 742-4202.

Another device, quite similar to the separator, fits under the 182's cabin floorboards. Designed by Skylane pilot Rodney Gross, who himself experienced a water-contaminated engine failure on takeoff in a 182, the system consists of two small reservoir tanks located near the fuel system low point in the aircraft's belly. These tanks allow water which was not drained during pre-flight sumping to settle, and are equipped with quick drains of their own, so that water can be eliminated from the system.

Gross's system has received a revised STC, and cannot be installed until the rest of the AD has been complied with. "These tanks are just an insurance policy," Gross

said. "They don't solve the problem."

Priced at $330, the system is available from Saturn Components Corporation, 15268 Earlham Street, Pacific Palisades, Calif. 90272, (213) 454-6714.

Speaking of water contamination, leaking and deteriorating fuel caps and seals are also likely avenues for aqueous invasion. Check them thoroughly for a tight fit.

Carb Ice

In figures released by the NTSB in 1977, an alarming number of accidents involving carb ice and 182s emerged. While the 182 isn't as prone to carb ice problems as some other designs (notably the C-150), anyone who regularly flies a Skylane in heavy weather should invest in a carb ice detector.

Crunch

When shopping for a used 182, examine the firewall carefully. The nose-heaviness of the 182, coupled with the airplane's heavy elevator forces, makes for frequent hard landings with a potential for gear-bending nose-low landings. The firewall is usually the first to suffer.

Another casualty of the 182's nose-heavy handling is the nosewheel assembly, with buckling and shimmies the usual result.

Overall...

Plenty of power, a big wing, heavy pitch forces, solid handling and a simple, safe fuel system (providing AD 84-10-1 has been complied with) make the Skylane one of the safest buys around.

Big, bulbous, and beefy describes the Cessna 182, shown here in its 1983 version.

Maintenance

The 182 is a simple, robust aircraft, with a healthy, but normal appetite for maintenance as the fleet ages. When we evaluated this airplane in 1979, readers reported annuals in the $250-$300 range. Today's readers have cited annuals in the $1,000 to $2,000 neighborhood. Looking at those numbers, it seems to us that the 182 line hasn't become any less reliable mechanically, but that maintenance and parts costs have gone through the roof. One reader calculated his hourly operating cost for labor alone at $25.

The Skylane shares the same McCauley/Hartzell prop AD that encumbers many aircraft designs, Cessna and otherwise, equipped with constant-speed propellers. With the exception of this and the fuel bladder problem, the AD scene for the 182 is relatively clear.

Powerplant

The Continental O-470 engine has a good record, although it doesn't seem to be as reliable as the four-cylinder carbureted Lycomings. TBO for the O-470 was 1,500 hours until 1983, when it was boosted to 2,000 for the O-470-U model.

A well-maintained engine should meet or exceed the TBO. The key to longevity on this engine appears to be a rigorous break-in period. "Firewall that sucker," is how one O-470 operator put it. The theory is that the heat of heavy initial operation seats the piston rings and valve seats firmly in place, cutting oil consumption and smoothing operation.

Some 1975 and 1976 Skylanes had special engine problems that used airplane buyers should be aware of. Aircraft built in those years bore the 182,° designation, and featured the O-470-S engine, which had a new ring design. Some of these engines had break-in problems, in some cases using as much as a quart of oil per hour. Despite its efforts, Continental apparently never really figured out what was wrong, and instead switched to higher-compression O-470-U in 1977. The most plausible theory offered to date is that the S-series engines were babied in break-in by well-meaning owners. Check for tell-tale high oil consumption on these engines.

Valve Problems

Earlier this year, Continental issued a mandatory service bulletin covering some 75 new and rebuilt O-470 engines evidently shipped with the wrong exhaust valves. It seems that soft, stainless steel valves were installed in the engines by mistake. This engine has hardened Nitralloy valve guides, which promptly chewed up the soft valves, a process resulting in stuck valves and metal particles wreaking havoc throughout the oil system. Proper valves for the O-470 engine carry part number 637781.

At roughly the same time, Continental sent out about 40 O-470 cylinder assemblies (P/N 646680) fitted with the wrong valves. By the time the problem was discovered, Continental had been sending these faulty assemblies out for almost a full year.

As of April, 1985, about 15 engines had been replaced due to extensive metal contamination of the oil. The rest were being reworked with the correct valves. During the valve replacement, valve guides must be reamed out to remove any metal build-ups.

The Skylane seems to have suffered less from 100LL problems than other 80-octane airplanes.

Nevertheless, the proven process of careful leaning, plug rotation, and 50-hour oil changes is the best policy, along with use of TCP should lead fouling be suspected.

Skylanes have paper induction air filter elements that can swell up in the presence of moisture and restrict airflow. Even worse, old paper filters can decompose to the point where they can be ingested by the engine. Such an ingestion was blamed as cause of a fatal Skylane crash leading to AD 84-26-02, which put a life limit of 500 hours on paper filters. The filter on the downed Skylane reportedly was more than 10 years old, and had accumulated 1,100 hours in the time of the crash.

This AD did not include foam induction air filters such as those made by Brackett Aircraft Co., which recommends their filters be replaced every 12 months or 100 hours if one inch thick, and every 200 hours if two inches thick. Since paper filters range in price from about $20 to over $100, the Bracketts might actually be cheaper to use. They are priced from $10 to a little under $60, and replacement filters cost even less. Brackett claims its filters stop potentially damaging particles down to 15 microns for a longer period than paper filters.

Aside from water and dirt, another factor that can cause great distress to paper, and maybe even foam

The first edition 182, a 1956 model with squared-off tail and rear-view window but no wheel pants. A workaday airplane destined to become the third-best selling lightplane in history.

filters is a ''backfire'' in the manifold system that belches flame out into the filter. This flame can burn portions of the filter into ashes and cinders that do no good for the engine. Suggestion: next time a backfire is encountered on startup, shut down, get out, and check the condition of the induction air filter.

Modifications

The marriage between airframe and powerplant has been such a happy one in the case of the 182, that there have been relatively few STC'd mods. EAA and Petersen Aviation both hold the autogas STCs for the 182 series, with Petersen's usable for both leaded and unleaded fuels (see Owner Comments for more on the difference in fuels). Robertson Aircraft, 839 West Perimeter Road, Renton, Wash. 98055, offers an extensive and expensive STOL mod. Less elaborate systems featuring new leading edge cuffs, sealed ailerons and stall fences are marketed by Horton STOL-craft, Inc., Wellington Municipal Airport, Wellington, Kan. 67152.

The major slick-up mods offered for the 182 line come from Charlie Siebel's Flight Bonus, Inc., located at Box 120773, Arlington, Tex. 76012, (817) 265-1650. Depending on the year of manufacture, Siebel's slick-ups promise to boost a 182's cruise speed from 12 to 20 mph and range in price from $2,485 to $3,425.

Skylane Club

There is a combination Skylane/Centurion Club headed by Bob Green, Box 75068, Birmingham,

Ala. 95253, (205) 879-7414. Annual dues are $20. Owners of 182s preferring more polyglot company might also join the Cessna Pilot's Assn., located at Wichita's Mid-Continent Airport at 2120 Airport Road, Box 12948, Wichita, Kan. 67277, (316) 946-4777. CPA also charges $20 a year.

Owner Comments

I own a 1981 Cessna Skylane 182R, and have put over 800 hours on it since new. There is a lot of good news about the plane, and a little bad.

First the good news: Performance.

The Skylane is a terrific instrument platform, both stable and forgiving yet able to fly fast approaches when mixing it up with the big planes at major airports. Its outstanding range adds flexibility for hard IFR.

Its short-field performance is exemplary, as are its load-carrying capability and, more important, its wide center-of-gravity tolerance. I can truly haul four people, full fuel, a panel full of avionics, and a little luggage, and be within both payload and CG limits.

Its controls, while not light, are balanced and authoritative, so that it handles crosswinds and turbulence very well. In fact, its smooth ride, coupled with generous inside space, make it a comfortable cross-country machine.

The Skylane's speed is consistently better than book, flying at over 140 knots at most altitudes and weights. Fuel burn is as advertised—12.5 gph at 75 percent.

There's plenty of room on the panel and in the payload for a full complement of avionics (King, Stormscope) and other options (standby vacuum pumps, carb ice detector). It's noisy; headphones and intercom are a must.

Now the bad news: Cost.

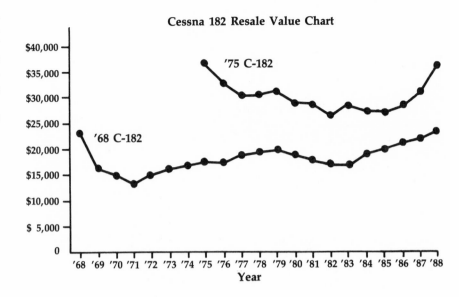

Cessna 182 Resale Value Chart

While parts availability and backup have presented no problems, I've had too many opportunities to find out. Annuals have cost from $500 to $1,800, even though painstaking maintenance is performed at every 50-hour oil change. Operating cost, exclusive of hangaring, insurance, and allowance for overhaul, exceeds $40 per hour. All three left-side cylinders needed rings and valves at 600 hours, although the subsequent reduction in oil use (from 4.5 hours per quart to nine) indicates there may have been a problem from the beginning.

Now the worst news: Reliability.

I'm on my seventh alternator control unit. It's no fun while IFR suddenly to be reduced to battery power, but it has happened so often that I carry a spare ACU so that at least when (and if) I land, I can get an immediate repair. Neither Cessna not my repair shop have a found solution.

In summary, the Skylane offers balanced performance, with a cost penalty. Buy a clean used one, but if the alternator control unit is over 10 months old, replace it immediately before venturing into a cloud.

Dr. Stephen J. Browne
Cambridge, Mass.

With Charlie Seibel's full-speed equipment I cruise 160-165 mph at 10,000 feet on 2,250 rpm and 18.5

inches at about 12 or 11.5 gph and use a quart of 50-weight Shell every three to four hours.

With RSTOL strips, 1,500-foot takeoffs are easily manageable.

Granted, it is a little ponderous compared to my Bonanza, but it's a wheels down grandpappy airplane and rock solid on VFR—very predictable when flying the numbers for climb, descent, approaches, etc.

Maintenance has been very predictable—no surprises, but then I'm meticulous. Nothing's too small for attention; therefore my $2,000 annuals are high. The 25-hour checkup and oil change is around $250 with no problems with either parts availability or backup.

My wife and I spent three weeks plus in the airplane last summer going to British Columbia, Alaska and the west, having plenty of room throughout—though packed stem to stern with camping, living and survival gear.

Henry G. Wischmeyer
Dallas, Tex.

We have owned a 1979 Skylane since 1981. This aircraft was purchased with 700 hours on it. It has an all ARC panel with the exception of a King 62A DME and a Sigtronics four-station intercom. In four years we have had minor navcom trouble four times—trouble that takes about $100 and three days to be corrected each time. No trouble at all with the 300 A/P or KN62A. We average 100 hours of pleasure flying per year. Annuals average about $350. One went to $600 because a jug had to be reworked at 1,000 hours. Seems Continental used a hammer to seat an exhaust valve guide. Other than that, the cylinders always hang in there at 72 to 76.

Our useful load is 1,146 as equipped. With a full load and 75 percent power at 6,500 to 8,500 feet we true at 135 knots. A light weights we reach 145 knots. It burns 12 gph and a quart of oil every four hours. For local flying we can get the burn down to nine gph.

Generally speaking, we like the overall performance and big plane feel it has over, say, a 172 or Cherokee. On the downside, we might wish for a little better fit and finish All of the door-to-airframe fits are atrocious, with very bad air leaks. We had a bad spell of water leaks which we finally stopped on our own through judicious use of silicon sealant.

I can say that after four years the paint and interior have held up real good. We keep it hangared.

There is one mod we were really interested in: the Seibel speed mod. But another Skylane owner at our airport did it, and the only good thing he had to say about it was that it didn't slow his plane down, which was kind of disappointing because we just know that the ol' 182 could be Mooney-ized a la 201.

Bob Billa, Jr.
San Antonio, Tex.

I purchased my 1979 Skylane II in the summer of 1983. The airplane has reportedly been hangared since new. The two navcoms, ADF, and encoding transponder are ARC equipment. Last February I installed an Rnav R20.

The ARC radios have naturally given me some difficulty, but a nearby shop knows them well and repairs them at what I think is a

reasonable cost. I had a sticking VOR needle, a problem left over from the previous owner who had installed three different VOR heads before I purchased the aircraft (repair cost $62). I had a comm transmitter go out (repair cost $125.00). I have also replaced a fuel gauge and sender unit. I have replaced the EGT gauge and have had the clock/timer rebuilt. The ADF antenna spontaneously snapped last week and is being replaced. I've also noticed that the static eliminators ''spontaneously'' break, and naturally I wonder. I've also noticed areas where the paint is peeling along with areas where filiform corrosion is appearing under the paint.

There was a problem with the control-mounted microphone switch wire, and I've replaced some panel lights which are outrageously priced by Cessna.

My annuals cost from $375 to $450. The first one uncovered some problems while last year's found nothing significant. I also have 100-hour inspections done, and I have oil analysis done when the mechanic remembers to submit the sample.

Although the 182 leaks like a sieve, I don't plan on leaving it outdoors or flying it in the rain anyway. I burn about a quart of oil every two hours. I get a lot of oil under the fuselage. I was told not to fill it to the nine-quart level unless I am going on a long trip. I do this and I have never seen the oil level go below eight quarts. I've wondered if the engine would quit using oil altogether if there were only eight quarts in the crank case; however, I'm not going to try that out.

It may seem strange that there appear to be so many faults with this aircraft; I've not named them all, yet I like it so much. I'm very picky.

John S. Ford, M.D.
Texarkana, Tex.

I bought my 1981 C-182 new for $58,500 complete with the Skylane II package and Narco DME. I wanted a full four-passenger fixed-gear that I could move into im-

mediately after getting my license, as well as one that would be a stable IFR trainer. I got my instrument ticket in the plane and my wife (she's also a pilot) and I have owned it for four years.

Total time is 450 hours and we have perceived no engine problems. I knew that huge oil consumption was a possibility, and true to form I use a quart every four hours —always have. I change the oil and filter every 50 hours and have an oil analysis done at every change. It shows normal.

Fuel economy has not been outstanding at 12-13 gph but it is outweighed by the 1,300 pound payload and 92-gallon tanks. My bladder is out well before the six-hour range. The comfort level is quite good, and coupled with headsets for all four seats, a four-hour trip to Mexico is quite pleasant at 142 knots true.

Besides the usual ARC radio glitches, squawks have included a broken carb heat control cable (my wife's heavy hand!) at 400 hours, a turn coordinator out at 410 hours, a new battery at 375 hours, three new tires at 390 hours, as well as new landing lights every 30 hours. Other than these items, we have been trouble free.

An annual inspection without any major problems runs a very healthy $1,500+. I've been told that late-model 182s normally run half this amount, but I've never seen it. As a result, my hourly maintenance costs clock in at $25 per hour.

My wife and I are happy with our airplane and have no plans for upgrading. We have a neighbor who has owned his 1962 Skylane since new and loves it still. We fly to our mountain home, where the airport elevation is 6,000 feet, a dozen times each summer, and have never had a problem taking off from the 3,000-foot strip even at gross. For us, the Skylane has lived up to our expectations beautifully. I'd buy another one!

Dr. Tom Bales
Novato, Calif.

Piper Dakota 235

The big dream of most pilots is to have an airplane that will go fast, haul a big load, fly forever without refueling and cost peanuts to maintain in the process. Subtract the one element—speed—and you have the formula for success of the Piper Dakota and its predecessors, the Cherokee 235, the Charger and the Pathfinder.

Together they form a singular class of aircraft in which you often can top off the fuel tanks to the point of spilling, load four good-sized adults along with a bunch of baggage and take off with a legal load. Since the gear is fixed, you won't break the sound barrier—so count on no better than 125 to 140 knots, depending on the model and the kind of wheel fairings. But with 82 gallons to burn over the course of six hours or so (or 72 gallons in the Dakotas), you can often beat faster, shorter-legged aircraft to your destination.

And since the gear is fixed, the electro-hydraulic engineering foibles of many retractables is eliminated, meaning generally cheaper maintenance costs. The 235-hp Lycoming O-540 engine, derated from 250 as used on the Aztecs and Comanches, is generally regarded as a relatively solid, free of glitches and quirks. Contributing further to repair economy, if maybe not fuel economy, are carburetors, rather than fuel injection.

History

The line began two decades ago, in 1964, as the Cherokee 235—a bigger-engined clone of the Cherokee 180. It was even certificated in the utility category at gross—which meant greater strength limits—and Piper salesmen liked to boast that it could carry its own weight in useful load. And, by gosh, it could.

With the Dakota came semi-tapered wings and better climb performance. Fuel capacity went down as two of the 235's four tanks were dropped.

The early models were really low-maintenance aircraft since not only was the the landing gear fixed, but even the prop was fixed pitch as standard equipment. A further cost-saving factor (back then, at least) was the ability of the powerplant to burn cheaper 80-octane fuel. The early B models had only 50 gallons of fuel in two wing tanks, standard, or 84 optional.

The 84-gallon standard configuration, using four tanks (two in the main wings and two in the tips), came in 1968 with the C model. The first significant change in the line came in 1973, however, with the Charger, thanks to a lengthened fuselage (like the Arrow's), which gave rear-seat passengers another welcome five inches of leg room. At the same time the useful load went up a paltry few pounds along with a 100-pound boost in the gross, reflecting the bigger cabin. Piper also widened the stabilator for better controllability with the extra fuselage length and longer loading envelope.

In 1974 the Pathfinder introduced mostly window dressing. Appropriately, part of this consisted of heavier, new one-quarter-inch-

thick windshields in an attempt to lower the cabin sound level. (Earlier models had one-eighth-inch-thick windshields.) A few other fillips were vertically adjustable front seats—by pushbutton, thank you—"cushioned nosewheel steering" (thanks to bungees) standard toebrakes on the right side and a supposedly more crashworthy seat design.

The Dakota

In 1974 the next "epic" change came to the line with the semi-tapered wings brought out by the Warrior a couple of years earlier, along with an engine variant designed to burn 100 octane. Since 80 octane was getting scarce, this was intended as a boon to eliminate lead fouling. But as the move to autogas for 80-octane engines gains momentum, it may in retrospect have been a mixed blessing. The good-looking new wings were not, however, outfitted with tip-tanks, so the fuel load dropped by 10 gallons' useful to a total of 74 in two main wing tanks.

Unfortunately, though the racy-looking new low-drag plastic wheel fairings offered as an option on the Dakotas (and other Pipers) raised the cruise speed by a healthy six to nine knots, in the beginning they were plagued with cracking and breaking problems. Piper replaced them with fiberglass ones intended to be better wearing.

There's no doubt that the higher-aspect-ratio wing on the Dakota gives the aircraft better climb performance than the Hershey-bar forebears. And pilots believe lateral control is nicer.

Even Turbocharging

Unafraid of mixing performance metaphors—i.e., a low-performance aircraft with a high-performance engine—Piper provided the ultimate option to the fixed-gear Dakota: turbocharging. In hindsight it took a gamble on reliability, however, by switching from the good-old trusty Lycoming to a lower-horsepower blown Continental—the 200-hp TSIO-360 that turned out to have more than its share of problems.

Performance and Handling

At equal weights, the 235, etc. will get 55 horses more performance than the Cherokee 180/Archer from which it is cloned—all of which translates into better climb and shorter runway demands (especially in high density altitude situations), along with more load and more speed. Its only natural competitor is the Cessna Skylane, with similar power and load-carrying ability. Our side-by-side tests conducted in 1979 suggested cruise speeds of these two aircraft were nearly identical; the Cessna could get in and out of shorter runways and had lower stall speeds, but the Piper could climb faster.

Aficionados of low wings like the extra stability during ground

handling in high winds, but the accident reports are far from devoid of pilots going awry landing or taking off in gusty crosswinds.

Nevertheless, the 235/Dakotas in most modes are benign aircraft that will shake themselves apart rather than stall precipitously, that have somewhat sluggish controls and that exhibit all the handling personality of a Chevy sedan. Like most Cherokees, they tend to wander during cruise, with a wing dipping on one side or the other, no matter how attentive the pilot is to balancing the fuel burn in the tanks.

Cockpit Design, Cabin Comfort

Three pleasant aspects to the 235 cockpit, to our mind, are the old-fashioned Cherokee hand-brake parking lever, which is the most secure in the business; the equally old-fashioned but delightful-to-use Johnson-bar flap lever (who needs electric flaps?); and the location of the fuel selector under the throttle quadrant where everybody can see it, rather than hidden behind the pilot's knee on the left wall. The Dakota, however, is the exception

The Pathfinder version of the Cherokee 235 has a thicker windshield for better soundproofing.

and has the fuel selector—guess where?

Our theory about the safety factor of having the fuel selector under the quadrant may be wishful thinking in the real world, however, since the 235s experience a goodly portion of accidents because of fuel mismanagement.

Location of the mp and tach near the pilot's knee is a bit less than ideal, but logical in one sense—that it's near the throttle and prop levers.

Naturally, choose the stretched models—Charger and later—for the extra leg room in the back. Owners also tend to rave about the comfort of the seats in these aircraft. "The well-designed bucket seats in the Dakota nicely fit my 'bucket,'" said one. "My nonpilot 200-pound husband has mentioned taking his right seat home for his den," she added. "Piper seats are very comfortable," said another. "I can fly for five hours without getting a backache."

Cost/Performance/Specifications

Model	Year	Number Built	Average Retail Price	Cruise Speed (kts)	Rate of Climb (fpm)	Useful Load (lbs)	Fuel Std/Opt (gals)	Engine	TBO (hrs)	Overhaul Cost
PA-28 235	1964-65	719	$18,750	136	825	1,404	50/84	235-hp Lyc. O-540-B4B5	2,000	$12,000
PA-28 235B	1966-67	320	$19,500	136	825	1,404	50/84	235-hp Lyc. O-540-B4B5	2,000	$12,000
PA-28 235B,C	1968-69	301	$21,500	136	825	1,404	84	235-hp Lyc. O-540-B4B5	2,000	$12,000
PA-28 235D,E	1970-71	106	$24,000	136	825	1,404	84	235-hp Lyc. O-540-B4B5	2,000	$12,000
PA-28 235F	1972	23	$25,250	136	825	1,404	84	235-hp Lyc. O-540-B4B5	2,000	$12,000
Charger	1973-74	285	$28,500	132	800	1,450	84	235-hp Lyc. O-540-B4B5	2,000	$12,000
Pathfinder	1975-76	316	$31,500	132	800	1,450	84	235-hp Lyc. O-540-B4B5	2,000	$12,000
Pathfinder	1977	89	$34,000	132	800	1,450	84	235-hp Lyc. O-540-B4B5	2,000	$12,000
PA-28 236 Dak.	1979-80	466	$50,000	143	965	1,366	77	235-hp Lyc. O-540-J3A5D	2,000	$12,200
PA-28 201T	1979	89	$35,000	154	902	1,321	77	200-hp Cont. TSIO-360-FB	1,800	$12,700
Dakota	1981-82	141	$60,000	143	965	1,366	77	235-hp Lyc. O-540-J3A5D	2,000	$12,200
Dakota	1983-84	25	$78,000	143	965	1,366	77	235-hp Lyc. O-540-J3A5D	2,000	$12,200

Safety Record

Although the NTSB was unable to sort out the Cherokee 235s and Dakotas from the great mass of PA-28s of all classes for us, we did examine five and a half years of accidents (146 in all) by Cherokee 235/Dakotas reported by the FAA from 1979 through mid-August 1984. Of course, they do not have the Safety Board's probable causes listed.

Among the Cherokee 235s (including Chargers and Pathfinders) the greatest two accident generators were engine failure and fuel

mismanagement, with 14 and 11 cases respectively. Next came groundloops or swerves—nine, followed by hard landings—six.

Among the Dakotas and Turbo Dakotas groundloop/swerves were blamed for the most damage along with various mechanical problems, with five cases each.

The 235's engine problems presented a fairly mixed bag, with no specific trend. Examples: fuel valve clogged with tank sealant, broken pin on drive shaft gear, broken exhaust valve, blown gasket, loose oil screen ("secured [?]by pilot"),

Though the fuel selector is under the throttle quadrant for easy viewing, the need to switch among four separate tanks may heighten the possibility for fuel management error, a common problem in this model.

Structural capacity of the baggage compartment is a hefty 200 pounds.

Tiny door allows access to the tire of Dakotas with snug modern speed fairings. Early plastic ones had cracking, breakage. Some owners of later fiberglass wheel pants claim similar problems.

even a field mouse nest in the carburetor air duct. There was one failed magneto impulse coupling, failing the drive gear. A series of engine stoppages on the 235 could not be explained when the powerplants were later inspected.

On the Dakotas, engine failures were attributed to such causes as a fuel leak at the wing root, and subsequent fuel exhaustion; loss of oil pressure from an oil leak at the base of the vacuum pump, connecting rod failure, a broken oil line and a mixture arm that came loose from the carburetor. In one case a Dakota experienced an engine fire on runup when the engine backfired and blew out the muffler. Exhaust gases were reported ignited by a leaky boost pump.

On the Turbo Dakotas engine stoppages were blamed on broken connecting rods in two instances, a cracked cylinder, loss of engine oil from an oil cooler leak, and loss of oil pressure because of a turbine seal failure.

Among the 235s, time and again the reports cited pilots going dry on one fuel tank while there remained fuel in others—and apparently neglecting to switch. The existence of four tanks to juggle in the 235s as opposed to just two in the Dakotas may explain the black mark on the former, even though the fuel selector is located right under the throttle quadrant where both pilots in front can see it.

The groundloop/swerve category that claimed so many victims among both the 235s and the Dakotas is a broadly mixed bag that encompasses everything from losing control because of "improper, inadequate braking" to losing directional control on the landing roll "when hit by gusty crosswind, veered off runway into a ditch." The lesson is that even with a marvelously "wide gear stance" and tricycle gear, the 235/Dakotas are not immune to mishandling, by a long shot.

Maintenance

In general, owners describe the 235/Dakota as presenting a modest maintenance burden. There are problems, however. Some criticize the brakes as "too light for the weight of the aircraft." One owner said he had to change them every year (or 100 hours). Also, alternator mounting brackets seem prey to an unusual degree of cracking and strain. This was the largest single problem area we noted in Service Difficulty Reports on the aircraft—and mostly on the Dakotas. Second worst: problems with the carburetor air boxes —separations, breaks, vibration.

To a lesser degree we noted reports of Bendix distributor blocks cracking and engine mounts cracking and breaking. A few complained of fuel vent hoses leaking and tank sealant in the fuel, causing blockages. As we noted above, at least one engine stoppage accident was blamed on a fuel valve clogged with sealant. Also, the "improved" fiberglass wheel fairings that replaced the original troubleprone thermoplastic ones (not always—check for them) still are prey to cracking according to some owners, and are expensive to replace.

On the Turbo Dakotas high cylinder head temperature was the bane of at least one respondent. "The gauge almost reaches the red on climb, even with full rich mixture," he noted. SDRs showed some cracking of turbo housings.

Airworthiness Directives

No big, devastating ADs have struck 235/Dakota owners over the past few years, except for one on the turbos. Most of the other ADs of any note and consequence appear related to fuel leakage problems. A 1979 AD called for removing the fuel tanks and modifying the vent system, for example, on both 235s and Dakotas. The Dakotas also were hit with an AD calling for a check and torquing of fuel fittings and unions to eliminate a fire hazard from fuel leakage. In 1978 Cherokee 235 owners were required to replace the fuel drain cover so it would not inadvertently drain fuel from the valve. And a year earlier another AD called for a check and possible replacement of fuel valves to prevent engine stoppage on 235s.

Mods & Improvements

Among the more useful STCs available to Cherokee 235 and Dakota owners are efficiency kits offered by Knots 2U and Laminar Flow Systems, providing gap seals on the ailerons and flaps, hinge covers, etc. Said one Laminar Flow installer, "We are making better time on our trips at 65 percent cruise (after the mod) than we did at 75 percent cruise before, and saving on gas." He added: "I have not given up the idea of a trade-in for a faster plane...Makes you wonder why Piper doesn't clean up the wings and do the same..."

Want better visibility at night? Devore Aviation in Albuquerque, N.M. will install vertical tail floodlights. Need better door sealing on a Dakota? Bob Fields Aerocessories in Ventura, Calif. has an STC on an inflatable door seal. Norton Co. of Akron, Ohio,

The Charger received a five-inch cabin stretch and a wider entry door, improving legroom and access for rear-seat passengers.

even has a radome kit for earnest weather busters.

Turbo Dakota owners might consider installation of Turboplus intercoolers and cowl flaps to cool down their powerplants (they are located at Gig Harbor, Wash.). S.G.H. Inc. of Auburn, Wash. has an STC for pressurized magnetos, as well.

Resale Value

As an investment, the Cherokee 235s and Dakotas are nothing to brag about. The typical resale value curve on the 235 and Dakota is a constant sag through the years, with no turnaround to account for inflation. Buyers should turn to the retractable singles for a more advantageous kind of curve. However, as a basic heavy hauler, the aircraft is matched only by the Skylane in its class, and anyone wishing more speed and equivalent useful load would have to lay out a fair amount more for a big retractable.

Owner Comments

I have been pleased with my '79 Dakota. It will take off in our average 90 degree weather in about 1,000 feet with four adults, full tanks and filled with baggage. Maintenance, apart from two ADs on fuel lines and mags, has been minimal. The greatest problem has been the brakes. They must be changed yearly. They are apparently too light for the weight of the aircraft. The aircraft is flown about 200 hours yearly.

The engine has proved flawless. It always starts instantly. We change oil every 25 hours. The interior finish is very well done and has held up very well in view of the fact that the Dakota is parked outside in our hot and humid Puerto Rican weather and constantly exposed to the broiling sun. The aircraft is now in need of painting. The paint is disintegrating and corrosion is starting on the left side of the aircraft only and the cabin top. The

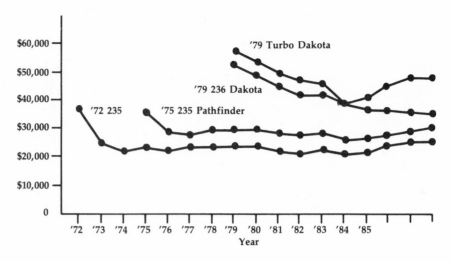

Dakota Resale Value Chart

right side shows little corrosion problem.

The plane was bought from Red Aircraft in Florida. They have been excellent in back-up. I have purchased several additions since new and simply by calling Red, they responded by sending parts and billing me later. I've written twice to Piper and they've never answered. Once I wrote regarding the possibility of installing a small children's seat in the baggage compartment, once regarding new gas tank screws. Never a response.

I was considering changing to a slightly faster plane last year, until I heard about Laminar Flow Systems in St. Thomas. Since it's only a short hop from San Juan, I flew over to speak to Robin Thomas. I was convinced. In short order they installed the system on the wings, gap seals on the ailerons, covers on the hinges, and Wow! It is like another airplane. The cruise has increased to about 150 knots or better. Drop the nose for a power glide and the airspeed drops into the yellow arc. It never did that before. We are making better time on our trips at 65 percent cruise than we did at 75 percent cruise before and saving on gas.

The takeoff has become almost unbelievable. With light loads—two and gas—it's lifted off in 500 to 600 feet. It will fly itself off the ground at 70 knots, which it never did before. It simply won't stay on the

ground. We increased our rate of climb about 200 feet a minute, and with a lower nose angle. The stall speed is somewhere down to about 50 knots as opposed to 59 knots before.

I have now given up the idea of a trade-in for a faster plane. By the way, we now pass every single flying in our area with the exception of Mooneys. The change to the plane with the laminar flow system has been startling. It's given us retractable performance with the simplicity of fixed gear. Makes you wonder why Piper doesn't clean up the wings and do the same as the Laminar Flow people.

In summation the product is great, the company that produces it seems uninterested in client relations. By the way, our averge yearly maintenance including the annual, has run between 800 to $1,000. I consider this reasonable.

Ronald Sobin
Guaynabo, Puerto Rico

My 1979 Dakota is turbocharged. It has a total 550 hours since new. It is pleasant to fly, and it is forgiving.

The major problem I have faced through the years is high cylinder head temperature. The gauge almost reaches the red on climb, even with full rich mixture. Sometimes I have to put the auxiliary fuel pump on. On 75 percent power cruise, gas flow is about 13.5

gallons per hour, speed about 140 knots.

Maintenance cost me $2,000 to change the turbo in compliance with the AD note last year. Annual inspection is between $500 and $700 if everything checked right.

I would appreciate your giving me any suggestion regarding the head cylinder temperature.

Nabil Koudsi, M.D.
Upland, Calif.

I have owned a 1979 Piper Turbo Dakota since September 1981 when it was a corporate aircraft with only 120 hours on it. At present, it has about 363 hours total time. Most of the time I cruise at altitudes between 9,500 and 13,500 feet.

As for performance, I climb at 105 knots indicated (for better cooling in warm weather) and set about 140 knots true in cruise at 65 percent power. Fuel consumption varies between 12 gph at low altitudes to about 13.5 gph at high altitudes on a warm day. The extra fuel is required to keep the cylinder temperature a few needle widths below the red line.

I have no real complaints about handling or comfort. But for long trips an autopilot is very desirable. Without it, the airplane will for sure wander off one way or the other, but not really more than most other similar airplanes. I have also flown the Saratoga, and it is more stable. Piper seats are very comfortable, for me anyway. I can fly for five hours without getting a backache. One minor complaint: the towbar is too short, and the little hooks do not provide a secure attachment to the nosewheel.

The Dakota's forte is its load-carrying ability. Mine is well equipped, including DME, but I can legally carry four FAA-sized people (including myself), 5½ hours of fuel and about 10 pounds of junk and not exceed gross weight or so out of CG.

During the 242 hours I've flown the plane, fuel has cost me an average

of $22 per hour of tach time, and out-of-pocket maintenance costs have cost me an average of about $28 per hour of tach time. The last annual cost me $1,800, including the cost of an overhaul on the turbocharger and calibrating the transponder, encoder, altimeter and static systems.

Within a year or so, I plan to upgrade to either a Saratoga SP or a Bonanza A36. But after having flown a turbocharged plane for almost three years, I have concluded that for the type of flying I do (VFR only), the benefits of turbocharging are outweighed by the penalties of increased fuel consumption and increased maintenance costs. My next airplane will be non-turbos, but I will opt for better low-level performance and retractable gear. And big double doors on the side, for all the junk I tend to carry.

Charles Pack
Los Altos Hills, Calif.

About two and a half years ago, I acquired a one-owner, well-equipped, well-maintained, clean 1979 Dakota, my first venture into ownership. It is one fine airplane, and I couldn't be more pleased. When I began to think seriously about buying, my analysis of my flying needs pointed me toward either a Skylane or a Dakota. Both possessed two critical characteristics: good reserve power and load carrying capability. Rereading the "Fly-off" comparison article in *Aviation Consumer* (June 1, 1979) was helpful and confirmed most of my own impressions.

The Dakota won out for the following reasons: 1) I had always felt more comfortable in low-wing airplanes (the "wing-under-me" and visibility in the pattern factors); 2) being 5'3" tall and non-gymnastic, I felt the Skylane presented two problems: visibility over the high panel and climb-on-top visual fuel checks; 3) the excellent reputation of the 2,000-hour Lycoming O-540 engine; 4) repeated experiences with minor glitches in ARC avionics becomes annoying—I wanted Kings; 5) I align with those who believe low-

wing, wide-stance planes are easier to land in gusty conditions and crosswinds; 6) the well-designed bucket seats in the Dakota nicely fit my "bucket"; and 7) an emotional reason—I just plain liked the Dakota's good looks.

I've logged over 500 hours in my PA28-236, in all conditions. The Lycoming has never missed a beat and at 1,150 hours shows no leaks, good compression, and clean oil analysis checks. Over the last 200 hours, fuel burn has ranged from 11 to 14 gph, with an average of 11.8. Note that most of my flying is done out of our 5,000 feet MSL airport, at 6,000 feet to 9,000 feet MSL. I currently have to add only two quarts of Aeroshell 15W-50 oil between changes every 40-50 hours.

Speed and climb? As advertised. Once, at 17,000 feet in quiet and cold morning mountain air, I was able to coax it into a 200 fpm climb with three people aboard and nearly full fuel. Even our oxygen masks smiled!

It is docile and easily handled in both cruise and slow flight, with slightly heavy (which I prefer) but smooth and positive aileron control. It will slowly drop a wing during cruise if you stop paying attention, and you cannot fly totally hands-off. Pitch control is easy with the electric trim. An unsolved rigging quirk in my Dakota is intermittent refusal to hold left rudder trim, and I have to spend a little more time than I would like twisting the somewhat inconveniently located rudder trimknob. Turbulence—and we get plenty of that out here—presents no significant problems.

A most comforting pleasure is to plan on loading up another couple and luggage and find that, after weight/balance and takeoff distance calculations, I can say to the lineman, "Top it off," before we head for wherever.

The Dakota fits my flying needs perfectly.

Bonnie Titley
Ft. Collins, Colo.

Cessna 185

From the North Slope of Alaska to the desert badlands of Australia, the Cessna 185 Skywagon reigns ubiquitous as the Marlboro Man of workhorse airplanes . . . tackling short bush strips, jungle rivers, or high-mountain snowfields with equal ease. As a potent taildragger, this plane has long been the "utility pickup" in Cessna's product line.

Like many of its automotive counterparts, however, the C-185 Skywagon has a lavish options list and suave enough manners in the air to appeal as well to the more hairy-chested end of the "family airplane" market.

History

The Cessna 185 first appeared in 1961 as a big brother to the 180, which the company had introduced back in 1953. Motivated by a 230-hp Continental, the 180 was limited in useful load with full fuel, so the 185 arrived sporting a 260-hp fuel injected Continental IO-470-F, toting 84 gallons of fuel, and offering 1,680 pounds of useful load . . . nearly 200 pounds higher than its basic empty weight.

Since the 180 and 185 were virtually identical in fuselage dimensions

Here's the typical 185 environment: mountains, grass strips, and snow.

(the 185 had a larger strake up front of the horizontal stabilizer), the 185's more sprightly performance was due entirely to his larger engine. In its workhorse role, this first 185 also offered optional Edo floats, skis, and a Sorenson spray rig. The next year a belly-mounted cargo pod with a 300-pound useful load was offered as a further utility option. All of these items are still available 22 years later on Cessna's current model.

With few exceptions, the development of the C-185 line has been evolutionary rather than revolutionary, so would-be purchasers have only a couple of major changes to bear in mind. Most of the cosmetic or functional improvements like the articulating pilot seats, standard "T" instrument configuration, better panel lighting, split electrical bus, Omni-flash rotating beacon, and Stabili-Tip conical cambered wingtips are retrofittable.

The first major change occurred in 1966 when Cessna offered the larger fuel-injected Continental IO-520-D engine as an option. This gave the 185 300 hp for takeoff (285 hp continuous), allowing a 100-pound increase in gross to 3,300 with only 10 pounds added to the empty weight. This switch also im-

proved cruise speed by about five knots, reduced the gross weight takeoff roll by about 200 feet, and raised the service ceiling to 17,300 feet. The 260-hp version was called the C-185E while its "big-bore" brother was the C-A185E. (The 1966 serial numbers from 185-0968 through 185-1149 don't give any clue to this engine swap.)

Customer response to this larger engine must have been favorable because Cessna made it standard the very next year, so all the '67s are C-A185E models, and this designation prevailed until 1973 when a major wing improvement was added. One other useful addition to the '67 bird, by the way, was a new aft baggage compartment. Along with this new storage space, an optional elongated cargo "stretcher" door was offered; this greatly facilitates loading long objects like bicycles or skis (not to mention stretchers) and is worthy of consideration as a retrofit to any of the 185's.

The 1973 model received a new Camber-Lift wing featuring the vaunted "fat leading edge" cuff originally developed by Robertson for their STOL kits. This change reduced the stall speeds in all configurations by about two knots, but it also improved the low-speed roll control, and rumor has it that this fatter leading edge is safer in icing conditions, though neither wing is approved for flight in known icing. This later wing can be added to earlier models by Robertson (see the information under Modifications) for purchasers who are otherwise enthralled by a pre-1973 skywagon.

The 1974 model year ushered in three options for the 185 that could be of interest to prospective users with special requirements for improved visibility: a pair of "bubble" side windows, extra windows built into the lower door panels, and a pair of amber-tinted skylight windows built into the ceiling above the cockpit.

Several changes were made in 1976, along with one seemingly regressive step. The first notch (10 degrees) flap extension speed was raised from 96 knots to 120, and a new three-position (Left/Both/Right) fuel selector switch was installed to replace the inherently more dangerous Left/Right/Off arrangement. Optional tailcone lift handles became available to ease manhandling the beast around on the ground. For the first time, primary airspeed readout was displayed in knots rather than miles per hour. But a puzzling change was made to the fuel system. The capacity of the fuel bladders in the long-range tanks was reduced from 81 to 74 gallons usable, which cut the plane's economy-cruise time aloft by 45 minutes.)

Over the next three years, several other notable changes were made to the C-185. In 1978, a new 80-inch three-blade McCauley prop became available as an option. It became standard in 1980 along with beefier engine mounts to damp its different vibration patterns. The former two-blade Skywagon props were very noisy at high rpm, emitting an awesome and unmistakable snarling howl at takeoff revs when the prop tips went supersonic. The wide-chord three-blade prop has a noise emission rating of only 77 db, which also helps to quiet things down inside the cabin.

The other major change was the switch, in 1979, to a new "wet" wing holding a total of 88 gallons . . . 84 of which is usable. Interestingly, Cessna still offers the old-style 40-gallon "twin-cap" bladder

tanks as an option; while somewhat prone to water-trapping wrinkles, especially if sloppily installed, these bladders over the long run may prove to be less leaky than the wet wing in really rugged environments, and there is some evidence to suggest that bladder tanks will retain fuel more reliably in a wing-deforming crash.

Since 1981, Cessna has made only token changes to the 185 line, (apart from raising the price by $18,110, seemingly an act of near-suicidal bravado that flies in the face of all recent market supply and demand figures). External cosmetics, to be sure, have been changed, and the ARC radios (always a hot item if not a hot seller) got two more revisions to their oh-so-necessary cooling fan. A new-design single-piece flex shaft connects the fuel selector to the main fuel valve, providing greater reliability and more positive detents (this in 1982), and for '83 a change (actually made by Continental) to the engine crankcase allows the use of the new short-cannister spin-on oil filter while eliminating the old two-pound filter adapter. A low-vacuum warning light was added to the instrument panel in 1983, and considering the notorious unreliability of Cessna's Airborne vacuum pumps in the past, we can only wonder why this particular gizmo didn't make an appearance sooner.

Performance

This is where the Cessna 185 shines. Other aircraft can fly faster, and a few smaller, lighter ones like

the Maule or the Super Cub can levitate in a shorter distance, but no other single-engine piston-powered taildragger can take off in 825 feet carrying four 220-pound adults, full fuel, and 170 pounds of baggage, show an initial rate-of-climb of 1,075 fpm and then cruise 800-plus nautical miles averaging 140 knots.

Maximum cruise speed at 75 percent and 7,000 feet is a very respectable 147 knots. The rpm "green arc" on the C-185 goes from 2200 rpm for cruising at 6,500 feet or below. This setting yields about 145 knots at average aircraft weights, and, depending on outside air temps, will burn anywhere from 14.3 to 14.7 gallons per hour of 100 or 100LL fuel.

Climb performance is robust. The 185 will still show upward mobility of at least 500 fpm at 10,000 feet at average weights, and the gross weight service ceiling for the current model is listed as 17,900 feet.

At higher altitudes (and consequent lower manifold pressures) the 185 becomes progressively less thirsty. Also, Continental allows leaning the IO-520 to peak EGT at 65 percent power or below, a condition reached naturally at about 8,000 feet at settings of 2400 rpm and (max available) 22 inches of manifold pressure. As in any airplane, the permutations and combinations of fuel flow versus power settings are many, but for example, at 12,000 feet/2400 rpm/18 inches, the C-185 will have a true airspeed of about 130 knots while burning only 10.3 gallons per hour. This is

Cost/Performance/Specifications

Model	Years Built	Number Built	Average Retail Price	Cruise Speed (kts)	Useful Load (lbs)	Rate of Climb (fpm)	Fuel Std/Opt (gals)	Engine	TBO (hrs)	Overhaul Cost
Cessna 185, A	1961-62	512	$19,000	145	1,680	1,000	81	260-hp Cont. IO-470-F	1,500	$10,750
Cessna 185B, C	1963-64	263	$20,500	145	1,680	1,000	81	260-hp Cont. IO-470-F	1,500	$10,750
Cessna 185D, E	1965-66	372	$21,500	145	1,680	1,000	81	260-hp Cont. IO-470-F	1,500	$10,750
Cessna A185E	1966-67	332	$23,000	146	1,785	1,040	81	300-hp Cont. IO-520-D	1,700	$11,250
Cessna A185E	1968-69	298	$25,000	146	1,785	1,040	81	300-hp Cont. IO-520-D	1,700	$11,250
Cessna A185E	1970-71	334	$28,000	146	1,785	1,040	81	300-hp Cont. IO-520-D	1,700	$11,250
Cessna A185E, F	1972-73	375	$31,000	145	1,785	1,040	81	300-hp Cont. IO-520-D	1,700	$11,250
Cessna A185F	1974-75	527	$34,500	145	1,785	1,040	81	300-hp Cont. IO-520-D	1,700	$11,250
Cessna A185F	1976-77	619	$40,000	145	1,785	1,040	74	300-hp Cont. IO-520-D	1,700	$11,250
Cessna A185FII	1978-79	479	$48,000	145	1,600	1,075	74	300-hp Cont. IO-520-D	1,700	$11,250
Cessna A185FII	1980-81	389	$60,000	145	1,600	1,075	84	300-hp Cont. IO-520-D	1,700	$11,250
Cessna A185FII	1982-83	NA	$73,000	145	1,600	1,075	84	300-hp Cont. IO-520-D	1,700	$11,250

Optional cargo pod increases luggage capacity but cuts speed.

respectable efficiency, especially considering that up to 1,100 pounds can go along for the ride in the cabin.

While Cessna does not formally tout the stock 185 as a STOL aircraft like the Helio Courier, the Skywagon sports four notches of manually-operated flaps (10-40 degrees in equal increments) which, along with the big engine and fat wing, contribute to splendid short-field performance. With full flaps and power off, the 185 stalls at an indicated airspeed of only 41 knots; with partial power and at lighter weights, this figure will be even lower, although somewhat academic because it would fall below the scale on the airspeed indicator.

The "book" landing distance for the 185 is just 585 feet, but this figure is relatively meaningless because in real life, planes rarely land at full gross or in dead calm air. Even more to the point, experienced 185 pilots regularly make true "bathmat" landings within 300 feet by dragging the plane in under partial power with full flaps at a nose-high altitude and 53 knots, then dumping flaps and braking assiduously right after the three-point full-stall touchdown. As with any aircraft, this technique is not recommended in gusty wind conditions when errant downdrafts could be lurking off the end of the runway.

Cabin Space and Comfort

The Cessna 185 is advertised and certified as a "six-passenger" airplane, but only the Marquis de Sade would commit even a small child to this airplane's third-row "seat," which hugs the floor of the standard baggage bay area (an area limited to 120 pounds) and offers only a vertical pad snapped to the aft bulkhead as a seat backrest. Unless they have very small and unusually pliant children, most 185 owners immediately chuck the worthless rear "seat," thereby assuring themselves of a comfortable four-place bird with a reasonably spacious baggage area in the normal location. This also allows insuring the plane as only a four-seater, which saves considerable money these days, especially in Alaska.

Seating in the 185 is quite comfortable for four adults. Both front seats can be purchased with hand-cranked articulating height and back-tilt adjustments, and the split rear bench seat, while lower-backed than the front seats, also has individual provision for reclining when the aft baggage load permits. Both legroom and headroom are ample up front, even for pilots up to 6'6" and legroom is adequate in the rear as well. Although the cabin is just under 41 inches wide, broad-shouldered crews up front can increase the comfort level in this dimension by staggering the seat positions.

Even with the three-blade prop, cabin noise in the Skywagon is fairly high, but much of it is high-pitched and seems to come, especially in the well-worn older birds, from air leaks around the doors, windows, and main upper air vent tubes (whose felt seals are notoriously flimsy).

Loading

In view of the "back-country pickup truck" primary role for this airplane, we remain mystified why Cessna hasn't done more engineering work to improve the loading access on the C-185. The two main doors on either side of the cockpit are adequate for loading people, but attempting to load anything large like a crate, trunk, or 55-gallon oil drum requires the removal of both the backseat and the copilot's seat along with the right front door. Unfortunately, the wing struts prevent the front doors from opening a full 90 degrees like those huge lovely doors on the old C-177 Cardinal, but at least the right-hand door on the 185 has "quick-pull" pins to expedite its removal, and the back (bench) seat also releases quickly from the floor.

The Skywagon's lone standard baggage door is only 18 inches x 20 inches . . . barely large enough for a case of Coors or a fat watermelon. Larger backpacks or hefty suitcases must routinely be manhandled back over the seats from the front doors with occasional scuffs to the headliner plus lots of sweat and swearing. A few years ago, Piper ran a nice ad showing a piano being loaded into a Cherokee Six; the only way a Cessna 185 could ever carry a piano would be strapped outside on the roof . . . and there might even be an Alaskan bush pilot somewhere crazy enough to try it. When we queried the factory on the subject of loading limitations, a marketing spokesman said, "If they want to carry oil drums or pianos, they should buy a 206." This corporate philosophy bodes ill for any major airframe improvements to the 185 in future.

Cessna does offer an optional external cargo pod that fastens to the belly of the 185 with myriad screws. This fiberglas pod is just over nine feet long and 14 inches deep with an 11x23 door in its left flank and another at the rear. While obviously not deep enough for bulky cargo, this unit is ideal for boards, skis, packs, or suitcases, and it is approved for retrofit installation on any of the 185 models. However, a brand new one costs over $5,000, plus installation, and cuts about four knots off cruise speed.

Handling Quirks

Once off the ground, the 185 is every bit as mild-mannered and pleasant to fly as any of its high-wing Cessna siblings. Aileron response is quite similar to that of the 182 and definitely much lighter in feel than the ponderous C-206. Pilots almost universally praise the manual flaps system for its quick and trouble-free operation. Float plane operators, in particular, often choose the 185 over the 206 just to get these speedy flaps which, when used adroitly, allow heavily loaded seaplanes to hop off the water faster. The controls in the Skywagon are well harmonized, so that very little rudder is required for turns. Rudder trim makes keeping the ball centered a cinch during the climb.

The 185 is quite sensitive to longitudinal trim changes, but the elevator trim wheel is geared very low. This means that about 15 backward swipes of hand-to-wheel are required to alter trim from normal cruise position to full aft for a three-point landing. Novitiates to the C-185 universally bemoan the lack of electric trim, but Cessna chose the present manual system for its low-maintenance reliability.

The Cessna 185 is not an easy plane to land. Like all other taildraggers, its c.g. is well aft of the main wheels, so the plane is ever ready to swap ends while in motion along the runway, especially in crosswinds. However, forward visibility is reasonably good (taller pilots can see directly over the nose while taxiing), and the 185 is not nearly as short-coupled as smaller planes like the Pitts. The secret to staying out of trouble in the C-185 (or any taildragger, for that matter) is constant attention and fast feet. C-185 pilots savor an extra bit of macho quotient for having mastered their mounts after an inevitable stint of bronc-busting work during the early flights.

Wheel landings are particularly difficult, partly because the C-185 has very springy steel gear legs. In gus-

ty conditions or when the pilot makes just a slight miscalculation of the proper instant for the "pin-on" forward stick pressure, a substantial bounce is almost certain. This can easily and rapidly develop into a disastrous series of phugoid kangaroo hops if not caught immediately with smooth steady back-pressure on the yoke to salvage a gentle three-point landing at the end of that first inadvertent balloon off the runway. There is also a critical period right after a successful two-wheel touchdown. If a crosswind gust hits the tail of the 185 during this crucial period of transition, only a quick and skillful application of downwind braking can save the plane from an expensive groundloop.

Most 185 pilots concur that a full-stall three-point landing (with the tailwheel locked for any bad crosswind or really rough field conditions) is the safest form of arrival because the airplane's speed is lower, stability is greater, and steering control is easier.

One final caveat . . . be very careful when attempting a go-around in a Skywagon. Once the flaps and full aft trim have been set for a three-point landing, the sudden application of full takeoff power will try to pull the nose straight up. It takes at least eight seconds to hand-crank the trim back to neutral, and you will feel like the proverbial one-arm paperhanger trying to dump a couple notches of

The 185 is a popular floatplane. Because its manual flaps allow more precise control, some bush pilots prefer it to a 206 for float flying.

flaps while slapping the trim wheel with the same hand. The best trick for coping with a last-minute go-around surprise is to add only partial power, which will arrest the descent without initiating an inadvertent Cape Canaveral climb profile.

Maintenance

Since the Cessna 185 is a derivative of the 180 (which, itself, evolved from the 170), it is no surprise that most major maintenance trouble spots or potential AD areas have been bred out of the bird. We have counted up ten AD notes that seem most significant, but of these, only three pertain to the airframe: 73-23-07 is a general call to check for defective spar attach fittings, 78-05-06 mandates a check for leakage of the Goodyear fuel cells installed between 1961 and 1971, and 79-10-14 requires a check on fuel tank venting with a possible need to switch fuel caps. Three more ADs have to do with the cylinder attach screws, activating pins, and possible blade shank failures on various of the McCauley props. One AD (72-20-02) specifies checking the older 470 series engines for H (heavy) cylinders, then the final three all refer to the IO-520 engines: 70-14-07 on fuel injection-by-pass needles, 77-05-04 for possible crankshaft failure due to scoring from oil pick-up hole in prop governor, and finally the ubiquitous 77-13-22 warning of possible crankcase cracks (which hit many other aircraft hard but never became much pf a problem in the 185 line).

Annual inspection base prices for the C-185 seem to run around $495 and bare minimum repairs on an average year with no major problems will add another $500. However, there are a number of airframe and engine spots that require vigilance. The Cessna exhaust mufflers and internal cones seem to crack or wear out at around 400 hours. The tailwheel bolt holding the fork assembly to the tailspring wears out or elongates its seating holes, which contributes to tailwheel shimmy. The McCauley wheels during sharp pivot turns, and quite a few pilots have reported the brake mechanisms pulling loose, rotating around, and cutting the brake line. The switch to Clevelands costs about $800 but is well worth the price in the long run.

The manual elevator trim is another potential trouble spot. At cruise speed, the elevator jackscrew can require 300 foot-pounds of torque, which puts a heavy strain on the roll pins that connect the trim wheel to the chain drive sprocket. They are very prone to shear, which leaves the trim jammed wherever it was set. While this is rarely lethal because it usually happens at a near-cruise setting, Cessna finally came up with a fix in 1981 that simply does away with the pins altogether and rivets the wheel to the sprocket . . . a worthwhile retrofit in our opinion.

Overall, the Continental IO-520-D engine has been quite reliable in the 185 (with the usual smattering of horror stories, to be sure). With large cowl flaps, spacious cowling, and no turbocharging, the engine rarely has any overheating problem, even while taxiing on a hot day. In fact, the greater danger is likely to be overcooling the powerplant during a power-off descent. Continental and Cessna blithely promise a 1,700-hour TBO for the IO-520 in the Skywagon, but most experienced owners consider this a joke. With frequent oil changes and some general pampering, the bottom end of the motor can usually make TBO, but the exhaust valves are the weakest link, and these cannot be expected to work properly much past 1,200 hours. Most conscientious owners end up doing a top overhaul at about this

Cessna 185 Resale Value Chart

time. Prospective 185 buyers should keep this in mind while shopping high-time planes and budget accordingly.

Modifications

Four companies (Bush, Horton, Met-Co-Aire, and R/STOL Systems) offer a variety of drooped tips, stall fences, fatter leading edges, and other related mods designed to increase the low-speed performance of the 185 wings. Owners of pre-1973 Skywagons would do well to consider updating to the "fat cuff" wing and the newer-style drooped wingtips, plus a set of aileron/flap gap seals, which make a noticeable difference in low speed roll control and add a bit to rate of climb. For normal (wheel) operations the C-185 does just fine without any esoteric STOL kits; however, when operating on floats or skis (where touching down at the lowest possible speed can mean a lot less wear and tear), these kits are a worthwhile addition.

The PeeKay division of DeVore offers a three-blade McCauley prop STC for all the pre-1979 Skywagons. PeeKay just sells the STC, and buyers must go direct to McCauley for the prop (which is part number D3A32C90/82NC-2).

Recently, an outfit up in Washington called Seaplanes, Inc., has started offering two interesting engine conversions: a swap to the

turbocharged TSIO-520 Continental (at 300 hp) or the very reliable 350-hp Lycoming TIO-540. In theory, either engine would give a performance boost to the 185, especially at higher altitudes, but the kits are so new that no reliable user reports or service data is yet available.

Since the 185 is still being produced, obtaining parts is no more difficult or expensive than for any other Cessna (which is not to say that the company's parts are either cheap or quick to arrive). Many non-structural replacement parts can be obtained from outside vendors: the Wall-Comnolloy exhaust muffler is a good case in point; it costs only half as much as the stock Cessna one and has proven to last more than twice as long.

A careful pre-purchase inspection by a disinterested mechanic with 185 maintenance experience is highly advisable. Many of these planes have done long years of yeoman toil out in rural operations where maintenance is sometimes skimpy. Obviously, if the plane has ever seen service on floats, corrosion is almost certain to exist somewhere in the airframe, and even a plane that has merely been tied down on a seaside airport for extended periods can have insidious corrosion problems. Most reputable shops will do a pre-purchase inspection just like an annual (and at the same price) without actually fixing any of the squawks.

Since the C-185 is mostly "standard Cessna," service is widely available, although mechanics in back-country areas tend to see more Skywagons and thus have more experience with the few unique maintenance problem areas, such as tailwheel shimmy-spring adjustment or cable tension on the manual trim system. If your mechanic at Teterboro or Long Beach has never laid hands on a Skywagon, you will pay extra for his experimental learning curve. On the other hand, up in Anchorage, where the C-185 is the unofficial state bird, half the people walking down the street could probably do a Skywagon oil change blindfolded.

Owners Association

The official International 180/185 Club is run by the President, C. E. ("Bomber") Bombardier, 4539 N. 49th Avenue, Phoenix, Ariz. 85031. The 180/185 Club currently boasts nearly 1,000 members, which is a respectable percentage of the nearly 4,500 C-185s that have been built to date.

Safety Record

While the overall accident rate of the Cessna 185 is about average, the fatal accident rate is quite a bit better than average. In fact, according to a special NTSB study of single-engine aircraft accidents between 1972 and 1976, the Cessna 185 was fourth best in fatal accidents of 33 aircraft compared.

Also, the Cessna 185 almost never has an in-flight airframe failure. A special study by Brent Silver of the 14-year period between 1964 and 1977 showed that the C-185 shared the best record with two other aircraft—the Cessna 172 and 175. During that period, the C-185 experienced not one airframe failure.

A computer run of C-185 accident briefs for the years 1979 through 1981 provided by the National Transportation Safety Board showed that by far the greatest portion of accidents stemmed from groundloops and swerves on land and water. There were no less than 40 of these. Since these aircraft,

Control wheels, not sticks, are standard equipment on this tail-dragger, of course. Don't look for an electric flap switch; flaps are manual. Watch out for ARC radios.

many of them outfitted with floats, often are used for bush operations, quite a few accidents occurred in rough terrain or on wilderness lakes and rivers with hidden sandbars, logs, etc. There was a sizable number of nose-over accidents as well: 13 of them.

The C-185 had its share of engine failure problems, as well, with 21 of those noted during the period studied. There seemed to be a mixed bag of causes, however, with no single obvious trend. There were a couple of cases of water in the fuel and of fuel mismanagement.

Aircraft Resale Value

The old 260-hp Cessna 185s seem to have fared better over the years in investment value than the new 300-hp models. We tracked a '65 D model as it climbed in value from 1969 to 1984—gaining about $5,000.

In 1969 the average resale price was about $12,900. Then in 1977 it suddenly jumped to about $18,300, where it has remained.

A 1975 F model we tracked showed rather lackluster investment performance, however, starting out at an equipped price of $40,200 and steadily sagging to its 1984 value of about $28,000. This aircraft did not

even exhibit the turn-around after four years or so that most popular models do.

Owner Comments

The 185 is an excellent and well-designed aircraft that is highly refined. I don't think it is appropriate for one to learn about taildraggers in, however. I had about 500 hours in a Citabria before I acquired the 185. While not vicious by any means, it requires constant attention and prompt correction, sometimes with a little muscle. It is often compared to the 206 in Alaska, but I prefer the 185 for personal transportation and aesthetics. There is no comparison on skis. Performance on the 206 is comparable and it offers better cargo carrying, but at 300 pounds more weight. Also, manual flaps on the 185 are infinitely preferable to electric, particularly on floats. Edo 2960 floats, which I have, are quite long and will dig their heels in if too much stick pressure is applied to achieve liftoff. An extra tug on the flaps accomplishes much the same as far as the wing is concerned without altering the planing angle of the floats. This maneuver requires feel and would be impossible with electric flaps.

Realistic flight plan block speed on wheels is 140 knots at 8,000 feet. Edo 2960's are relatively fast floats

With this 1979 model, the 185 got a wet wing with 84 gallons usable.

in the air but will still take 20 knots off at the same altitude. At normal float operation altitude 115 knots is more realistic at 24/24.

I always lean 50° rich of peak on the EGT at either 23 to 24 inches of manifold pressure and 2400 rpm for cruise. I plan for 15 gph with 14 as a good actual overall average at altitude. Some operators do not feel the IO-520 should ever be leaned below 14 gph.

At 450 hours total time on the engine I switched to AeroShell 15/50 and within 20 hours thereafter noticed vibration. Inspection of the oil filter revealed metal that was diagnosed by Continental as bearing material. The engine was replaced.

The choice of floats depends somewhat on fresh water or salt. I prefer Edo floats myself although PeeKay makes a good float which doesn't get off smooth water quite as well but is more suited for ocean operation. The 1960 floats are listed on the Cessna equipment list and provide the best combination of speed in the air and performance on the water. Most commercial operators seem to prefer the Edo 3430s where airspeed is not a factor and overloading is. Aqua floats are noted for their leaking and do not have a particularly good reputation. CAP floats are not seen very much any more and have a reputation for porpoising in a step turn, a not really necessary maneuver.

I use Landes wheel penetration skis, which are a good compromise

ski and half the price of retractable skis, which are superior, however. The penetrating tire gives a surprising amount of drag. I do not like straight skis myself as it limits the aircraft's utility, particularly in areas around sea level. The 185 is simply too heavy to manhandle on the ground like a Super Cub.

I found that the best way to land a 185 in most circumstances is with an approach speed of 65 knots, three or four notches of flaps, trimming full aft when ground effect is felt, and timing the full retarding of the throttle with touchdown in the three-point altitude. Wheel landings have more style and are unquestionably the way to go in gusty winds. In the last several years my landings have been evenly divided between wheel and three-point.

I have owned a 180 and not ground-looped either plane, or any taildragger for that matter, yet. I don't feel that a groundloop is inevitable as it can be avoided in most cases. I have abandoned several landing attempts, however, where I felt that there was a definite possibility of losing control. In gusty crosswind conditions it is not unusual to use full rudder, and a pilot should be ready with a touch of brake, which is usually quite effective. Twenty to 25 knots is the most direct crosswind that I would care to attempt. Also be careful of a left crosswind on takeoff as, when the tail comes up, full rudder will probably be needed. If I had to land in conditions with the wind stronger I would land into the wind across the runway.

Robert H. Wagstaff
Anchorage, Alas.

I had my doubts about the IO-520 engine before we bought our 185. It is amazing how actually owning an airplane changes your point of view. I have really grown to resent Continental's attitude, both to their customers and as exemplified in the poor engineering and a pinch-penny attitude in assembling their products.

We recently lost a cylinder on our 400-hour IO-520. Continental's comment was, ''Oh Gee, you must be doing something wrong, that's not a problem anybody else has.'' Now that we were feeling properly guilty and had resolved to run the engine three points rich of peak lean instead of the recommended two, we removed the cylinder and took it to the machine shop. The machinist was not at all surprised to hear that the cylinder was from a 400-hour engine. He told me from which position (#) it had to come, and said that this was quite normal. Starting at about 500 hours, I could expect to replace at least three cylinders before a major would be necessary at 1,200 hours!

The problem with this particular cylinder (in addition to its location at the right rear of the engine) was bad seating in the exhaust valve, caused by excess guide clearance and lack of seating at the factory. Continental assembles all heads at the maximum allowable clearance, so the TSIO heads can be interchanged with the IO heads. The result is excess clearance for IO heads when they are new. Continental's somewhat unique views on seating valves and balancing engines are too well known to be worth any long comment.

In addition to sloppy assembly there is a design problem with the engine (in addition to the weak crankcases), in the area of top cylinder cooling. There are not nearly enough cooling fins in this area, and (it must be assumed) for reasons of cost Continental refuses to use sodium cooled valves, a combination that ensures overheating and rapid wear in the upper-cylinder and valve area.

Name Withheld

Cessna 206

As a utility workhorse, the Stationair 206 is a handful to land gracefully when lightly loaded. Engine problems cause the greatest number of accidents and incidents.

Trucking on down through the years, Cessna's 206 and 207 have earned a reputation as workhorse utility haulers that will carry almost anything that will fit inside.

Where the average airplane topped with fuel might grudgingly allow three-quarters of the seats available to be occupied before going over gross, in the big Cessna Stationairs you can normally fill all six or seven seats with people, carry a full load of fuel and still remain legal.

And the occupants can be FAA-sized 170-pounders, too.

Easily removable rear seats and big double doors add to the flexibility and double-duty nature of the aircraft as a people or cargo hauler.

Model History

With only modest changes along the way, Stationairs, or Super Skywagons, have been rolling out of Cessna factory doors for over two decades, starting in 1964. (The line was halted with the rest of the Cessna piston-engine fleet in 1986, of course.) Probably the most significant change along the way has been a small hike in horsepower for the normally aspirated model in 1968 (from 285

hp to 300 hp) and on the turbo model in 1977 (from 285 hp to 310 hp).

The early models used to be called Super Skywagons. In 1970 they were renamed Stationairs. Then in 1972 the line was outfitted with cuffed leading edges—call them "camber-lift wings" in merchandising lingo—that added extra stability and controllability at lower speeds. Also that year the baggage compartment was stretched an extra seven inches to the rear. In 1975 a set of more streamlined wheel fairings and a cowl flap cleanup hiked the cruise speed about six mph. And in 1978 club seating was offered on the Stationair 6s, as they now were called, and 28-volt electrical systems

Double doors open over 3½ feet wide for easy access to the rear cabin.

were added. In 1979 an optional anti-icing package was offered for props and windshield, but not wings. Naturally, it was not approved for flight into known icing.

The model was stretched in 1977 to bring out the Stationair 7 or 207 with a truly monster cabin that would seat, naturally, seven. It had a max. useful load maybe 30 pounds greater than that of the 206. A year later an eighth seat became available in the rear for the Stationair 8, its latest moniker.

Load Carrying and Cabin Comfort

The Stationair's 1,600-to-1,700-pound useful load, long c.g. envelope and big rear cargo doors—over 44 inches wide—make it an outstanding load carrier. In the ''U'' version it comes with just a pilot's seat, in fact, so the remainder of the flat floor (flat except for small ''dimples'' in the floor for the rear-seat passengers' feet) can be used to stow various kinds of gear and cargo. Special kits were offered to use the aircraft as an aerial ambulance, photo ship, skydiving plane, glider tow and

casket hauler. Also, the floor height makes for easy loading of the cabin.

Cessna used to boast in its brochures that the Stationair could load six adults, 200 pounds of baggage, full fuel, 100 pounds of options and still be under gross weight—and by gosh they were right. Don't assume, however, that although six (FAA-size) 170-pound adults can go along, they all will be sitting in the lap of luxury. The rear two seats are a bit on the cramped side—as in the Cessna 210s, because the ceiling is lower and the sidewalls narrower at the rear.

But if you're willing to live with the aesthetic compromise of an optional under-plane cargo pod, you can at least carry six people and lots of baggage quite conveniently.

Performance and Handling

Look for top cruise speeds of 143 to 148 knots, burning lots of gas—15 to 16 gph or so. One owner said he was content to throttle back to where he got 135 knots more economically at 12.5 gph, however.

Naturally, carrying so big a load, the Stationairs are not going to have feather-like handling qualities. Pilots who have stepped up the Cessna ladder, though, say the transition is not too difficult, but it may take a while. One owner said it was as rock steady as a tank in rough weather, and landed pretty much like a heavy 172. Another described control pressures as

In a typical Cessna panel, engine instruments and fuel gauges are on the right side.

Like the C-210, the Stationair will handle six riders, but it offers only modest room for the two passengers in the rearmost seats.

"heavy, but very positive." A third, a CFI who had lots of Skylane time, said it took him about 50 hours to feel comfortable flying the Stationair.

Like other big Cessnas, the airplane is reluctant to stall and has heavy pitch forces at slow speeds. Like other aircraft that have a big c.g. envelope, it can be nose heavy in the landing flare unless there's weight in the rear. And the massive flaps, which can crank down to 40 degrees, will bring the big bird down like a freight elevator on final approach. It's difficult to envision overshooting in this aircraft, without aggravated overspeeding.

The giant 207 also is a handful to flare that final few degrees to avoid getting a hard three-pointer. But though the pitch forces are heavy, the ailerons are quite light. The 207, unlike the 206, also has a forward baggage loading compartment to help balance the load.

Rear passengers also note: the rear double doors will not come open with the flaps lowered. (One flier who often flies over water observed that this might pose an exiting problem during a ditching emergency.)

Vs. Piper's Saratoga
The six-place Stationairs are almost an exact match for Piper's Saratoga

The 1975 Stationair II

The 1984 Stationair 6

and Cherokee Six in power and loading ability, and it might be a tough choice to make between the two. Advantages of the Piper are 300 extra hours of engine TBO (2,000 hours vs. 1,700) and a little more room for the rear-seat passengers, plus the extra baggage space in the nose of the aircraft—which also helps in balance as well as load.

Safety Record

The Cessna 206 Stationairs share with the other fixed-gear Cessnas a generally excellent safety record. Among all four- to six-place fixed-gear aircraft they had the third best fatal accident rate, after the Cessna 180 and 172, according to National Transportation Safety Board figures tallied in 1979. In a special study of 33 light aircraft, the Cessna 207 ranked fifth best, and in total accident rate it came out seventh best—or overall in the top quarter of the fleet. Only in the hard landing category did the C-206 come out in the worst half of the fleet, and even there it was 12th down from the top—i.e., better than 11 others.

Our own study of data provided by the FAA for the years 1983 through 1985 showed that engine related problems caused the greatest number of accidents and incidents on both the 206 and 207—with 29 cases for the C-206 and 19 for the C-207. Of the 20 accidents/incidents for which a specific cause was named, basic engine hardware failures were involved in the largest proportion—11. Of these, the biggest bunch (five cases) involved connecting rods—rods separated, rod bearing failed, rod bolt or nuts failed.

Second largest number of failures—four—involved broken crankshafts. Also, in a couple of cases cylinders separated, and in four cases there were oil problems of various types.

Second highest accident/incident category for the Stationairs was hard landings, with 15 of these logged in the past three years. The aircraft, often loaded heavily as a utility craft, is a natural candidate for this kind of problem, especially thanks to its barn-door flaps and the high rate of sink the careless pilot can encounter on final. In several instances pilots also came to grief trying to go around without retracting the flaps—and with that much drag, good luck.

If there's not enough weight in the back, fliers might also have trouble flaring the aircraft properly. A number of 206 pilots managed to damage the nosewheel by failing to touch down on the mains first, or by porpoising, according to the accident statistics.

Various groundloops, swerves and runway handling problems contributed the third largest category for the Stationairs, with a dozen accidents. In several cases the aircraft was actually blown over onto a wingtip by high side or

Cost/Performance/Specifications

Model	Year	Average Retail Price	Cruise Speed (kts)	Useful Climb (lbs)	Fuel Std/Opt (gals)	Engine	TBO (hrs)	Overhaul Cost
206, A	1964-66	$28,000	142	1,800	65/84	285-hp Cont. IO-520-A	1,700	$12,000
206, B/C/D	1967-69	$31,000	142	1,800	65/84	300-hp Cont. IO-520-F	1,700	$12,000
T206, A/B	1966-68	$30,000	147	1,650	65/84	285-hp Cont. TSIO-520-C	1,400	$13,500
206E/F	1970-72	$29,000	142	1,700	65/84	300-hp Cont. IO-520-F	1,700	$12,000
T206E/F	1970-72	$35,000	147	1,650	65/84	285-hp Cont. TSIO-520-C	1,400	$13,500
206F	1973-75	$32,000	142	1,760	65/84	300-hp Cont. IO-520-F	1,700	$12,000
T206F	1973-75	$35,500	147	1,660	65/84	285-hp Cont. TSIO-520-C	1,400	$13,500
206G	1976-78	$43,000	147	1,690	65/84	300-hp Cont. IO-520-F	1,700	$12,000
T206G	1976-78	$49,000	152	1,610	61/80	310-hp Cont. TSIO-520-M	1,400	$13,500
206G	1979-81	$61,000	147	1,690	61/80	300-hp Cont. IO-520-L	1,700	$12,000
T206G	1979-81	$71,000	152	1,610	61/80	310-hp Cont. TSIO-520-M	1,400	$13,500
206G	1982-84	$90,000	147	1,690	61/80	300-hp Cont. IO-520-L	1,700	$12,000
T206G	1982-84	$105,000	152	1,610	61/80	310-hp Cont. TSIO-520-M	1,400	$13,500
206G	1985-86	$129,000	147	1,690	61/80	300-hp Cont. IO-520-L	1,700	$12,000
T206G 1986	1985-86	$146,000	152	1,610	61/80	310-hp Cont. TSIO-520-M	1,400	$13,500

quartering tailwinds on the runway or taxiway—sometimes hitting the prop with expensive damage done.

Finally, Stationair pilots managed to run out of fuel or run a tank dry 10 times in the current study, for the fourth largest accident category.

Maintenance Considerations

There's little doubt that the Continental TSIO/IO-520 power-plant has come in for more than its fair share of problems in the Stationair line, judging from Service Difficulty Reports filed with the FAA. As we saw above, this was corroborated by the accident reports.

Cylinder, crankshaft, crankcase and valve problems noted in the SDRs can be added to the list of connecting rod problems that came to light in the accident reports. In the 407 SDRs surveyed from 1984 to Aug. 1986, we noted 18 instances of cracked or separated cylinders, 11 of cracked crankcases, seven of broken or worn crankshafts and a dozen valve problems of various types.

We also spotted nine cases of exhaust stack cracking or breaking, and seven instances of the fuel selector valve having a free play of anywhere from 20 to 50 degrees. An AD (85-02-07) deals with this problem.

One subtle item to check when looking over a potential buy is corrosion on the trailing edge of the elevator from the inside. Apparently the styrofoam filler inside collects water and the moisture causes the problem. Some SDRs noted severe corrosion inside that could not be spotted easily from outside.

The Stationairs also have the by now notorious bladder fuel tanks, and thus are prey to all the grief concerning wrinkles trapping water inside.

In the last decade there were two Airworthiness Directives of special interest. One (77-16-05) called for inspection of fuel selector valves to prevent inadvertent fuel shutoff, and the other (79-08-03) required work to prevent an electrical system failure that might cause smoke or fire from the wires behind the instrument panel. We noted several instances of smoke in the cockpit in the accident/incident reports.

Modifications

There is a raft of STCed mods for the 206 line. Naturally, it's a popular model for water work, and various manufacturers provide floats and amphibious landing gear. To improve its STOL capabilities,

Horton STOL-Craft in Wellington, Kans. offers a kit consisting of wing leading edge cuffs, drooped tips and stall fences. Bob Williams in Udall, Kans. offers another similar kit.

For longer range, the buyer can look toward Flint Aero in Sangee, Calif. for installation of a pair of wing tip tanks.

For observation or camera work, Ryan Int'l, Airways Corp in Wichita, Kans. has an STC for installation of blister windows and camera ports.

And of course Bob Fields Aerocessories in Ventura, Calif. will

Cessna 206 Resale Value Charts

provide inflatable door seals to keep out wind and water and excess noise.

The Jungle Aviation and Radio Service located in Waxhaw, N.C. and known for its work in designing crashworthiness features has an STC for installation of seats and seat tracks, although it is moot whether they can offer those to the public because of potential liability problems. They also have a mod for replacement and relocation of the pre-select flap switch with a continuous input one that allows simultaneous pilot operation of the throttle and flap controls.

Resale Value

Through the years the Stationairs have tended to hold their value fairly well. Like other aircraft held in reasonably high esteem, they rose in resale value slightly during the inflationary years of the late 70s, and then slipped a bit in '79 and '80. But they've soldiered on fairly steadily since then, losing only a fraction of their value. If anything, the 207s have tended to keep a bit higher value in the last half decade than the 206s.

For Support

The Cessna Pilots Assn. is the one to join for information and help. They're in Wichita, Kans., (306) 946-4777.

Owner Comments

I feel that the 206 is perhaps the most under-appreciated airplane in the Cessna line-up—under-appreciated by everyone except someone who owns one.

I started looking for my first airplane in late 1980. I had no real idea what I wanted, but it had to be big enough to carry my wife and three kids or cargo for my company, or at least be able to cope

with the Sierra Nevada mountains without "squeaking over." I had already crossed the Sierras and Rockies a few times in C-150s and 172s with some white knuckles to show for it.

I looked at older 182s and even 210s. I was just about to make an offer on a 210 when someone on the line asked me how I would like to look at a 206. "A 206? You've got to be joking," I thought. "They are pigs, burn lots of fuel, get run over by 210s, which have the same amount of room, and just plain aren't the 'in thing.'" But . . . they do have factory cargo doors, carry an honest six passengers, don't burn much more fuel than a 182, go reasonably fast, can climb to 16,000 feet (if you have some time), and don't cost much to annual since the legs have rigor mortis.

After flying this aircraft for an hour, I bought her and still own her more than five years later. My 206 has a cargo pod (factory version). In 1982 I put in a "new" ARC radio package myself (I work in electronics for a living) with supervision. The whole package cost me $4,000 plus some DC-to-DC power converters to change over my 14 VDC power to the 28 VDC that the RT-385As required. I have not had a radio failure in four years except for one display element that is intermittent.

I paid $14,800 for the plane mainly because the IO-520-A had about 1,600 hours SMOH. When I bought the plane, that was TBO, but Continental raised it to 1,700 hours early in 1982. I kept a close watch on the engine, changed the oil every 25 to 30 hours, and kept flying until this year. The engine is now being overhauled for about $14,000 firewall forward, including a replacement prop. I am waiting for word from the FAA on whether I can put the new Ritter & Iverson camshaft in the IO-520-A. It is approved for the later models.

The old engine ran fine except for the need for quite a little technique in restarting the engine after a couple of hours of flight. I adopted the old "turn on the electric fuel pumps, flood it, and then go through the flooded start procedure" routine. This takes practice in jockeying the mixture and throttle controls to get it started before the battery croaks. Luckily, I guess, the previous owner had installed a battery jumper cable connection on the port side of the engine compartment. More than once did I need a boost from a friendly pickup until I learned the technique.

I burned an honest 12.5 to 13.5 gph of 100 LL. This was despite hauling around a cargo pod all the time. I cruised at a dependable, though not really speed-burning 155 mph. I climb generally from sea level at 750-900 fpm, depending on load and how hard I push it. With a high-time engine, I tend to baby the power settings. Off the deck at 2700/31, at 500 feet kill the flaps; once stabilized, pull manifold pressure back to top of redline and continue to climb. Somewhere around 2,000 feet agl I pull the prop to 2,450 unless I am in a hurry to get more altitude. Then I adjust for best climb.

I got hit by the fuel bladder AD in 1984 while the plane was being readied for new paint. I did not need new bladders, but some wrinkles were pulled out, the newer quick drains were installed. (They are lousy; they have always leaked since installation. Cessna has told me where to go to get ones that work, but I don't like sulphur smells, and my old style already on the plane before the AD never leaked.) And now I see more water in my sump checks than ever before. For $675 I don't know if they did me any favors.

Since I use the plane primarily for business travel, I can attest to its ruggedness and suitability. I would say that the Cessna 206 is perhaps the best single-engine plane for a small business that has to move fairly big, somewhat heavy equipment from point A to point B at a reasonable cost. I have been from Tracy, Calif. to Houston, Tex. twice at full gross in about 14 hours. It's not the quietest ride, but when you fly a truck, you expect to suffer a little. With 80-gallon tanks, I regularly get five to 5.5 hours between stops with reasonable reserves. I can fly from Tracy to Tacoma Narrows Airport in Washington nonstop without any worry.

They say that the cargo pod cuts five knots from my cruise, but my actual figures seem to be about what the book says. The pod gets a lot of looks. People ask me if it is radar, some science project, or a special fuel tank. The pod lets me put 300 pounds of baggage essentially under the pilot's feet. This does not increase useful load or gross weight (you really lose because the pod weighs about 40 pounds) but it allows you to move some of that extra weight forward on the c.g. so you don't become tail heavy at gross. It also makes trips with passengers more comfortable by cutting down on cabin clutter.

I like the way the 206 handles, since I trained in 172s. It feels like a tank in rough weather, and lands pretty much like a heavy 172. It is cheap to run at 12.5 gph @ 155 mph. I generally spend about $350 per annual since I participate in the work.

During the rest of the year I have only experienced some minor problems with leaky brake seals (fixed on the last annual). I also had a seat rail crack, so I replaced that.

I could buy a newer plane, but I still haven't found one that can compete in the price/performance range of the 206. The next step up in any category would seem to require either a retractable or twin. Then the maintenance, annual and insurance costs would go up dramatically. I pay $1,700 per year now for insurance.

Galen Flinn
Tracy, Calif.

I own a 1981 U206G. I've owned the airplane for two years. In my opinion it is the finest high-wing aircraft Cessna has designed.

Annual and 100-hour inspections average about $600-$650. Insurance, with the hull covered to $60,000 costs me $3,200. Last year it was $1,800—a 178-percent increase over 1985, with no claims and the safest year in general aviation history. Also, the 1981 C-206 probably has the lowest AD rate of all the 206s built.

Performance is excellent, but the airplane will lap up the 100 LL if not leaned aggressively. If not leaned properly, the fuel consumption can be as high as 16 gph, but oil consumption will go to a surprising one quart per engine hour, due to the excess fuel washing the oil right off the pistons and out the exhaust.

Takeoff run with full fuel and 10 degrees of flaps on a standard day is about 700 feet. The normally aspirated 206 will do fine to 10,000 msl, but pack a lunch to attain the 14,800-foot service ceiling. Climbout is excellent at 1,100 fpm, medium load.

The aircraft is very stable at MAC; the control pressures are heavy, but very positive. The aircraft is difficult to stall like other high-wing Cessnas, but altitude loss is minimal, sometimes less than 50 feet. A takeoff departure stall is next to impossible, cranking out 300 horses and almost having to stand the airplane on its tail to do so.

Excellent visibility for a big high-wing aircraft. Interior room is great. I have standard, but club seating does offer a tad more if you like to fly backwards.

Used 206s are becoming very popular—particularly in the Houston area. Pilots are discovering the great advantages of its big useful 1,100-pound carrying capacity plus full fuel. Smart 206 owners know what they have and are not giving the 206 away.

Glenn MacConnell
Sugar Land, Tex.

SINGLE-ENGINE RETRACTABLES

Piper Malibu

A sleek, long-winged high-flyer, the Malibu is in big demand on the new and used-plane market.

Piper's PA-46 Malibu pressurized single is one of the few bright spots in general aviation these days. Introduced in 1984 as the first new clean-sheet-of-paper design in nearly a decade, the Malibu had excellent performance, and a huge six-place cabin. It was an immediate hit, selling like hotcakes at close to list price—in dramatic contrast to the moribund sales of every other airplane model.

The first used Malibus are now on the marketplace, and they offer the used-plane shopper the ultimate in single-engine capabilities—but the price of entry into this rarified stratum is still high.

Used-Plane Marketplace

The Malibu market is still strong, but by late 1985 it cooled off somewhat from the heady days of 1984, when the new-plane order book was backlogged for months. "That's a thing of the past," commented one big used-plane broker.

According to one dealer, the main factor in the price of a used Malibu is radar. Most Malibus were factory-equipped with wing-mounted Sperry color radar, which requires a special "radar wing" with a compartment to accept the dish. The radar cannot be retrofitted, and non-radar Malibus have limited appeal for most pilots of this class of airplane, who consider radar a virtual necessity for high-altitude all-weather flying.

According to the dealer, many of the used Malibus on the market are non-radar airplanes being dumped by owners who want to buy radar-equipped Malibus. Be prepared to pay a premium of at least $15,000 to get a radar-equipped airplane. Likewise, the "known-icing option" (boots, prop, windshield de-ice) is worth at least $10,000.

The used-Malibu market is small. By late 1985, total Malibu production had amounted to about 180, and we estimate that no more than a couple of dozen used or demonstrator Malibus are for sale. So far, at least, the owners seem to like them. One dealer said he sent letters to every registered Malibu owner expressing an interest to buy their planes, but said he got only one reply.

Performance

The Malibu is the hottest-performing single-engine airplane on the market. The book numbers are impressive, and Malibu owners consistently report that their aircraft meet or exceed the book.

The Malibu is a heavy airplane (4,100 pounds gross weight) to be dragged around by 310 hp, so take-off performance won't snap any vertebrae in your neck. But once aloft on that huge 43-foot wing, the Malibu comes into its own. Initial climb rate is listed as 1,143 fpm, and owners report the climb to 25,000 feet (the plane's max certified altitude) takes about 27-28 minutes at typical weights. An old Cessna P210N, by contrast, takes ''about eight days'' to climb that high, according to an owner who's had both. Unlike the P210N, the Malibu is a true high-altitude airplane, with the power and the wing to fly high routinely.

Owners report max cruise speeds of about 215 knots at 25,000 feet, with typical fuel burns of only about 16 gph. It may seem odd to put such emphasis on fuel efficiency in a $300,000 airplane (sort of like a guy who buys a $40,000 Mercedes turbodiesel and brags because it gets five mpg better than the gas model, thereby saving him $100 per year), but the Malibu's high mpg enables it to fly very long legs non-stop. Several owners mentioned six-hour legs with comfortable fuel reserves, and the max range at 75 percent is over 1,300 nm—almost double that of a P210N.

Payload/Range
Most Malibus, very well equipped with dual everything, de-ice boots, radar and air conditioning, have useful loads between 1,300 and 1,400 pounds, enough for a full 120-gallon load of fuel, three 170-pound people and 100 pounds of baggage. Like virtually all airplanes, the Malibu requires pilots to trade fuel for payload.

With a full cabin of baggage-carrying passengers (assume 200 pounds each), fuel will be severely limited, to perhaps 30 gallons—only enough to go a couple of hundred miles with a decent reserve. Things get more reasonable with more normal loads, however. Three non-fat couples with overnight bags would leave enough for perhaps 90 gallons—sufficient to fly 800 or 900 nm.

Owners praise the roomy front and rear baggage bins, which provide plenty of space, weight capability and balance flexibility.

Creature Comforts
Here's where the Malibu stands alone among single-engine aircraft. The big-plane feel starts with the rear air-stair door entry and continues with the huge rear cabin, which is nearly the match of a Navajo. By comparison, the P210 is claustrophobic. Pilots rave about the Malibu's smoothness and low noise level.

Only drawback noted by owners is the insufficient cabin heat. Rear-seat passengers shiver at high altitudes in winter, particularly at night. One owner reports that he installed his own insulation under the rear floorboards.

By all reports, the Malibu's pressurization system is excellent. Owners love it, but their enthusiasm may be partly attributed to the fact that most are step-up buyers who have never flown pressurized aircraft before. But the Malibu's system is far superior to the P210's, and the equal of some bigger piston twins.

The 5.5 psi differential allows a comfortable 8,000-foot cabin at 25,000 feet. (By contrast, the P210—even the new R model—provides a borderline 12,500-foot cabin at 23,000 feet.) Pressurization is rate-controlled.

Handling Qualities
Owners praise the way the Malibu flies. Despite the long wings, aileron control is crisp and precise. Pitch control is also light for a plane this big, especially compared to the old 210s. ''It's a one-hand airplane,'' commented one Malibu pilot approvingly.

Trim stability in pitch is fine—only minor changes due to power and airspeed adjustments. Lateral trim can be a problem, however. Because of the long wings, a small fuel imbalance shows up in the controls quickly. Plan on switching tanks back and forth at least every hour. The bungee-style rudder trim is judged inadequate by several owners. During high-speed let-downs, there's not enough left rudder trim to keep the plane coordinated, so strict ball-in-the-center purists will have to ride the left rudder at times.

Some owners have also complained about poor yaw stability in turbulence. This isn't too surprising considering the Malibu's long wing and proportionally stubby fuselage. A yaw damper might be a nice

Cost/Performance/Specifications

Model	Year	Number Built	Average Retail Price	Cruise Speed (kts)	Rate of Climb (fpm)	Useful Load (lbs)	Fuel Std/Opt (gals)	Engine	TBO (hrs)	Overhaul Cost
PA-46 310P	1984	88	$254,000	186	1,100	1,509	120	310-hp Cont. TSIO-520-BE	2,000	$20,000
PA-46 310P	1985	N/A	$270,000	186	1,100	1,509	120	310-hp Cont. TSIO-520-BE	2,000	$20,000

option, but none is available as far as we know.

Stall speed is a modest 58 knots, but the "book" approach speed is a rather hot 90 knots. Pilots tell us that the plane floats forever at that approach speed; a more reasonable number would be about 75 or 80.

Engine

The Malibu's 310-hp Continental TSIO-520-BE has some unusual features. With precise induction tuning, it is designed to be leaned very aggressively, to 50 degrees on the lean side of peak TIT. In fact, it *must* be leaned that way; the pilot is forbidden to use any other procedure. Continental has largely taken engine management out of the pilot's hands. For example, only three power settings are authorized for cruise—55, 65 and 75 percent: most owners report that they follow the book procedures to the letter, and few had any complaints.

Cowl Flaps

The Malibu doesn't have any. That makes for less pilot workload, but it also means the engine tends to run hot in the climb, despite Piper's stern dictum that all climbs must be made with full rich mixture. Several owners report near-redline CHTs in climb at speeds below 120 knots (best-rate-of-climb speed is 115 knots). At a climb speed of 130, however, CHTs come down, and most Malibu owners use fairly fast cruise-climb speeds.

We also got reports of high CHTs in high-altitude cruise. One owner reports he flirts with the red line at 75 percent power on warm days at 25,000 feet, when density altitude is 27,000 or 28,000 feet. He has to reduce power to keep CHT in the green. Cowl flaps would be useful in such situations.

Because the normal flow of cooling air through the cowling must be high to provide adequate cooling in the climb, the Malibu engine is quite sensitive to overcooling on descent. Owners describe careful letdown procedures that must commence more than 100 nm from the destination. However, for quick letdowns, the landing gear can be extended at high speed—much like the speed brakes on a jet—and a good rate of descent results, even with the engine partially powered up to keep warm.

A used-Malibu buyer should quiz the previous pilot/owner about his letdown procedures. If the guy says "Huh?" when you mention shock cooling, beware.

Getting the Bugs Out

Most used Malibus in late 1985 were 1984 models with low serial numbers. That posed a dilemma for the used-plane buyer: with any new aircraft model, it takes a while to get the bugs out, and these early airplanes don't have the benefit of design and engineering refinement.

A prime example is the hydraulic system. It was a maintenance disaster from the beginning, and Piper will reportedly switch from hydraulic to electric flaps in the 1986 Malibu. Piper has made earnest attempts to Band-Aid the hydraulic systems of the earlier airplanes, buy any used Malibu up for sale is virtually guaranteed to have had hydraulic problems.

As long as Piper keeps fixing them for free, as they have been doing, the hydraulic problems will be bearable. But the company's largesse certainly won't last forever. "My first four hydraulic pumps were paid for by Piper," writes one owner. "I have a feeling the next one will be paid for by me." We also wonder if Piper will be as generous and supportive of second-hand Malibu owners as they have been with their factory-fresh customers.

Hydraulic Solutions

Piper has issued several service letters and bulletins that apply to the hydraulic system. Any used Malibu considered for purchase should have them all. Here are the most important ones:

• SL 965—Addition of hydraulic accumulator.
• SL 792—New fitting in hydraulic pressure gauge line.
• SB 808—Replacement of hydraulic actuator seals.

The new actuator seals are particularly important; the original ones were apparently incompatible with hydraulic fluid (!) and leaked badly, causing the pump motor to run constantly and eventually burn out.

Service Bulletins

The Malibu has suffered non-hydraulic glitches, of course. In fact, Piper has issued a blizzard of service letters and bulletins (we counted nearly 30) on the airplane. During 1985, the vast majority of all service letters and bulletins issued by Piper applied to the Malibu.

Again, anybody contemplating the quarter-million dollar purchase of a used Malibu should make sure all have been complied with. (Remember that not all the bulletins necessarily apply to every individual Malibu. But the early models most likely to be on the used-plane market will probably be affected by most of them.)

The Malibu bulletins, considered mandatory by Piper, are the following:

• SB 780—Flap drive
• SB 782—Magneto switch guard
• SB 783—Elevator binding
• SB 784—Pressurization outflow lines
• SB 786—Brake cylinders
• SB 790—Turbo oil scavenger reservoir
• SB 791—Oxygen Light
• SB 792—Fuel line
• SB 793/808—Nosegear
• SB 794—Fuel boost pump
• SB 796—Wing rivets

- SB 799—Landing gear safety switch
- SB 810—Gear safety solenoid

The service letters, which Piper doesn't consider mandatory (but Malibu buyers should) are these:

- SL 938—Baggage door
- SL 967—Airstair door
- SL 968—Oil filler door
- SL 970—Landing gear doors
- SL 971—Engine cooling baffles
- SL 973—Cabin door
- SL 974—Cowling replacement
- SL 975—Cabin door seal
- SL 976—Seat pan

Judging from owner reports, SL 974, which offers a new, reinforced cowling to replace the original crack-prone one, should be a high priority. Several owners report bad cracks, and one said a three-inch hole developed in his cowling.

In every case, Piper has offered the retrofits or mods described in the service letters at no cost, but only for six months from the date of the service letter. The freebie offers on many of them may have expired by the time this appears in print, so second-hand buyers may have to foot the bills themselves if the mods haven't already been accomplished.

Service Difficulty Reports

In addition to the problems addressed in the aforementioned service letters and bulletins, and in reports to *The Aviation Consumer* from owners, FAA service difficulty reports reveal several interesting patterns.

Although hydraulic and landing gear problems have garnered the most attention, in the SDRs the largest number of problems reported deal with the exhaust and turbocharger systems. We counted over 17 of these. Several of these concerned cracked exhaust tee assemblies, while several others reported leaking crossover tubes that melted the aluminum heat shield.

There was also a clutch of reports on cracking turbo intercooler mounting flanges.

Among the electronic problems reported were two bizarre ones involving the starter being engaged when the master switch was turned on. One explained this happened because the protective cover activated the starter. In one case the alternator broke up and damaged the cowling and prop spinner after the backup alternator cooling failed.

In connection with the various landing gear problems were four instances of bent or cracked engine mounts resulting from the nose gear hitting it.

Malibu pilots might also check that their emergency exit door is not difficult to open because of blockage by upholstery, as reported by one Malibu operator. They might also make sure the fuel cap gasket is secure, since there were two reports of water getting into the fuel tank. One resulted in an engine stoppage at over 16,000 feet. The engine was successfully restarted, however.

Overall, the Malibu's first year has not been a good one from the maintenance/reliability point of view. In fact, it is unpleasantly reminiscent of Piper's last new clean-sheet-of-paper design, the Tomahawk, which had a rash of ADs and service bulletins soon after its introduction. But the Malibu is far more complex than the Tomahawk, and Piper has done a superb job of supporting the plane—even to the point of encouraging owners to fly back to the factory for free fixes of service-bulletin items. Piper is clearly trying hard, and we feel the second year will be better than the first.

Safety

We're aware of only one fatal accident in a Malibu, in August 1984. The aircraft mysteriously dove into the ground at a steep angle during an ILS approach to

Keene, N.H. Weather was reasonably good (1,000-foot broken ceiling with five miles visibility). No probable cause has been officially pronounced yet, but investigators found an electrical plug disconnected in the autopilot/trim system.

We noted a total of 15 nonfatal Malibu accidents through mid-October 1985. The greatest number of accidents—seven—involved nose-wheel collapses for one reason or another.

In one instance the aircraft veered off the runway as the nose gear touched down. The nose gear rotor broke, allowing the gear to rotate. On another the nose gear simply collapsed on landing, and in a third a Malibu taxied over a barrier and the gear collapsed. The retract strut attach bolt was broken. In yet another case the nosegear collapsed when the pilot retracted the flaps on rollout and moved both the flap and gear levers since the "tubing was too close." In another instance the aircraft veered left off the runway after landing and the nose gear collapsed. It was noted in that context that there is a service bulletin out on the steering horn.

Some pilots seem to be landing the aircraft hot or long, since three accidents were the result of overshoots with pilots landing long and/or fast.

There was only one reported case of an engine failure, this one during a climbout after a turbo drain reservoir broke at the weld and all the engine oil was lost. There was an "uneventful" forced landing, however.

Maintenance Costs

It ain't cheap to run a pressurized six-place airplane. Fuel costs about $40 per hour, routine maintenance about $12 per hour (owners report annual and 100-hour inspections run in the $1,000 to $1,500 range).

Engine overhaul reserve is about $8 per hour (all 1985 prices).

Malibu owners have suffered through a lot of bugs, but since Piper had been fixing everything for free, the hourly cost has been zero. Obviously that won't last forever. Once Piper's munificence subsides, the potential exists for catastrophic maintenance expenses if you get a lemon (as it does with any big, expensive airplane). The Malibu's early problems give us pause for the future, however.

Typical insurance bills run around $5,000 per year, and hangaring can cost as much as the owner is willing to pay.

One owner toted it all up to $200 per hour, including interest and monthly payments. Sounds about right.

Depreciation

The early popularity of the Malibu and its current healthy value on the used-plane market bode well for future resale value. A new 1984 Malibu that listed for $340,000 in late 1985 was worth perhaps $280,000—about 82 percent of new after one year. If Piper can work out the new-design bugs, and if the engine holds up over the long run (few Malibus have more than 400 hours) and if no major delayed disasters surface (as they did with the P210), then the Malibu has every chance to become a blue-chip used-plane investment like the Mooney 201 or A36 Bonanza.

Owner Comments

I picked up my PA-46 Malibu (serial number 36) on May 1, 1984. To date it has 460 hours. It has full de-ice, radar, Stormscope and the best King avionics.

Performance: I went through the Malibu school at Vero Beach and fly the plane strictly by their numbers.

75 percent power is 31 inches/2,400 rpm and 15.5 gph; 65 percent is 28/2,300/13.5 gph; 55 percent is 25/2,200/11.5 gph. At a given power setting, fuel flow is the same, regardless of altitude, so on trips of any distance at all, I fly high to maximize true airspeed.

At 75 percent and 15.5 gph, my TAS at 25,000 ft. is 215 kts, 22,000 is 210 kts, 17,000 is 200 kts and 12,000 is 190 kts.

During full-power climb, fuel flow is 38 gph, and I can average 1,000 fpm though the mid-teens and 850 fpm into the low 20s, usually 200-400 pounds below gross weight.

In August, my son and I flew from Anniston, Alabama to northwest British Columbia. We covered 6,000 nautical miles in 28.2 hours, with six takeoffs and climbs in the 20-23,000-ft range. Average block-to-block groundspeed for the entire trip was 212 kts, with fuel consumption averaging 17.5 gph. We flew from Anniston to Vancouver with one stop, and on three occasions we flew at 75 percent power for more than six hours, and landed with more than 45 minutes fuel on board each time. I never fill the plane to the full 120-gallon capacity—usually 110 or 115.

Comfort is about like a cabin-class Navajo or 400-series Cessna. Air conditioning is mandatory in this airplane, or you would simply burn up in the Southeast nine months of the year. Noise level is good and there's little vibration. The seats could be a little wider. Leg room in back is fantastic. Luggage space fore and aft is great.

Handling: The Malibu is simple to fly. Power management is full throttle to cruise altitude, set cruise power and lean to 50 degrees lean of peak TIT (a two-minute job). Descent planning is critical; I usually start down from the 20s about

100-110 miles out. Big reason is supercooling of the engine. I don't mind the CHT going from 390 to 220 in descent, but I'm very concerned about how quickly it drops. I start the descent very slowly (200-400 fpm) until CHT starts to move, and then slowly increase rate of descent to 1,000 fpm, still maintaining 75 percent power.

Maintenance: Piper and my local dealer, Anniston Aviation, have been absolutely super. I've had few delays for parts, and support from Piper has been wonderful, even after the warranty has expired.

Here's a list of my major unscheduled maintenance items:

1. Starter adapter broke (50 hours).
2. Hydraulic piston in landing gear (twice in first 100 hours).
3. Replace top cowl (twice in first 200 hours).
4. Replace nose cowl (100 hours).
5. Alternator bracket broke (400 hours).
6. Exhaust bracket broke (200 hours).
7. For the first 50 hours, hydraulic pump would cycle 20 or 30 times per hour. Flaps were found to be badly out of rig. Plane went back to Vero Beach and flaps were rerigged and motor replaced. Pump now cycles about four times per hour. Better, but not perfect.

To sum it up: Even though by buying one of the earlier Malibus I got hit by several service bulletins and early hydraulic headaches, I'm very proud and pleased with the airplane. For this kind of performance and pressurization, and operating economy (not to mention sex appeal), I would not consider any other airplane currently built in this price range (single or twin).

Cliff Clegg
Anniston, Ala.

Having flown my Piper Malibu for 16 months and 400 hours, I'm happy to share the following with you:

Performance: I get consistently six knots over book at the upper altitudes (FL 180 to 250). At first, I religiously flew 75 percent power, which gave me 216 knots at 16 gph. However, like most new Malibu pilots, I failed to consider density altitude. If you file for FL 250 in the summertime, it can easily put you at 28,000 density, resulting in cylinder temps running above the green. Piper and Continental seem to have nailed the 75-percent-power altitude limit at precisely 25,000 ft density and not a nickel's worth higher. At that point, CHT will stay in the upper part of the green.

I'm still a little spooked by running right at the top of the green, even though Piper and Continental have assured me that "green is green." After many hours of experimenting, I have found that 29.5 inches m.p. and 2,350 rpm results in extraordinary smoothness, super-quiet cabin, and great fuel mileage, plus lower CHTs. This looks like about 70 percent power, although Piper charts show only 55, 65 and 75 percent. This power setting gives me 14 percent better range, and only four percent loss in speed. Running lean of peak is a snap—no transition problems there.

Handling: superb roll response, hands-off stability superior to anything I have ever flown (mostly Bonanzas).

Maintenance: Other than oil changes, nothing to speak of. Squawks have been landing gear actuator rods, hydraulic pump and persistent cracking of the main cowl. Piper has done a superb job of handling all warranty claims, including service bulletins, and a final fix for the cowl cracks is promised to be forthcoming. Most of the squawks have been vendor products. Considering that the Malibu is an entirely new design, I

am pleased how trouble-free the airframe and engine have been. Annual inspections run no more than other airplanes in this class.

Comfort: The pressurization is marvelous, at FL 200 to 250 you're above virtually all the weather, and an 8,000-foot cabin gives you an airline-quality environment. The cabin size is perfect. The greatest asset of the Malibu cabin is the ability of the pilot to leave his seat after two or three hours, walk to the rear, stretch, have a Coke, stretch again, talk with the folks in back for a few minutes, and then go back up front. From the fatigue point of view, pilot time seems to start again from zero at that point. It's a great feeling.

Rear passengers love the legroom, and the six-hour non-stop run I usually make from Denver to the East Coast leaves everybody fresh and ready to go. The very quiet ride and lack of vibration contribute greatly to that fact. The Malibu is by far the quietest recip I have ever flown.

Shortcomings: Nobody bats 1,000, but Piper came pretty close in designing the Malibu. The landing gear handle is too stiff. The cabin light controls are jammed together unnecessarily (there's lots of room elsewhere on the panel). The rear cabin is too cold. (I put three bucks worth of insulating batts under the floorboards of mine).

Bill Prymak
Broomfield, Colo.

I have owned a Piper Malibu for 11 months and 250 hours. I rate the performance and handling as excellent, maintenance as good, comfort excellent, parts availability poor. The last 100-hour inspection was $1,400.

I was very pleased with the plane until I started adding up the squawks.

1. The plane had a missing weld in the right intercooler which caused backfiring at high altitudes until discovered and replaced with a completely welded intercooler.

2. The hydraulic pressure gauge has read either zero or over the red line since the plane was new. This was corrected when the landing gear selector lever was replaced.

3. There was a crack in the scavenger pump oil reservoir requiring replacement of the entire reservoir.

4. The mechanical fuel pressure failed to provide normal fuel pressure until it was replaced.

5. The nosegear steering horn was broken by the ground crew while towing the airplane and was replaced with a redesigned steel unit. (The old one was cast.)

6. The tachometer continues to have occasional fluctuations and will be replaced by the factory.

7. The low vacuum annunciator light comes on with power reduction and stays on for several hours in spite of resumed high-power operation. This is also to be replaced by the factory when the parts are available.

8. The entire front cowling had to be replaced due to cracks around the air inlets and oil filler door.

9. I had a dual vacuum pump failure, apparently caused by a selector valve that jammed, causing both pumps to pump against a closed system. I think that an electric artificial horizon is a necessity in this airplane.

The performance is better than book. We recently flew fully loaded non-stop from Reno to St. Paul, Minn. The advantages of the airplane far outweigh the above list of problems.

Lawrence H. Foster
S. Lake Tahoe, Calif.

I took delivery of my Malibu in 1984. It's the 26th model off the production line. It has 334 hours on it, and performance has been nothing short of superb. It is probably the best-handling airplane I've ever flown.

As with any newly conceived design, there are going to be glitches. All my flying buddies warned me about flying a new design, advising me to wait a few years until the bugs were worked out. I ignored them and have not been sorry, although there are times when I've questioned my decision.

For example, I have now had the opportunity of having my fourth hydraulic pump, and I suspect there will be a fifth and a sixth. The first four were replaced under warranty, but I worry that the fifth and sixth won't be. (They cost $1,500 apiece.) I have written to Piper requesting a one-year warranty on newly-installed pumps, which should protect me, since they don't last anywhere near a year.

I was told there was a "fix" on newer models, but a friend of mine just bought a new Malibu and his pump failed within 100 hours. I would happily swap this eight-pound unit for a 20-pound unit out of a Navajo or a Cheyenne that has historically had good reliability.

Aircraft finish and workmanship are excellent. I would hope that the white cloth material in the interior would be changed to another color and texture so it wouldn't attract so much dirt. It takes continued effort to keep mine clean.

Oil consumption is nil. My engine usually runs 15-20 hours before I have to add a quart. I have been using 15W-50 Shell, which has caused problems with the O-rings in the propeller. I had them changed.

There are 11 Malibus at my home field of San Jose airport, so I'm well tuned in to all of the problems they've been having. One big one is cracking in the exhaust manifold. I'm assured that a fix has solved the problem, but that remains to be seen.

The bottom line is that if I had it to do over again, I'd do it exactly the same way. But if Piper support for the Malibu had not been as good as it has been, I probably would not be making these positive remarks. The Lear-Siegler people have been very good about supporting this aircraft, and I hope they continue to do so.

Arthur Holmboe
Los Gatos, Ca.

Cessna Cardinal RG

By many accounts, Cessna's 177 RG Cardinal has survived the ravages of time and a defunct production line quite well. It perhaps now can even be considered the queen of the used economy retractables, at least in terms of near tag sale prices.

It is less doggy in performance than similar aircraft like the Piper Arrow and Beech Sierra, and though still 10 knots or more slower than the Mooney 201, costs a small fortune less. For example, where a 1978 Mooney 201 is going for a handsome price of around $49,000 these days, a '78 Cardinal RG can be fetched for a relatively paltry $29,000 or less, according to *Aircraft Bluebook Price Digest* figures.

Cardinal RG owners don't seem to complain too much about parts availability, though the line was closed down in 1978 after only eight years of production. And they rave about its looks and novel design features. They even seem rather inured to the aircraft's Achilles heel—its trouble-plagued landing gear system. Owners who reported to us this time sounded off a lot less bitterly on the gear problem than they did for our last

The rearward location of the wing provides the pilot with a rare high-wing glimpse of sky and traffic inside the turn. The notch in the fuselage for the main landing gear can be seen on the belly in the wing's shadow.

call for user feedback on the 177 RG in 1980.

Peer Pressure

In comparison with the Piper Arrows, Mooneys and Beech Sierras that have the same 200-hp powerplant, the Cardinal RG is fastest, except for the Mooney, of course. It is roomiest, except for the Sierra. And it can carry the best useful load of all of them, by a small margin. In terms of price, it is $5,000 cheaper on the average than the Arrow on today's used market (for a '78 model), and even about $1,000 cheaper than the Sierra.

In General

Although the 75-percent book cruise speed for the Cardinal RG is supposed to be a sizzling 148 knots/170 mph, in the real world most owners talk about speeds closer to 140-145 knots/161-167 mph. But on the other hand, they boast of economy gas burns of eight to nine and a half gph. And

with a generous 60-gallon fuel capacity on all but the '71 RGs, range is superb.

Owners report the Cardinal RGs ride well in turbulence, have nice-handling controls, provide a "stable instrument platform" and behave well in slow flight. "It is like driving a sports car compared to the cumbersome Skylane," said one owner. "Handling is superb."

Cabin Load and Comfort

As a safety-enhancing corollary to the spacious cabin, owners say the aircraft is almost impossible to load out of the cg envelope. But the baggage compartment is a strange one, since it is bisected by the hump that accommodates the retracted landing gear. This means suitcases that fit through the horizontally mounted baggage door then must be finessed into one of the two vertical slots on either side of the wheel well hump.

Said one owner, however, "The much maligned baggage compartment swallows an enormous amount of luggage, despite the hump. A useful load of 1,025 pounds works out to four adults, 120 pounds of baggage and enough fuel to fly four hours with IFR

From the '71 through '75 models, the aircraft had a "left-handed" panel (photo on left) that was more notable for styling than for instrument space. The '76 model corrected this with an enlarged panel. In a rare bit of human engineering, the suction gauge is placed on the top left corner of the panel, where the pilot can see it, rather than way over on the right, as is common practice.

reserves. It is a true four-place single."

Whistling in the Wind

The four-foot wide cabin doors are everybody's pride and joy for ease of access, and they can catch the wind like sails to open a full 90 degrees to the fuselage. (Watch out.) Along with the benefits come some drawbacks, however, since owners still complain about door sealing problems. One said he solved the problem by simply removing the "hardened original seals" and replacing them with new ones.

But we remain skeptical in the light of comments by Bob Fields (of Bob Fields Aerocessories in Santa Paula, Calif.). Instead of providing inflatable seals for what we figured would be the ultimate solution to the problem, Fields told us he threw up his hands in frustration at getting any seals to work on the Cardinal RG, even though numerous owners came to him for help. "The variation in space between the doors and the fuselage is terrible," he said. "Some portions of the doors fit too tightly, others too

loosely, so when you get one part of the seal to inflate properly, another is pinched off." Fields attributed the awful fit to poor quality control.

Wet and Wild

If the doors can leak air, it stands to reason they can leak water. And so owners testify. The windshields tend to leak as well. But then Cessnas as a class seem prey to leakage problems. One Cardinal RG owner said he solved his leaky windshield problem simply by applying a bead of clear RTV around the outside of the windshield. As a final line of defense for the pilot, however, he suggested covering the pilot's left leg with a plastic chart.

Many aircraft also are noted for poor heating of rear seats in winter. The Cardinal RG tackled that problem by running heating ducts in back through the big doors. Alas, owners report little hot air makes it as far as the rear seats.

History of Model Changes

The aircraft has experienced a few modest changes through its eight-year production life. Though none is terribly significant alone, perhaps the collective improvements through the years to the landing gear system and its many idiosyncracies amounts to something. The 1972 model gained a few knots in cruise and a slightly better climb rate thanks to a new prop. Also, the fixed cabin steps were dropped. They tended to expose the bottom of the fuselage to even

more grief when the aircraft landed gear-up (as they did with some regularity). Instead, small foot pads were placed on the main gear struts. In addition, landing and taxi lights were mounted in the nose instead of the wing.

The '73 model received a slightly redesigned nose cowl and an extra 10 gallons in usable fuel—up to 60 gallons. The fuel selector system was changed from one limited to "off" and "both," to one that also provided "left" and "right" positions. The problem on the earlier model was that one tank could be depleted more rapidly than the other, since the pilot could not select either a right or a left wing tank. This often meant unbalancing the aircraft.

In 1976 the instrument panel was redesigned and enlarged, and a simplified landing gear hydraulic system was offered, along with a stronger nose gear trunion.

For the '77 model, the aircraft received a fuel selector that gave it commonality with other Cessna singles, had a more positive detent and was supposed to be more easily maintainable.

And finally in 1978 the aircraft received a 28-volt electrical system and an improved gear retraction power pack that cut retraction time in half to six seconds.

Resale Value

Despite inflation, the Cardinal RGs on the whole exhibited rather mundane resale curves, never soaring up as highly valued aircraft do. Instead, they merely sagged to a certain level in the standard four years after new, then remained pretty much on a plateau through the years. Thus, the original '71 model dropped from about $31,000 to around $20,000 and remained within a couple thousand dollars of that through the years. The last model, the '78 ship, dropped from about $54,000 to $29,000 in the classic four-year span, and remained in that vicinity to the present.

Safety Record

A study of accident rates in the decade 1972 to 1981 by *The Aviation Consumer* gave the Cardinal RG an excellent ranking in terms of fatal accidents and a slightly better-than-average rate in total accidents. In fatal accidents, the Cardinal RG came out third best after the Cessna Skylane RG and the Beech 33 Bonanza/Debonair and tied with the Beech 36 Bonanza with 1.5 fatal accidents per 100,000 hours. In total accidents it was seventh out of seventeen with 7.8 accidents per 100,000 hours. (See the May 1, 1984 issue.) The study compared single-engine retractables.

What kind of accidents predominate among Cardinal RGs? A study of NTSB accident records for the years 1979-1980 by our sister magazine *Aviation Safety* showed the most—slightly over 37 per cent —involved engine failures. But there seemed to be no particular pattern. Of those in which the problem could be determined, the most—three—occurred after breaks in oil hoses, but all different hoses going to different parts of the aircraft. One engine failure occurred when the oil pump impeller gear broke. This was later the sub-

ject of an Airworthiness Directive, but we noted in a three-year runout of the FAA's Service Difficulty Reports (up through September 1981) at least a dozen problems involving broken oil pump gear teeth.

Landing accidents accounted for the next highest category, with nearly 12 percent, with hard landings and groundloops leading the way in unpleasantness.

Gear Nemesis

As for the traditional nemesis of the Cardinal RG—landing gear problems—the two-year study showed it only third in the rankings along with a host of other problems like fuel management, takeoff accidents and weather-related problems. Nevertheless, failure of the gear to extend or actuator failure brought three RGs to grief.

Our earlier detailed study of 78 Cardinal RG accidents covering the five-year period from 1973 to 1977 showed once again that engine failures predominated, with about 34 percent of the accidents. These

That big carpet-covered hump squarely in the middle of the baggage compartment is not a picnic box, but a receptacle for the retractable main gear. Otherwise, the cabin is gorgeous and roomy.

were seldom fatal. That time, though, gear-up landings and gear collapses and retractions accounted for second place or about 20 percent—or a total of 16 accidents. Some of these were pilot error, however.

Stall/spin/mush accidents in the Cardinal RG were fairly infrequent. In the five-year period there were two in-flight airframe failures. One occurred in weather and was fatal. In the second the pilot overstressed the aircraft and bent the wings, but actually managed to land safely. In general, despite the lack of wing-strengthening struts, the aircraft has a good record of in-flight airframe failures.

Maintenance

Powerplant accessories and brakes were the main problem areas reported on our most recent feedback from Cardinal RG owners.

Cost/Performance/Specifications

Model	Year	Number Built	Average Retail Price	Cruise Speed (kts)	Rate of Climb (fpm)	Useful Load (lbs)	Fuel Std/Opt (gals)	Engine	TBO (hrs)	Overhaul Cost
Cessna 177 RG	1971	213	$22,500	144	860	1,170	50	200-hp Lyc. IO-360-A1B6D	1,800	$10,600
Cessna 177 RG	1972	70	$23,500	148	925	1,155	50	200-hp Lyc. IO-360-A1B6D	1,800	$10,600
Cessna 177 RG	1973	150	$25,000	148	925	1,140	60	200-hp Lyc. IO-360-A1B6D	1,800	$10,600
Cessna 177 RG	1974	160	$26,500	148	925	1,140	60	200-hp Lyc. IO-360-A1B6D	1,800	$10,600
Cessna 177 RG	1975	195	$28,500	148	925	1,120	60	200-hp Lyc. IO-360-A1B6D	1,800	$10,600
Cessna 177 RG	1976	264	$30,500	148	925	1,093	60	200-hp Lyc. IO-360-A1B6D	1,800	$10,600
Cessna 177 RG	1977	215	$32,500	148	925	1,093	60	200-hp Lyc. IO-360-A1B6D	1,800	$10,600
Cessna 177 RG	1978	100	$34,500	148	925	1,106	60	200-hp Lyc. IO-360-A1B6D	1,800	$10,600

But most seemed to feel that maintenance required for the aircraft was reasonable, in general. A recent maintenance survey yielded average hour maintenance costs for the Cardinal RG of around $17 an hour and annual inspection costs averaging a bit under $800. Unscheduled yearly airframe and engine costs together averaged about $600.

We received nowhere near the litany of complaints we did on our last survey several years ago, when owners railed about chronic maintenance problems. Biggest problem areas then were alternator failures, Bendix magneto breakdowns, cracking exhaust pipes, malfunctioning fuel quantity gauges, breaking alternate air induction doors, leaking fuel caps, hot-running engines, landing gear horn malfunctions and malfunctioning landing gear mechanisms, especially hung-up nosegear.

A check of Service Difficulty Reports from 1979 through most of 1981, however, suggests some troublesome areas. A few were: stabilator problems such as loose bolts, worn bushings and cracked brackets; cracked and broken prop spinners; cracked crankcases; broken engine oil pump gear teeth (mentioned before); Bendix magneto failures; and throttle cable malfunctions.

Focus on Landing Gear

Though some owners this time around reported problems with the notoriously quirky landing gear system, the complaints were by no means legion as before. It would appear that the constant focus of attention on the problem by pilots and maintenance shops, and by Cessna's own progressive series of fixes, have diminished its impact significantly. And this comes in the face of the '81 SDR breakdown showing page after page of gear problems. (One must temper this finding, however, with appreciation for the fact that so many of Cessna's *other* retractable-gear aircraft through the years have experienced more than their share of gear problems.)

Through the eight years of its production, the Cardinal had four different landing gear systems, as Cessna strived to correct all its quirks. The first, most problem plagued one on the '71 and '72 Cardinal RGs, was a Rube Goldberg combination of electrical and hydraulic components whose weakest link was its electrically actuated main gear downlocks. The '73 Cardinals got hydraulic downlock actuators that improved reliability. Then on the '74 aircraft the gear selector handle itself was turned into a hydraulic valve and hydraulic pressure was routed not directly but through a panel-mounted valve controlled by the handle. This system also eliminated the remote electrical control unit.

Finally, with the '78 models the 12-volt Prestolite hydraulic power packs were eliminated in favor of a 24-volt power pack of Cessna's design. This has proved to be the most satisfactory of all the systems and, of course, would be the one to choose if cost considerations permit. At any rate, potential buyers should check to see which, if any, of Cessna's recommended service instructions have been applied to whichever model they are looking at. There are at least eight of them, including numbers 71-41, 72-26, 73-28, 74-26, 75-25, 76-4, 76-7 and 77-20.

The aircraft has a rather brief Airworthiness Directive history, with only six ADs against it from 1972 through 1979. And we already mentioned the Lycoming AD (81-18-04) affecting IO-360 engines and calling for replacement of the oil pump impeller and shaft to prevent oil pump failure.

Modifications

Among the STCs published for the Cardinal RG are the following: Wing leading edge cuffs and vortex generators on the vertical stabilizer, by Horton STOL Craft, Wellington, Kans.; chrome-plated brake disc installation, by Engineering Plating & Processing, Kansas City, Kans.; installation of an air/oil separator, by Walker Engineering Co., Los Angeles,

Calif.; and recognition lights on the horizontal stabilizer, by Devore Aviation, Albuquerque, N.M. Also, Silver Instruments and Shadin have STCs for fuel computers.

What to Join

The Cessna Cardinal Club is located at 1701 Saint Andrew's Drive, Lawrence, Kan. 66044 and its president is Beth Harrison. Also, Cardinal owners can contact the Cessna Pilots Assn., P.O. Box 12948, Wichita, Kans. 67277, (316) 721-4313.

Owner Comments

The average cost over the life of my '74 Cardinal RG (purchased when it was one year old) is about $40 to $45 an hour. (That includes direct operating and and fixed costs, flying about 175 hours a year.) This may be higher than average, but I spare no expense on maintenance. The aircraft is maintained by Howard Aircraft Service, at Craig Field in Jacksonville, Fla., and Bob Howard is a real nitpicker. My annuals run from $1,500 to $2,000. My hourly maintenance cost for 1984, the highest ever, worked out to $28.06.

Mechanically, the aircraft has presented only one major problem. Following a fast, no-flap landing, the nose gear collapsed as the aircraft turned off the runway. An improperly adjusted nose gear linkage was found to be at fault. Apparently the aircraft left the factory in that condition and flew for two years before the accident. At normal landing speeds, the hydraulic system apparently could overcome the air pressure on the nose gear. At high speeds this was not the case. Result: a new prop.

Brake pads also were a constant problem. I should have installed chrome disks years ago. Parts, however, are no problem.

I flight plan for 140 knots at about eight to nine gph. It is a fine cross-

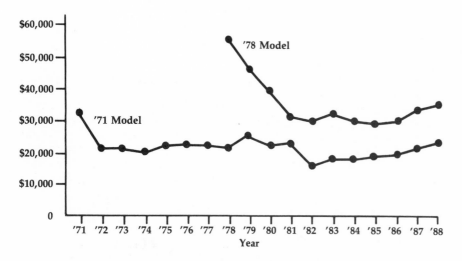

Cardinal RG Resale Value Chart

'78 Model

'71 Model

country machine for my purposes. I usually fly the aircraft with an average of two people aboard. The handling characteristics are outstanding. The controls are firm, crisp and effective. The aircraft has the feel of a much heavier machine, more like a 182 than a 172. The stalls are mild with prompt recovery. The placement of the wing is one of the characteristics of the aircraft that I dearly love, since you are forward of the leading edge, which gives you outstanding visibility.

The avionics are ARC. What more can I say! One of the avionics people that worked on the radios said, "You really have to be wealthy to fly with ARC equipment," and I believe her. I had two problems: finding someone who would work on them, then finding someone whose repairs would hold up until I got back to my home base. I am going to install new avionics following completion of the new paint job.

All in all, I am very fond of the aircraft. Frankly, I don't find any of the aircraft of the same class being marketed today comparable to a Cardinal RG.

John D. Shea, Jr.
St. Augustine, Fla.

Early in 1980 I read *The Aviation Consumer's* Used Airplane Guide

on the Cardinal RG, and decided the aircraft had the performance and range I was looking for. Later that year I bought a 1973 model which had been operated by a flying club in Wisconsin. I selected this particular craft, which had about 2,300 hours on the airframe, because someone had the good sense to install a complete Collins Microline avionics package. This has proven to be a reliable set of equipment during many hours of IFR cross-country flying.

After purchasing the airplane, I gave it new paint, new interior and a zero-time engine and prop. Also, I replaced the horrible plastic instrument panel cover and glove box door with a hardwood panel. The cheap plastic panel does make a good template for laying out its replacement.

The airplane pretty much meets book speeds and delivers 165 mph cruise at 70 percent power. I always plan nine gph from takeoff to touchdown. Sixty gallons works out to six and a half hours of fuel on board. I was surprised that with two on board, it is relatively easy to get to 14,000 feet if you just increase the rpm to 2700 during the climb after leaving 8,000 feet. The book permits this power setting from sea level.

There seems to be a lot of additional power in the last 200 rpm, which is also nice when the bird

starts to collect a little ice. It sees a lot of IFR and is a good IFR aircraft.

On two occasions, the gear down-and-locked indicator would not illuminate without a few cycles of the landing gear. After spending hundreds of dollars at repair stations where they found nothing, I was looking at the connections to the microswitches in the end of the main gear struts during an annual, and found the inline connectors to be loose on the wires. After five minutes with a soldering iron, there have been no more gear indicator problems. I suggest examining these little connectors whenever you have a chance.

I've spent some time trying to reduce the noise level in the airplane even though it is fairly quiet for a single-engine machine. I found that some thin cork with adhesive backing made by Sound Coat of Santa Ana, Calif. applied on top of the glareshield running to the windshield was more effective than other sound absorbent material on the floor or in the ceiling panels, etc.

I had a Walker Engineering Air/Oil Separator added to the engine breather, and this has helped tremendously in keeping the bottom of the airplane clean.

Maintenance on the airplane is not too far out of line. The aircraft has settled into about an $800 annual, with no big surprises during the year except maybe an alternator—due, I feel, to the vibration of the IO-360. Small inspections throughout the year and a hangar have done a lot to keep maintenance costs down.

I was considering moving to a T210 for more speed and the ability to climb up through the clouds here in western Oregon, but the Cardinal RG is much more economical, very comfortable, and has been pretty darn reliable—in five years only two delayed trips—so I plan to keep it for some time.

John Desmond
Vice-president, Engineering
Flight Dynamics, Inc.
Hillsboro, Ore.

Mooney M20

Mooney's M20 series is one of the most enduring elderly aircraft on the used-plane market. More than 4,000 M20s were built between 1955 and 1977, and they are beloved by their owners for their speed and efficiency, if not cabin room. (This article will discuss only the M20s built until 1977, when the M20J and M20K versions—popularly known as the 201 and 231—were introduced.)

History

The M20's history is a complex one, and only fanatical Mooney buffs seem to know all the changes of nomenclature and corporate parentage. We will refer mainly to the type certificate nomenclature (M20A, M20B, etc.) rather than the various labels affixed by succeeding marketing departments.

The first M20 appeared in 1955. It had a 150-hp Lycoming engine and wooden wing and tail, a throwback to the M18 Mite, the all-wood single-placer from which the M20 was derived. In 1958, the M20A was introduced with a 180-hp Lycoming.

The first all-metal Mooney was the 1961 M20B, called the Mark 21. It retained the popular 180-hp engine. The next year, in 1962, gross weight was raised from 2,450 pounds to 2,575, and the designation changed to M20C. The M20C also had electric flaps (M20B's were manual) with 11 degrees more travel, and it had more rudder power. This general configuration (known variously as the Mark 21 and Ranger) was continued until the late 1970s. It is the most economical of the four basic Mooney models.

In 1964, Mooney added a souped-up 200-hp version called the M20E.

It lasted until 1975, and was known as the Super 21 or Chaparral. It is the fastest of the pre-201 Mooneys.

In 1967, Mooney bowed to the wishes of the marketplace and offered a version with a 10-inch stretch in the cabin. This, at last, turned the Mooney into a true four-place airplane. This long-cabin fuselage was offered with the 200-hp engine (M20F Executive) in 1967, and with the 180-hp engine (M20G Statesman) in 1968. The M20G lasted only three years, but the M20F was an immediate hit, selling more than 500 the first year and prompting Mooney to drop the Super 21 for 1968. (It returned as the Chaparral in 1969.) It survived until 1977, providing the starting point for the aerodynamically refined M20J—the current production 201.

Mooney also made a little-known fixed-gear model, the M20D Master, in 1963 and 1964. It was simply a fixed-gear version of the 180-hp M20C. Nearly all Masters have been converted to retractable gear, however. The economic argument is compelling; a Master is worth about $13,000, and it costs about $3,000 to convert it to retractable gear. The result, virtually an M20C, is worth about $18,000. Now you know why there are so few original Masters. In any case, if you are shopping for a 1963-64 so-called Mark 21, check the serial

The Executive has a longer cabin and an extra window. This is a 1975 model built by Republic, and today worth about $26,000.

number plate to assure that it is not in fact a converted Master.

Adding to the confusion of all the model changes were several changes of ownership. The original Mooney Aircraft Corp. was eventually taken over by Butler Aviation in 1969—just in time for a big recession that severely depressed aircraft sales. Butler didn't help itself much; among other things, it attempted to jazz up the Mooney's looks by grafting a bizarre-looking appendage to the top of the tail. This triggered widespread derision and immediately became known as the "Butler buttonhook." Few, if any, survive. After selling less than 50 planes in 1971, Butler folded its tent, and it wasn't until three years later that Republic Steel came to the rescue and bought the line. Production resumed in 1974, setting the stage for the introduction of the 201 in 1977 and the company's ascent to the dominance of the four-place retractable market that it holds today. Then, in 1984, the firm was purchased by a partnership led by, Alexandre Couvelaire, head of Euralair of Paris, along with Armand Rivard, president of Lake Aircraft. Production of the Mooneys continues at Kerrville.

Best and Worst

Mooney connoisseurs tell us the best Mooneys ever built were the 1966-67 models. These had most of the airplane's desirable features—the square windows, flush-riveted wing, retractable step, optional manual landing gear (preferred for its simplicity by many Mooney nuts), good corrosion-proofing and the "wide-deck" engines. "The 1966 E models seem to have the smoothest wings I ever saw," comments long-time Mooney mechanic Charlie Dugosh. The long-cabin Executive also became available for the first time in 1967.

Around 1968, the company started running into financial problems, partly due to the disastrous M-22 Mustang program, and partly due to some financial chicanery that eventually landed the company president and secretary/treasurer in prison for 13 counts of fraud. The company was sold to American Electronics Laboratory in 1968, and to Butler Aviation a year later. Both companies naturally tried to cut down on expenses, and the 1968-1971 Mooneys showed signs of economizing: fixed steps, round-head rivets on the under side of the wing leading edge, exposed inspection plates, reduced corrosion-proofing, etc. As a result, Butler-built Mooneys were consistently two to four knots slower than the earlier models. And reliable sources tell us that some Butler-built airplanes had improperly shaped wing curvature, due to lack of attention to detail in the jigging/building process. This had no structural effect, but could disrupt laminar airflow and increase drag noticeably. Mooney modifier Coy Jacob says he's seen one Butler-built airplane that flew 13 knots slower than an otherwise identical earlier model. If you're considering a 1968-1971 model, flight test it carefully to make sure performance is up to snuff.

Beware of Wood

If the 1966-67 models were the cream of the crop, the dregs were certainly the early wooden Mooneys. We can sum up our view on the wooden-tailed airplanes very succinctly: don't buy one. One Mooney expert we consulted took a slightly softer position: "Well, I suppose if you wanted a unique-looking flower planter for your front yard, it would be all right."

The M20 and M20A have the worst record of in-flight breakups of any airplane, almost entirely the result of failures of the wing and tail. A prohibitively expensive AD requires a pull-test of the vertical fin every six months, at a cost of $500 or more. (To put that cost in perspective, the whole airplane is only worth about $9,000.)

Some mechanics doubt the AD's effectiveness. Mooney guru Charles Dugosh says, "I won't do the pull test. You could break a glue joint without even knowing it, and later you'd have a catastrophe. I won't do any work at all on a wood-tail airplane. I don't want my signature anywhere in the logbook."

As a result of the AD, most M20s and M20As have been retrofitted with metal tails, at a cost of about $5,000. This still leaves the question of wooden wings, however. The wood-wingers are the cheapest of the old Mooneys, and very likely have been left outside in the weather by an owner who couldn't afford hangar rent. An AD on the wooden wing requires a yearly inspection (about five hours of labor). Dugosh believes that a *properly inspected* wooden wing will not fail prematurely. But finding a mechanic who's intimately familiar with wooden Mooney wings and knows where to look for the tell-tale signs of wood rot could be a problem. We'd advise buying a wood-wing Mooney only with extreme caution, and only if it passes the careful scrutiny of a mechanic with long experience looking at wooden Mooney wings.

Appraisal Points

• Windows: Curved side windows are the hallmark of a truly elderly Mooney. In 1965, they were replaced by square ones. That was fine for the rear seat passengers, who got more visibility to help cure the claustrophobia of the rear seats, but the pilot's visibility actually declined out both the side front window and the windshield. Nevertheless, the square windows are the most obvious way to tell very old Mooneys from merely old ones.

• Landing Gear: Early Mooneys had manually operated landing gear. Electric gear became available in 1966, and standard in 1969. Surprisingly, most owners of manual-gear Mooneys seem to prefer them that way. "I love the simplicity and reliability of the manual gear," one Super 21 owner wrote. Maintenance and inspection costs on the gear should also be less. A manual-to-electric conversion kit is available, but not many are sold. According to one Mooney dealer we talked to, the manual-gear airplanes sell for just as much—if not more—than comparable electric-gear airplanes. Nevertheless, the

Performance/Specifications

Model	Gross Weight (lbs)	Cruise Speed (kts)*	Fuel (gals)	Engine	TBO** (hrs)	Overhaul Cost
M20	2,450	143	35/52	150-hp Lyc. O-320	2,000	$8,000
M20A	2,450	157	35/52	180-hp Lyc. O-360-A1A	2,000	$9,000
M20B	2,450	158	52	180-hp Lyc. O-360-A1A	2,000	$9,000
M20C	2,575	143-158	52	180-hp Lyc. O-360-A1D	2,000	$9,000
M20E	2,575	160-163	52	200-hp Lyc. O-360-A1A	1,800	$11,000
M20F	2,740	156	64	200-hp Lyc. IO-360-A1A	1,800	$11,000

Book cruise speeds are considered optimistic in early models.
** *TBO assumes half-inch valves in 180-hp engines (1,200 hours if not); and large dowel pins and updated camshaft in 200-hp engines (1,200 and 1,400 hours if not).*

manual gear does take a hefty heave, and is not recommended for small or weak pilots. "It's a barrel of laughs to watch even a contortionist try to raise the gear the first few times," one owner writes. "A veteran manual-gear Mooney pilot could probably scratch his right elbow with his deformed and scarred right hand."

• Instrument Panel: Through 1968, Mooney panels were awful, from 1969-71 merely mediocre; and from 1975-77, pretty good. Several companies refit instrument panels, however, and many older aircraft have improved panels. Try to find one.

• Engine: Early 180-hp Mooneys used the O-360-A1A; in 1962, the switch was made to the -A1D version, which had the "shower of sparks" magneto. Until about 1965, that engine had a 1,200-hour TBO, but larger valves extended TBO to 2,000 hours. Make sure the engine has been updated with the larger half-inch valves.

The 200-hp engine has been the IO-360-A1A since the beginning, but early versions proved troublesome. Check that any M20E or -F considered for purchase has been overhauled with improved connecting rods (Service Bulletin 439) and large main bearing dowel pins (S.B. 326). Lycoming also recommends that the camshafts in early IO-360s be replaced (Service Instruction 1263), but one big overhaul shop told us they've seen no difference in service life between the two camshafts. The updated part, however, does allow a 200-hour TBO extension.

Generally speaking, the 180-hp Lycoming engine is one of the two or three most reliable aircraft engines currently in production. The IO-360, although uprated somewhat, also has a pretty good record, assuming that the aforementioned updates have been made.

• PC: A unique feature called Positive control (or PC) was standard on Mooneys for a while in the 1960s. PC was simply a full-time wing-leveler autopilot linked to the electric turn coordinator. A button on the yoke allowed it to be disengaged for maneuvering. But unless the button is depressed, the airplane will fly more or less straight with its wings level.

Theoretically, this is a fine safety feature, and may well play a role in the Mooney's extraordinarily low rate of in-flight airframe failure. (Most breakups are triggered by the pilot's losing control of the aircraft and diving into a high-speed spiral.) But some Mooney pilots dislike PC intensely, and go to great lengths to defeat it. (A rubber band to hold down the button is a popular ploy.) Our advice: stifle your macho pilot tendencies and look for an airplane with PC installed and operating.

Performance

Here is the big selling point of the old M20 line. The hot performer of the group is the 200-hp short-cabin M20E, whose owners report cruise speeds of around 140-150 knots on a fuel burn of about 10 gph. The 180-hp M20Cs are generally about four to nine knots slower, as are the long-cabin M20F and M20G.

Several owners commented that the 180-hp Mooneys are underpowered near gross weight. "It doesn't exactly snap your neck on takeoff," comments one owner. Perhaps recognizing this, Mooney lowered the gross weight of the 180-hp long-cabin M20G by 50 pounds, perhaps assuming that since there was finally room to put a couple of big people back there, overloading would be more likely.

Listed climb rate ranges from a rather mediocre 800 fpm for some M20C models to 1,125 for the M20E. Book cruise speeds range from 143 to 163 knots, but these are hopelessly optimistic. We're told that in those days Mooney fudged its speed figures by measuring them at very light weights. Airspeed calibration was also questionable.

Mooney owners prize the airplane's efficiency, with fuel burns of only about 8-9 gph for the 180-hp models and 9-10 gph for the 200-hp versions. Fuel capacity is 52 gallons in most models. (Exceptions are the M20 and M20A, which had 35 gallons standard and 52 optional, and the M20F Executive, which carries 64 gallons.) The M20C with full tanks is good for about five hours cruising with a small reserve, or about 750 miles. The 200-hp Mooneys can fly about the same distance in a little less time.

Safety

The M20 has a good—but not excellent—safety record. According to an *Aviation Consumer* study covering the years 1972-76, the Mooney ranked fifth among the 13 most popular single-engine retractables. Its fatal accident rate was 2.4 per 100,000 flight hours. (The range among the other 12 aircraft was 1.0 to 4.2.) Total accident rate was 11.3, in a range of 4.6 to 16.8.

According to an NTSB report covering the same period, the M20 ranked about average in engine failures, overshoots and undershoots, and good or excellent in stalls, in-flight airframe failures, ground loops and hard landings. In no category listed by the NTSB did the Mooney rank poorly.

For owners concerned about airframe integrity, the Mooney is virtually in a class by itself. We're aware of only two fatal in-flight airframe failures in the past two decades. Legend has it that Republic Steel, before it bought the line in the early 1970s, decided to test a wing to destruction just to see how strong it was. What they ended up doing was testing the test rig to destruction; the hydraulic jacks finally broke at 11 Gs, with the wing doing just fine. The fuselage is also practically bulletproof; a steel roll cage surrounds the cabin, in addition to the normal aluminum airframe. Such quaint conservatism of design would be considered too expensive and heavy these days, but we don't hear too many Mooney owners complaining.

The Mooney's great structural strength is no surprise; one of the structural designers who converted the original wooden Mooney to the all-metal configuration was Ralph Harmon. (Harmon was also president of the company for a time.) Harmon had also played a major role in the structural design of the Beech V-tail Bonanza, whose old models have the highest fatal in-flight break-up rate of any metal airplane, and none come under fire for alleged structural shortcomings in the wings (early 1947-48 models) and tail. Apparently Harmon learned his lesson, and an "overbuilt" Mooney is the result.

Creature Comforts

In a word, they're lousy. Only the M20F Executive and M20G Statesman are what we'd call real four-adult airplanes—and large folks might even argue with that. The short cabin airplanes (M20, M20A, M20B, M20C, M20E) are horribly cramped in back. "The plane is excellent for one or two people, but when long-legged front occupants slide the seats all the way back, it gives the impression the rear seats were designed for double amputees," comments one Ranger owner. Cabin noise is very high, as it is in virtually any old plane. (Or new one, for that matter.) Wear your E-A-R plugs.

Handling Qualities

While generally a decent-flying machine, the Mooneys do have some odd qualities. Pilots generally describe the aileron controls as stiff (perhaps the result of the pushrod linkage). Response is quick, however, despite the high forces. The airplane is reasonably stable and makes a decent instrument ship, particularly with the PC feature. Without the PC, though, "You really gotta fly it IFR," reports one owner.

The long-body M20F Executive and M20G Statesman should theoretically be more stable because of their extra length. (If the tail is moved farther away from the wing, stability generally improves.) Stall characteristics can be abrupt, and you certainly wouldn't want to spin one, either accidentally or on purpose. Compared to an Arrow, Skylane or Cardinal, a Mooney is not a good staller.

Landings can be tricky if the pilot doesn't use the right technique. (This is complicated by the rather mediocre flaps, which make steep approaches impossible.) Owners tell us that 65 knots is about the right approach speed, never any faster than 70. At light weights, even 60 knots leaves plenty of energy for the flare. Some pilots pop the flaps up during the flare, but this is unnecessary if approach speed is on target.

Landing gear and flap extension speeds are very low, which limits the pilot's flexibility during descent, particularly with the manual gear. One owner reports it's virtually impossible to operate the manual gear much above 80 knots. Because of the Mooney's relatively clean airframe and high-aspect-ratio wing, rapid descents are difficult without overcooling the engine.

Crosswind capability is only fair. Very early models (M20, -A and -B) had more limited rudder travel and even less crosswind ability—only about 12 knots, according to one owner.

The Mooneys are rather awkward on the ground. "It takes about 40 acres to turn one around," comments one owner. Mooneys are also somewhat skittery on takeoff, although any competent pilot will adjust quickly.

Maintenance

The average mechanic will groan

Mooney cowling is a mechanic's—and an aerodynamicist's—nightmare.

when an old Mooney rolls into the hangar door for maintenance. The planes were not designed to be easy to work on. The cowling, for example, is attached with hundreds of screws; unfastening them all takes a lot of mechanic's time (and owner's money). Engine access is difficult because of the tight cowling, and working behind the instrument panel can be a nightmare.

Mooneys are not as common as Cessnas and Pipers, and the average mechanic may not be familiar with them. Advises one owner, "Find a good Mooney mechanic—otherwise, you'll be paying for a lot of on-the-job training." We echo that advice: the Mooney is one airplane that should not be taken to any old mechanic. If there's a Mooney specialist in your area, seek him out. In the case of a wooden M20 or M20A, our advice would be even stronger: Entrusting your airplane to a mechanic who doesn't have long years of experience with wooden Mooneys could be fatal.

The premier Mooney maintenance center in the country is Charles Dugosh Aviation in Kerrville, Tex. Dugosh has worked on Mooneys for decades, and is based right on the same airport as Mooney headquarters, and so has a very close working relationship with the factory. If the factory learns something about maintenance, it's likely that Dugosh will know it a day later.

We've also received good reports on Wittenbrook Flying Service, Barnsville, Ohio; Coast Aircraft in San Diego; Aero Venture, Robbinsville, N.J. and Wilmar Aviation, Wilmar, Minn. Mooney service centers in the Northeast are Conn Mooney, Danbury, Conn. and Weber Aircraft in Lancaster, Pa.

Service Problems

Letters from Mooney owners and FAA service difficulty reports highlight several areas of concern

Used Aircraft Guide

for the used-Mooney shopper. Among them:

• Leaky fuel tanks. The fuel sealant in the tanks of older Mooneys, designed for 91- and 100-octane fuel, apparently breaks down after long contact with 100LL fuel, which is high in aromatics. This has created a real problem for Mooney owners, many of whom have had to reseal their tanks. ("And those that haven't, will," comments one Mooney expert.) Any Mooney shopper should check very carefully for leaks. A reseal job can cost anywhere from $500 to $3,000, and it's difficult to do the job right.

• Dented or broken nose gear struts. The Mooney nose gear design allows very limited nose-wheel steering travel before something bends or breaks. Unfortunately, the nation's linemen don't seem to have gotten the message yet, and towing limits are routinely exceeded.

• Corroded fuselage tubes. Although not widespread, some cases of tube corrosion have been reported, primarily in the lower longerons. Replacement can be hideously expensive; one owner reports he spent over $6,000 replacing corroded tubes. Moral: check carefully before buying.

• Hartzell prop AD. This hated directive is not limited to Mooneys, of course, but is nevertheless a major expense. The AD requires a complete prop overhaul every four years. Initial date of the AD was 1977, and the first wave of repeat overhauls is already past, with the next one due in 1985 on many aircraft. Incidentally, the M20B model has a McCauley prop and is not subject to the AD.

Modifications

The "modifications" section of most of our used-plane reports merits only a paragraph or two, but the Mooney is different. M20 loyalists have developed a vast array of mechanical and cosmetic modifications that can turn virtually any old Mooney into a very good approximation of a 201. The mods include

This 1964 Super 21 sports the round windows that are the tipoff to the truly ancient Mooneys.

a bewildering array of fairings, seals, covers, windows, windshields, and cowlings that can boost speed by up to 17 knots and make the plane look virtually brand-new. You can drop $15,000 so fast it'll make your head spin.

There are two main purveyors of Mooney mods. Summa Sales, Inc., 4551 Commerce, High Ridge, Mo. 63049, 800-325-9445, offers a 201-style cowling ($7,200), a 201-style windshield ($2,097), 201-style instrument panel ($4,375), a speed fairing and gap seal kit ($1,975) and other smaller mods. Coy Jacobs, head of the self-proclaimed "Mooney Mod Squad" has a gorgeous 1967 M20E that is virtually indistinguishable from a new Mooney 201—and flies even faster, according to Jacobs. Reports we've received describe the workmanship on these mods as excellent.

Another modifier is Paul Loewen of Lake Aero Styling and Repair, Box 545, Lakeport, Calif. 95453, 707-263-0412. Lake likewise has a 201-style cowling and windshield, but no instrument panel. Lake also offers a dozen different aerodynamic mods that, in combination with the cowling and windshield, provide 201-like performance. The third firm offering Mooney mods is Miller Air Sports, San Marcos, Tex. 78666, 512-353-7422. Miller offers a 201-type cowling and a 201-style windshield. Summa- and Lake-modified 201s earned awards at the

national Mooney fly-in in 1981 and 1982.

McCauley Aviation, Pine Bluff, Ark., sells a speed fairing kit and chrome brake discs.

Owner Club

The Mooney Aircraft Pilots' Association is one of the best of the owner group/fan clubs. They publish a monthly (rather primitive) newsletter, hold regional and annual conventions, and, most importantly, can provide sound advice on service problems. Any owner should know as much as possible about his airplane; even if you disdain the rah-rah Mooney boosterism and down-home good fellowship, we'd recommend joining the MAPA simply for its pool of knowledge about maintenance problems. Mooney Aircraft Pilots Association, 314 Stardust Dr., San Antonio, Tex. 78228; 512-434-5959.

Owner Comments

In deciding to purchase our 1965 "C" model Mooney, I rejected all earlier models because they used machine screws rather than quick-release Dzus fasteners to attach the cowling and they had "old-style" windows. I also liked the smaller cooling-air inlet used in 1965 compared with the later models. The '65-'67 models also have superior flush riveting and fasteners, a vacuum-retract step, cowl flaps, and smooth elevator and rudder skins. The manual gear and hydraulic flaps are elegantly simple.

The older short-fuselage Mooneys respond beautifully to the same aerodynamic clean-up and attention to detail that the 210s and 231s received. Modifications to N1PF include Mooney 201 flap gap fairings, flap hinge fairings, horizontal stabilizer root fairing, and a plexiglass landing light fairing that were installed in accordance with John Porter's STC. Aileron lower gap seals, brake rotation, a 231 style dorsal fin, and hinge covers for the rudder and elevator were also installed in accordance with Paul Lowen's STC. Other modifications included cleaning up the antennas, removing the belly strobe and replacing it with wing-tip strobes, removing the OAT gauge, installing a 201 tail skid, and re-rigging the flaps and ailerons. These modifications netted a speed increase of at least 10 knots.

As much as I like our Mooney, I do curse some during maintenance procedures such as replacing a starter motor, resealing fuel tanks, adjusting the trim stops on the horizontal stabilizer, or removing the hundreds of screws that fasten access panels. Lubricated stainless steel screws help somewhat, but a power assisted screwdriver is essential.

Expert advice regarding Mooney maintenance is readily available. At the Mooney factory, Ed Penney is very knowledgeable and helpful. Mooney Service Centers such as Charlie Dugosh, on the Kerrville airport, and Paul Lowen's "Lake Aero Styling and Repair," at Lakeport, Calif., are outstanding.

Many Mooney fuel tanks do leak avgas. I attribute this problem primarily to 100LL avgas and I avoid it like the plague. Our right wing tank leaked like a sieve when we bought our plane. I resealed it several years ago using the methods and materials specified in the Mooney maintenance manual and it has sealed perfectly since then. Resealing the fuel tanks is not particularly difficult but it is very tedious and time consuming. I found it too depressing to keep

track of the time I spent, but it was about 100 hours for one wing. There is no substitute for removing *all* the old sealant. This means physically scraping around all rivets and fasteners. Solvents, such as MEK, are not useful, and they could cause problems later if they seep into the cracks and attack the new sealant from the underside. My main sustaining thought while resealing the tank was that the only thing worse than resealing it the first time would be redoing the job if it were not done properly.

One of my highest priority maintenance items is periodically checking and adjusting the preload that holds the landing gear linkage in its "over-center" position that maintains the landing gear in the down-and-locked position. The Service and Maintenance Manual (section S.F. 2&3) and Service Bulletin M20-35A describe how to measure and adjust the preload.

Our records show that we have spent $5,942.60 maintaining our aircraft during the last 602.7 hours of flight for a cost of $9.86/hr.

Pilots of carbureted Mooneys should pay careful attention to Mooney's Service Bulletin M20-64 and Service Instruction M20-14. They detail inspection and maintenance procedures for the carburetor heat box. We had owned our airplane less than one

year when our butterfly broke loose and blocked the carburetor air inlet. The engine was running at cruise power and sucked up the loose valve, and it blocked the air inlet. The engine would lose about 500 rpm before the valve would drop, and the cycle would repeat.

The ground-handling qualities of the aircraft are definitely inferior to the flight-handling qualities. The neoprene rubber discs that Mooney uses to absorb the shock of normal taxiing and landing are undamped and require some pilot adaptation. The turning radius of a Mooney is large. Mooney pilots seem to accept the inferior ground handling qualities presumably because of the many good features of the airplane.

I would particularly recommend pre-201 Mooneys to pilots who are both mechanically inclined and who value the speed and efficiency benefits enough to outweigh the annoyance of maintaining items inside the compact airframe.

Maurice McEvoy
Berkeley, Calif.

Our Statesman Flying Club has operated a 1968 Mooney M20G Statesman for five years and finds it the ideal aircraft for our use. It travels at 140 knots and burns 8.3 gph, the perfect combination for economical trips or training and

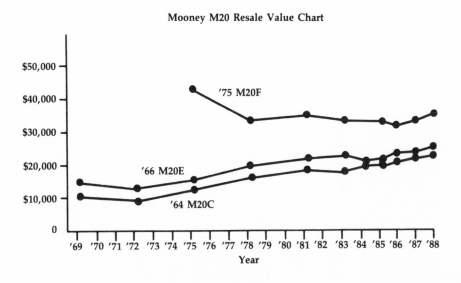

Mooney M20 Resale Value Chart

practice. What's more, it has the long body (10 inches more in the rear seat than the C&E models), the supremely reliable carbureted O-360 engine, the ease and assurance of the "PC" wing leveler and, best of all, the failure-proof manual gear. It is exquisitely designed and crafted, although mechanics often curse the cramped engine compartment.

Our plane flies 300 hours per year and has cost 8, 6, 9, 7, and 10 dollars per hour for maintenance in each of the respective years we've run it, for an average of $8 per hour. This includes minimal avionics repair (about $0.75 per hour) as well as semi-annual inspections. The inspection labor runs about $400 and the associated repairs typically lift the cost to $800. Thus, the other $800 per year in maintenance is unscheduled. The engine was overhauled last spring by Lycon in Mesa, Ariz. for less than $5,000 using Superior parts and has performed admirably in its first 75 hours, using one quart of oil each 12 hours after ring seating on the chrome cylinders.

Periodically we think of replacement, but there is no competition. The Tiger is extinct, the Arrow is not as efficient, the Archer slow and the Cessna RGs lack quality. Even the Mooney 201 is not as economical as our '68, and it only completes a one-bladder trip a half-hour quicker. I only hope our Statesman can fly on as long as there's avgas.

R.B. Sherwood
Torrance, Calif.

I have owned a 1965 Mooney M20C for the past three years. It is a

Tubular construction is used in the front half of the Mooneys, semi-monocoque in the rear. Check for corrosion in the lower longerons.

strong, comfortable IFR airplane that turns out 145 knots TAS at nine gallons an hour and gives a nominal range of 550 nm with IFR reserves. The useful load with full fuel (52 gallons) is 682 pounds, even though it is well equipped for IFR.

For a 180-hp airplane, the Mooney M20C exceeds or matches the real-world performance of all the current 200-hp retractables except for the Mooney 201. I chose it, in large part, based on articles in *The Aviation Consumer* over the years and because of the Lycoming O-360-A1D engine, which is well characterized as very reliable.

My first annual cost $982 plus two days of my own work. However, this included several overdue repairs: new main gear shock discs, air box rebuild, brake pads, new tail pivot bolts, oil return line, strobe toggle switch and shimmy dampener rebuild.

The next two annuals averaged $283 plus two days of my own labor. I have managed to keep the inspection costs in line by promptly correcting problems as they arise. Fortunately I have an A&P friend who has been willing to supervise and sign off my work when it has been within my own capabilities.

The manual gear is great. A little learning is required, but once mastered it seems very natural. At the annual inspection it is neces-

Cost Comparison

Model	Year	Average Number Built	Retail Price*
M20	1955-58	200	$10,500**
M20A	1958-60	500	$13,250**
M20B	1961	222	$18,000
M20C	1962	336	$19,000
(Mark 21,	1963	328	$20,000
Ranger)	1964	183	$21,000
	1965	379	$22,000
	1966	280	$23,000
	1967	147	$24,000
	1968	196	$25,000
	1969	97	$26,000
	1970	88	$27,000
	1971	9	$28,000
	1974	37	$30,000
	1975	39	$31,000
	1976	33	$33,000
	1977	25	$35,000
	1978	15	$37,500
M20E	1964	368	$22,000
(Super 21,	1965	361	$23,000
Chaparral)	1966	474	$24,000
	1967	62	$25,000
	1969	73	$27,000
	1970	54	$28,000
	1971	23	$29,000
	1974	36	$31,000
	1975	19	$32,500
M20F	1967	539	$26,000
(Executive)	1968	206	$27,000
	1969	92	$28,000
	1970	72	$29,000
	1971	12	$30,000
	1974	65	$32,500
	1975	126	$34,500
	1976	126	$36,500
	1977	6	$38,500
M20G	1968	164	$26,000
(Statesman)	1969	20	$26,500
	1970	6	$27,500

* Price assumes dual navcom, VOR, glide slope, marker beacon, transponder, ADF single-axis autopilot, mid-time engine, good paint and interior, no damage history. Subtract 15-20 percent for wholesale prices.
** Price assumes aircraft has been converted to metal tail.

sary to check the over-center gear lock torque during the retract test. This requires only a few minutes.

The scheduled maintenance works out to $516 per year and unscheduled to $491 per year. Total maintenance works out to $12.58 per hour, not counting avionics.

Tim Jensen
Minneapolis, Minn.

Cessna Skylane RG

The Skylane RG has won favor in the used-plane market as an economy retractable that is strong on room, load and comfort and quite a bit less expensive than the bellwether Mooney 201. It is, however, nagged by mechanical and airframe shortcomings that warrant close inspection.

Most prominent of these is the landing gear system, which, judging from the FAA's Service Difficulty Reports, carries on a long Cessna tradition of retractable-gear bedevilment manifested in both its singles and twins. Prospective buyers should also be on the lookout for airframe quality control shortcomings like leaking windshields and doors.

Despite a sizable proportion of prangs due to gear problems, the airplane has an excellent safety record compared to other aircraft in its class when it comes to fatal accidents.

History

The aircraft has undergone no major changes over the years since it was introduced in 1978. But there have been lots of little ones that are significant in correcting a myriad of glitches. Buyers should make a close check of service bulletins that were complied with, or ignored, on this airplane—especially those concerning the various components of the landing gear system.

The biggest changes to the line occurred in 1979 when the bladder tanks (and all their well-known problems) were dropped in favor of integral fuel tanks of larger capacity. Also, that year the turbo model was brought out.

Among the smaller changes made through the years were—in 1980—a new door latch and pin system designed to help seal the doors better, an electric fan for the avionics, to help cool the radios while taxiing, and redesigned wing root ventilators. (Some owners of '79 models complained that these would simply pop open during high-speed flight.)

In 1981, the Skylane RGs got improved battery access along with a new muffler for better heating (rear-seat passengers complain about cold feet in '79 models) and an improved fuel selector valve with more positive detents. (At least one fatal crash was reported where the pilot had the selector positioned between tanks.)

In 1983, the extension speed for the first 20-degrees of flaps was raised from 95 knots to 120 knots, as an aid to slowing down the aircraft. A low-vacuum warning light was offered, as an electric six-cylinder primer system replacing the manual one for easier starting. Also, the landing gear "up" indicator light was replaced with a red "gear unsafe" light. This goes on whenever power goes to the gear pump motor, or when the gear is in transit.

Struts and all, the RG clips along at 155 knots or better. Light weights give disproportionate speed advantage.

In addition, the nose gear doors were redesigned so the door skins overlapped the lower cowl skin, eliminating butt joints. Service Difficulty Reports show three instances where the nose gear doors interfered with proper operation of the gear. Thankfully, the main gear has been spared door problems—because it has no doors.

In 1984, the Skylane RGs received new "improved" composite fuel caps, and rear-seat shoulder harnesses were made standard equipment instead of options. (The SDRs suggest that leaking fuel caps have been a problem with the R182s.) Also, the copilot got a standard control wheel and rudder pedals, so these would not have to be purchased as extra-cost options.

Performance

Since the Skylane RG is most often compared with the Mooney 201, it should be noted up front that although the Mooney can be expected to beat out the Cessna in a flat-out, full-power heat at altitude it won't do so by an embarrassing margin. In fact, when the Cessna climb all the way to 20 grand with full power and could pull 750 fpm nicely on a cruise climb. Said another, "I have climbed through 14,000 feet with an inch of ice at 900 fpm, and I'm here to tell you this is the true value of a strong turbocharged engine."

Range of the Cessna is nothing to sneeze at, either. With 81 gallons usable on '79 and later models, that's enough fuel for six hours of flying at high cruise speeds.

Handling

The aircraft is typical Cessna—i.e., heavy on the pitch controls, especially in the landing flare, but stable as a rock in cruise. Said one owner: "Once trimmed, it will stay put. I don't feel a real need for altitude hold on autopilot, even in hard IFR." Said another, "I lift weights for a hobby, but still had trouble holding full aft control wheel in a full stall." But he added that as an aerobatic pilot he felt he had completely explored all its flight characteristics and found them to be "fault-free." Nevertheless, the big, effective flaps do create pitch changes that require retrimming.

One flier summed it up: "It makes no unusual demands on pilot

Stacked up against the Mooney 201, the RG falls short by a few knots in a race at altitude, despite its extra 35 horses. But in airport performance, it outshines the low-winger.

182RG is lightly loaded, it will give away only maybe three to four knots to the low winger.

Big loads, on the other hand, seem to have a more significant retardant effect on the Cessna than with other aircraft. One owner plotted the phenomenon as giving the Skylane RG a boost of two knots for every 100 pounds it was below gross weight.

The Cessna by no means is completely overshadowed by the Mooney 201. In a side-by-side flyoff by *The Aviation Consumer* between the two aircraft (when both had two aboard and about three-quarters fuel) the Cessna showed itself to have the better climb rate and to be much more adept at getting into and out of airports than the Mooney. On top of that it showed off much more agile ground handling.

Owners of the nonturboed R182s talk about getting a healthy 150 to 160 knots at top cruise (75 percent power), burning 12 to 14 gph. Turbo owners report getting 160 to 165 knots at 9,000 to 13,000 feet with about the same fuel burn. One turbo owner reported getting 178 knots on 66 percent power at 19,000 feet with light weights.

With its 235 hp, the RG also climbs well. Full power is available on the turbo all the way to 20,000 feet. One turbo pilot said he got a 1,000-fpm

Cost/Performance/Specifications

Model	Year	Number Built	Average Retail Price	Cruise Speed (kts)	Useful Load (lbs)	Fuel Std/Opt (gals)	Engine	TBO (hrs)	Overhaul Cost
R182	1978	583	$45,000	157	1,200	56/75	235-hp Lyc. O-540-J3C5D	2,000	$11,300
R182	1979	729	$49,000	157	1,200	88	235-hp Lyc. O-540-J3C5D	2,000	$11,300
TR182 (turbo)	1979		$53,000	173	1,150	88	235-hp Lyc. O-540-L3C5D	2,000	$11,500
R182	1980	314	$55,000	157	1,200	88	235-hp Lyc. O-540-J3C5D	2,000	$11,300
TR182 (turbo)	1980		$60,000	173	1,150	88	235-hp Lyc. O-540-L3C5D	2,000	$11,500
R182	1981	169	$62,000	157	1,200	88	235-hp Lyc. O-540-J3C5D	2,000	$11,300
TR182 (turbo)	1981		$68,000	173	1,150	88	235-hp Lyc. O-540-L3C5D	2,000	$11,500
R182	1982	129	$74,000	157	1,200	88	235-hp Lyc. O-540-J3C5D	2,000	$11,300
TR182 (turbo)	1982		$79,000	173	1,150	88	235-hp Lyc. O-540-L3C5D	2,000	$11,500
R182	1983	44	$86,500	157	1,200	88	235-hp Lyc. O-540-J3C5D	2,000	$11,300
TR182 (turbo)	1983		$92,000	173	1,150	88	235-hp Lyc. O-540-L3C5D	2,000	$11,500
R182	1984	25	$98,000	157	1,200	88	235-hp Lyc. O-540-J3C5D	2,000	$11,300
TR182 (turbo)	1984		$108,500	173	1,150	88	235-hp Lyc. O-540-L3C5D	2,000	$11,500
R182	1985	NA	$110,000	157	1,200	88	235-hp Lyc. O-540-J3C5D	2,000	$11,300
TR182 (turbo)	1985		$120,000	173	1,150	88	235-hp Lyc. O-540-L3C5D	2,000	$11,500

Fail-prone instrument panel eyebrow lights are a constant source of frustration for some RG owners.

ability. It is a very safe, forgiving and rugged aircraft.''

Cabin Load and Comfort

Skylane RG pilots rave about the ability of the aircraft to haul people and baggage—in spades. And they love the roominess. One six-foot-four pilot whose wife is six-two said, ''We are able to stretch out and be comfortable even with four people in the plane. Even the A36 Bonanza cannot match the Skylane in interior comfort on a long trip, in my opinion.'' They talk about a loading envelope that would be hard to exceed and mention useful loads with IFR-equipment of over 1,100 pounds.

On top of that, the double doors allow easy entry for front and rear seats, and headroom is good both front and rear.

The handicaps on the RG, on the other hand, are a loud cabin din, occasional leaky doors and

windows, cold rear seats and, as we mentioned before, wing root air vents that sometimes pop out at higher speeds and provide unwanted air conditioning. Some RG pilots also complained of uncomfortable engine vibration at cruise.

Safety Record

During the first five years of production, the Skylane RG logged a marvelous safety profile compared with other single-engine retractables in its class—when it comes to fatal accidents. When stacked up with 17 other aircraft, the RG came out best by far, eclipsing even that longtime safety star, the Beech 33. The one fly in the statistical ointment, however, is that the Skylane RG has not flown enough hours to compare with others of the group like the Piper Arrow or Bonanza.

And in the last few years fatalities have been chipping away at the RG's clean record. We tallied 23 fatal accidents through 1985. But most of these resulted from factors that couldn't be blamed on aircraft

shortcomings. Nine were weather related and three stemmed from medical problems—hear attack, stroke, alcohol. Another two were blamed on buzzing, and details from three others were still missing. Equipment failure apparently caused another fatal crash after the pilot departed IFR with a defective gyro horizon and later lost control on a missed approach. And we mentioned above the accident involving the fuel selector.

The total accident record of the Skylane RG is not, however, so golden. The Beech 33 comes out ahead in this category. Our survey of accident causes shows that landing gear problems were major factors in the greatest proportion of nonfatal RG accidents. We counted 21 of these from 1978 through 1985.

The greatest number involved the failure of the gear to extend, or a collapse on landing or takeoff. On only a small portion of these was the pilot blamed for inadvertently retracting it during touch-and-goes. And, interestingly enough, we noted no instances where the pilot simply forgot to extend the gear on landing.

Next largest nonfatal accident category for the RGs involved hard landings. We tallied 15 of these. The typical scenario involved a bounce, damaging the prop and possibly running off the side of the runway. On almost half of these the nosegear eventually collapsed.

Third biggest category was engine problems—we counted a dozen. Over half the stoppages occurred after takeoff. Three were blamed on magneto problems—the cam screw coming loose—and an Airworthiness Directive was issued to address the matter. Three others were related to internal malfunctions, one to water ingestion, and another quit after changing tanks on letdown. It's worth noting that none of the engine failures resulted in a fatal accident in the RG.

The RG cabin is a strong suit for roominess and comfort, if not for the at times leaking doors and windows. The baggage compartment gear door hump is at the rear of the cabin.

The next largest accident category involved fuel exhaustion—eight cases were noted. In a couple of cases fuel had siphoned out because of "unsecured" fuel caps.

Maintenance Considerations

The Skylane RGs are plagued with a sizable number of problems that merit buyer attention. Here's a list gathered from owner reports and FAA Service Difficulty Reports:

• Landing gear malfunctions. The litany of problems with the gear chronicled by the SDRs almost defies description. It's actually difficult to isolate any one or several main causes. Whereas most SDR problems usually can be tallied in singles or maybe tens, we counted over nine pages full of gear-related problems—with about a dozen cases on each page. Consider that maybe only a tenth of the cases in the field even get reported to the FAA, and you have some idea of the apparent magnitude of the Skylane RG gear problem over the years.

Some examples: main landing gear actuator bolts loose, broken or

sheared; chafed hydraulic line completely failed, pilot unable to lower gear and lock; rudder cable rubbed hole thru emergency hand pump gear down line; control cable to carb heat rubbed thru hydraulic line to power pack; nose landing gear actuator hose ruptured in flight; downlock actuator leaking, found piston rod assy. scored; relay became intermittent, causing landing gear to fail to operate either up or down; landing gear failed to extend due to screw missing from gear motor circuit breaker; hydraulic hose on nose landing gear actuator has a tendency to kink in the crease and stop the flow of fluid; solenoid struck closed, causing hydraulic pump to run continuously until circuit breaker popped; nose landing gear door grabbing on fuselage skin when it tried to open, etc. etc., *ad nauseam*.

• Shimmy dampeners. Problems were legion, involving broken clamp pins, broken attach bolts, worn bellcrank bolts, cracked barrels, etc. At least one Cessna Service Bulletin (80-67) was aimed at correcting the problem with a modification kit. Two pilots, however, said they found a cure to

The 1983 Skyland RG.

nosewheel vibration by increasing tire inflation to 55 psi.

• Balky throttles. At least five different service bulletins and mod kits were put out to cure the problem, and any used RG should have them installed.

• Instrument panel "eyebrow" lights that flicker out quickly. Multiple replacements seem to be the rule. Said one owner, "I buy them by the dozen. If anyone can figure out a fix, I'll happily buy the STC."

• Cabin and Water Leaks. Service bulletins address the chronic Cessna problem of leaks around the windshield and wing roots. "Repeated applications of silicone only retuned the sound of the air leak," said one owner. "Finally, they removed the windshield to discover about a six-inch gap in the sealing gasket."

• Other problems noted included turbos leaking oil, vacuum pump drive shafts shearing, aileron hinge cotter key holes badly aligned, Bendix starters failing, exhaust stacks cracked and alternator mounting bolts worn.

AD History

Despite the arduous roster of problems just tabulated, the Skylane RG has managed to get by with relatively few Airworthiness Directives, so far. And most of those that were issued affected engine accessories like the Bendix magnetos (six ADs called for inspections and mods) and the Slick magneto (one AD). An inspection was also required of the Stewart-Warner oil cooler for leakage.

Much-publicized ADs called for inspection of fuel tank caps for leakage, and for inspection of bladder fuel tanks on '78 RGs for wrinkles and installation of quick drains. Others required inspection of aileron hinges for the correct location of cotter pins. Replacement

of certain Marvel-Schebler carburetors and Airborne vacuum pumps was called for—as it was on many other aircraft.

Modifications

R/STOL Systems, Inc. has taken over the full list of Robertson mods. They are at Everett, Wash., (206) 355-2736. Charles Seibel of Flight Bonus, the wizard of fixed-gear Skylane cleanups, can provide wing strut fairings and flap and aileron gap seal and cowl closures, but these give only three and a half mph or so extra speed—nowhere near the improvement achieved by cleaning up the gear. Nevertheless, he's located at Arlington, Tex., (817) 265-1650.

Resale Value

After an encouraging rise in equity for RG owners in 1981, the aircraft has disclosed a desultory curve in resale value to the present, with their worth holding nearly level or sagging with time. At least they are, therefore, cheaper than their big competitors, the Mooney 201s. Hence, in 1986 a 1980 RG could be purchased for about $48,000

Skylane RG Resale Value Chart

according to the *Aircraft Bluebook Price Digest* vs. about $56,000 for the Mooney 201.

Owner Organization

Check with the Cessna Pilots Assn. at Wichita Mid-Continent Airport, P.O. Box 12948, Wichita, Kans. 67277, (316) 946-4777.

Owner Comments

We have owned and operated three 182RGs—one normally aspirated and two turbos. We have found them to be among the best aircraft to put on our rental line of all those Cessna has built.

But magnetos tend to cause ignition noise on radios. The engines vibrate a fair amount and cause general loosening of parts, including beacons, landing light bulbs, alternator filters and avionics.

The starter Bendix is weak engaging, particularly in cold weather. The windshields leak around the base during flight in rain, and the black instrument deck covers warp.

Despite the above, we recommend the aircraft highly.

Field Morey, President
Morey Airplane Co.
Middleton, Wisc.

The only problems I have had so far on my one-year-old Skylane RG are the electric flap switch and the No. 2 comm radio—both repaired under warranty. I have been very well pleased with this aircraft. The strong points are the roomy, comfortable cabin, excellent stability in rough air and smooth, six-hour cruising range, easy cold-weather starting, good load-carrying ability, a great-performing Lycoming O-540 engine and excellent shortfield performance.

Also, it makes no unusual demands on pilot ability. It is a very safe, forgiving and rugged aircraft.

On the down side is the rather poor visibility, a too noisy cockpit that requires either ear plugs or a headset, mediocre Sperry avionics and heavy pitch forces—especially in the landing flare. It must be properly trimmed in all flight attitudes.

It cruises at 140 knots true at 65 percent power, burns 11-12 gph and uses one quart of Aeroshell 15-50 each 10 hours. Insurance is $2,000 per year and includes liability, property damage and hull.

I felt the $930 cost of a recent annual was rather excessive for a new aircraft with no serious glitches.

T. Gorman
Yarmouth, ME

My '79 Skylane RG has been highly reliable and quite comfortable, especially on long trips. I am 6'4" and my wife is 6'2", and we are able to stretch out and be comfortable even with four people in the plane. Even the A36 Bonanza cannot match the Skylane in interior comfort on a long trip, in my opinion.

Maintenance has run about $1,000 to $1,300 a year, including parts. I do my own oil changes and have assisted on annuals several times. In five years I've got about 1,100 hours on the plane. I've had to replace a flap motor, the brake drums with chrome discs, the turn-and-bank indicator and the vacuum pump. I am now on the third battery; they seem to die at about 18 to 24 months, despite my best efforts. I've also had the DG go out in the first 500 hours. And the Bendix starter broke this past month and cost about $250 to get fixed.

The plane has Cessna radios. Both navcoms have been reliable. The

ADF has had an intermittent problem that's been worked on four times over the years. It worked reliably for the last two years, but is now back in the shop for a fifth time. The transponder has required three trips to the shop.

I figure the plane's hourly operating cost in the $45 to $50 range.

Kenneth B. Carpenter, M.D.
Knoxville, Tenn.

Dealer warranty support on my 1979 Turbo Skylane RG was good, as far as the factory would allow. Cessna's support was fair for some things, but poor on others. Parts availability has been poor some of the time, and the prices often seem unrealistic.

We normally like to cruise between 9,000 and 13,000 feet and use 2300/23", which is 65 to 73 percent, depending on temp. Fuel consumption will be 12.5 to 14 gph and TAS from 155 to 165 knots at near gross. Performance has been good right up to maximum operating altitude of 20,000 feet.

As equipped (with a full panel of King digital avionics and a Century IIB autopilot), the useful load is 1,160 pounds. With full 88 gallons of fuel, that leaves 630 pounds payload. As with all Skylanes, the loading envelope is good, and it would be hard to exceed with normal people and cargo loads. Range with fuel and comfortable reserves is more than 700 nm.

I'm a big person (6'3" and 200 pounds) and enjoy the large roomy cabin with plenty of headroom. The doors allow easy entry for both front and rear seats. The full articulating front seats adjust to tall and short as well as giving comfortable positions for long flights. Rear-seat headroom and legroom is good. Noise level is fairly high. Cessna's doors and windows are not fitted and sealed very well. The ventilation system is good; however the front wing root vents tend to come open unexpectedly at high speeds. (It was a good system for 120-knot Skyhawks.) Heating is okay for front seats, marginal in back, especially with the air leaks and high, cold altitudes. Carry a blanket.

Handling is typical Skylane—very stable with moderately balanced controls. Once trimmed, it will stay put. I don't feel a real need for altitude hold on autopilot, even in hard IFR.

It has very effective flaps both for extra lift and high drag. They do produce pitch changes which necessitate retrimming. Rudder control is adequate for pretty heavy crosswind landings.

The Lycoming engine requires much different procedures than the Continental O-470 in the fixed-gear Skylane. Throttle linkage and adjustment is very critical for the turbo model, to operate both carburetor and wastegate properly and smoothly. The modification kit available from Cessna took three or four times as long to install and adjust as Cessna estimated. The air intake flange on the carburetor air box broke off at about 300 hours while in flight, resulting in loss of turbocharging and drop in mp. The replacement box has a riveted flange rather than a crimped one and should hold up better.

Be real careful about using carb heat on the ground. The box with the flapper valve has big holes that can allow solid matter to enter, then go into the turbo when carb heat is applied. Cessna disputes this and wouldn't pay for a new turbo-charger.

Incidentally, as long as I operate at high enough power settings to keep turbocharger activated, I have not had any carb ice problems. Engine

temperatures normally run on the cool side of the green. Even at 18,000-20,000 feet and high cruise powers the temperatures stay low even with cowl flaps closed. I have had no vacuum pump problems yet, but will likely install the cooling kit available from the Cessna Pilots Assn.

We have had no gear problems, and so far no evidence of corrosion under paint. (The aircraft is hangared in Sacramento, Calif. with hot, dry summers and cool, damp winters.) The fuel caps are still sealing fine, but I will replace with vendor-produced new metal caps this winter as a precautionary measure.

We're on the third alternator control unit. This one, however, has been operating for about 350 hours. The windshield had a bad air and water leak when delivered. Repeated applications of silicone only retuned the sound of the air leak. Finally they removed the windshield to discover about a six-inch gap in the sealing gasket. Annuals and other engine/airframe maintenance runs about $1,200 to $2,000 per year.

In summary—the Turbo Skylane RG is like all Skylanes—a big, comfortable four-seat airplane. It loads easy and flies easy. It handles dirt and sod strips almost as well as the fixed gear, but has the additional speed and altitude capabilities. I like the airplane and basically have been pleased with performance and reliability of most systems.

James W. Elliot, D.D.S.
Sacramento, Calif.

In the 15 months that I have owned my '78 Skylane RG, the average price for a similar airplane has appreciated about $4,000—not bad for an investment, although the new equipped price is about $120,000, which makes used planes very attractive.

Cost per hour in the last year, including engine, hangar, insurance, replacements, repairs and maintenance comes to $22.65 per hour.

The Lycoming O-540 engine is simply great. It has 1,620 hours on it and I haven't put a dime into it, and the lowest compression reading taken recently was 75 over 80. It burns a quart in about 10 hours.

The high performance and low stall speeds make it a safe airplane for people who don't fly professionally. The minuses are the usual Cessna leaky windows and doors and the average interior and appointments. The nosewheel gave me a periodic chatter problem on landings and takeoffs, with constant bushing replacements required, until I realized that we mistakenly kept the air pressure in the tire too low. Increasing tire pressure to 55 psi seems to have solved that problem. The other problem is the constant need to change nav and red panel lights.

Donald S. Prusinski
Hales Corners, Wisc.

My '79 Skylane RG had some filiform corrosion when I got it; so I invested in a new paint job, complete with the epoxy primer it should have had all along. I also put on chrome brake discs. I specifically shopped for a '79 or later to avoid the fuel bladders.

The maintenance has been entirely reasonable. The most recent annual, with my assistance, was $650. This included a starter drive gear and a seat rail. I budget $10 an hour for maintenance, and put in lots of my own time on preventative items.

I have already purchased the new-style fuel cap kit ($73 for both sides). Your article on that subject was correct; it will be a lot of labor to install them, involving draining the tanks and removing access panels, since the new adaptors install from inside the tank. However, in a six-year-old airplane like this, the adaptor necks for the flush-style caps are getting rusty, and would need replacement soon, regardless.

The turbocharged Lycoming O-540 engine shakes at idle; it runs so rough at runup that one wants to taxi to the nearest mechanic, but it is remarkably smooth and quiet at the top of the green (2400 rpm). It would appear that the turbo is a very effective muffler. I always cruise at 2400 rpm, and any attempt to reduce the cruise rpm below that results in a noticeable increase in vibration. My point of reference is the Continental O-470 in my '74 Skylane that idled very smoothly but was an ear bruiser at cruise.

It appears that the turbo throws a small amount of oil into the induction air stream. This shows up as an oil leak at the junction of the induction duct and the carburetor air box. When I first got the plane, I had the turbo rebuilt to eliminate this, but it did not help. So I sealed the joint with silicone, and now the oil passes into the carburetor instead of onto the belly.

Peter F. Hebb
Peterborough, N.H.

Prior to my Skylane RG ownership I bought a 1979 Cessna 180 Skywagon. The most noticeable difference between the 180 and the 182RG was in engine roughness. The O-540 Lycoming was rougher and louder than the Continental O-470. It had a "beat" at cruise that caused the visors, compass and panel to vibrate.

In spite of careful leaning, I was never able to get the fuel consumption below 14 gph except at high altitudes (10,000 to 12,000 feet), when it would pull only 18" mp and 13 gph. After the contamination scare, I went to Shell semi-synthetic oil and the consumption decreased dramatically. As an engineer, I am doubtful of miracle cures, as well as an engine that doesn't use oil, but I didn't add but one quart between 50-hour changes afterward.

My main recollection of the engine, however, was its hard starting characteristics. I heard the same from other owners. (I moved up to a light twin after 500 hours and two years with the RG.) We blamed the sidedraft HA-6 carburetor—too many cubic inches for the carburetion, etc. Lots of throttle pumping usually did the trick, but after the easy-starting O-470-U engine, I have my doubts about the big Lycoming. Cessna and

Lycoming people were no help. According to them, the problem didn't exist. I left it at country airports on two occasions because of this.

I had the carburetor overhauled to comply with the metal float AD, the primer lines and nozzles checked repeatedly, and careful spark plug gapping and maintenance. All to no avail. Upon selling the plane, the mechanic doing the prepurchase examination noted that the impulse coupling was worn. It was replaced, and the engine started easily. So much for my local mechanics' diagnostic abilities.

Despite the starting stubbornness, however, the engine ran strongly, and gave a measure of reassurance in those heavy weather and dark night excursions that it would keep running as long as it got its share of 100LL. I never have had problems with carb ice as I did with the O-470 Continental.

Overall the Skylane RG is hard to beat. I'm going on to a Baron, but know if I have to come back in the future, it will be like welcoming an old friend once again.

Charles D. Haynes, P.E.
Tuscaloosa, Ala.

Mooney 201/231

The Mooney 201 has been on the market since 1977, the Mooney 231 since 1979. Both aircraft have established excellent reputations and inspired tenacious owner loyalty, judging from the reader reports we received. In fact, we can think of no other aircraft in the Used Airplane Guide series that has won such acclaim from owners. Typical comments: ''Finest plane imaginable,'' ''superb,'' ''greatest airplane I've ever owned,'' '' a sweetheart.'' The 201 and 231 are prized mainly for sterling performance and economy, along with first-rate quality control.

The other side of the coin for used-plane buyers, of course, is the high prices commanded by used 201s and 231s. A 1977 201 has a *Bluebook* price of $42,500. Compare that with the $32,000 value of a 1977 Piper Arrow. (Both aircraft sold new for about $47,000 with normal equipment.)

History

The M-20J (201) was first introduced in 1977 as a modification of the stalwart M-20F Executive, which had been in production since the 1960s. Aerodynamic and cooling refinements increased cruising speed by an astonishing 15 knots. The 201 has continued in production since then with no major changes. Among the minor improvements were a repositioned fuel selector and an improved instrument panel in 1978. Generally, though, the model year of a 201 is virtually no factor for the used-201 shopper; the condition and history of each individual aircraft is what counts, depreciation patterns aside. Likewise, the 231 has had virtually no changes during its two-year production run. The ma-

Identical except for the engine and a few details, the 231 (left) and 201 are highly prized by their owners. As a result, used-plane prices are quite high.

jor difference betwen the 201 and 231 is the engine: the 231 has more power and is turbocharged. The 200-hp Lycoming four-banger in the 201 is replaced by a six-cylinder 210-hp turbo Continental TSIO-360 in the 231. The 231 also has some aerodynamic refinements that the 201 originally lacked, along with changes in the control system to accommodate the new engine and a prop shaft extension designed to give the 231 a racy shark-nose look. The performance of the two airplanes is very similar at low altitudes, but the turbocharged 231 is of course superior above 10,000 feet or so. (Its maximum ceiling is 24,000 feet.)

In 1984, the firm was purchased by Mooney European distributor Alexandre Couvelaire and Armand Rivard, who owns Lake Aircraft. Both the 201 and 231 continue to be produced in Kerrville, Tex.

Resale Value

The 201 is definitely blue-chip; its resale value rivals that of the hallowed Beech Bonanza. A 1977 201 is today worth 78 percent of its new price, a proportion only slightly less than a 1977 V35B. Normal aircraft depreciation patterns show a ''valley'' after about four years; after that, most aircraft hold their value or increase slightly (in

inflated dollars, of course). A 1977 201 reached its maximum depreciation in just two years.

Performance

The 201 and 231 are truly superior performers, far better than competitive aircraft. The 201, for example, outpaces its 200-hp four-place competition by more than 20 knots, using the same amount of fuel. (It may be no coincidence that the Rockwell 112B and Cessna Cardinal RG were dropped after falling far behind Mooney in the 200-hp sales race.) The 201, in fact, can nip at the heels of a Beech Bonanza or Cessna 210 while using only two-thirds of the fuel.

Owners consistently report that the 201 meets or exceeds its book performance figures. (This doesn't surprise us; Mooney's performance testing and measuring procedures put the rest of the industry to shame.) At 75 percent power, 201 owners report speeds approaching 170 knots. At a more conservative 65 percent power, cruise speed is 160 knots or so, according to owners. Fuel consumption ranges from 9 to 12 gph, depending on power and mixture settings. *Aviation Consumer* pilots have confirmed these astoundingly good numbers on their cross-country trips.

Range is also excellent; the high speed of the 201 combined with a generous 64-gal. fuel supply allow trips of up to 1,000 miles with a small reserve. Practical IFR range

Fuel gauges are right in front of the pilot's nose, which is great, but engine gauges are way on the right.

for the 201 is about 900 miles at 75 percent power.

The 231 is no faster than the 201 up to about 10,000 feet, and burns about two gph more fuel. At extremely high altitudes, however, the 231 can rack up airspeeds exceeding 190 knots at light weights. At the more normal 12,000-18,000-foot cruising altitudes preferred by most 231 pilots, 180 knots is about right.

In the real world, however, the performance of the 231 is not all that much better than the 201's, except for high-altitude climb. The 231's impressive 190-knot speeds are often theoretical. In warm weather at very high altitudes, the engine tends to run hot. That requires either the use of cowl flaps, which reduces speed by about five knots, or running an ultra-rich mixture, which burns excessive fuel. The 231 engine also tended to "miss" or "stumble" at high altitudes until pressurized mags were retrofitted by the factory free of charge. Turboplus, Inc. offers an intercooler designed to keep engine temperature lower, however.

Although the 231 is faster and carries more fuel than the 201, range is about the same. The 231 burns more fuel and must climb very high to achieve its maximum speeds, which decreases range.

Takeoff and landing performance of the 201 is about average for this class of aircraft. It requires precise speed control to achieve the short landings promised by the book. Pilot technique is also critical to achieve the published density altitude takeoff performance; a difference of a couple of knots in lift-off and climb speed can lengthen takeoff by 1,500 feet at 10,000 feet in the 201, for example.

The 231, because of its higher gross weight, higher stall speed and huge cowl flaps, has a rather long takeoff roll—nearly 50 percent longer than the 201's. The turbo-

charging naturally closes this gap at higher field elevations.

Handling Qualities

The 201 and 231 don't have the innate grace of control of aircraft such as the Bonanza. Aileron control is rather stiff, although better than in the older Mooneys. The only other major handling quirk of the 201 and 231 stems from their low drag: it's hard to get slowed down during descent. As one owner puts it, "Because the 201 is aerodynamically slick, it is absolutely the wrong plane to be in when you're cleared to land, close to the end of the runway and 3,000 feet above the ground. There is no sane way of losing altitude and slowing at the same time."

On the ground the 201 and 231 are rather awkward. Turning radius is large, and the nosewheel steering rather heavy.

By the standards of other nosewheel aircraft, the 201 is rather squirrelly on takeoff, particularly in those last few seconds when the airplane is deciding whether it wants to fly or not. The 231, because of its different weight distribution and pitch control system, seems more stable on the takeoff roll.

Both aircraft are "floaters" on landing if approach speed is a bit too fast. This fact, combined with the landing gear geometry and pitch response, cause a tendency to "porpoise" or "wheelbarrow" on

the nosewheel if the pilot is not sharp. The knack of landing smoothly comes quickly in most cases, however.

Loading

Both aircraft have useful loads of 950-1,000 pounds with the usual IFR equipment. Thus, as with most aircraft, it's impossible to carry full fuel, full seats and a good load of baggage. But the 201 will carry three 170-pound adults in most cases. Because the 231 needs more fuel to go the same distance, cabin payload will be less for a given trip, but not by much. The aircraft are not particularly sensitive to balance; any reasonable load will be within the c.g. envelope.

Accommodation

The 201 and 231 have a reputation for snugness that is not totally justified. The cabin is 44 inches wide, about the same as the Piper Arrow's. However, the seats are much lower to the floor and the instrument panel closer to the pilot; this no doubt creates the impression of snugness, as it does in a sports car. As one reader puts it, "You don't get into a Mooney, you put it on." This is somewhat of an exaggeration; another 201 owner writes, "Many people fault the Mooney on room, but I am 6'2" and 200 pounds, and I do not have any problem ..." Another writes, "We fly frequently with another couple on cross-continent flights in full comfort. The leg room, shoulder room and rear seat room are quite comfortable for the usual four-hour legs we fly.'' Although certainly less spacious than, say, the Bonanza, the 201/231 does not suffer by comparison to most other 180- to 200-hp four-placers.

Safety

Unfortunately, both the 201 and 231 are too new to have amassed enough flight time and accidents to establish a strong pattern. However, the older Mooneys (the Rangers, Executives, Super 21s and so forth) have a fairly good overall safety record. Fatal accident rate for the period 1972-76, according to NTSB figures, was 2.4, which ranks fifth best among 13 retractables in a recent *Aviation Consumer* study. The older Mooneys rank exceptionally high in structural integrity (only two documented in-flight airframe failures in the aircraft's history). In stall/spin accidents, the older Mooneys rank 16th best out of 31 aircraft studied between 1965 to 1973.

Naturally, the 201 and 231 are different aircraft from the earlier M-20 models, but the family resemblance is strong enough to suggest the 201 and 231 accident rates may be comparable.

One safety point: do not spin a Mooney. It loses altitude by something like 1,000 feet per turn.

Maintenance

Generally, the 231 and 201 are reliable, low-maintenance air-planes. One owner reports his last annual inspection turned up absolutely no discrepancies and cost a grand total of $230. Typical comment: ''Super airplane. What problems I've had to date are very minimal ...''

No airplane is perfect, of course, and there are certain trouble spots a potential 201 or 231 buyer should check closely:

• Landing lights. The 1977 model 201 in particular had landing light problems, due mostly to vibration. The 1978 model had an improved light mount, and a retrofit mod is available for 1977 models. Check to see if this mod has been installed.

• Cowl flap hinges. The 1977 and 1978 models have a poor design that causes trouble. In 1979 a stronger hinge, larger bolt and bushings were added. This may not have solved the problem, however; we got one report of loose cowl flaps on a 1979 model as well. A retrofit mod kit is available to beef up the flap hinge on 1977 and '78 models.

• Landing gear motor. The 1977 had an unreliable Dukes motor. Later models have a much superior one.

• Nosewheel and strut. It's easy to ''porpoise'' a 201 on landing, and that's hard on nosewheels. Replacement is quite expensive, so have a mechanic check it carefully. Also check the logbook for prop repairs; ground strikes caused by the same porpoising tendency are fairly common.

• Fuel tanks. The fuel tank sealant used in the 201 and 231 is apparently vulnerable to the aromatic compounds in 100LL fuel, and there have been several reports of tank leaks.

All of the above, of course, are in addition to Airworthiness Directives, which should be complied with in any aircraft you consider buying. Major airframe ADs required replacement or rework of the static system and oil cooler (77 model only), landing gear brace bolts and the Bendix fuel injector (1977-78 models); and auxiliary fuel pump and oil pressure transducer (1977-80 models). (The listed year models are approximate; check serial numbers in the ADs against the particular aircraft you're looking at.) There are also other ADs common to many aircraft, such as the Bendix dual magneto, Airborne vacuum pump and lithium-battery ELT directives. Any well-maintained 201 or 231 should have these ADs complied with.

The 231 has a special maintenance problem that can be annoying: a high-altitude ''miss'' in the Continental TSIO-360 engine. The thinner air at high altitude has less electrical resistance, which can result in ignition system arcing that momentarily cuts out the spark plug. More than half the 231 owners we queried for this article reported the problem. Careful maintenance of the ignition system and massive-electrode spark plugs

Cost/Performance/Specifications

Model	Year	Number Built	Average Retail Price	Cruise Speed (kts)	Rate of Climb (fpm)	Gross Weight (lbs)	Useful Load (lbs)	Usable Fuel (gals)	Engine	TBO (hrs)	Overhaul Cost
M-20J (201)	1977	377	$45,500	170	1,030	2,740	1,100	64	200-hp Lyc. IO-360-A1B6D	1,800	$ 9,250
M-20J	1978	385	$49,500	170	1,030	2,740	1,100	64	200-hp Lyc. IO-360-A3B6D	1,800	$11,250
M-20J	1979	136	$53,500	170	1,030	2,740	1,100	64	200-hp Lyc. IO-360-A3B6D	1,800	$11,250
M-20J	1980	136	$58,500	170	1,030	2,740	1,100	64	200-hp Lyc. IO-360-A3B6D	1,800	$11,250
M-20J	1981	175	$63,500	170	1,030	2,740	1,100	64	200-hp Lyc. IO-360-A3B6D	1,800	$11,250
M-20J	1982	112	$68,000	170	1,030	2,740	1,100	64	200-hp Lyc. IO-360-A3B6D	1,800	$11,250
M-20J	1983	90	$76,000	170	1,030	2,740	1,100	64	200-hp Lyc. IO-360-A3B6D	1,800	$11,250
M-20K (231)	1979	246	$58,000	192	1,080	2,900	1,100	73	210-hp Cont. TSIO-360-GB	1,800	$12,750
M-20K	1980	199	$63,500	192	1,080	2,900	1,100	73	210-hp Cont. TSIO-360-GB	1,800	$12,750
M-20K	1981	165	$69,000	192	1,080	2,900	1,100	73	210-hp Cont. TSIO-360-GB	1,800	$12,750
M-20K	1982	104	$76,000	192	1,080	2,900	1,100	73	210-hp Cont. TSIO-360-GB	1,800	$12,750
M-20K	1983	62	$85,000	192	1,080	2,900	1,100	73	210-hp Cont. TSIO-360-GB	1,800	$12,750

are some help, but Mooney has decided to use a different magneto and harness for the 1981 model 231. The new ignition setup has been available free for retrofit to older 231s.

We have also received reports of induction icing problems in the 231. One owner reported a complete stoppage and lost 5,000 feet before restarting.

One concerned 201 owner reported a vexing maintenance problem. "I may be dreaming," he wrote, "but it seems that birds have a strange attraction for my airplane. They love to sit on the tail and leave droppings all over it. My 201 is parked in a row of perhaps 50 aircraft, from an MU-2 to a Cub, and mine is consistently the only airplane to suffer this disfigurement. I was talking to another 201 owner recently, and he described precisely the same problem. Something is going on here."

Perhaps the solution to the bird problem is an AD requiring a large doo-doo shield to be permanently affixed to the 201 tail. This would certainly discourage the birds, and shouldn't cause a speed loss of more than 20 knots or so, although further flight tests might be necessary to ensure no adverse effect on stability and handling qualities.

Service

Although the 201 and 231 seem to be reliable, well-built aircraft, if you do have a problem, you'd better find the right mechanic to work on it. Average Joe Mechanic may never have worked on a 201 or 231 before, and financing his learning curve could be expensive. As one owner writes, "Phone calls to non-Mooney shops have left me with nightmares ..."

By almost universal acclaim, the top Mooney service center in the country is Dugosh Aviation in Kerrville, Tex. (the same field as the Mooney factory). According to the Mooney Pilots Association, four other top Mooney shops are Willmar Air Service, Willmar, Minn.; McCauley Aviation, Pine

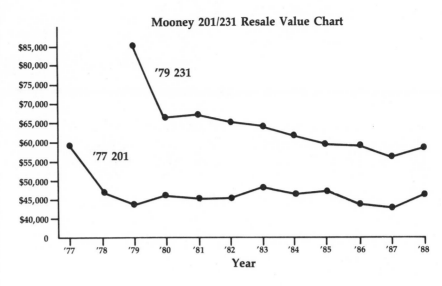

Mooney 201/231 Resale Value Chart

Bluff, Ark.; Performance Aircraft in Long Beach, Calif.; and Daytona Beach Aviation in Daytona Beach, Fla.

Unfortunately, the Mooney dealer network is one of the weak links in the system. They are few and far between, and some are rather small-time operators. (A couple of years ago, one Mooney Marketing Center accepted full payment from a customer for a brand-new 201, but never sent the money on to Mooney, and then went out of business. When the buyer showed up at the factory to pick up his plane, he got a sad surprise.) One 201 owner wrote, "Very happy with the plane, very unhappy with the dealer." Another complained that his mechanic (not a Mooney dealer) encountered delays ordering parts from the factory because the nearest dealer, through whom the parts had to be channeled, was hundreds of miles away.

We were not exactly showered with compliments about Mooney factory support. The company rarely pays for ADs or service bulletins beyond the warranty period, even in cases of obvious design defects, such as the cowl flaps and landing lights. In this respect, Mooney lags behind the rest of the industry, which has gradually begun to pay for certain ADs on late-model aircraft even

beyond the warranty period.

Owner Club

The Mooney Aircraft Pilots Association is closely allied with the Mooney company, and we would recommend membership to any 201/231 owner. Address is 314 Stardust Drive, San Antonio, Tex. 78228; phone: 512-434-5959.

Owner Comments

The 201 does everything the book says. It is common to get cruise speeds of 155-160 knots at 4,000-8,000 feet using 63-68 percent power. The 64 gallons usable fuel gives great IFR range and flexibility.

The ADs on the magneto, boost pump, cowl flaps, and spinner are a source of irritation. The greater irritation is that the cowl flaps are not a permanent fix, and I've had to have the tanks on my '77 201 completely resealed due to aromatics in fuels. Ouch!

Four people and any baggage can compromise some fuel. With full fuel I am limited to 595 pounds. Two 850-mile trips to Florida used

10.2 gallons per hour at 160 knots. Like an albatross, it is cumbersome at other than high-speed flight. On the ground it has a large turning radius, and when trying to "grease it on" it floats forever until *it* wants to land.

I've had my maintenance performed by Byerly Aviation in Peoria, a Mooney dealer, and had excellent service. Phone calls to non-Mooney shops have left me with nightmares of what would happen at other than a Mooney dealer or someone very familiar with Mooneys.

●

The speed for the 201 is about as advertised but the 231 will exceed Mooney's claims. I've confirmed this with other 231 owners. Up to 8,000 feet I see no difference between the 201 and 231. Over 8,000, the 231 really begins to shine! Most of my flying is in the 10,000-14,000-foot range. It's good to have a plane that doesn't feel "slushy" at those altitudes. I used to think 6,000-8,000 feet was plenty high. But when you get used to being above much weather, getting better reception and selecting favorable winds, higher altitude becomes second nature.

I have 200 hours on my 231 and have had little maintenance. However, there is a slight "miss" problem somewhat common to 231s. This is attributed to the fine wire plugs. Both Mooney and the dealers state that going to the massive electrode plugs corrects this, and I hear Mooney is considering switching to massive electrodes. I had this miss but had the plugs cleaned and rotated, and it appears to have stopped.

I bought a new 201 in 1978. It is a superb flying machine. Aside from the fact that several days after delivery it was down with an AD on the mags, it has been healthy and working well. The 201 is economical and handles like a dream. It is a great instrument platform and very comfortable. Maintenance and parts have been good.

However, I am disappointed with the aircraft industry's lack of

The 231 has a propeller shaft extension to give it a sleeker look.

responsibility on ADs. If they make a mistake in the manufacturing of a product, I certainly don't feel I should be responsible for their blunder.

I'm extremely well satisfied with my 201's performance, handling, roominess and low repair and operating costs. My only complaint is the fuel tank valve between my legs on the floor. The newer 201s corrected that problem.

The 231 is a quality airplane, well put together and gives every impression of durability and strength. There have been a few minor problems so far, two which I consider to be serious.

The first and most difficult to cure is induction ice. If the temperature is below freezing and there is visible moisture, you will very shortly suffer a loss of manifold pressure, the turbine inlet temperature will drop, and you will start trimming the nose up to maintain altitude. You could open the alternate air door, but there will be a marked loss of power.

●

I have over 500 hours in my 1978 201. Couldn't be more pleased. It is an excellent instrument airplane. Cruise speeds and fuel burn are by the book. I often load full fuel, two couples and baggage and am within weight and balance limits. Workmanship is excellent. Had trouble with fuel pressure gauge several times. Other than that, no serious problems. With today's fuel prices, this is the airplane to own if you plan on doing a lot of flying and don't own your own refinery.

Maintenance has been reasonable and minimal. I have only had to cancel one trip in two years due to mechanical problems. Of course I have the services of the best Mooney mechanic in the country (Charlie Mathews, Mathews Aircraft, Riverside Airport, Tulsa, Okla).

●

My 231 is the greatest airplane I've ever owned. That includes seven airplanes, Piper and Cessna.

I purchased my airplane last September with 350 hours TT. Since then I've flown the plane 45 hours. Nothing has needed fixing. The 100-hour was an inspection and oil change only. Cost: $480.

The performance of the plane meets or exceeds the book figures. The quality of the Mooney workmanship far exceeds Piper and more so Cessna. The paint job is far superior. It will carry a good load of ice and is a superb IFR platform. When it rains, the Mooney does not leak. The plane can be hot on landings, and persons without Mooney experience must adjust.

Over 15,000 feet the plane has a miss in the engine. The local Mooney dealer is experimenting with different spark plugs.

Another problem inexperienced Mooney pilots have is porpoising when a hard landing is made if power is not added. If the nose is forced over after a bounce, you will surely end up with a prop strike.

Piper Comanche

The luster of the Piper Comanche, with its superb roominess, great old Lycoming engine and modest price tag, has dimmed slightly with the passage of time. Though parts availability is generally reported as good despite the production halt of the entire line in 1972, some airframe parts take longer and longer to get, and two decades' accumulation of Airworthiness Directives adds to the psychological and fiscal burden of ownership.

Countering these deficiencies is a superb owners' association—The International Comanche Society—along with an energetic mod shop—Knots-2U—with an intriguing roster of update revisions that keep the old birds' performance and looks up with the times.

History

Piper manufactured five different single-engine models between 1958 and 1972. The arrival of the cheaper-to-build Arrow and a great flood that swamped the Lock Haven plant ended the Comanche line, however. The various models were built in these time spans:

- Comanche 180, from 1958 to 1964.
- Comanche 250, from 1958 to 1964
- Comanche 260, in 1965.
- Comanche 260B, from 1966 to 1968.
- Comanche 260C, from 1969 to 1972.
- Comanche 260C turbo, from 1970 to 1972.
- Comanche 400, from 1964 to 1965.

General Value Points

The powerplants of all the different models are characterized by owners almost universally as outstandingly troublefree. With optional fuel of 86 gallons usable translating into around seven to nine hours' flying time, the Comanches have unbeatable range. All the Comanches have fine roomy cabins that are several inches wider than those in the later Arrows. The 260B and C models actually have six-place seating, with two rather cozy seats in the baggage compartment.

The aircraft will climb at a good rate, and most pilots praise its short-field characteristics. Control reaction is crisp and pleasant, with a generous slam-bang warning stall buffet. There is good parts availability for accessories and engines. And prices for this kind of high-performance aircraft are quite decent in this day and age. Figure on from $20,000 to $40,000 for the later models.

On the debit side, all the Comanches are bears to land with finesse, the doors fit poorly, the instrument panel is archaic and nonstandard, and acquisition of airframe parts may require a good wait. Also, the Comanches have suffered a string of ADs—a good number of them repetitive ones—over the years—11

The barrel-chested Comanche 400 has demonstrated phenomenal climbing ability both in the air and in resale value over the years. This relatively rare bird evidently has already become a collector's item.

in the last decade alone. The 250 model by itself has accrued over 25 ADs since it was first built.

Comanche 180

The Comanche 180 is highly regarded for its economy, but naturally cannot haul great loads or operate effectively at high density altitudes heavily loaded. Max useful, nevertheless, is around 1,000 pounds, which should allow a full 60 gallons of fuel and three or four passengers. Owners report speeds of 135 to 140 knots, burning 8.5 to 9.5 gph. Rate of climb is 700 to 900 fpm at gross weight.

The 180 came with just a hand brake until 1960; after that, most were built with optional toe brakes. We noted at least one accident related to the use of hand brakes during the checkout of a pilot unfamiliar with this system. The optional 90-gallon fuel tanks became available in 1961 (60 gallons were standard). A full load of 90 gallons yields a phenomenal nine-hour endurance but limits payload to a couple of people and baggage.

Electric flaps were introduced in 1962, but some pilots consider this a step backward over the simple, quick-acting manual flaps. The 1960 and 1961 models are best for conversion to the 250-hp engine.

Our choice of 180s: a 1961 model with 90 gallons, toe brakes, manual flaps—approximate cost is $18,000.

Comanche 250

The 250 is the classic Comanche, probably one of the best airplanes available today for under $25,000. Even the 1962 Beech Debonairs (225-hp) are going for about $28,000, as are 1960 Bonanzas with the 250-hp engine.

Preferable models are 1961 and later, which had 100 pounds more gross (up to 2,900 lbs.) and useful load, 90-gallon fuel tanks and optional toe brakes.

Owners report cruise speeds in the 154-160-knot area on 12 to 14 gph. Climb rate is strong: about 1,000 to 1,400 fpm, according to owners.

The carbureted 250-hp Lycoming engine is a good one, presuming it has the half-inch valves. TBO is then a healthy 2,000 hours, and users report engine times several hundred hours longer.

Comanche 260

The 260-hp model was introduced in 1965, but the big change didn't occur until 1966. The '65 model is thus unique—the only four-seat carbureted 260-hp model. Because of its smaller gross weight, it has the highest book rate of climb of any Comanche except the 400: a robust 1,500 fpm.

In 1966 with the B model the fuselage was stretched slightly to allow for two extra (little, padded) seats that were actually in the baggage compartment, along with extra windows. In addition, fuel injection was provided and the gross weight raised 200 pounds to 3,100 pounds. Because of the extra gross weight, book speed is only slightly higher than that of the older 250s; but with the same load, the Comanche B is about four knots faster than the 250, according to reader reports.

The B is also presumably a bit quieter than the plain 260 because of a thicker windshield and side glass. And the 260's slightly longer fuselage is reported to give it better longitudinal stability than the 250 has—an advantage for autopilotless cruising and IFR flight, of course.

The 260C model, the ultimate refinement of the breed, was introduced in 1969. Recognizable by its shark-nose cowl, it had another 100

pounds' gross, which raised the standard useful load to a whopping 1,427 pounds. In order to avoid aft c.g. problems, however, the prop was moved forward several inches, resulting in the nice-looking streamlined nose. The C model also introduced cowl flaps and an aileron-rudder interconnect. The latter has the unfortunate side effect of making the ailerons heavier.

Turbo Comanche C

The turbo model was introduced in 1970 and built for three years until the Comanche line expired in 1972. The "second throttle" dual Rajay turbo system boosted high-altitude (25,000 feet) speeds to 198 knots at 75 percent and 182 knots at 55 percent. At more reasonable altitudes of 12,000-15,000 feet, the Turbo Comanche will true about 174-183 knots on some 16 gph.

The Turbo's modified exhaust system results in a noticeably quieter cabin, especially at altitude. The engine itself is beefed up to take the higher turbo temperatures, though the Rajays did not ground boost manifold pressure, but merely "normalized" to deliver a full 29 inches up to 25,000 feet. The pilot has to crank in the extra turbo boost manually.

Comanche 400

The Comanche 400 appeared in

Cost/Performance/Specifications

Model	Year	Number Built	Average Retail Price	Cruise Speed (kts)	Rate of Climb (fpm)	Fuel (gals)	Engine	TBO (hrs)	Overhaul Cost
PA-24-180	1958-59	1,176	$19,000	139	910	60	180-hp Lyc. O-360-A1A	2,000	$ 8,500
	1960-61	1,366	$20,000	139	910	60/90	180-hp Lyc. O-360-A1A	2,000	$ 8,500
	1962-63	713	$21,000	139	910	60/90	180-hp Lyc. O-360-A1A	2,000	$ 8,500
	1964	129	$21,750	139	910	60/90	180-hp Lyc. O-360-A1A	2,000	$ 8,500
PA-24-250	1958-59	1,476	$22,000	157	1,350	60/90	250-hp Lyc. O-540-A1A5	2,000	$11,100
	1960-61	1,366	$24,000	157	1,350	60/90	250-hp Lyc. O-540-A1A5	2,000	$11,100
	1962-63	713	$26,000	157	1,350	60/90	250-hp Lyc. O-540-A1A5	2,000	$11,100
	1964	129	$27,000	157	1,350	60/90	250-hp Lyc. O-540-A1A5	2,000	$11,000
PA-24-260	1965	299	$29,000	158	1,370	60/90	260-hp Lyc. O-540-E4A5	2,000	$11,000
PA-24-260B	1966-67	451	$32,000	161	1,370	60/90	260-hp Lyc. IO-540-D4A5	2,000	$11,500
	1968	51	$33,000	161	1,370	60/90	260-hp Lyc. IO-540-D4A5	2,000	$11,500
PA-24-260C	1969-70	147	$38,000	161	1,320	60/90	260-hp Lyc. IO-540-D4A5	2,000	$11,500
	1971-72	50	$42,500	161	1,320	60/90	260-hp Lyc. IO-540-D4A5	2,000	$11,500
PA-24-260TC	1970-71	50	$43,000	198	1,320	60/90	260-hp Lyc. IO-540-N1A5	2,000	$12,500
	1972	28	$45,500	198	1,320	60/90	260-hp Lyc. IO-540-N1A5	2,000	$12,500
PA-24-400	1964-65	145	$45,000	185	1,600	100/130	400-hp Lyc. IO-720-A1A	1,800	$19,000

1964 and disappeared after only a year on the market, for some good reasons. A total of 145 were built, and they have become something of a collector's item. The 400 has the basic four-seat Comanche airframe, but the engine is a monster 400-hp eight-cylinder Lycoming IO-720.

The engine and airframe marriage was not a happy one, however, for the Comanche 400 is a nose-heavy gas guzzler with performance only a little better than the Comanche 260's. Cruise speed is listed at 185 knots, and owners report an honest 174-183 knots at 75 percent cruise—but at an excessive fuel flow of about 20-22 gph. At 10,000 feet and 65 percent power, speed drops below 174 knots and fuel consumption is about 18 gph, according to owner reports.

Compared to a 1969 Comanche C (260 hp), which sells for $7,000 less, the $39,000 (the recent average going price) Comanche 400 rates poorly except for its specialty value. Gross weight of the 400 is 400 pounds higher than the 260's, but since the 400 weighs 337 pounds more empty, the useful load advantage is only 63 pounds.

Because of the 400's voracious appetite for fuel, the cabin payload is actually less than the 260C's for any flight of more than about 300 miles. With the optional 130-gallon tanks full, in fact, an IFR Comanche 400, for all its brute power, is a three-passenger airplane.

The original Comanche 400 gained a reputation for being notoriously hard to start, especially when hot. The problem was the Bendix 700 magneto used on early versions of the IO-720 (it tended to slip out of proper timing). Lycoming solved the problem on later engines by going to 1200 mags, but all Comanche 400s originally had the troublesome 700 ones. Presumably most or all have been converted to the 1200 series. Naturally, we

The Comanche 180. Note the short main gear legs and nose-high attitude. Owners advocate pumping up the main struts to simplify landing.

wouldn't advise buying one without the conversion.

Other points to bear in mind: an average IO-720 overhaul will cost about $18,000, compared to about $10,000 for the 260-hp model.

Despite its hefty operating costs, the 400 has a loyal cadre of owners, most of whom see the plane as a classic collector's ship. The plane is a delightfully stable IFR platform, exceptionally smooth, and its rate of climb is matched by few conventional single-engine aircraft.

Handling Qualities

The most notorious handling idiosyncrasy of the Comanches is the way they land. It's extremely difficult to make greasers consistently without some special magic. The aircraft tend to float during the flare, then pay off jarringly.

Special techniques for landing Comanches could fill a book. Some pilots use half flaps until committed to the landing, then lower them all. Other pilots counsel never using flaps at all. One pilot advises he makes golden landings by approaching at 104 knots and coming over the lights at 90 and flaring at 74 knots. Another asserts, "70 knots is just right." Years ago we used to make a normal approach with full flaps and then, when smoothly into the flare inches above the runway, retract the flaps and settle in. To each his own.

An almost universally condoned practice to improve landings is to pump up the main gear oleos and

bleed off the nose strut to change the landing attitude. The Piper Arapaho that was designed to replace the Twin Comanche (but never did) had whopping large main struts to counter the problem.

Along with landing problems come takeoff problems when pilots attempt to hold the aircraft on the ground in gusty conditions. The reason is the aircraft has a tendency to wheelbarrow in this kind of situation. Once in the air, however, the Comanches have a good reputation for handling, with light ailerons and a docile stall.

One operating quirk to watch for: When the Comanche landing gear is raised, the emergency gear handle between the seats pivots from a vertical position to a horizontal one against the floor. If a chart case or other object gets in the way, the gear will jam, the circuit breaker will blow, and serious gear problems may arise later.

Safety Record

According to a special NTSB study of accident rates of single-engine aircraft (over the years 1972-1976), the Piper Comanche PA-24 line came out quite a bit worse than average in only one category: overshoots. The Comanche was fourth worst in all 32 aircraft compared, after the Grumman Traveler, Cessna 195 and the Beech 23. This might suggest that either Comanche pilots are coming in too hot, or that the flaps are deficient in allowing a good angle of descent.

Despite the Comanche's notoriously poor cockpit visibility, the Comanches had only a slightly higher than average record of midair collisions and ranked ninth out of 25 aircraft.

On the other hand, in a separate study by Contributing Editor Brent Silver of fatal in-flight airframe failure accidents, the Comanche showed up very poorly. In the span of 14 years between 1964 and 1977 the Comanche had the fifth worst breakup record of 29 fixed-gear and retractable-gear aircraft. In fact, it trailed just behind the V-tailed Bonanza. The other four worst records went to the wooden Mooney, Bellanca 14-19, 17-30, 17-31 and the Navion.

A study by *The Aviation Consumer* of Piper Comanche accidents briefs provided by the National Transportation Safety Board (for the years 1979 through 1981) showed the biggest problem was engine failures because of some mechanical breakdown.

There were 22 such accidents (out of a total of 147), plus another two engine stoppages attributed to carburetor ice. In three other instances engine failure was caused by water in the fuel. Hence, although Comanche owners characterize their powerplants as troublefree, there appears to be a problem with poor or inadequate maintenance on these older aircraft.

Second biggest accident generator was fuel mismanagement, with 19 cases where pilots either exhausted the fuel totally or ran a tank dry and crashed or made forced landings.

Third biggest accident problem with Comanches was gear-up landings caused by the pilot's either inadvertently retracting the gear on landing or failing to make sure it was down and locked. There were 13 of these. In several instances, however, the problem was compounded by some kind of electrical failure, a low battery or popped circuit breaker; and the pilot didn't notice the electrically operated gear wasn't down and locked. Another eight cases of gear collapse were attributed to maintenance problems.

Fourth biggest problem area concerned stalls, stall/mushes or spins. There were 10 of these, with at least half related to pilots expecting better short-field performance than they got or tackling high density altitude situations.

As for the problems disclosed by the other studies we mentioned above—in-flight airframe failure and overshoots—we tallied six Comanche breakups. Five of them occurred in thunderstorm areas, one with a gyro failure in IFR conditions. And we counted eight cases of overshooting.

Despite the Comanche's reputation as a tricky lander, there were only three accidents blamed on hard landings, and in one of those the aircraft had a load of ice. And poor cockpit visibility or not, there was only one midair among the roster.

Maintenance Considerations

Since the Comanche is not exactly a vanished species, there are quite a few mechanics around the country who were weaned on them. But it is imperative to find knowledgeable ones, or pay the Piper(!). There are reportedly quite a few capable shops around the country, and lots of inexpert ones. For a good one in your local area, we suggest you get in touch with the International Comanche Society.

As for gurus, we suggest Maurice F. Taylor, the Society's technical advisor, at either 704-963-5529 summers, or 813-439-2792 winters. He, in turn, suggests that one of the most knowledgeable Comanche people is Robert Gift of Lock Haven Airmotive in Lock Haven, Pa., 717-748-5582.

As for maintenance costs, another Pennsylvania shop that says it has been working on Comanches since way back (Penn-Air, Inc. at Altoona—Blair County Airport in Martinsburg, Pa., 814-793-2164) provided the following average costs for annual inspections, including parts, labor, fluids and state sales tax in 1983:

- PA-24-180—$795.
- PA-24-250—$835.

When the Rockwell 114 came out, the "old" Comanche C outraced and outclimbed it despite powerplants of similar size.

- PA-24-250, -260 fuel injected—$885.

Service Manager Danny R. Claycomb also said that a 50-hour oil change, lower plug cleaning, tire service along with a check of lights, brakes, and clean up would amount to from $225 to $250. However, if an aircraft came in without the records summarized and up to date, this could take the IA another eight to 10 hours to accomplish.

Parts Availability

Almost all the Comanche owners who provided us with feedback staunchly maintained that parts were no problem whatever. Even the International Comanche Society said Piper was doing a "superb job" for an aircraft out of production as long as the Comanche. Owners said if the dealers can't get the parts from Piper, then the Society can help scrounge them up.

We did get a few contrary signals from some Piper dealers, however. These said service was quite poor, and the delay in actually getting parts delivery could be months long. One old-timer in the business suggested that actually right now the parts situation was at its nadir, and that the time was ripe for an outside supplier like Univair or Wag-Aero, perhaps, to pick up the rights to make parts.

Maurice Taylor of the Society said that the hard-to-get parts are not the kind that ground the airplane, but are more likely to be items like inside moldings for windows or perhaps parts that local shops can fashion with a Form 337.

Service Difficulties

A survey of five years of SDRs for Comanches showed the landing gear system to have caused by far the greatest number of problems, often resulting in belly landings or gear collapsing. Typical callouts involved lower drag links binding; bungee arms cracked, broken or bent; and circuit breakers popping a "chronic problem with PA-24s." Mention was made of installing 30-amp circuit breakers in place of 25-amp ones according to Piper instructions, to alleviate the problem.

Next biggest problem area concerned the powerplant, with a varied assortment of problems involving everything from bearings and valves and cylinders to crankshafts and crankcases.

Third worst problem involved exhaust stacks and muffler components cracking and breaking.

Lesser problems involved magnetos, cracked aileron nose ribs (per AD inspections) cracking and rusting engine mounts and cracked wing skin around rivets where the stringer crosses the ribs. Still other problem areas were cracking control wheels and fuel cells that had collapsed, deteriorated or were leaking.

Airworthiness Directives

The AD that caused most consternation among Comanche owners recently was 82-19-01, which called for inspection of the main wing spar for cracks. This was issued after a Comanche in Canada lost its right wing when the pilot pulled

Comanche Resale Value Chart

up in a climbing left turn after flying over a friend's house. Transport Canada found the failure had been caused by a fatigue crack in the spar, and it found similar fatigue cracks in the other wing. The aircraft had experienced minor damage previously, but nothing significant that would have affected the wing's integrity, we were told. This runs counter to rumors that the aircraft had sustained serious wing damage earlier.

The AD called for the mechanic to cut out a small piece of metal skin to allow acccess for the inspection. What rankled owners is that some shops apparently charged four to 11 hours for what should have been no more than a one-hour $80 to $100 job.

The FAA reports that so far no cracks have been discovered as a result of the AD-mandated inspections. However, during the inspections another potential problem was discovered in the form of chafing of the wing spar lower cap where the spar enters the fuselage.

As a result, Piper issued a Service Bulletin (No. 751) in May 1983, calling for inspection to detect any chafing that might have occurred. This, Piper maintained, might in turn affect the structural integrity of the spar cap. At last word, the FAA was considering issuing an AD making the SB mandatory.

To further burden Comanche owners, the spar crack inspection AD was made a repetitive one, to be performed each 100 hours. We counted eight other repetitive ADs on the Comanche airframes (there may be more on accessories, engines, etc.), some of which can be terminated with installation of a corrective Piper kit.

Modifications

One of the notorious problems on the Comanches is poor door sealing. Owners who wish to add another latch (overhead, as on the Cherokees) to enhance door closing and security should contact the International Comanche Society for details of a mod for which they received one-time approval via a Form 337. Another possible solution to the problem is an inflatable door seal, provided by Bob Fields Aerocessories in Santa Paula, Calif.

Knots-2U can provide several performance boosters such as aileron and flap lower (and now upper) seals for $1,450 installed or $1,050 in kit form; wing root fairings for $425 installed or $355 kit; and a removable fiberglass dorsal fin to allow access to antennas for $1,080 installed or $895 kit; plus installation of the cabin air vent in the dorsal fin for $400. Contact Jim Bradshaw (312) 256-4807.

One-piece windshields have been

Piper Comanche

STC'd by several different organizations. Among them are Beryl D'Shannon Aviation Specialties, Atlanta, Ga.; Wayne Airframe, Inc., Van Nuys, Calif., Cee Bailey's Aircraft Plastics, Long Beach, Calif.; Great Lakes Aero Products, Flint, Mich. Users say they do a marvelous job of eliminating some of the tunnel-like qualities of the cockpit. Knots-2U also has one.

To help diminish the coat of oil on the underbelly, an air-oil separator is available from Walker Engineering Co., Los Angeles, Calif.

If extra range is desired, 15-gallon tip tanks are available from H.S. Osborne, Oro Grande, Calif.

In addition, R/STOL Systems, Bellevue, Wash. can provide STOL equipment in the form of recontoured wing leading edge, stall fences, drooped ailerons and new wing tips.

Since the older Comanches have generators that poop out at low rpms, owners might wish to upgrade to an alternator. InterAv in San Antonio, Tex., 512-344-2785 sells a kit for about $500.

Organization to Join

As we've mentioned above, the International Comanche Society, Inc., is highly touted by Comanche owners for its support, expertise and its *Comanche Flyer* newsletter. Their latest address is Box 468, Lyons, Kans. 67554-0468, 316-257-5138. The Society also publishes a special booklet of maintenance tips that owners say is extremely useful.

Investment Value

We plotted the resale value of each of the lines, and interestingly enough, the Comanche 400 showed the most dramatic climb in equity. After bottoming out at about $15,000 in 1971, it took off to where it has more than doubled in 1984, to $39,000, according the *Aircraft Bluebook Price Digest*. The 260B model showed the next best climb in value over the years, with all the others plodding slowly upward, driven by the pressures of infla-

tion, except for a brief plunge in 1980 and 1981.

Owner Comments

Comanches have accrued in value. Some things to look for are one-piece windshields, center stack radios, brake drums on wheels turned around so that they retract up *into the wheel well*. Other neat things are gap seals, wing root fairings, and others. I've replaced the 1955 vintage airscoops with 'NASA' scoops for improved cooling.

Although I enjoy and use my Comanche, I have a definite problem: lack of certain critical parts. Lack due to an "out of production" airplane. Piper helps where they can—but it is usually "sorry—out of production."

The mere mention of certain AD notes makes me mad. The gear AD at about $500 was bad enough. The prop AD at about $600 was understandable. The aileron nose rib AD was ridiculous. I personally requested the FAA for a variance on this one. All the supporting data, documents, letters, etc. FAA said no. And now it's every 100 hours inspect the aileron nose rib.

In September 1982, another AD. In the next 20 hours, said the AD, cut a hole in the wings and inspect for cracks.

C. Lamar Carlton
Sebring, Fla.

I have gone on many long trips in this plane and I really don't think there is a better-performing plane for load carrying, speed, density altitude, or economy on the used-plane market. Compare the numbers with say a new RG-182, then the price and you'll get what I am driving at.

My 250 has the Brittain tip tanks, 15 gallons each, and 30 gallons in each wing tank. The end-plate effect of the tips allowed an increase of 200 pounds in gross weight. The nice thing is that the 200 pounds does not have to be in fuel. Keep the tips

empty, and you get the 200 pounds in the cabin. Gross weight is now 3,000 pounds with tips.

Density altitude is always a concern out west and the Comanche gives excellent D/A performance. The owner's manual is the pits on figuring out D/A, and some other things, so each pilot ought to be conservative on his first trials. However, with 60 gallons, four real-size passengers, I can get out of a 2,200-foot paved strip, D/A of 4,000 feet with no real problems.

With just pilot and full fuel, you are right up at the very front of the c.g. envelope—nothing dangerous, but gives you a decided nose-down feeling at cruise. Might just be an illusion, but you are right up at the front of the envelope.

Comfort can't be beat. I am a big person and I still have plenty of room. Noise level is a bit high, mainly due to poor door sealing—a generic fault in Comanches, unless fixed, and this is usually expensive. I usually use 143 knots for flight planning.

Carlton S. Yee
Eureka, Calif.

The Comanche 250 will fly an honest 160 knots, and I have had mine to 20,000 feet to get over weather. I generally burn 13 to 14 gallons per hour at 2400 rpm, full throttle, leaned, at altitudes between 12,000 and 15,000 feet.

Handling is generally very straightforward, and control pressures are average, in my opinion. The airplane does have two idiosyncrasies: first, it can be a difficult airplane to trim, and in rough air the airplane will not stay easily at a given altitude. Second, when the airplane is landed, a pilot must be very alert to his airspeed for touchdown. The airplane will make perfect landings time after time if flareout is done at the correct airspeed. Alternatively, the airplane will jar your teeth if you are three knots too fast or three knots too slow.

Jeffrey Bowen
Denver, Colo.

Lake Amphibian

If you're looking for a reasonably-priced land-or-water personal plane, the Lake LA-4 amphibian is virtually your only choice. For 40 percent less money, the Lake offers much better payload and similar performance to a hulking Cessna 185 on amphibious floats.

A Lake won't haul a moose or a 55-gallon oil drum, but that doesn't matter much to the typical individual buyer looking for a used amphibian for pleasure and/or business. Rather than, "Which amphibian should I buy?" the question becomes "Which model Lake?"

History

The Lake first appeared in the early 1950s as the Colonial C-1 Skimmer, a 150-hp three-placer developed by a couple of ex-Grumman engineers named Dave Thurston and Herb Lindblad. In 1958, power was increased to 180 hp, seating capacity increased to four, and the result was called the C-2. In 1960, the Skimmer got a major facelift, including a longer bow, a stretched wing, and a new name, the Lake LA-4. About 250 Skimmers and LA-4s had been built when production shut down in 1962.

The Lake was revived in 1963 under a new marketing arrangement whereby the aircraft were built by one company, Aerofab, and sold and serviced by another, Lake Aircraft. In 1970, the 180-hp engine was replaced with a 200-hp fuel-injected Lycoming and the aircraft was renamed the Buccaneer. A small number of turbocharged models have been built over the years, and there was even one straight seaplane version built. The marketing company changed hands in 1979, and two new models have been introduced

When all the cold, rational analysis is finished, this is what hooks pilots on the amphibian: the idyllic summer lakeside setting.

since. The Buccaneer got an extended propeller shaft and other modifications in 1983 and was rechristened the EP, and an enlarged 250-hp five-place version called the Renegade has been certified. This report will not deal with the EP or Renegade.

Used-Plane Market

A first-time Lake buyer should be cautious. The market is fairly small (a recent issue of *Trade-A-Plane* lists fewer than a dozen for sale), and prices can vary all over the place because watercraft are much more susceptible to such value deflaters as corrosion or damage history. The Lake factory has also gotten into the refurbishing business in a big way, and now sells a dozen or so spruced-up used Lakes every year.

Because the Lake is rare and unusual, we'd strongly recommend a thorough prepurchase inspection by a knowledgable Lake mechanic—not just the guy down at the airport who has maintained your Cherokee for years. A good Lake man, for example, would know to check the hull bulkhead at station 97 for hard-landing damage. Not many Cessna wrenches would know that, we'd wager.

Performance

The price of doing land-water double duty is rather anemic performance by landplane standards. A 200-hp Buccaneer performs about on par with a typical 150-hp landplane. Lake used to advertise a max cruise speed of 130 knots but this was notoriously optimistic, as the present company admits. Most owners report cruise speeds in the 105-115-knot range. Unfortunately, fuel consumption matches that of other 200-hp planes at about 10 gph, so fuel mileage is a very poor 10 nmpg or so. A Mooney will fly 40 or 50 knots faster than a Lake on the same fuel. (On the other hand, you don't see many Mooneys landing in the water; those that do certainly don't take off again.)

Performance of the 180-hp Lakes is less by about 4-8 knots.

The Lake has a big wing that helps make up for the high drag, so book climb rate is a respectable 1,200 fpm. Several Lake pilots report, however, that at heavy weights it is rather sluggish getting "on the step" and in climb. The 180-hp airplanes should be considered two-place airplanes off the water, unless the takeoff area is huge.

At light weights, the Lake could almost be called a STOL plane. Owners report ground rolls of under 400 feet on land, and approach speed is a Cessna-150-like 57 knots.

Useful loads average about 800 pounds for a VFR 180-hp airplane to about 950 pounds for the 200-hp models—quite comparable to 200-hp landplanes. One loading quirk to look out for: as more passengers are added, c.g. moves forward. The Lake tends to be nose-heavy anyway (that's why the heater is on the ceiling instead of in the nose), and we read one Lake accident report in which the craft was loaded more than an inch ahead of the forward c.g. limit.

Fuel capacity is one shortcoming of the Lakes. Standard tanks hold 40 gallons, good for about three hours with a small reserve. At slow Lake speeds, that's just over 250 nm range. Auxiliary tanks in the wing sponsons can increase fuel capacity to a reasonable 54 gallons. Try to find a Lake with the extra tanks.

Creature Comforts

Inside room is adequate in the front seats, but rather tight in back. Two large adults will be very cozy in back. (L.L. Bean types tell us, however, that it's entirely possible to sleep two people in a Lake with the seats folded down.) The rear baggage compartment is small and accessible only through the two front clamshell doors—a "class A pain in the butt," according to one owner. The Lake's cargo/baggage limitations and docking problems are the main reasons it is rarely used by bush pilots.

Despite the location of the engine up and away from the fuselage, the interior is very noisy, according to owners. "I really need my David Clark headphones," commented one owner. The Lake factory now offers an interior soundproofing kit that is claimed to reduce the roar to some extent. Cosmetically, most Lake interiors are reminiscent of 1956 Nash Ramblers.

Handling

One of the Lake's worst features is ground handling. There's no nose-wheel steering, so the pilot must steer by differential braking. While this **approach works reasonably** well in some planes, like the Grumman Americans, in the Lake it's lousy. Comments one owner, "It will quickly, and without warning, swerve to either side and become a monster to get straight again...I consider it dangerous for the novice."

On the water, the Lake is slow to get on the step with a heavy load. (One owner describes how rear seat passengers have to hike forward even at sea level in smooth water.) But once skimming along the surface, the Lake is exceptionally agile by seaplane standards, prancing through spray-soaked gyrations that would leave the typical floatplane pilot scared to death, if not upside down six feet under water.

In the air, the Lake has rather mediocre handling. The ailerons are nice and light, owners tell us, but the rudder is a thigh-crusher. Stalls are gentle, with good control from the huge rudder, and come at about 43 knots indicated. A maneuver favored by Lake demo pilots is the free-falling anvil descent: power off, gear and flaps down, and push over the nose. Thanks to the aforementioned Peterbilt aerodynamics, astounding descent rates can be achieved without building up excessive airspeed—and a good thing it is, since red line airspeed is only 127 knots.

One handling quirk of the Lake is its pitch response to power. Push the throttle sharply forward, and the nose goes down for a moment. Pull it back and the nose rises. (This, of course, is due to the high engine position, which generates big pitching moments with power changes.) Also, takeoff requires a definite rotation by the pilot to overcome the high-power low-speed noseover tendency. Such unairplanelike traits might shock the Lake novice at first, but owners tell us they adjust quickly and find them no problem.

Overhead Engine

New Lake owners will have to adjust to the overhead engine controls. (Four levers in the turbo models.) Another oddity: because of the engine location, exhaust heat can't be used to heat the cabin. Heavy, expensive maintenance-hog gasoline heaters are unfortunately the only alternative. Up through 1973, Lakes had the troublesome Janitrols, which are subject to an AD requiring complete overhaul every two years. After 1974, Lake switched to Southwind heaters that were more reliable, but had only two positions, on or off. "You either cook or you freeze," is the way one owner put it. The 1983 models have an improved Janitrol that is supposed to be fantastic.

Maintenance

The Lake is a rather complicated airplane, with more than the usual number of systems. Gear, flaps and trim, for example, are all hydraulic. When the great bugaboo of all water airplanes—corrosion—enters the picture, the possibility arises for truly nightmarish maintenance prob-

On the water, Lakes take a surprising amount of abuse. Brake steering makes for awkward ground handling, however.

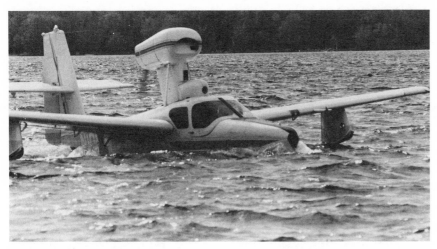

Early models had negligible corrosion proofing—a critical matter on these aircraft. Bulge at base of engine pylon is a gas heater.

lems in old or poorly kept-up Lakes, particularly those operated in salt water. Many used Lakes will be advertised as "never flown in salt water," but they should nevertheless be meticulously inspected for corrosion.

Corrosion-proofing deserves special attention. The 180-hp airplanes built during the '60s had no zinc chromate treatment, and some didn't have Alodine, either. "As far as we can tell, there was no pattern on the Alodining," says Bruce Rivard of Lake, who was part of the new regime that took over Lake marketing in 1979. "Some of them had it, some didn't." Alodine treatment has a faint gold tint; look for it in the interior structure on any pre-1970 airplane. Even with the Alodine treatment, the lack of the green zinc chromate primer makes those airplanes susceptible to corrosion. "A 180-hp Lake that's been in salt water is bad news," comments Rivard.

Starting in 1970, all Buccaneers were Alodined and zinc chromated. Starting with the 1983 models, an additional polychromate primer was used.

One mechanic described to us a $10,000 repair job on a corroded 1969 LA-4. (*Bluebook* price of a 1969 LA-4 is about $19,000 or so.) A bad case of corrosion in an old airplane can make it virtually worthless.

Water operations can also be hard on the hull structure. Hard landings on the water are fairly common because of unpredictable wind and waves, not to mention submerged sandbars and logs.

Carefully check the fuselage/hull structure for internal damage, especially the bulkhead at station 97. (This was strengthened in 1982 models.)

Once again, we recommend Lake specialist for this inspection. One owner reports sadly that the two mechanics he hired to do a prepurchase inspection of a used Lake missed $2,000 worth of internal damage, along with some leaky hydraulic lines.

Our check of FAA service difficulty reports revealed no major problem areas. We did notice several reports of nose gear malfunctions, and an odd reoccurrence of exhaust cracks at the number two cylinder, however. And one report caught our eye: "During taxi, engine fell over on wing."

Maintaining a Lake will probably be more expensive than taking care of a comparable 200-hp landplane—after all, you are keeping it both airworthy and seaworthy. At the right shop, however, the bill shouldn't be too high. One owner reports a $450 flat fee for the inspection alone, with additional repairs bringing the total bill to $850. The Lake factory has an unusual service for owners: they'll do an annual right at company headquarters (Laconia, N.H. in the summertime, Kissimmee, Fla. in

the winter). Flat rate is $400, with repairs extra, of course. "We'll give the owner a detailed list of problems so he'll know what he's getting into," comments a Lake spokesman.

Unfortunately, the factory doesn't like to do prepurchase inspections.

Here is a list of recommended Lake shops. (Just because a shop doesn't make our list is no cause for alarm. These just happened to have been recommended; other equally good, or better, shops may not have come to our attention.)

Ed Nelson, E&H Aircraft, Seattle, Wash. (206) 762-9285.

Mark McKinney, Midwest Airmotive, Plainfield, Ill. (312) 759-3988.

Elton Townsend, Gravenhurst, Ontario, Canada(705) 687-4343.

Alexander Aircraft Sales, Peoria, Ariz.

Frank Persson, Frank's Aircraft Service, Tulsa, Okla. (816) 836-3396.

Engines

The 180-hp Lycoming O-360 generally has a better service record than the fuel-injected 200-hp version. The IO-360 had some problems in the early 1970s, and Buccaneers of that vintage should be checked to make sure they have updated valves, camshafts and piston pins. TBO of unmodified early engines is only 1,200 hours, although this was increased to 1,400, then 1,600, and finally 1,800 hours if the improved parts were retrofitted.

Lake claims that the IO-360 runs cooler in its pylon installation than in any other aircraft, and that as a result engine life is longer. Lycoming has not officially endorsed this claim with a longer TBO specifically for the Lake, however.

Service Support

We get reports of uneven service support. One owner told us it was excellent; another described a four-month wait for a flap. A mechanic reported, "Some days it's good, some days it's bad, you can never tell." One buyer of a new 1983 airplane reports he had to replace a nose gear strut, a main gear strut, and a battery, and has had problems with a cracked cowling, magneto housings and the encoding altimeter. The plane was down for six months during its first year. He reports that Lake seemed unenthusiastic about providing service info or financial aid.

Other owners report good reliability, however, and our impression is that the small Lake sales/service organization can be responsive at the top levels. (The disgruntled 1983 Lake owner reports things improved after he called Lake president Armand Rivard.)

Safety

Our scan of NTSB records shows a total of 51 accidents during the period 1978 through 1981. Ten were fatal. About 43 percent of the accidents involved water operations. (This number is a bit uncertain, since the exquisitely vague language in the NTSB accident briefs sometimes didn't make it clear whether the accident occurred on the water or a land runway. The NTSB computer cleverly covered its butt by referring to "ground/water loop/swerves" on several occasions.)

The FAA has no hours-flown data on the Lake, so we are unable to calculate a precise accident rate. However, figuring that there are about 600 or so Lakes flying, and assuming an average of 150 hours per year for each airplane, we can make a rough guesstimate of 2.8

fatal accidents per 100,000 flight hours, and about 14 total accidents per 100,000 hours.

Both of these guesstimated numbers are fairly high in comparison to other single-engine retractables, which have fatal rates ranging from 0.8 to 3.3. Total accident rates of other retractables range from 4.6 to 15.0. The Lake seems to rank near the bottom of the safety standings among its peers. (Some may argue that the Lake's only peers are other amphibians. We don't have numbers for other amphibs, but our impression—an impression backed up by insurance rate numbers—is that amphibs as a class have far more accidents than comparable landplanes.)

The Lake's poor accident statistics are no big surprise, considering the unpredictability of water operations and the limited water experience of most Lake pilots. Of the 24 pilot-related water accidents in Lakes during the four-year period, just one involved a pilot with more than 200 hours time in type. Half the pilots had less than 50 hours in Lakes. "An amazingly high percentage of Lake accidents occur to new pilots in their first few hours of water flying," one insurance adjuster told us.

The message is clear: If you can get through the first couple of hundred hours in your Lake, the chances of a water accident go way down.

The water accidents we surveyed covered the predictable gamut—bounced landings, noseunders,

swerves and spinouts. Although splashily embarrassing and spectacular, Lake water accidents rarely hurt anybody. Only three were fatal—about 13 percent of the total. But water accidents did bend a lot of metal; every water accident listed by NTSB resulted in either destruction of the airplane or "substantial" damage.

Total flying experience seems almost irrelevant when it comes to flying a Lake safely. One fellow, for example, had nearly 9,000 hours total time, but only 10 hours in Lakes. He misjudged the distance required for a glassy water takeoff (apparently forgetting that the hull tends to "stick" longer to glassy-smooth water) and hit trees.

Lake pilots seemed to have their share of troubles taking off and landing on *terra firma* as well. More than half (16 out of 27) of the non-water crunches occurred on takeoff or landing. We also counted two engine failures, and two Lake pilots ran out of gas.

The secret to flying a Lake safely is to get a thorough checkout from an experienced Lake instructor. We're not talking an hour of touch-and-goes here; the factory usually spends 10 to 15 hours checking out purchasers of new Lakes. The factory also offers a check-out program for used-Lake buyers or owners, and we would strongly recommend it.

Insurance

Besides common sense and self-preservation, there's an economic

Cost/Performance/Specifications

Model	Year	Number Built	Average Retail Price	Cruise Speed (kts)	Rate of Climb (fpm)	Useful Load (lbs)	Fuel Std/Opt (gals)	Engine	TBO (hrs)	Overhaul Cost
C-1	1957	23	$10,250	97	700	790	30/39	150-hp Lyc. O-320-A2A	2,000	$8,000
C-2 IV	1958-59	128	$15,000	117	800	830	30/39	180-hp Lyc. O-360-A2A	2,000	$9,000
LA-4	1960-65	82	$20,000	114	800	850	40	180-hp Lyc. O-360-A2A	2,000	$9,000
LA-4	1966-69	102	$24,500	114	800	850	40,	180-hp Lyc. O-360-A2A	2,000	$9,000
LA-4	1970-71	26	$27,500	114	800	850	40	180-hp Lyc. O-360-A2A	2,000	$9,000
LA-4-200	1970-71	53	$31,500	130	1,200	1,065	40/55	200-hp Lyc. O-360-A1B	1,800	$11,000
LA-4-200	1972-75	232	$37,500	130	1,200	1,065	40/55	200-hp Lyc. O-360-A1B	1,800	$11,000
LA-4-200	1976-77	150	$41,000	130	1,200	1,135	40/54	200-hp Lyc. O-360-A1B	1,800	$11,000
LA-4-200	1978	70	$43,000	130	1,200	1,135	40/54	200-hp Lyc. O-360-A1B	1,800	$11,000
LA-4-200	1979	52	$46,000	130	1,200	1,135	40/54	200-hp Lyc. O-360-A1B	1,800	$11,000
LA-4-200	1980	24	$50,000	130	1,200	1,135	40/54	200-hp Lyc. O-360-A1B	1,800	$11,000
LA-4-200	1981	49	$55,500	130	1,200	1,135	40/54	200-hp Lyc. O-360-A1B	1,800	$11,000
LA-4-200	1982	8	$63,000	130	1,200	1,135	40/54	200-hp Lyc. O-360-A1B	1,800	$11,000
LA-4-200EP	1983	N/A	$73,000	130	1,200	1,135	40/54	200-hp Lyc. O-360-A1B6	1,800	$11,000

incentive to get a factory checkout: lower insurance rates. Amphibious airplanes are notorious for high insurance rates. In Alaska, hull rates are so outlandish that most bush pilots do without. In the lower 48, a floatplane pilot may pay over 10 percent per year for hull coverage.

Luckily for Lake pilots, one insurance company has taken a special interest in Lakes. Alpha Aviation (800-526-0415) insures more than 200 Lakes, nearly half the fleet. The company gives an 18 percent discount to any pilot who has completed the factory training. And it generally charges lower rates than for comparable amphibious-float-equipped aircraft.

For example, the cost to insure a 1980 Lake Buccaneer flown by a pilot with 750 hours, 100 hours of Lake time and a factory checkout might be four to five percent annually. This would be about 30 percent higher than a comparable Mooney or Piper Arrow, but only about half that of a Cessna 185 on amphibious floats.

A low-time pilot with a fresh seaplane writing and a late-model airplane would pay about eight percent for hull coverage, perhaps $6,000. Thus the 18 percent discount for a factory checkout would amount to a savings of $1,000-plus the first year—enough to pay for the checkout.

"Our loss experience with the Lake has been excellent in liability and about average for hull," comments Frank Brown of Alpha. "Virtually every loss is water-related."

Turbochargers

Several dozen Lakes have been delivered with turbochargers. We'd advise buying one only if you plan to operate regularly out of high-altitude lakes. The airplanes are so slow that it's hardly worthwhile to climb high for speed. And the normal reasons people use to justify a turbo—the ability to climb above weather, maintain altitude over mountainous terrain, and to maintain altitude with a load of ice—just don't apply, since a Lake really has no business in such con-

Lake Amphibian Resale Value Chart

ditions in the first place.

Balanced against the improved takeoff performance at altitude is the price of higher maintenance. The add-on Rajay turbos don't have a very good reliability history; 500 to 800 hours is considered to be a normal turbo life span. And of course the turbo makes the engine itself run hotter.

The turbo Lakes use manual wastegates. While this adds a fourth lever to the power quadrant and requires more pilot workload, it is more efficient and easier on the engine than the fixed-wastegates used in other Rajay installations like the Turbo Arrow, Seneca and Mooney 231. The Lake turbo is only a normalizer; that is, it may be used only to restore normal manifold pressures at high altitude. Max manifold pressure is still the normal 30 inches.

The turbo installation weighs about 40 pounds, and high-altitude flight requires a heavy-duty heater. Useful load is reduced to the point that an IFR Turbo 180 is a two-place airplane, and a Turbo Buccaneer not much better. And the small fuel supply limits the turbo's utility even more. Face it, the Lake is basically a low-altitude fun machine, and not even a turbocharger will turn it into a cross-country cruiser.

The original C-1 Skimmer built from 1956 through 1960 had a bow

two feet shorter and a wing four feet shorter than later Buccaneers. Consequently, the Skimmer tended to porpoise a lot, and climb rate was rather sickly. Only a handful of the 150-hp C-1 Skimmers are still flying, and perhaps a few dozen 180-hp C-2 Skimmers. They rarely come up for sale; the few that are left tend to be prized as antiques by doting owners. Value can range from $7,000 to $15,000, depending on condition.

The LA-4-180 can be a good bargain. There simply is no cheaper way to carry four people in an amphibian, although performance with four full-size adults is marginal. LA-4s generally run in the $15,000-20,000 range, although a factory-refurbished airplane with all the latest updates could go for as much as $27,000.

Most Lakes on the used-plane market are Buccaneers. There were no major changes in the Buccaneer until the 1983 EP model, but minor evolutionary changes over the years are worth looking for. Examples: the 1981 model has more grease fittings, polychromate primer, an improved canopy and better, more rust-resistant cabin vents. The 1975 model has improved grease fittings in the landing gear.

STC Mods

The only STC mod we're aware of is the Causley Super Lake, which appeared in 1982. But the company is apparently now out of business (the phone was disconnected when we called). The mod consisted of wing root fairings, float fairings, wheel well fairings, sculptured wingtips, trailing edge fillets called "batwings," a dorsal fin and new prop spinner. The aerodynamic improvements were claimed to add nine knots of cruise speed and "drastically" increase climb rate.

The Lake company itself is now the main purveyor of retrofit mods. It has taken over the "batwing" mod of the Causley STC, which Lake says helps improve flow around the pylon and propeller and provides more lift, particularly in ground (or water) effect. Cost: about $3,000.

Lake also offers the "Hydro-booster" hull mod, which consists of four external strakes. In addition to reinforcing the structure, the strakes are claimed to reduce water drag and make the craft more stable in turns. At a price of $1,580, the mod is "worth 10 times its price in what it does for the airplane," according to Bruce Rivard. The Lake factory can also retrofit improved canopies, instrument panels, interiors, soundproofing kits, wingtip foam flotation kits, and seven-gallon sponson fuel tanks.

The float tanks can be easily retrofitted to 1972 and later models, which already have the internal fuel lines in place. Cost is $4,032, or $3,537 if the old floats are in good shape and can be traded in. (Note, however, that full sponson tanks affect water handling and reduce buoyancy.)

Lake also can retrofit the cargo door it designed for the Renegade. Cost: $2,015.

Owner Comments

I have operated a Lake LA4-200EP about 300 hours since December of 1982. I have been more than pleased by my experience with this aircraft. The performance is truly phenomenal, and the aircraft is straightforward and easy to fly. I have found the performance claims of the manufacturer to be conservative.

In 300 hours the only parts replacement that was not part of the scheduled annual inspection was a trim actuator which the manufacturer cheerfully replaced under warranty.

The annual inspection was $580 with a standard labor cost for the inspection of $450.

Handling on both land and water is better than any other aircraft that I know.

Other new aircraft I have operated required constant attention for up to two years before all the "bugs" were removed.

John G. Kehlar
McLean, Va.

This is my second Lake Amphibian, which has to say something about my feeling for it. I have well over 1,000 hours in the aircraft. One sort of needs it. It is a difficult airplane to fly. It is a demanding aircraft. Very heavy rudder, for example.

The engine has performed flawlessly. And, as a matter of fact, there have been no real problems with the structure of the aircraft (except one real lousy water landing I once made).

It is sort of junky: It should be cleaned up for higher speeds. I

Extra cabin door, as on the Renegade here, can be retrofitted on older Lakes.

have the Q-tip propeller and it seems to help with the high noise level. I also use the David Clark headsets, which I think are vital against the noise.

Gerald R. Dillon
Minneapolis, Minn.

We purchased a 1981 demo approximately one year ago.

The aircraft was flown over 200 hours between April and October of 1983. Its performance was as expected: true airspeed at cruise (5,000-7,000 ft.) is 123-126 knots. climb rate 750 fpm; functional ceiling 8,000-9,000 ft. (where it runs out of strength). In almost all configurations we generally burned under 10 gph.

There is no question, however, that the Lake is the best thing going for water work. Once you have experienced the "greased swish" of a Lake landing, dry-land landings are of little further interest. As a watercraft, it excels. The only real drawback is docking; that is definitely easier on floats. The payload also lives up to expectations; with full fuel (54 gals.) we can still handle three good-sized souls (180 pounds) and 100 pounds of luggage within gross and c.g. limits.

All of this good commentary must be tempered, however, by serious servicing problems on this aircraft. From the day we purchased the Lake, we have experienced continuing problems with the nose strut, electrical systems and other items detailed in our correspondence to Lake Aircraft Co. While the staff at Lake was generally helpful, the fact remains that the aircraft underwent a factory annual at the time of purchase, a 100-hr. inspection during the month of July (1983) and a recommended second annual in November (1983) that was only just completed last month because of the aforementioned problem areas. We realize that an airplane is a big hole in the sky in which you pour money, but this has been ludicrous.

J. A. Germ
Naperville, Ill.

Piper Turbo Arrow

Although it occupies a marketing niche as a bargain-basement turbo single, the Piper Turbo Arrow is the ultimate refinement of the classic four-place Cherokee series—certainly the most popular low-wing airplane class ever. The turbocharged, retractable member of the Cherokee line was introduced in 1977 as a companion to the best-selling Arrow III, and it has proven very popular. In 1982, for instance, the Turbo outsold the standard Arrow by nearly five to one, proving once more that sophistication and performance are bigger selling points than reliability and low maintenance.

While the Turbo Arrow does have some reasonable performance numbers, and can be picked up on the used market for as little as $35,000, potential trouble spots under the cowling deserve serious consideration by any used-plane shopper.

History

The Turbo Arrow's genealogy so far has been fairly brief and not very eventful. When it first appeared in 1977, there were some eyebrows raised at the 200-hp six-cylinder Continental TSIO-360 engine. The standard Arrow had received good service from the four-cylinder 200-hp Lycoming, and the logical progression would have been to turbocharge that powerplant. But Rockwell had already taken that approach with its 112TC, with very poor results. And Piper had already used the Continental TSIO-360 for several years in its Seneca II, so it chose virtually the same powerplant for the Turbo Arrow.

Turbo Arrow is distinguishable from its non-turbo brother (rear) by sharp spinner and landing light pod below the cowl. These are 1978 models.

After two years on the marketplace, the Turbo Arrow III underwent a facelift—or rather tail-lift—to become the Turbo Arrow IV. The standard, boring, quiche-eating tail was discarded in favor of a bold new T-tail. It was strictly a cosmetic move, designed to fit Piper's new T-tail motif (already established by the Tomahawk, Lance II and Cheyenne III). The 1979 Turbo Arrow IV also got a new version of the TSIO-360 with a beefier crankshaft, denoted by the suffix '-FB' instead of the previous '-F.' That change increased TBO from 1,400 hours to 1,800. Other than engine and tail, changes have been minor.

Used-Plane Market

The market for Turbo Arrows is fairly active. "They're a popular plane," one big broker told us. Real-world prices generally start at about $30,000 for a 1977 model with a high-time engine, and climb to upwards of $75,000 for a cream-puff loaded 1983 model. A typical 1980 Turbo Arrow with a few IFR goodies would go in the low forties. The T-tail version suffers a bit in today's rather depressed market compared to the "old-fashioned" low-tail models. "I wouldn't pay one scratch more for a '79 T-tail than a '78 low-tail," the broker commented. "That's because my customers won't pay any more, either." The T-tail penalty on the Turbo Arrow, however, is nowhere near as heavy as that on the T-tail Lance, which is a real dog on the market because of its poor handling qualities compared to the standard Lance (and subsequent Saratogas).

One reason Turbo Arrows are so popular is that prices are comparatively low. Compare the Turbo Arrow to the Mooney 231, for example. Both are four-place retractables powered by identical engines. Yet the Mooney commands a far higher price on the used-plane market, a measure of the relative esteem in which the two airplanes are held by the flying public. While a 1980 Turbo Arrow IV can be had for just over $40,000, you'll need better than 60 grand to take home a 1980 231. The Turbo Arrow is worth $5,000-$10,000 less than even the non-turbocharged Mooney 201, which has similar performance. Compared to the standard Arrow, the Turbo version commands from $3,000 to $8,000 more, depending on the year.

Performance

The Turbo Arrow has reasonably good, although by no means sizzling, performance. Most Turbo Arrow owners fly in the 10,000-13,000-foot altitude range, just below the point where oxygen becomes necessary. At these altitudes, the airplane turns in cruising speeds ranging from about 165 knots at 75 percent power and about 14 gph to 150 knots at 65 percent power and 11 gph. Several owners report speeds well in excess of book figures, although Piper airspeed indicators are often optimistic.

The maximum book cruise figure is 172 knots at 19,000 feet. The only owner we heard from who's flown that high reported achieving 167 knots at 65 percent power—right on the book number.

Owner-reported power settings are not very reliable, however, because of the primitive and incorrect power charts Piper supplies with the airplane. The Turbo Arrow book says that at a given rpm, the same manifold pressure will give the same power output at any altitude from sea level to 20,000 feet. This is nonsense, of course; exhaust back pressure and compressor discharge temperature vary with altitude, and both of these factors affect power output. (Mooney's power chart for the same basic engine shows up to three inches variation in manifold pressure for constant power at various altitudes. Even Piper notes such variations in the power charts for its Seneca III, which uses essentially the same engine as the Turbo Arrow.) The Turbo Arrow owner is thus very poorly equipped to set power precisely. At 14,000 feet, what he believes to be 75 percent power "by the book" is in reality closer to 83 percent power.

Turbo Arrow cruise speeds are about 20 knots below those of the Mooney 231. It's slower than even the non-turbocharged Mooney 201 at any non-oxygen altitude. But the Mooneys are unusually fast; compared to other competitive airplanes, like the Rockwells and Cessnas, the Turbo Arrow stacks up pretty well.

Climb rate is a creditable 950 fpm at sea level and gross weight. As with any turbo aircraft, rate of climb is maintained constant (or nearly so) at altitude, and owners report climb rates of 1,000 fpm with typical loads (below gross) all the way up to 10,000 feet. At moderate weights, ROC is still 500 fpm at 20,000 feet. While this is quite good by non-turbocharged standards, it again falls well short of the Mooney 231, the only directly competitive airplane. Under the same conditions, the 231 will climb 840 fpm.

Range of the Turbo Arrow is good. It has big 72-gallon tanks, enough for about five hours normal cruising with a small reserve. At an average cruise speed of 160 knots, that's nearly 800 nm. (Max cruise at rich mixtures reduces this range appreciably.) Throttled back to 55 percent power at 10,000 feet and 9.2 gph, the Turbo Arrow is good for seven hours at 135 knots—better than 900 nautical. Basically, the Turbo Arrow will take you about as far as you'd want to go in one hop. (Unfortunately, that nasty ol' 231 is still there to embarrass the Turbo Arrow; the Mooney will fly about 100 miles farther.)

Loading

The Turbo Arrow has a gross weight of 2,900 pounds. Real-world empty weights of IFR-equipped airplanes typically run around 1,900-1,950 pounds, leaving a useful load of about 950-1,000 pounds. With full fuel, that's 550 pounds for payload—three people and 10 pounds of carry-on. A cabin full of people and luggage will cut fuel capacity to 30 gallons, enough for perhaps 200 nm with IFR reserves. Such loading numbers are typical of four-place retractables.

Piper makes a big deal out of the

Cost/Performance/Specifications

Model	Year	Number Built	Average Retail Price*	Gross Weight (lbs)	Useful Load (lbs)	Cruise Speed (kts)	Fuel (gals)	Engine	TBO (hrs)	Overhaul Cost
PA-28R-201T (III)	1977	427	$34,000	2,900	1,200	172	72	200-hp Cont. TSIO-360-F	1,400	$13,000
PA-28R-201T (III)	1978	427	$38,000	2,900	1,200	172	72	200-hp Cont. TSIO-360-F	1,400	$13,000
PA-28RT-201T (IV)	1979	310	$41,500	2,900	1,200	172	72	200-hp Cont. TSIO-360-FB	1,800	$12,750
PA-28RT-201T (IV)	1980	178	$45,500	2,900	1,200	172	72	200-hp Cont. TSIO-360-FB	1,800	$12,750
PA-28RT-201T (IV)	1981	167	$51,000	2,900	1,200	172	72	200-hp Cont. TSIO-360-FB	1,800	$12,750
PA-28RT-201T (IV)	1982	68	$60,000	2,900	1,200	172	72	200-hp Cont. TSIO-360-FB	1,800	$12,750
PA-28RT-201T (IV)	1983	48	$71,000	2,900	1,200	172	72	200-hp Cont. TSIO-360-FB	1,800	$12,750

*Price assumes dual navcom and VOR, localizer, glideslope, markers, transponder, encoder, ADF, two-axis autopilot, oxygen, 750 hours on engine. Wholesale prices about 20 percent less.

Turbo Arrow's load-carrying abilities, claiming in magazine ads that it is superior to that of the nemesis Mooney 231. This is hogwash. The 231 has useful load numbers very similar to the Turbo Arrow's.

Loading balance is no problem in a Turbo Arrow unless it is equipped with air conditioning. The heavy (60-lb.) rear compressor limits rear-seat and baggage loading, according to two different Turbo Arrow owners who responded to our survey. The air-conditioning option moves the c.g. back by nearly an inch, or about seven percent of the envelope. Without air conditioning, however, a typical IFR-equipped Arrow demands only normal everyday attention to c.g. matters.

Handbook figures for the 1978 T-Arrow III and 1979 IV version suggest that the IV has dramatically better takeoff performance. At 7,000 feet and 20° C., for example, the book says a Turbo Arrow III will clear the obstacle in about 5,700 feet at gross weight. For the T-Arrow IV, the figure is 3,400 feet.

Why the astounding difference? Should a mountain dweller insist upon only a T-Arrow IV? Not necessarily. Piper engineers admit that there is no actual performance difference between the two airplanes, side-by-side on the same day. Apparently Piper simply changed its procedures for measuring (and extrapolating) takeoff data. So which figure reflects reality? We have no idea. The lesson for Turbo Arrow shoppers: Don't take the handbook numbers very seriously.

Creature Comforts

The Turbo Arrow rates about average in cabin roominess. The Cherokee was originally designed not to be *too* wide, in order not to make the top-of-the-line Comanche look bad. So the Turbo Arrow gets stuck with a fairly narrow 42-inch cabin. Headroom is pretty good, with a floor-to-ceiling distance of 48 inches, very typical of single-engine airplanes and four inches more than the low-slung Mooneys. Legroom in the rear is

good, the result of a fuselage stretch given the whole Cherokee line back in 1972.

Flying Qualities

Turbo Arrow owners praise their craft for its benign and solid handling, particularly in IFR conditions. It has no unusual vices that we're aware of. There are some differences between the later T-tail models and the earlier low-tail versions, however. According to one owner who has flown both extensively, the primary difference is in the planes' reactions to gear and flap lowering. Putting down the wheels causes no pitch change in the T-tail and a nose-down pitch in the low-tail. Flaps trigger a sharp nose-up surge in the low-tail, and nose-down action in the T.

Runway traits are also different. The T-tail airplane does not rotate as quickly on takeoff, and does not have as good pitch authority at low speeds. (The low tail sits in the prop blast and is therefore more responsive.)

Engine

The heart of any airplane is its engine, and beneath the cowling of the Turbo Arrow beats a heart of . . . well, it's not gold by any stretch of the imagination. The TSIO-360-F and -FB are hot-running, high-vibration engines that have had a host of problems. (For details, see the March 1, 1983 issue of *Aviation Consumer*.) And we're not just talking maintenance headaches. The fixed-wastegate TSIO-360 series as installed in the Turbo Arrow, Turbo Dakota, Seneca III and Mooney 231 has an engine-failure accident rate eight times

higher than the Bonanza's, for example. FAA data shows 26 Turbo Arrow accidents or incidents stemming from powerplant failures in a recent five-years period. (The Turbo Dakota, essentially a Turbo Arrow with fixed gear, is even worse; seven percent of the fleet had engine failures in only three years.)

Here's a laundry list of major Turbo Arrow engine problems:

• Broken connecting rods. Apparently a batch of improperly heat-treated rods found their way into some engines built around 1979. Failures in Turbo Arrows have resulted.

• High-altitude "missing." Above about 12,000-15,000 feet, the thin air has markedly less insulating effect. Therefore, magneto current is more likely to leak out and "arc," causing possibly severe misfiring. Keeping the ignition system in perfect shape and plug gaps tight can help, but the real solution is to pressurize the magnetos. Mooney fixed the same problem on its 231 a couple of years ago (offering free retrofit kits to owners), but Piper so far has ignored it.

• Cylinder, piston and valve problems. Generally caused by running too hot at too high boost. The fixed-wastegate design means that the turbocharger is always running,

This aircraft with good IFR equipment was able to carry full fuel, 200 pounds in the baggage compartment, plus two 170-pounders in front and a 123-pounder in the rear seat and remain within limits.

whether it's needed or not. This increases stress on the engine and raises inlet air temperatures. That, combined with poor cooling, causes all sorts of upper-end distress.

• Turbocharge cracking. This has been the subject of a recent (and very expensive) AD. Turbos must be inspected every 200 hours and replaced if cracked (many have been found that way). Cost to replace a housing: about $1,000.

• Poorly designed breather tubes. They can freeze up, causing all the oil to be vented overboard. At least one accident has resulted. Check Service Bulletins M80-18 and M79-19. Applied to 1977-78 airplanes only.

• Oil pump tach drive. Improperly torqued bolts cause oil pumps to break. Major AD in 1981.

In addition, there have been literally dozens of service bulletins on the engine.

All this is not to say that the TSIO-360-F or -FB cannot be a safe, reliable powerplant. Several Turbo Arrow owners reported no problems at all over hundreds of hours. The secret seems to be to keep the engine cool and to avoid high-boost conditions.

Cooling Problems

The Turbo Arrow's engine reliability woes are partly a result of poor engine cooling. Many owners report that cylinder head temperatures run right at the redline in warm weather, and find they must use special procedures—climbing flat and fast, running rich mixtures, and foregoing high altitudes—to avoid overheating the engine. Piper designed the Turbo Arrow without cowl flaps, apparently in a misguided effort to save money and keep the price down. As a result, the Turbo Arrow runs very hot in climb, yet during cruise on cold days the engine can actually be overcooled. This wastes several knots of cruising speed.

The cooling problem also wastes a lot of money, since pilots must

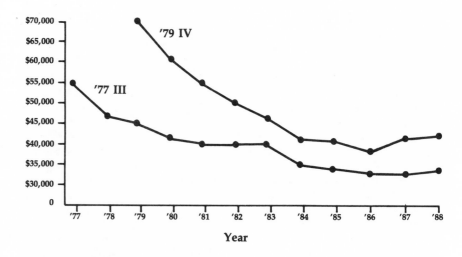

Turbo Arrow Resale Value Chart

often run extra-rich fuel mixtures just to cool the engine. An extra gallon an hour can easily add up to over $500 in fuel per year (assuming 300 hours annually). Some Turbo Arrow pilots find that even full rich mixture is not enough during climb, and have taken to turning the fuel boost pump on to force even more excess fuel through the overheated cylinders.

The integrity of the cooling baffles is absolutely critical to Turbo Arrow engine health. Check them carefully, particularly the rubber seals. We'd also recommend installation of an optional Piper cooling kit. It consists of new baffles and extra louvers in the bottom of the cowling. (It's kit number 764-152V, listing at $458.36.) Installation is estimated at eight hours. Piper for some reason seems almost to keep the kit a secret, describing it only in an obscure "Service Spares Letter" (No. 388) rather than the normal service bulletin/service letter network to which most mechanics and some owners routinely subscribe. (The kit is available for 1977-79 models, but not, as best we could discern, for 1980s or 1981s. The cooling mod was a factory option in 1982, and was made standard equipment for 1983.)

There is a flip side to the cooling kit, however. Because more air is flowing over the cylinders at all times, the airplane will be more prone to overcooling during descent, which can cause engine

damage due to thermal shock. (At least one engine expert dismisses thermal shock as an old wives' tale, however.) In any case, pilots of Turbo Arrows with cooling kits installed should resign themselves to the loss of a couple of knots of cruise speed and be very careful on descent.

Operating Quirks

To assess the Turbo Arrow's role as an economy turbo—it is in fact the cheapest turbocharged airplane currently in production—Piper decided on a fixed wastegate. The gate is stuck part way open at all times. Sure, it's cheaper to build that way, but such a primitive system has some disadvantages. First, the turbo works all the time, even when it's not needed. Second, minor changes in speed, altitude or rpm cause big swings in manifold pressure, even with the throttle fixed.

As a result, takeoff procedures are weird; the pilot advances the throttle only to about 35 inches to start the takeoff roll. As the plane accelerates, mp shoots up to the redline of 41 inches all by itself. During climb, mp drops off with increasing altitude. And any rpm change results in huge mp variations. In fact, we once flew a Turbo Arrow in which power was increased for climb by *reducing* the throttle. The previous rpm adjustment had already caused the mp to zoom up above the redline by itself.

Starting the TSIO-360 can be a problem on cold mornings. Try to buy an airplane with the optional priming system. We once had to leave an airplane (not equipped with the primer) sitting for several days when it absolutely failed to start in 30° weather. One owner describes the priming system as "worth its weight in gold."

Safety

We have no overall fatal accident figures for the Turbo Arrow alone. However, the Arrow series in general had a fatal accident rate of 11.3 per 100,000 flight hours for the period 1972-76. (This acocunts for fatal accidents from all causes.) The 11.3 figure is about average, ninth among 13 retractable singles sampled by *Aviation Consumer*. (The rates ranges from 4.6 to 16.8.) Considering that the Arrow is often a "step-up" retractable flown by less experienced pilots, that is not a bad record.

The Turbo Arrow differs only in the engine, and as we have already said, the engine failure accident rate is very high. Fortunately none of those engine failures have yet resulted in fatalities.

The T-Arrow has one good feature that reduces embarassing runway crunches: the famous automatic landing gear. The autogear works, there's no doubt about it; the Arrow series has a gear-up accident rate less than a third of the Cessna Cardinal's. Some pilots dislike the auto-gear intensely, however, mostly because it can stay down too long on takeoff, or possibly extend inadvertently in a steep climb situation if improperly calibrated or adjusted. The system can be overridden, however, and some pilots choose to do that. Nevertheless, we feel the Arrow automatic gear system is a praiseworthy safety feature.

Maintenance

A Turbo Arrow is almost certain to be far more expensive than a standard Arrow to maintain. A factory remanufactured TSIO-360-FB costs about $14,000. Pro-rated over the 1,800-hour TBO, that's nearly nine

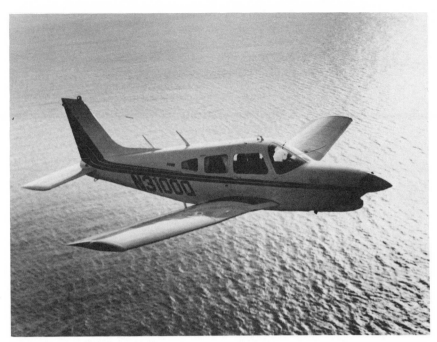

Turbo Arrow is a bargain basement turbo, but a combination that can sometimes spell trouble.

dollars per hour. For the 1,400-hour -F engine on 1977-79 T-Arrows, the number is a formidable $11 per hour plus. (Incidentally, according to one owner, Continental will not accept an older -F engine in exchange for an -FB reman. He was forced to either buy a reman engine with a crankshaft of questionable strength, or spend $6,400 extra to buy an -FB engine outright, with no trade-in.)

Annual inspection costs for the Turbo Arrow can be high. Typical costs reported by owners ranged from $1,100 to $3,400, although one fellow reported $500. (He apparently didn't bother with any AD notes.) Hourly maintenance costs seem to run in the $15-$25 range.

The only major relatively recent AD is that on the Rajay turbo housing. Try to buy an airplane with a late-model, ductile ni-resist housing that does not need repetitive 200-hour inspections and is less likely to crack. Naturally, all ADs should be complied with on any airplane considered for purchase.

A recent service bulletin recommends an inspection for cracked nosegear link and brace assem-

blies. Determine whether this has been accomplished on any plane under consideration.

Modifications

Knots 2U Inc., (312) 256-4807, offers aileron and flap gap seals for about $1,000 plus installation. These are said to increase cruise speed by about five knots; reduce stall, takeoff and approach speeds by about four knots; and provide crisper aileron control. "It makes a whole new airplane out it," one Turbo Arrow owner told us.

Turboplus Inc. (800) 742-4202, has developed an extensive engine mod for the Turbo Arrow that should go a long way toward solving the overheating and reliability problems. It consists of an improved induction system, a turbocharger intercooler, pressurized magnetoes, cowl flaps and improved engine instrumentation. Cost of the mod kit is $4,995 plus installation by your local mechanic. Or Turboplus will install it for you at a cost of $6,495.

Frankly, Turboplus appears to be doing what Piper should have been doing all along. Currently, the Turbo Arrow can be characterized as an excellent airframe with a poor engine installation. The Turboplus mod promises to make the Turbo Arrow an all-around good airplane.

Owner Comments

I have owned my Arrow for 20 months and have flown 225 hours during that time. My aircraft now has a total of 660 hours. I fly out of Colorado Springs at an altitude of 6,175 feet and find the turbo a necessity. I average 10.4 gph block to block cruising at 65 percent power at usual altitudes between 10,000 and 15,000 feet. I file for a TAS of 155 knots and believe this aircraft offers an excellent balance between speed, efficiency, and payload. The plane is a stable instrument platform and has a generous center of gravity envelope. The optional electric primer makes starting even in cold weather a snap, and I consider this feature a must. The cabin is average for this class of aircraft, but even with my wife and two children under three, we get along comfortably on long trips.

The fixed-gate turbo means constant throttle adjustments are necessary while climbing and descending. This does not create a problem for a regular user, but I would not recommend this aircraft for rental pilots without a *thorough* checkout.

My maintenance has been expensive. My first annual cost $1,721. This did include a complete review of all the maintenance history and a costly fuel tank inspection. My last annual cost $3,401. However this included a recurring propeller overhaul (a real aggravation since the AD is irrespective of hours flown) and the recent Rajay AD compliance, which fortunately for me was published while my aircraft was down for the annual.

Thanks to a great maintenance facility (West Aire, Inc., Colorado Springs, Colo., Verlin Schauer, chief of maintenance) I was able to have one of the few improved "04" housings available installed, which relieves me of repetitive inspections. This alone accounted for approximately $1,200 of my annual costs, and the prop overhaul cost approximately $700. My direct operating costs have been $57 per hour. This does not include insurance, tie down, new radio equipment (Stormscope or heat shields), or overhaul reserve.

The two other items: I used to have a problem with cylinder head temperatures rising into the red, but I have found that using continuous LO fuel boost pump during climb-out and a slightly higher or richer mixture has practically eliminated this problem. I figure the slight increase in fuel consumption will offset the possibile earlier overhaul.

Also, I have been spoiled by the turbo capabilities, and if I ever move from the Rockies, I believe I will still want a turbocharged aircraft for its tremendous performance and reserve power. Also I feel a turbocharged aircraft is one of the best defenses against unexpected icing. I love my plane.

David S. Lennon
Colorado Springs, Colo.

I have owned a 1978 Turbo Arrow III for the past 18 months. It is simply the best four-place aircraft that I have flown. While not as fast as the Mooney 231, it does offer the following:

• Comfort. The cabin is large enough for six-footers without cramping.

• Cruise performance of 165 to 170 knots at 12,500 feet.

• A good useful load (1,090 pounds on mine), leaving a payload of 670 pounds with full fuel.

• An honest 1,000-fpm climb at gross weight below 10,000 feet.

Since buying this aircraft, I have had no turbo-related problems. The engine does run hot, and the leaning can put the CHT into the red if one is not careful. In the summer additional fuel is burned (1-1½ gph) to cool the engine. Pulling 75 percent power on a hot day will

Interior space is adequate, if not sensational. "Luxury" velour interior was an extra-cost option on this 1978 model.

burn about 15 gph. Starting is easy. The manifold pressure must be monitored on takeoff and minor prop variations in speed can change the boost by two to three inches.

Would I buy another Turbo Arrow? Yes, if it was not a T-tail. It beats the tacky interior and complicated landing gear of the Turbo Skylane and provides room for large people, unlike the Mooney.

Michael G. Salish
Lakeside, Calif.

I have owned a 1977 Turbo Arrow for the past two years. I have also flown extensively a 1980 T-tail Turbo Arrow. In regard to flying characteristics, I have found that the major difference between the two is the trim control. In the low-tail version, lowering the gear causes a nose-up attitude that can be only partially compensated for with 10 degrees of flaps. The T-tail model shows no sudden trim changes with gear extension. It does require, though, full back trim with full flaps on landing. Both planes are extremely easy to fly and do very well in IFR conditions and crosswind landings.

Cost of owning the airplane has been quite dear. Two ADs have alone cost $1,600 over the past year. One was for a nose gear overhaul and the second for the oil pump torque adjustment. The other major cost has been leaking fuel-sending devices, requiring gasket replacement and 16 hours of labor. The last annual cost $2,200, which does include the above mentioned torque adjustment AD, but not the nose gear. The plane has cost $60 an hour, dry, to fly. There is currently an AD against the turbocharger. If ours has a crack, I am looking at another $1,400 for a replacement.

The engine now needs a major overhaul at 1,500 hours. Will I do it? Perhaps. I am also looking at a Mooney.

Gerald R. Moress
Salt Lake City, Utah

I recently purchased a 1979 Turbo Arrow and am very pleased with it. It is a very stable, good-handling airplane. My T-Arrow trues at 146 knots at lower altitudes and 156 knots at higher altitudes at 65 percent power, and burns 11 gph. The annual inspection cost $497.

All in all, the T-Arrow is a pretty good airplane, it is faster than some and slower than others, but it does a pretty good job for me. Outside of cosmetic purposes, I don't see much of an advantage of the T-tail over the low tail. I like Piper's soundproofing package. The quiet ride is the first comment that Cessna drivers make.

Mike Casey
Lewis, Iowa

To date I have logged 60 hours in my 1977 Turbo Arrow, bought used in October 1982. I am very satisfied with the stability, handling and overall performance, with the following observations:

One of the first modifications was to pressurize the Bendix mags. At 17,500 feet the engine was smooth as silk, no roughness. But I could not operate above 55 percent power at this altitude due to CHT overheating. Perhaps a richer mixture would have helped, but economy would suffer. Perhaps an intercooler. Turboplus, maybe?

At 15,500, no problems. About 165 knots TAS at 65 percent power gave about 11 gph (30 inches at 2400 rpm).

Only mechanical problem so far was the gear retraction hydraulic

pump. An "O" ring failed and the gear would not retract. Repair cost was $202.

Robert Doenges
Rancho Palos Verdes, Calif.

The recent AD on Rajay turbos turned up an interesting situation. If your repair station orders the casting from Continental, you'll be charged about $650 for the part. However, if the part is ordered from Rotomaster for a turbocharger that fits a Lycoming engine (same part number), the price is $477. Combs Gates at Arapahoe Airport has replaced more than a dozen castings at the $477 price, while nobody else around here has caught on.

The speed and fuel consumption is acceptable to us—we figure on 11.5 gph and plan for 155 knots. Our maintenance reserve is high because of our experience with Continental's optimistic estimate of TBO. Annuals are in the $500 range, and we fly about 150 hours per year.

Philip Williamson
Aurora, Colo.

My plane is a 1978 model I bought new and by fixing and modifying as needed. I have a very satisfactory plane. We took delivery and had to argue with the dealer that the loose horizontal stabilizer was not designed that way—he wanted to charge me to tighten the hinges.

Most cooling problems have involved careless assembly of the rubber baffles, which I got hard-nosed about. I finally added the optional cooling kit, which now gives me a very normal operating temperature.

I had a high-altitude missing problem from day one, and it would *almost* go away with a very careful tune-up, but gets worse very quickly. In desperation, I started to completely replace the magnetos, and lo-and-behold, guess what! The mag shop discovered a hairline crack in the distributor cap. After replacing the cap, no more high altitude missing. I wonder how

many misfiring Turbo Arrows have cracked caps?

Vibration and shaking from the two-blade prop on that six-cylinder Continental had always bothered me. Three power pulses for two prop blades are impossible to balance. So six months ago I had a new full-size 76-inch three-blade prop put on. What a difference! I should have done it sooner. It changed the character of the plane completely, but for the better. Very smooth, super acceleration on takeoff, much quieter, faster cruise at low rpm and much steeper closed-throttle approaches for obstacle clearance.

Merrill D. Martin
Emeryville, Calif.

As an owner of a 1978 T-Arrow, I have been very happy with its performance. I have not kept specific records of maintenance and hourly costs, but I consider mine to be about average. I have replaced my attitude indicator two times and DG once, however.

I have not experienced the heating problems that have been mentioned, but I did experience the engine roughness at high altitude. The roughness was corrected by my FBO. It was found to be a faulty mag condenser. I generally fly 10,000-13,000 feet on long trips, and it has been fine so far.

My only real complaint has to be the numerous ADs on the airplane and a 100 percent lack of support from factory and/or parts manufacturers. I have very strong feelings that the ADs are due to faulty manufacturing and installation and should be borne by the companies, as the ADs are not due to lack of maintenance and performance of my part. These have been very costly: 1) gas line replacements and gas valve problems, 2) heat shield, 3) mags, 4) Rajay turbo cracks, 5) nose wheel, and more. I have been told by my FBO that Piper will not do any repairs or accept responsibility on out-of-warranty items. *This is wrong.*

David A. Gray, Jr.
Sacramento, Calif.

Rockwell 114

The Rockwell 114 is a sad story—a fine-looking, well-built aircraft that survived only four years in the marketplace. The 114 doesn't fly very fast and guzzles a lot of gas, but perhaps its most damaging liability is the fact that it was marketed by Rockwell, which never was successful in the single-engine plane business and finally packed it in for good in 1979, taking the 114 with it, of course. Fewer than 500 Model 114s were built. "They're hard to sell," one big used-plane broker told us, "but there's still a following for the airplane."

History

The 114 is an outgrowth of the 112, introduced in 1972. The 112 was developed after marketing studies showed that customers wanted zippy styling and comfort above all. The 112 had all that, but was so underpowered with its 200-hp Lycoming that it could barely get out of its own way. As a result, the 112 is a slug on the used-plane market (we heard of one changing hands for $12,000 back in 1982). In 1976, Rockwell introduced the 114, which was simply a 112 with a 260-hp engine. The 114 is commonly characterized as "the plane the 112 should have been in the first place."

The 114 was in production only four years, with no model changes of consequence. The 1977 model had aerodynamic improvements resulting in slightly improved performance, plus better soundproofing and fixes for earlier compass interference and trim-tab freeze-up problems. In 1979, the "Gran Turismo" version was offered, with a three-bladed prop, new cowl flaps, a fancy interior—and an outrageous price. The $95,000 price

tag (more than the bigger, faster, more powerful Cessna 210) was apparently a desperate attempt by Rockwell to recoup some of its losses, but the strategy backfired, and 114 sales declined sharply in 1979. Shortly thereafter the entire Rockwell single-engine line was aborted.

Used-Plane Market

The 114 is not exactly a gem on the used-plane market. In the current depressed single-engine market, a 114 can be had for anywhere from about $30,000 for a 1976 model to about $40,000 for a 1979 Gran Turismo.

Currently, 114s of almost any vintage are worth only a little better than half their new-plane price tags—a very low figure. Used blue-chippers like the Mooney 201 and Bonanza are worth 75-85 percent of their new prices. (We should point out that the 114's new price tags were ridiculously inflated, and that most new 114s were sold at heavily discounted prices, so the picture is not quite as bad as the numbers portray.)

Performance

The 114 is a mediocre performer, considering its power. Owners report cruise speeds in the 150-knot range, not very fast for 260 hp. The Mooney 201, and Cessna Skylane RG both fly faster on

One of the few low-wingers with two doors, the 114 is noted for its creature comforts.

less power (the Mooney dramatically so). When the 114 was introduced, *Aviation Consumer* pilots flew the aircraft in a side-by-side test with a 1972 Piper Comanche, which had the same 260-hp engine. Results: the Comanche was not only faster, but climbed better and stalled slower to boot. Book max. cruise figure is 156 knots for the 1976 model 114, and 161 knots for later versions.

Fuel efficiency is directly related to speed, and again the 114 looks bad compared to its main competition, the Mooney and Skylane RG. Owners report fuel flows of 12-14 gph at moderate cruise speeds, for an mpg rating of about 12-13. In these days of $2 per gallon avgas, it is rather hard to justify such poor fuel efficiency (particularly in a retractable). At the prevailing $1 a gallon price when the 114 was first introduced, fuel efficiency was not so critical, but every fuel price increase particularly hurts the 114. (In the last few years, of course, there has been talk of oil gluts, and crude prices have actually fallen, and many soothsayers predict fuel prices will hold steady or decline for several years to come. That is good news for 114 owners, who can almost watch their plane's resale value curve mirror the spot-market crude price zigzags.)

Climb performance and range are both adequate. Listed rate of climb is just over 1,000 fpm for the 1976 model, and 1,160 fpm thereafter, comparable to performance by the Mooney and Skylane RG's, and superior to that of the economy 200-hp retractables such as the Arrow, Sierra, Cardinal RG and, of course, the sickly 112. Range is 600 nm or so, well short of the Mooney's and Skylane RG. The 68-gallon fuel supply is enough for four hours or so at high cruise and five-plus hours at low cruise, but the 114 lacks the huge reserves of endurance of the Mooney and RG, both of which carry more fuel and burn it at a slower rate.

Creature Comforts

If Rockwell salesmen didn't like to dwell on performance, they positively glowed when talking about the 114's cabin. It is 47 inches wide, wider than that of any other single and a lot of twins. Owners invariably cite the roomy cabin as a prime reason for buying the airplane and, particularly in the later models, the 114's interior trim complemented the roominess. The rear seats, however, are a bit short on legroom. Linebackers should love the 114; power forwards maybe not.

Early 114s were quite noisy, but Rockwell has offered a sound-proofing kit to cut a few decibels from the cockpit din. Later models are quieter, but still typical of the horribly noisy (90-95 dBA) cockpits of virtually all light aircraft.

Loading

While the 114's useful load is rather low for a 260-hp airplane (it's about 350 pounds less than the Cherokee Six 260, for example, and less than a 260-hp Bonanza or Comanche), the fact that the 114 is limited to four seats and 68 gallons of fuel makes it one of the very few full-seats-plus-tanks-plus-baggage airplanes flying today. This is a fine safety factor. A 114 owner virtually never needs to think about gross weight limits, unless he is hauling cement blocks or circus fat ladies. "I have been comfortably able to travel with four adults, baggage,

The Commander 114 is one of the few low-wing aircraft to have a "both tanks" position on the fuel selector—a good safety feature.

skis, ski boots and full fuel for five and a half hours' flying time," reports one owner. Another reports a cabin payload of 773 pounds with a well-equipped IFR airplane with full fuel.

There is one flaw in the 114's rosy loading picture: a zero fuel weight limit of 2,732 pounds. This limits cabin payload to about 750 pounds in typical aircraft. That's ample for most flights, but doesn't allow for extreme situations like four 200-pounders. The zero-fuel weight limit is unusual among single-engine aircraft, and makes you wonder about the supposed structural superiority of the 114 due to its highly touted certification under Amendment 7 regulations. A zero-fuel limit means that the wing spar's bending load limit may be exceeded when the gross weight is safely below limits. We wonder how many 114 owners are even aware of the zero-fuel weight limit and its significance.

Resale Value

Resale value for both the 1976 and 1979 Model 114 are down, down, down. Normally, an aircraft will bottom out after three or four years, and then either hold its value or appreciate slightly (in inflated dollars, of course). The 1976 Model 114 has declined in value every year since 1976, with no sign of leveling off. In 1982, it was worth $36,000; two years later the value was down to $33,000. The 1979 model, meanwhile, lost nearly half its value in three years, to com-

mand only $62,000 in 1982; it brought around $45,000 in 1984.

Handling

The 114 is a fine-flying airplane in most respects. The controls are well-harmonized and the aircraft has a nice "feel." The 114 shows remarkable speed stability with gear and flap extension; virtually no trimming is necessary even if flaps and gear are thrown out at the highest permissible speed. This is a very nice feature during IFR let-downs and approaches. The only black mark is a tendency to wallow in turbulence.

The 114 is universally praised for being easy to land. The plane's pleasing controllability and ultra-forgiving trailing-link landing gear make greasers routine, a fact that no doubt sold a lot of 114s, since pilots like to impress passengers (and themselves) with smooth landings. Crosswinds are a problem, however; the 114 has insufficient rudder to handle crosswinds much above 15 knots. The same rudder insufficiency can make crosswind takeoffs a bit dodgy, particularly when the wind is from the left.

The 114's panel is well arranged. The fuel system also deserves praise: it is one of the few low-wing aircraft to have a "both" position on the fuel selector, an important safety feature.

Styling

Normally, we don't comment on an aircraft's styling, but in the case of the 114, we'll make an exception. It's a nifty-looking airplane, with a gracefully tapered wing, pleasing fuselage lines and a nicely-proportioned tail. The good looks of the 114 will certainly help its resale value in the years to come. "I've sold a couple of them on looks alone," one used-plane salesman told us. More than most pilots care to admit, styling plays a big role in the choice of an aircraft. A man's personal aircraft is a statement, an ego extension and a status symbol; Rockwell played on the 114's good looks by marketing it as a "class" item—expensive, but worth the price for those who could afford it.

Maintenance

The 114 has no outstanding maintenance problems that we're aware of. The engine is the very reliable 260-hp Lycoming IO-540, which has an excellent track record in the Comanche 260 and a 2,000-hour TBO. There have been only a few airframe ADs on the 114, but it shares with dozens of other aircraft the across-the-board ADs on the Hartzell prop, Bendix fuel injectors and magnetos, Lycoming fuel diaphragms, Airborne vacuum pumps, Aerosonic fuel flow transducers, plus the ubiquitous lithium battery ELT directive.

Nevertheless, as with any aircraft, there have been a number of maintenance glitches on the 114. Here is a list of some 114 service bulletins:

• 114-1: Rerouting of aileron control chain to prevent possible binding/interference and/or excessive wear. This applies only to very early 1976 model aircraft.

• 114-2: (September 1976; applies to approximately first 100 aircraft): Inspection and/or modification of the throttle control cable to prevent throttle malfunction.

• 114-3: (October 1976; approximately first 100 aircraft): Inspection of main landing gear retract cylinder bearing. Came as a result of landing gear problems in early aircraft, a not unusual occurrence in a new design.

• 114-4A (March 1978; serial number 1-134): Replacement of fuel selector valve. Although not an AD, this is one service bulletin that should be complied with.

• 114-5B (December 1977; approximately first 150 aircraft): Modification of seat and seat belt. The seats and shoulder harnesses were a bit of a trouble spot on the 114, and it took three bulletins to get it right. This one eventually became an AD. Incidentally, the 114 shoulder harness is a very poor design from the crashworthiness standpoint. The harness is anchored to the seat back itself rather than a hard point on the cabin framework. This makes a neat, cosmetic installation, but is virtually useless in a crash, since the crash forces are transmitted through the harness and seat back to the seat mounting brackets, which, like virtually all aircraft seats, are prone to rip loose from the floor.

• 114-6 (November 1976; s/n 1-158): Modification of cabin air vent system to prevent carbon monoxide gas from entering the cabin. This also became an AD.

• 114-7 (January, 1977; s/n 1-155): Inspection of the main landing gear orifice assembly. Through poor quality control, some of these were installed improperly at the factory, resulting in possible gear problems.

• 114-8 (February, 1977; s/n 1-214): Modification of the engine

breather tube to prevent ice buildup.

• 114-9 (March, 1977; s/n 150-199): Installation of placard on seat headrest.

• 114-10 (August, 1977; s/n 1-282): Replacement of clamp on parking brake valve. Designed to prevent slippage of cable and inadvertent release of parking brake.

• 114-11 (November, 1977; s/n 1-319): Replace main gear rod assembly pin retaining screw. This is the third service bulletin dealing with potential landing gear problems.

• 114-12 (November, 1977; s/n 1-318): Modification of vertical fin rib to prevent cracking.

• 114-13 (December, 1977; s/n 1-149): Another modification of the seat/harness, this one to correct a problem in the first series of bulletins.

• 114-14A (May, 1978; s/n 1-376): Inspection and replacement (if necessary) of aileron hinge supports.

• 114-15 (March, 1978; s/n 1-367): Modification of passenger seat locking pin. Designed to assure the locking pin locks into the seat track properly, thus preventing seat slippage at a critical moment. Another crashworthiness item.

• 114-16 (May, 1979; s/n 1-513): Replace prop governor. Leaky governors were a common problem; although not an AD item, it should have been done to any 114 considered for purchase. Cost is listed at $390 in the service bulletin, but take inflation into account

Cost/Performance/Specifications

Model	Year	Number Built	Average Retail Price*	Cruise Speed (kts)	Rate of Climb (fpm)	Gross Weight (lbs)	Useful Load (lbs)	Fuel (gals)	Engine	TBO (hrs)	Overhaul Cost
114	1976	134	$38,500	157	1,050	3,140	1,235	68	260-hp Lyc. IO-540-T4B5D	2,000	$13,000
114	1977	169	$41,000	162	1,160	3,140	1,235	68	260-hp Lyc. IO-540-T4B5D	2,000	$13,000
114	1978	98	$43,500	162	1,160	3,140	1,235	68	260-hp Lyc. IO-540-T4B5D	2,000	$13,000
114A Gran Turismo	1979	40	$48,500	162	1,160	3,140	1,235	68	260-hp Lyc. IO-540-T4B5D	2,000	$13,000

* Price includes dual navcom with VOR, LOC, glideslope, transponder, encoder, ADF, Century III autopilot, soundproofing mod, strobes, all ADs complied, 700 hours SMOH. Wholesale prices are 15-20 percent lower.

when figuring current costs.

• 114-17 (July 1979; s/n 1-511): Modify aileron bellcrank doubler to prevent cracks. This is third bulletin dealing with aileron system; check it carefully before purchase.

There were only two service bulletins issued from May 1979 to April 1982, about the time production was suspended and Rockwell got out of the single-engine business. We presume this is not because 114s have become suddenly trouble-free, but rather that the Rockwell service department no longer had time to issue service bulletins unless they were really critical.

Backup Support

We've received mixed reports on Rockwell's product support for the defunct single-engine line. Several 114 owners say they have had no problems at all getting parts, but one fellow said that Rockwell support was "zero" and that he was forced to scrounge parts up himself. In any case, Rockwell service dealers are few and far between. The secret seems to be to find a mechanic experienced with the airplane; it's rare enough that not every A&P has even seen one.

Service responsibility for the 114 has been taken over by Gulfstream American. "We're trying our best to continue supporting the airplane," said a spokesman of the Commander single-service department. He concedes that some parts now have to be built to order, presumably at very high costs and after a long wait. There are only 13 service centers for the Model 114 around the country, so a prospective owner might do well to establish a good rapport with the factory's main main. The phone number in Bethany, Okla. is 405-789-5000. For extra help and advice, contact the 112/114 owners association at Box 406, Woodbury, Conn. 06798, (203) 266-4554.

Safety

Because so few 114s were built,

Rockwell 114 Resale Value Chart

there is not enough of a statistical base for a valid safety analysis of that particular model. However, the 112 and 114 series combined, of which about 1,500 were delivered, had a fairly mediocre fatal accident rate of 3.1 per 100,000 flight hours during the period 1972-1976. This is about average for the single-engine retractables as a group; fatality rates ranged from 1.0 for the Beech 33 Bonanza to 4.2 for the Bellanca Viking.

The 112 and 114 accidents show no particular pattern; there were a total of 12 fatal accidents in the 112/114 up through 1978. But just two of these involved the 114; one was the result of the pilot running out of fuel. The other occurred when the aircraft hit trees off the end of the runway after a downwind takeoff on a soggy grass runway. (The pilot hadn't bothered to taxi all the way to the end of the runway for takeoff.)

One problem involving seat harnesses was revealed early in 1985. The Rockwell singles came from the factory with front seats featuring an unusual shoulder harness installation. Rather than attach the harness to the fuselage structure, Rockwell designers chose the seat backs themselves as the attach points. In what is undeniably a convenient, if unorthodox location, the harness retracted into the seat backs when released.

Perhaps Rockwell designers were attempting to encourage shoulder

harness use by making the harness easy to find and stow. The attempt unfortunately didn't work. An AD issued in March, 1985 called for relocation of the shoulder harness attach point from the seat back to the cabin wall just aft of the door.

This AD was in response to a pair of accidents involving a 112A and 114 in which two people died and another was severely injured due to failures of the front seat rollers which caused the seats to release. With the shoulder harnesses integral to the seats themselves, there was no secondary system that would hold the seats in place.

However, after howls of protest arose from owners over the $1,500 mod, AOPA took up up the cause and filed a petition urging the FAA to reconsider the AD. The petition was successful, and the AD, which would have required relocation of the harness attach points and modification of the front seat base, was suspended.

Owner Comments

We own a 1976 114 and couldn't be happier. More than enough cabin room for four big people and the reclining seats make even all-day flying comfortable. It is the most forgiving airplane I have ever flown. You can load it *full* with baggage, fuel, and people and not worry whether it will fly or land. The trailing beam gear allows you to dive into the ground when landing and cut down on the flare.

Also, landing this way allows you plenty of control, because (as everyone knows) the rudder isn't all that great.

The noise level is probably excessive to passengers, but a good headset almost puts the pilot to sleep in cruise. At 55 percent power and optimum altitude (8,000 feet) we get an honest 13 gph fuel flow including takeoff and climb. We changed to Shell 15W-50 about two years ago and now average a quart every 5-6 hours.

We are fortunate to live in a town that has a twin Commander dealership, and so parts and labor have never been a problem. They know the airplane well and handled the in-warranty problems as well as any manufacturer. Our last annual was $500.

C.L.M.
Indianapolis, Ind.

We bought our Rockwell 114 Commander in November of 1979. I have put an average of 400 hours per year on it, and we have been extremely pleased with the overall characteristics of the airplane.

Performance—We found the 114 highly superior to the 112 due to the larger engine. We are able to carry approximately 950 pounds of useful load with full fuel and have approximately five and a half hours fuel and cruise at 140 knots, making the airplane very useful.

Handling—The 114 handles far better than any other high-performance plane in its class. The cruciform tail configuration makes it a very stable plane to fly in any weather condition. The trailing-arm landing gear makes even the most novice an expert during landing.

Maintenance—The maintenance expense has been in line with Cessna or Piper products. The only thing I found out of line is that there have been three muffler replacements within the 1,000 hours that we have flown the airplane.

Comfort—The plane is touted as

Though the 114 is one of the few aircraft that normally can hold full fuel, four riders and baggage, some owners describe baggage space as minimal.

being the "cabin-class single," and it lives up to the claim. I like the two large doors, one on either side, for easy access and the spacious interior as well as large luggage compartment. The seats are comparable only to something in the cabin-class category.

Parts Availability—So far, parts availability has been no problem.

Backup—My selling dealer in Shelby County, Ala. has maintained excellent backup support for all the single-engine Rockwell line. Mechanics at Beechcraft, Piper and Cessna dealers have been anxious to do any repairs needed on the 114, saying everything is well laid out and accessible.

During 1981 maintenance costs amounted to about $3,900 for 387 hours, just about $10 per hour. Insurance was $1,230. We figure about 12 gallons per hour for fuel, totalling about $24 per hour. Depreciation in 1981 was $9,000, hangar and tiedown $4.12. Total operating cost came to $62 per hour, including depreciation (but not including overhaul reserve, which would add about $4 per hour).

W.E. Ogburn, Jr.
Gulf Breeze, Fla.

I have a 1979 114A. The aircraft is identical to the 114 except for a three-blade prop, cowl flaps, door-locking mechanism and sound insulation.

Performance: at 5,000 feet, 152 knots, burning close to 15 gph. Rate of climb at sea level in excess of 1,200 fpm. At 8,000 to 10,000

feet, 142 to 144 knots at 12 gph. Range a comfortable five hours.

Handling: Strong crosswind take-offs can be hairy unless no flaps are used. Airplane will not take crosswind landings in excess of 20 knots. Apart from that, superb handling on the ground and in flight, the Commander is a very stable instrument platform and with its good climb rate can also climb through moderate icing. There is absolutely no trim change when flaps or gear are lowered, which makes the Commander very easy to handle in busy airports.

Maintenance: No problems except nose gear shimmy damper and trim controls, which have a tendency to freeze.

Comfort: Very comfortable for two or four. Our plane was flown to Puerto Rico and back to New York with four people and bags. The only incovenience was the slow cruising speed and the heat on the ground.

Parts availability and backup: Poor at the beginning, presently zero. The dealer network is non-existent in the Northeast.

Average cost of annual: $500 to $600.

We are very pleased with the comfort and the loading capabilities of this very strong, well-built airplane, but not too happy with the speed and fuel consumption. We are now considering trading her for a Mooney 231 or a Baron 55.

Erik Larsen
New York, N.Y.

Beech Debonair/F33

The F33A is the ultimate refinement of the 33 breed. It is now more sought after on the used-plane market than the classic V-tail Bonanza.

Beech's Model 33, called both Debonair and Bonanza in its various versions, has emerged in the past few years as perhaps the most prestigious blue chip on the used-aircraft market. While the value of most used planes has fallen precipitously during general aviation's recent hard times, the Bonanza and Debonair have held virtually all their value. Ironically, the increasing demand for the 33 has come about mostly because of the slumping value of its V-tailed stablemate, the 35 Bonanza, due to worries about its high in-flight breakup rate. The 33, along with the larger A36 model, has become known as "the Bonanza that doesn't break up."

Used-Plane Market

The turnaround in the relative value of the V-tail and straight-tail Bonanzas has been startling. In 1979, before the V-tail's breakup record was widely known, the 35 reigned supreme. In those days, a two-year old 1977 V35B was valued at $84,000, while a 1977 F33A —identical in every way except for the tail—commanded only $77,500. By 1982, the tide had started to turn; that same 1977 V35B had dropped $15,000 to $69,000, while the F33A had lost only $10,000 and was still worth $67,500. By 1985, the V35B had declined another $4,000, to $65,000, while the F33A had *increased* in value to $73,000. That's a $14,500 turnaround.

Over the entire six-year period, the 1977 V-tail lost 22 percent of its value, while the straight-tail F33A declined just six percent. The premium price pilots used to pay for the looks and "prestige" of a V-tail now goes for the better safety of the straight-tail airplane. That sounds like a step in the right direction to us.

The 33 still looks good compared to other aircraft, too. We're aware of only one late-model single or light twin that's held its resale value better than the F33A over the past five years: its big brother the A36 Bonanza. Not even the Mooney 201, a darling of the used-plane market since its introduction in 1977, can match the F33A's resale record.

Geneology

The straight-tail 33 was an outgrowth, of course, of the original V-tail Bonanza. The V-tail was introduced back in 1947, and had the high-performance single-engine market sewed up until the late 1950's, when Piper brought out the Comanche, and Cessna introduced the 210—both at prices way below the Bonanza's.

Rather than lower the price of its cherished prestige flagship, Beech fought back against the 210 and Comanche with the model 33—an "economy" Bonanza without the distinctive V-tail and with a 225-hp engine instead of the Bonanza's then-250-hp. To avoid sullying the Bonanza's regal moniker by association with a less expensive airplane, Beech named the new economy model the Debonair. It debuted in 1960. List price of that first Model 33 was $19,995, about the same as the Comanche and a bit less than the 210. (The "real" Bonanza listed at $25,300.)

Beech lost little time refining the Debonair. The A33, introduced in 1961, featured a small third cabin window in the rear, and a hat shelf behind the baggage compartment. Gross weight was increased 100 pounds, from 2,900 to 3,000 pounds. In 1962, the B33 was fitted with the standard 74-gallon Bonanza fuel tanks, a big advantage over the previous four-tank system, which had less capacity (63 gallons) and required dangerously arcane fuel management procedures. (More on this in the Safety section.) The B33 also had a much-improved instrument panel, along with a fillet in the vertical fin to give it a more flowing look. Since the B33 is the oldest model with the big tanks, higher gross weight and the new panel, some owners consider the 1962-64 models the best bargain of all the 225-hp Debonairs.

With the C33 in 1965 came a couple of cosmetic changes: a larger third window and a still sleeker dorsal fin. Gross weight was bumped up another 50 pounds to 3,050 while convenience features like rear bucket seats (no more bench), a new ram's-horn control wheel, a bigger hatshelf and an improved heater were added. The E33 and F33 (vintage 1968 and 1970) had no significant changes, except the dropping of the name "Debonair." At last, the 225-hp straight-tail airplane was officially welcomed into the "Bonanza" brotherhood.

In 1966, Beech decided to add another Debonair to the line. In addition to the 225-hp C33, it introduced the 285-hp C33A—essentially a full-fledged "big" Bonanza with a straight tail instead of a V-tail. (For psychological and marketing reasons, however, the straight-tail airplane carried a slightly lower price tag.)

To add to the nomenclature confusion, Beech also called the C33A a Debonair until 1968, when it changed the name of the 285-hp airplane to Bonanza as well. Also in 1968, it introduced a short-lived aerobatic 285-hp version called the E33C. Both the aerobat and the 225-hp airplane were phased out in 1970. By 1971, there was only one standard-body straight-tail Bonanza: the 285-hp F33A. (The stretched 36 Bonanza had been introduced in 1968, but that's another story.)

The "economy" Bonanza made a brief comeback in 1972-73, however, with the 260-hp G33, but from 1974 on, only the F33A remained. By this time, Beech had abandoned the pretense that the V-tail was somehow more desirable, and it set the prices of the V-tail V35B and straight-tail F33A exactly the same. Throughout the 1970's, the V-tail outsold the straight-tail by about a two-to-one margin, but in 1980, shortly after the V-tail breakup controversy became public, the F33A pulled even in the sales race, and in 1981 and 1982, the F33A outsold the V35B by two-to-one. The V-tail, soundly repudiated in the market-

Efficiency-minded connoisseurs prefer the later 225-hp versions. This is a C33.

place, was laid to rest in 1983, while the F33A continues in production.

Performance

The 33 series, in the Bonanza tradition, has excellent performance. The 225-hp airplanes will cruise at 148-156 knots on 11.5 to 12 gph, while the more powerful 285-hp models will top 165 knots on about 15 gph. (If the plane has been modified with the Smith Speed conversion, an aerodynamic slick-up mod, these speeds will increase by 13-17 knots.)

Rate of climb is listed at about 900 fpm for the various 225-hp models and about 1,200 fpm for the 285-hp versions. Not surprisingly, the 260-hp G33s fall in the middle, at 1,060 fpm. As with most aircraft, in the real world, these figures are rarely matched, but pilots and owners report strong climbing abilities under most conditions. The 225-hp airplanes, however, are sometimes judged wanting in high-altitude climb and high-density-altitude takeoffs.

Again, climb performance is substantially improved with the Smith Speed Conversion.

Payload-Range

Standard useful load of the 225-hp Debonairs is about 1,200 pounds, but a well-equipped IFR airplane would have about 1,000 pounds available for payload and fuel. With the 74-gallon tanks full, payload is only about 550 pounds —three average people and not much baggage. Because of the limited loading, says one Debonair pilot, "All Deb owners habitually overload their aircraft, especially those planes with the large tanks."

The small-tank (50-gallon) A33 has an extra 120 pounds' payload with full fuel, but the straight 33, with its lower gross weight, is comparable to the B33 and later airplanes in full-fuel payload (with less fuel, of course).

The 285-hp Debonairs have enough extra load-carrying ability to make them four-pax-plus-luggage airplanes from the poundage standpoint. But watch the center of gravity! The entire Bonanza series is notorious for its limited c.g. envelope, and the stretched A36 model was developed primarily to solve this problem. The 33 series has a wider c.g. envelope than the otherwise-identical V-tails (the straight tail does a better job of stabilizing and therefore permits more aft loading), but the 33s are still somewhat limited. In most cases, it's simply not legally possible to put two adults in the rear seats and a bunch of bags in back.

The balance situation is complicated by the fact that all fuel is carried in front of the c.g. As fuel burns off, c.g. shifts aft. That means that for takeoff on a long flight, a Debonair must be well forward of the rear limit to account for the aft shift as fuel burns off.

Handling Qualities

The Bonanza series has always been a pilot's favorite. The handling is delightfully quick and smooth in the air, with controls well harmonized in all three axes. "My Debonair is the best-flying airplane I've ever flown," crows one typical owner.

But the other side of the "light and responsive" coin is poor stability in IFR conditions. As one Debonair owner put it, "The model 33 is not a particularly good instrument airplane. The same qualities that make it such a pleasure to fly turn it into a handful on instruments. It has almost neutral stability, and one must devote a great deal of attention to just controlling the aircraft. If any serious instrument flying is anticipated, a reliable autopilot should be a high priority."

The 33 is not particularly stable in the yaw mode, although it does not have the stomach-wrenching Dutch roll in turbulence that the V-tail has.

Landings are particularly easy in the Debonairs; most pilots agree that the Deb has an excellent combination of handling qualities and landing-gear geometry. However, a 1966 NASA "secret" report on the handling qualities of various general aviation aircraft criticized the A33 Debonair it tested for poor lateral stability in the landing configuration. NASA test pilots also criticized the A33 for awkward crosswind takeoffs because of the rudder-aileron interconnect.

The 33s, like the 35s, stall rather sharply, particularly with gear and flaps down and power on. Watch the go-arounds and base-to-final turns. However, the 33 is apparently not so violent as the 35; the NASA test pilots criticized the V-tail stall traits in the 1966 report but found no fault with the A33's.

Cabin and Cockpit

Bonanzas have won fame for their roomy, airy cabins, and the 33 model is no exception. There's so much headroom that a pilot of average height looks like a midget from the outside. Forward visibility is excellent out the panoramic windshield, and, in the later models with the three large cabin windows, out the sides as well. Noise is about average for this class of aircraft—that is to say terribly noisy.

The 285-hp Debonair is listed as a six-seater, but this is an optimistic delusion of the Beech sales department. The optional fifth and sixth seats are tiny and claustrophobic,

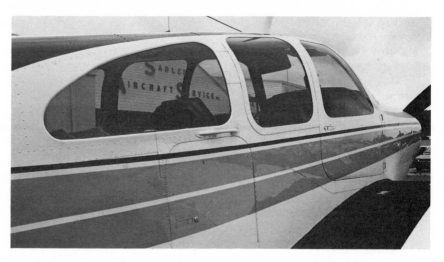

and are virtually impossible to use because of c.g. restrictions anyway. Unless you have four little kids to haul around, consider all the 33s to be strictly four-place airplanes.

The B33 and earlier 225-hp models have old-fashioned bench-type rear seats, but they are surprisingly roomy and not really a liability from the practical standpoint.

From the pilot's point of view, the 33 line has the traditional Bonanza ergonomic quirks. A single throwover control wheel was standard equipment on the Debonairs, although many have been fitted with optional dual controls. The massive control bar connecting the yoke or yokes to the center control column can block the pilot's view of parts of the panel and get in the way of the engine controls.

In the older models, the mixture knob is located below the throttle instead of to the right of the prop control, as in most airplanes. And the landing gear and flap switches are reversed from their normal positions in most aircraft, a quirk that has caused many embarrassing (and expensive) gear retractions on the ground. (During the years 1974-78, in fact, inadvertent gear retractions were the leading cause of non-fatal accidents in 225-hp Debonairs.) These quirks aside, however, the post-1963 Debonairs have generally good instrument panel layouts.

The fuel selector is less than ideal, located low on the cockpit side wall by the pilot's left knee. Thus, to

The bigger rear window first appeared in 1965 on the C33 model. It can be easily retrofitted to older aircraft.

switch tanks, a pilot must crane his neck and reach down in a rather awkward cross-hand manner. Also, there is no "both" position on the selector, which assures that the pilot will be switching tanks at least once during a long trip. (From the safety point of view, the less tank-switching a pilot has to do, the better.)

Operating Costs

Fuel efficiency of the Debonairs is good, with fuel costs running from $25 to $30 per hour. (That's figuring gas at $2 per gallon.) Owners of 225-hp Debonairs can cut their fuel costs dramatically, however, by using auto fuel. With the proper STC paperwork (available for $112.50 from Petersen Aviation, Rte. 1, Box 18, Minden, Nebraska 68959, (308) 832-2200) it's entirely legal to use either lead-free or leaded regular autogas in the 225-hp airplanes, which normally burn 80-octane avgas.

Typically, liability insurance coverage runs $400 to $500 a year, with hull insurance ranging from perhaps $1,000 a year for an old 225-hp B33 to $2,000 for a late-model F33A.

Engine overhaul reserve amounts to about $6 per hour for both the 225-hp and 285-hp models. (Oddly, the smaller IO-470 costs very nearly as much to overhaul as the bigger IO-520.) Count on about

$9,000 to overhaul either engine; the 285-hp powerplants have 1,700-hour TBOs, compared to 1,500 hours for the 470s.

Adding it all up, assuming 200 hours per year, operating costs—excluding maintenance —should run from $40 to $50 per hour. Whether *total* operating costs end up at $50 or $100 per hour depends, of course, on the unpredictable and potentially disastrous maintenance bills.

Maintenance

According to owner reports and conversation with mechanics, Debonair maintenance costs can run from pretty low to pretty outrageous, depending on hourly utilization, the owner's mechanical aptitude and blind luck. While the well-proven, solidly built airframe has stood up well over time, three potential bugaboos haunt the Debonair owner: cracking crank-

cases, leaking fuel bladders, and Beech's high parts prices.

Assuming nothing major goes wrong—and in many cases it doesn't—Debonair annuals are reasonable. "Annual inspections run around $400 unless additional parts and labor are required," said one owner. To date (I've owned it three years) there have been no surprises at annual time." The owner put his total maintenance cost at an extraordinarily low $2 per hour. Others disagree. "Maintenance costs are very high, if not exorbitant," writes one. "We try to keep everything working, and that costs a lot." Echoes another, "The Debonair is not a high-maintenance airplane, but it *is* expensive to maintain. This is because...anything purchased from Beech is outrageously expensive."

Cracking crankcases have been a continuing problem in the 285-hp

Debonairs (along with many other aircraft). The so-called "heavy" cases introduced in the mid-1970's didn't help much, and cracks continue to crop up despite all manner of design and material changes over the years. Case cracks usually aren't immediately dangerous, and small ones can be lived with until overhaul, at which time the crack can be welded up and the case heat-treated. (Cost: typically, $500-$700.) If the crack is bad enough to ground the plane (an AD sets out the guidelines), an owner faces two expensive options: overhaul the engine prematurely (about $9,000, plus the cost of case repair) or completely disassemble the engine and repair the case ($4,000 or so, mostly for assembly/disassembly labor and the extra new parts required when the engine is put back together again).

Moral for F33A shoppers: check with microscopic care for crankcase cracks.

Cost/Performance/Specifications

Model	Year	Number Built	Average Retail Price	Cruise Speed (Kts)	Rate of Climb (fpm)	Useful Load (lbs)	Fuel Std/Opt (gals)	Engine	TBO (hrs)	Overhaul Cost
33	1960	233	$ 25,500	156	1,010	1,170	44/63	225-hp Cont. IO-470-K	1,500	$10,750
A33	1961	152	$ 27,500	161	960	1,250	44/63	225-hp Cont. IO-470-K	1,500	$10,750
B33	1962	200	$ 30,000	161	960	1,250	44/74	225-hp Cont. IO-470-K	1,500	$10,750
B33	1963	137	$ 31,000	161	960	1,250	44/74	225-hp Cont. IO-470-K	1,500	$10,750
B33	1964	89	$ 32,000	161	960	1,250	44/74	225-hp Cont. IO-470-K	1,500	$10,750
C33	1965	157	$ 35,000	161	980	1,200	44/74	225-hp Cont. IO-470-K	1,500	$10,750
C33	1966	86	$ 36,000	161	980	1,200	44/74	225-hp Cont. IO-470-K	1,500	$10,750
C33	1967	62	$ 37,000	161	980	1,200	44/74	225-hp Cont. IO-470-K	1,500	$10,750
C33A	1966	102	$ 43,000	174	1,200	1,525	44/74	285-hp Cont. IO-520-B	1,700	$11,250
C33A	1967	77	$ 43,500	174	1,200	1,525	44/74	285-hp Cont. IO-520-B	1,700	$11,250
E33	1968	81	$ 40,500	161	930	1,200	44/74	225-hp Cont. IO-470-K	1,500	$10,750
E33	1969	34	$ 42,500	161	930	1,200	44/74	225-hp Cont. IO-470-K	1,500	$10,750
E33A	1968	69	$ 45,000	174	1,200	1,375	44/74	285-hp Cont. IO-520-B	1,700	$11,250
E33A	1969	41	$ 48,000	174	1,200	1,375	44/74	285-hp Cont. IO-520-B	1,700	$11,250
E33C	1968	13	$ 43,000	174	1,200	1,380	44/74	285-hp Cont. IO-520-B	1,700	$11,250
E33C	1969	12	$ 46,000	174	1,200	1,380	44/74	285-hp Cont. IO-520-B	1,700	$11,250
F33	1970	20	$ 43,500	161	930	1,375	44/74	225-hp Cont. IO-470-K	1,500	$10,750
F33C	1970	5	$ 48,500	174	1,200	1,380	44/74	285-hp Cont. IO-520-B	1,500	$10,750
G33	1972	45	$ 49,000	168	1,060	1,365	44/74	260-hp Cont. IO-470-N	1,500	$10,750
G33	1973	5	$ 49,000	168	1,060	1,365	44/74	260-hp Cont. IO-470-N	1,500	$10,750
F33A	1970	20	$ 52,000	172	1,200	1,300	44/74	285-hp Cont. IO-520-B	1,700	$11,250
F33A	1971	34	$ 54,000	172	1,200	1,300	44/74	285-hp Cont. IO-520-B	1,700	$11,250
F33A	1972	52	$ 57,000	172	1,200	1,300	44/74	285-hp Cont. IO-520-B	1,700	$11,250
F33A	1973	63	$ 60,000	172	1,200	1,300	44/74	285-hp Cont. IO-520-B	1,700	$11,250
F33A	1974	71	$ 64,000	172	1,200	1,300	44/74	285-hp Cont. IO-520-B	1,700	$11,250
F33A	1975	75	$ 68,000	172	1,200	1,300	44/74	285-hp Cont. IO-520-B	1,700	$11,250
F33A	1976	62	$ 72,000	172	1,200	1,300	44/74	285-hp Cont. IO-520-B	1,700	$11,250
F33A	1977	69	$ 77,000	172	1,200	1,300	44/74	285-hp Cont. IO-520-B	1,700	$11,250
F33A	1978	82	$ 83,500	172	1,200	1,300	44/74	285-hp Cont. IO-520-B	1,700	$11,250
F33A	1979	68	$ 89,000	172	1,200	1,300	44/74	285-hp Cont. IO-520-B	1,700	$11,250
F33A	1980	45	$ 95,000	172	1,200	1,300	44/74	285-hp Cont. IO-520-B	1,700	$11,250
F33A	1981	49	$101,000	172	1,200	1,300	44/74	285-hp Cont. IO-520-B	1,700	$11,250
F33A	1982	36	$107,000	172	1,200	1,300	44/74	285-hp Cont. IO-520-B	1,700	$11,250
F33A	1983	10	$115,000	172	1,200	1,300	44/74	285-hp Cont. IO-520-B	1,700	$11,250
F33A	1984	32	$125,000	172	1,200	1,300	44/74	285-hp Cont. IO-520-B	1,700	$11,250

Fuel bladders are another weak spot in the Debonairs. The Goodyear tanks in older airplanes are particularly prone to cracking; Uniroyal bladders are a better bet, experience has shown. If the bladders do develop leaks, the tab can be $2,000 or more for replacement, according to owners. The 33 and A33 with the four-tank systems have an even bigger potential for disaster.

Another Goodyear product—the brakes on early models—are also short-lived and trouble-prone. Many Debonair owners have replaced them with Cleveland brakes, which have proven superior. Look for Clevelands on any Debonair you buy, or anticipate putting them on soon.

The 225-hp models are susceptible to lead-fouling of the spark plugs if 100-octane fuel is used instead of the 80-octane the engine was designed for. (Even "low-lead" 100 has four times the lead of 80 octane.) If 80 is unavailable, try unleaded auto fuel.

Beech parts prices are the demon that haunts any Debonair owner. The buyer of a new $200,000 A36 may not balk at a $2,000-plus price tag for a control wheel yoke assembly, but that amounts to nearly 10 percent of the value of a 1961 A33. That's the problem with new replacement parts—they cost the same whether the plane is old or new, cheap or expensive.

Safety

Here's the best news: the 33 series has the lowest fatal accident rate of any single-engine retractable, according to *The Aviation Consumer* statistics for the period 1972-81. The 33's fatal rate was only 1.4 per 100,000 flight hours, compared to an average of 2.3 for 16 other single engine retractables. (The Cessna 210, for example, had a fatal rate of 2.3; the Mooney M20J 2.4. The Piper Comanche had a rather high 2.9.)

By comparison, the late-model V-tail Bonanzas (1964 and later) had a fatal rate of 1.7, and the older

Debonair Resale Value Chart

V-tails (1947-63) a rather terrible 3.3.

Where the straight-tail 33 really shines is in-flight breakups. An *Aviation Consumer* study for the years 1977-83 shows that the 33 (and 36) have a break-up rate just one-tenth of the V-tail's. We're aware of only three in-flight breakups of 33 series Beeches, compared to more than 200 for the V-tails.

The reasons for this big difference aren't entirely clear. The 33 has slightly better pitch stability and heavier pitch forces than the 35, and so may be less prone to pilot loss of control and overstress. The straight tail also provides slightly better lateral stability, reducing the tendency to enter a "graveyard spiral" in instrument conditions. The straight tail also gives better yaw stability, reducing Dutch roll gyrations in turbulence.

Another possibility: the straight tail is simply stronger and stays intact through all manner of high-speed dives, pullouts and turbulence that may break a V-tail. The V-tail has been criticized for the excessive "overhang" of the stabilizer ahead of the front spar, and at least three companies offer kits to beef up V-tails structurally.

Beech Aircraft's official position is that there's really little difference between the 33 and 35. Pilots of both aircraft occasionally lose con-

trol in IFR conditions or severe turbulence, says Beech, pushing the aircraft beyond its airspeed and/or g-load limits. It doesn't matter much, according to the Beech theory, whether the plane breaks up before it hits the ground (35) or hits the ground in one piece (33). Either way, the occupants are dead.

We disagree with Beech's interpretation. When we examined NTSB records of both in-flight breakups and "uncontrolled impact with ground" crashes for the 33 and 35, it turned out that the 35 still had a rate of fatal loss-of-control accidents—either breakups or uncontrolled impacts—nearly three times higher than the 33.

Although they have an excellent overall record, the early Debonairs have a quirk or two to watch out for. Pre-1970 models had no baffles in the fuel tanks, which allowed fuel to slosh away from the fuel line pickup in slips, skids or during fast turns on the ground (such as those preceding a hurried takeoff). Beech was aware of the fuel unporting syndrome (which affected Debonairs, Bonanzas and Barons) as far back as 1961. It issued a service letter warning that a turning-type takeoff could result in a "momentary power interruption" at "about the same time the airplane becomes airborne." The letter assured owners that "...this does not create a hazard."

But the FAA identified 16 fuel-unporting accidents by 1971, and issued an AD prohibiting takeoffs with tanks less than a quarter full. Beech installed baffles in 1971 and later models and retrofit kits for the older airplanes, but few have been retrofitted. We'd consider the fuel tank baffles a must in any Debonair considered for purchase.

The early Bonanzas had a bad record of fuel mismanagement accidents, and the early 33 and A33 Debonairs have similar fuel systems, with multiple tanks that require lots of switching, an out-of-the-way fuel selector that's hard to see and a gauging system that makes it easy to read the wrong tank.

Modifications

When it comes to airframe and cosmetic mods, Debonair owners are in hog heaven. Literally dozens of mods are available to make an old Debbie look new: windows, windshields, panels, spinners, interiors, etc. Chief purveyor of Debonair cosmetic mods is Beryl D'Shannon Aviation Specialties, P.O. Box 840, Lakeville, Minn. (612) 469-4783.

The aforementioned Smith Speed Conversion includes a series of detail aerodynamic improvements that typically improve cruise speed by 13-17 knots. Smith also offers a modified cowling that is claimed to improve cooling, cut drag and allow better engine breathing for more power at high altitudes. Mike Smith Aero, Stanton County Airport, Box 430, Johnson City, Kans. (316) 492-6840.

Bonanza Society

Perhaps the most active of the owner groups is the American Bonanza Society, P.O. Box 12888, Wichita, Kans. (316) 945-6913. The ABS publishes a monthly newsletter with technical info and how-to tips, along with the usual rah-rah stuff about members' creampuff planes. While the ABS is sometimes timid about confronting safety problems head-on (it likes to maintain good rapport with Beech), the club is still a good source of info and a good bet for any 33 owner. (Yes, the Bonanza boys do allow straight-tail owners to join their ranks.)

Owner Comments

I have had a Model 33 for six years. I usually fly it at 60 percent power using 2300 rpm. It uses 10.8 to 11.2 gph and trues out about 135 knots. As you can see, it doesn't come up to the handbook data, but it is a sturdy, comfortable but noisy bird. Annuals run $600 to $900. The original 600 x 6 tires were replaced with 700 x 6, and their life is considerably longer, with no clearance problems. The tail does waggle like the V-tail, but by holding the rudder so it doesn't move, you can stop the waggle. (The same technique worked on the V-tail I had before the Debonair.)

Of the light aircraft I've flown, the 33 has the best visibility, and as far as I'm concerned is the safest and best-built of the lot

Newton Kerr
Olmstead, Ohio

A year and a half ago, I purchased a 1962 B33 with 1,600 hours total time and 350 hours on a chrome major. The Deb is one of the smoothest planes I've ever flown. It's a good instrument ship as long as you're wide awake, stay ahead of the airplane and maintain proficiency. Load-carrying and range (over 1,000 nm) are good as long as you realize that the c.g. moves aft as fuel burns off.

My Deb has the speed-slope windshield and aileron gap seals, and I have removed the step. I climb and cruise better than book numbers, 180 mph cruise on 12 gph or less. Stall speed with everything hanging out is 50 mph indicated. I wonder what's being built this year that will match it in speed, range, comfort and safety record?

Cost of operation runs about $25 per hour for gas, a quart of oil every six hours, $1,000 a year for insurance, $400 for annuals. In 200 hours and 19 months, the only problems have been with the prop control and propeller lubrication. My only complaint is a universal one: the high cost of Beech parts.

Raymond McDonald
Ferndale, Wash.

My partner and I have owned a 1964 B33 Debonair since October 1981. It's been a pleasure to own and fly, providing us with 200 to 300 hours a year of safe, reliable transportation.

Because of the quick and smooth roll characteristics, an autopilot is recommended for serious IFR flying. The Deb can be a handful in turbulence. We can carry four

Double control bar arrangement can be used on the Model 33 instead of the throwover wheel, but this makes control access more awkward.

The B33, circa 1962-64 is recognizable by the small rear window. Though the cabin is short, it is high, beamy and quite comfortable for four.

passengers and baggage for as long as we're able and still have a reserve. Rear c.g. is the only thing to watch carefully, as the c.g. shifts to the rear as fuel burns off. We count on burning 12 gph while averaging 165 mph.

In 1984 we flew 318 hours with maintenance costs of $13 per hour for mechanical and only $1.00 per hour for radios. Our annual ran an additional $500, which is typical unless we let some things go until the annual. The 1968 Cherokee 180D I owned previously cost about the same amount per mile to operate. Our insurance runs $1,018 per year for $30,000 hull and $2 million liability.

As far as the IO-470-K engine goes, it has been all routine so far. We have 1,200 hours on it and expect to get TBO without a problem. We run platinum plugs to avoid the lead-fouling problems we have with 100 LL gas. We are now considering the autogas STC. Leaky exhaust gaskets have always been a problem. We recently had all the studs removed and the cylinder seats resurfaced, and that has solved the problem so far. Oil consumption is about a quart every two or three hours because of improper break-in.

Like most Beech owners, we have many mods, including one-piece windshield, Beryl side windows, Beryl rear air exhaust, Cleveland brakes, three-inch gyros, alternator and instrument post lighting.

Gary Otto
Duluth, Ga.

Three partners and I own a 1966 C33. We spent $10,000 on it in 1982 for a complete firewall-forward overhaul, including propeller.

Performance has been by the book in all phases of operation. We consistently get 158-160-knot cruise speeds at 6,000 to 8,000 feet with fuel burn of 13.5-14.0 gph. I try to

lean the mixture to about 25-50 degrees on the rich side of peak EGT.

I find the Deb very enjoyable to fly, with light, harmonized controls. Longitudinal stability is adequate, whereas lateral/directional stability is somewhat weak. The cabin is as comfortable as anything in its class. The only problem I've found is that the landing gear geometry leaves a very lightly loaded nosewheel if the plane is near the aft end of the c.g. envelope. There have been times when I thought the tail would hit the ground. (It hasn't actually happened yet.)

After 19 years and 3,100 hours on my aircraft, Beech quality is apparent. Other than spark plugs, batteries, tires and brakes, we've had very few mechanical expenses. Checking the numbers for the past 300 hours of operation, the average hourly cost works out to about $41 (not including avionics or reserve for overhaul). Maintenance accounts for about $2 of this figure. Annual inspections run around $400, plus whatever parts and extra labor are required beyond the inspection.

Jerry Jordan
Leawood, Kans.

As an airline pilot with extensive general aviation background, I believe the Beech 33 is the most satisfying cross-country single-engine airplane I've ever flown. The early Debonair provides an outstanding combination of economy and performance. The

Continental IO-470 engine at 65 percent power will burn 11.5 gph at 10,000 feet and give an honest 150 knots. I flight-plan one gallon of fuel for every five minutes of flight time, and can usually tell the line person how much fuel the tanks will hold to within half a gallon.

The Debonair is a real four-place airplane. My full-IFR airplane will *legally* carry four 170-pound adults, 100 pounds of luggage and 50 gallons of fuel (full tanks in my plane), enough for three hours plus a reserve. That's as long as I can stand to sit in a light airplane cabin, anyway. VFR, I plan 500-mile legs. IFR, I would like to have more fuel capacity. Factory-installed aux tanks on the early 1960-61 models are of limited value because they only added about 20 gallons but increased weight substantially. The Flight Extender tip tanks made by Beryl are a better choice.

Cabin comfort improves with each year up to about 1967. In my plane, ventilation is better than a Comanche, but not nearly as good as a 210. Visibility is excellent. Noise level is average (high).

The Model 33 is not a particularly good instrument airplane. The same qualities that make it such a pleasure to fly visually make it a handful on instruments. It has almost neutral stability, and one must devote a great deal of attention to just controlling the aircraft. If any serious instrument flying is anticipated, a reliable autopilot should be a high priority.

Bellanca Viking

Riding on the wooden wings of yesteryear, the Bellanca Viking is an airplane Howard Hughes would have approved of. The spruce-and-mahogany wings, the Dacron-coated fuselage, and quaintly bestrutted empennage, combine to give the Viking a charm all its own (not to mention the drag coefficient of a flying boat).

But persistent concerns about wood rot, and a general perception of the airplane as an orphaned design (production was suspended in 1980), have kept resale values extraordinarily low: A 1976 Super Viking with good avionics can be had for $33,000, while an F33A Bonanza of the same year commands $66,000. And in most cases, used Vikings come with low total airframe time. Apparently, few enter any kind of commercial service.

As with most oddball (er, distinctive) aircraft, the Bellanca Viking has its own loyal cadre of boosters and supplicants, who literally praise it to the skies as "the best all-around high-performance single." Owners mention easy handling, simple systems, and cruise speeds in the 160-knot ballpark as reasons for continued ownership; and routine maintenance seems to require no special connections with the International Monetary Fund. Owners consistently report annuals in the $350 to $700 range, although some said parts—while easy to get—were "high." (Non-routine maintenance is another matter: Several operators cited wing repair bills that were, in their words, "sufficient to cause heart attack" and "impressive.")

Group Characteristics

When Viking owners talk of their planes' family "tree," they're not just speaking figuratively. The

Bellanca mahogany wing dates to before World War Two; and the last of the Super Viking wings, produced in 1980, differs little from the original. The same glass-smooth, curvacious wing that marked the Cruisaire (the Viking's forerunner) as a "hot ship" in the Forties still draws praise from owners today as "the most perfect wing of any modern light aircraft." Nary a rivet-head protrudes to ruin the airfoil's perfect contour.

Unfortunately, the rest of the Bellanca is not so slick aerodynamically. The bottoms of the wings sprout ugly, drag-producing wheel bumps; the horizontal stabilizer has struts (a la Curtiss Robin), and the fuselage is a bit slab-sided, for a "high-performance" plane. As a result, the plane turns in no better than Mooney Executive performance on 300 horsepower (even though the Bellanca's fuselage is no wider than the Mooney's). An efficiency queen, the Viking definitely is not.

Efficiency isn't everything, of course, and there are other reasons for buying an "old-fashioned" airplane like the Bellanca. Its methods of construction demand a high level of craftsmanship, and in this area, Bellancas excell: Owners report unusually fastidious workmanship throughout the aircraft, especially inside the typically well-appointed cabin. The fit-and-finish is far above industry standards for this size aircraft.

Exposed nosewheel and bulbous main-wheel bumps under wings contribute to draggy performance. The 300-hp Viking delivers real-world cruise speeds of 150 to 160 knots.

How do the various year models differ? For the most part, they don't. Since the first Viking's appearance in 1967 (which marked the end of the triple-tailed, 260-hp Cruisaires), subsequent models have differed externally only in paint scheme. A variety of powerplants can be found under the hood, however. The original staple engine was the 300-hp Continental IO-520-D (TBO 1,700 hours), which could be supplanted (at customer request) by a 290-hp Lycoming IO-540-B (TBO 1,200 hours, normally aspirated) or IO-540-G (TBO 1,400 hours, turbocharged). Post-1970 models sported either the 300-hp Continental IO-520-K or the 300-hp Lycoming IO-540-K (TBO 2,000 hours), which—for $8,000 extra—could be fitted with dual Rajay turbochargers. Most Vikings have the Continental engine.

Performance and Handling

"Performance," according to one owner, "is adequate but not outstanding." Except for the Super Turbo models, which one owner says trues out at 186 knots at 12,000 feet, the Vikings are sluggish cruisers compared to Bonanzas and 210s. One operator reported 170 knots at 10,000 feet; another said he flight-plans 140 knots, based on 60-percent power and block-to-block fuel burns of 15 gallons per hour. Apparently, there is considerable variation among individual airplanes, due to rigging and vagaries of construction over the years.

Owners are less than enthusiastic about the airplane's short legs: Standard fuel tankage is a mere 60 gallons (three hours plus reserves), all in the wings. The 15-gallon fuselage aux tank is a common option; but even with 75 gallons, it's difficult to fly a 700-nm trip without stopping for gas.

On the plus side, owners offer nothing but euphoric praise for the Viking's handling, one (typical) owner describing it as ''an absolute joy to fly.'' Ailerons are said to be light and creamy-smooth; rudders heavy but responsive; pitch forces, moderate to challenging, depending on c.g. location. Flaps do not betray any rude behavior, nor does gear deployment (at the manageably high speed of 124 knots). Gobs of drag and a 3,000-lb.-plus gross weight combine to give very steep descents for the unwary, however.

Useful loads for well-equipped Vikings (which most are) run around 900 pounds—a bit less than you'd expect for a 300-hp low-wing retractable (and far short of the Cessna 210's 1,500 pounds). Given the poor payload, it's perhaps a blessing that the airplane was not given larger fuel tanks, or a more capacious interior.

Speaking of interiors, owners are generally complimentary of seats, fabrics, etc. (which is good, since it diverts passengers' attention from the lack of shoulder and leg room), but the noise level is almost universally regarded as too high—no doubt a consequence of the large engine and fabric-skinned fuselage construction. ''The airplane has got to have the highest noise level of any modern production aircraft,'' one owner observes, adding: ''Headset, ear plugs, and intercom should be go/no-go items.'' Factory engineers surely must have considered additional soundproofing at some point; we can

The Viking panel is sensibly laid out, which is something you can't say for most used planes. View is obstructed by steel tubes (as in the Piper Aztec, which, like the Viking, has a tube-truss fuselage).

only wonder if they didn't rule it out on the basis of weight, since payload is already critical. We'll never know for sure.

If stealth is a consideration, one owner reports that the Viking exhibits an extraordinarily poor primary radar return—no doubt the result of mahogany's elusive X-band signature.

Systems

Like many older designs, the Viking betrays a number of idiosyncrasies which a new pilot would do well to study. The absence of cowl flaps on most models is a plus point, at least in terms of pilot workload (although it may compromise cylinder and accessory life). The prop, throttle, and mixture controls are all vernier types—with the prop knob directly above the mixture knob—which may cause some vertigo for all but Bonanza pilots, who wouldn't be caught dead in a Bellanca anyway.

Then there's the fuel system. On some early models, there were two fuel selectors with eight possible combinations of selector settings;

later models have just one selector (between the front seats, at knee level) with four positions, of which one can be used in level flight only. Fuel quantity is read on vertical-readout gauges which owners say are highly non-linear—i.e., accurate only in the ''full'' and ''empty'' extremes. The three-position boost pump rocker switch is also a source of confusion, as reflected in pilot's statements in accident reports. Many pilots are not aware that the Viking's boost pump is so powerful that it can flood the engine, preventing easy restart. What's more, pump usage varies according to the type of engine installed. Obviously, it behooves the pilot to get a thorough checkout, and study the handbook.

Until May 1968, Vikings had an unusual combination flap-and-gear actuation system that worked off the engine-driven hydraulic system and was located between the pilots' seats. In 1968, electric flaps were substituted for hydraulic, and control levers mounted on the front lower panel, in convention arrangement (gear left, flaps right).

Panel layout is good, with flight instruments where they should be, nav heads in midpanel, radios in a stack on the right, and autopilot-cum-miscellany to the far right, above the flap switch and circuit breakers. (Visibility through the one-piece windshield, however, is compromised by the presence of two steel tubes at ten and two o'clock, a la Aztec.) Reclining seats are optional.

A pneumatic switch in the landing gear circuit forms the basis of something called "Auto-Axion," which automatically lowers the landing gear at an airspeed of 83 knots (which is about what you'll indicate in cruise going over the Rockies). To our knowledge, it has caused owners no grief, and may actually be preventing gear-up accidents: in a recent three-year period, we could find in NTSB files only four gear-up landings involving Bellancas—two of which were pilot-induced, not mechanical.

The fuel drain knob is under the cowling, but it only drains the tank you've selected, so count on lots of walking between cabin and cowl to get all points drained.

One owner reports that his alternator belt always slips in heavy rain.

Maintenance

Although miscellaneous airframe parts are expensive (e.g., $80 for flap cables), and repair costs for replacement of the Viking's "lifetime fabric" or wings can rival the Polish national debt, routine upkeep is said by owners to be quite reasonable. Extensive annuals can run upwards of $2,500, but the average inspection seems to come in at $700—about the same as the tab for a Bonanza, 210, etc.

Several important repetitive Airworthiness Directives apply to the Bellanca Viking. The most important (and notorious) of these is AD 76-08-04, the 1976 directive on wood rot. Under the terms of this AD, the Viking wing must be inspected for moisture content in accordance with Part I of Bellanca Service Letter 82A at each annual inspection. Since not all shops are familiar with Bellancas, it pays to seek out expert counsel for this type of work. Owners recommend Tom Witmer at Cap Aviation in Reading, Pa.; Miller Flying Service in Plainview, Tex., and Dave Poole at Dennis Martin Aircraft at Ft. Lauderdale Executive Airport. (Miller is also a good source of Viking info, in general.)

The wing moisture check should be a starting point for any pre-purchase inspection. Don't take the word of the previous owner nor a logbook entry; actually have a qualified shop check the wings prior to delivery. Special tools are required for this; it requires more than "an eyeball and a screwdriver" (as one man states)—unless, of course, you open the inspection covers and find, as one owner did, "mushrooms growing in right wing."

Other important ADs are 76-23-03 on exhaust failure (an inspection is required each 100 hours); 77-22-02 on nose landing gear engine mount sections; and 75-20-06 on vertical side fuselage tube cracking in the tail section (repetitive inspection each 100 hours until Service Kit

SK1234789-0004 is installed). Additional ADs may apply to individual accessories installed on various airplanes (certain magnetos, Lycoming oil pump impellers, etc.); make sure to have an A&P do a complete AD listing for the particular plane you intend to buy.

In 1983, the Viking line went back into production, with first deliveries to Miller Flying Service. This should, of course, have a positive effect not only on parts availability, but aircraft resale value as well. The new manufacturer is Bellanca Inc., P.O. Box 964, Alexandria, Minn. 56308 (phone 612/762-1501). Their distributor: Miller Flying Service, P.O. Box 190, Plainview, Tex. 79072 (phone 806/293-4121).

Accident Record

The Bellanca Viking was one of several aircraft spotlighted as having a particularly poor safety record in the National Transportation Safety Board's 1979 study of accident rates by aircraft type. (Other poor-showing airplanes included the Grumman AA-1 series and the Cessna Skymaster.) Shortly after the NTSB released its report, Bellanca Aircraft Corp. sent a cheer-up letter to aviation editors, defending the Viking's safety record. As it turns out, the Safety Board did lump Viking data together with Cruisaire (i.e., early-Bellanca) data to arrive at its findings. And this did produce a skewed result, at least for non-fatal accidents—the Crusaire series

Cost/Performance/Specifications

Model	Years Built	Number Built	Average Retail Price	Cruise Speed (kts)	Useful Load (lbs)	Rate of Climb (fpm)	Fuel Std/Opt (gals)	Engine	TBO (hrs)	Overhaul Cost
Viking 17-30	1967-70	290	$18,000-$20,000	163	1,300	1,840	58/92	300-hp Cont. IO-520-D	1,700	$ 9,800
Viking 17-30A	1971-74	419	$22,000-$27,000	163	1,108	1,085	60/75	300-hp Cont. IO-520-K	1,700	$ 9,800
Viking 17-30A	1975-77	129	$29,000-$39,000	163	1,108	1,085	60/75	300-hp Cont. IO-520-K	1,700	$ 9,800
Viking 17-30A	1978-80	106	$45,000-$57,000	163	1,108	1,085	60/75	300-hp Cont. IO-520-K	1,700	$ 9,800
Super Viking 17-31A	1969-70	34	$18,000-$21,000	164	1,375	1,800	60/75	290-hp Lyc. IO-540-G1B5	1,400	$12,000
Super Viking 17-31A	1971-74	104	$21,000-$26,000	164	1,190	1,800	60/75	300-hp Lyc. IO-540-K1E5	2,000	$12,000
Super Viking 17-31A	1975-77	23	$28,000-$38,000	164	1,100	1,170	60/75	300-hp Lyc. IO-540-K1E5	2,000	$12,000
Super Turbo Vik. 17-31ATC	1969-70	11	$23,000-$24,000	204	1,305	1,800	72/92	250-hp Lyc. IO-540-G1E5	1,400	$12,000
Super Turbo Vik. 17-31ATC	1971-72	23	$26,000-$29,000	294	1,190	1,800	72/92	300-hp Lyc. IO-540-K1E5	2,000	$12,000
Turbo Viking 17-31ATC	1973-75	75	$30,000-$34,000	193	1,053	1,170	60/75	300-hp Lyc. IO-540-K1E5	2,000	$12,000
Turbo Viking 17-31ATC	1976-77	17	$38,000-$44,000	193	1,053	1,170	60/75	300-hp Lyc. IO-540-K1E5	2,000	$12,000
Turbo Viking 17-31ATC	1978-80	16	$50,000-$57,000	193	1,053	1,170	60/75	300-hp Lyc. IO-540-K1E5	2,000	$12,000

(mostly taildraggers) had many more non-fatal accidents than the Viking, on an apples-to-apples exposure basis. However, the *fatal* accident rate for the Viking and Cruisaire is the same: (4.5 fatal accidents per 100,000 flight hours)—about twice the rate of the Mooney M20 series (2.4 per 100,000 hours), and quite a bit worse than the Beech Bonanza (at 2.6). In a nutshell, the Viking does not compare well with its peers for safety.

The Viking's non-fatal accidents seem to be lumpable into three categories: a broad category subsuming all the more-or-less ''expected'' bad-luck events that befall all planes more or less equally (hard landings, crankshaft failure, water in the fuel, and so on) . . . engine failure for undetermined reasons . . . and fuel mismanagement. In a review of data covering the years 1979 through 1981, we find that out of 37 total Viking accidents, 32 were non-fatal; and of those, six involved unexplained powerplant failure, while ten involved fuel mismanagement, and the rest fall into the grab-bag category. It's clear that fuel mismanagement and engine problems loom large in the Viking's accident picture. A possible reason seems to be that Viking pilots—once they encounter water contamination, vapor lock, or fuel starvation (from not switching tanks) in the air—are not able to restart the engine easily. Simple restart procedures that work in other airplanes don't always work in the Bellanca, apparently (a problem compounded by a too-effective boost pump, as explained earlier).

In the fatal-accident category, we find that about half of the accidents are attributable to VFR pilots who blunder into IFR weather. More ominously, looking at the 56 fatal Viking accidents that have occurred through 1981, we find that *one out of eight* fatal Viking crashes involves in-flight airframe failure. On an equal-exposure basis, this makes the Viking's in-flight breakup rate not much different from that of the Beech Bonanza. (Remember that there are only 1,000 Vikings on the civil registry, compared to 10,000 Bonanzas; and the

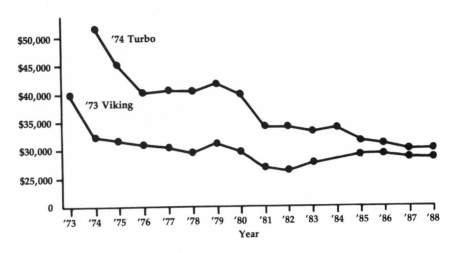

Viking Resale Value chart

'74 Turbo

'73 Viking

Year

Viking's flying history starts in 1967, whereas the Bonanza's starts in 1947. Thus there is greater statistical significance to the Bonanza's breakup data.)

The Viking is a strong airplane. But contrary to the bold rhetoric of the factory a few years ago (when Bellanca claimed that there had *never* been an in-flight structural failure of a Viking), there *have* been breakups—eight fatals, in fact. Most have been weather-related. But it is interesting to note that of the eight fatal Viking breakups on record, six happened in 1969-70 model airplanes. (There has been only one breakup of any Bellanca made after 1970.) This strongly suggests structural problems in a small batch of airplanes. Former Bellanca factory personnel say, however, that there were absolutely no changes in materials or methods of construction in the Viking line over the period in question.

In sum, it appears that the Bellanca Viking—while not gifted with a particularly superb safety record—need not be a particularly hazardous plane to own if pilots will simply avoid aerobatics, invest in good maintenance (particularly of the wing and fabric), take time to understand the fuel system (including in-flight restart techniques), and stay clear of thunderstorms and/or weather for which the pilot is not prepared.

Owner Comments

I have owned three Bellanca Vikings since 1973 and have found them to be an exceptional value and one of the last vestiges of craftsmanship in American manufacturing. In particular, the last two new Bellancas were very well built. Everything was working and tight when I picked the airplanes up from Miller Flying Service in Plainview, Tex. The interior and exterior finishes are particularly nice. The crush velour with leather (or vinyl, I'm not sure which) has held up well. The Imron paint has stayed new-looking with very little attention. No unscheduled maintenance was required in the first 200 hours on either airplane.

My direct operating cost including gas, oil, maintenance, insurance and hangar have run about $40 per hour. In 1,500 hours of flight time spanning seven years, other than routine maintenance, I have required replacement of a propeller governor, an overvoltage relay, and a nose gear strut seal.

The aircraft is an absolute joy to fly. The handling is very responsive. It is especially nice in the banked maneuvers such as steep turns and chandelles. With very little effort one can imagine he is at the controls of a WWII fighter instead of a good stable cross-country airplane. In any large, powerful aircraft proper attention to speed management is important, and this aircraft is no exception. Speed and power must be controlled on approach in order to prevent excessive sink rates. Power off, C-150-type landings require considerable pilot technique, but power-on landings are very easily one. The aircraft is especially good in a crosswind. The low wing, large flaps, and wide gear make it very stable at touchdown.

The cross-country profile is good. I generally plan 500 nautical mile legs in 3.25 hours and have a 100-mile reserve. My airplane will carry two couples, overnight baggage and four hours of fuel and be well within its weight limit. The airplane is very stable in instrument conditions and has no tendency to fall off into a spiral. The panel layout is good and the radio options are quite varied. I have a two-axis autopilot but seldom use it because the airplane is so stable.

In general, I am quite pleased with my Bellanca. I was delighted to hear that the aircraft is back in production. I plan to buy another one if the present one ever wears out.

Bill Bass, Jr. M.D.

I purchased my 1975 17-30A Continental Super Viking in June 1976, as a dealer's demo with about 200 hours on it. I have put about 1,000 hours on it since then. My use is 100 percent business, traveling from Ohio to Montana and south as far as Missouri and Kansas. The plane has done all that was asked of it and some that wasn't, such as carrying a whale of a load of ice into South Bend one winter day.

It is a good solid airplane, steady instrument platform, and reasonably fast. I flight plan 140 knots. Fuel consumption leaned at 22/23 is 12.5 gph. Try as I may, block to block, it works out to 15 gph.

Handling is superb; it is very responsive but will hold a course, hands-off without use of autopilot, with tinkering. Trim changes on

Fabric covering can cost several thousand dollars to replace.

gear/flap extension/retraction are noticeable but easily controlled with the electric trim button on the yoke. I have managed significant wind shear and crosswind situations that even caused tower personnel at a large (DTW) airport to comment on doing a better job than the large commercial jets. The Viking responds to being flown like a light twin—carry a little power right down to the flare.

I don't take my plane into unapproved fields—the fiberglass main wheel doors don't take kindly to abuse. Full-flap slips are permitted and you can really get down in a hurry but need power to stop the sink. Overall, it does a fine job, but I would caution against low-time or occasional-use pilots trying anything unusual. This is a heavy, powerful, high-performance airplane that takes time and experience to get the most out of.

The cabin is tight for four, but so well done that you really don't notice. Workmanship is just what you would expect from an almost custom hand built plane; i.e., it is terrific!

Maintenance between annuals is minimal if plane is properly cared for. I change the oil every 25 hours, Philips X/C 20W-50W, capacity is 12 qts.; however I run one new quart through it and add 11 qts. since the 12th quart always seemed to end up on the belly anyway. Between changes I'll add two qts. and be a quart low (10 qts.) when the next change comes up. I've replaced one vacuum pump (about

700 hrs.) and one exhaust valve. Compression is 70 to 75 over 80.

Needless to say I am very pleased with the plane, and since Continental raised the TBO from 1,500 to 1,700 hours, I feel it is better to keep it than to sell and then try to replace it. I understand they are starting to build them again which should help the resale value. In the meantime, I think a properly maintained, well kept Viking is the best buy on the market.

Dean I. Grauer, Jr.
Allen Park, Mich.

My latest Bellanca is a 1976 Super Viking. I have owned this plane for four years and have never had any difficulty. The annuals are done by Miller Flying Service, and the cost runs from a low of $590 to a high of just around $700.

I did Microlon the engine when I first got it at a little over 300 hours. It now has approximately 1,000. There have been no problems in starting the Lycoming engine. I true out at about 186 knots at 12,000 feet.

If there is anything to complain about concerning the Bellanca, in my opinion it would be the room on the inside. I am 5'9'' and weigh approximately 210 pounds and make a number of trips cross-country.

I am probably prejudiced, but I sincerely believe this to be the best-flying and best-handling of any plane this size.

Ellis B. Qualls
Show Low, Ariz.

Meyers 200

The high-domed canopy on the Meyers 200 is cleanly faired for low drag and offers all-around visibility.

In the late '50s and early '60s, Meyers Aircraft Co. pieced together aerodynamically clean shells over massive tubular frames and turned out a few dozen stout and speedy four-seat airplanes. Then, Aero Commander spent a small fortune trying to mass-produce Al Meyers's design. In 1987, nearly 100 Meyers/Aero Commander 200s were still flying, and their owners swear that they are the best airplanes ever made.

Without batting an eye, they go so far as to call their airplanes the Ferraris of the sky. They boast that they can run circles around a Cessna 210 of the same vintage and pull away from a Bonanza.

Owners are fond of pointing out, too, that there has never been an AD on the airframe (although they do complain bitterly about the ADs that have been issued against the engine and propellers).

Should you need further proof of the airplane's stoutness, Meyers devotees will note that the airplane's bridge-like center section required no beef-up when the 200 was transformed into a 300-knot turboprop.

The airplane's reputation for speed and durability—carefully nurtured, no doubt, by its zealous admirers—and its rarity have kept prices high. If you have a yen for a Meyers 200, figure on shelling out between $30,000 and $40,000 for an average example of the breed, much more for one in exceptional condition—if you can find an owner willing to sell.

Evolution

The 200 was Allen H. Meyers's third design. At the age of 28, after working at the Glenn Martin, Chance Vought and Stinson factories, Meyers had set up his own shop in Tecumseh, Mich. The shop was an aircraft design and manufacturing facility, an FBO and, later, a boat-building yard.

On his own in 1935, he began work on his first design: a biplane called the Meyers OTW (Out To Win), which earned Uncle Sam's blessing for use in the Civilian Pilot Training program. When the program ended, the Meyers Aircraft Co. made ends meet by building such things as aluminum boats, tops for Jeeps and galleys for cargo ships. During this time, Al Meyers designed a two-place, retractable-gear, low-wing airplane called the Meyers 145.

Only about six Meyers 145s were built, and the design eventually was modified into a four-seater, the 200. The prototype Meyers 200 flew in 1953, but it wasn't until five years later that the airplane received its type certificate. At that time, the prototype's carbureted, 225-hp Continental O-470-M engine was replaced with a fuel-injected, 260-hp IO-470-D.

Meyers Aircraft Co. built about 11 Model 200As in 1959 and 1960, and then introduced the 200B, which incorporated only minor changes, including an improved instrument panel. Seventeen were built in the next two years; then the 200C was unveiled.

C Model Improvements

Visibility and creature comfort were greatly improved in the C model. It had a higher cabin roof and a larger windshield than its predecessors, and its interior was plusher. With only nine built, the Meyers 200C is the rarest of the breed.

In 1965, the Meyers 200D was introduced. Among the most noteworthy changes were its 285-hp Continental IO-520-A engine and flush-riveted wings. Meyers Aircraft built only eight of these airplanes before financial troubles caused the company to sell the rights and tooling to Aero Commander the next year.

That company moved production of the Meyers 200D to Albany, GA, believing that the cheaper labor costs there would facilitate production of the "Bonanza-killer." But that was not to be. After building 77 Aero Commander 200Ds and flying a prototype six-seat, swept-tail E model, the company called it quits in 1967. (The 200E prototype now is owned and flown under an Experimental certificate by Californians Richard Morgan and Vinson G. Vanderford.)

Held by Prop-Jets

Legend has it that Aero Commander spent $4 million building $3 million worth of airplanes and was forced to sell the Meyers design when its parent company, Rockwell-Standard, merged with North American in

1967. The rights to the Meyers/Aero Commander 200 were acquired by Interceptor Corp., which certified a turboprop version, the Interceptor 400 (more on that later). The company eventually went bankrupt and was reformed under a holding company, Prop-Jets, Inc.

Prop-Jets is owned by Peter Paul Luce of Boulder, Colo. Ten years ago, Luce struck a deal with Branson Aircraft of Denver to bring the 200 back into production, but the deal fell through.

Accounts vary on how many Meyers 200s are still flying. But, the latest FAA records show 99 of them (nine As, 11 Bs, seven Cs, 71 Ds and the one E) were registered in this country two years ago. About a dozen are thought to be flying overseas.

Design and Construction

The Meyers 200 can best be described as a very sophisticated homebuilt. Many observers contend that Al Meyers never intended the airplane to be mass-produced, which could explain Aero Commander's lack of success.

"Meyers was in the FBO business," recalled one observer. "When there were no orders for a 200, they pulled the little jigs and fixtures up into the rafter to free up some floor space for repairs."

At the heart of the airplane's design and reputation are welded, 4,130 chrome-alloy steel tubes that form the fuselage and center section. The structure runs from the firewall to the rear fuselage bulkhead and out into the wings, where it supports the main landing gear assemblies. The rear fuselage section is of semi-monocoque design and construction.

The landing gear and Fowler-type flaps are hydraulically actuated, and the flight controls incorporate push-pull tubes. There are two emergency gear-extension systems: a hand-pump to supply hydraulic pressure and an uplock-release mechanism. Fuel is carried in two main tanks and two auxiliaries. Each holds 20 gallons of fuel, and total usable capacity is 74 gallons.

The passenger seat and the two rear seats were designed to be removed

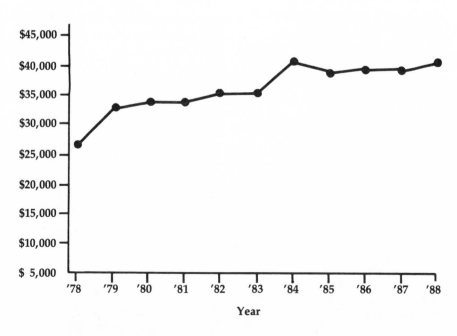

Meyers 200D Resale Value Chart

Cost/Performance/Specifications

Model	Year	Number Built	Average Retail Price	Cruise Speed (kts)	Rate of Climb (fpm)	Useful Load (lbs)	Usable Std/Opt (gals)	Engine	TBO (hrs)	Overhaul Cost
200A	1959	5	$32,000	170	1,150	2,150	40/80	260-hp Cont. IO-470-D	1,500	$11,500
200A	1960	6	$32,000	170	1,150	2,150	40/80	260-hp Cont. IO-470-D	1,500	$11,500
200B	1961	7	$33,500	170	1,245	1,025	40/80	260-hp Cont. IO-470-D	1,500	$11,500
200B	1962	10	$33,500	170	1,245	1,025	40/80	260-hp Cont. IO-470-D	1,500	$11,500
200C	1963	6	$35,000	170	1,245	1,025	40/80	260-hp Cont. IO-470-D	1,500	$11,500
200C	1964	6	$35,000	170	1,245	1,025	40/80	260-hp Cont. IO-470-D	1,500	$11,500
200D	1965	6	$40,000	183	1,450	1,015	80	285-hp Cont. IO-520-A	1,700	$12,250
200D	1966	69	$40,500	183	1,450	1,015	80	285-hp Cont. IO-520-A	1,700	$12,250
200D	1967	20	$41,000	183	1,450	1,015	80	285-hp Cont. IO-520-A	1,700	$12,250

quickly to accommodate cargo. But the airplane cannot haul much—legally, that is.

Beefy Bird

Throughout production of the relatively heavy airplane, gross weight remained at 3,000 pounds. With equipped empty weights typically tipping the scales at about 2,100 pounds, useful load is a mere 900 pounds. Add full fuel, and you can fit only about 450 pounds of people and baggage into the airplane and remain within certified weight and balance limits.

As one owner commented, the four-place Meyers 200 really is "a legal two-place airplane." Although Aero Commander completed testing to raise the gross weight to 3,350 pounds, the paperwork was never submitted to the FAA for approval.

Performance and Handling

The airplane's forte, of course, is speed. Maximum cruise speed of the original models is 195 mph—as fast as the V-tail Bonanzas produced during the same period, and five to 10 mph faster than contemporary Cessnas 210s.

With its bigger engine and flush-riveted wings, the 200D is even faster: 210 mph at max cruise. This is a good five mph faster than S- and V-35 Bonanzas and 20 mph faster than D- through G-model 210s.

Never-exceed speed of the 200A is 208 mph, and its maximum structural cruising speed is 165 mph. Starting with the B model, these limits were raised to 236 mph and 210 mph, respectively. Thanks to relatively high gear- and flap-extension speeds, the slippery airplane can be slowed quickly to mix with traffic in the pattern. In the 200A, the gear can be lowered at 165 mph, and the flaps at 125 mph. Gear-extension speeds for the B, C and D models are 170 mph for normal operation of 210 mph in an emergency (Good-bye, gear doors).

No Featherweight

The controls are relatively heavy, thanks both to the push-pull tubes and to the rather skinny yoke. Owners say that, due to a bungee arrangement in the control systems, little or no trim changes are required when the gear and flaps are extended.

Owners report that the airplane generally is easy to fly. But newcomers, especially those with little experience in heavy, high-performance singles, should get a thorough checkout by an instructor who knows the airplane. On take-off and climb, there is quite a bit of torque to contend with, due to the airplane's design. Al Meyers chose not to offset the engine or horizontal stabilizer to lessen low-speed, high-power torque effects. As a result, almost full right rudder is needed on takeoff and initial climb.

Owners say, though, that if there is anything on the airplane that might cause a pilot to come to grief, it is the fuel system. (And, as we shall see later, accident records bear this out.) A single selector controls flow from each of the four tanks, and there is only one gauge, which shows the amount of fuel remaining only in the tank selected. Fuel management, therefore, requires constant attention and a good memory.

Another system that requires some getting used to is the elevator trim control. The dual trim tabs are positioned by a control knob on the panel. And it is quite sensitive, requiring only a slight twist this way or that to relieve control pressure.

The Fowler-type flaps are very effective; stall speeds are 67 mph clean, and 54 mph with gear and flaps extended. However, owners report that the airplane will sink quite rapidly if airspeed and power are not managed properly on final approach.

Safety Record

As reported in the Sept. 15, 1980, issue of *The Aviation Consumer*, fuel system problems and fuel mismanagement were the leading causes of accidents that occurred from 1974 through 1978. Several incidents have been triggered by deteriorated fuel lines. However, the Meyers Aircraft Owners Assn. did a good job in getting the word out on this problem, and most owners have had their lines replaced.

A recent check of FAA records shows that nine Meyers 200s were involved in accidents from 1980 through June 1987. It is interesting to note that only one of the accidents involved injury. The pilot died when his 200B crashed out of control in Texas last year. The cause of the crash has not been determined.

Fuel problems played a role in three of the accidents. In one, a 200D had only minor damage in an emergency landing following fuel exhaustion. Another landed short of a runway and ran through a fence after its engine lost power when the pilot switched tanks in the pattern. The engine in a third 200D failed to respond due to low fuel pressure on short final, and the gear collapsed on landing.

Five of the accidents involved gear problems. A 200B was slightly damaged after its pilot forgot to extend the gear for landing. A 200D's landing gear retracted while taxiing, due to an improperly positioned gear handle, according to the FAA. The left main gear on another 200D retracted while taxiing, but in this case investigators failed to determine why.

In the fourth gear-related accident, a pilot struck a stake while taxiing and then cycled the gear after takeoff when the nose-gear-up light failed to illuminate. Apparently the nose gear fell off the airplane during takeoff or while the gear was being cycled, and the 200D eventually landed on the mains, only. Nevertheless, damage was reported as minor. Another Meyers 200D had minor damage when its nose gear failed to extend during a landing, for unknown reasons.

The accident record also included a pilotless 200B that crashed into a hangar. The engine inadvertently

had started when the pilot moved the propeller, unaware that the magnetos were hot.

Maintenance

Although there have been no ADs on the airframe, a few have targeted the propellers and engine. Three ADs on McCauley props have required replacement of their attach bolts and inspection of their blades and hubs for cracks. The Hartzell props have drawn two directives. One required blade replacement; the other, issued in 1985, called for replacement of blade clamps.

Another AD, issued 12 years ago, required inspection of IO-520 crankcases for cracks. Magneto impulse couplers on these engines have drawn three separate directives.

Recurrent maintenance is mandated by two directives. AD 84-26-2 requires replacement of paper induction air filters every 500 hours; and AD 86-13-4 requires the cylinders in Meyers 200D engines to be pressure-checked every 50 hours until they are replaced.

Recent Service Difficulty Reports included two nose-gear maintenance discrepancies. A broken nosewheel horn in a Meyers 200A prevented the wheel from extending fully; and a broken cable in a 200D allowed the gear to cock and jam in the wheel well. There were two SDRs on frayed rudder cables found in 200Ds.

Potential Problems

According to owners we spoke with, the Meyers 200 is not a maintenance-intensive airplane. However, they did reveal two potential sources of grief.

One is the cabin door. It is constructed of aluminum and fiberglass and does not hold up well to use and abuse. Most owners say their doors do not fit properly

anymore, and leaking air creates quite a racket. Many have had their doors pop open in flight.

Landing gear bushings are another problem. Each airplane has about 52 of them, and they require regular replacement. One owner said he has had to replace his bushings every 250 hours.

Deterioration of plastic seat components has been another problem. However, fiberglass replacements are available from My-Com Development, 18 Williamsburg Lane, Chico, Calif.

My-Com, owned by Vinson Vanderford and Richard Morgan, also offers Hoerner-style wing tips and a kit to relocate the rotating beacon from the top of the vertical tail to the airplane's belly. Turbulence created by the beacon reportedly detracts substantially from the rudder's effectiveness.

The Parts Situation

Owners report that so far they have had no problems getting parts for their airplanes. They say that most parts requiring regular replacement are used on many other aircraft, so there is a good supply.

Paul Whetstone's Million Air facility at San Antonio International has, by far, the largest inventory of parts for the Meyers 200. Because the FAA was not on hand to observe the transfer of the inventory to San Antonio, the parts are not yellow-tagged. That means that it is up to the mechanics who install the parts to determine their airworthiness.

According to Whetstone, landing gear parts may soon become a problem. "I've only got a couple sets of landing gear, and I'm running out of torque links," he said. Since the links are cast aluminum, it is doubtful that any more will be manufactured, unless the airplane is returned to production.

The Interceptor

Although the few attempts to take up where Aero Commander left off did not go far, there is still some hope that production of the Meyers 200 will resume. Whetstone, who also is president of Prop-Jets, Inc., currently is attempting to arrange for production of the Interceptor 400 overseas. Once the turboprop is in production, he says, it would be easy to start building 200s again, too.

The Interceptor 400 received a type certificate in 1971, but only two of them were built. One survived two accidents—a ditching off the coast of California after the fuel pump cavitated, causing the engine to flame out, and a crash into trees on short final after another flameout caused by fuel unporting—only to be destroyed in a hangar fire. (No one was hurt in the accidents.)

Whetstone owns the other Interceptor, which, he claims, cruises at more than 300 knots (345 mph) while burning 240 pounds of Jet-A per hour. Rate of climb is 2,000 feet from sea level to 24,000 feet. The Interceptor was designed by a group of former Aero Commander engineers headed by Don Long, who had a hand in designing the Jet Commander. Thicker fuselage skins were used to allow pressurization of the fuselage to 3.0 psi, providing a 13,000-foot cabin at 24,000 feet.

During the conversion, the wings and rear fuselage were substantially modified, and a new vertical tail and rudder were incorporated. The tubular center section, however, required no modification. The Interceptor, which is powered by a Garrett TPE engine, flat-rated to 400 hp, was certified at a gross weight of 4,050 pounds.

Prop-Jets, like Aero Commander many years ago, apparently believes low labor costs are the keys to success with Al Meyers's design. "If you could build that airplane in a country where labor is inexpensive, you'd have a winner," Whetstone said. He noted that plans call for marketing the airplane as a military trainer, but added that the Interceptor would also be "the ultimate businessman's airplane."

Whetstone predicts that if the Interceptor is built overseas, the price will be about $600,000. "And if that is in production, it would be a piece of cake to build some 200s, too," he said.

Buyer Checkpoints

There are probably three good reasons for buying a Meyers/Aero Commander 200. The first is speed. The airplane can outrun just about anything else in its class. The second reason is the strength of its construction. Several of the airplanes have survived harrowing accidents with only minor damage.

But for the prices the airplanes currently are commanding, there is quite a lot to choose from on the used aircraft market. For example, a Mooney M20K is just as fast and far more efficient.

In terms of strength, Meyers owners may sneer at the relatively thin skins used on, say, a Bonanza, but they cannot deny that the Bonanza was certified in the Utility as well as the Normal category. It, too, is a fairly tough airplane.

And while Bonanzas and 210s may be a little slower and, perhaps, not as stout as a Meyers, they can legally carry much more payload. So, we get to the third and probably the best reason to buy a Meyers 200—because it is a Meyers 200. In many ways, it is a unique airplane — an attention-grabber. You're hard-pressed to spot one at even the most crowded general aviation airport.

But prospective buyers of the "Ferrari-of-the-sky" should know what they're getting into. As we mentioned earlier, there have been no ADs on the airframe, but several have been issued on the engine prop and other systems. Evidence of compliance with these should be in hand before any deal is consummated.

Owners say they're easy to fly, but they are certainly no baby carriages. The fuel system and potentially high sink rate could spell trouble for the unwary. And, while parts may not be hard to find now, there is concern about the diminishing supply of some landing gear components. Some owners believe that in the future it may not be possible to rebuild a substantially damaged 200.

200 Club

The Meyers Aircraft Owners Assn. is a rather informal but tightly knit group of some 200 owners and admirers. The association holds an annual fly-in at various parts of the country and publishes a "semi-regular" newsletter.

Bill Gaffney, the association's secretary, is handling correspondence at 26 Route 17K, Newburgh, NY 12550, (914) 565-8005.

Owner Comments

I own a D model and am a partner, with Dr. Richard Morgan, in the only E model ever built. It has a big swept tail, and the engine sits 12 inches farther forward. But it has the same engine and wing as the 200D. The fifth and sixth seats are where the baggage compartment used to be. It's a good-looking airplane, and it flies nicely.

Dr. Morgan also has a D model. It's the only turbocharged 200 around, and it works well. At 18,000 feet, you can get about 245-250 mph. We got a one-time STC on it; but if you copied everything we did exactly, you'd have no problem getting it approved. And the Meyers has such a big engine compartment, it's easy to work in there. We used a 310-hp TSIO-520-M Continental in it; we took the entire unit from a 210.

The Meyers is just an overgrown homebuilt. When you work on them, you find that no two are exactly alike. I owned a C model for 14 years, and I think it's the best airplane Meyers built. It was the first one with a raised cabin and a big windshield. I put a 285-hp engine in it, and I found it was only, maybe, four miles per hour slower than a 200D.

The Meyers is probably one of the strongest airplanes ever built. One guy had an engine failure coming into Reno and didn't quite make the airport. He hit going crossways on a road around the airport perimeter. A curb took all the gear off. Then, he went through a Cyclone fence, tore that off and came out the other side in a rough field. He finally came to a stop in a cloud of dust, opened the door, and he and his wife and little boy stepped out without a scratch on them. And the airplane was still all together.

The airplane is really strong, but it also is heavy. Most of them go about 2,100 pounds, empty, with equipment. That really cuts down on useful load.

It's still one of the fastest, nonturbo'd singles in the sky today. I flew it against a Viking 300 the other day. He was at 25 square, and I was down to 2,200 rpm and 19 inches to stay alongside of him. It's about six mph faster at the same power setting as the Beech Bonanza, which has the same engine.

Another nice thing about it is that when you extend or retract the flaps, you don't have to touch the trim. It's got a series of bungees in there on a little bellcrank that automatically takes up a little

tension on your elevator when your flaps go down.

If you have to make a go-around, you simply come in with full power, retract the gear and hit the flap handle. The flaps will come up from 40 to 20 degrees and stop there, so that you don't end up dumping all your flaps off.

But, again, it's a heavy airplane, and you don't want to get behind the power curve. You fly it kind of like a twin and hold a little power until right over.

Considering that they're retracts, I haven't had many maintenance problems with the 200s I've owned. The old oil-impregnated, carbon bushings used in the landing gear didn't last too long. We finally went to oil-impregnated, bronze bushings, and they seem to be working out well. Now, there are new ones out that are Teflon-impregnated steel, which really ought to work great.

Of course, the doors never did fit right on the 200s that either Meyers or Aero Commander built. Maybe, one in 20 close and do not leak air. But if a guy takes the time, about 100 hours of labor, he can rebuild a door and make it fit.

Vinson G. Vanderford
Yuba City, Calif.

I bought my Model 200D new in 1967. I expect you'll find most of us who have owned the airplanes that long are pretty happy with them. I think its a real fine airplane. It's built strong; there are almost no ADs on the airplane. It stalls slow, cruises fast, and it's very stable—a good instrument platform.

I owned Tri-Pacers, Cherokees and a Comanche, and flew a friend's Bonanza before buying the Meyers. I thought the Comanche was a good airplane, but the Meyers handles and feels a lot better. It also has a shorter wing, which means

you don't have to scuff one when you're trying to put it in a hangar. I think the Meyers was made very well, though some people feel it was made too heavy.

Most owners have had to replace their gas lines and some of the hydraulic lines, but I'd consider that normal maintenance. I've had some problem with my nose wheel shimmying. It doesn't have a damper, and I've had to replace all the bushings.

The only problem I can see for somebody who gets in one for the first time is that it's kind of short-coupled, and with its big engine and pretty big prop, you get some torque; and you have to use a lot of right rudder to keep it lined up for takeoff. Other than that, there really isn't too much wrong with the airplane.

Bill Claytor
Winchester, Va

I bought my 200D in 1976. It's a super airplane. It's fast—I file 165 knots when I go IFR—and, with 80 gallons of gas, it has good range. I've measured 13 gallons an hour at 8,000 feet. If you lean it out, it will go 1,100 miles.

It has the same size tires on the mains as on the nose, and there's plenty of prop clearance, which makes it a good airplane for grass strips. I've been using mine on a 1,500-foot strip for 11 years. Of course, I don't fly four people out of there…

There are no ADs on the airframe, but there was one of those across-the-board ADs on McCauley props some time ago. All the 210s, Bonanzas and Meyers had to have their props taken off if they had more than 1,200 hours, whether they were bad or not.

When Meyers designed it, he used parts from airplanes that were being built by other manufacturers. Some of the parts are from Bonanzas, some are Aztec parts. The fuel gauges are from automobiles. The arm rests are out of Pontiacs.

The only big parts problem I can foresee would occur if you had major damage to the airplane. You might not be able to get a wing or center section. You'd have to rebuild them. But bushings and bearings are easy to find, and the tires, the propeller and the engine are standard equipment on many other airplanes.

Larry Brandenburg
Rising Sun, Md

Beech Bonanza 35, 36

The word "legend" is tossed around rather freely when people talk about airplanes, but the Beechcraft Bonanza probably has a better claim to legendary status than any other modern lightplane. The Bonanza was the first high-performance post-war design (it was introduced in 1947). Its various models have been in continuous production since then, and are still considered by many to be the best single-engine airplanes flying.

The most innovative postwar aircraft to emerge on the civilian market, the early Bonanza 35 is inspected by Walter H. Beech and Olive Ann Beech.

The Bonanza's astonishing success is the result of excellent performance, sleek good looks, responsive handling and a "Mercedes of the air" image. The loading limitations, high parts prices and cracking crankcases are not part of that legend, however.

For many years, the Bonanza enjoyed a blue-chip reputation on the used-plane market. Because of high demand and huge inflationary price increases of new Bonanzas during the 1970s, it was routine for a decade-old Bonanza to be worth more than its new selling price. Owners reported paying top dollar for a used Bonanza, then selling it a few years later at a profit.

But the V-tail version of the airplane has in recent years suffered a sharp decline in value because of its bad record of in-flight breakups. (More on that later.) A V-tail is now worth about 10 percent less than an equivalent straight-tail 33 Bonanza; a few years ago the reverse was true. The generally bearish used-plane market of the mid-80s has hurt resale value of virtually all other aircraft, but the 33 series has taken over from the 35 the role as the best resale investment among light aircraft.

A prospective Bonanza buyer should carefully examine his motivation for buying. On a coldly rational cost-effective basis, a used Cessna 210 or Piper Comanche will generally provide more airplane per dollar. But pilots seem to be more impressed by macho appeal, plush interiors and the "feel" of the airplane. In this realm the Bonanza is supreme. We wonder how many used-aircraft buyers choose to buy Bonanzas after objective comparisons with other makes. Most, we suspect, simply decide to buy a Bonanza and don't even look seriously at other types. For those buyers, the question is merely which used Bonanza is the best buy?

Models

There is a bewildering variety of Bonanza models. There are three basic types: the Model 35, the classic V-tail form of the aircraft that was in continuous production from 1947 until 1982, with power ranging from 185 to 285 hp; the Model 33, introduced in 1960 with a conventional tail and engines ranging from 225 to 285 hp; and the Model 36, a "stretched" six-seat conventional-tail version introduced in 1968 with a 285-hp engine. (Adding to the confusion is the fact that the 33 model was called the Debonair for seven years.)

Engines

Early Bonanzas up through the G35 in 1956 had Continental "E" series engines. Although the powerplants are reasonably reliable, the supply of parts and knowledgeable mechanics for these engines is rapidly dwindling. Continental no longer makes remanufactured E series engines, and there are no more crankcases or crankshafts being made. Other parts are generally available, but rapidly becoming more expensive as production dwindles. Cost of an overhaul for an old Bonanza is about $8,000, hefty fee considering that the airplane itself may be worth only $15,000, even with a fresh overhaul.

Later Bonanzas have either the IO-470 or IO-520 Continental engines. Prior to 1970, both these engines were rated at 1,200 hours TBO. In 1970, the valves were improved, and TBO went up to 1,500 hours. Older engines overhauled with the better valves also have the 1,500-hour TBO. This should be a major checkpoint for buyers.

Cracking Cases

Literally thousands of Bonanza owners have suffered the "Curse of the Cracking Crankcases," either directly or indirectly because of overhaul considerations.

IO-520-B and -BA engines built prior to mid-1976 have a severe problem with crankcase cracking. The overhauling of those engines has virtually ceased because no reputable overhauler will sign off without a new post-1976 "heavy" case. The cost of case replacement added to normal overhaul cost is about the same as the cost of a remanufactured engine from the factory, which now includes the heavy case. The result has been a bonanza (sic) of reman IO-520 bus-

iness for Continental, and the elimination of the option of a lower-cost standard overhaul. The factory does offer some credit for cracked cases on trade-ins for remanufactured engines, but in most cases, "light case" Bonanza buyers will find themselves paying a couple of thousand dollars more than the usual overhaul cost when their engines are due for rebuilding.

Incidentally, beware of the phrase "heavy case" in advertisements for used Bonanzas. There have been at least three "heavy" case versions designed to combat the cracking problem. The first two didn't work. Only those engines manufactured or remanufactured after July 1976 have the true "heavy" case.

However, even the "heavy" cases aren't immune to cracking. A 1983 *Aviation Consumer* study showed that heavy-case engines had a

record nearly as bad as the "light" cases. Crankcase cracks continue to be a problem in Bonanzas.

Maintenance Problems

The other two major Bonanza maintenance checkpoints are shared with various other aircraft: the Hartzell prop AD and the leaking Goodyear rubber fuel tanks. The prop AD — which applies only to IO-520-powered Bonanzas — generally costs $1,000.

The fuel tank AD is not as expensive in most cases, since only an inspection is required. However, if a leak is discovered, replacement can be costly. There is no consistent pattern, but most Bonanzas built between 1961 and 1975 are subject to the Goodyear AD. All Bonanzas have rubber bladder tanks of some sort, and their life expectancy is six to eight years. Replacement cost

Cost/Performance/Specifications

Model	Year Built	Number Built	Cruise Speed (kts)	Rate Climb (fpm)	Useful Load (lbs)	Fuel Std/Opt (gals)	Engine	TBO (hrs)	Overhaul Cost	Average Price
Bonanza 35	1947-48	1,500	150	950	1,092	39/60	185-hp Cont. E-185-1	1,500	$10,000	$ 16,000
A35	1949	699	148	890	1,075	39/60	185-hp Cont. E-185-1	1,500	$10,000	$ 16,500
B35	1950	479	148	890	1,075	39/60	196-hp Cont. E-185-8	1,500	$10,000	$ 17,000
C35	1951-52	719	152	1,100	1,050	39/60	205-hp Cont. E-185-11	1,500	$10,000	$ 18,000
D35	1953	297	152	1,100	1,050	39/60	205-hp Cont. E-185-11	1,500	$10,000	$ 18,250
E35	1954	705	160	1,300	953	39/60	225-hp Cont. E-225-8	1,500	$10,000	$ 18,750
F35	1955	392	160	1,300	978	39/60	225-hp Cont. E-225-8	1,500	$10,000	$ 19,500
G35	1956	489	160	1,300	1,003	39/60	225-hp Cont. E-225-8	1,500	$10,000	$ 20,500
H35	1957	464	165	1,225	1,080	39/60	240-hp Cont. O-470-G	1,500	$10,000	$ 22,750
J35	1958	663	174	1,250	1,080	39/60	250-hp Cont. IO-470-C	1,500	$10,750	$ 25,000
K35	1959	435	169	1,170	1,118	49/70	250-hp Cont. IO-470-C	1,500	$10,750	$ 26,000
M35	1960	399	169	1,170	1,118	49/70	250-hp Cont. IO-470-C	1,500	$10,750	$ 27,000
N35	1961	279	169	1,150	1,270	50/80	260-hp Cont. IO-470-N	1,500	$10,750	$ 28,500
P35	1962-63	467	169	1,150	1,270	50/80	260-hp Cont. IO-470-N	1,200	$10,750	$ 30,000
S35	1964-65	665	178	1,200	1,385	50/80	285-hp Cont. IO-520-BA	1,200	$11,300	$ 34,500
V35	1966-67	625	178	1,135	1,485	50/120	285-hp Cont. IO-520-BA	1,200	$11,300	$ 38,000
V35TC	1966-67	555	195	1,225	1,450	50/120	285-hp Cont. IO-520-BA	1,400	$13,000	$ 43,500
V35A	1968-69	468	177	1,136	1,440	44/74	285-hp Cont. IO-520-BA	1,200	$11,250	$ 42,250
V35A-TC	1968-69	252	200	1,225	1,373	50/120	285-hp Cont. IO-520-BA	1,400	$13,000	$ 47,750
V35B	1970	142	172	1,167	1,313	44/74	285-hp Cont. IO-520-BA	1,500	$11,250	$ 46,500
V35B-TC	1970	110	200	1,225	1,373	50/120	285-hp Cont. IO-520-BA	1,400	$13,000	$ 50,500
V35B	1971-72	185	172	1,167	1,313	44/74	285-hp Cont. IO-520-BA	1,500	$11,250	$ 50,000
V35B	1973-74	285	172	1,167	1,313	44/74	285-hp Cont. IO-520-BA	1,500	$11,250	$ 54,000
V35B	1975	128	172	1,167	1,313	44/74	285-hp Cont. IO-520-BA	1,500	$11,250	$ 58,000
V35B	1976	131	172	1,167	1,313	44/74	285-hp Cont. IO-520-BA	1,500	$11,250	$ 62,000
V35B	1977	120	172	1,167	1,313	44/74	285-hp Cont. IO-520-BA	1,500	$11,250	$ 66,000
V35B	1978	109	172	1,167	1,313	44/74	285-hp Cont. IO-520-BA	1,500	$11,250	$ 72,000
V35B	1979	123	172	1,167	1,313	44/74	285-hp Cont. IO-520-BB	1,500	$11,250	$ 78,000
V35B	1980	50	172	1,167	1,313	44/74	285-hp Cont. IO-520-BB	1,500	$11,250	$ 84,000
V35B	1981	28	172	1,167	1,313	44/74	285-hp Cont. IO-520-BB	1,500	$11,250	$ 90,000
V35B	1982	20	172	1,167	1,313	44/74	285-hp Cont. IO-520-BB	1,500	$11,250	$ 96,000

can run between $1,500 and $2,500, depending on the model.

Several *Aviation Consumer* readers mentioned vacuum pump failures, and the Airborne pumps used in many Bonanzas have a poor record. Failure of the vacuum pump in IFR conditions, of course, can be fatal.

Safety

The Bonanza's safety record is generally good — with a couple of important exceptions. According to *Aviation Consumer* studies of NTSB and FAA statistics for the period 1972-76, the 33 and 36 models have excellent records (see the list of single-engine retractable accident rate at the beginning of the book). The 33, in fact, has the lowest fatal accident rate of any single-engine airplane, and the 36 is not far behind.

The V-tail 35 model is another story. Newer V-tails, including the 1964 S model and later models, all with 285-hp engines, have a reasonably good fatal accident rate, but the older models rank very poorly, with a fatal accident rate nearly twice as high as the later V-tails and nearly quadruple that of the 33 series.

In-Flight Breakups

A major reason for the poor fatal accident rate of the older V-tails is the relatively very high rate of fatal in-flight airframe failures in those models. Over the years, there have been more than 230 Bonanza in-flight breakups, in which we estimate some 500 people have died. We have reprinted here a chart of the in-flight breakup rates of the various Bonanza models. As you can see, the old ones are the worst, with the 1947-48 "straight 35" having an especially high breakup rate. (The lower percentages for late-model V-tails are a bit misleading, however, since they haven't had enough time to build up a high number of accidents.)

What makes the V-tail's high record of in-flight breakups all the more ironic is the very low breakup

How well will this 1975 V35B hold its value? Until the V-tail breakup record became widely known, used Bonanzas appreciated in value. However, a 1975 model has lost $20,000 in value over the past four years.

rate of the straight-tail 33 and 36 models, which are essentially identical to the 35 except for the tail. The V-tail's breakup rate, according to one study, is 24 times higher than the straight-tail's.

The typical scenarios of a V-tail breakup is this: the pilot gets into bad weather and/or heavy turbulence, the airplane gets away from him, and comes apart in the ensuing high-speed dive and/or pull-out, which exceed the structural limits of the plane. The reasons for the high breakup rates of V-tail Bonanzas are not crystal clear, but

Bonanza 35 Fatal Inflight Airframe Failure Accidents·

Model	Number FIFAFAs	Number Produced	Percent FIFAFA
35	71 .	1500	4.8
35R	0	13	0.0
A35	17	701	2.4
B35	11	480	2.3
C35	20	719	2.8
D35	14	298	4.7
E35	10	301	3.3
F35	6	392	1.5
G35	7	476	1.5
H35	2	426	0.4
J35	5	396	1.3
K35	4	436	0.9
M35	10	400	2.5
N35	4	280	1.4
P35	7	467	1.5
S35	7	667	1.1
V35	5	622	0.8
V35A	5	470	1.1
V35B	3	n.a.	n.a.
Total	208		

*Through 1979.

we believe the problem has two major facets: structural weak points and handling qualities.

Structural problems most likely play a big role in the high break-up rate of the 1947-48 model 35. Those years, the Bonanza had unusually thin wing skins and no shear web in the outboard leading edge —structural shortcuts designed to save weight. Although the break-up problem abated somewhat after Beech beefed up the wings in 1949, it did not go away, particularly in the A through E models. The problem seemed to move back to the tail; while the majority of "straight 35" breakup involved wing failures, the majority of failures in later models occurred in the tail. Some critics have faulted Beech for the front spar design in the stabilizers, particularly after the "overhang" in front of the spar was increased with the C model. Accident investigators report a pattern of tail failures in which the stabilizer skin fails and folds over the spar.

Any airplane will fall apart in the air if pushed far enough past its airspeed or g-load limits, and Bonanzas usually don't break up unless pushed past their limits. The question is, why do the pilots of older V-tails allow their craft to exceed speed and load limits so much more often than pilots of other airplanes?

The answer, we believe, may lie in the handling qualities of the V-tail Bonanzas.

The V-tail airplane has very light ailerons and low lateral stability — what the test pilots call high spiral divergence. Once a wing drops a little, it tends to keep going. In instrument weather and turbulence, this low rolling stability can put the pilot into the "graveyard spiral" quickly.

The V-tail airplane is also very light on the controls in the pitch axis. This low longitudinal stability means turbulence or pilot inattention will cause larger, quicker airspeed and altitude excursions. The light controls also mean that just a moderate pull on the wheel results in a sharp pullup and high g-forces.

The V-tail Bonanza's low longitudinal stability is exacerbated by the rather narrow center-of-gravity envelope. (Some models even have 30 pounds of lead in the nose to counter the balance problem.) With any passengers in the back seat, a Bonanza can be very close to its aft c.g. limit, and it's not uncommon for V-tails to be flown illegally beyond their aft limit. An aft c.g. further reduces the V-tail's already low longitudinal stability, making the airplane even more sensitive in pitch and making wheel forces even lighter.

The low stability in the roll and pitch axes can team up against the pilot. A typical scenario: pilot looks down at chart while gust drops right wing. Airplane begins rolling to the right, simultaneously dropping the nose and picking up speed. Pilot looks up from chart, notes very high airspeed, and pulls back on the wheel abruptly. Airplane pulls six g's and breaks off the wings or tail.

The famous "Bonanza waggle" may also play a role. The V-tail has very poor Dutch roll (yaw) characteristics in turbulence. In extreme cases, severe turbulence may yaw the plane to such high angles that the tail could literally be blown off, particularly at high speeds, according to some engineers.

The poor stability in all three axes is due mainly to the design of the V-tail itself. The straight-tail 33 and 36 Bonanzas have much better stability, and an almost perfect record of in-flight breakups (only two that we're aware of).

Another factor may be the sensitivity of the V-tail ruddervators to flutter. The V-tail Bonanza's margin of flutter is fairly small, and tests have shown that as little as two ounces at the trailing edge of the ruddervator — a piece of ice, or even a repaint job — can cause flutter under some conditions.

Stall/Spin

Older Bonanzas also show up poorly in stall/spin and fuel mismanagement accidents. According to NTSB accident statistics for the period 1965-73, the Bonanza had a fatal stall/spin accident rate of 0.68 (per 100,000 flight hours) — second only to the Beech 23 series (Sierra, Sundowner, etc.) among modern aircraft. By comparison, the Cessna 210 had a fatal stall/spin rate of only 0.24 — only about a third as high.

The Bonanza does have a sharp stall, often accompanied by a wing drop. There is little aerodynamic buffeting as warning of an impending stall. Some pilots have reported severe wing drops, even to the point of ending up on their backs in certain situations. We asked a former Beech engineer about the Bonanza's stall, and he said that no two Bonanzas stall alike. "Even at the factory, some of them were very straightforward in the stall, while others dropped off rather abruptly."

Another major cause of design-induced accidents is fuel mismanagement. Again, the older Bonanzas are near the top of the list in fuel mismanagement accidents. According to a 1964 CAB report on fuel mismanagement, the Bonanza ranked second worst (to the Piper Tri-Pacer) in fuel mismanagement accidents that year. An NTSB study for the years 1965-69 ranks the Bonanza as having the highest incidence of fuel starvation accidents of any light aircraft. And a study of fuel starvation accidents during 1970-72 puts the Bonanza in the "higher than average" group along with three other aircraft.

The reason for the Bonanza's high incidence of fuel mismanagement accidents is presumably due to the placement of the fuel selector and the rather odd fuel pump operation in older models. The selector valve is on the floor under the pilot's left leg, which forces the pilot to crane his neck and divert his attention from the windshield and instrument panel to change tanks. Consequently, Bonanza pilots may switch tanks by feel, a riskier procedure. Also, the selector detents are poorly defined in some models, and it's possible to hang up the selector between tanks, which shuts off the fuel.

If an engine does quit from fuel starvation, the Bonanza pilot faces a dilemma: turn on the boost pump or not? If he doesn't according to a CAB study, the engine may take as long as 35 seconds to restart. If he does, he may flood the engine if the pump is left on too long. The owner's manual of one model Bonanza instructs the pilot to turn on the boost pump "momentarily" when switching from a dry tank. The pilot must tread a narrow line between a fuel-starved engine on the one hand and a flooded-out engine on the other hand. Not a happy choice.

The 1957 Bonanza incorporated a major series of wing and tail strengthening features.

And then, of course, there is the notorious "fuel unporting" syndrome that has resulted in numerous Bonanza accidents and lawsuits against Beech. In extended slipping or skidding maneuvers or in fast turning type takeoffs in pre-1970 models, fuel would slosh away from the fuel pickup if the tank was less than half full. Beech issued a service letter as far back as 1961 on the fuel unporting phenomenon. It warned that fuel unporting was a possibility after a turning takeoff, and stated that in such a case the air bubble in the fuel line would "reach the engine at about the same time the airplane becomes airborne and could cause momentary power interruption." The letter went on to say, "This does not create a hazard . . ." We think a lot of people would argue with that statement.

In any case, the FAA had identified 16 accidents caused by fuel unporting by 1971, when an AD was finally issued. The AD required no modification of the fuel system, merely a yellow arc on the fuel gauge and an admonition not to take off or slip or skid excessively if the fuel was in the arc. Beech did modify the tanks in 1970, and offered a retrofit kit for older Bonanzas, but only a handful of the retrofit kits were sold. Thousands of pre-1970 Bonanzas still have the unmodified tanks and are susceptible to fuel unporting. We would strongly urge any buyer to check whether the baffle kit has been installed, and to install it himself if it has not been done.

Summing up, while the straight-tail 33 and 36 models and the more recent 285-hp V-tail airplanes have good to excellent safety records, the older V-tails rank poorly. These older less-than-$30,000 Bonanzas are an attractive buy, but they are not for the overconfident or underqualified. More than 30 percent of the fatal accidents in older V-tails are in-flight breakups, and the stall/spin and fuel mismanagement accident rates are also quite high. Clearly, the older Bonanzas demand the pilot's full attention and adequate skills.

Loading

Early 185- and 225-hp Bonanzas have useful loads of about 900 pounds with normal equipment, and equipped useful load has grown over the years as horsepower increased to about 1,200 pounds in later 285-hp models. (The all-time Bonanza lifting champ is the 1968-69 straight 36 model, which had a standard useful load of 1,620 or about 1,400 with normal equipment.) Although 1,200 pounds is a fairly creditable figure, it is well short of the later Cessna 210s. Standard useful load of the 35 model took a big jump in 1961 with the N35 and another in 1964 with the S35, paralleling horsepower increases to 260 and 285. Generally speaking, Bonanzas are not full-seats-and-full-fuel airplanes with baggage, even the 285-hp four-placers.

However, most owners find that their loading is limited by c.g. restrictions before gross weight restrictions. The 35 models have especially narrow c.g. envelopes and it is very easy to load them aft of the limit, even with the 30-pound lead weights that some Bonanzas have in the nose for ballast. In many cases, it simply isn't possible to put two adults and significant baggage in the rear of a Bonanza, no matter how much fuel is off-loaded. In fact, c.g. problems become more pronounced with less fuel because the Bonanza's leading edge fuel tanks are ahead of the c.g. As a result, c.g. moves aft as fuel is burned off. This can be quite tricky for the pilot, who may be entirely legal when he takes off, but could find himself well out of the c.g. envelope to the rear as he approaches his destination after a long flight.

One of the results of a too-far-aft c.g., of course, is decreased pitch stability and lightened stick forces. Considering the Bonanza's already light pitch control forces and its tendency to build up speed quickly, an out-of-c.g. Bonanza can really take a pilot by surprise. If you plan to buy a Bonanza for four-person weekend outings, be sure to do some same weight-and-balance computations for each particular airframe you look at.

Performance

Here is where the Bonanzas shine. The first ones totally outclassed all the competition in performance, and there's still no non-turbo-charged single-engine airplane in production today that will catch a good clean V35B. All Bonanzas deliver excellent speed for their horsepower and therefore good fuel economy. Book speeds range from 148 knots for the old A and B models to 178 knots for the V35 (and a snorting 200 at altitude for the turbo-charged V35 TC). Real-world speeds may be somewhat lower than the book (and sometimes the airspeed indicators) say, but owners nevertheless report good speeds: 165 to 174 knots for the 250-, 260- and 285-hp models, and 152 to 161 knots for the Bonanzas with the 225- to 240-hp engines. Fuel consumption runs from a high of about 16 gph with the 285-hp models to 10 gph with the E-185.

Rate of climb is also energetic, with only the very oldest Bonanzas climbing less than 1,000 fpm at gross weight (by the book, at least). Bonanzas are excellent short-field aircraft, partly because of their good performance, partly because of the rugged landing gear. The gear, incidentally, is so beefy that virtually the same gear is used for the Baron, which weighs a ton more.

Creature Comforts

Again, the Bonanza is strong in this respect. The cabin is quite large, especially in terms of headroom. (In fact, most pilots look like midgets while flying Bonanzas because of the high roof and window line.) Back-seaters aren't quite as well off because of the fuselage taper, but room is still adequate. Excellent visibility from broad windows accentuates the feeling of roominess of the airplane.

Interior appointments are traditionally excellent in Bonanzas. Beech apparently believes that a man who pays five or ten times the price of a Cadillac expects to have a quality interior — a philosophy apparently shared by few other manufacturers. Interior plushness is an important part of the Bonanza mystique.

Rear passengers in V-tail Bonanzas are usually miserable in turbulence, however. The V-tail looks neat and is the shining symbol the Bonanza line, but it does a lousy job as a tail. In turbulence, the V-tail models fishtail excessively, usually requiring several oscillations to recover from a good jolt. (See the "Modifications" section

for a report on the Airskeg yaw damper, which apparently works decently.)

The 36 and A36 Bonanzas have a "club car" seating arrangement, with two pairs of rear seats facing each other. With three or four people aboard, this is a wonderfully roomy compartment, but a fifth and sixth person makes things chummy indeed. Virtually no one ever flew six full-sized people in an A36 (until the '79 models) because there was no room at all — literally none — for baggage. A small baggage compartment was added in 1979.

Many models of the 33 and 35 Bonanzas are called five- or six-seaters, but this is an optimistic delusion. A fifth or sixth seat, if installed, fits in the luggage compartment and is suitable only for very young children. In most cases, c.g. and/or baggage loading considerations make it impossible to use the rear seats, even given a supply of willing children with cast-iron stomachs.

Handling

The Bonanza has a uniquely fortuitous blend of aerodynamics and ergonomics that results in marvelous flying characteristics. Pilots praise it for well-harmonized and responsive controls, and many owners have told *The Aviation Consumer* that the Bonanza is the easiest of all planes to land. (Our own personal experience tallies with those opinions.) The "feel" of the Bonanza is another major element of the airplane's legend.

Cost/Performance/Specifications

Model	Year Built	Number Built	Cruise Speed (kts)	Rate Climb (fpm)	Useful Load (lbs)	Fuel Std/Opt (gals)	Engine	TBO (hrs)	Overhaul Cost	Average Price
Bonanza 36	1968-69	184	168	1,015	1,620	50/80	285-hp Cont. IO-520-BA	1,200	$11,250	$ 54,000
A36	1970-73	291	168	1,030	1,443	44/74	285-hp Cont. IO-520-BA	1,500	$11,250	$ 68,500
A36	1974-75	288	168	1,030	1,443	44/74	285-hp Cont. IO-520-BA	1,500	$11,250	$ 75,000
A36	1976-77	385	168	1,030	1,443	44/74	285-hp Cont. IO-520-BA	1,500	$11,250	$ 85,500
A36	1978	228	168	1,030	1,443	44/74	285-hp Cont. IO-520-BA	1,500	$11,250	$ 90,500
A36	1979	222	168	1,030	1,443	44/74	285-hp Cont. IO-520-BB	1,500	$11,250	$ 97,000
A36	1980	171	168	1,030	1,443	44/74	285-hp Cont. IO-520-BB	1,500	$11,250	$107,000
A36	1981	165	168	1,030	1,443	44/74	285-hp Cont. IO-520-BB	1,500	$11,250	$124,500
A36	1982	117	168	1,030	1,443	44/74	285-hp Cont. IO-520-BB	1,500	$11,250	$135,000
A36	1983	60	168	1,030	1,443	44/74	285-hp Cont. IO-520-BB	1,500	$11,250	$145,000

Beech Bonanza 35, 36

Modifications

There is a welter of airframe modifications available for Bonanzas, and many owners have modified their older aircraft to the point that they're virtually indistinguishable from brand-new '78 models. Among the more popular Bonanza mods:

• Airskeg aerodynamic yaw damper, which supposedly improves V-tail wagging in turbulence. (Walker Engineering Co., Los Angeles, Calif., 213-272-1248.)

• Maybe a better answer to the yaw problem is a $1,495 electronic damper made by S-Tec Corp., Mineral Wells, Tex., (817) 325-9406.

• Cosmetic mods include one-piece windshields, late-model side windows, baggage doors, pointed spinners and a host of other interior and exterior touch-ups. Biggest of the specialists in this field is Beryl D'Shannon Aviation Specialties, Inc., in Lakeville, Minn., (800) 328-4629.

• The Smith Speed Conversion is a wide-ranging aerodynamic cleanup that increases speed by 13-17 knots. Smith resets the wing incidence, installs flap gap seals and performs a myriad of other small aerodynamic cleanups. But taken altogether, their effect is large. A modified cowling is also available that cuts drag, improves cooling and allows better engine breathing. The mods aren't cheap, however; the full speed treatment is $13,000, with the cowling an additional $5,250. Smith Speed Conversions, Box 430, Johnson, Kans., 67855, 316-492-6840.

• Smith also developed an internal beefup kit to strengthen the V-tail. It costs $1,975 installed by Smith; the kit costs only $825. For cost-cohscious Bonanza owners not so concerned about appearance, Smith also offers an external cuff to support the leading edge of the V-tail stabilizer. It's $595 installed, or $395 for the kit alone. A second external cuff-type V-tail beefup is offered by Knots 2 U, Inc., 1941 Highland Ave., Wilmette, Ill.

60091, 312-256-4807. Cost of the kit is $575, plus three to four hours installation time. A third kit is offered by B & N Cameron Park Airport, 3280 Cameron Park Dr., Shingle Springs, Calif. 95682, 916-933-1367.

• Numerous engine conversions are available to upgrade older Bonanzas to 240-, 250-, 260- or 285-hp engines. Also, an STC allows conversion to a 300-hp Lycoming, which has the uncracking crankcase and a 2,000-TBO. Continental conversions are done by D'Shannon (address above); Lycoming mod is by Machen, Inc., Spokane, Wash., 509-838-5326.

Here's a quick rundown of the "milestone" Bonanza models with which major changes occurred:

35	Original airplane, 185-hp engine, 2,550-pound gross weight.
A35	Thicker wing skin, heavier spar carry-through.
C35	205-hp, 2,700-pound gross weight, larger tail with wider-angle V.
E35	225-hp.
F35	Third side window, stronger tail.
H35	First of "second generation" Bonanzas with O-series engine. 240-hp, gross weight 2,900 pounds, major structural beefup.
J35	Fuel injection, 250-hp.
N35	260-hp, third side window enlarged, fuel capacity increased to 74 gallons.
P35	New instrument panel.
S35	First of "third generation" Bonanzas, 285-hp, extended cabin. Very close to current configuration.
V35TC	Turbo-charged model, 132 built 1966-70.
V35B	Last production V-tail model.
33	First straight-tail model, 225-hp, named "Debonair."
C33A	285-hp.
E33	Renamed Bonanza.
E33C	Aerobatic model.
36	Straight tail, lengthened fuselage, cargo door, 3,600-pound gross weight.

American Bonanza Society

Perhaps the best of all the owner groups is the American Bonanza Society. Membership is nearly 7,000, and accounts for more than half of all Bonanza owners. The Society's newsletter is relatively sober and technically oriented, without so much of the gushy effusiveness of other aircraft owner association newsletters. Anybody shopping for a used Bonanza should get in touch with the American Bonanza Society, Box 12888, Wichita, Ks. 67277.

Owner Comments

The Bonanza is excellent for cross-county flight in smooth air. In turbulence you quickly find that yaw stability leaves much to be desired. Rear-seat passengers find the well-known Bonanza tail wag to be particularly objectionable.

Weight-carrying capability of the Bonanza is good, but it is nearly impossible to load it to gross weight without exceeding the aft c.g. limit.

The Bonanza is fun to fly. It handles nicely and offers ample performance. All of us had previous experience in high-performance singles, and little trouble was encountered in learning to fly and land the Bonanza smoothly. Some undesirable characteristics deserve mention, though. Low-speed aileron control becomes sluggish, making for interesting encounters with gusts on short final. Stalls call for an alert pilot, since the plane tends to drop its left wing abruptly at the break. In this circumstance the pilot finds himself looking for more rudder control, as he does during landings in strong crosswinds. Also, in the transition from landing approach to go-around, the pilot finds himself straining to keep the nose down while he takes out the high degree of nose-up trim used in the approach. The bungee interconnect in the controls gets criticized from time to time, particularly after

Bonanza 35, 36 Resale Value Chart

crosswind landing and other maneuvers performed using cross-controlling.

Hot starts of the fuel-injected Continental engine can be exasperating. When cold, it generally starts after the first few blades.

Parts are extremely expensive. The Beech dual control yoke costs $1,800. The new fuel cell costs $1,252, but by the time it was installed we were out $1,600. We found this out after discovering that one cell leaked and could not be repaired. The cell was replaced, but the replacement also leaked and it was, in turn, replaced. The FBO applied for reimbursement credit from Beech, and was finally applied four months later. The reimbursement covered the parts and installation but did not cover some $40 in freight charges. The FBO said we were fortunate since Beech generally does not make reimbursements that complete. We did not consider ourselves fortunate at all.

After the fuel cell, the second most expensive of these maintenance items was replacement of the vacuum pump. This makes the fifth vacuum pump on the plane since new, indicating a history of problems in the pressure system. We recently replaced the pressure regulator as well.

As with most older aircraft, performance is somewhat less than published figures after antennas, rigging and engine age impose their penalties. Our F model (225-hp) trued out at 163 mph while our M model (250-hp) gives an honest 182 mph. Twenty-five additional horsepower gives 19 more miles per hour. We have often wondered whether Beech did more than just increase power. The additional power, speed and perhaps a bit of redesign also provided a firmer IFR platform.

●

We asked Bill Guinther, former president of the Bonanza Society, to offer a few tips for buyers of used Bonanzas. Keeping in mind that Bill is both very knowledgeable about these airplanes and at the same time a professional Bonanza booster, we offer his comments:

When Beech engineers started to make plans for a civilian single-engine high-performance airplane after World War II, they asked military pilots what should be included in a civilian airplane. The answer that came back was 'very light control forces.' Most of the 'fighter pilots cited the Spitfire's balanced controls as most desirable, stating that the newer P-51 Mustang, with its bigger engine, had very heavy stick forces. Therefore, the engi-

neers at Beech decided that the airplane they planned would have balanced surfaces with very little force changes through the whole range of airspeed.

The 1947 'straight' 35 is still one of the finest-flying, best-feeling airplanes ever designed. Of course, in those days most of the pilots had military background flying high-performance airplanes, so the light control pressures were not a detriment.

The first Bonanza, having a gross weight of 2,550 pounds, had a very low stall speed (46 mph) which meant it had outstanding short-field performance. Today's Bonanza, with an increase of more than 100 hp and 1,000 pounds gross weight, requires more takeoff and more landing space.

The first engine on our 1968 V35A went to 1,750 hours and was showing good compression. Oil had been changed every 25 hours since new, but we got nervous about paying the core charge if the crankshaft or case went bad. The engines have needed a cylinder or two topped because of valve guide and exhaust wear, but we count on 1,600 per engine.

An S or V model Bonanza is an excellent buy because the style hasn't changed in 19 years — the performance stays the same and they can be updated to look like new.

In terms of performance, my 1973 F33A delivers book or above speeds and climb rate; that is to say, 175-177 knots true at 75 percent power and 172-174 knots true at 65 percent. Timed rates of climb average 900 fpm at altitudes below 3,000 feet. The quality and workmanship are second to none and suggest an attention to detail that is simply not available in any similar aircraft.

As in every airplane, there are areas for improvement. Of primary importance to me are the Continental crankcase AD, the Hartzell prop AD, and the fuel cell AD. (My fuel cells turned out to be Uniroyal, so I'm okay for now.) The engine burned or spilled an inordinate amount of oil, but the installation of a Walker Airsep has cured that. My pet peeves are two: the price of parts is astronomical; i.e., $165 for an ammeter.

Beech loves to issue service letters. I have received no less than 10 in the year I have owned the airplane. While I admire their concern for safety, the cost of the various retrofits and inspections has amounted to a considerable sum.

Having flown both models, I feel the F33A is more stable in yaw response in turbulence than the V-tail, but still displays some fishtailing.

Overall, other expenses have been reasonable, with annuals going for about $600. While a Bonanza is a more expensive aircraft to own in terms of initial cost and parts, it offers superior performance and a quality of construction second to none. It is a rugged, dependable machine which holds its value very well.

●

Takeoffs and landings require no special effort or techniques. Good landings are relatively simple to achieve. Short-field takeoffs and landings equal, or even better than what we have been able to get from a Cessna 182.

The well-known yaw is there occasionally, in certain air conditions. Riding the pedals eliminates most. The Airskeg is also an aid toward reducing yaw.

When modifying a Bonanza, don't expect to get all of your money back. Windows, panels, cabin interiors, wing lights and paint can be changed but you will still be flying an older Bonanza that looks pretty with essentially the same performance as before. If you do modify, our recommendation is to use only Beech parts. When turning a plane over to a modifier, insist on a written completion time. We had our F-35 tied up for four months on one accasion and seven weeks on another. My number one recommendation is to save the money you would put into a major modification and trade up.

The original Model 35 has had a much worse than average record of in-flight airframe failures.

In order to more fully understand the cost, performance and specification difference between the various models we made an analysis of true value based on weighted age, speed, range, useful load and cost. The results were fascinating: In the $20,000-$30,000 bracket the K and M models were outstanding. The J model was dragged down by range limitations.

Why own a Bonanza? The answer is simple. For $30,000, a 19-year-old aircraft will outperform the new Skylane RG and Rockwell 114 costing twice the Bonanza investment. The performance differences are even greater when compared to the Skylane or Dakota costing approximately one and one-half times more. Justifying an aforementioned new aircraft with its high initial depreciation is difficult in the face of Bonanza performance, dependability, resale value and flexibility for modification.

The performance of the S35 Bonanza is excellent, but not quite as advertised. Although my partner and I are used to cruising at 75 percent power on Lycoming-engined aircraft we have owned before, we have chosen to fly our Bonanza at 65 percent power for greater engine smoothness and reduced noise level. This consistently produces block-to-block speed to 160 knots, and the altitude chosen seldom changes this.

The Bonanza handles more smoothly than any Piper or Cessna product I have flown. I find no other characteristics to be unusual

except for the tail-waggle in turbulence. The Bonanza is the easiest airplane to land smoothly consistently of any aircraft I have flown. This feature alone is probably reason enough to buy the airplane.

Maintenance for us has been no big problem since we have owned the airplane only 600 hours and many problems have yet to arise. The big maintenance problems are the two AD notes out on engine crankcase cracking and Goodyear fuel tank bladders. Our aircraft did have one crack problem, but in several hundred hours since the crankcase was replaced we have had no additional problems. Any pilot contemplating purchase of a Bonanza absolutely must insure that the engine has the new heavier crankcase, and has had new fuel bladders installed. The only maintenance problem which has not been resolved is the large amount of oil thrown off by the wet vacuum pump. The pump works adequately, although vacuum is almost always on the low side, but there is always oil along the firewall and belly of the airplane. So far, we have not been willing to bear the expense of converting to a dry-type vacuum pump. It has had no effect upon the operation of the aircraft but it is bothersome.

We found that the best insurance coverage was available through Don Flower and Assoc. in their group insurance policy available for members of the American Bonanza Society. They indicated to us that time in type was more important that obtaining an instrument rating in order to reduce premiums. But how do you accumulate 25 hours of Bonanza time when none are available for rent?

Cessna 210

They laughed at Cessna's fetish for high-winged airplanes way back in 1959 when the company took a Cessna 180 airframe and, in a most unconventional manner, retracted the landing gear into the fuselage. Later, the evolution of that airplane, the Cessna 210 Centurion, became the world's best-selling large single by far. But it also has been one of the most problem-plagued.

History

Though not able to trace its ancestry back as far as the Beech Bonanza of the post-World War II epoch, the 210 has a 25-year history that encompasses three different engines and cabins and two different wings plus a host of other systems modifications.

Since the first model appeared in 1959, the gross weight has risen nearly half a ton from a modest 2,900 pounds to a hefty 4,100 pounds, making the airplane the heaviest single in production for general use. The horsepower has risen from 260 hp to 325 hp and the cruise speed peaked out just under 200 mph/174 knots.

A turbocharged model introduced in 1965 has gone on to outsell its normally aspirated sibling by nearly a two-to-one ratio.

Major Evolutionary Changes

In 1962 the cabin was enlarged slightly and given rear windows. But basically the airplane remained a four-placer. Then in 1964 a major engine change was made, going up from 260 hp to 285 hp. The first turbo model appeared in 1966. In 1967 another significant change involved replacing the strut-braced wing with a cantilever one, while boosting fuel capacity from 65 gallons to

90. The airplane cabin still could not be considered a six-placer, however; it was, at best, a four plus two (kids).

Then in 1970 a major cabin modification provided six adult seats with extra baggage space in the rear, and the gross weight was raised by 400 pounds to 3,800 pounds. Next, in 1971 takeoff horsepower was raised to 300. And in 1972 the old engine-driven hydraulic system was replaced with an electro-hydraulic system. The pressurized P210 was introduced in 1979.

Naturally, 1970 and later models are desirable for the extra cabin space and extra load-carrying ability, and '67 and later models for the extra 25-gallon fuel capacity.

With the 1977 model, the turbo 210 finally got a boost in horsepower from 285 up to 310 hp. And in 1985 the turbo received even more power as the rating went up to 325 hp.

Earlier, in 1979, the 210 underwent a landing gear simplification operation that did away with the main gear doors. Instead, the main wheels were simply tucked into a slot in the fuselage, eliminating a lot of nuisance and complication on a gear system that had gone through its share of problems over the years. Evidently, the move sacrificed no measurable speed, either.

Also in 1979, the gross went up one more time to 4,000 pounds with the

The turbo 210s are among the few singles with approval to fly in known icing. Even though equipped with boots, nonturbos are not.

210N model, and in '85 it went up to 4,100 pounds with the 210R.

In 1982 Cessna offered optional dual alternators and vacuum pumps. Then, with the 1983 turbo models certificated for flight in icing conditions, Cessna incorporated dual vacuum pumps as standard equipment. So either vacuum system alone could provide power for deice boots along with vacuum-powered instruments. In view of the failure rate of vacuum pumps, especially when burdened with the need to power deice boots, this is an invaluable option.

Also on the '83 model, the company began installing new Slick pressurized magnetos to give more protection against misfiring at high altitudes.

In 1984 Cessna increased the engine TBO from 1,400 to 1,600 hours and made shoulder harnesses standard equipment on all seats.

Performance and Handling

Speed, useful load and range are the 210's strong suits. With a top cruising speed of 196 mph/171 knots, the later model 210s yield a range with reserve of nearly 1,000 sm — greater than any other single aside from the Mooney 201, to our knowledge.

With an IFR-equipped, full fueled payload of about 970 pounds, the late-model Cessna 210 can haul the astonishing load of five adults and about 22 pounds of baggage for each rider. No other single comes close except the Piper Lance, which is still about 70 pounds shy. To accommodate all this weight, an unusually broad center of gravity envelope tolerates loading extremes that would cause aerodynamic havoc in other airplanes.

Of course, the rear two seats are a bit cramped for long flights, and they pose entry and exit problems —but they are available if needed. Furthermore, there is a separate baggage compartment in the rear.

Left and right front-seat cabin doors provide extra flexibility for the forward four seats.

In terms of handling, as the heaviest airplane in its class at gross, the 210 must be treated with respect — something quite a few pilots neglect to do, judging from the accident reports provided later on showing overshoots and hard landings. For so large an airplane, however, the airplane should not be faulted on its aerodynamic agility, since it has very quick, light ailerons. The airplane is heavy in pitch control, however, and with its limited elevator is difficult to maneuver into a full-stall break, but naturally, it will mush with the best of them at low-power, low-speed situations.

Despite windows all-around, visibility is limited by the high wing inside a turn; and the instrument panel is so high that when the average pilot has cranked his seat high enough to see over it, he can't see out to the left without ducking his head under the window jamb.

Cabin Comfort, Finish

A fairly common complaint among 210 owners is that the general quality of the cabin interior is not commensurate with the caliber of the airplane as a prestige top-of-the-line product. Though the Royalite material on the instrument panel is

Cost/Performance/Specifications

Model	Year Built	Number Built	Cruise Speed (kts)	Useful Load (lbs)	Rate of Climb (fpm)	Fuel Std/Opt (gals)	Engine	TBO (hrs)	Overhaul Cost	Average Retail Price
210	1960	610	165	1,160	1,300	65	260-hp Cont. IO-470-E	1,500	$10,800	$ 19,000
210A	1961	171	165	1,160	1,300	68	260-hp Cont. IO-470-E	1,500	$10,800	$ 21,000
210B	1962	281	160	1,220	1,270	65/84	260-hp Cont. IO-470-S	1,500	$10,800	$ 23,000
210C	1963	156	160	1,220	1,270	65/84	260-hp Cont. IO-470-S	1,500	$10,800	$ 23,500
210D	1964	283	166	1,260	1,210	65/84	260-hp Cont. IO-520-A	1,700	$11,300	$ 24,000
210E	1965	224	166	1,260	1,210	65/84	285-hp Cont. IO-520-A	1,700	$11,300	$ 25,500
210F	1966	101	165	1,435	1,115	65/84	285-hp Cont. IO-520-A	1,700	$11,300	$ 27,000
T210	1966	147	191	1,335	1,280	65/84	285-hp Cont. TSIO-520-C	1,400	$14,000	$ 29,000
210G	1967	122	167	1,440	1,000	90	285-hp Cont. IO-520-A	1,700	$11,300	$ 28,500
T-210G	1967	104	194	1,350	1,115	89	285-hp Cont. TSIO-520-C	1,400	$14,000	$ 30,000
210H	1968	125	167	1,440	1,000	90	285-hp Cont. IO-520-A	1,700	$11,300	$ 29,500
T-210H	1968	65	194	1,350	1,115	89	285-hp Cont. TSIO-520-C	1,400	$14,000	$ 31,500
210J	1969	136	167	1,440	1,000	90	285-hp Cont. IO-520-J	1,700	$11,000	$ 30,000
T-210J	1969	45	194	1,350	1,115	89	285-hp Cont. TSIO-520-C	1,400	$14,000	$ 32,500
210K	1970	181	164	1,552	800	90	300-hp Cont. IO-520-L	1,700	$11,300	$ 31,000
T-210K	1970		190	1,620	930	90	300-hp Cont. TSIO-520-H	1,400	$14,000	$ 34,000
210-KII	1971	171	164	1,552	860	90	300-hp Cont. IO-520-L	1,700	$11,300	$ 33,000
T-210K	1971		190	1,620	930	90	300-hp Cont. TSIO-520-H	1,400	$14,000	$ 36,000
210LII	1972	220	164	1,552	860	90	300-hp Cont. IO-520-L	1,700	$11,300	$ 35,000
T-210L	1972		194	1,476	1,030	90	300-hp Cont. TSIO-520-H	1,400	$14,000	$ 38,000
210LII	1973	351	164	1,552	860	90	300-hp Cont. IO-520-L	1,700	$11,300	$ 38,000
T-210LII	1973		194	1,476	1,030	90	300-hp Cont. TSIO-520-H	1,400	$14,000	$ 41,000
210LII	1974	474	164	1,552	860	90	300-hp Cont. IO-520-L	1,700	$11,300	$ 41,000
T-210L	1974		194	1,476	1,030	90	300-hp Cont. TSIO-520-H	1,400	$14,000	$ 44,000
Centurion II	1975	531	164	1,552	860	90	300-hp Cont. IO-520-L	1,700	$11,300	$ 44,000
T-210II	1975		194	1,476	1,030	90	300-hp Cont. TSIO-520-H	1,400	$14,000	$ 47,000
Centurion II	1976	520	171	1,552	860	90	300-hp Cont. IO-520-L	1,700	$11,300	$ 47,000
T-210II	1976		197	1,476	1,030	90	300-hp Cont. TSIO-520-H	1,700	$11,300	$ 51,000
Centurion II	1977	719	171	1,552	860	90	300-hp Cont. IO-520-L	1,700	$11,300	$ 51,000
T-210II	1977		197	1,476	1,030	90	310-hp Cont. TSIO-520-R	1,400	$14,000	$ 57,000
Centurion II	1978	680	171	1,552	860	90	300-hp Cont. IO-520-L	1,700	$11,300	$ 56,500
T-210	1978		197	1,476	1,030	90	310-hp Cont. TSIO-520-R	1,400	$14,000	$ 62,500
Centurion II	1979	685	171	1,552	860	90	300-hp Cont. IO-520-L	1,700	$11,300	$ 61,500
T-210N	1979		197	1,476	1,030	90	310-hp Cont. TSIO-520-R	1,400	$14,000	$ 68,500
210N II	1980	494	170	1,580	950	90	300-hp Cont. IO-520-L	1,700	$11,300	$ 67,000
T-210N II	1980		221	1,700	930	90	310-hp Cont. TSIO-520-R	1,400	$14,000	$ 76,000
210N II	1981	399	170	1,580	950	90	300-hp Cont. IO-520-L	1,700	$11,300	$ 77,000
T-210N II	1981		221	1,700	930	90	310-hp Cont. TSIO-520-R	1,400	$14,000	$ 88,000
210N II	1982	236	170	1,580	950	90	300-hp Cont. IO-520-L	1,700	$11,300	$ 91,500
T-210N II	1982		221	1,700	930	90	310-hp Cont. TSIO-520-R	1,400	$14,000	$102,500
210N II	1983	49	170	1,580	950	90	300-hp Cont. IO-520-L	1,700	$11,300	$110,000
T-210N II	1983		221	1,700	930	90	310-hp Cont. TSIO-520-R	1,600	$14,000	$123,500
210N II	1984		170	1,580	950	90	300-hp Cont. IO-520-L	1,700	$11,300	$135,500
T-210N II	1984		221	1,700	930	90	300-hp Cont. TSIO-520-R	1,700	$14,000	$150,000

218

light and conveniently removable, it in particular often comes in for criticism as looking "cheap."

A number of owners also complain that their 210s are not weather-proof, that they leak rainwater through the cabin, pasenger doors and baggage doors. We are unable to tell whether, on this score, the 210 is any worse or better than other airplanes, since aircraft door sealing and weatherstripping has always been an occult art, with mixed success on many models.

Cabin width (44 inches in the middle) and height (47 inches) makes for sufficient passenger and pilot comfort in the front four seats, and in the cantilever-wing models the wing carry-through beams are located behind the front-seat passengers where they are out of the way.

Comparison

Stacked up against the Piper Lance and the Beech A36 Bonanza, the late model 210 is a speck faster than the A36 and about 15 knots faster than the Lance. The 210 carries a useful load about 130 pounds over that of the A36, but about 13 pounds shy of the Lance. The 210's cabin is two inches wider than the A36 at the widest, but again comes out second best to the Lance by about four inches. The 210 comes out second to the Lance in baggage space and baggage structural capacity.

Maintenance

The biggest problem reported by owners is the landing gear system, especially in the pre-1972 models with the engine-driven hydraulic system, as opposed to the later electro-hydraulic one. The task of maintaining these older ones, with accumulator, power pack, filter and hydraulic pump, was described by one mechanic as "a pain in the ass."

Owners reported long delays in getting gear system parts for the older models, too, when the gear saddle A.D. triggered a rash of repairs, though this may have eased off somewhat lately. Parts are

Instrument panel for a '75 turbo 210, with fuel gauges at the right of the radio rack.

also available through salvage houses. An independent IA mechanic we often consult with (John Dennis of Poughkeepsie, N.Y.) characterized the landing gear system on recent models as relatively robust and simple and requiring comparatively little maintenance.

Though some owners complained about the high cost of parts, Dennis said he felt Cessna's (and Piper's) were not high compared with other manufacturers like Beech and Rockwell.

He warned prospective purchasers of pre-1964 models 210s to have a mechanic make a thorough inspection or face the possibility of spending "big bucks" to make extensive corrections, especially in the gear system. Like all large, sophisticated airplanes, the 210 takes care and money to keep operating properly.

A.D. History

The one dark shadow lurking over the purchaser of a used 210 is the notorious landing gear saddle problem, which affects all 210s built from 1960 to 1969. Fatigue cracks began showing up in alarming numbers in the early seventies, usually after the airplane had accumulated 1,000-1,200 hours. FAA records show 181 cracked saddles from 1970-75, and there were possibly hundreds of other unreported cracks.

Typically, the cracks would be found during annual inspections. If they weren't, the saddles would eventually break altogether. The pilot then would discover his problem when one landing gear leg would hang up in the half-way position. Ten messy, expensive gear-up landings by 210s with broken saddles were reported in one 30-month period.

An AD was finally issued in 1976. Immediate saddle replacement was required for 1960 and 1961 models, but the replacement saddles themselves must be replaced every 1,000 hours — the replacement saddle is just as defective as the original. Cost of replacement is about $1,000-$1,500, so any purchaser of a 1960 or 1961 model should count on at least $1 per hour for saddle replacement. And be sure to check how soon the replacement is due — the owner may be trying to sell the plane just before his saddle replacement is due, and you could be stuck with the bill a few hours later. In all cases, inspect the saddle closely to insure that it hasn't cracked already.

The 1962-67 models had the same original defective saddles as the '60 and '61s, but differences in the retraction system allow an improved saddle to be fitted as a replacement. But there's a kicker. The "improved" saddles, it turns out, aren't much better than the originals, and we have reports of replacement saddles breaking in as few as 300 hours. According to an FAA report, "The so-called 'improved' saddles have served only to extend the life of the part, rather than eliminate the cracking/breaking problem . . . the problem has persisted and now includes airplanes with the improved saddles." The AD still requires a dye-penetrant inspection annually once the replacement saddle has accumulated 1,200 hours.

Nineteen sixty-eight and 1969 models had the "improved" saddles as original equipment, and they must be inspected at 1,200 hours and annually thereafter. Expect them to break eventually. In all cases, the saddles should be closely inspected.

In 1970, the landing gear system underwent a major redesign, and there has been no recurrence of the problem that we know of.

Potential buyers of 1960-64 210s should also be on the lookout for other gear problems. Another 1976 AD required replacement of the hydraulic landing gear actuators on those models — a $2,000 job. Make sure that AD has been accomplished. There have been no reports of recurring actuator problems, so an airplane with modified actuators should be all right.

Filiform Paint Problem

Buyers of used Cessna 210s should also be particularly careful about the paint jobs on aircraft built between 1977 and 1982 and later based in hot, humid seaside areas like Florida. Some of these appear to be subject to filiform corrosion because of Cessna's method of preparing the aluminum surface for the Dupont Imron paint.

Cessna chose to use only a wash primer, no Alodyne, and no epoxy primer barrier coat, as Dupont recommended when Cessna switched to Imron in 1977. As cases of filiform corrosion began turning up, Cessna, without publicity, began correcting some of them by paying customers for new paint

Cessna 210 Resale Value Chart

jobs. This program has long since expired, however. And Cessna began using Alodyne in 1982, but did not use the epoxy primer.

Safety Record

The Cessna 210 has a very poor accident rate in comparison with other single-engine retractables. In fact, it has the third worst out of 17 aircraft whose accident rates were computed for the decade 1972 through 1981. Only the old Piper Comanche and the Beech 24 Sierra had worse accident records for that period.

In terms of fatal accidents, the C-210 fares better, however, coming out only eighth worse out of the 17 aircraft, or almost in the middle of the pack. Engine stoppage is the single most common cause of accidents in the 210, accounting for 58 out of 181 accidents during the 10-year period. But only about half the stoppages were related to mechanical problems; the rest resulted from fuel exhaustion or starvation. Vapor lock problems may have contributed to the stoppages.

Among the salient facts disclosed by a study of all the Cessna 210 accidents reported by the NTSB for the two years, 1975 and 1976, out of 181 accidents reported, fully 32 percent, or 58, were related to engine stoppages. Other large tolls were related to gear-up landings (22 or 12 percent), improper IFR operations (20 or 11 percent) and

all-around poor pilot judgment (30 or 17 percent).

Since 28 engine stoppages (or 15 percent) were caused by a malfunction of some sort, pilots might give some attention to the causes reported in the NTSB listings.

The greatest number of failures — four — was caused by engine crankshaft failures. Three stoppages were caused by failure of the throttle control in some fashion (throttle control shaft broke at rod end; throttle link failed because of throttle control rod end pin; uniball rod end allowed bearing to slip off ball over washer.)

Two more stoppages resulted from mixture control failures (mixture control bolt missing, lock nut found in nacelle; mixture control assembly broke — FAA advisory circular 20-7N).

And another pair occurred when the oil quick drain opened during flight, causing the engine to lose all its oil.

Seven engine stoppages were for undetermined reasons.

Gear-up Landings

Of the 22 gear-up landings, a little over half occurred because pilots were distracted or simply forgot to lower the gear; however, in three of these instances pilots had some excuse in that the gear warning horn was not working.

220

There seemed to be no obvious pattern in the gear-up malfunctions, except that in two cases the gear actuator or actuating cylinder failed.

Fuel Mismanagement

The large number of fuel mismanagement problems might come as a surprise to anyone familiar with the typical "infallible" high-wing Cessna fuel system that normally allows the pilot to dispense with tank switching. However, until the 1982 model Centurions came along, a "both" tanks position was not available, and pilots had to switch from left to right tank in the conventional manner.

According to the NTSB accident reports, two engine stoppages resulted when the pilot inadvertently allowed the one tank to run dry, and then was unable to restart the engine, despite the fact there was sufficent fuel in the other tank.

In one of the instances the Safety Board said the pilot, who had low time in the 210, did not turn on the electric fuel pump when switching from the dry left tank to the right tank. Evidently, the gravity feed is not sufficient to do the job, though fuel injection engines are usually difficult to restart when starved of fuel.

What is surprising is that most pilots tagged with fuel mismanagement simply used every drop of available fuel and were obliged to make forced landings. Since there is a generous 89 usable gallons of fuel available — enough for five to six hours at high cruise speeds — it's mystifying why so many pilots apparently wanted more.

One possible contributing factor might be the poor location of the fuel gauge on the right side of the instrument panel rather far away from the pilot for easy viewing. Only starting in the '78 model 210s has this situation been altered by locating the fuel gauges down on the lower throttle pedestal directly above the fuel tank selector switch.

Pilots are warned in the operating handbook to avoid prolonged slips

with fuel tanks less than one-quarter full. Since one pilot actually "flamed-out" in this condition while slipping for a crosswind landing approach, the warning should be heeded.

It also behooves 210 pilots (and all others, of course) to drain the fuel tanks for water and sediment — a fairly simple exercise on the high-wing Cessna. Six of the Cessna 210 engine stoppages resulted from water contaminents in the fuel.

Fuel Bladders

Buyers of Cessna 210s built up until the late 1970s that have bladder fuel tanks instead of integral tanks should keep an eye out for possible trapping of water in the tank wrinkles. An Airworthiness Directive was issued in 1984 mandating checking of the bladders for wrinkles that might trap water and lead to an engine stoppage.

Some aircraft in which a guarantee could not be given that the water problem was eliminated were given placards telling pilots to rock and roll the aircraft before flight to dislodge extra water trapped by the wrinkles. These aircraft must be inspected once every 12 months for wrinkle formation and overall fuel cell condition.

Although 20 crashes (all but one fatal) occurred when pilots got in over their heads in IFR weather, only two cases were reported of severe structural damage from overstressing the airplane. In one of these the airplane tumbled out of a thunderstorm in pieces; in the other the pilot brought the airplane back to base with bent wings after approaching within five miles of a thunderstorm. The 210 has a much better record than the Bonanza in this respect.

In-flight Breakups

In the past few years, the Cessna 210 has shown a marked increase in in-flight breakups. In fact, since 1976 late-model Centurions were breaking up about as often as late-model V-tails. Compared with its peers in the heavy single category, the 210 came out third worst in a

comparison of breakup rates between 1977 and 1983. The Piper Lance was worst with 6.5 breakups per million hours; the Beech 35 next with 4.8 and the Cessna 210 third with 3.3. Safest of all in terms of breakups was the Beech 33/36 with a rate of only 0.5 breakups per million hours.

Vapor Lock Shock

Cessna 210s and P210s share with Cessna 206s vapor lock problems that have caused engine interruptions and engine failures. At the end of 1981, Cessna brought out kits designed to eliminate the problem, by incorporating vapor return lines. Service Bulletin SE 81-33 deals with the matter and applies to 1976-79 T-210s and P210s, which Cessna believed had the worst of the vapor problems. Make sure the aircraft you are considering has this improvement.

The new vapor line mod is similar to the fuel system in 1962-63 models, which have had few vapor lock problems.

Although prop clearance (with a three-bladed prop) is a better-than-average 10.89 inches, 210 pilots caution that the geometry of the airplane seems to make for a greater-than-average danger of striking a prop when taxiing over uneven surfaces, as from sod to ramp.

Most of the other problems in the 210 reported in the two-year NTSB rundown involved undershooting or hard landings or groundlooping, all of which suggest poor pilot judgment and inability to properly handle a big, heavy, high-performance airplane. In two cases, the airplane actually was blown over onto its nose from high winds while taxiing.

Modifications

One way to help keep the engine running cooler on the turbo model 210s is to have an intercooler installed by Turboplus in Gig Harbor, Wash., (800) 742-4202. The price is $5,995 installed. The company also can install speed brakes for $4,645. These will, conversely, help keep the engine from being overcooled on descent.

Flint Aero in Santee, Calif., (619) 448-1551, can provide wingtip tanks for the cantilever wing 210s, adding an extra 33 gallons. The price is $4,250.

R/STOL Systems, Inc. in Everett, Wash., (206) 355-2736, has taken over the Robertson mods and can install them for $7,950. One of the most elaborate STOL kits available, it includes drooped ailerons when flaps are down, recontoured wing leading edge, stall fences and gap seals.

If you fly your 210 in hot climates, Parker Hannifin Corp.'s Airborne Div. in Elyria, Ohio, (216) 871-6424, will sell you an air-conditioning kit for $6,283.

If you are concerned about oil spilling out all over the belly of your Centurion, consider contacting the Cessna Pilots Assn. for a free (for members) set of so-called Baylock drawings (named after the fellow who devised them) that reposition the crankcase breather line.

And if you don't mind spending $800 or so and another 10-15 hours of installation time, you can get rid of the gear doors and associated hydraulic paraphernalia on your 1970-78 210 with a Uvalde gear door removal kit from Mark Huffstutler in Uvalde (of course), Tex., (512) 278-4481.

To prepare for the unpleasant possibility of loss of vacuum pressure, a number of companies have STCs providing auxiliary vacuum pump systems. Parker Hannifin Corp. has one; Allison-Coffer, Azle, Tex. has an STC for an electrically-driven pump as a standby. Also, Precise Flight, Sunriver, Ore., (503) 593-1484, offers a standby vacuum system that works without any external pump.

Societies

The National 210 Owners Assn. is located at 9959 Glenoaks Blvd., Sun Valley, Calif. 91352. Contact Bill Kitchen at (213) 875-2820. They publish a quarterly newsletter. Another good source of information is the Cessna Pilots Assn., Wichita Mid-Continent Airport, 2120 Airport Rd., P.O. Box 12948, Wichita, Kans. 67277. John M. Frank, (316) 946-4777, is editor of the association's slick, four-color monthly newsletter.

Owner Comments

The performance and handling of the aircraft are very good. The only thing that has to be watched is to plan your descent since the aircraft is aerodynamically clean and needs time to descend from IFR cruising altitudes without reducing the power too much. Comfort in the cabin is very good. There is enough room to sit upright as opposed to feeling like you are sitting on the floor, and the cabin is well heated and ventilated.

Maintenance costs have been high. One problem has been the cylinders and five of the six had to be replaced for low compression; one for a stuck ring which wore the cylinder, and the other four for leaking exhaust valves. Other high maintenance items are the Cessna 300 series avionics. Parts availability from Cessna has been adequate, but a number of times Cessna has failed to get a part out as promised, leaving the aircraft stranded on the ground. Parts availability from Van Dusen has been good, when they stock the item.

The most prominent idiosyncrasy is water leakage around the baggage door. Regardless of the maintenance hours devoted to this problem, the door still leaks in heavy rain. Cold weather starting is nearly impossible below 10 degrees F unless the sun has been on the airplane during the day.

•

We purchased a new Cessna 1975 Turbo 210 II which was fully equipped with Cessna 400 avionics.

When we picked up the aircraft at Wichita, the paint was literally falling off. Flying from Cessna's field to Wichita Int'l., the autopilot 'ran wild' when switched to approach couple mode, the DME was inoperative, the number two navcom was erratic, the pilot's door and baggage door leaked, the ADF was inoperative and the approach control did not receive our transponder. We could not arrange for repairs at the Cessna factory, so decided to return to Oregon for warranty work. Unknowingly, we decided these were routine 'new car' problems.

In the ensuing 18 months and 450 hours, everything that could go wrong proceeded to do so. By then the aircraft had been painted three times; had two KN65 DMEs installed, but *never* had one operative (remember, DME is required at or above 18,000 feet and this was a turbo); had two encoding altimeters; two altimeters; two vacuum pumps; two top overhauls (including replacing two cylinders due to manufacturing defects); two baggage doors; totally new wing root seals; door seals; window seals; and a complete return trip through the factory to solve the water problem. In all the time we owned it, it leaked.

Water ran through the top shoulder harness attachments, down the shoulder harness, onto the carpet and wicked throughout the plane. At any time, you could remove the floorboards and find standing water.

While the avionics and instruments continued to deteriorate, we continued to pay. Cessna refused to pay for top overhaul number one but did pay part of number two. Most avionics repairs were paid for by us, but regardless of who paid, we *never* had a DME. The airplane was used 90 percent for business, but by the end of our first year we figured that our 200-mile average commute would have been twice as fast by car if we counted the number of missed days due to downtime.

Finally we sold the plane. Our only bright note is that some sucker paid us $1,000 less than our original cost. We will never buy another new Cessna aircraft.

•

Perhaps my best reaction to ownership of a 210 is the fact that I traded my 1969 model plus $35,000 for a new 1978 model. I feel that this is the finest single manufactured. It is is the only true six-placer.

Characteristics are: good speed, fantastic payloads, and the best instrument platform around. No weight and balance problem as with the Bonanzas.

But there are some shortcomings: the typical Cessna ten-cent-store plastic panel, noise, and less than desirable visibility.

Maintenance costs have been good. I spend more on my King Avionics than the airplane. I replaced first engine with factory reman at 1,250 hours; never had a gear or engine case crack. But I would strongly recommend three-blade prop in lieu of two-blade on older models due to noise problem.

•

I purchased a used 1961 Cessna 210A in 1975 and was advised to replace the main gear actuator shaft and gear assembly and the main gear saddles. No other problems were apparent with the aircraft, from log book studies and a current inspection.

With the exception of replacement of the gear actuators and saddles, the first year's annual inspection cost $1,074.

The second year's annual, with the exception of a fuel cell which leaked in cold weather, cost $866.

In terms of performance, I am delighted with the airplane. I frequently fly with one or two passengers at 2350/2400 rpm. Consistently, true airspeed checks out at 169/171 knots, seven or eight knots above the speeds shown in the

The 210 cabin carries an amazing load, but the rear seats are tight.

Cessna 210

book. Numerous ground checks, combined with winds aloft, verify the accuracy of that speed.

At approximately 6,000 msl, fuel consumption is 12 to 12.5 gph. At 12,000 msl fuel consumption approximates 10 to 10.25 gpm.

The gear has been totally reliable for extension and landing, although on occasion, either on landing or after takeoff, the gear doors have failed to close because of a problem with a switch in the gear console. This switch has been adjusted once ($30) and replaced twice in 350 hours of use.

Rate of climb is excellent with one or two on board — 1,500 feet per minute near sea level in moderate weather is normal at full throttle. Rate of climb of 1,000 fpm is standard throughout most of the year, at an airspeed of approximately 130 IAS.

We consistently flight plan 160 knots, and usually find we are closer to 165 in actual practice on IFR work.

The only objection is that shoulder room in the front seat is a little less than desirable with two 200-pound men up front. Other than that, it's an ideal one-to-four person airplane, a remarkably economic plane for its speed and range.

•

Both 210s we've owned (a '68 and a '73 model) consistently performed at and above book specs in all categories, particularly speed. Gas consumption of the later model was a constant problem, with the engine burning 16 gph at 66 per-

cent, with the book calling for 14.5. Two Cessna dealers were unable to correct the problem.

The 210 is not a responsive aircraft on the controls, but can be relied upon to provide very few surprises in most flight regimes. Ground nosewheel steering is stiff, sluggish and difficult, with brakes always being needed.

Our '68 model was good. The '73 was another story. The aircraft was assembled poorly, with obviously poor workmanship and components. On one flight, I had the turn and bank fail, the vacuum pump go out, and, upon landing, the starter motor went bad. Our annual inspection was over $1,800, with very little AD work. Maintenance bills were high, even though usage was less than 250 hours per year operating two- to four-hour flights at 66 percent power. We seldom had a flight where some cheap little part didn't fail.

The landing gear on the 210 is not cheap to maintain. For a system as complex as it is, however, the gear is remarkably reliable.

Our 1971 model does not have a saddle problem, but it does have an engine-driven hydraulic pump which has given us some grief.

Proper rigging of the gear is very important, and this takes a lot of maintenance time.

The weight-carrying ability of the plane is superb. I have done many weight-and-balance calculations and have found very few realistic situations which would put the aircraft out of balance.

Beech Bonanza A36TC

The Beech A36TC Bonanza is a handsome, roomy, slick-flying machine with an eccentric fuel system some regard as its Achilles' heel. It also has the distinction of being just about the most expensive used piston single on the market. In fact, a 1979 model today demands some $27,000 more on the used-plane market than a Pressurized Cessna 210 of the same vintage, according to book figures.

And both aircraft started out life at about the same new, average-equipped price of $135,000. It might be little consolation to potential used-plane buyers, but considerable solace to owners, that the A36TC retained its value unusually well. Thus, we plotted a loss in resale value of only about 14 percent for the top-of-the-line Bonanza vs. 35 percent for the Pressurized Cessna 210.

Production Mystery

Anyone trying to assess the market attitude toward the A36TC may have a hard time simply because there are so few ships for sale out there, and many brokers have never laid hands or eyes on one. This stems from two factors, one obvious, the other theoretical. The first is that not many of the turbo Bonanzas have been built, compared with, say, Cessna T210s. The second is that presumably many owners like the birds, have learned to cope with their idiosyncrasies, and see no reason to part with them.

Since 1979, when the A36TC was introduced, through 1981, we count just 270 delivered from Beech. By contrast, almost twice as many normally aspirated A36s were shipped out to dealers—567. This is exactly the reverse of the situation with the Cessna top-of-

the-line single T210, which outsold the nonturbo 210 during the same period by 1,082 aircraft to 414, or better than two to one.

There have been no significant evolutionary changes in the A36TC since its debut in 1979. The B36TC brought out in '82 had four-foot-longer wings accommodating an extra 28 gallons of fuel, bringing the capacity up to 102 gallons—30 more than the T210 carries. This was coupled with an extra 200 pounds of gross weight.

A Matter of Popularity

Clearly, the big Cessna turbo single has been king of the roost in the marketing world for some years, and has garnered a following of sizable dimensions. It was therefore natural that Beech would try to get a bit of the action. Intriguingly, both manufacturers started out even in 1966 with turbo versions, but while Cessna went on to achieve great success with the T210, Beech simply dropped its V35TC in 1970 after only five years of production.

The big Cessna obviously has a lot going for it, including an equipped useful load some 300 pounds greater (among 1980 models) than

The turbo model has louvers instead of cowl flaps for engine cooling, so lots of fuel is used in the climb.

the turbo A36TC Bonanza's and about an hour's greater range, thanks to an additional 16 gallons of fuel capacity. On top of that, the big Bonanza costs almost one-third more than the Cessna new. (The new B36TC made up some of those differences, except price, of course.)

Handling and Performance

The aircraft has magnificent handling typical of the Bonanza line, without the tail-waggle of the V-tails. Pilots describe it as responsive, yet stable and fun to fly. Like all its clan, it is flatteringly easy to land and exhibits the kind of control response that makes flying the bird more than just a matter of driving from point A to B.

The A36TC's performance is quite similar to the T210's in cruise speed, takeoff and landing distances over an obstacle and even stalling speeds—when measured at each aircraft's gross weight. Off-load the several hundred pounds of extra useful load the T210 can carry, and when both aircraft get off at the same weight, the T210 comes away with a nice performance edge in most categories.

Comfort and Loading

The aircraft has seats for six riders, and a minuscule rear baggage compartment of only 10 cubic feet with a 70-pound capacity. Beech therefore likes to consider the rear pair of seats as part of the baggage compartment, and duly notes in its spec sheets that this offers a 400-pound capacity. We calculate that a decently equipped IFR model should be able to carry full fuel and five 170-pound riders with nothing left over for baggage.

That's about all the passenger load you'd want to carry in this aircraft, however, unless you were hauling a couple of kids or small adults in the back seat, because shoulder room there is cramped. But there's plenty of room in the front four and, like the other Bonanzas, the A36TC has marvelous big windows and a high ceiling for a good feeling of spaciousness. Naturally, the double rear entry door and club seating add a classy touch to the stretched 36 model Bonanzas.

As for staying inside the weight and balance envelope, pilots report nothing like the rear-loading problems of the V-tailed Bonanzas. But naturally they try to load from the front first. On the other hand, in a well equipped aircraft, some pilots report they can run into problems at the front of the envelope if they're flying solo, load something in the rear. Count on a useful load of about 1,250 pounds after packing the panel with avionics.

Engine Management

The one operational quirk most A36TC pilots comment on is engine management on takeoff and climbout. The aircraft has an

Turbo in this case denotes not only extra performance, but an extra degree of attention demanded to monitor the electric boost pump system on takeoff.

unusual electric boost pump system with two separate switches. One has three positions: off, low and "high/low" or "auto," depending on the serial number of the aircraft. The other is an emergency switch. On takeoff at full throttle the fuel flow rate is supposed to be between 32.5 and 34.2 gph. If the flow is not high enough, the pilot should feed in low boost pump to make up the difference. If that's not sufficient, he is instructed by the pilot's operating handbook to switch to the high/low (or auto) boost and then manually lean to the correct amount.

Some pilots characterize this as more manipulation than they care to worry about on takeoff, while others describe it as a serious safety hazard.

While the POH tells the pilot leaning is required to prevent "excessive fuel flow and possible engine roughness," it doesn't warn about the possibility of flooding and possible engine stoppage.

One pilot told us he was checking out another flier in the aircraft when they noticed the too-low flow rate on the takeoff roll, leaned over and snapped on the high/low boost, and the engine stopped pronto before they got around to leaning it.

The B36TC comes with a revised fuel system arrangement and simplified procedures that presumably are designed to reduce problems. It has enlarged fuel lines and eliminates the automatic high position in favor of a simple "high" position. (We have no indication that any of this is retrofittable to the A36 line, however.)

On the B36TC the pilot is not bothered with the need to use the auxiliary fuel pump in either the low or the high position to achieve the correct fuel flow, according to the POH. By contrast, he is specifically warned not to take off with the aux fuel pump on "HI," because, according to the manual, "Excessively high fuel flows can cause engine combustion to cease during the takeoff roll." That's a clinical way of saying the engine may stop dead.

And during the climb when encountering reduced fuel flow with high fuel temperatures, whereas the A36TC pilot is told to turn on the Hi/Low (auto) position and lean as required, the B36TC flier is counseled only to select the low position. And if the fuel flow continues to drop, instead of switching to high, he should level off and reduce power until fuel temperatures drop. Thereby the possibly risky, and at the least, bothersome, procedure of having to both add boost and lean the mixture is done away with.

Another modification in the B36TC

Cost/Performance/Specifications

Model	Year	Number Built	Average Retail Price	Cruise Speed (kts)	Rate of Climb (fpm)	Gross Weight (lbs)	Useful Load (lbs)	Fuel (gals)	Engine	TBO (hrs)	Overhaul Cost
A36TC	1979	32	$112,500	194	1,165	3,650	1,388	74	300-hp Cont. TSIO-520-UB	1,600	$16,000
A36TC	1980	125	$119,000	194	1,165	3,650	1,388	74	300-hp Cont. TSIO-520-UB	1,600	$16,000
A36TC	1981	114	$130,000	194	1,165	3,650	1,388	74	300-hp Cont. TSIO-520-UB	1,600	$16,000
B36TC	1982	50	$160,000	190	1,049	3,850	1,512	74	300-hp Cont. TSIO-520-UB	1,600	$16,000
B36TC	1983	55	$177,500	190	1,049	3,850	1,512	74	300-hp Cont. TSIO-520-UB	1,600	$16,000

Beech Bonanza A36TC

fuel boost system: the second, emergency auxiliary fuel pump is eliminated completely.

The so-called high/low automatic function of the aux pump carries with it another operational quirk that annoys some pilots. On the pretakeoff runup, the manual requires ginning up the engine to 30 inches mp and putting on the high boost. Pilots say the resulting thunder and possible squeal of brakes can be a bit too dramatic for passengers, and is better done only on occasion.

In the Climb: Fuel to Burn

There's also been a lot of discussion about how much fuel needs to be pumped to the engine on the climb to altitude in the A36TC. Aviation magazine articles evaluating the aircraft talked about fuel burns of 30 gph all the way to level-off, to keep the engine running cool at reduced forward speeds. (The A36TC has no cowl flaps; and while this lessens pilot workload, one can't help but wonder whether extra cooling fuel is needed to compensate.) But that means using up a lot of fuel in the climb to altitude in what has to be a not too long-legged bird to begin with.

Owners we talked to reported using various power settings, with fuel burns on climbout ranging from 22 gph to 28 gph. One said he uses 34 inches mp and 2,600 rpm, drawing 28 gph in a normal climb. However, he said he leans to between 25 and 26 gph fuel flow, noting that "factory people" said this was okay as long as the temperature levels were all kept in the green. (They asked not to be quoted.) Another pilot said he normally climbed at 29 inches mp and 2,500 rpm, and this yielded about 22 gph of fuel flow.

According to the A36TC book, cruise climb should be made at a fuel flow of 28 to 31 gph up to the critical altitude, or about 22,000 feet (the point when the turbocharger wastegate is fully closed at a given throttle setting). And then the fuel flow can be reduced according to manifold pressure setting. So the

This shows what you can load into just 10 cubic feet of baggage space, balance considerations permitting.

aircraft does gulp lots of fuel on the climbout.

Turbo Centurion pilots, by contrast, are told by the manual to keep 30 inches mp and 2500 rpm in the climb, leaning to 120 lbs/hr (20 gph), with the cowl flaps open as required, and using the auxiliary fuel pump to hold that fuel flow on hot days, if needed. The T210 engine is rated at 310 hp for takeoff and 285 hp for max continuous power. The powerplants on both aircraft are variants of the Continental TSIO-520. (Recommended fuel flow at takeoff, incidentally, in the T210 is a healthy 29 to 31 gph, though not quite as high as in the A36TC.)

Safety Record

Accident briefs provided by the National Transportation Safety Board showed a paucity of reports on the A36TC in the first two years. In fact, there were only two accidents listed, one of them involving a fatality. But in our view both accidents had significant ramifications. One other accident has come to our attention, and we'll discuss that, too.

Of the two listed by the Safety Board, one was attributed to a partial power loss, resulting in a "stall/mush" during a forced landing just after takeoff. The pilot, however, was accused in the NTSB's probably cause findings of

improperly set mixture and boost pump. No novice, he was an experienced test pilot with 24,750 hours of flying time and 250 hours in type. In fact, the purpose of the flight had been to start spin testing the aircraft to certify Brittain tip tanks installed on it.

The other accident also occurred during takeoff, when fire broke out in the engine compartment. The plane crashed, killing a passenger and seriously injuring the pilot. It is believed that in that accident, which occurred in March 1980, raw fuel was sprayed against the unshielded turbocharger, with the resulting flame and smoke incapacitating the pilot before he could make a controlled emergency landing.

Beech telegrammed the 146 A36TC owners on file at that time, instructing mechanics to check for a leak at the mixture adjustment screw. A drain hose was then to be installed leading from the adjustment screw out to the cowl flap, to vent overboard any future fuel leak from that area.

Airworthiness Directive 80-21-02 made the correction mandatory. The third accident came to our attention in a letter from a subscriber. He told us he was taking off in his A36TC Bonanza and had climbed about 100 feet off the ground when he noticed the fuel pressure gauge doing strange things. The needle had arced completely off its half of the gauge into the manifold pressure segment of the gauge where it was indicating 10 inches of mp. The engine quit cold from flooding, according to the pilot, and in the intervening five or so seconds before he hit the ground he tried the usual emergency moves like hitting the electric boost pumps, etc.

Ironically, as he describes it, if he'd been aware that the problem involved getting too much fuel rather than too little, he conceivably could have salvaged the situation by leaning quickly to stop the flooding. As it was, both the pilot and his passenger were seriously injured.

The pilot said the engine was a new

one, too, had only four hours on it before the crash and had been given to him by Beech and Continental because the first engine was found to have a hole in the crankcase. As a sidelight, he told us, "What got me the new engine was probably your article. I Xeroxed the article on the cracking IO-520s and gave it to them and said it was obviously a casting defect and was an ongoing thing... So for my trouble I got a new engine that nearly killed me."

On the other hand, the pilot praised both Continental and Beech for their backup in his two crises. "Beech stood 100 percent behind the product." When he had his first engine problem, Beech offered to come and pick up the airplane and to lend him a brand-new V-35 Bonanza in the interim.

Summing up, he said: "Continental and Beech have been completely nice about this thing. I had all kinds of problems with leaking fuel cells, also, and had to replace them when brand new. I think, finally, I just got a lemon."

Operational Considerations

Pilots transitioning into the A36TC from other makes of aircraft should be aware of the unorthodox positioning of the gear and flap levers (the reverse from other manufacturers) and of throttle quadrant controls (with the mixture below the throttle).

After the crash of the test pilot on takeoff, investigators found the prop positioned half-way back from takeoff pitch. The question arises: could the pilot have inadvertently pulled back the prop instead of the mixture control? Though he had a lot of time in Bonanzas, he constantly flew many different kinds of aircraft.

However, there are many circumstances that blur accurate determination of the accident cause. The pilot, Lyle Flick, was seriously injured and experienced traumatic amnesia after the crash. Also, as he made his takeoff run, another pilot on a taxiway nearby observed smoke coming from the Bonanza

The model B36TC has longer wings and additional fuel, along with a revised and simplified fuel system.

and called out this fact in the blind over the radio. Finally, rescuers at the crash scene turned off switches in the aircraft to prevent a fire, and thus altered the cockpit configuration.

Naturally, there is some interest in the pre-crash position of the auxiliary fuel pump switch in the aircraft, and whether the engine could have stopped because of flooding from an overboost.

The electric boost pump switch is located in an awkward area, hard to see, below the central control column on the Bonanza. As mentioned before, if the high position is selected, the pilot may run the risk of flooding the engine unless the mixture is leaned correctly. This arrangement has been characterized by some experienced pilots as "ridiculous, ergonomics-wise," and a safety hazard.

Maintenance

Figures we received from A36TC owners in 1982 indicated that so far they were spending about $1,000 on the average for annual inspections. The cost ranged from a low of $600, on a first annual, to $2,000, with most of them ranging between $1,100 and $1,400.

Owners characterized maintenance costs on the aircraft as high, but some seemed to feel it's part of the game. "As to parts and service," said one, "the price *is* high. But the quality is worth it, and the reliability is quite good, in my experience." Few chronic problems surfaced in the owner comments, except that one said he

had to keep replacing landing lights.

There were not a lot of service difficulty reports in the FAA roster on this aircraft at the time, either. But there were two instances of cracked crankcases, which suggests the problem on this TSIO-520 engine has not gone away.

The only other mildly repetitive problems we noted concerned a missing safety clip in the rudder cable turnbuckle, leading to excessive play in the rudder control (two cases); cracks in the vertical stabilizer skin (two instances); the fuel intake tube chafing against the turbo heat shield (two cases reported).

There was also a handful of turbo-related problems: a crack on the turbo exhaust inlet assembly (two cases noted); oil leaking past the turbo oil seal and a broken turbo inlet above the EGT probe, burning cylinder head and oil temperature wires. In addition, in one case a V-clamp failed, allowing exhaust gases to burn a hole in the cowl.

Airworthiness Directives

There have been less than a dozen ADs on the aircraft, but two early ADs were important ones relating to fire hazards. The first one (80-21-02), called for installation of a drain hose over the idle fuel adjustment screw to prevent fuel leaks in the engine compartment. The second one (81-24-06) required retorquing the through bolts of the engine-driven fuel pump to prevent fuel leakage.

Modifications

Tip tanks, gap seals and thicker windshields for extra soundproofing, and safety, are offered for the A36TC by Beryl D'Shannon Aviation Specialties, Inc., Lakeville, Minn. Kit price for the 15-gallon tips is $3,350, not including installation. Gap seals: $1,595 installed. Windshields: $1,219 to $1,419, depending on thicknesses, which go up to one-half an inch.

Smith Speed Conversions, Inc. at Johnson, Kans. provides a whole range of cleanup improvements that yield an extra 16 to 17 knots, at a price of $11,700.

Osborne Tank & Supply, at Oro Grande, Calif. has obtained an STC for its Brittain tip tanks, which will hold 20 gallons each.

For the ultimate in upgrades, the A36 owner can have an Allison turboprop installed under an STC the company was aiming for by December 1985. This gives the bird 167-knot cruise speeds at anywhere from 12,000 to 25,000 feet. Cost is about $250,000.

For the Joiners

The American Bonanza Society, now located in Wichita, Kans., publishes a handsome newsletter and provides a platform for the exchange of information among Bonanza fliers of all persuasion.

Owner Comments

I have owned an A36TC for two years. I bought the aircraft new. Since then I have logged 400 hours with no difficulties whatsoever. This is not my first Bonanza, and from previous experience I have expected and gotten extreme reliability and usefulness from each product. I have had no problems with the avionics or radar installation.

My aircraft is equipped with tip tanks, giving me 104 gallons total useful fuel. This is enough for 6½ hours of flying time. Cruise speeds

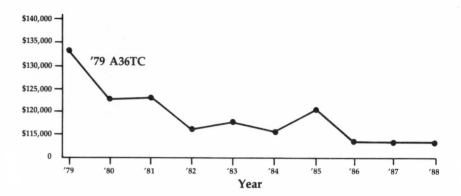

Bonanza A36TC Resale Value Chart

'79 A36TC

between 11,000 and 13,000 feet have always been in the 190-knot range. I fly approximately 10 percent of the time at altitudes above 20,000 feet, and obtain well over 210-knot true airspeeds. The aircraft is stable, and handles turbulence rather well, and particularly handles ice rather well. I fly approximately 150 days out of the year in all kinds of weather, and have come to realize that the A36TC can handle 1½ in. of ice all over without any untoward results, other than a decrease in airspeed of approximately 15 knots, and an increased stall speed of approximately 15 knots as well.

The only unusual difficulty encountered with this airplane comes on very hot days, after a very short engine shut-down, when the engine and the fuel system are rather hot. During those times it is necessary (when taking off from airports above 4,000 to 6,000 feet above sea level) to use a high boost pump and/or emergency pump, with the engine lean for takeoff power (32 gallons fuel per hour). Unless this is done, you may find that the engine may not be able to retain the required fuel flow and manifold pressures required for takeoff.

Annual inspections have been expensive, ranging from approximately $1,100 to $1,400. There has been no extra maintenance done between annual inspections. The

Continental engine has been flawless, consuming approximately half a quart of oil (15W50) every 15 hours.

G.D. Castillo, M.D.
Champaign, Ill.

I purchased my A36 in May 1981, as a dealer demonstrator with about 60 hours on the tachometer; I have put over 200 hours on it since. My average stage is 250 nm, over 85 percent on business.

In the areas of performance, handling and comfort, all the superlatives I had read about Beech airplanes were borne out. For some reason, I have never been able to hit the book fuel consumption figures at a power setting, but the airspeed variation leads me to the conclusion that the power gauges are somewhat inaccurate. The variation is small and consistent, so I've ignored the discrepancy.

My plane is equipped with club seating with table, and I've been unable to find a procedure to reverse the middle seats without gouging the table's trim at the bottom. Perhaps someone else has solved this?

As to parts and service: the price *is* high. But the quality is worth it (I've owned all the majors, except Mooney), and the reliability is quite good, in my experience. AOG means Air Freight parts (no charge to me). Overall, it has been a great plane to own, from all standpoints.

As averages: maint./hr.—$4.50; annual $1,250.

John R. Segerstrom
Pendleton, Ore.

In July of 1981 I purchased an A36TC from Beechcraft West in Hayward, California, after having been an owner of Piper products for some 10 years. I told the sales personnel that they would have a difficult time convincing me of the justification for the cost of a Beechcraft product. After having a demonstration in June of 1981 of the A36TC, I fell in love with the handling and performance characteristic of the A36TC as well as the comfort and appearance. I have some 350 hours in the 36TC and I have participated in the round-table discussions at the Bonanza Society meetings on the A36TC.

The A36TC performs in excess of the owner's handbook specifications, and will not disappoint any owner. Handling characteristics are extremely good. On short fields in IFR conditions, and unstable and turbulent air, the A36TC performs far beyond the best of any single-engine aircraft I have flown. My experience covers almost all models of the Piper line. The aircraft I flew prior to the purchase of the A36TC was a Turbo t-tail Lance.

In comfort, the A36TC receives many compliments. All materials used in the aircraft are top quality and craftsmanlike fitted. On long trips the A36TC does very well. If it were possible, I would like to see the cabin widened just a bit to be equivalent with the PA32 models of Piper. One finds himself sharing his elbows with his co-pilot in the cockpit.

The one area that I have found to be quite expensive in a Beechcraft product is the maintenance. Since the aircraft was first delivered, we have complied with 50-hour inspections and have had a few items that have needed constant reminders to the dealer for correction.

Recognizing the fact that sparkplugs and three tires were replaced in accordance with our annual inspection and we were given a $200 credit as a promotion from Beechcraft towards maintenance, the total bill for the annual would have come to nearly $2,000.

On an aircraft with 302 hours on its tach, my partners and I found the annual cost to be excessive. We have no qualms with the quality of the Beechcraft facilities and mechanic; however, next year we will look for an equally qualified but less expensive operation for performing our annual. As an example of the expensive parts, we had a cargo passenger compartment door handle malfunction on us, and it cost $78.25, exclusive of labor. We have not run into any difficulty acquiring parts.

As for other operational idiosyncrasies, the engine requires a fuel flow of 32 to 34½ gallons for take-off. If this amount of flow is not achieved, then use of the low/high fuel boost pump is necessary, and if fuel flow is not stabilized with the use of this setting, then one turns it to the high position. An extremely crucial problem with turning it to high is that the pilot must then lean the engine back to within the 32- to 34-gallon range; otherwise overboost of fuel or flooding could occur. Perhaps a more refined procedure on this particularly crucial item is needed.

Also, we have now gone through six landing lights and use the aircraft a limited time at night. The dealer has now informed me that a different wattage bulb should cure the problem. We are hoping this to be true as we have purchased more landing lights for this aircraft than all previously owned combined.

Overall, if I were to choose another single engine turbocharged aircraft, without any question it would be the A36TC Bonanza. Just recently I flew the B36TC and found it to be an equally fine performer. Not having the need for the large amount of fuel aboard, I

In all the 36 Bonanzas, the club seating is top drawer.

find the A36TC to meet all of our corporation needs.

Thomas A. Mantz
Oakdale, Calif.

Dale Johnson of Flightcraft, the Beech dealer in Portland, Ore., suggested I respond to your request for information on the A36TC. Our company has a 1980 A36TC which we bought new. We average a bit over 300 hours a year, with approximately 50 percent of that IFR. After working out some bugs when the plane was new, we have been well satisfied. We have 100-hour checks which at times become annuals. Average cost of an annual runs around $600.

To give you some idea of costs I've gone through our invoices including 100 hours and annuals, added them up and then divided by the hours on the plane. I have not included avionics costs, but have included strobe costs, which have been considerable. They have a problem, but can't seem to identify it. The invoices do include the cost for the oil change. Average maintenance cost runs at a bit over $14 an hour.

Our maintenance is done at a private shop which takes pride in its work, and a personal interest in our plane. Dates of all items which come up for renewal, e.g., ELT batteries, are on their computer.

I'm a corporate pilot. Of all the single-engine aircraft I've flown, the A36 is by far the best.

Charles R. Young
Portland, Ore.

Mooney 252

The Mooney 252 TSE - the big changes over the earlier Model 231 are mostly inside the front cowling, where greatly improved engineering solves a multitude of problems.

The redesigned turbo Mooney delivers sizzling performance at altitude while staying cool under the cowl.

The ability to cruise at nearly four miles a minute with close to 18-mpg efficiency is enough to please almost any pilot—if, that is, he doesn't mind slapping on an oxygen mask and traveling light. The 252 is incredibly fast and efficient at altitude, but it's no load-hauler or luxury tourer.

With full tanks, there's enough left in the W&B envelope to accommodate only two 170-pounders and their bags; and Mooney airplanes always have been notorious for being relatively short on elbow and leg room. But for a 252 devotee that doesn't matter. What matters is speed. Some owners have gone so far as to equip their planes with long-range tanks, so they can fly fast longer.

The 252 has been out only a couple of years, and the few to be found on the used-plane market still carry rather sizable price tags. It is possible, however, to get one that's still under warranty (the owners we talked with gave very high marks

to their warranty service). And for the price, you're likely to get a lot of airplane. A typical 252 is crammed with enough equipment to make an airline pilot envious.

Hot Start

Mooney Aircraft Corp. introduced the turbocharged Model M20K in 1979. Originally called the 231 for its top speed in miles per hour, the airplane initially hit it big in the marketplace. But it soon struck out in the shop. The cooling system for the 210-hp Continental TSIO-360-GB was inadequate, and the fixed waste gate turbo system demanded a deft hand on the controls and nearly constant attention to power management. Even with proper power management, engines in early 231s ran hot and were likely to misfire at altitude. To their dismay, pilots found they had to fly at lower altitudes and reduced power settings, keeping the mixture rich and cowl flaps open. Frequent top overhauls became commonplace.

As word got out about the 231's problems, sales plummeted. The problems did not persist, however. A switch to pressurized magnetos in 1982 took care of the misfiring glitch, and many of the engine problems were solved when an improved version of the TSIO-360, the -LB1B, made its appearance under the 231's cowl two years later. (See the April 15, 1987 issue for a thorough report on the 231.)

Redesign

About five years ago, Mooney's engineers began plotting a redesign of the M20K. Their goals were to boost electrical capacity, improve high-altitude performance, reduce

The 1986 Mooney 252.

drag and spiff up the interior. The result of their efforts was the 252. That they did their work well is evidenced by the fact that the redesigned bird can cruise at its predecessor's all-out top speed.

Mooney switched from a 14-volt to a 28-volt electrical system—a necessary upgrade for airplanes that usually roll out packed to the gunwales with optional equipment. The change increased available power from 850 to 2,000 watts. At the same time, a dual alternator setup was added to the options list to boost available juice even further, to 4,000 watts. Dual alternators are a must in a 252, in our opinion, and are a big improvement over the standby generator—capable of keeping only "essential" equipment alive—that previously was on the M20K's options list. (The new alternator used in the 252, by the way, is capable of providing a full 70 amps. The "70-amp" alternator that came with the 231 can put out only 60 amps, tops, due to the way it is geared.)

A loadmeter was added to the 252's panel to provide useful information on what's going on in the electrical system, and it's a welcome addition to the two idiot lights that had to suffice in the 231. Another benefit of the 252's electrical system is extra engine-cranking power from the 24-volt battery, which comes in quite handy for cold starts.

Pump Jump

The M20K uses a vacuum pneumatic system to spin its gyros. While a bit less complicated and easier on the gyros than a pressure system, the vacuum setup does tax the pump, making it run hot, especially at altitude. As a result, the airplane used to be plagued by more than its fair share of pump failures. According to Mooney, though, that problem has just about gone away. One of the company's engineers told us that the failure rate has declined substantially since they switched to Sigma-Tek's aluminum-rotor pump.

As a backup, the 252 also has a standby vacuum system. It comprises an electrically driven pump installed in the tail cone. The standby system provides enough vacuum to keep the gyros and autopilot going, should the primary pump give up the ghost.

Flow Control

Rather than taking the easy route and stuffing a bigger motor under the cowl, Mooney improved the M20K's performance by making several changes in methods of moving air around and through the engine. The biggest change was replacement of the Roto-Master (formerly Rajay) fixed waste gate turbo system with a new setup comprising a Garrett turbocharger, variable waste gate, intercooler and "tuned" induction manifold.

The automatic waste gate control unit senses throttle position and compressor air discharge pressure, and maintains desired manifold pressure by adjusting oil pressure on the waste gate actuator. Hot induction air spun from the turbocharger compressor loses roughly half its heat as it passes through the intercooler—basically a 42-square-inch radiator—and into the induction manifold. According to Mooney, the temperature drop is about 60 degrees F. at low altitudes and 120 degrees up high.

Because the induction air is cooler and, therefore, denser, the 252's TSIO-360-MB1 engine can produce its rated 210 horsepower at 36 inches of manifold pressure and 2,700 rpm from sea level to about 23,000 feet. Maximum operating altitude is 28,000 feet, where 78.6 percent power can be maintained for cruise. This is a substantial improvement in performance over the -LB en-

gine, which can maintain 210-hp— at 40 inches and 2,700 rpm—only up to about 15,000 feet. Max altitude for the 231 is 24,000 feet; but, above 20,000 feet, a raucous 2,700 rpm is required to maintain 75 percent power.

Tune-Up

Tuning the induction system involved adjusting the sizes of the individual tubes to deliver nearly identical air/fuel charges to each of the six combustion chambers. According to Mooney, this resulted in a smoother running engine—one that can be leaned more "aggressively." Indeed, 252 manuals contain no performance data for best-power—only best-economy (leaned to peak turbine inlet temperature or 1,650 degrees, whichever comes first), and the company recommends that the engine be run, leaned-out, at 78.6 percent power...even at FL 280. (There's a choice of four power settings for this. They range from 28.5 inches and 2,400 rpm to 26.0 and 2,700.)

Air enters the 252's engine through a NACA duct on the right side of the cowl. It includes and "inertial separator"—basically, a 90-degree turn in the ducting; air can make the turn easily, but snow, ice and water droplets cannot. Therefore, the threat of induction system icing isn't as great as in the 231, which takes in its induction air through a separate channel in the cooling-air inlet. Also, the new inlet is much bigger than the old one, and the manually adjustable, three-position split cowl flaps were replaced with a one-piece, electrically driven flap that can be adjusted to any position between closed and fully open.

Mooney said the cooling-air system was designed to keep the engine within temperature limits during a max-performance climb from a sea-level runway, sweltering in 100 degree heat, all the way up to 23,000 feet—the "critical altitude." (We've made a few such climbs ourselves in 252s and know the company wasn't just blowing smoke.)

Performance

It's ironic that a lot of 252 owners muck about below the altitudes at which the airplane really hauls tailfeathers. If you're going to stay low, you'd probably be better off with a naturally aspirated 201 or 205. Pulling 70 percent power at 8,000 feet, for instance, a 201 can do 162 knots on 10 gph. That's a couple knots faster and nearly two gph more efficient than the blower bird. If you goosed the 252 to 78.6 percent power, it would go six knots faster than the 201 at 8,000 feet, but it would be burning three more gallons of fuel in an hour to do so.

The 252 is meant for high-flying. Above 12,000 feet, it really starts hauling. Holding 78.6 percent power will get you 175 knots at 12,000 feet, 185 knots at 18,000, 193 at 22,000 and 202 at 28,000. Fuel flow will be just a tad under 13 gph. Our experience with the airplane indicates that, even on hot days, the -MB1 engine runs cool enough to accommodate a quick climb to altitude to take advantage of a tail wind. Under standard conditions, rate of climb at full power and 96 knots (Vy) tapers off from 1,080 fpm at sea level to 450 fpm at FL 280. For a more leisurely cruise climb and better visibility over the nose, 32 inches and 2,500 rpm, and

Cost/Performance/Specifications

Model	Year*	Number Built	Average Retail Price	Max Cruise (kt)	Rate of Climb (fpm)	Useful Load (lb)	Std/Opt Fuel (gal)	Engine	TBO (hrs)	Overhaul Cost
252	1986	66	$154,000	202	1,080	1,100	75.6/—	210-hp Cont. TSIO-360-MB1	1,800	$14,500
252	1987	91	$177,500	202	1,080	1,100	75.6/—	210-hp Cont. TSIO-360-MB1	1,800	$14,000

105 knots gives 780 fpm at sea level, 350 fpm at max altitude.

What Goes Up...

Descents and pattern work always have been problematic in Mooney airplanes, but the optional speed brakes (another "must" option, we think) greatly improve a 252 pilot's abilities to get the airplane down without overcooling the engine and mill about with the various flying roadblocks in the pattern. Without brakes, about 750 fpm is the best you can do without building up too much speed or shocking the engine. With brakes, 1,000 to 2,000 fpm can easily be achieved.

Gear speed is 140 knots, eight knots higher than the 231. In an effort to cut drag, the main gear were modified to fit fully into their wells (the mains protrude slightly on the 231) and inboard gear doors were added. We understand this negligibly reduced drag; but one slight benefit is that the doors also close after the mains are extended and do cut down on noise and vibration somewhat.

Handling

Flight controls are relatively heavy, thanks to use of push-pull tubes, rather than cables. Though not as light and crisp as the controls of a Bonanza, or even an Arrow or Skylane, the heaviness adds a degree of stability, which comes in handy in rough weather or while shooting an approach. Lack of rudder trim has always been a drawback (those long climbs to altitude can be rough on right-thigh muscles). We have found electric pitch trim in 252s to be almost unbearably slow; it does, after all, have to move the entire empennage, rather than a couple of tiny tabs. Pitch changes are rather pronounced as gear and flaps are extended or retracted; and with a forward c.g., it takes a good pull to keep the nose up while flaring for landing.

The airplane is far from graceful on the ground. Rubber-disk suspension makes for a rough and bouncy ride on uneven taxiways and runways. And the 252 requires some room for maneuvering. Minimum turn radius without brakes is 41 feet—10 feet wider than either a Turbo Arrow or Beech B36TC.

And, while we're griping, we should mention the POH. The manuals for all Mooney airplanes leave much to be desired. They fall far behind the POHs provided by Beech, Cessna and Piper in terms of legibility and organization of information.

Tight and Light

One of the trade-offs for speed and fuel-efficiency is a relatively small cabin. Comfort is, of course, subjective. If you enjoy driving sports cars, you'll love flying a Mooney. And, unless you're exceptionally tall or short, you'll probably find a 252 quite comfortable. Those with the "Special Edition" option have lush carpeting and upholstery, armrests, adjustable seats and headrests, and inflatable lumbar supports.

As we indicated earlier, the 252 is no load-hauler. Mooney posts empty weight at 1,800 pounds, but a typically equipped 252 is more likely to weigh in the neighborhood of 2,030 lb. With full tanks (close to five hours worth at max cruise), legally there's room left for only a bit over 400 pounds of people and bags. Fill the seats with FAA-standard people and max-out the baggage compartment and hat shelf with 130 lb, and you can legally load enough fuel to fly for, maybe, 20 minutes with VFR reserves.

Safety Record

Production of 252s totaled 157 in 1986 and 1987. NTSB records indicate that, as of the end of last year, only one 252 had crashed. The

airplane was demolished, and two people were killed, when it hit trees and crashed about 500 feet below the summit of a 3,000-foot mountain in Vermont last November. NTSB had not completed its investigation at press time, and few details were available. Though no flight plan was filed, it is believed the airplane departed from Long Island and was enroute to an airport a few miles north of the crash site.

A weak cold front had passed through the area, and conditions near the airport were "up and down" all day, according to one witness. A commuter pilot, who landed a few minutes after the accident occurred, reported a 2,500-foot ceiling south of the airport with lower-running fog and scud. NTSB's preliminary report indicates that the pilot, who had purchased the 252 in May, did not have an instrument rating.

NTSB records include four fatal accidents involving 231s in the past three years. One crashed, killing four people, while doing aerobatics at low altitude. Four died when another 231 struck powerlines while scud-running. Another crashed, killing three people, when the pilot lost control in a thunderstorm. The fourth hit powerlines on final approach, killing one person, who had neither a pilot license nor a medical certificate. A prominent scenario among nonfatal 231 accidents was a hot, high approach to a short runway, followed by an overrun or a blotched go-around by a pilot with relatively low time in type.

Maintenance

Tight working space under the cowl and behind the panel is among mechanics' favorite gripes about any Mooney airplane. With extra equipment, such as the intercooler and dual alternators, the 252 is a bit more difficult to work on. However, several shops specializing in

Mooneys (Dugosh Aircraft Service in Kerrville, Wittenbrook Flying Service in Barnesville, Ohio; and Weber Aircraft in Lancaster, Pa.) told us that 252s, so far, are requiring much less maintenance than 231s. They attribute this to the improved turbocharger and cooler-running engine. Costs for annual inspections range from about $500 to $900 (1988 prices).

Only three ADs apply, so far. They are: 77-12-6, which requires replacement of Hartzell Y-blades and clamps; 84-26-2, replacement of paper induction air filters every 500 hours; and 85-25-2, modification of servo mounts in certain King autopilots. However, there has been a flurry of service bulletins. Among components affected by the bulletins were: cowl flap hinge bolts and arm assemblies; altimeter setting-knob locks; circuit breakers; voltage regulator; engine cowl heat shield; induction system flange; waste gate oil-supply hose; inboard gear door hinge pin; and turbocharger check valve clamps. Another bulletin recommended sealing the tailcone to keep rain out. In addition, the infamous service bulletin on tube-frame corrosion also affects 252s that have been flying more than two years.

Modifications

An electric aileron trim system kit is available for $595 from AeroTrim, 1130 102 St., Bay Harbor, Fla. 33154, (305) 864-3336. The company says the system can be installed in about 3.5 hours. AeroTrim also offers plastic gas cap covers, which ward off rain, for $12.95 a pair, and is expecting approval soon of an STC for a rudder trim system.

Long-range tanks are available from Monroy Aerospace and from Mooney Mod Squad. The Monroy mod comprises a 17-gallon auxiliary tank (16-gallon tank, if the airplane has speed brakes) in each wing that feeds directly into the main tank. Installation by Plane Doctors in Fort Lauderdale costs $3,600, or $4,000

on 252s with speed brakes. Monroy also sells aux-tank kits for brakeless airplanes, only, for $1,390 and estimates about 70 hours for field installation. Monroy Aerospace Corp., P.O. Box 8217, Coral Springs, Fla. 33075. (305) 344-4936. Though similar to the Monroy setup, Mooney Mod Squad's aux tanks have electric pumps to transfer their fuel to the mains. The modification can be performed on 252s without speedbrakes for $2,995 to $3,495, depending on the condition of the main tanks, at the company's facilities near St. Louis and in Venice, Fla. Thicker windows, which cut down on interior noise, also are available. The prices are $1,100 for quarter-inch side windows (replacing the eighth-inch originals) and $975 for a three-eighths windshield (replacing three-sixteenths). Worthy of note are "firewall-forward" conversions available for 231s. The company says it can change an -LB engine into an -MB1 for $29,000; replacement of earlier -GB engines with factory-new MB1s will cost around $39,000 to $45,000. (All prices are 1988 figures.) Mooney Mod Squad, Inc., 11 Robin Lane, Fenton, MO 63026, (800) 325-9445.

Kohlman Aviation was expecting approval of an STC to install a TKS ("weeping-wing") deice/anti-icing system on 252s and other Mooney models. The company said installation of TKS components on the tail surfaces, wing, prop and windshield will cost $21,650. Kohlman Aviation Corp., 319 Perry St., Lawrence, KS 66044, (913) 843-4098.

Togetherness

As we've said before, the Mooney Aircraft Pilots Association is one of the best. The club publishes an informative monthly newsletter and organizes regional get-togethers and technical sessions, as well as an annual fly-in at Kerrville. MAPA, 314 Stardust Drive, San Antonio, Tex. 78228, (512) 434-5959.

FlightSafety is developing training programs for buyers of used as well as new Mooneys. A proficiency program comprising seven hours of ground school and up to six hours of flight training already is running twice a month in San Antonio, and additional training sites are being established. The cost is $1,500. For information, call FlightSafety at (800) 227-5656.

Summing Up

As a high-flying, economical speed-ster, a 252 is in a class of its own. It is not as roomy as would-be competitors, such as the Turbo Arrow or Turbo Skylane, nor can it carry as much; but performance comparisons are almost ridiculous. A 252 is 20 to 30 knots faster and about a gallon per hour less thirsty than the Piper and the Cessna. Probably the closest competitor, up high, is the B36TC Bonanza, which can hit 200 knots at 25,000 feet, burning nearly 17 gph, while carrying a payload with full fuel equal to the 252's max useful load. Before getting bit by the Bonanza bug, however, figure paying an extra $100,000 over a 252's price to pick up a late-model B36TC. For that matter, consider that the prices for used 252s are not that much lower than the stickers on new ones, which come with full warranties. Owners we've talked with have raved about their warranty service. Though the 252 has few peers up high, a 201 or 205 is a better choice, in our opinion, for those who want speed and economy but don't want to mill about in the nose-bag altitudes. Down low, the naturally aspirated Mooneys are faster and more economical than the blower birds, and they can carry a bit more. Purchase and maintenance costs, too, are lower.

Owner Comments

I've put 600 hours on my 252 since I traded in a 231 for it in 1986. The

252 runs much cooler; the 231 was always up near red line. I typically fly as high as I can; anyone who wants to stay low is better off with a Cherokee. Why buy the airplane if you're not going to take it up to altitude? At 28,000 feet, I get 205 knots on 13.2 gph at 78 percent power.

I have the Monroy long-range tanks and highly recommend them. I've gone to Denver nonstop and regularly make Florida in less than six hours. The tanks give me nine hours endurance at 78 percent power. Without them, you have only about 4.5 hours. I have the 115-cubic-foot oxygen system, which gives me about 13 hours worth, flying alone.

Although I've found the airplane to be reliable, I think Continental's engine stinks. I've had cracked induction tubes four times. The tubes are as thin as paper. Also, the valve guides were not put in properly at first; so, after 300 hours, I had to have a top overhaul. But, Continental did pay for the work. I've also gone through four sets of tires on the mains; they don't seem to wear as well as the tires on the 231 I owned. I've also had numerous problems with the King KAP 150 autopilot; the KFC 200 in my 231 was much more reliable.

But, none of these criticisms would deter me from buying another 252. There's no other single-engine airplane that can compare. Mooney makes good airplanes. The criticisms about comfort—or, the lack of it—in Mooneys, I think, are unfounded. I'm six-foot-two and have plenty of leg room without putting the seat all the way back. I would like to see them put in a deicing system and up the gross weight of the 252, though; and I'd also like to see them get rid of the Continental and put in the 280-hp turbo Porsche engine when it's ready.

My experience with the 252 has, overall, been favorable. I'm very happy with the factory and with Conn Mooney (in Danbury, Conn.). They've taken care of warranty problems and paid the bills with no complaints.

Jack Herrick
Jericho, N.Y.

I purchase my M20K last July from Lake Aircraft in Renton, Wash. It was a demonstrator, with 200 hours on it, and had been used to break the speed record from St. Louis to Washington at 384 mph. I have added over 150 hours, many in transition and instrument training. Virtually all of my previous flying—1,000 hours over 17 years—was VFR in Cherokee 140 and 180 models. In transitioning to the high-performance 252, I found only a few hours of uncomfortable flying, all with an instructor at my side.

There have been a few squawks, all minor. I've had two alternator cooling shrouds crack. After a new alternator was installed, there were no further problems. A defective TIT gauge was replaced. The malady that concerned me the most was that the engine would die on roll-out or while taxiing after landing in hot weather. This would happen only when the throttle was retarded to the stop. I could control the problem by being cautious about throttle management or by turning the low-boost fuel pump on immediately after landing. The nuisance was solved permanently by careful adjustment of the engine-driven pump to Mooney specifications. Once, oil temperature went to red line, and I thought I had a serious engine problem.

However, it turned out that a piece of paper had been sucked onto the oil cooler during a takeoff or landing in the San Juan Islands.

I've spent virtually no money correcting these squawks; every enigma was covered by warranty. This is the first new airplane I've owned, and it has been a pleasure not to be writing a lot of checks for unscheduled maintenance. I have nothing but immense praise for the factory and, especially, Lake Aircraft. I get the impression that they are extremely customer-conscious and have a passion for excellence.

Performance is incredible. (I think I'd be impressed with the 252's performance even if I had transitioned from a twin.) The vernier power controls are a dream and make for precision adjustments. Takeoffs require a lot of right leg, but I activate my yaw damper shortly after lift-off. I highly encourage prospective buyers to add this to their options list. The ailerons feel quite stiff, compared to the PA-28.

Even on the hottest day, rate of climb at Vy (96 knots) is over 1,000 fpm at gross. On cool days, I've seen 1,400 to 1,500 fpm. Speed is where this airplane excels. On short (under 200 nm), low hops, I file for 175 KTAS, but up high is where you can consistently see 200-plus knots. It'll go to FL 280—and get there quickly—so you can play the winds like a Stradivarius.

The 252 is snug but comfortable. After all, it is a Mooney, and with four adults, you'd better all be friends...and use Right Guard. I like the vertically adjusting seat; and there is a lot of leg room, though a few of my taller passengers have not been thrilled with entry and exit techniques. If a pilot is under 5-10, as I am, rudder pedal extensions are a necessary but inexpensive option. Arm rests, front and rear, feel and look great.

Bulb-inflated lumbar supports in each of the front seats seem like a silly add-on, but they really help on a long flight.

I do have a few minor beefs. (1) There is a blind spot in the right-front of the cabin that makes flying right-hand traffic patterns difficult. (2) I've yet to discover the trick to hot starts, and often have to ask my drop-off passengers to deplane while the engine is idling. (3) There is a lack of cockpit pockets, pouches, glove boxes, etc. My sunglasses and check lists often come cascading down onto my lap from the glareshield during takeoff. (4) The fuel drains are difficult to get to. Crouching on hands and knees in a business suit is really very disturbing.

Despite these petty gripes, I think the 252 is an outstanding flying machine. It's easy to fly, so long as you've had adequate training. I believe pilots are drawn to this airplane because of its performance, and I'm no exception. Descending recently with VFR flight following, I heard the following ATC transmissions: "Mooney 252YD, traffic at 12 o'clock, same direction, a twin Cessna, also descending. You're overtaking." "Twin Cessna 4224R, be advised traffic at six o'clock, three miles, a Mooney, overtaking." I could just see the twin driver lower his nose and push the throttles forward...

Michael Williams
Gearheard, Ore.

I purchased a Mooney 252 in April 1986 and have been quite happy with the airplane. On warranty, at no charge to me, the following work was performed by Mooney Aircraft Corp. and by Performance Aircraft of Hayward, which sold me the airplane: cowling heat shields were replaced; gas cap seals were modified; frame corrosion was repaired and insulation replaced; gear door hinges were modified;

and landing light heat shield was replaced.

The following engine parts were replaced: vacuum pump (after 55 hours of ownership); exhaust pipe clamp; induction tube flanges; and the No. 3 cylinder induction tube. We also took care of the oil-hose waste gate actuator according to Mooney Service Letter 87-1. All of this work was done under Continental's warranty, with no charge to me.

Also, we had a porpoising problem with the King KFC 150, which was solved by replacing the attitude gyro and realigning the autopilot. This, too, was done on warranty. The only other maintenance the airplane has required were an annual inspection and 50-hour oil changes. The annual cost: $1,195. The 50-hour services have run about $350, including parts and labor. In addition, both strobes burned out and had to be replaced last November for $204.

Total down time was 45 days; and, though this may seem like a lot of maintenance, I must commend both Mooney and Performance Aircraft for their support of the airplane.

Normally, I fly with two people aboard; but, occasionally, I have taken as many as four people and light baggage by off-loading 20 or 30 gallons of gas and flying 2.5 hours between refueling stops. I fly frequently into major airports, and the Mooney's ability to keep the airspeed up on long instrument approaches has been appreciated not only by me but, I am sure, by controllers and other pilots. To make landings easier, I have left the speed brakes up through the flare.

Being the owner of a Piper Arrow for about six years, I found the change to the Mooney superb. After 10 hours of instruction, including a BRF and an instrument competency check, I felt well

checked-out in the plane. If I had to do it over again, I would buy another 252. I am pleased with the airplane. Support from the Mooney and my FBO has been excellent.

Bruce Valentine, D.D.S.
Modesto, Calif.

We have owned our Mooney 252 TSE since June 1986. In speed and economy we have been very pleased with the airplane. We typically get performance of about 185 knots true at lower altitude and 200-205 knots true at higher altitudes on 12.8 to 13.3 gph at 78% power settings. Climb performance at gross with 120 knots indicated is about 750 fpm, and we can count on this right up through the higher altitudes.

Handling on the Mooney is excellent with the exception of go-arounds, which require special attention to coordination of trim during retraction of the flaps and gear.

Our first maintenance problems occurred shortly after the airplane was delivered to us. The voltage regulator failed and required replacement. This was just the beginning of our maintenance problems, which have included replacement of fuel manifold valve, rewiring of corroded wires in No. 2 nav, vacuum pump replacement, repair and/or replacement of marker beacon cable and antenna, replacement of encoder twice, replacement of ADF, replacement of mechanical fuel pump, primer valve, intercom volume potentiometer twice, TIT probe twice, and airspeed indicator, vacuum pump twice and right engine baffle.

Also, service bulletins or special letters required us to have circuit breakers replaced, landing light lens retrofitted, inspection of fuselage tubular structure, engine induction system inspection, inspection of alternate air door rigging, replacement of turbocharger wastegate oil supply hose assembly, revision of main gear door rigging, replacement of heat shields on lower cowling, inspection of fuel filler cap seals and replacement of turbocharger rubber clamps.

The biggest of our maintenance problems by far has been the continuous troubleshooting, removal and replacement and service on the King KAP 150 autopilot. This began just two months after purchase of the airplane. It has required the plane to be flown to Hayward, Calif., Phoenix, Ariz.,

Kerrville, Tex. and finally to the King factory in Olathe, Kans. The onboard computer has been replaced three times.

King service bulletin requiring retorquing of servos was performed, the autopilot gyro was replaced twice and the aural trim alert was replaced. This was all a result of dynamically increasing pitch variations during autopilot use. The problem was finally diagnosed at the King factory to be a faulty horizon gyro and bearings.

All told, the maintenance required on the airplane has resulted in a total of 28 weeks out of service and

numerous flights to factory authorized service locations.

In spite of these problems, Mooney's and King's warranty policies have covered the majority of maintenance costs to date.

Summing up, performance and economy of this aircraft are excellent, while dependability has been disappointing. Our concern lies in the possibility that these maintenance nightmares will continue to occur beyond the warranty deadlines of both Mooney and King.

O.S.
Las Vegas, Nev.

Cessna P210

As a used-airplane buy, Cessna's pressurized P210 is a tantalizing paradox. The plane has one of the worst reputations of any airplane in recent years — and deservedly so, for it has plagued owners with a seemingly unending series of mechanical problems. As a result, value of the P210 on the usedplane market is relatively low.

In fact, we saw an ad not long ago placed by a P210 owner who wanted to trade his six-place pressurized P210 for a four-place non-pressurized Mooney 231 — and he was willing to trade even. However, because of the P210's depressed value, a canny buyer can get a good bargain *if* he finds the right airplane. After seven years of trial and tribulation, it appears Cessna finally made enough changes so that it's possible to get a reasonably trouble-free P210 — but only if the buyer chooses carefully.

Troubled History

The P210 is a pressurized outgrowth of the ancient 210 line. It first appeared in 1978 as the only pressurized single on the market. (It held that distinction until the Piper Malibu arrived on the scene in late 1983.) The P210 was heralded as a great, daring leap in technology, and its later problems were excused by many on the grounds that, "Well, that's the price you pay for advancing the state of the art." This is a major misconception. The P210 was indeed a daring *marketing* leap, but technologically it was nothing new. The airframe was a quarter-century old, the basic TSIO-520 engine had been around for years, and the pressurization system was lifted straight from the pressurized Skymaster. "New" features like the fixed-point controller for the turbo wastegate were in fact technical

Little windows identify the P210, which is certified for known icing. Radar pod is under the wing.

steps backward designed to cut costs.

But the marketeers certainly had done their homework; the P210 sold well from the beginning. Nearly 400 were built the first two years, and most owners seemed happy. Things looked good for the P210.

Then, during the summer of 1980, two P210s crashed after engine failures resulting from detonation. The FAA issued emergency ADs requiring ultra-rich mixtures to keep the engines cool, along with other performance-robbing anti-detonation measures. There followed a long period of technical turmoil at Cessna which has only died down in the past few years. A new turbocharger was fitted, and announced with much hoopla as the "Performance-Plus" package that would solve the detonation problems. That it did, but the "Performance-Plus" label was rather farcical; performance in fact declined dramatically, and most P210 pilots found they could not maintain manifold pressure or cabin pressurization above 16,000-18,000 feet. For six months, P210 owners screamed and fumed in frustration, while Cessna tried vainly to come up with a solution. Finally, in late 1981, Cessna announced its fix: A new air induction system, retrofitted free by Cessna, restored the lost performance. The P210s original induction system, it turned

out, had been poorly designed all along.

During all the detonation/turbocharger goings-on, P210 owners were reporting all sorts of other engineering and quality-control problems: leaky, warped exhaust systems, failed vacuum pumps, overheating avionics, engine surging due to vapor lock, and landing gear malfunctions. Many pilots also complained about poor instrumentation that left them ill-equipped to operate the complex high-performance aircraft correctly.

Choice of model year shouldn't be a major concern for the P210 shopper; most important mods have been retrofitted to the older models, making all pre-'82 airplanes essentially identical, except for the landing gear. The 1978 P210 had gear doors, whereas on later models Cessna dropped main-gear doors altogether, thereby cutting manufacturing costs (and maintenance costs for the owner). The loss of gear doors did not affect cruise speed — although gear-lowering speed did go up a whopping 25 knots in the doorless post-'79 birds, to 165 KIAS.

The 1982 and 1983 models (actually they're all 1982s; the "1983" P210 is a leftover 1982 airplane with a new paint job) did get some major nonretrofitable (for the most part) improvements that deserve attention. Among them:

• New turbo controller. The "fixed-point controller" on 1978-81 aircraft is an economy measure that maintains an upper deck presure — the pressure between the turbo compressor and the throttle butterfly — of 35 inches, even when the engine only needs 25 inches. This causes the turbo to work a lot harder than it has to, which results in more exhaust back pressure and hotter induction air. Both sap performance and reliability. The 1982-83 P210 has a "slope controller" which maintains deck pressure at a steady two inches above manifold pressure, and takes a lot of unnecessary load off the turbo.

• New fuel system. The vapor-lock-prone system of earlier P210s was discarded in favor of an excellent left-right-both system with proper vapor-return lines.

• Engine improvements. The valves, rings and valve guides were improved, and the engine designation changed from TSIO-520-P to TSIO-520-AF. In the process, TBO went up 200 hours, to 1,600 hours.

• Dual vacuum pumps and alternators were made available as options.

• Cowl flaps were improved to reduce the chances of overcooling on descent.

• A TIT (Turbine Inlet Temperature) gauge was added, along with a restriction of 1,650 degrees TIT. This serves to limit leaning and keep exhaust temperatures down.

Summing up, there are two kinds of P210s: the "Mark I" airplane built from 1978-81, and the "Mark II" that appeared in 1982. P210 buyers should make every effort find a 1982 or 1983 model if the pocketbook allows.

Used-Plane Market

Currently, the P210 is in good supply at rather depressed prices. "It's a buyer's market," one big broker told us. "A P210 shopper shouldn't have to compromise. The well-equipped airplanes are out there."

And, as we said, prices are low. A 1979 P210 can be bought for about the same price as a comparable T210 or even a normally aspriated A36 Bonanza of the same vintage. In effect, the pressurization comes free on the used-plane market. (The current retail difference between a new P210 and a T210 is about $50,000.) The used-plane buyers thus can benefit from the huge depreciation loss suffered by the poor fellow who bought it new.

Current P210 prices run from about $70,000 for a 1978 model with ARC avionics and no de-ice equipment to $120,000 for a 1982 model. This is an improvement since 1983, when one P210 owner sadly confirmed a $100,000 ceiling price; he tried to sell his loaded 1981 model (it had even been updated with the dual vacuum and alternator systems) and the best offer he could get was $95,000 — precisely half what he paid for it new one year earlier.

Performance

The performance of the P210 can be considered from two angles. Compared to other big, turbocharged, single-engine airplanes, it has adequate performance. But compared to other pressurized aircraft such as the Cessna 340A or Baron 58P, it falls well short.

Because of the power drain of pressurization, P210 performance is slightly less than that of the T210, which has the same airframe and power. Maximum certified ceiling of the P210 is 23,000 feet, but owners report that because of the mediocre climb performance, cruising altitudes above 20,000 feet are impractical unless the plane is very lightly loaded and the trip a long one. Time-to-climb to 23,000 feet is listed as 31 minutes at max available power, but a more reasonable figure is the 39-minute climb to 20,000 feet at normal climb power. That's a long time, and it explains why many P210 pilots prefer to stay in the 15,000-18,000-foot area.

Cruise speeds range from about 170-190 knots, depending on altitude and power setting. However, one P210 pilot reports he gets over 200 knots consistently at light weights.

The 90-gallon fuel supply is not exactly generous. By the book, it's good for a range of about 700 nm with a 45-minute reserve at 70 percent power. Throttled back to 55 percent, book range climbs to over 800 nm. However, these range figures require leaning to rather high exhaust gas temperatures, and prudent P210 pilots prefer to run richer mixtures. This results in higher fuel consumption (by about two to three gph) and range reductions of about 100 nm. A good conservative rule of thumb is 20 gallons per hour, block-to-block, at high cruise speeds. With IFR reserves, that's only about three hours cruising time.

Cost/Performance/Specifications ———————

Model	Year	Number Built	Gross Weight (lbs)	Useful Load (lbs)	Cruise Speed (kts)	Fuel (gals)	Engine	TBO (hrs)	Overhaul Cost	Average Price
P-210N	1978	150	4,000	1,600	187	90	310-hp Cont. TSIO-520-P	1,400	$13,250	$ 74,000
P-210N	1979	235	4,000	1,600	187	90	310-hp Cont. TSIO-520-P	1,400	$13,250	$ 82,000
P-210N	1980	204	4,000	1,600	187	90	310-hp Cont. TSIO-520-P	1,400	$13,250	$ 95,000
P-210N	1981	169	4,000	1,600	187	90	310-hp Cont. TSIO-520-P	1,400	$13,250	$115,000
P-210N	1982	50	4,000	1,600	187	90	310-hp Cont. TSIO-520-AF	1,600	$13,000	$134,500
P-210N	1983	22	4,000	1,600	191	90	310-hp Cont. TSIO-520-AF	1,600	$13,000	$158,000

Takeoff and landing performance is comparable to heavier twin-engined aircraft; about 2,200 feet is necessary to take off over a 50-foot obstacle at gross weight under standard conditions. Stall speed with flaps down is 61 knots right at the FAA-imposed upper limit for single-engine airplanes.

Creature Comforts

Here, of course, is where the P210 shines. The pressurized cabin makes all the difference in the world above 12,500 feet, eliminating the need for cumbersome and uncomfortable oxygen masks. But once more, compared to pressurized twins, the P210 is rather anemic. Pressure differential is only 3.35 pounds, the lowest of any current pressurized airplane. The P210's pressure system has no rate controller; it simply starts to pressurize at the altitude selected by the pilot, maintains that cabin altitude as long as it can, and then maintains the maximum differential as the climb continues. As a result, pilot and passengers are subject to more ear-popping than they would be in, say, a Cessna 421. Such is the price of the "economy" pressurized airplane.

The front four passengers have reasonable — although not lavish — room. Cabin width is a modest 42 inches, but there is lots of headroom for the pilot to sit comfortably upright. The two rear seats, however, are horribly cramped, and recommended on long trips only for children, midgets or contortionists.

Cabin quiet is one of the P210's strong points. The turbocharger muffles the exhaust roar, and the tightly sealed cabin keeps out most of the slipstream noise.

Loading

The 210 series is renowned for its big load capacity and wide c.g. envelope. The P210 generally lives up to those traditions. When it was introduced in 1978, the P210 was the heaviest 210 of them all at 4,000 pounds, 200 more than the Turbo 210. (The T210 has since been

Cessna P210 Resale Value Chart

boosted to 4,000 also.) Typical operating weights run around 2,500-2,600 pounds for well-equipped aircraft, including de-ice equipment. That leaves a healthy 1,400-1,500 pounds of useful load. With 90-gallon tanks full, there's still about 900 pounds left for payload. That's five standard 170-pound people, or four plus baggage.

The P210 pilot is more likely to find himself loaded out the front end of the center-of-gravity envelope rather than the rear, particularly on well-equipped airplanes with full panels and dual alternator/vacuum systems.

Handling Qualities

The 210 series is known for very heavy controls, and the P210 is the most ponderous of the 210s because control cables must be routed through tight-fitting air seals where they pass through the pressure vessel. The P210 will be perceived as a stiff-handling dinosaur, both on the ground and in the air, by pilots stepping up from smaller single-engine planes. But on the other hand, the P210 is rock-solid in turbulence and IFR conditions, the environment in which it will presumably spend a lot of time.

Pitch control is particularly heavy. This makes landing with two people in front a challenge to the

biceps, but it does have the safety plus of limiting the pilot's ability to apply high G-loadings and overstress the airplane. (The 210's record of overstress-induced inflight breakups is surprisingly poor, however — 16 in the five years up to 1983. Three P210s have broken up in flight.)

Safety Record

We have no statistics on P210 accident rates, but the 210 series in general ranks about average or slightly below when compared to other single-engine retractables during the period 1972-1976. The 210's fatal accident rate was 3.1 per 100,000 flight hours, in a group that ranged from 1.0 to 4.2.

A look at P210 accidents, however, reveals some unusual trends. A surprisingly large percentage of accidents are related to mechanical malfunctions, design defects or poor human engineering of the aircraft. Of 30 accidents reported by the NTSB during the period 1978-81, only about a third were pure and simple pilot blunders. (Only one involved weather.) Thirteen of the 30 were engine failures. Of those 13, six were fuel mismanagement crashes. (These figures confirm our earlier findings of very high fuel mismanagement accident rates for the 210 series in general.) Of course the pilot must take some blame in any fuel mismanagement accident, but the design of the fuel system plays a big role, too — and the P210's fuel system apparently needed the big improvements it finally got in 1982. Several accident reports mention misleading fuel gauges.

The other seven engine failures were your basic internal crap-outs: two from detonation, with various other exhaust fires, cylinder blowoffs, and undetermined causes. The notorious vapor lock syndrome caused one crash, and another was triggered by excessive fuel from a runaway boost pump.

Another fertile ground for P210 accidents: landing gear problems. FAA accident/incident records show 19 P210 gear crunches of various sorts through 1982, more than half of them due to mechanical malfunctions. The FAA records — which appear to be more complete than NTSB data — list a total of 75 P210 accidents or incidents since 1978. That amounts to about 10 percent of the fleet.

In all, we're aware of ten fatal P210 accidents. Of those, three were inflight breakups (one triggered by a vacuum system failure). One resulted from a cylinder blowing off the engine, another came after the pilot reported a loss of elevator control over the Gulf of Mexico.

Buyer's Checklist

We've covered the P210's myriad technical problems in detail in the past, and touched on them earlier in this article. Rather than describe the problems again, we'll concentrate on solutions. What follows is a P210 buyers' checklist which, if followed closely, will give the buyer a fighting chance at getting a safe, reliable airplane that won't drive him to the poorhouse.

• *Exhaust system.* Do not buy a P210 without the new Inconel exhaust system. (Or at least plan to retrofit it immediately after purchase.) The P210 exhaust system is, in our view, an engineering disgrace, made of unsuitable material. As a result, the P210 exhaust system has been notoriously troublesome since the beginning and carries a 50-hour AD inspection for cracks.

Slash in the side of the engine cowl exhausts air from the TurboPlus intercooler mod.

Retrofitting the Inconel system is expensive. Cessna has a "special deal": the $3,200 cost of the replacement Inconel system will be reduced by $1.17 for every hour below 1,400 hours on the aircraft. For example, the owner of a 400-hour airplane would get a $1,170 price break, and pay *only* about $2,000.

• *Fuel system.* Ideally, one should buy a 1982 airplane with the redesigned fuel system. If not, make sure that the airplane is fitted with Cessna's vapor-return line fix. (See service letter SE81-42.)

• *Vacuum system.* We'd recommend the dual vacuum system, which can be retrofitted to all P210s. It is mandated by AD for any P210 equipped with the known-icing option.

• *Dual alternator system.* 1982 aircraft were available with dual 60-amp alternators, and some 1980 and 1981 models were retrofitted at the factory. (That program was terminated in 1983, however, so it's too late to retrofit a plane after purchase.) Electrical redundancy is a must for an all-weather plane like the P210; we'd recommend the dual system. Some earlier P210s have a small emergency standby generator. This is better than nothing, but get the dual 60-amp system if you can.

• *Induction system.* Don't buy a P210 without the bigger intake scoop and improved plenum chamber introduced in 1982. Most aircraft should already be retrofitted, since Cessna paid the bill for it.

• *Avionics.* Cessna's in-house ARC line reached an all-time low in quality and reliability in 1977-78, and although things seem to be improved later, most people consider a panel full of ARC avionics to be a major liability in a P210. Look for King or Collins equipment. Also consider retrofitting the improved avionics cooling fan introduced on Cessna's single-engine line. The previous cooling fan was poorly designed and very unreliable, and when it quits, the marginal ARC radios are even more likely to malfunction.

• *Instrumentation.* Standard factory engine instrumentation on 1978-81 P210s is, in our opinion, pathetically bad. We believe every P210 should be equipped with, (1) a six-probe EGT with absolute temperature scale, (2) six-probe cylinder-head temp gauge, (3) Turbine Inlet Temperature (TIT) gauge, (4) accurate digital fuel-flow gauge. Look for a plane with this equipment (any serious pilot should already have it installed). If you can't find one, plan to install it immediately after purchase.

• *Engine.* The TSIO-520-P has a poor reliability record in the P210. Cylinder problems are common, partly a result of excessive heat. Check compression carefully, and have mechanic inspect the condition of the valves and valve guides. Check the cooling baffles with great care. Look at maintenance records closely. The engine has a nominal TBO of 1,400 hours, but few engines have reached that mark without major problems.

• *Cabin leaks.* Poor quality control at Cessna's Pawnee plant has shown up in leaky cabins, particularly the door seals. These problems manifest themselves in reduced pressure capability and loss of manifold pressure. Check the outflow valve carefully; if it's defective, a replacement valve costs more than $5,000.

Modifications

In addition to the previously listed mods, which we would consider virtually mandatory, there are other aftermarket products available for the P210. Among them:

• *R/STOL Systems kit.* Drooped ailerons decrease stall speed by about six knots, while stall strips and wing fences assure a gentle, controllable stall, according to R/STOL. A modified aileron control system with special low-friction pressure seals greatly reduces aileron control forces and increases roll rate by about 50 percent. Cost is $8,500, downtime about two weeks. R/STOL claims eye-opening takeoff performance improvements, but these are apparently based on a takeoff speed five knots below power-off stall speed — not a wise procedure, in our opinion. R/STOL, Snohomish County Airport, Everett, Wa. 98204 (206) 355-8700. R/STOL also offer wing-mounted RCA color radar for the P210.

• *Turboplus intercooler, speedbrakes.* One way to help keep the engine running cooler is to have an intercooler installed by Turboplus in Gig Harbor, Wash. for $6,695. The company also can install speed brakes on the aircraft for $4,645. These will, conversely, help keep the engine from being overcooled on descent.

• *Air American engine conversion.* This Wilkes-Barre company (717) 457-6736 will install a 350-hp Lycoming engine with a 2,000-hour TBO and an intercooled turbocharger for $73,500. Also part of the package is extra strengthening, bracing and weighting to reduce the chance of flutter, along with dual vacuum pumps and alternators. The company also sells an auxiliary fuel tank that provides an extra 20.5 gallons usable. This fits in the baggage compartment and transfers to the right main tank.

• *Flint long-range tanks.* Two tip tanks add 33 gallons' fuel capacity and a couple of feet of wing span for better climb performance. Range is increased by about 250 nm. Cost: $4,250, Flint Aero, 8665 Missouri Gorge Rd., Santee, Calif. 92071.

• *Riley Turboprop conversion.* Noted aircraft souper-upper Jack Riley

has a PT6 P210 conversion. The Riley P210's cost is about $260,000, triple the value of any used P210 on the market.

Owner Comments

As a former owner of a 1968 E33A Bonanza and a 1974 F33A Bonanza, I must say that after 550 hours in a P210, it would be hard to give up the pressurization and icing capabilities. It is truly a comfort on long trips. We used to spend $10 to $20 to fill our oxygen tanks. Now I spend it for the extra fuel for the P210. But we have the extra comfort.

Beech's A36TC costs the same or more than the P210, and offers no pressurization or de-ice capability. A used P210 with all the options is a good buy today.

Howard Hermel
Mankato, Minnesota

I have experienced continuing heat-related problems and avionics malfunctions to the extent that, as of this date, I still have not had all avionics working at the same time. On the positive side, I am very impressed with the stability of the aircraft for IFR purposes and for landing. I have a Robertson STOL kit which I am very impressed with. The pressurization system makes flying much more comfortable than I had given it credit for. Overall, if I can get the avionics problem sorted out, I am certain I am going to be very satisfied.

Roger O. Weed
Anchorage, Alaska

In April 1979, I purchased a new 1978 P210 from Coronado Skyways, an authorized Cessna Dealership in Albuquerque, New Mexico. The aircraft received the full Cessna Warranty Program. I began flying the aircraft regularly (approximately 30 hours per month)

and put the aircraft under a 100-hour inspection program with Sky Scenes, the new Cessna dealership.

Approximately every 25 hours, I have had an oil analysis, and from the beginning, the oil analysis revealed a high chrome and iron content in the oil. The Cessna regional manager was informed and requested Continental to look at the engine, which they did. The Continental representative examined the cylinders with a boroscope; and stated the cylinders showed evidence of corrosion, and concluded the corrosion was the cause of the high iron and chrome in the oil.

The Continental representative, the Cessna representative, and the shop foreman who maintains the aircraft, all agreed that the regular flying of the aircraft while in my possession ruled out the possibility that the corrosion developed after I purchased the aircraft.

Cessna Aircraft Company has refused to make further investigation or repairs under their warranty program. Cessna responded that the corrosion was caused from conditions beyond the control of Cessna, and declined warranty participation.

Philip J. White
Albuquerque, New Mexico

Access for all six seats is through a single door on the left. On the right an openable double-window hatch is hinged from the top for emergency exit. Baggage is loaded separately in an unpressurized rear compartment.

Piper Saratoga SP

Anyone sorting through the mixed bag of used planes for a machine that will carry six, not four, people in greater comfort and frugality than any other will probably seize upon the Piper Saratoga as the solution.

But add speed to the equation, and you have destroyed the rationale, for there is a covey of faster six-place singles and twins. However, all of the competing singles and a good number of the multis sacrifice *Lebensraum*.

Add safety as a further element to the equation, and doubts may cloud your mind, since the Saratogas have an uninspiring accident record, compared with their peers.

History

The fixed-gear Saratoga and the retractable-gear ''SP'' appeared upon the scene in 1980 as the third major evolution in nomenclature and, to some extent, construction and aerodynamics of the old fixed-gear Cherokee Six. The Six, which started out in 1965 with 260- and 300-hp models, was followed by its retractable clone, the Lance, in 1976.

This, in turn, was succeeded by a T-tailed version, the Lance II, in 1978. After earning an unsavory reputation for awkward handling qualities during a brief two-year sentence on the market, the T-tail was unceremoniously dumped for the Saratoga line.

As judged by all who have flown the old and the new models, the Saratogas are an improvement of real magnitude and deserve special consideration by anyone looking for a genuine six-seat used aircraft with decent handling qualities. But naturally the Saratogas—fixed and retractable, turbo and nonturbo—have not been on the market long

enough to compete with the old Sixes and Lances in price. The latter are dirt cheap, by comparison.

Peer Pressure

When classed with their slightly more cramped but speedier peers, the Beech A36 Bonanza and Cessna 210 Centurion, the Saratogas are still sometimes the cheap relatives the Lances used to be. Thus, where you can pick up a 1980 C-210 for around $78,000, the Saratoga SP of equal vintage will set you back around $67,000, on the average. Don't expect to latch onto an A36 for less than $110,000, though.

The main claim to fame of the Saratoga line is its wing, which was lengthened and tapered to give greater aspect ratio, but not burdensome extra wing area. Add to that a pair of Frise ailerons for more sprightly lateral control, and you have an aircraft that operators boast gets off more easily than the Sixes and Lances, flies faster and handles better.

As one Saratoga SP owner said, ''During takeoff with the Lance, the subjective feel was that the plane just did not want to fly on lift-off and had to almost be forced into the air. The feeling of the Saratoga is completely different. The plane has the feel of almost wanting to leap off the runway, even though

The Saratogas abandoned the traditional Hershey bar wing for a tapered one with Frise ailerons and much improved control.

the power available is the same in both aircraft.''

The new wing also allowed addition of extra fuel—to the tune of eight more gallons, with new bladder tanks in the outer portion. The inner wing retained its two 38.5-gal. metal leading edge tanks. Together, they provide a healthy total of 102 gallons of usable fuel.

Fuel Consumption and Performance

The extra fuel is not exactly a luxury in the Saratoga, since the airplane's big 300-horse Lycoming is a thirsty beast that will consume from 16 gph when flown conservatively in its normally aspirated version, to maybe 18 gph in the turbo version.

The high fuel consumption, which does not happen to be paired with blazing speed, is most often cited by owners as the one thorn in their side. In fact, with a typical 65-percent-power cruise of around 150 knots, the nonturbo Saratoga SP can expect to be passed by the likes of the Mooney 201, and left standing still by the A36 and C-210. Owners stress, therefore, that the

Saratogas are most sensibly used as long-range machines, to carry big cabin loads. Said one pilot, "The only drawback that I can think of is the high fuel consumption if the plane is used for local flying, such as recurrent training, touch-and-goes or local airport hopping."

Load Capacity

Not only do the Saratogas provide bountiful cabin room for six, often with club seating in the rear, they also allow plenty of room for luggage. And with a 100-pound compartment in the nose and another of equal capacity in the rear, the pilot is given an excellent opportunity to keep the aircraft balanced. With an equipped useful load of about 1,500 pounds in the retractable version, pilots can figure on carrying six adults, a full 200 pounds of baggage and still have enough fuel (47 gallons) to fly for almost three hours without reserve.

Or with full fuel, they can count on carrying five adults and some 38 pounds of baggage. The 100-pound lower useful load on the fixed-gear model will lower those figures, of course.

If the beamy Saratogas are fuel guzzlers, what's the alternative? An equally roomy twin will burn nearly twice the fuel with maintenance bills may be double or so. So there is good logic in the choice.

Handling

As mentioned above, the Saratogas are much more pleasant, facile aircraft to maneuver than the earlier Sixes and Lances, thanks to the improved wing. The stall remains vintage Cherokee, with lots of buffet and mushing, but small chance of a big wing drop and stall break. Not only is the takeoff more eager, but when landing heavily loaded, the Saratogas are less likely to come down final like lifting (or nonlifting) bodies. Pilots seem to like the manual flap system, since it is quicker than an electric one.

In turbulence, the Saratogas tend to yaw some. Therefore, passen-

gers riding in the rearmost seats during turbulence will be subjected to an annoying amount of tail waggling, but not as badly as in the earlier T-tailed Lance.

Safety Record

The retractable-gear Lances and Saratogas collectively do not have an enviable accident history. Of 17 single-engine retractables we compared for the decade 1972 through 1981, the big Pipers shared the worst fatal accident rate with the old (35-P35) V-tail Bonanza of 3.3 fatal accidents per 100,000 hours. By comparison, the Beech A36 shared the third best fatal record with the Cessna Cardinal RG of 1.5 fatals per 100,000 hours; and the Cessna Centurion came in about half way down the list (10th) with a 2.3 rate.

In total accident rate, the Lance/ Saratoga showed up somewhat better, in 12th place, actually outshining the Cessna 210 by three ranks, but being bettered once again by the A36 Bonanza, which has an excellent (low) overall accident rate.

NTSB Briefs

An accident listing provided by the Safety Board for the years 1980 and 1981, which included all fixed-gear and retractable models of the PA-32 and -32R class, disclosed that engine failures were the most common type of problem, with 28 tallied, with fuel mismanagement accounting for a large proportion of those: 11. However, the greatest

The Saratoga's main claim to fame: a beamy cabin, club seating and room for six, plus baggage.

number of fatal accidents—nine— was attributed to pilots inadvertently flying from VFR into IFR conditions.

Second highest fatal accident cause, with seven cases, involved in-flight airframe failure. Four of the breakups were in fixed-gear models; three in retractables. Most involved bad weather with thunderstorms in the area; one was in snow and ice, and another was related to spatial disorientation at night by a low-time pilot.

Third highest fatal accident cause was improper IFR operation and fourth, engine failure.

Engine Failures

As mentioned above, while engine failures claimed the biggest number of accidents among the Saratogas, Sixes and Lances, a major portion of those occurred because of fuel mismanagement. Nearly all of these were logged by pilots who had low time in that type of aircraft. The fuel selector system is quite straightforward, and located under the power quadrant where it is easy to see and reach by both pilots. However, unlike most other systems, it has a selector knob that is moved left and right rather than rotated. Although there are two tanks in each wing, there is only one position for each wing. And by the same token, there are only two fuel gauges, one for each wing.

244

To assist the pilot in loading fuel, there are sight gauges in each wing.

As for mechanical problems blamed for engine failures, there was no discernable trend, simply miscellaneous breakdowns involving: fuel line nut, oil exhaustion, valve failure, primer failure and resulting fire, cylinder crack, oil pump gear, valve broken, air in fuel.

A large proportion of nonfatal accidents was attributed to overshoots: 13. In many of these, pilots with low time in the aircraft simply misjudged the approach and went off the runway with unpleasant mechanical results (there was only one fatal in this category). Only half as many undershoots occurred in this type aircraft. Both types of accident are fairly common in big, heavy high-performance ships.

A fairly sizable number of accidents were blamed on ground loops and swerves—a good number of them in snow or gusty wind conditions—only two because of bounced landings and improper use of brakes.

Gear Stress

As with other big, heavy aircraft, often operated on rough strips, there are likely to be hard landings and gear failures. The big Pipers had their share of hard landings (six) and gear failures (seven). And despite the existence of an auto-

matic gear-lowering feature, the aircraft managed to land gear up on four different occasions during the two-year study period—twice because of mechanical problems. The device can nevertheless be rated a boon, though pilots must learn how to operate the override during takeoff to prevent the gear from dropping when the pilot wishes it to remain up.

Dangerous Retractables?

Can any trends be spotted from among the two years of briefs to suggest design problems among the retractables, which have such a miserable accident record? Not really, though with only a two-year run we were unable to get the big picture. In each category of accident we were able to scan, there were normally fewer accidents among the retractable Pipers, presumably because there are fewer in the fleet. The most dangerous

Oval intake scoop and cooling vents on the cowl are hallmarks of the turbo models.

category among the retractables was flying from VFR into IFR conditions, with six fatal accidents, vs. seven for the fixed-gear models.

The one area where the retractables seemed to have a worse record was in undershoots, with five accidents vs. only two among fixed-gear models. But only one of those retractable accidents was fatal, and the pilot had alcohol in his blood.

Maintenance Considerations

The nose gear on the retractable models appears to have accounted for the most trouble in a maintenance sense. The FAA's Service Difficulty Reports show several cases of the nose gear extending in flight (when it was not asked to do so) because of failed rod ends on

Cost/Performance/Specifications

Model	Year	Average Retail Price	Cruise Speed (kts)	Rate of Climb (fpm)	Service Ceiling	Useful Load (lbs)	Fuel (gals)	Engine	TBO (hrs)	Overhaul Cost
PA-32-301	1980	$ 68,500	150	990	16,000	1,667	102	300-hp Lyc. IO-540-K1G5	2,000	$14,750
PA-32-301T	1980	$ 70,500	165	1,075	20,000	1,612	102	300-hp Lyc. TIO-540-S1AD	1,800	$20,000
PA-32R-301	1980	$ 75,000	158	1,010	16,700	1,579	102	300-hp Lyc. IO-540-K1G5D	2,000	$14,750
PA-32R-301T	1980	$ 83,000	177	1,120	20,000	1,537	102	300-hp Lyc. TIO-540-S1AD	1,800	$20,000
PA-32-301	1981	$ 73,000	150	990	16,000	1,667	102	300-hp Lyc. IO-540-K1G5	2,000	$14,750
PA-32-301T	1981	$ 76,000	165	1,075	20,000	1,612	102	300-hp Lyc. TIO-540-S1AD	1,800	$20,000
PA-32R-301	1981	$ 87,500	158	1,010	16,700	1,579	102	300-hp Lyc. IO-540-K1G5D	2,000	$14,750
PA-32R-301T	1981	$ 95,500	177	1,120	20,000	1,537	102	300-hp Lyc. TIO-540-S1AD	1,800	$20,000
PA-32-301	1982	$ 81,000	150	990	16,000	1,667	102	300-hp Lyc. IO-540-K1G5	2,000	$14,750
PA-32-301T	1982	$ 88,500	165	1,075	20,000	1,612	102	300-hp Lyc. TIO-540-S1AD	1,800	$20,000
PA-32R-301	1982	$100,000	158	1,010	16,700	1,579	102	300-hp Lyc. IO-540-K1G5D	2,000	$14,750
PA-32R-301T	1982	$108,000	177	1,120	20,000	1,537	102	300-hp Lyc. TIO-540-S1AD	1,800	$20,000
PA-32-301	1983	$ 93,000	150	990	16,000	1,667	102	300-hp Lyc. IO-540-K1G5D	2,000	$14,750
PA-32-301T	1983	$104,000	165	1,075	20,000	1,612	102	300-hp Lyc. TIO-540-S1AD	1,800	$20,000
PA-32R-301	1983	$112,000	158	1,010	16,700	1,579	102	300-hp Lyc. IO-540-K1G5D	2,000	$14,750
PA-32R-301T	1983	$120,000	177	1,120	20,000	1,537	102	300-hp Lyc. TIO-540-S1AD	1,800	$20,000

the hydraulic cylinder. An Airworthiness Directive was issued to correct the problem. Also, another Piper Service Bulletin was issued to replace the nose gear actuator attach bolt, which was bending and breaking.

The greatest number of complaints among SDRs dealt with problems in the Bendix magnetos. Other areas where problems developed: exhaust system, turbo system (with several instances of wastegates warping and seizing); rusted, corroded and cracked engine mounts; and cracks in the ailerons, usually at the balance weights or screws in the leading edge. We noted two instances of cracking crankcases on the Lycoming 540 engines.

One owner also reported his biggest problem was with the front door seal, which stayed deformed during cold weather and would not seal properly, despite numerous replacements. He finally solved the problem by installing an inflatable door seal sold by Bob Fields Aerocessories (Santa Paula, Calif. 805-525-6236).

Resale Value

All of the Saratogas tracked since their introduction in 1980 have showed the standard plunge in resale value, ranging from a loss of 20 percent in the fixed-gear turbo model to almost 30 percent in the retractable turbo. The curves seem to be flattening out, however, and the several models actually appears to be starting to rise in value.

Owner Comments

I have put approximately 450 hours on the plane, averaging about 150 hours per year. Prior to purchasing this 1981 SP, I owned a 1976 straight-tailed Lance.

While the Saratoga is marginally faster, there is a marked difference in how the two planes handle, especially during takeoff. The wing changes made on the Saratoga

Saratoga SP Resale Value Chart

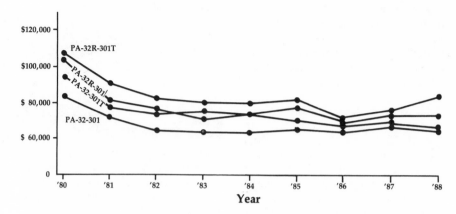

markedly improve the takeoff feel of the airplane.

During takeoff with the Lance, the subjective feel was that the plane just did not want to fly on liftoff and had to almost be forced into the air. The feeling of the Saratoga is completely different. The plane has the feel of almost wanting to leap off the runway, even though the power available is the same in both aircraft.

In cruise or landing, I can find very little difference in the handling characteristics of the two aircraft.

James M. Rich, Jr.
Asheboro, N.C.

I have a 1983 Piper Turbo Saratoga SP. It was one year old as of March 15, 1984. I purchased it new and during the first 12 months of ownership I put 350 hours on the tach.

Overall, the aircraft has been absolutely superb with very few problems. It has been used for many long-distance cross-country trips. The plane has seen virtually all flying weather extremes.

On this aircraft, Piper's quality control was excellent with no squawks the first 100 hours. The interior quality, appearance and comfort with club seating and cabin size for a single is unmatched in its class.

If I could change anything on the

aircraft to make it better and/or easier to fly, I would make the following suggestions:

1. Move mp and rpm gauges up into easier pilot view.
2. Rudder trim should be more easily reached without having to bend over and reach so far forward.
3. Flap handle should have a second flaps-up position to click into after the pilot is seated so that it could be used without bending down and forward.
4. Do something with the absolutely ridiculous inside-the-cockpit fuel drain setup. It should never take two people to pre-flight an airplane, and yes, the wind is always blowing, so setting the bucket on the ground under the sump is quite a task. Finally, dumping fuel on the ramp is not nice.
5. Higher quality, larger display and more convenient positioning of EGT. It is fine in its present location if your copilot is of the opposite sex and attractive because you have to place your head in the copilot's lap to read the gauge accurately.
6. Fuel quantity, oil pressure and cylinder head gauges should be larger and with more gradations for better accuracy.
7. A small fan is needed to better push heat to passenger area of cabin.

Ralph D. Maltby
Newark, Ohio

TWIN-ENGINE PISTON

Cessna T303 Crusader

Six years ago, the T303 was considered by many in the industry to be the prototype of a new family of aircraft that would leap the gulf between Cessna's two engineering and manufacturing companies— the Pawnee and Wallace divisions.

For a period of time, there was a third marketing and support organization: Cessna Citation, but it was brought into the fold as a part of the Wallace operation. This was considered beneficial, since in design and manufacturing techniques and philosophies, the two were so different that they did not seem to be arms of the same corporation. There apparently was little if any exchange of ideas or information.

The Crusader, as it was later named, would be the first application of lessons learned in aerodynamics, systems, human factors, materials, methods and manufacturing on the military T- and A-37 jets and the 500 series of Citations—many of which had let to significant changes in the 400 series of piston and turboprop twins— down through the rest of the line.

Trickle-Down Hopes
More importantly for buyers, it offered hope that more modern design and construction was finally trickling down through the ranks towards the woefully derivative single-engine line. As successful as these products had been, they were variations on a theme that had been cast between the late 1930s and '40s, their growth in size, performance and capability more the product of bolt-on and paste-on adaptation than of engineering pro-

gress and general technological advance.

As is well known, the first Model 303 was a very different airplane from what was introduced as the T303 in late 1979 and which was finally put on the market in late 1981. It was still called the Clipper—the name change was forced by Pan American after the design was radically redone—but instead of a very light twin to compete with the Cougar, Duchess and Seminole, it was a turbocharged baby cabin twin. The company hoped to position it somewhat above the successful Piper PA-34 Seneca and Beech B-55 Baron and just below Piper's PA-31 Navajo and Cessna's own 400 series unpressurized piston twins.

To its credit, Cessna had recognized during the heady sales successes of the late 1970s that the small-twin market was not a large one, in part because the add-on systems necessary to give that category true utility could not successfully be carried on the diminutive twins and leave any room or power for payload and performance. Demand for a training/personal, nice weather twin was insufficient to pay back a development program. The

The mid-mounted horizontal tail: a thing of beauty designed to reduce propwash vibration and improve elevator effectiveness. But watch out for overrotation on takeoff. Also, several fixes were needed to prevent rudder oscillation in icing.

existing 300 series twins, the 310, 337 and 340 (although the latter continued to be offered through the 1984 model year) were increasingly incompatible with the design, manufacturing and materials philosophies and techniques of the company.

Handmade
They were labor intensive to build. In fact, there was still a great deal of hand rather than tool or process forming involved. The 400 series had been transitioned to more modern airfoils and construction techniques as well as to much better-organized, less work-intensive systems and cockpits. None of the improvements were being added to the 300 series, particularly the venerable 310, and speculation had begun in the late 1970s that it had reached the end of the line.

So the T303, renamed the Crusader, should be considered both an end run around the bottom of the twin market philosophy of the competition and a hoped-for successor to the 310/320/340 family that would conform more closely with the new design and manufacturing direction at Cessna.

In the Beginning

Much of the coverage of the T303 has focused on it and the very light, "entry level" twins or between it and the PA-34. In those categories it does quite well. Considered as a 310 replacement, however, it is very much a mixed bag, to be generous. Despite the production economies of the T303 over the 310 airframe and the relative cost of the powerplants, the Crusader hit the market with a substantial price differential. In practically every performance category save runway requirements, the 310 outperforms the T303 by a hefty margin. However, in ease of operation, including the transition time required to safely operate and in design-induced traps, overall pilot workload, and—most important for many operators—passenger acceptance, the Crusader wins hands down. That is to be expected for a

Trailing beam landing gear smooths landings, but the gear has had its share of mechanical problems.

new design; but so are performance improvements.

In brief, Cessna's planners positioned the airplane in one segment of the market. The market positioned it a bit further down the line.

A Cabin Twin that Shrank in the Wash

The airplane has been thoroughly described in previous issues (February 1, April 1 and October 1, 1982; and a Used Aircraft Guide in the October 15, 1984, edition), so we will just highlight some features here.

At a glance, the T303 does not resemble any other Cessna, particularly anything produced at the Pawnee Division. On closer inspection, there are many features of the 500 and remodeled 400 series: bounded, clean wings incorporating integral, wet fuel tanks rather than the troublesome fuel bladders; and beefy-looking trailing beam or link main landing gear that smooths-out rough fields and less-than-perfect landings. One visible departure is the cruciform tail.

The horizontal tail is mounted approximately one third up the

vertical stabilizer. The design objectives were to minimize vibration from the disturbed air generated by the propellors (one early claimed benefit is the ability to operate at low rpm—down to 2,100, at which speed noise and vibration are very low), improve elevator effectiveness and to minimize pitch changes with power or configuration changes. One trade-off is a tendency to overrotate during a liftoff. (Some observers think a cruciform tail would have more effectively solved the empennage problems of the 340, 425 and 441.)

Cessna design engineers, led by David R. Ellis, spent a lot of time tuning the aerodynamics and the relationships demanded by high and low-speed flight and clean landing configurations. Solutions resulted in airflow control devices on the vertical tail, at the fuselage/wingroot juncture, the engine nacelles and on the upper flap surfaces. Designers also spent a fair amount of work on the airframe to improve service and maintenance access.

First Counter-Rotating

The T303 is the first Cessna twin to feature counter-rotating engines/propellors. As part of the weight-management program, Cessna selected a special variant of the Continental IO-520, the L/TSIO-520 AE, which saved 65 pounds each over the normal version. AiResearch turbochargers are bolted on at the Cessna plant.

In addition to being lightened, the Continentals were tuned to run at a fairly high compression ratio as aircraft engines go, 8.5 to 1, as part of the goal to reduce fuel consumption. One result of that is that maximum continuous power is established at 71 percent to preclude detonation. To calm fears in the marketplace over yet another light (read troublesome) engine, it was delivered with a recommended

The 1982 Crusader.

TBO of 2,000 hours, a full warranty for six months or 240 hours and pro-rata to TBO. Visual and aural fire warning detection systems were also standard (fire suppression devices were not). Cooling is by a variation on updraft; instead of cowl flaps, there are internal shutters to reduce aerodynamic drag.

The gear-actuating system is based on the electrically actuated hydraulic one that has caused so much grief for operators of retractable singles. (To get a bit ahead of ourselves, it has been comparatively trouble-free on the Crusader, in which a free-fall emergency extension mode has been incorporated.)

Other good trickle-down systems include dual bus main and avionics electrical systems that include pull-off circuit breakers rather than the typical Cessna reset-only, lower cost version.

The fuel system and fuel management is simpler (on, off, crossfeed) and located within easy reach and fairly easy sight on the base of the power quadrant.

Cockpit organization reflects much of the good planning established in the Citation and is a boon to pilot workload. There is enough room for an independent set of copilot flight instruments with its own pitot/static system.

Early Success

The market for new general aviation aircraft was well on its way to the worst crash ever when the T303 was introduced, but all things considered (and remembering the sales shot that a still-large dealer network represented to predictable orders for the company), it started breathing down the volume neck of the most popular twin selling, the Seneca.

According to official factory figures, 31 airplanes were delivered in 1981 (as '82 models); 131 in 1982; 57 in 1983; 65 in 1984; 11 in 1985; and 2 in 1986. Most of the aircraft delivered in 1984 through '86 were probably assembled in '83. By late 1987, a total of 297 aircraft had been delivered (although serial numbers through T30300315 were set aside). Whether those last 18 assigned serial numbers reflect aircraft built and put in storage somewhere, or whether production was terminated at 00297 is an interesting question. Keep in mind that factory deliveries reflect distributor/dealer sales, not necessarily retail sales. Many Crusaders stayed in dealer inventory and were used as training/air taxi/charter aircraft.

Light as in Flimsy

In any event, the new twin got off to a good start, particularly considering market conditions.

However, the first year of field experience disclosed that light twin meant light (some would say flimsy) in some design, material and manufacturing elements. Typical of all manufacturers' general aviation aircraft, real-world use was disclosing some shortcomings. Certain areas, such as the turbocharger mount, copilot's door hinges, main gear shock struts and a few other bits and pieces of the airframe were beefed-up.

In its second model year, the Crusader also received known icing certification and a few operational options (one, fuel pressure limiting switches, was later made standard). An aft cargo door, which more than doubles the width of the opening and slightly increases baggage space (from 22.5 to 26.5 cubic feet) due to relocation of the aft cabin bulkhead, was also offered in 1983.

In the first year of field experience, quite a few operators were mentioning that they liked the airplane, but it was spending too much time in the shop. One said that something seemed to break on practically every trip. This brought back echoes of the unfortunate 411 to many, and presaged the experience many people had with the Malibu in later years.

At first glance and first flight, most people were impressed with the diminutive Crusader, even line boys and mechanics who admired some of the service-oriented features. But despite the thousands of hours of testing and evaluation by the factory, real-life use was disclosing shortcomings in just a few hours. Quite a few of them were traced to poor performance on the assembly line, but increasingly design or materials defects were showing up.

To its credit, Cessna worked hard to support the product, but some fixes did not work or transferred problems to another part of a given system. Operators were becoming frustrated because many proposed fixes were not true fixes, and shortcomings disclosed early on were recurring.

Service History

In the first three years of service, operational experience with the Crusader resulted in more than 60 service bulletins and an even larger number of service letters and advisories. Service difficulty reports (SDRs) supported the field experience. Some of the problems identified back then have been continuing, as the 278 SDRs issued in the interim reveal. These include vertical fin attachment, main and nose landing gear, and turbo and exhaust mounting systems.

The service bulletins, kits and letters have continued to be issued, as well. Cessna has continued to try to resolve the problems. For instance, last year the company was working on a second totally new turbo and exhaust mounting system.

Landing gear and turbocharger-related problems are the biggest continuing issues on the T303. Magneto problems are next, followed by alternator troubles, especially a tendency to throw or break belts and instances of cracking cases. Maintenance people suspect a combination of poor alignment and vibration as the major factors in quite a few of the service difficulties experienced, including numerous reports of cracked engine mounts.

Quality Control Problems

Most of the others are traced to poor quality control. For instance, several reports of loose vertical fin attach bolts reported as a result of in-flight vibration were attributed to improper assembly and torquing at the factory. These resulted in an airworthiness alert.

The turbo/exhaust problems also triggered an airworthiness alert. They have also led to engine mount, turbo heat shield and mounting rust and corrosion problems and to quite a few other heat-related problems within the engine compartment. There has also been continuing difficulty in aligning the turbo exhaust outlet with the tailpipe.

A lot of people expected the lightweight engine to result in many difficulties, but it has performed surprisingly well. There have been some cylinder and valve corrosion and galling or spalling in the valve train. Most of the deterioration appears to be a product of aircraft stored without proper preparation of the powerplant. This situation is not peculiar to the T303 and TSIO-520 AE, as many purchasers of low-time or nearly-new aircraft from field inventory have discovered in the past few years. The only protection against this expensive headache is a thorough internal inspection before purchase.

Nineteen of the current batch of SDRs report cracking and failure in the main landing gear retraction arm and assembly; several others relate to side braces and downlock assemblies. The nose gear shimmy damper, actuator and its attach bracket, steering bellcrank and retraction stop have also experienced continuing difficulties. Cessna beefed up the main gear doors after several instances of cracks occurring at the hinge.

Shimmy Shock

One former operator of a fleet of five has a host of incident horror tales related to the shimmy damper. Its failure while in motion, particularly after landing, results in almost uncontrollable vibration that has broken instruments in the cockpit, and in one occurrence, resulted in the instrument panel flopping out onto the controls.

Some of the alternator-related SDRs suggest that electrical power demands of the systems, particularly with the smaller, 60 amp alternators, are too high (a shortcoming shared with the Seneca). T303 shoppers should put the larger capacity 95 amp alternators that are standard with deice-equipped models on the list of must-halves.

Magnetos are troublesome items on most aircraft. Quite a few of the SDRs suggest that pressurized mags, while they cure some operational problems, may create new ones, particularly moisture contamination that leads to arcing, and filter and other material breakdown, including bearing seizure. In turn, this suggests that regular inspection and replacement of filters should be part of the preventive maintenance program.

Umbrella Needed?

Another headache that could result in a serious problem, particularly if you experience an emergency after takeoff, is a result of water leaks. There were five reports of circuit breaker disconnect traced to water leaking over and into the panel mounted on the side wall below the pilot's side window. In two of the experiences, the gear could not be retracted because the breaker had disconnected internally and could not be reset. (We have encountered this problem three times, in 400 series Cessnas. In each case it was the gear circuit breaker that popped.)

Operators of aircraft that are regularly stored outside should be

Cost/Performance/Specifications

Model	Year	Number Built	Average Retail Price	Cruise Speed (kt)	Rate of Climb (fpm)	Useful Load (lb)	Std/Opt Fuel (gal)	Engines	SE Ceiling (ft)	TBO (hr)	Overhaul Cost
T303	1982	162	$135,000	180	1480	1,870	155	TSIO-520-AE	13,000	2,000	$14,500
T303	1983	57	$160,000	180	1480	1,870	155	TSIO-520-AE	13,000	2,000	$14,500
T303	1984	79	$195,000	180	1480	1,870	155	TSIO-520-AE	13,000	2,000	$14,500

particularly alert to the problem, especially if they start a trip during or after heavy rain. Look for a trail of water from the ice window down the side wall to the panel. This is a place where the company should do a better job of sealing, or at least deflecting water.

Based on experience with other Cessna aircraft, there were surprisingly few squawks reported on the ARC avionics gear that was standard kit for it and most other Cessnas until just before the end of production, when some optional systems from other suppliers were offered.

Airworthiness Directives

Given the operational and service record of the Crusader, there have been surprisingly few ADs issued. There are a total of five, most of which relate to accessories (dratted magnetos and air filters, for instance). One was for a mandatory inspection for turbo-related problems. An early one covered the counterweight bolts on McCauley propellors. The big one (two, actually—85-11-5 and 86-1-1) lifted known-icing certification from properly equipped T303s. Cessna developed a fix and an associated kit that, together with some operational and configuration limitations, restored approval effective last October.

Cessna documents describe the effect of ice accumulation at the juncture of the horizontal and vertical stabilizers as resulting in '' . . . a mild oscillation of the rudder/rudder pedals when the airplane is configured for final stages of a landing approach . . .

and possibly a slight nose down pitch change. The extent of this phenomenon varies with certain combinations of airspeed, power setting, flap deflection, sideslips and type of icing conditions.'' Pilots who have encountered the phenomenon may want to embellish that description a bit.

The airframe fix is the addition of more vortex generators below the horizontal stabilizer, a new fairing shape covering the leading edge of the stabilizers at the cruciform junction, a flow control fence at the bottom of the left horizontal stabilizer and a flow energizer on the vertical fin just below the horizontal tail.

Operational recommendations are to reduce airspeed, reduce power, reduce flaps and to coordinate flight (reduce slip). Operational restriction in the final fix is a maximum of 10 degrees of flaps, which makes sense when you are carrying a load of ice on any airplane.

Safety Record

The accident record is quite good, too. By late 1987, there were a total of 25, of which two were fatal (a total of six fatalities) and three involving injuries. The worst one, in terms of fatalities (five), was a result of flight into known icing conditions, during which the pilot reported heavy vibration. Three non-injury accidents were attributed to gear failure, one during taxi because of a violent nose wheel shimmy and nose gear collapse.

One horrendous incident that resulted in no damage was caused by a vacuum pump failure that led

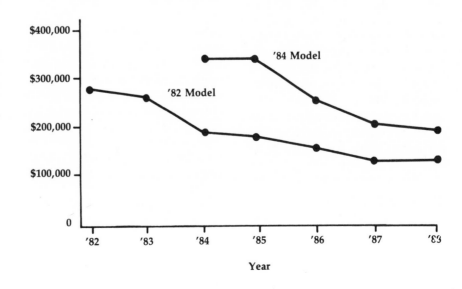

Crusader T303 Resale Value Chart

to loss of control and stall in the clag. The airplane fell out of the overcast in an inverted spin. At 500 feet agl, the pilot recovered and landed.

The other accidents do not appear to bear any relationship to the nature and character of the design.

Is There a Bargain Here?

Average equipped list prices for the Crusader ranged from just under $275,000 in 1982 to about $318,000 in 1984. In 1987, asking prices ranged from about $135,000 to $195,000. Average airframe time is right on 1,000 hours. (The highest-time T303 we noted had a reported 1,600 hours on it, although there are undoubtedly some with more than that.)

While we can't prove it, a higher-time copy might be preferable to a cherry low-time airframe/engine combination. If it has been carefully maintained and all the bulletins followed and fixes applied, that is. The theory is that most of the items that have been failing will have been corrected except for those that recur, in which preventive maintenance and careful inspection must be the rule.

Given the level of support Cessna has given to the aircraft, it appears that the Crusader might be a better bet than older, out of production aircraft. However, the prudent potential buyer of any aircraft not currently being built might better assume himself an orphan and secretly hope for a pleasant surprise. Given the availability and increasingly outrageous price charged for relatively simple bits and pieces, that would seem to be the safest strategy.

The Good Part

Pilots drawn to twins should be disabused of any belief that two is better than one, unless they are regularly trained to the highest possible level of proficiency. Only turbine equipment has the sufficiently high surplus of power needed to climb or accelerate-go out of an engine failure. And even if the engine goes during a comfortable cruise, good systems management and proper technique will extend the range of your landing options in a piston twin, nothing more. The accident record continues to suggest that the decision-making and technique skills required of piston twin operators are very high.

The Crusader is average, which means marginal, in single engine capabilities and characteristics. What it has going for it is a well organized cockpit, good visibility (except at night, when reflections in the side windows from the panel are bothersome because of a skimpy glare shield), generally better designed systems that provide more options if something goes awry, and light, reasonably well-harmonized controls and good basic flying characteristics.

The trade-off of light control forces is more work in turbulence. While Cessna originally touted the good longitudinal stability of the design, it jiggles and twiggles a lot in rough air. Therefore, a yaw damper should be on your shopping list (check to make sure that everything is rigged right and the yaw damper hasn't gone to sleep in your pre-acceptance inspection).

Another of the nice big airplane features of the T303 is three-axis trim. But in our initial single engine work in the airplane several years ago, it was apparent that there was enough rudder trim to remove the control pressure required to maintain minimum slip flight after an engine-failure. Your leg will get tired (and you need a big input at initial failure to keep the airplane headed in the right direction), as we can attest from a night, IFR, for-real engine shutdown.

In addition to its very nice all-around flying qualities, the design has high gear and flap speeds that make operations in high density areas, or quick descents, far easier to accomplish and far easier on the powerplants than in many competitive alternatives.

Loading Flexibility

The array of baggage places gives the operator considerable loading flexibility, both in terms of cabin clutter and weight and balance. The only caveat here is that the cubes far exceed the legal carrying capacity, and careless loading can lead to an out of cg condition.

As a light twin with a bit more panache and some very good operational features, the Crusader is a very real option. It would be even better if Cessna had definitely fixed all of the weaknesses that are the bad side of "light" twin and would finally learn something about quality interior materials and finish.

Anyone in the market for a light twin right now should definitely put the Crusader on his or her list. But spend a few nights reading the volumes of service letters and bulletins, and ensure that your heart's desire had them all handled. P.S. Make sure your mechanic takes his borescope with him for the inspection.

Owner Comments

We have owned our Cessna 303 since January 1986. As president, CEO and chief pilot of our company, I have flown the aircraft about 250 hours. The aircraft currently has about 880 hours, with 880 on the left engine, and 280 on the RE reman.

We had the latest "mandatory" service bulletin done (turbine mounts), at which time bolts on turbos were frozen in, and turbos were cracked getting the bolts out, resulting in two new turbochargers being required, which Cessna didn't pay for.

The 400 radios have spent many hours on the bench and are the worst equipment on the plane.

The aircraft flies like a sweetheart—comfortable, roomy, stable (once you get past the hop on takeoff) and very forgiving.

Little things [on the aircraft] are junky. Tumbles on baggage compartment locks are "pot metal." You have to use lock-tite to hold a tiny screw that retains the locking arm that holds the tumblers in. I've dropped two over Northern Mississippi (tumblers, that is). Air stair cables frayed and had to be replaced after 600 hours (how many openings and closings?). Ashtrays are all corroded. Little things, I know, for something that lists around $250 M, you'd expect a little more. Why cut corners on a 50¢ item?

I normally cruise at eight to 10 M, top of the green on MP and 2200 rpm, get 155-160 TAS, and burn 25 gph. Climbout @ 2400 rpm and 115 knots IAS for about 700 fpm.

SE performance won't set the world on fire, but it is docile. No heavy rudder pressure required if you tip the right way, and will hold altitude and give some climb when you get it all cleaned up, but most important is that it's easy (no rapid loss of heading, no heavy pitch up or down) to control. SE approach is easy, and the greatest danger seems to be delaying your descent to be conservative, and overflying the runway. The fact that the wheels come down at 175 seems to help control temps—leave these rpms up, come down fast (approach control appreciates it), drop the wheels and land.

Overall statisfaction—very good. Comfort—outstanding. Flyability—

great. Electronics—poor . . . Little things—poor.

Richard L. Kanary
Portland, Ore.

I have owned and operated my Crusader since January 1985. I purchased it as a factory demonstrator directly from Cessna with 214 hours on the plane. Terms of the purchase also included an annual inspection, which turned out to be the best thing that ever happened to me. When the annual was completed, significant corrosion was found on all cylinders on the left engine, and the compression rating on the No. five cylinder was just below 13 psi. The ;right engine also had light to severe corrosion on five cylinders. One was pulled from the left engine for a more detailed inspection, and a casting flaw on the engine block was also dicovered, which necessitated a complete new left engine.

By the time everything was completed and the plane was back in flying order, I ended up with a completely new left engine and entire new "top" on the right engine. Total cost came to $50,272, of which Cessna and/or Continental paid $48,264. This covered all parts, engines, pro-rated labor, etc.

I now have about 940 hours on the plane. Other problems I have experienced were as follows:

1) Replacement parts are extremely expensive. For instance, I had to replace a tachometer at 618 hours, at a cost of $1,560. This seems outrageous to me.

2) At 762 hours I discovered something which at the time caused me great concern, and still worries me. On an annual inspection it was determined that the left flap was unairworthy due to extreme heat

damage. In trying to determine the cause of the problem, it became evident that the fuel tank drain valve is located immediately outboard of the exhaust pipe. When the system was installed at the factory, apparently a washer was missing, which caused a "minute" gas leak.

At some time in landing configuration with full flaps extended, the heat given off from the exhaust system was sufficient to ignite a small amount of fuel from the drip, causing a blowtorch effect on the flap. As far as I am concerned, location of the fuel tank drain valve directly behind the exhaust pipe is an extremely poor one, and incredibly dangerous. Total cost to replace the flap also amounted to approximately $3,000. In addition, the plane was grounded for almost one month.

3) At 775 hours during work on an exhaust system AD which necessitated pulling both turbochargers, it was determined that one of them had casting flaws, and cracks had developed. This required replacement of both turbochargers at a cost of $3,500.

In addition to the above items, I have had a continual recurring problem with the Slick pressurized magnetos on the plane. To date I have suffered four magneto failures, including one almost simultaneous failure of both mags on the right engine just after rotation with the plane at max gross takeoff weight and ISA + 10 conditions. Fortunately, I was on a 15,000-foot runway and was able to land straight ahead.

Aside from the above problems, I thoroughly enjoy the plane. It is an absolute delight to fly and is extremely stable in all weather conditions. Being located in the Pacific Northwest, I log a significant number of IFR and night operations and have found that the plane flies well in all conditions.

At the time I purchased the plane, the factory estimated that direct operating costs would be about $78.92 an hour. To date my figures have averaged $113.24 per hour. Fuel and oil have averaged $54.40 per hour, and maintenance costs $58.84 per hour. Maintenance costs are almost twice the cost of the factory estimate, but I believe this is due to the dramatic increase in the price of airplane parts since 1984.

After factoring in replacement reserves of approximately $25 per hour, I end up with a cost per flight hour of $138. This compares to Cessna's estimate of $103 per hour based on 1984 figures.

I maintain my plane to FAR 135 conditions, and normal 50-hour inspections run about $285 plus parts, while 100-hour inspections (annuals) have averaged $1,380 plus squawks.

Overall, I have been extremely pleased with the plane and its performance. Its short-field characteristics are excellent, and the trailing link landing gear system makes it almost impossible to botch a landing. In addition, compared to other light twins in its class, the stairway entrance door, large cabin area and emergency exit located by the copilot's seat are real plusses. The plane can also carry a tremendous amount of luggage, people, etc. and still remain safely within all CG and gross weight requirements.

Overall, I would rate the plane a solid eight on a scale of one to 10, and other than having to pay the extremely high cost of replacement parts, I have thoroughly enjoyed the plane over the last 700 hours.

William J. Allred
Portland, Ore.

Grumman Cougar

The Grumman American Cougar.

The macho aura that used to surround double-breasted airplanes has pretty much faded away into aviation's folklore, but the two-of-everything afforded by light twins remains a powerful attraction to many pilots.

The Grumman Cougar is a rare bird that offers systems redundancy for operating costs that are nearly on par with those of high-performance singles, and it provides good performance and flying characteristics, to boot.

Owners speak in near reverence of the low maintenance requirements of their Cougars and the continued support of the orphaned airplanes by Gulfstream Aerospace. Though they worry about how long the support will continue, there seems to be a fairly good supply of parts for the airplanes, at least for the near future.

The Cougar's relatively good, economical performance and forgiving flying characteristics also are points of pride among owners. They note

that the airplane is nearly as fast and efficient as the venerable Twin Comanche with none of that light twin's control problems, particularly the Piper's tendency under certain loading and asymmetric power conditions to enter a flat spin.

Indeed, some flight instructors believe that, because of its docility, the Cougar is unsuitable as a multi-engine trainer; it just doesn't have the bite to give students a proper glimpse of the potential white-knuckle experiences in multi-engine flying.

Into the Void

Grumman American's announcement that it was developing a light twin from scratch came late in 1974, two years after the demise (some would say premature) of the popular but quirky Twin Comanche. A Cougar prototype flew early in 1977 and won its type certificate in the fall. Deliveries of the Model GA-7 began in February 1978.

The Cougar was on the market only seven months before Grumman American Aviation Corp. was pur-

chased by Allen Paulson of American Jet Industries. Paulson made no bones about the fact that he had bought the company to acquire suitable facilities and trained workers to build his dreamplane—a weird bird called the Hustler, which had a turboprop engine in the nose, a jet in the tailcone and ultimately, went nowhere.

The Cougar's single-engine stable-mates (the T-Cat, Lynx, Cheetah Cheetah and Tiger) immediately were given the axe, but the light twin received a brief reprieve. All told, the Cougar remained in production for only about two years, and only 115 of the airplanes rolled off the assembly lines at Savannah (71 in 1978, 44 the next year).

In 1987, the sleek cats generally were fetching prices in the $35,000 to $45,000 range. Of course, you could pay less for a much-used-and-abused trainer that has been parked outside in the sun and rain all its life and still has the original Narco radios in its panel. On the other hand, we saw one pampered and unusually well-equipped Cougar whose owner hinted that he he might sell if someone waved $60,000 at him.

Points of Departure

Grumman American and Beech Aircraft Corp., with its Duchess, were head-to-head in the race to deliver a new light twin in the late 1970s, and Piper Aircraft Corp. was hot on their heels with the Seminole. Eventually, these airplanes, too, would have truncated production runs; but both the Duchess and Seminole outnumber the Cougar more than three to one.

In several ways the Cougar is different from the other two light twins. Rather than having lapped and riveted skins, the Cougar's sheet metal is bonded to the bulkheads and ribs forming its fuselage, empennage and wings. The result is a slicker airframe, a much smoother appearance and, as reported by owners, few problems with corrosion. In addition, the lower portions of the cabin fuselage are made of strong but lightweight aluminum honeycomb.

But the biggest difference is, of course, the Cougar's 160-hp Lycoming O-320 engines. The Duchess and Seminole have 180-hp O-360s. They also have counter-rotating propellers, which eliminate the critical-engine bugbear. Both of the Cougar's props turn clockwise; therefore, a pilot theoretically should have a tougher time dealing with a failure of the left (critical) engine, since the right prop takes a bigger bite and produces more asymmetric thrust than the left.

One Fan Fare

The Cougar, Duchess and Seminole are much alike in one area: single-engine performance. All three perform miserably after losing an engine on takeoff. The Cougar POH indicates that, at sea level on a standard day and at its gross weight of 3,800 pounds, the

airplane will climb at about 200 fpm on one engine, if the pilot does everything right (cobs the good engine, feathers the bad, gets the gear and flaps up, and so on). If a 200-fpm rate of climb doesn't sound all that bad, consider the Cougar's single-engine performance another way: that is, in terms of climb gradient. Under the conditions outlined above, the airplane will struggle upwards a mere 140 feet for every mile it travels over the ground.

With their 180-hp engines, the Duchess and Seminole don't do much better. Their single-engine rates-of-climb and climb gradients are, respectively: 235 fpm and 166 feet per mile; and 217 fpm and 148 feet per mile. That meager performance comes under standard conditions; lose an engine in any of the airplanes on takeoff from Denver on a hot day, and the numbers likely would have negative signs in front of them.

At gross and with one fan feathered, a Cougar will climb 50 fpm at 4,250 feet, maximum, under standard conditions. In comparison, the single-engine service ceilings of the Duchess and Seminole are 6,170 feet and 4,100 feet, respectively.

Good Manners

Although it does not perform well on one engine, the Cougar has good control characteristics, due to

Owners rave about cabin room, and even rear-seat passengers have more-than-average legroom. The aft seats fold down to handle up to 340 lbs. of baggage.

a large extent to the airplane's huge tail. Vmca, the minimum control speed with an engine out, is 61 knots—two knots below stall speed with landing gear and flaps extended. Stall strips on the leading edges of the modified laminar-flow NACA 63A-415 wing cause the wing roots to stall long before the tips.

We were given a demonstration of the Cougar's docile manners by Gil Stout of Flying Tigers in Marietta, Pa., a former Grumman dealer whose specialties still include Cougar sales and service. At 1,500 feet on a warm day, Stout shut down the right engine, feathered the prop and made a 45-degree turn into the dead engine. No problem. Then, he pulled the nose way up. The stall buzzer shrieked as the Cougar shook like . . . well, a wet cat. One wing dropped, then the other; but Stout was able to pick them up with the rudder each time. Meanwhile, we were sinking at about 500 fpm; but, throughout the demonstration, the airplane never gave any indication that it was about to do something nasty.

Because of limited elevator travel, it is difficult to stall a Cougar without abrupt control deflection. There is a trade-off, however. According

Although the props are not counter-rotating, the aircraft has extremely benign engine-out handling abilities.

to owners, a pilot making a power-off landing with full flaps in an airplane loaded toward its forward cg limit can run out of elevator authority in the flare and plunk down on all three wheels, especially if airspeed is a tad too high on approach.

Short-Field Standout

Despite this idiosyncrasy, owners report excellent short-field capabilities. One said he operates a Cougar regularly on a 1,490-foot grass strip. According to the POH, the Cougar can lift off and climb over a 50-foot obstacle within 1,850 feet; 1,330 feet are required for a landing over an obstacle. This performance is predicated, of course, on proper technique and on having both fans turning. Unfortunately, the Cougar's POH provides no data on accelerate-stop or accelerate-go performance. Such information is provided in Duchess and Seminole POHs, though.

Taxiing on crowded ramps and taxiways is a snap. The nosewheel can be steered with the rudder pedals to a deflection of about 17 degrees; beyond that, the nosewheel steering mechanism unlatches, and very tight turns can be made with differential braking and power.

Performance

Due to the normally aspirated, carbureted 160-hp engines, the Cougar delivers its best cruise performance down low. For example, the POH shows that in standard conditions at 6,000 feet, true airspeed is 156 knots at 75 percent power with a fuel burn of 16 gallons per hour when leaned to peak EGT. At 65 percent power, airspeed drops about 10 knots and fuel consumption about three gph.

A total of 114 usable gallons of fuel can be carried in the wing tanks. That's enough for a little more than six and a half hours of flying at 75 percent cruise power with an hour's worth of fuel for reserves.

Relatively high gear- and flap-extension speeds help in slowing the slippery airplane in the terminal area. The gear and 10 degrees of flap can be extended at 145 knots, indicated. At 110 knots, the flaps can be lowered all the way to 30 degrees. Pitch changes are nearly undetectable when the gear and flaps are operated. The Fowler-type flaps are electric, and the landing gear are operated by an electrically actuated hydraulic pump.

Creature Features

Owners rave about the spacious cabin, which provides plentiful head and elbow room, and even ample leg room for rear-seat passengers. All four seats have lap

belts and shoulder harnesses. Visibility through the large windows is excellent.

The Cougar has two baggage compartments. A maximum of 175 pounds can be carried behind the rear seats, but loading bulky items through the 14- by 28-inch door might pose a problem. The rear seats also can be folded to accommodate up to 340 pounds of baggage. The other baggage area is in the nose and has a maximum capacity of 75 pounds. A 24-inch-wide door on the right side of the nose provides access to the baggage area, as well as to the battery and any electronics equipment housed there.

The baggage areas and the large fuel tanks provide plenty of leeway in loading the airplane. Most Cougars have a useful load of about 1,230 pounds, enough for four passengers, their baggage and enough fuel for 3½ hours of flying.

Maintenance Considerations

As previously mentioned, owners report that their airplanes require very little care beyond normal maintenance and inspections. However, one airworthiness directive requires overhaul or replacement of the Hartzell propeller blades every five years or 1,500 hours in service. Two other ADs require periodic inspection and replacement of Bendix magneto blocks and paper induction air filters. In addition, the Cougar's type certification data sheet shows one life-limited component: the inboard wing spar assembly, which is limited to 5,705 hours.

Parts availability seems to be no problem at present. Gulfstream Aerospace maintains a stock of Cougar parts. A company spokesman said that although a buyer still is being sought for the orphaned light airplanes, Gulfstream will continue supporting the Cougar

Heir apparent to the Twin Comanche. Like it, the Cougar has 160-hp powerplants, but a better reputation for handling, and better landing qualities.

supporting the Cougar "as long as necessary." Other parts sources include Air Mods Northwest in Snohomish, Wash., Fletcher Aviation in Houston, Flying Tigers in Marietta, Pa., and Wag-Aero in Lyons, Wisc.

Only 33 service difficulty reports have been filed by Cougar mechanics in the six years from 1981 to 1987. Among them were several reports of cracked rudder bellcranks and elevator horns, deteriorated fuel transmitter floats and malfunctions in the landing-gear position-indicating system.

In addition, Ken Blackman of Air Mods NW told us he found a badly frayed elevator trim cable while installing soundproofing in a Cougar's tailcone. He said the damage probably would not have been spotted during a routine annual inspection. Blackman also advised that prospective Cougar buyers should inspect the wheelwells

carefully for rust. It appears that the wells in some of the airplanes were not primed correctly and can start to rust when water is slung into them by the wheels.

Poor craftmanship reportedly led to paint problems on many of the AA-1, AA-5 and GA-7 airplanes that were built in Savannah. "I rejected one airplane three times until the factory repainted it," one former dealer recalled. "It looked as if a drunk had laid out the stripes. And I have seen paint chipping off many of the airplanes Grumman American made."

Safety Record

NTSB had only two Cougar accidents in its files for the seven years from 1980 to 1987. One airplane crashed into Corpus Christi Bay, killing all four people aboard, during a night business flight in May 1980. The airplane was never recovered, and the probable cause of the accident remains undetermined.

The other accident occurred in November 1982 in Nebraska. The Cougar was on an air taxi flight

with two people aboard when it struck trees and crashed in a meadow during a VOR approach. The crash occurred on a dark night with a 200-foot, obscured ceiling and six-tenths of a mile visibility in fog and drizzle. The pilot suffered minor injuries; his passenger was killed. NTSB determined that the Cougar had dropped below the published minimum descent altitude during the approach and was then climbing when it hit the trees.

A check of the FAA's records revealed seven incidents during the past seven years. One Cougar settled and struck its props on a runway when the pilot retracted the gear on takeoff; but the damage was minor, and the pilot was able to bring the airplane around and land. Another airplane was not aligned with the runway when it touched down on a training flight, and it ground-looped and struck a VASI light.

One incident involved a Cougar that taxied into another airplane after being hand-propped. There were no injuries nor damage when another Cougar had a complete electrical failure on takeoff after

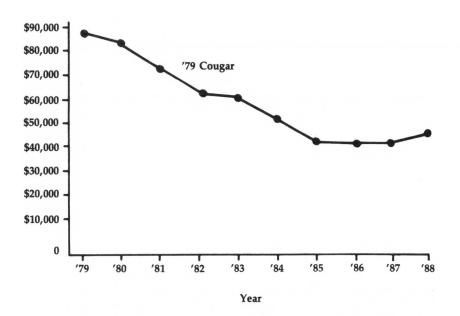

Cougar Resale Value Chart

'79 Cougar

Year

having been jump-started due to a dead battery. A broken gear-door hinge prevented the left main gear from locking on one airplane; the gear collapsed on landing, causing minor damage. Another Cougar made an uneventful single-engine landing during a training flight in which a propeller would not come out of its feathered position. The last incident also involved a single-engine landing; the pilot had shut down his left engine after a broken connecting rod punched a hole in the crankcase.

Belling the Cat

Systems redundancy—and the peace of mind that comes from having two alternators and two pneumatic pumps while shuttling about at night or in weather—probably is the best reason to

consider buying a light twin. And the Cougar seems to offer a lot of bang for the buck in this respect. In comparison, its more powerful contemporaries, the Duchess and Seminole, just don't seem to provide a sufficient edge on performance to match their higher acquisition, operating and maintenance costs.

However, the Cougar is an airplane in limbo. Although owners paint a rosy picture of current maintenance needs and costs, that picture could change. There's no way of telling if and when Gulfstream Aerospace will pull the plug on supporting its orphan airplanes. If that should happen, current stocks of parts for Cougars could dry up quickly.

And though the Cougar has earned an excellent (and in our opinion,

overstated) reputation for its docile handling qualities, its performance on one engine is no better (and in some cases, worse) than any other light twin. If you brush elbows with Cougar cognoscenti long enough, you're bound to hear of how so-and-so took off, circled the pattern and landed using only one engine. Such tales, even if true, deceptively ameliorate the exposure to high risk that a pilot of any piston twin is subjected to between lift-off and 50 feet above the runway. Prospective buyers should keep in mind that an engine failure on lift-off would require flawless pilot technique and result in definitely meager climb performance.

Therefore, a prospective buyer would be wise to weigh systems redundancy against the relative merits of a sophisticated single, such as an A36 Bonanza or Centurion of the same vintage, which cost about the same on the used market but fly faster, burn less fuel and carry more payload. But, if you just have to have a light twin, the Cougar certainly deserves a close look. Owners are supported by the American Yankee Assn., P.O. Box 11757, Fresno, Calif. 93774.

Owner Comments

My partner, Norman Radin, and I have had our Cougar about six years now. We traded up from a Twin Comanche because we were concerned that the airplane was just getting too old. We were having difficulty getting parts, and the avionics needed to be upgraded, which would have been very

Cost/Performance/Specifications

Model	Year	Number Built	Average Retail Price	Cruise Speed (kt)	Rate of Climb (fpm)	Std/Opt Load (lb)	Fuel (gal)	Engines	TBO (hr)	Overhaul Cost
GA-7	1978	71	$42,000	160	1,160	1,230	118	160-hp Lyc. O-320-D1D	2,000	$9,000
GA-7	1979	44	$44,500	160	1,160	1,230	118	160-hp Lyc. O-320-D1D	2,000	$9,000

expensive. When we decided to trade up, we looked for an economical light twin.

We looked at the Duchess and the Seminole and even considered an older one, the Travel Air. But we decided against the Travel Air, because I had owned a B-55 Baron earlier, and it proved to be a relatively more expensive airplane to maintain. The Duchess and Seminole did not seem to have the extra performance that would justify the maintenance on their larger engines. The Cougar appeared to offer more value.

We are very pleased with the Cougar. We had only one major problem in all the time we've had it, and that was damage to the rudder caused by a wind storm. It took a little longer than we would have liked to have the rudder replaced, but Gulfstream eventually came through with the parts. There was a problem at the factory, and it took about six weeks to get the parts. We also had a minor problem with water leaking into the nose baggage compartment. Other than that, we have had no problems. We have had very low maintenance costs on that airplane—unbelievably low.

I usually fly between 8,000 and 11,000 feet, the most efficient altitudes for the airplane, as close to 75 percent power as I can get and lean it back to the economy range. Almost always, I make my filed airspeed, 155 knots, and burn somewhere between 15 and 16 gallons an hour. And that's very close to what we used to get with the Twin Comanche; the numbers are very similar in terms of performance.

The Cougar is a much more stable airplane than the Twin Comanche and easier to fly. When it came to landings, the Twin Comanche seemed to have a mind of its own; you just couldn't grease it on every time. The Cougar is a very forgiving

airplane; it does just what you want it to do. The stall characteristics are very docile, and I really don't think you could spin the airplane, even if you wanted to. It's very light on the controls and lands very easily. It's also a wonderful instrument platform. Our insurance people told us the Cougar is the safest light twin flying, and they give a reduction in rates because of that.

It is a true four-place airplane. You can load four people and their baggage, and still carry enough fuel to have good range capability. The Cougar has a big cabin; it feels a lot like a Baron. You sit up high, and visibility is excellent. There's a lot of leg room, but, unfortunately, the rear seats don't recline.

We like the systems redundancy you get with a twin; and we're going to stick with the Cougar, because there is really nothing else that compares with it. The only thing I don't like is that it has only one landing light, which is on the nose gear. Therefore, you can't always show a light when you want to. I wish someone would offer an additional, recognition light in the nose or wing.

Allen Rothenberg
Washington, D.C.

I purchased my GA-7 in February 1986 with 1,060 total hours on the airframe and engine. Current TTA&E is 1,300 hours, and my total time to date is 500 hours. I transitioned to this twin from a Beech Sundowner, my first airplane, in 10 hours. I wanted a light twin for safety and security reasons (real or imagined), and I felt a light twin couldn't cost any more to fly than two singles. The GA-7 has had very few ADs, but this may reflect the small size of the fleet, rather than any real design and engineering superiority.

My Cougar has been a pleasure to own and easy to fly and maintain, compared to the other airplanes in

its class. Over all, workmanship and quality are on par with Piper and Cessna's airplanes, but certainly not up to Beech standards.

The Piper Seminole is much smaller, and the Beech Duchess wags it tail in turbulence like a Bonanza and is a maintenance hog.

The GA-7 is a large aircraft with room to spare in the cabin and rear-seat area, and it's fast. I trued out at 170 knots at 8,000 feet, firewalled with two people and half fuel on a cool day. At 24 inches and 2,400 rpm, it averages 145 to 155 knots. It does everything well on one engine, except climb fast.

In 250 hours, I have had to replace both vacuum pumps (originals), and a starter solenoid stuck, broiling the starter. That was my fault for not shutting off the master switch after takeoff, but I needed my lights as it was a night flight. I've also installed new brake linings, new tires and a new strobe power pack. I used a Whalen, which works fine; the original Grimes would have cost three times as much to replace. I was plagued by absent and erratic oil pressure indications until I discovered the gauge cluster wasn't grounded properly and added a separate ground wire, solving the problem.

I've changed the oil filters and oil every 50 hours, using both Aeroshell and Phillips multi. During the past 100 hours, I've used Shell in the right engine and Phillips in the left; the airplane uses 10 percent less Shell, and the oil stays cleaner longer. I changed the lower spark plugs to a long-reach type, which seem to have solved a problem I had with fouling on 100 LL avgas.

The plane actually has cost very little to own and maintain. It uses between 16 and 19 gph; and it is a pleasure to fly and easy to land. In my estimate, the Cougar is probably the best light twin ever built.

Parts have not been a problem. Gulfstream Aerospace supplied plastic wing root fairings within two to three weeks and claims to be able to supply any other parts I may need. Wag-Aero and Dave Fletcher also have a good supply of parts, so I don't think there will be any worse parts problem with the Cougar than with any other aircraft.

As you may have guessed by now, I am very happy with my GA-7 and would buy another one. They are certainly a good value on the used market.

E. Weitzman
Medford, N.J.

I purchased a 1978 Grumman Cougar in May 1985 and sold the plane in June 1987. During the time I owned the airplane, it was flown approximately 250 hours. The Lycoming 160-horsepower O-320 engines required no maintenance other than routine oil changes and air filters. One muffler developed a small crack, which I discovered while examining carbon deposits on the heater hoses. I removed the muffler and had it welded for $20.

Other repairs to the aircraft were fairly minor. There was considerable wind noise from the door, so I had an FBO order and install a door seal. They put it on backwards, so I ended up doing the job over again. In addition, I had to have the struts aired, the wheel bearings repacked, the brake pads replaced twice and the spark plugs changed. The Hartzell two-blade propeller has an AD that requires inspection or overhaul every five years. I had an overhaul done by Hartzell in Piqua, Ohio; the cost, including removal and reinstallation, was just over $2,000.

Annual inspections, which I helped to do with the assistance and guidance of an A&I, cost $200 per year. I removed all inspection covers, the tail cone, engine cowlings, etc. The A&I merely had to inspect the various components.

Operating costs during the two years I owned the Cougar are summarized below:

	Year 1	Year 2
Insurance	$2,577	$2,562
Parts and repairs	$455	$911
Radio repairs	$238	$276
Annual inspection	$200	$200
Hangar rental	$2,400	$2,400
Total	**$5,870**	**$6,349**
Cost per hour (125 hr/year)	$46.96	$50.79

The figures above do not include a propeller overhaul. Compliance with the AD would merely have required an inspection, which would have cost approximately $700. The purchaser, however, wanted the prop overhauled before he bought the airplane.

During the two years I owned the Cougar, I found the airplane easy to fly, stable and forgiving. The autopilot made cross-country flying a breeze. I flew the airplane at 23 inches and 2,300 rpm, or about 70 percent power, because I found higher power levels substantially increased noise in the cockpit. Fuel consumption averaged 14 to 16 gallons per hour, and the aircraft burned about one quart of oil every 20 hours.

Overall, it would be almost impossible to beat the Cougar in terms of reliability, economy and safety. It probably is the best "first twin" to own.

Name withheld by request

Maybe I'm a bit of a rebel, but I always go for airplanes that give the best performance for the dollar.

Therefore, I go with the Grummans, the Mooneys and the Aerostars. In my opinion, the Cougar is the best buy for the money. Overall, the costs of operating a Mooney 201 and a Cougar are about the same. A Cougar burns about four gallons more gas an hour for approximately the same speed.

For the extra fuel, you have complete systems redundancy, and on top of that, it takes less maintenance. The 201 almost never makes it to its 1,800-hour TBO; 1,500 hours is more likely. On the other hand, the Cougar's Lycomings usually have no problem getting to 2,000 hours or more. I think anyone in the market for a used Mooney ought to take a good look at the Cougar, first.

We service about 15 of them here at Flying Tigers. To date the only airframe parts we've put in have been tires, brakes, light bulbs and batteries. I still have almost the complete inventory of parts I was required to buy from the factory back in 1977 to be a Grumman dealer. The only thing I've used out of that is one throttle cable so far. I've been in this business going on 30 years, and I've never had any problem getting Grumman parts. To be honest, the Grummans use fewer parts than any other airplane I've maintained.

We use our own Cougar for multi-engine training. It's got 2,000 hours on it and has never been in the hangar. The paint is chipped and faded; but, mechanically, it's excellent. We change the oil every 100 hours, put in a new set of spark plugs every 400 hours, replace the brake linings about every 200 hours and, occasionally, put in a new light bulb or battery; but that's it. It's got Lycoming O-320-Ds, which are just excellent engines. The Slick magnetos require no more maintenance than Bendix mags; except that, when they were introduced, they were a throwaway mag, and there are too many mechanics who still consider them as throwaways and don't take a good look at them, first.

The Cougar was designed from the beginning as a twin; the other so-called light twins are adaptations of singles. The Seminole is an Arrow they put two engines on; the Duchess is a twin Musketeer. The Cougar has a lot of things the others don't have. For instance, if you lose both the mechanical and the electrical fuel pump in the right wing, you can keep both engines running by going to double cross feed. The pumps correspond to the tanks, not to the engines.

When I get out of this business, I'm going to take a Cougar and rebuild it from the ground up to keep as my own personal airplane.

Gil Stout
Marietta, Pa.

Piper Seminole

One of the few light twins still in production, the Piper Seminole is a delight to fly and serves a valuable purpose as an economical twin for multi training. But potential buyers should be aware of a flaw in its makeup: It shares the engine tappet deterioration problems that has caused so many maintenance headaches in the Cessna Skyhawk's O-320-H powerplant.

The Seminole has nice lines and pleasant handling qualities. The fuel tanks are in the engine nacelles. The nose compartment carries a heater but no baggage and no radar.

Introduced in 1979 as a multi version of the T-tailed Arrow, the Seminole was rolled out the factory doors at Vero Beach, Fla. in numbers that were never to be matched in following years. Piper delivered 142 that first year; 55 the second, and 37 in 1981, but only three were sold during the first seven months of 1984. In 1980, a turbo version was brought out; about 70 of these were built the first two years, but only seven were delivered in the first seven months of 1984.

The Multi Rationale

Except for twin-engine training, justification for a small twin like the Seminole (and the Beech Dutchess, for that matter) flunks the test of reason. With only a 161-knot cruise, the Seminole is slower than the single-engine Mooney 201, Beech Bonanza, Cessna 210 and Piper Lance, for example. Its max useful load of 1,462 pounds (51 pounds higher in the turbo version) is surpassed by that of the Beech A36 Bonanza, Cessna 210 and Stationair 6, Cherokee 6 and Lance, to name a few. And all these singles burn less fuel and are saddled with half the engine and prop maintenance and overhaul expenses.

Investment Value

Most aircraft worth their investment salt bottom out in about four

years and begin to move back upward. A 1979 Seminole, which cost $105,195 (average equipped) when new, might bring $45,000 in 1985; and a 1982 turbocharged model that originally sold for $169,940, would command about $93,000.

Handling and Performance

The aircraft reacts pleasantly to the pilot's touch. The ailerons are light and the controls nicely harmonized. Pitch trim is very slow, however. Positioning the flaps either up or down induces no change in aircraft pitch. The flaps, incidentally, are set by means of Piper's traditional manual lever, which is effective, simple and sensible.

Since multi training is likely to make up a large part of the Seminole's regimen, student pilots will be happy to learn they can forget about the critical engine on this aircraft because the engines are counter-rotating. Vmc minimum control speed is a low 56 knots, though Piper provides a healthy 26-knot margin to Vsse safe single-engine speed. This is the speed below which Piper says no practice engine-out work should be initiated. Stalls give plenty of warning buffet, and that little T-tail actually has the authority to get a real stall break.

To achieve its rather sensational promotional spec numbers for takeoff performance over a 50-foot

obstacle, however, Piper employs a rather smaller margin, using a liftoff speed of only 63 knots at gross, and 25 degrees of flaps. Result: a stupendous 1,400-foot takeoff distance for obstacle clearance, vs. a much more modest 2,119-foot distance for the Seminole's big competitor, the Beech Duchess. The Duchess figures, however, are predicated on normal takeoff procedures, lifting off at 71 knots.

The Seminole's 1,400-foot landing stretch over the obstacle cannot be argued away, however, since the 75-knot approach speed calls for a very similar 76 knots on approach. And the landing figures over an obstacle for the Duchess are a much lazier 1,881 feet.

To be fair, it must be conceded that the Seminole has a good, effective set of flaps that can provide a nice, steep approach—not that this is anything special for most twins, of course. Count on a little over 700 nm range in this bird with full tanks and reserves.

Load and Comfort

The Seminole is not quite as beamy

and airy as the Duchess, and it lacks the nice triple-entry doors (one on each wing and a cargo/cabin door on the left rear of the Beech twin). In fact, it has standard Piper Arrow dimensions. The baggage compartment also is identical, and takes 200 pounds structurally in the rear of the cabin. There is no baggage compartment in the nose.

However, our calculations showed that the aircraft would be difficult to load beyond the weight and balance envelope toward the rear. On one sample aircraft we computed that a full 200 pounds of baggage could be loaded aft, then a full load of fuel pumped in, a single pilot plumped down on the front seat, and the rear pair of seats burdened with the remaining 272 pounds of useful load—and still be within limits. That's reassuring.

Accident History

Inspection of accident and incident data from the National Transportation Safety Board and FAA files shows the greatest number of problems on the Piper Seminole stemmed from inadvertent gear-up landings. We counted 14 of these prior to 1982, with a significant proportion relating to mixed-signals during dual flight instruction. In three cases the instructor had pulled the landing gear circuit breaker as a test of emergency procedures. In another instance the gear had been left up, and forgotten, as part of a simulated single-engine landing.

Second largest number of accidents was generated by collapsing landing gear, mostly the nose gear, with seven of these noted, and attributed to mechanical problems.

Specific failures noted were: three

Seminole Resale Value Chart

'79 Seminole

cases of a broken bolt in nose gear linkage; elongated drag brace bearings, nose gear retract piston out of rig, and bolt missing from drag link assembly. On top of that there were two hard landings, one of which resulted in the wheel being broken off and props damaged.

Then came a small number of engine problems—four—with half of those not traced to any specific mechanical problem. In one instance the aircraft had made a forced landing after an oil leak was noted in the right prop. In another case a precautionary engine shutdown was made due to low oil pressure. In those crashes where no mechanical engine problem could be traced, one pilot attempting a go-around experienced a rough engine, and another detected a power loss during a maximum-performance takeoff and landed before the gear had extended.

In two cases Seminoles crashed when the instructor pulled an

engine on takeoff during an emergency test. There were also two crashes because of fuel exhaustion, one undershoot, and several taxi accidents.

We counted only three fatal accidents, altogether. One occurred when the pilot, wearing a cast on his right hand, flew into the ground on a visual approach with fog and rain in the area. Another Seminole struck some trees and crashed. It was over gross, there were thunderstorms in the area, and it had been stolen and was on an illegal drug flight. The final fatal crash occurred when the aircraft ditched into the ocean after fuel exhaustion.

Despite the fact that the aircraft is equipped with carburetors instead of fuel injection, we found no accidents related to carburetor icing.

Mechanical Problems

The predominant area of mechanical shortcomings in the Piper

Cost/Performance/Specifications

Model	Year	Number Built	Average Retail Price	Cruise Speed (kts)	Useful Load (lbs)	Rate of Climb (fpm)	SE Rate of Climb (fpm)	SE Ceiling (ft)	Fuel (gals)	Engine	TBO (hrs)	Overhaul Cost (each)
PA-44-180	1979	142	$40,500	161	1,462	1,340	217	4,100	110	180-hp Lyc. O-360-E1AD	2,000	$ 9,000
PA-44-180	1980	26	$45,000	161	1,462	1,340	217	4,100	110	180-hp Lyc. O-360-E1AD	2,000	$ 9,000
PA-44-180	1981	7	$51,000	161	1,462	1,340	217	4,100	110	180-hp Lyc. O-360-E1AD	2,000	$ 9,000
PA-44-180T	1981	59	$65,000	180	1,513	1,290	180	12,500	110	180-hp Lyc. TO-360-E1A6D	1,800	$11,500
PA-44-180T	1982	NA	$74,500	183	1,513	1,290	180	12,500	110	180-hp Lyc. TO-360-E1A6D	1,800	$11,500

Seminole appears to be one made notorious by the O-320-H engine in the Cessna Skyhawk: spalling tappets and camshafts. It turns out that the Seminole's Lycoming O-360-E engines have the same tappets used in the by now much publicized Lycoming O-320-H.

The FAA's Service Difficulty Reports for the Seminole disclosed that tappet and camshaft spalling problems formed the largest single entry block of user problems, with 43 cases, and another 11 instances of camshaft spalling, lobes flattened, etc. and discovery of metal shavings in the oil filters.

If one applies the FAA's rule of thumb suggesting that only about 10 percent of actual problems are reported, some 430 engines or 215 aircraft conceivably could be affected, statistically, at least. Of course, only some 246 Seminoles were built and delivered, by our count, when the report was issued.

Indeed, Airworthiness Directive 80-04-03 suggests that the Seminole engine may be prey to at least some of the catalog of grief that has befallen the O-320-H engines. This AD brings the Seminole's O-360-E engines under some of the same corrective orders, "to prevent excessive wear and oil system contamination associated with hydraulic lifters spalling . . ." Required are addition of Lycoming's special lubricant every 50 hours and inspection for metal contaminants in the oil every 100 hours.

Since Lycoming has brought out larger hydraulic lifters (tappets) to combat the spalling problems, along with "improved" crankcases to house them, this now confronts Seminole owners with the same unhappy decision O-320-H owners face at overhaul time: Should they risk overhauling an engine with the old tappets, or spend more on the new tappet/crankcase combination?

In terms of sheer volume, at least, the Seminole's number two problem area suggested by the Service Difficulty Reports involves cracked carburetor air boxes (37 reports)

and carburetor heat shrouds cracked (16 reports).

Number three is leaking landing gear actuator cylinders (24 reports), and four is landing gear trunions cracked, sheared and worn (23 reports). Next come 22 reports of elevator trim cables fraying, many of the problems occurring in the tail cone near the electric trim motor and windlass. In a couple of instances mechanics suggested there was too much tension on the cable and that perhaps a limit switch was needed. The next largest category involves cracked or broken engine mounts, with 18 reported.

Pilots shopping for used Seminoles might also take care to look for instances of cracking aileron spars, ribs or rib noses, since there were 15 reports of this type of problem, along with another 10 telling about loose aileron control attach fittings or the spars themselves moving at the pushrod attachments.

Other potential problem areas spotlighted by the SDRs: nose cone spar assemblies cracking (in six of the 11 cases reported this occurred at the bottom holes for the drag brace mounting plate); cracked firewalls (12 cases reported); fuel primer lines broken, cracked or chafed (eight instances); as well as the discovery of pieces of the fuel pump return spring found broken in the prop governor cavity and fuel pump cavity (10 cases). Shoppers should also be on the lookout for problems with throttle cables binding, breaking or seizing (13 reports) and finally crankcase cracks (10 of these noted).

An awkward power gauge arrangement splits the tachometers to the left of the throttle quadrant, the manifold pressure gauge to the right. The cowl flap levers below the throttle bank are well suited to the pilot's touch, however.

Airworthiness Directives

A significant portion of the problems revealed by service difficulties in the field, which we discussed above, have been dealt with by ADs. Hence, there are ADs on the following topics: binding throttle control cable fix, fuel primer mod kit (to prevent a fire hazard from leaking lines), replacement of the downlock hook and bushing to prevent nose gear retraction on landing, a fix to prevent binding of the aileron push rod and possible loss of aileron control, a mod of the nose cone spar to prevent cracks and possible malfunction of the landing gear, a mod to reduce aileron spar deflection and cracking and loss of aileron control, and reinforcement of aileron skins to prevent cracks on the outside leading edges.

In addition to the engine AD for the tappet problem we already discussed, there is another AD calling for replacement of certain types of upper exhaust valve spring seats to prevent valve failure. And one calls for replacement of the oil pump impeller and shaft to prevent pump failure.

Service Bulletins

Along with Piper SBs corresponding to the above ADs, there was one other worth noting, calling for replacement of the carburetor air box rivets. The SB notes that if the attach rivets shear in the carb air box flapper valve bushings, the heat flapper valve could jam, putting the carb heat out of action.

In addition, a service letter was issued by Piper providing for reinforcement of engine baffles, to prevent cracks; replacement of the nose landing gear micro switch bracket to improve the reliability of the gear position indicating system by reducing the need for frequent adjustments of the up-limit micro switch. Buyers might check to see if these nonmandatory fixes were incorporated.

Owner Comments

We were probably among the first FBOs to put the Seminole on the line as a working airplane. Prior to the PA44, the alternative for a twin trainer was either an Apache, the 310, or possibly an early Seneca I. For a variety of reasons all are unacceptable. The Seminole proved to be the perfect airplane for twin training, rental, and light charter work. Our maintenance costs have been quite low, the machine is exceptionally easy to fly, and has proven to be the *safest* light twin imaginable.

Our observations: Performance: In most areas the PA44 will better the handbook specs. We have consistently flown the airplane at max gross weight with no noticeable decrease in performance. The 1,400-pound useful load is exceptional. It is not unusual to achieve 1,400-1,500 fpm climb rates at full gross weight. With two pax, cruise at 75 percent will run 172 KTAS and about 18.5 gph, using the EGT. Landing and takeoff distances can be improved by 10 percent or so with good pilot technique.

Handling: Exceptional. The smoothest flying light twin I've ever flown. The airplane is as easy

Toujour velour, the interior is posh, but the optional headrests play havoc with rearward visibility.

to land as the Warrior, which I consider to be the truest airplane to land on the market. Single-engine handling is straightforward and honest. Go-arounds are a piece of cake from any point in the approach—a considerable change from the sweaty-palm go-rounds in the Apache, etc.

Comfort: Our bird is the plush version with soundproofing, which creates about the lowest cockpit noise level I've experienced. The low sound level makes the PA44 particularly suited for instruction, also a nice touch for charter customers.

Maintenance: Our airplane has been virtually maintenance-free. The engines are now above 1,900 hours and we have not topped the first cylinder. Compression and oil consumption would indicate we'll get at least 2,200 hours or so before overhaul will be required. (Excepting our Part 135 use, of course.) Parts, since the PA44 is mostly a conglomerate of other Piper planes, have been absolutely no problem. The only unique problem we've encountered was the replacement of the left engine throttle cables, which grounded the airplane one day!

In the maintenance area the Seminole has been a most pleasant surprise. We find the cost of a 100-hour inspection to be about that of an Arrow; i.e., in the $600-$800 range.

Turbo Seminole: Although we are not operating a Turbo PA44, I think the machine worth particular mention. Through our sales work with the turbo version we were all quite impressed by its cruise speed and range. It is not uncommon in a mid-weight airplane to see cruise speeds in the 190-knot area, and at a fuel flow of approximately 19-20 gph when leaned using the EGT. And 190 knots on 19 gph definitely is not bad!

All in all, the PA44 is a fine airplane for what it is intended. It *is not* a heavy IFR airplane when icing is about. It *is not* a big, roomy airplane like the Seneca or Saratoga series. What it is is a comfortable, quiet, four-place bird, with excellent speed and outstanding range.

It is a shame that the machine did not carve out a better niche for itself with the flying public and FBO operators. For the "sophisticated single" owner who's looking for a "step-up" airplane I can't imagine a better choice.

Our bird has averaged over 55 hours/month and has, on occasion, flown over 100 hours/month with an absolute minimum of worry. It is also one of the few twins I'd feel comfortable renting--even to "qualified" customers.

Jack Doub, Pres.
H&D Aviation, Inc.
Terre Haute, Ind.

Beech Duchess

In 1974, Beech's designers — beset with the task of creating a step-up plane for the Beech Aero Centers — started laying the groundwork for a simple, yet advanced, light twin based on the Beech Sierra design. The prototype sported a T-tail, two doors (a la Sundowner), and a pair of conventional-rotating 160-hp Lycomings (which were later replaced by counter-rotating 180-hp engines). Forty-four months after its inception, the Model 76 Duchess attained FAA type certification and began rolling off the Liberal, Kansas assembly lines.

No sooner had the Duchess hit the market, of course, when the light-twin arena suddenly became quite crowded, what with the Grumman Cougar's debut in 1978 and the arrival of Piper's Seminole in 1979. (Cessna's T303 Crusader — nee Clipper — was to have been an entrant in the light-light-twin derby, but Cessna thought better of the move at the last minute and reconfigured the T303 as a Seneca-class medium hauler.) Nonetheless, Beech's Aero Centers quickly placed orders for over 200 of the bonded-construction T-twins; today, there are more than 430 Model 76s in operation, though none were sold in 1983 or 1984.

Novel Construction

Although the Duchess's lines clearly relfect its Musketeer ancestry, the Model 76 is anything but a double-breasted Sierra in actual construction. The Sierra's outward-retracting gear design was abandoned in the Duchess, for example, along with the Mooney-style rubber shock biscuits. (The Duchess displays a pair of mega-

lithic oleo shocks on the main gear, while the nose strut is taken *in toto* from the A36 Bonanza.) Like the Sierra, the Duchess has bonded wet wings; but unlike the other Aero Center airplanes, the Model 76's main tanks extend to the wing-tips, carrying 50 gallons usable (each). Also, the Duchess's ailerons are bigger (and travel farther) than the Sierra's.

In the fuselage, extensive use was made of honeycomb-sandwich construction techniques, to produce a light, crashworthy, and at the same time, vibration/noise-resistant cabin. A feature unique among twins is the Duchess's cabin door configuration (borrowed from the Sierra): there are doors and walkways for both pilot *and* co-pilot, plus a large baggage door on the left aft fuselage behind the wing.

T-tail Trade-offs

The Duchess's most distinctive design hallmark, however, is its T-tail. Although considered by many to be merely a stylistic (i.e., marketing) device, the T-tail actually contributes in meaningful ways to the airplane's performance. Because the horizontal surfaces are out of the propellers' slip-streams and sit far to the rear atop a *swept* tail fin, their effectiveness is enhanced; and as a result, the horizontal tail area can be reduced — with a commensurate reduction in drag — at no penalty in pitch control. (In fact, the pitch authority of the Duchess tail is so great than the

The first (and most expensive) of the new-generation light twins, the Duchess is now available on the used market at prices under $75,000 (for 1978 models) — less than half what a fully equipped 1982 Duchess costs.

original prototype experienced problems with excessively high nose angles in stalls. This problem was ameliorated, however, with the switch to heavier, 180-hp engines from the earlier 160-hp Lycomings.) As a side benefit, prop-wash buffet is also eliminated.

The real-world payoff of the T-tail for the Duchess can be measured in terms of pitch control in the flare (excellent), allowable c.g. range (10.9 inches total), versus 8.3 for the Sierra), and the amount of trim change needed after gear or flap deployment (little, if any). The T-tail's end-plate effect also contributes to rudder effectiveness, providing a low single-engine minimum control speed (Vmc) of 67 knots CAS, which is one knot below the airplane's clean stall speed (Vs) of 68 KCAS. (In a twin-engine plane, it is desirable from a safety/controllability standpoint to encounter the stall at an airspeed higher than Vmc.) Of course, these benefits do not come without a modest weight penalty for the added structure needed to carry the lofty horizontal stabilizer — estimated by Beech, in this case, at 15 pounds.

Since the Model 76's introduction, few substantive design changes have been made (although myriad minor adjustments have been incorporated in later models and published as service bulletins; see below). In early 1979, improved door locks became standard and cowl flap hinges were changed from aluminum to steel; in mid-1980, an improved engine mount was introduced; in 1981, a landing gear horn muting system (to keep the horn from sounding prematurely during high-speed power-off letdowns) was introduced. For 1982, Beech increased the number of static wicks from five to 12. Overall, the design of the Model 76 remains virtually unchanged since 1978 — a testament, perhaps, to the airplane's basic soundness.

Performance

Owners praise the Duchess as a capable medium-range cross-country machine, with 75-percent power cruise speeds typically in the 160-knot region at fuel flows of just under 10 gallons per hour per engine. To underscore the plane's economy-of-operation appeal (for a twin, at least), Beech, in 1982, appended a "super economy" cruise performance page to the Duchess handbook, claiming a 142-knot speed at 14,000 feet, with props at 2,100 rpm and manifold pressures at 18.0 inches (fuel consumption: 6.8 gph/engine). We doubt that anyone would choose to operate the plane in that fashion, but the point is well taken: this *is* a bona fide economy twin.

With a maximum takeoff weight of 3,900 pounds (100 pounds more than the normally aspirated Piper Seminole — 25 pounds *less* than the Turbo Seminole), the Duchess turns in rather mediocre takeoff numbers; to wit, a sea level ground roll of 1,017 feet and a 50-foot

obstacle clearance distance of 2,119 feet — no better than the Travel Air (Beech's original 180-hp twin) and actually quite a bit worse than the competition (Piper's Seminole gets off and over in 880 feet and 1,400 feet, respectively, assuming we can believe Piper's numbers).

On landing, the comparisons with Brand 'P' are even more striking: the Duchess rolls a full 1,000 feet after touchdown at gross weight, versus the Seminole's 590 feet. With heavy-duty brakes, the Seminole will — according to Piper — roll a mere *383 feet* after a no-wind touchdown. One wonders whether Piper's tape measures are made in the U.S.

Rotation speed in the Duchess comes at 71 knots, which corresponds with Beech's "intentional one engine inoperative speed" (Vsse) as well as with the two-engine best angle of climb speed (Vx). Upon attaining 85 knots (the best rate of climb speed for single- *or* all-engine operation), a full-throttle climbout yields a 1,248-fpm rate of ascent initially, decaying to 1,000 fpm at 4,000 feet.

The Duchess's single-engine performance specs are nothing to write home about — although, of course, the same is true for other twins in this category. On one engine, the Duchess turns in an anemic 235-fpm sea-level climb rate at gross (vs. a complexion-whitening 217 fpm for the Seminole and 180 fpm for the Turbo Seminole). The climb dwindles to 50 fpm at the single-engine service ceiling of 6,170 feet (vs. 4,100 feet for the lighter-gross-weight Seminole — again, a question of whose numbers you believe).

The usable fuel capacity of 100 gallons gives the Duchess an en-

durance, at 75-percent cruise, of around four hours with IFR reserves. The published range (with reserves) varies from 623 nautical miles to upwards of 800 nautical, depending on whether 75-percent cruise or "super-economy" power settings are used.

All in all, the Duchess's performance is on a par with — and in most cases no better than — that of the 1958 Travel Air. Which raises the obvious question: Why would Beech go to the trouble and expense of certifying a *new* 180-hp light twin when it could just as easily have revived the Travel Air, a proven (and much-loved by some) design?

When we put this question to a Beech spokesman some years ago, he answered by saying that the Travel Air was and is a complicated design, expensive to produce (as are Barons that derive from that same type certificate); the Duchess employs state-of-the-art materials and construction techniques, affording a lighter airframe (by about 200 pounds, compared to the Model 95); and in designing the Duchess, Beech had the opportunity to create a twin with truly superior slow-speed handling characteristics.

All of which is true. We can only lament the fact that Beech's efforts did not result in a twin with a lower price tag. A new 1982 Duchess sold for a whopping $171,875 (average-equipped) — two and a half times the cost of a comparably equipped new Travel Air in 1968.

Handling and Comfort

The Duchess is nothing if not comfortable. Although the cockpit tapers noticeably just forward of the pilots' thighs, the Bonanza-like

Cost/Performance/Specifications ─────────────

Model	Year	Number Built	Cruise Speed (kts)	Useful Load (lbs)	Rate of Climb (fpm)	SE Rate Climb (fpm)	SE Ceiling (ft)	Fuel (gals)	Engine	TBO (hrs)	Overhaul Cost	Average Price
76	1978	72	115	1,450	1,248	235	6,170	100	180-hp Lyc. O-360-A1G6D	2,000	$9,500	$43,000
76	1979	213	115	1,450	1,248	235	6,170	100	180-hp Lyc. O-360-A1G6D	2,000	$9,500	$48,000
76	1980	84	115	1,450	1,248	235	6,170	100	180-hp Lyc. O-360-A1G6D	2,000	$9,500	$53,000
76	1981	55	115	1,450	1,248	235	6,170	100	180-hp Lyc. O-360-A1G6D	2,000	$9,500	$58,000
76	1982	11	115	1,450	1,248	235	6,170	100	180-hp Lyc. O-360-A1G6D	2,000	$9,500	$68,000
76	1983	None	--	--	--	--	--	--		--	--	--

head room and 44-inch cabin width (the cabin is wider, amazingly, than that of the Baron) contribute to the feeling that one is actually flying a much larger airplane. The accommodations are strictly first-class.

Pilots transitioning to the Duchess from single-engine aircraft will appreciate the fact that the plane's panel layout (with the exception of the vertically displaced tachometers) is both logical and eye-pleasing. Gear and flap switches are where they should be — gear on the left, flaps on the right — as are the power levers (mercifully, Beech abandoned the irksome center-panel ''prop/throttle/mixture'' grouping found on the Barons and placed these controls in the standard TPM arrangement in the Duchess).

Starting the Duchess's carbureted O-360s is easy enough if you remember to press *in* on the ignition switch while cranking, to engage the primer (a solenoid-operated system which, mysteriously, feeds fuel only to cylinders one, two and four of each engine).

On the ground, the Duchess handles a bit differently from its Piper counterpart. The slow damping action of the main gear oleos — combined with the plane's large spanwise mass distribution — gives the Duchess a curiously ponderous feel while taxiing, even setting up a Dutch-roll-like oscillation as one goes around corners. Likewise, the slightest touch of the brake pedals tends to collapse the nose oleo. These idiosyncracies are basically harmless, however.

On takeoff, the Duchess requires a positive tug on the yoke to break ground (not too much, though, or you'll overrotate). Thanks to the counter-rotating props, there is no need to correct for torque or P-factor. In the air, visibility is excellent. In fact, the nose slopes away so precipitously that it is difficult, at first, to judge the plane's angle of attack.

Unlike the Aero Center singles upon which the Model 76 design is

Twin doors make for easy entry and egress — and twice the opportunity for in-flight door openings, although the Duchess has had no problems in this area as yet. A third door (for cargo) is located aft of the left wing.

based, the Duchess has no rudder-aileron interconnect — nor is one needed. The controls are light (as twins go) and well-harmonized, inviting comparisons with such single-engine aircraft as the Bonanza and Saratoga. Stability is excellent in the pitch and roll modes; yaw is less good, with some tendency toward short-period waggle in turbulence. Overall, however, the plane is decidedly well-behaved.

An interesting quirk of the airplane is its maximum gear-*raise* speed of 113 knots, occasioned by the design of the forward-retracting nose strut. Once the gear has been lowered (as a speed brake, say), it cannot be raised again until airspeed has been allowed to bleed off to under 113 knots.

Safety

According to NTSB records, as of 1982 there had been only six accidents involving Duchesses since the aircraft was introduced in 1978, two of them fatal. (Interestingly, only one of the six pilots involved was over the age of 33.)

• One Duchess was destroyed (and the two persons aboard killed) on a VFR flight from Long Beach to

Ramona, Calif. when the aircraft encountered zero-visibility weather and collided with the ground in a controlled descent.

• A Duchess sustained heavy damage on a training flight from Little Rock, Ark. when the flight instructor allowed his student to land gear-up.

• Confusion in the cockpit resulted in another gear-up landing (again with substantial damage) —this time in Sioux City, Iowa — when an instructor told his student to cancel a practice single-engine go-around. The CFI landed the plane wheels up.

• Inclement weather claimed a noninstrument-rated Duchess pilot with 20 hours in type on a flight from Wyoming to Salt Lake City. The aircraft crashed out of control at night, in icing conditions.

The Duchess panel is visually quiet, with a place for everything and everything in its place. Power levers are in the standard throttle-prop-mixture arrangement. (Flap switch, not visible, is next to the copilot's yoke.)

• A hard landing in icing conditions caused major damage to a Duchess on a January nighttime arrival in South Bend, Ind. Four people escaped serious injury.

• Fuel exhaustion and fuel mismanagement were mentioned in the description of "probable cause" for a double-engine-stoppage accident. The 24-year-old pilot had departed Monmouth, N.J. for West Chicago, Ill., nonstop, against undetermined headwinds; substantial damage occurred when the plane, out of fuel, made an off-airport landing near its intended destination.

Note: Perhaps it's worth mentioning that none of the 12 persons involved in the four non-fatal accidents cited above suffered serious injuries. (Perhaps it's worth observing, too, that although weather radar is available as an option on the Duchess, anti-icing equipment of the type that might have prevented two of these accidents is not.)

Slow-Speed Traits

True to the designers' original intentions, the Duchess excels at low-speed controllability — with or without both fans turning. Pitch, roll, and yaw control remain crisp at speeds near blue-line (85 KIAS), and — thanks to the presence on the center pedestal of trim knobs for ailerons, rudder, *and* elevator — the plane trims up quickly for hands-off flight after shutting down either engine. (Handling is the same with either engine out, of

course; there is no "critical" engine.)

Stalls are conventional in all respects, except that the controls remain surprisingly effective at vanishingly low airspeeds. With both engines developing power, the airplane can be flown well below 50 knots IAS, dirty, without stalling.

One of the nice aspects of the T-tail is that, since it sits high above the wing's wake, it doesn't "feel" disturbances caused by lowering/raising the gear or flaps. On deploying the landing gear (at up to 140 knots) or flaps (up to 110 knots), there is no noticeable change in pitch attitude.

Maintenance

From a reliability standpoint, the Duchess has one thing going for it that the Seminole does not: namely, the A-series Lycoming O-360 engine. Unlike the E-series O-360s installed in the Seminole, the Model 76's O-360-A1G6D engines are among Lycoming's oldest and most proven O-360 variants, utterly worthy of the 2,000-hr. TBO bestowed upon them. The Piper Seminole's O-360-E1A6D engines, on the other hand, are a more recent design with valve train components common to the infamous O-320-H "Blue Streak" engine of Skyhawk fame. As almost everyone knows by now, the O-320-H has had a history of severe tappet-spalling problems. (The spalling — which seems cold-weather related — is partially preventable by the use of Lycoming's special LW-16702 oil ad-

ditive.) What you may *not* know is that the O-360-E (and TO-360-E) engines on the Seminole are also experiencing tappet-destruction problems. The problem is so acute, in fact, that Lycoming requires regular use of the LW-16702 "mystery oil" as a prerequisite to warranty coverage for O-360-E engines. (The oil additive is *not* required for the Duchess's engines.)

This is not to say, of course, that the Duchess does not have its share of maintenance problems; seven AD notes and 45 service bulletins issued by 1982 say otherwise. For the most part, however, the Duchess's maintenance glitches are minor. Most of the ADs, for example, involve one-time inspections or fixes applicable to early-serial-number aircraft. The only important repetitive AD affecting the aircraft (other than the one targeting the plane's Janitrol combustion heater) is a 1980 AD (80-19-12) requiring 50-hr. checks

Duchess pilots need to monitor cowl flaps for overheating and carburetor heat for overcooling. There is no fuel injection.

of the engine mounts for cracks. Unfortunately, the AD names all Duchess's from S/N -1 to -415.

Space prohibits an exhaustive listing of Duchess-related Service Instructions here. Most of these bulletins involve minor product improvements or non-mandatory inspections. Some, however, are of major importance (such as S.I. 1147 — revised in March 1982 — pertaining to engine mount replacement; and S.I. 1166, regarding improved main gear doors). Prospective Duchess buyers would be well-advised to crosscheck aircraft logbooks against the Beech S.I. Master Index (publication 98-34774B, available through any Beech dealer) to see whether applicable service bulletins have been complied with.

Duchess Resale Value Chart

Owner Comments

Our company presently operates two Duchess aircraft. They both have exceeded our expectations in all aspects of their operation. The handling characteristics are very good, although the elevator seems to be a bit light. True airspeeds vary between 155 and 160 knots at 65 percent power setting with a fuel flow of 19 gallons per hour. Our direct operating cost averged $53.24 per hour with no engine reserves. These figures were for a seven month period during which the aircraft flew 506 hours. We generally operate these aircraft between 650 and 700 hours a year. Their normal load is one and, occasionally, two passengers and we average about 150-mile stage lengths.

Our only major unscheduled problem was one engine overhaul at 1,400 hours, due to a lifter that disintegrated. As far as the airframe is concerned our problems have been the gear doors, which tend to develop cracks, and an engine mount inspection at 50-hour intervals. We had one cracked mount. Beech provided a fix for the gear doors and has given us very good product support.

Single-engine performance is a little better than average for this class of aircraft, and handling characteristics on one engine are very good. Our aircraft serial numbers are ME-12 and ME-31 with 1,400 hours and 2,000 hours respectively, so we are affected by virtually all the service bulletins.

I would like to add that from a pilot's point of view, these aircraft are a delight to fly, and from an accounts standpoint, easy to feed.

Marvin Pippen
Wharton, Tex.

I selected the Duchess as a moderate range business machine and feel that it will handle that task well. The visibility is good and the handling predictable. It is a little noisier than the Seminole but the visibility gain makes up for it. Also, the two entry doors are a decided convenience. Handbook figures on fuel consumption and speed appear to be accurate. I will need more time to establish *how* accurate.

The prospective purchaser will want to get the beefed up engine mounts (standard on later models) or else a repetitive AD inspection will have to be made every 50 hours. There apparently was some cracking of mounts on some of the earlier models; hence, the AD. Al-though I had the heavy mounts installed, the AD has not officially been lifted.

The Duchess pilot will want to take special care when securing after a flight. The rudder trim should be rolled full down and the rudder locks installed. They're hard to figure out, but do it anyway. The elevator surface droops naturally at rest and will damage the rudder if the rudder is allowed to swing in the wind.

Last, but not least, have a set of "starter engaged" indicator lights installed on the panel if the airplane doesn't already have them. As I learned, extended cranking will cause the starter relay to hang up, keeping the relay engaged. The result of all this is that the starter will be damaged (probably destroyed) and the battery run down, the trouble being that you don't know it. A volt-meter would be handly at times like this. (The lesson here is to get familiar with the electrical system.) Incidentally, I have to give high marks for the position of the circuit breakers and engine instruments in the Duchess. All handy and well laid out.

Garwood Burwell
Madison, N.J.

Mine is a 1980 aircraft which has proved to be fairly satisfactory.

If the beholder equates newness with beauty, then the Duchess is handsomer than the old Travel Air, but no better a performer.

There were considerable problems with the gear actuators which required replacement six times. They continually leaked and blew seals. Also, the passenger windows are now showing stress cracks where they are riveted. Beech is supposed to be looking into this.

Handling qualities are very satisfactory and landings and takeoffs are to the book. Speed on the average is 165 knots at 75 percent power. Fuel burn is 7 gallons/hour per side. The carbureted system is easy to start. The interior is very roomy and comfortable. There is easy access through the plane's twin cabin doors and large rear cabin door.

The annuals run around $1,200 with approximately $125 per month for general maintenance. The avionics panel is small, limiting equipment choice and the yoke doesn't accommodate sufficient space for wiring of push-to-talk buttons or remote ident switches, etc. Sound in the cabin could be better and a prop synch would be nice. Visibility is excellent and loading is adequate.

In summary, I would like to see more horsepower to obtain a cruise of 185 to 190 knots. Range is good, but with larger engines or turbocharging this could be increased. In all, a good economical twin with fine handling characteristics — a high-quality aircraft.

Nathan Goldenthal
Peoria, Ariz.

The Beech twin offers fliers the luxury of not only a pitch and rudder trim, but an aileron trim as well.

The elevated elevator may be out of reach for a walk-around inspection, but it also is out of the way of propwash buffet.

Piper Apache

"With the introduction of the Piper Apache into the utility airplane field," said the opening lines of the PA-23 Owner's Manual, **"a new era in the development of personal and business aviation is presaged."** And indeed it was so. In an 11-year production run beginning in 1954, Piper unleashed more than 2,100 Apaches on the world, demonstrating for the first time the viability of a type of plane that had never before been produced in quantity: the light twin.

Cursed by many for its poor single-engine rate of climb and generally unhurried performance, the Piper Apache is nonetheless revered by flight schools and owners alike for its easy flying qualities, spacious interior (the cabin structure—which is the same as the Aztec's—is wider than a Baron's, at 44 inches across), rugged construction, and reliable—not to mention miserly with fuel—Lycoming O-320 engines.

Today, 28 years after the Apache's introduction as the world's first true "light twin," the PA-23 is still in demand on the used market—largely because it holds the dubious distinction of being the least expensive used twin available. Doggy older versions of the twin can be had for under $10,000, while average-time, average-equipped 160-hp models can be bought (often with many STC'd options installed) for $15,000 to $20,000.

Whether the old bird is truly a bargain is certainly debatable, however. The Apache comes with a number of curious (and complex) mechanical quirks—not to mention a string of repetitive-inspection type ADs—resulting in upkeep costs equivalent to those of a light twin costing upwards of $150,000.

History

To airplane genealogy buffs, it will come as no surprise to learn that the roots of the Apache's family tree lead not to Piper, but to Stinson. In 1952, Stinson built and flew a prototype "light twin" with two rudders (a la Ercoupe), a pair of Lycoming O-290-D2 engines rated at 135 hp, and retracting tricycle gear. The 3,200-lb. (gross) aircraft cruised at 130 knots, hauled 1,250 pounds of useful load, and was able to fly 625 nm on 72 gallons of fuel—outstanding fuel economy for a twin, even by today's standards. Target price for the Twin Stinson was pegged at $25,000, in 1952 dollars.

When the Stinson company fell on economic hard times, Piper agreed to take over the Twin Stinson design and—discarding its twin tail in favor of a single fin, and replacing the O-290-D2s with a pair of O-320-A1s—type certificated the airplane as the PA-23-150 "Apache" (the first of many Indian monikers to follow). In 1954 dollars, the original Apaches sold for $32,500 basic —$36,235 equipped.

The first 750 or so Apaches off the line—those built between 1954 and 1957—came with 150-hp engines and a 3,500-lb. gross weight (a

Even doted-over Apaches with shiny new paint jobs aren't worth much more than $15,000.

combination that was good for no more than 240 fpm rate of climb on one engine at sea level on a standard day). In mid-1957, the Apache got a higher-compression version of the O-320 engine with 10 additional horsepower; gross weight also went up, to 3,800 pounds. The bench-type rear seat was also replaced, in 1957, with two individual seats, and a five-place interior was offered as an option.

In 1959, the instrument panel (heretofore a crazy-quilt of dislocated gauges, switches, and boxes) got a facelift, with radios positioned in a center stack and flight gauges mercifully clustered on the left. The following year, a large third side window made its appearance with the debut of the PA-23G, which also featured a welcome increase in gear-down speed to 130 knots (from 109 knots) as well as an increase in flap speed to 125 mph (from the previous absurdly low 87 knots).

After a production run of only 28 airplanes in 1961, Piper reintroduced the PA-23 as the "Apache 235" in 1962. This version of the Apache was, in fact, merely a re-engined Aztec with carbureted, low-compression six-cylinder O-540-B1 engines. (It should be noted that the Aztec, which debuted in 1960, was originally an outgrowth of the Apache, and in fact shared the same basic type certificate.) Unable to sell more than a handful of the larger models, Piper axed the Apache 235—and with it, the Apache name —in 1965, having delivered at that time only 117 PA-23-235s (but more than 600 Twin Comanches).

Performance

Owners are divided on which of the Apache models (other than the large-engined 235) offers the best performance. Current hangar mythology holds that the early Apaches—with their 150-hp engines—are generally doggiest, with exceptionally low single-engine rates of climb (the book says 240 fpm at sea level). But in fact the higher gross weight of the 160-hp models resulted in a *higher* power loading (not to mention wing loading) for 1957-1961 models, and a *lower* single-engine climb rate (180 fpm). Single-engine performance is thus generally poor for the series—but no worse, on balance, than many other light twins. (In fact, the 150-hp Apache's engine-out climb rate is actually better than that of the Seneca II or Cessna's T303 Crusader.)

Everybody agrees on one thing: the Apache is not exactly overpowered. Speed simply is not the airplane's strong suit. The 1956 Owner's Manual claims a cruise speed of 152 knots at full throttle and 2400 rpm at 6,000 feet (roughly 75 percent power); but, as one owner remarked wryly, "The performance charts in the Owner's Manual were probably written by

the marketing department." Owners typically report Skylane-like cruise figures of 135 knots true at 65 to 70 percent power, with fuel flows in the 15 to 16 gallon per hour range, for 150-hp models; about two knots more for the 160-hp versions (and up to 20 knots more for the highly modified, 180-hp turbocharged Geronimos). Economy cruise is in the 120 knot area, yielding 14 gph. These speeds are at gross weight, however, and owners claim that cruise figures go up about one knot for every 100 pounds of fuel or baggage offloaded.

Considering the airplane's respectable 1,250-lb. useful load and relatively tiny engines, the Apache returns fairly incredible short-field performance, with takeoff rolls of 990 feet at gross on a standard sea-level day (680 feet at 3,200 pounds), and landing distances of a mere 670 feet at gross (or just 600 feet at 3,200 pounds). These are no-wind figures. Obstacle-clearance numbers were not stated in the aircraft Owner's Manual. (Likewise, accelerate-stop distances had not been considered important in 1954.)

Once an Apache is airborne, a best rate of climb speed of 87 knots yields a creditable 1,350 fpm climb rate at gross (according to the book), diminishing to 1,000 fpm at 5,000 feet, with full throttle. And although single-engine rates of climb are poor at full gross weight, the offloading of 300 pounds of cargo and/or fuel results in a book climb figure of 330 fpm with one engine (we're not told which one) caged. Likewise, the single-engine absolute ceiling rises from 6,750

feet at 3,500 pounds gross weight (for the 150-hp Apache), to 8,000 feet at 300 pounds below gross, operating on the critical (left) engine.

Standard fuel capacity on the Apache was 72 gallons, in midwing fuel cells. Factory long-range tanks, installed in the outboard tips, however, boosted total fuel capacity to 108 gallons. For even more range, an owner can add STC'd Met-co-aire tip tanks, to give a grand total of 144 gallons of fuel—enough to make the airplane's endurance compete with the pilot's. (One owner tells of making nonstop flights from Wichita to the West Coast, bucking 20-knot headwinds.) With any more than 100 gallons of fuel on board, however, the Apache becomes a less-than-four-persons (assuming no baggage) airplane.

Handling Characteristics

What the Apache lacks in speed and sex appeal, it more than makes up for in comfort and easy handling, according to owners (who characterize the ship as "very forgiving," "a stable instrument platform," and "a delight to fly"). Control forces are light and well balanced, as twins go. Stalls, likewise, are docile, although one instructor-owner admonishes that plenty of right rudder will be required during power-on stall recoveries.

Docile demeanor aside, the Apache nonetheless displays several potentially irksome quirks in the air. Like the Aztec, the Apache has an annoying tendency to pitch up with the initial deploy-

Cost/Performance/Specifications————————————————————

Model	Years Built	Number Built	Average Retail Price	Cruise Speed (kts)	Useful Weight (lbs)	Engine	TBO (hrs)	Overhaul Cost (each)
PA-23-150	1954	115	$13,500	148	3,500	150-hp Lyc. O-320-A1A	2,000	$ 8,000
PA-23-150	1955-57	626	$15,500	148	3,500	150-hp Lyc. O-320-A1A	2,000	$ 8,000
PA-23-160	1957-58	754	$16,500	150	3,800	160-hp Lyc. O-320-B3B	2,000	$ 8,500
PA-23-160	1959	368	$17,500	150	3,800	160-hp Lyc. O-320-B3B	2,000	$ 8,500
PA-23-G	1960	141	$18,000	150	3,800	160-hp Lyc. O-320-B3B	2,000	$ 8,500
PA-23-H	1961	28	$18,500	150	3,800	160-hp Lyc. O-320-B3B	2,000	$ 8,500
PA-23-235	1962-63	82	$23,000	166	4,800	235-hp Lyc. O-540-B1A5	2,000	$12,000
PA-23-235	1964-65	34	$24,000	166	4,800	235-hp Lyc. O-540-B1A5	2,000	$12,000

ment of flaps. (Piper finally got around to fixing this in 1976 and subsequent Aztecs. It was never corrected in the Apache.) And in pre-1960 models, the flap speed is fixed at a bothersomely low 87 knots, which requires quite a bit of nose-up trim to achieve in the first place. New pilots would be well-advised to anticipate the nose-up reaction as they reach down (way down on the center pedestal) to hit the flap lever.

In reaching for the trim, however, the new Apache pilot will face another quirky feature: the airplane's overhead crank-type trim knobs (a quaint Piper tradition with airplanes of the time). Let's see now, is it counterclockwise to trim nose-up, or clockwise? And which handle do we want? (There are two trim handles: one for rudder, another for pitch.) It's best to become thoroughly acquainted with this system on the ground, naturally, before tackling single-engine work—or pattern work, for that matter.

Another quirk: with the gear down, the rudder becomes heavier, since the shimmy dampener is a friction collar, which adds a lot of friction to the rudder pedals. This, according to one owner, takes some getting used to during crosswind landings.

The Apache's gear selector—located on the right side of the center pedestal—incorporates an effective (if infuriating to students) safety catch, a kind of thumb-switch that must be moved to the side before the gear lever can be moved upward. If the pilot attempts to yank the lever up without stowing the catch, the lever jams on the catch, and to be freed, the lever must first be lowered at least a half inch. Gear retraction thus takes some effort. (The catch constitutes a mechanical "squat switch," preventing inadvertent retraction of the hydraulic landing gear while on the ground.)

Despite the laudable attempt at making the gear handle difficult to raise while taxiing, Piper's designers for some reason decided to place the flap selector on the left

Apache Resale Value Chart

'61 PA-23H
(New price: $46,000)

'56 PA-23-150
(New price: $38,000)

Year

and the gear selector on the right—a nonstandard arrangement that subverts the original intent of the safety catch.

Another annoying gear problem: retraction time, at 11 seconds, is painfully long, particularly if you need the gear up fast in preparation for a single-engine climbout. Depending on which engine you lose, the gear retraction time could actually be 11 seconds or infinity; the hydraulic pump works off the left engine only, and while the pump will still function with the prop windmilling, the drag caused by the windmilling is more than enough to cancel any rate-of-climb gains that would accrue to raising the gear.

The bottom line: if you intend to hold altitude after the left engine fails, you'll need to feather the prop. (It will feather automatically in the event of oil pressure loss, but that's another matter.) At that point, however, you won't be able to raise the gear without pumping it up manually—30 to 40 strokes of the emergency pump handle (located in the center of the control pedestal). By Piper's own estimate, raising the gear this way takes 20 to 30 seconds. In an emergency, that may well be 19 to 29 seconds too long.

Since the flaps are hydraulically actuated, they, too, depend for proper function on the left engine's

turning. But at least here, selecting flaps up while airborne results in the wind blowing the flaps up. (Getting them down again would, of course, require manual operation of the emergency pump handle after left-engine failure.)

Standard equipment on the original Apaches included a single 35-amp generator driven by the left engine, and a single vacuum pump driven off the right engine. Fortunately, most Apaches were delivered with the optional dual generators and dual vacuum pumps, providing an acceptable measure of systems backup—an important part of what light twins are supposedly all about. Still, there are some single-generator, single-pump Apaches flying, and it behooves buyers to screen potential purchases carefully in this regard, particularly if serious instrument work is contemplated.

One other peculiarity that potential Apache buyers would do well to keep in mind: In a recently updated bird with lightweight digital electronics, the 30 pounds or so of avionics power supplies that came in the nose of the plane originally will be gone—leading to possible aft-c.g. loading problems. (The problem is aggravated by the absence, in the Apache and early Aztecs, of a nose baggage compartment. The Apache's baggage area is behind the rear seats.) What's more, the Apache, one owner

Apache owners love to doll up their old birds with various mods. This one has a pointy nose and a square tail, and looks almost like an Aztec.

warns, does not fly well when tail-heavy.

Safety Record

In a special study by the National Transportation Safety Board of light twin engine failure accidents from 1972 to 1976, the Piper Apache fared very badly, ranking as the airplane (out of 24 light twins studied) having the worst incidence of accidents following engine failure. The actual rate of engine-failure accidents was found to be 6.91 per 100,000 flight-hours—more than triple that of the Twin Comanche, at 1.98 per 100,000 hours, and more than seven times that of the Aztec.

This is not to say that the Apache's *engine-failure rate* is high; there are no statistics on this, since—for one thing—nobody keeps records on how many engine failures occur that *don't* end in an accident. The NTSB study merely says that *if* you lose an engine in an Apache, your chances of crashing are higher than would be the case if you were flying almost any other popular light twin. Why is the Apache's engine-out accident rate so high? Apparently, it has little to do with the aircraft's Vmc (74 knots) or single-engine performance, which are nearly identical to the Aztec's. (The published single-engine ROC figures for the 1981 Aztec F and 1956 Apache 150 are 235 fpm and 240 fpm, respectively.) So why should the Aztec have one-seventh the engine-out accident rate of the Apache? The Safety Board laid blame to the Apache's high power loading (11.8 lbs./hp, versus the

Aztec's 9.6). We tend to think that the airplane's role as multiengine trainer has something to do with it, too.

An *Aviation Consumer* review of NTSB accident statistics covering a recent one-year period revealed that of 42 accidents involving Piper PA-23 aircraft, 16 (or 38 percent) were fatal. Of the fatals, about half involved continued VFR flight into adverse weather, with a surprising number of the pilots instrument-rated. (Three others involved pilot incapacitation for medical reasons.) The nonfatal accidents formed several distinct patterns. Among them: landing overshoots after engine failure (by far the largest category), loss of control after in-flight door opening, and accidents involving botched single-engine climbouts or go-arounds, where the aircraft simply wouldn't gain altitude.

Several gear-up landings were listed in the NTSB's recent records (one of them after total hydraulic failure combined with non-functioning of the emergency CO_2 blow-down system). Ironically, the PA-23's "half-in, half-out" wheel wells—designed specifically to allow tire rubber to cushion the impact of a gear-up landing and thus minimize damage—failed to keep these gear-up incidents out of the "substantial damage" column of the NTSB's accident printouts.

One accident (not fatal) involved a double engine failure over water as the pilot was descending on the auxiliary fuel tanks (which are placarded for level flight only).

Two hours of fuel were left in the mains when the engines quit. The aircraft sank off the coast of Florida.

Carburetor icing shows up with regularity in the NTSB's Piper PA-23 accident reports. The Apache's engines are notorious for breeding venturi ice in humid conditions, and more than one pilot has gone down after *both* engines have begun to run rough from carburetor freeze-up.

If there are lessons to be learned from the PA-23's accident record, they are: [1] Don't lose an engine. But if you do, be ready to land; and be current. [2] Don't even think about executing a go-around with one engine dead. One shot is all you've got. [3] Be ready for the door to pop open at any time—and don't let it bother you (just fly the airplane). [4] Don't climb or descend on auxiliary tanks. [5] Anticipate carburetor ice, and remember that if it comes, it will very likely affect both engines at once.

Airworthiness Directives

Like most aircraft of its vintage, the Apache has racked up quite a number of airworthiness directives over the years (23 on the airframe, nine on the O-320 engine, and sundry other ADs affecting accessories, such as the South Wind heater). Many of these ADs no longer apply. Some, however, are perpetual and repetitive. For example:

AD 63-12-02 requires repetitive 100-hour inspections of elevator butt rib P/N 17058-3 (and its doubler plate) for cracks, until a late-model, improved elevator assembly is installed.

AD 63-26-02 requires repetitive 100-hour visual inspections (and 500-hour dye penetrant inspections) of elevator and rudder castings for cracks. The replacement of affected castings with forgings eliminates the inspection requirement—but many Apaches still have the castings.

AD 71-12-01 mandates 100-hour inspections of a control pedestal support bracket until such time as an improved part is installed.

AD 78-08-03 requires 1,000-hour dye penetrant inspections of upper and lower rudder hinge bracket assemblies. No improved parts are available.

AD 80-18-10 requires 100-hour magnifying glass inspection of fuel control cable and valve assemblies, with mandatory 1,000-hour overhauls of the fuel control unit.

AD 80-26-04 required a beefup of the fuselage structure surrounding the cabin entrance step, with 100-hour inspections of the area thereafter. As it turns out, the portion of fuselage truss to which the cabin step bracket attaches also carries critical rudder cable pulleys; thus, when excess weight is placed on the cabin step, the structure deforms, causing misalignment of the rudder cable pulleys and binding of the rudder. (This AD applies to the Aztec as well.)

A sweeping AD on the PA-23 flap system (AD 81-04-05, revised February 5, 1982) requires repetitive 100-hour inspections of the flap-spar-hinge attachment areas and bellcrank for cracks, as well as one-time beefing up of the flap torque tube bearing block bracket in accordance with Piper Service Bulletin No. 671.

Where the Lycoming O-320 engines are concerned, the most important ADs are probably those affecting the oil pump. A 1973 AD required the replacement of Woodruff-key drive type oil pumps with square-drive components. In 1981, a controversial AD (81-18-04) required the replacement, at 2,000 hours after major overhaul or before, of sintered-iron type oil pump impellers. Almost every engine remanufactured by Lycoming (and quite a few of those overhauled in the field) between 1970 and 1980 got the sintered iron impellers, which have shown a tendency to crumble in extended

Stubby Apache is very unstable with aft center of gravity. Even NASA pilots found it tough to fly instruments under such conditions. Noseheavy, it's okay.

service. (They've been crumbling since 1970, but the problem was masked for years by the Woodruff key drive failures.) Compliance with these ADs is essential; check maintenance records carefully when considering a potential purchase.

Additional ADs have come out targeting combustion heaters made by Stewart Warner and Janitrol. Since all Apaches and Aztecs have either a Stewart Warner or a Janitrol heater, compliance with the repetitive inspection and overhaul requirements of these ADs is mandatory for any Apache owner. Figure on a $400 to $600 heater rebuild every 500 hours.

Parts and Service

Despite the Apache's age and its being out of production for practically two decades, owners report little or no problem obtaining replacement parts. One operator reports that when he needs an Apache part fast, he orders from Seguin Aviation (see below); when time is not of the essence, he orders from Piper.

Direct hourly operating costs in the $30 to $50 range (extremely low for a twin-engine plane) are frequently cited by owners, who lay much of the credit to the Apache's 2,000-hour-TBO Lycoming engines. These engines are, by industry standards, arguably the most reliable and economical to operate of any modern "flat, opposed" aircraft engine. (Note: The 2,000-hour TBO applies only to engines with half-inch valves. A few 7/16-inch valve engines are still in the fleet; these are limited to 1,200 hours be-

tween overhauls. Check engine records carefully.)

The engine cowlings, alas, are something else again. Due to what one owner calls "extremely poor cowl and baffle design," the cowls take a long time to remove for service, and are subject to repeated vibration cracking. Virtually every Apache cowling you come across is riddled with patches and stop-drill holes. (One operator suggests that perhaps this is how the Apache got its name: "You got a patch here, and a patch here, and . . .")

Access to the rest of the plane's systems is relatively good. An A&P owner of a highly customized Apache estimates that he spends 35 hours working on the plane for every 100 hours of flying time. Annuals range from $80 for the A&P-licensed owner with a no-squawks bird . . . all the way to $4,000, in the case of one M.D. who said he brought his many-squawks 1959 model to Seguin for its annuals.

The original Apaches came from the factory with Goodrich expander-tube brakes, which some owners characterize with Walt Disney adjectives. A sizable portion of the Apache fleet has since been converted to Cleveland brakes, however—a definite improvement, maintenance-wise.

The hydraulic power pack was mentioned by some owners as an item occasionally needing work. The most common failure mode involves sticking of the pressure relief valve, and bending of its retainer plates (with no loss of hydraulic fluid or danger of gear-up landing).

Mods and Clubs

A glance at the FAA's *Summary of Supplemental Type Certificates* shows no less than 157 approved STCs for the PA-23 series, covering everything from autopilots to dual brakes (most Apaches have brakes on the pilot's side only) to extra seats and emergency exits—not to mention such more-or-less standard mods as one-piece windshields, added side windows, square wingtips, full wheel enclosures, dorsal fins, long noses, bigger engines, and turbocharging.

The most important Apache modifiers are Nayak Aviation (206 East Terminal Dr., International Airport, San Antonio, Tex. 78216), which offers extra windows, baggage compartments, gross weight increase, and engine mods. J.W. Miller Aviation (P.O. Box 16203, San Antonio, Tex. 78216), with its dual brake mod, one-piece windshield, rear picture window, fiberglass nose mods, wheel well doors, and Franklin engine conversion . . . and, of course, Seguin Aviation (Rt. 1, Box 225, Seguin, Tex. 78155), home of the famous Geronimo conversion. Seguin will sell you individual STC'd kits, or a complete Geronimo treatment with 180-hp engines and a total airframe rebuild. If Seguin doesn't have it—you probably can't get it.

For camaraderie, there's the Flying Apache Association, Inc., 67 Brierbrook, Milton, Mass. 02186. The group, founded in 1978, has about 200 members.

Owner Comments

As the owner of an original Apache with 150-hp engines and no mods, I find the airplane inexpensive to own and operate. It burns 15 gph at what I call high cruise, 135 knots. When I'm not in a hurry, I use a low power setting, getting 117 knots and 14 gph.

The Apache is well known to be a two-engine twin, especially at gross, and I highly agree; however, with only two seats in use and no fuel in the aux tanks, it will actually fly the pattern on one engine (a big pattern), or climb 100 to 150 fpm at 6,500 feet in average temperatures.

The structure of the Apache (and its big brother, the Aztec) are something today's manufacturers have neglected to hold onto. One distinction I can claim, which I'm sure puts me in a small membership, is that I had occasion once to

Apache is notorious for lousy single-engine performance. In the real world, with any load aboard, an Apache will not maintain altitude on one engine.

smash the wings from an Apache (which had crashed in a forest) to dispose of them. My weapon was a 25-ton Northwest crane. Not owning a demolition ball, I used the weight of the crane to crush the wings—or tried to. To my amazement, the crane just crawled up on top of the wing and sat there. I had to be exerting 12½ tons, or half the crane's weight, as I could only get one track on the wing at one time. I stopped the crane, got off, and examined the wing. I hadn't dented it. I was amazed, to use the same adjective twice.

Piper, please don't throw away the fat Hershey-bar wing jigs. Maybe you could turn them over to Seguin Aviation.

I should mention the roominess of the cabin. It is one feature that I certainly enjoy. One bad feature that constantly bothers me, however, is the noise level in the cabin. (Without earphones, I couldn't take it.) I wish someone would come up with a cure.

●

My wife and I have owned a 1958 PA-23-160 since September 1976. We use it both for personal transportation and in our part-time flight instruction business. I am a licensed A&P, and perform almost all maintenance myself.

The most costly maintenance items I've faced, other than prop and engine overhauls, were a cracked engine mount, and welding required to beef up the truss structure in the area of the cabin entry step as required by AD 80-26-04. I have experienced a few problems

with the nosegear downlock mechanism, but I attribute these mainly to the fact that the plane is used as a trainer, cycling the gear all the time.

The hydraulic power pack malfunctioned once, when the main relief valve did not release the pressure surge at the end of the retract cycle and was forced out of its mounting hole, bending the retainer plates. According to John Dean of Midwest Piper in Wichita, that failure mode constitutes 90 percent of all power-pack failures in Apaches and Aztecs.

I purchased a new Southwind heater in 1979, and that unit has been a lemon, requiring repeated cannibalizing of the old heater to keep it going. Since glow plugs burn out quite regularly, it would be advisable to keep spares on hand.

Parts and outside labor probably average $7 an hour for me, and since I do all my own work my annual inspections run around $80 (for the IA to inspect the opened plane and sign the paperwork).

The performance charts in the Owner's Manual probably were written by the marketing department. Single engine performance is a far cry from the book figures (I estimate 70 fpm less than published); the only comfort is that the O-320-B3Bs have an outstanding reliability record, and shouldn't quit in the first place.

Cruise performance is approximately 135 knots true at about 10,000 ft. density altitude, with a fuel flow between 15 and 16 gph. It varies with weight, though, as in any airplane. Cruise increases about one knot for every 100 pounds less weight.

With the Metco tip tanks, the Apache is a two-seater with room for baggage and fantastic range. I've made several flights of almost 10 hours, going nonstop from Wichita to the West Coast bucking 20-25-knot headwinds. No-wind range is around 1,300 nautical, but you better stop at Sears and buy a Port-A-Potty.

Piper Twin Comanche

While it's been over a decade since Piper halted production of the PA-30 and PA-39 series, collectively known as the Twin Comanche, the aircraft continues to soldier on. All told, some 2,150 Twin Comanches rolled off the Lock Haven line in the years 1963-1972.

Anyone searching for a twin with the economics of a single almost — should give the Twin Comanche a closer look. As unveiled in 1963, the Twin Comanche was intended to fill the hole in the general aviation market created by the demise of the PA-32 Apache. In some ways the two aircraft are similar; sharing what was fundamentally the same 160-hp Lycoming O-320-B3B powerplant (except the PA-30's engine was designated the IO-320-B1A, due to the introduction of fuel injection).

History

The Twin Comanche could boast better speed and range with virtually identical cabin capacity as the Apache, and the buying public seemed to appreciate some of the sportier styling features of the new twin. The aircraft rested slightly aft on its tricycle landing gear, and the so-called ''tiger shark'' engine nacelles and optional wing tip tanks gave it a speedy look A top speed just over 170 knots enhanced the twin's sporty image. Accordingly, the airplane sold well to both private owner/operators and charter/flight school operations.

Tarnished Image

This image was soon to be tarnished by a series of fatal flight training mishaps, bringing to light what came to be called the ''stall/spin syndrome.'' Flight schools came to regard the Twin Comanche as perhaps not the best light twin for training purposes.

Closer inspection revealed the real fault was an over-design of the airplane.

Rather than suffer from a lack of control at low speeds, the Twin Comanche suffered from almost too much. The originally placarded Vmc speed was quite low, due mainly to the airplane's oversized rudder, so low in fact that at low altitudes, Vmc and stall speed were nearly the same. Add to this the fact that FAA was recommending Vmc maneuvers be performed at as low an altitude as possible to take maximum advantage of asymmetric power and that the Twin Comanche's high aspect-ratio wing tends to dump all its lift at once in stall, and the reasons for the series of training accidents becomes clear.

In these low-speed conditions, symmetric lift could roll the airplane suddenly, with a spin a likely result, a maneuver that tends to be terminal at low altitude.

Piper's Fix

Piper took two steps to fix the problem, one voluntary, the other less so. An AD called for the placarded Vmc to be increased to 72 Knots. The company then developed a stall-strip kit which was offered to Twin Comanche customers at no charge. The strip gave more predictable stall performance by ensuring initial flow separation over the inboard wing sections. The strip became standard on the

PA-30 models like this one do not have counter-rotating props like the later PA-39 versions, which improve engine-out traits.

PA-39, the Twin Comanche variant with counter-rotating props.

The Stretch

The year 1966 saw the introduction of the PA-30B, an airplane that can't truthfully be called six-place for anything but the shortest flight because the addition of the extra seating eats up the baggage space and the useful load of 1,390 lbs. allows just a half load of fuel if all six seats are filled and a reasonably equipped instrument panel goes along. An additional window on each side gives these back seat flyers something to look out of.

Also new to the PA-30B were the factory-installed Rajay turbochargers, as was a 125-lb. boost in gross weight to 3,725 lbs. Tip tanks became standard on the turbo Twin Comanches. Rajay Turbochargers were used to normalize the engines' performance, that is, to restore sea-level manifold pressure, not to increase pressure above the normal 30 inches Hg.

The result is that the turbocharged airplanes are no more powerful than normally-aspirated ones and actually sacrifice a small amount of performance until altitudes are reached at which the normally-aspirated plane can no longer maintain 75 percent power. Turbo Twin Comanches are capable of cruise speeds of up to 190 knots at high altitude.

Turbocharging

The Rajay turbocharger installation is straightforward. Each turbo wastegate is controlled directly by a mechanical cockpit handle. A cheap, simple, and generally reliable system, the Rajay turbos impose additional pilot workload due to extra controls and the lack of an automatic controller, allowing major fluctuations in manifold pressure due to changes in airspeed, temperature, or mixture, or the presence of turbulence.

Some readers have reported turbocharger wastegate control cables burning out due to their proximity to exhaust heat. Whatever maintenance glitches turbo Twin Comanche owners do experience, it's a fact that they will have to overhaul their engines slightly more often than owners of their crafts' normally aspirated brethren. TBO is 1,800 for the turbocharged powerplants, 2,000 for the non-blown version.

Wending its way down the Piper production line in 1969, the PA-30C was different in incidental ways from its predecessors. The interior was cleaned up, most noticeably by a new instrument panel with offset radio rack and flight instrumentation in the venerated "sacred six" pattern.

End of the Line

The opening years of the '70s saw the eventual end of the Twin Comanche line. They also saw the creation of the final, and to a lot of Comanche fans, the finest of the line, the PA-39 series. New counter-rotating engines eliminated the critical engine, and marked the beginning of Piper's love affair with this configuration, which would later appear on both the Seneca and Navajo C/R series.

Older Twin Comanches can be converted into counter-rotating aircraft through the purchase and installation of the proper engines, props and related kits from the manufacturer. The prime caveat here is cost. Such an expensive conversion would only be really useful if the aircraft is to be used for instruction.

Performance

Prospective buyers can expect cruise speeds around 165 knots, with a fuel burn of 16-17 gph, although some Twin Comanche owners have reported even leaner burns. This puts the airplane in the same performance class as some single-engine models, all with the benefits of twin-engine flight, although some of those benefits may seem remote when engine overhaul time comes.

As introduced in 1963, the basic Twin Comanche was much like the single-engine Comanche of the period: four-place seating with baggage space aft of the rear seat. Four wing tanks held 90 gallons of fuel; tip tanks could increase that to 120 gallons, 114 of which is usable.

While overall handling for the Twin Comanche is conceded as good, many pilots report somewhat tricky behavior on landings. The airplane shows a marked resistance to greased landings, preferring to pay off with a jolt at the end.

Maurice Taylor, Twin Comanche enthusiast and de facto historian for the International Comanche Society, agreed that landing was often something different in this twin. ''The airplane had funny landing characteristics that I think were partly due to its attitude on the landing gear. It sat back on the gear, sort of like a DC-3. That made it difficult to make it a good landing. It would be a safe landing but not a good landing, not a comfortable landing.

''Still, nothing has taken this plane's place. To build something comparable today, well, the cost would just be prohibitive.''

Taylor doesn't hesitate when asked about the Twin Comanche's good side. ''The airplane has a very good engine. The IO-320 is a reliable engine and one of the first with a 2,000 hr. TBO.''

Pricing

Price performance for the Twin Comanche line has become predictable too. A 1969 PA-30C carried a price tag of $52,725. That same aircraft can be had today for about $38,000 inflation-weakened dollars. As shown on the accompanying graph, Twin Comanches have largely leveled off in terms of price in recent years.

When inflation is figured in, the aircraft seems to be trapped in a buyer's market, with sellers taking what they can get. The 1972 vintage PA-39C/R has proved to have

Cost/Performance/Specifications

Model	Year	Average Retail Price	Cruise Speed (kts)	Rate of Climb (fpm)	SE Ceiling	Useful Load (lbs)	Fuel Std/Opt (gals)	Engine	TBO (hrs)	Overhaul Cost (each)
PA-30	1963-65	$28,500	169	1,460	5,800	1,390	90/120	160-hp Lyc. IO-320-B1A	2,000	$10,500
PA-30B	1966-68	$34,500	169	1,460	5,800	1,350	90/120	160-hp Lyc. IO-320-B1A	2,000	$10,500
Turbo B	1966-68	$39,000	194	1,290	19,000	1,317	120	160-hp Lyc. 320-C1A	1,800	$11,250
PA-30C	1969	$38,000	172	1,460	7,100	1,330	90/120	160-hp Lyc. IO-320-C1A	2,000	$10,500
Turbo C	1969	$43,000	209	1,290	17,000	1,309	120	160-hp Lyc. IO-320-C1A	1,800	$11,250
PA-39C/R	1970-71	$42,000	172	1,460	7,100	1,370	90/120	160-hp Lyc. IO-320-B1A	2,000	$10,500
Turbo C/R	1970-71	$48,000	192	1,290	12,600	1,309	120	160-hp Lyc. IO-320-C1A	1,800	$11,250
PA-39C/R	1972	$44,000	172	1,460	7,100	1,370	90/120	160-hp Lyc. IO-320-B1A	2,000	$10,500
Turbo C/R	1972	$50,000	192	1,290	12,600	1,309	120	160-hp Lyc. IO-320-C1A	1,800	$11,250

Twin Comanche Resale Value Chart

a fairly stable market value in recent years after taking a bit of a nose dive in the years immediately following manufacture. Costing $66,715 new, the 1972 model maintained a fairly steady price until 1984 when it dipped slightly into the low $40,000 neighborhood.

Safety Record

In terms of statistical safety, the Twin Comanche series stacks up as slightly better in some categories, slightly worse in others. In a NTSB study examining the safety performance of 20 light twin models over the years 1972-1976, the Twin Comanche emerged roughly average in terms of fatal accident rates at 1.91 per 100,000 flight hours. Engine failures resulting in fatalities are somewhat rare in this type, a testimonial to the reliability of the IO-320 engine. Just 0.14 deaths per 100,000 flight hours were reported due to engine failures.

On the dark side, however, the NTSB figures show the Twin Comanche well above average in terms of total accidents per 100,000 hrs., with 11.76 mishaps reported, compared to an average to 6.94. But when compared to the fatality figues, it looks like your chances of walking away from a Twin Comanche mishap are better than for a lot of other twins.

Of the 100 more recent Piper PA-30/PA39 Twin Comanche accidents cited by NTSB between 1977 and 1982, 53 were attributed to conditions unrelated to aircraft systems; i.e pilot error. Of the remaining mishaps, 11 involved failure of the Twin C's landing gear due to mechanical failures of retraction tubes, bent or broken rod-end bearings on main gear, electrical systems failures blamed on excessive alternator wear, landing gear connecting arm failures, and overall electrical power failures.

Even when not beset by internal woes, the Twin Comanche's legs proved somewhat shaky in the sort of rough landings the aircraft is notorious for, with ground-loops, hard landings and over-shoots racking up 12 Twins. Gear retractions and collapses of undetermined cause resulted in seven more mishaps.

A handful of Twin Comanche accidents were attributed to miscellaneous causes. A fire in flight and a fire on the ground claimed an aircraft apiece, while engine-out situations downed five Twins. One broke up in a thunderstorm, while another became the victim of a triple threat: an alcohol-impaired, VFR-only pilot who took off into IFR conditions and broke up in a thunderstorm.

Airworthiness Directives

Indeed, evidence of the powerplant's reliability is given in the small number of ADs dealing with it, even the turbocharged version. By far the bulk of Twin Comanche ADs focus on the airframe. In them are a number of potentially expensive structural notes, including replacement of the nose gear actuator tube, rebalancing of the stabilator, inspection/replacement of the stabilator torque tube bearings, and beefing up the aileron nose bulkheads. A 1983 AD calls for inspection of the lower spar cap for damage and possible cracks where the spar enters the fuselage at the lower wing root fairing.

Service Difficulties

As far as service problems go, the Twin Comanche has a number of trouble points that bear watching. Structural ADs have dogged the aircraft almost from its inception, and the situation bears even more careful monitoring as the fleet ages further. Reports from the field indicate the aileron spars are especially fragile components, with cracks developing under the hinge brackets.

An AD (77-08-01) deals with the problem, but cracks have been detected even after the notice has been complied with. That particular AD called for the fitting of replacement hinge brackets, after which the 100-hr. inspections are dispensed with. Reports would indicate, however, that continued examination of the area is the safest route to travel.

Watch Those Fuel Pumps

Fuel pumps seem to come and go quickly in some Twin Comanches. According to one report, a total of 15 pumps from six airplanes had to be replaced. One aircraft went through five pumps! Most failures happened within a few hours of overhaul, blamed on the lower parting surface on the pump, which leaks. One leaking pump resulted in an aircraft fire.

Similar complaints have come in from the field on fuel pumps in general. Frequent failures have been cited among pumps that apparently have been sitting on parts shop shelves for extensive periods—eight years in one case. While the shelf life of parts with rubber components depends to a large extent on the storage techniques, wise buyers will check the dates on both new and rebuilt parts.

Engine Mounts

Corrosion problems in engine mounts have become a serious matter, especially on the turbo Twins, where exhaust heat tends to weaken the metal. Heat fatigue on engine mounts has been reported on the normally aspirated models as well.

Reports indicate a number of other spots to watch, such as: resin leaks on the magneto coil due to overheating; burned or cracked heat exchangers, the subject of an AD that requires a 500-hr. overhaul many Twin C owners find expensive and troublesome; and problems with the spinners on the Twin C's Hartzell props.

Useful Options

Among the most useful options are the tip tanks, prop de-ice (although prospective owners should be cautioned that the Twin Comanche is not certificated for flight into conditions of known icing), and avionics packages such as factory-installed three-axis fully coupled autopilots.

Miller Mods

J.W. Miller Aviation, Inc. at Horseshoe Bay Airport, Box 7757, Marble Falls, Tex. 78654, (512) 598-2556, is a major source for Twin Comanche mods, leading off with a 200-hp Lycoming powerplant to give the Twin a real kick in the pants: 174-knot cruise, 1,900 fpm climb along with 500 fpm single-engine climb. Price tag will come to $53,000 for the normally aspirated, $56,511 for turbos, and the mod comes with a dorsal fin and new nacelles.

Miller also offers a nose job for the Piper twin, only this one adds to the plane's proboscis, instead of subtracting from it. The new nose

Miller modification adds a swoopy new snoot and bigger 200-hp engines. Cruise speed is well over 200 mph.

affords seven cubic feet of baggage space capable of accommodating 130 pounds of baggage for $4,855. Nacelle baggage lockers from Miller can hold 75 pounds apiece, and cost $5,085 for both. Those who want to give a Twin Comanche longer legs can get the integral fuel tanks that boost fuel capacity by 38 gallons (19 gallons each in two separate tanks) while adding 180 pounds to the aircraft, and deducting $8,900 from the owner's bankroll.

R/STOL Systems

Up in Everett, Wash., R/STOL Systems offers a STOL mod that gives PA-30s and 39s some rather muscular capabilities, such as a 40 percent overall reduction in takeoff and landing rolls. Costing $9,000, the R/STOL mod allows a PA-30 to clear a 50-foot obstacle in 1,120 feet, a PA-39 in 1,050. Approach speeds can be as low as 65 knots, down from the standard 78 to 82 knots for this type. Vmc for the STOL-modified Twin Comanche is back where it once was, at 70 knots.

An earlier AD issued to R/STOL on the mod called for a cable to replace a bungee cord used for flap retraction. Piper used the bungee cord as original equipment but failure of the cord in a R/STOL mod left the aircraft in a dangerously symmetrical flap configuration. Failure of the cord in a stock Twin Comanche still leaves the aircraft with sufficient roll control in the eyes of the FAA.

Knots 2U

If Twin Comanche owners want to boost the performance of their

birds without resorting to brute force, they can turn to the service of Knots 2U, Inc., a company specializing in slicking up older airplanes. The Knots 2U mod comes in several parts, and all or part can be installed, either by the owner in kit form, or by professionals.

Gap seals for the ailerons and flaps cost $1,050 for the kit and will come to $1,450 installed. Wing root fairings are $355/kit and $425/installed and a removable dorsal fin hiding a pair of comm antennas is $1,080/ installed or $895 for the do-it-yourselfer. Neither of these last two mods is approved for use on R/STOL twins. Installation of the antennae themselves is another $450.

Additional mods cover areas of high aerodynamic drag, such as the engine nacelle exhaust ports ($980/kit, $1,350/installed).

Knots 2U also has a one-piece windshield for the Twin Comanche that extends nine inches further into the roofline for better visibility. It is one-quarter-inch thick and tinted and costs $950 for the kit or $1,900 installed.

And what does all this buy the Twin Comanche flyer? Improved performance overall, some more docile behavior on landing, some eight to 12 knots better cruise speed, along with the better handling that entails a 200 to 300 fpm increase in climb speed, along with slightly better fuel consumption.

Knots 2U, Inc. is at 1941 Highland Ave., Wilmette, Ill. 60091, (312) 256-4807.

Maintenance Expert

Those looking for the ultimate maintenance guru for their aging Twin Comanche need look no farther than Robert Gift of Lock Haven Airmotive, Lock Haven, Pa., (717) 748-5820. Gift was service manager at Piper at the time of Twin Comanche production and is widely acknowledged as the expert in type.

The Society

For a good, eclectic (if not exactly impartial) information source on the Twin Comanche, get in touch with the International Comanche Society. While ICS's main concern is the single-engine cousin of the Twin, they also list a large number of Twin enthusiasts in their ranks. Home for the ICS is Box 468, Lyons, Kans. 67554. Telephone (316) 257-5138. Don't be put off if the person answering the phone doesn't immediately identify the place as the ICS; the organization shares office space with a print shop.

Owner Comments

I have owned a 1963 PA-30 for six years. It is by far the most reliable, cost effective aircraft I have ever owned or even been near. Cruise at 65 percent power, peak EGT, is 15 knots while burning 13.5 gph total. None of the new light twins can come close, and they are built like Spam cans; the PA-30 is solid. And it only cost me $27,000 in 1977! With the standard tanks (84 gals.) zero wind range is about 800 nautical miles with an hour's reserve.

If you are thinking of buying a PA-30/39 or a PA-24, you should join the International Comanche Society. Their monthly magazine, the *Comanche Flyer,* contains much useful information on both the

singles and twins. There is also a compilation of past information called ''Tips'' which can be purchased.

Keith F. Kelly, Jr.
Dallas, Tex.

Growing up in Lock Haven, I watched the development of the PA-30 with more than casual interest, spent a lot of time in them, was involved in the manufacture and new model refinements in the late '60s early '70s, disagreed strongly with the decision to curtail its production, and recently was a part-owner of a 1968 Turbo Twin Comanche.

Therefore, my comments might be somewhat prejudiced. However, I believe that the Twin Comanche remains one of the best airplanes every built by Piper; certainly one of the prettiest planes in the sky, fast, economical and a delight to fly, but it is not a toy. It is a small, high-performance airplane that must be flown as such.

For what it's worth, I've listed what stand out to me as the major pluses and minuses of the Twin Comanche:

Pluses:
Ecomony—both operating and maintenance. Quiet cabin—even by today's standards. Performance—especially cruise and takeoff performance. Appearance. Simple systems—fuel, landing gear, flaps, fresh air. Very solid construction, especially the wing spars. Easy access to the engines for maintenance. Flat, uncluttered floor. C.G. range and load carrying capability. Responsive, well-balanced controls. Convenient

Turbo Twin Comanche is beloved for high speed, economy, and purring quiet, but watch out for those pesky Rajay turboes.

storage areas under front seats. Stable platform for instrument flying. Range. Those sleek, low-drag nacelles. Handy check lists and power setting charts on visors.

Minuses:
Landing characteristics, especially with full flaps. Lack of easy access to engines for preflight. Stall characteristics. Visibility, especially compared to newer aircraft. S/E performance. Heavy nose gear steering on ground. Props that don't like to stay in synch. The instrument panel is busy, crowded, poorly arranged in early models and has too many placards. Fresh air inlets are noisy and inadequate on hot days.

With regard to service and support, our experiences were that Piper still supports the airplane quite well with sheet metal and interior items. However, when we checked on buying new engine mounts, both the price and the lead time were prohibitive. The main problem areas, though, are vendor-supplied parts and systems, such as the STCd turbocharger, avionics and the heater.

After all these years, the Twin Comanche remains one of, if not the most, efficient twin-engine aircraft available. It has its faults and must be flown with respect. It is so clean that it can pick up speed quite rapidly in even a shallow dive, and with its abrupt stall characteristics, maintaining proper airspeeds on approach and in the pattern is a must. Nevertheless, it is a pleasure to fly and certainly one of the most economical and practical cross-country planes for one to four people ever produced.

John R. Piper
Culver, Kans.

I have been the owner of a 1971 PA-39 (counter-rotating prop) model for two-and-one-half years. This is my third Comanche over a 15-year period, starting in 1968 with the PA 24-180 model, upgrading to the 250 and then the Twin. My experience with Comanche Singles' excellent reliability, comfort, load carrying ability, simplicity of systems, and cost effectiveness continues, with the PA-39 Twin.

My aircraft has 1,530 hours total time, the cylinder heads have never been off, and the original engines are running perfectly with no less than 73 lbs. pressure per cylinder. Oil consumption is reasonable for engines with over 1,500 hours, averaging one quart (per engine) for every 10-12 flight hours.

In terms of range and flexibility, I've found this aircraft to be nothing short of fantastic. With 120 gallons total fuel capacity (tip tanks), practical range exceeds seven hours duration and 1,300 miles, leaving a reasonable 15-17 gallon fuel reserve. Maximum range (reflecting speed improvements due to the Knots-2U installation) is about 1,550 miles. Trying for max range is too much for my constitution, but it is nice to know when planning 1,300-mile legs that there's lots of reserve.

Regarding the Knots-2U installation, performed by Jim Bradshaw's group, the results are exceptional for what I consider to be a very fair installation price and quality workmanship. I spent approximately $2,000 to have the aileron/flap gap seals and the wing-root speed fairing installed in 1982. An accurate estimate of the increased airspeed is six knots. Together with a very capable 17,000-hour total time instructor, I have put this plane through its

Miller mod also offers nacelle baggage bins. No worries about balance; they're located very near the center of gravity.

paces in all flight regimens. As a result of the Knots-2U installation, it typically exceeds the manufacturer's specification by 30-40 fpm for single-engine rate of climb, and the power-off stall speed appears to be reduced by at least a knot or two.

Another important result of the Knots-2U installation is marked improvement of landing characteristics. While my total Twin Comanche time is only 250 hours, I have over 2,000 hours in single-engine Comanches which, with controlled release of manual flaps, could always be brought in for a smooth landing. The Twin Comanche, however, is somewhat more difficult to "grease in," particularly with full-flap settings. My instructor, and other high-time Twin Comanche pilots I know, either use half-flap settings to achieve smooth landing consistently or resign themselves to about a 50/50 chance of pre-landing stalls six to eight inches above the runway.

Dropping it in form a height of six to eight inches should have minimal impact on the longevity of the landing gear, but is not a great way to impress your passengers. As a consequence of the Knots-2U installation, I can count on a perfect landing 95 percent of the time with half flaps and with full flaps and careful speed control, ("a steady 82 knots on the final approach seems best"), I can get a greaser about 75 percent of the time. Prior to the Knots-2U installation, I had given up on full flap landings except in short-field situations where I was willing to accept the minor adverse consequences.

As to speed, I can consistently rely on 168-170-knot cruise speeds at 6,000-8,000-foot altitudes with a fuel burn of about 17 gallons per hour. For more range, I use lower power settings and get about 160 knots on 15 gph. I have met other Twin Comanche pilots who contend they get similar speeds burning up to two gallons per hour less fuel, but I do try to run the engines at 25%-50% below peak EGT.

I bought this aircraft for $42,000 in 1981 and have put approximately $18,000 of capital improvements into it for new paint, interior, avionics, etc. While I had expected to buy a set of new engines, my mechanic informs me that Twin Comanches typically run to their 2,000 hour TBO and advised me to stick with the existing engines since compression tests, oil analysis, and overall operating performance indicate that they are in perfect condition.

Considering the extra fun of flying a twin ("fist-full of throttles/macho syndrome"), the reliability of those little Lycomings, the high airspeed in relation to the horse-power/fuel consumption equation, etc., I am exceptionally pleased with the Twin Comanche. There is no new light twin on the market that can match the fuel economy, performance, range and flexibility even at three to four times my total investment. When you have something as good as the Twin Comanche, why switch? I would advise anyone interested in a PA-30 or -39 to hurry out to buy one before that flying public wakes up to their exceptional value, and the remaining number get bid up substantially compared to today's bargain basement prices.

Joseph E. Sichler
Simsbury, Conn.

Piper Seneca

As heir apparent to the Twin Comanche, the Piper PA-34 Seneca has been an enormous marketing success since it burst upon the scene in 1972. But used-plane buyers should be aware that there's a difference of night and day between the models that were built before and after 1975.

The first Seneca had normally aspirated Lycomings in blunt nacelles. Handling qualities were quite deficient.

The pre-1975 models had no turbocharging and possessed an absurdly low single-engine ceiling along with what many pilots regard as abominable handling characteristics both in the air and on the ground. Coupled with short range and a lackluster payload, these qualities made the airplane ripe for a wholesale redesign.

Piper came through with just that in the 1975 model, by replacing the four-cylinder Lycoming IO-360s with turbocharged six-cylinder Continental TSIO-360s. This provided the Seneca with a more than respectable single-engine ceiling, a significant increase in payload — and better aesthetics, to boot, since the new powerplants were housed in much better looking streamlined cowls.

On top of that, the aircraft's control system was modified to eliminate its awkward handling characteristics.

Nevertheless, the newer Continental powerplants have not been without their problems, and they have received mixed reviews from owners and maintenance and overhaul shops.

The Early Models

The 1972 Seneca first on the scene was an ill suited adaptation of the Cherokee Six fuselage and wings to multi configuration. The nose gear steering was ponderously heavy, partly because the rudder was tied in with the aileron system, and every time the pilot kicked in left or right rudder, the ailerons responded as well, adding to the tug on the pedals.

This characteristic, engineered to satisfy the need to be able to raise a wing in flight with the rudders alone, gave the aircraft equally ponderous flight controls. The aircraft was at its worst in turbulent IFR work and in gusty crosswind landings, when the pilot could find himself banking left and right in great pendulum swings, as he attempted to keep the wings level.

Promoted as an ideal, simple step-up machine for single-engine pilots, the early Senecas were anything but that.

To make up for a serious deficiency in load-carrying ability, Piper in the 1973 model pulled a mostly paper-work exercise that boosted the gross and useful load by 200 pounds, but it did so at the sacrifice of an already low single-engine ceiling — which dropped from 5,200 feet to 3,650 feet.

A Rash of Fixes

The pre-75 models also were plagued with potentially expensive fixes that unleashed a series of service letters, bulletins and Airworthiness Directives. The main landing gear support structure was hit with such an AD in '73 and the outer wing spars in '74.

Piper came out with kits allowing installation of skin and rib reinforcement doublers in '74 after "wing skin irregularities" were found under the wings outboard of the main landing gear wells in some aircraft. They also brought out a reinforcement kit to buttress the aft wing assembly after cracks were found at the juncture of the main landing gear with the aft false spar.

An exhaust system that turned up serious cracking problems was replaced in '73 by a completely new, "vastly superior" (said Piper) exhaust system of longer life, that eliminated the repetitive inspections required on the earlier system. This was offered as a retrofit.

During the first year of operation, some Senecas also were found to have loose balance weight assemblies on the stabilator tips, and an AD was issued on this. There have since been at least two, and possibly three Seneca crashes due to stabilator failure. (Incidentally, Piper's first prototype Seneca crashed during testing when the stabilator failed.)

In 1975 the usable fuel dropped form 95 to 93 gallons, and it was found that possible rough finish on the landing gear oleo struts might have been causing the struts to bind, putting extra load on the wing in landing, and causing wing cracks.

Buyers looking at the older model Senecas should keep all these pointers in mind during their inspection of the aircraft.

The New II — A Whole New Ballgame

The 1975 Seneca II wrought major changes in the flying personality of the airplane. The turbocharged Continentals removed the onus of the low single-engine ceiling and boosted it up to 13,400 feet. The powerful downspring that made the original Seneca awkward in the landing flare was replaced by a less potent one and a bobweight. Also, the rudder-aileron interconnect was removed, and a bungee smoothed out rudder steering during taxi. Furthermore, lateral control was improved by lengthening the ailerons.

Whereas the original Lycoming-powered model had seemed extremely noisy and vibration-prone, the new Continental package quieted and smoothed things down significantly. The "poor-man's" automatic turbo control also made its debut on this airplane. Equipped with a simple by-pass valve and an overboost relief valve, it eliminated the need for a sophisticated automatic wastegate. However, at the same time, it demanded more attention from the pilot on takeoff to prevent excess spoolup as the throttles were advanced. In addition, the manifold pressure was extremely sensitive to minor changes in rpm, airspeed and altitude; consequently, precise power management could be a real chore. This, of course, compounded the problems of pilots transitioning from singles, though the handling qualities of the aircraft were greatly improved.

Along with a jump in gross weight, the Seneca II offered an additional 186 pounds in useful load which the airplane desperately needed to take advantage of its truly commodious six-place cabin and 200-pound baggage capacity.

Pilots should be aware, however, that the Seneca II has a zero fuel weight limitation of 4,000 pounds. Therefore, anything above 4,000 pounds, up to the 4,570-pound gross weight must be in fuel only, not people or baggage.

In 1982, Piper spruced up the airplane once more and called it the Seneca III. Changes were not quite so dramatic as in the changeover from I to II, but the improvements were nevertheless worthwhile: an engine uprate that increased power from 200 hp to 220 hp, a 180-pound increase in gross weight, a wing beefup that increased the zero-fuel weight to a more reasonable 4,400 pounds, and a new windshield, along with other minor improvements.

Loading

A nice feature of the Seneca's baggage loading format is that half can be loaded in the nose compartment to ease weight and balance problems if need be. And everyone who talks about the airplane give high marks to the both-sides, front-and-rear door configuration for loading and unloading of people and cargo. Also, club seating adds a little variety to the passenger format.

High Safety Marks

The National Transportation Safety Board's comparative accident figures show the Seneca to have the lowest fatal accident rate of seven popular classes of twins surveyed. Its total accident rate, however, placed it right in the middle of the pack.

If any one category of problem dominates the NTSB accident roster from 1971-1975, it is collapsing landing gear. Out of 57 reports, 15 dealt with this. Some of them were attributed to simple overload failures because of hard landings, or landing hot and attempting to turn off at too high a speed, but several were tracked to component failure.

The nose gear drag link bolt failed or was pulled from its fittings in two of these accidents.

The second largest problem area was related to engine failure or diminished power output from one or both engines — with 10 of those reported. On no less than four of these, dual instruction was involved, where the flight instructor yanked the mixture on one engine, and a problem developed on a go-around. In one case the wrong sparkplugs were used, and in another there was a problem relating to valves and plugs.

Cost/Performance/Specifications

Model	Year Built	Number Built	Cruise Speed (kts)	Rate of Climb (fpm)	S.E. Service Ceiling (ft)	Useful Load (lbs)	Fuel (gals)	Engine	TBO (hrs)	Overhaul Cost	Average Price
PA-34-200	1972	360	163	1,460	5,200	1,414	93	200-hp Lyc. IO-360-C1E6	1,400	$11,000	$ 28,000
PA-34-200	1973	353	163	1,360	3,650	1,614	93	200-hp Lyc. IO-360-C1E6	1,400	$11,000	$ 29,000
PA-34-200	1974	214	163	1,360	3,650	1,614	93	200-hp Lyc. IO-360-C1E6	1,400	$11,000	$ 31,000
PA-34-200T	1975	327	177	1,340	13,400	1,800	93	200-hp Cont. TSIO-360-E	1,400	$13,000	$ 41,000
PA-34-200T	1976	371	177	1,340	13,400	1,800	93	200-hp Cont. TSIO-360-E	1,400	$13,000	$ 44,000
PA-34-200T	1977	433	177	1,340	13,400	1,800	93/123	200-hp Cont. TSIO-360-E	1,400	$13,000	$ 48,000
PA-34-200T	1978	474	177	1,340	13,400	1,800	93/123	200-hp Cont. TSIO-360-E	800	$13,000	$ 54,000
PA-34-200T	1979	530	177	1,340	13,400	1,800	93/123	200-hp Cont. TSIO-360-E	800	$13,000	$ 62,000
PA-34-200T	1980	367	177	1,340	13,400	1,800	93/123	200-hp Cont. TSIO-360-E	800	$13,000	$ 71,000
PA-34-200T	1981	85	177	1,340	13,400	1,800	93/123	200-hp Cont. TSIO-360-E	800	$13,000	$ 83,000
PA-34-200T	1982	179	177	1,400	12,300	1,900	93/123	200-hp Cont. TSIO-360-KB	1,800	$13,500	$115,000
PA-34-200T	1983	115	177	1,400	12,300	1,900	93/123	200-hp Cont. TSIO-360-KB	1,800	$13,500	$125,000
PA-34-200T	1984	178	177	1,400	12,300	1,900	93/123	200-hp Cont. TSIO-360-KB	1,800	$13,500	$150,000

On the older Senecas two pilots were distracted enough by a cabin door opening in flight to crash. One occurred on an aborted take-off; the other forgot to put the gear down before landing. The newer Senecas have improved door latches.

Powerplant Record

The Seneca's II's weak spot is engine reliability. The Continental TSIO-360 with the fixed wastegate has not proved very reliable in the field, suffering a number of cylinder and valve problems related to overheating. (The same engine in the Turbo Arrow and Turbo Dakota has a poor record, partly due to the very poor cooling in those aircraft.) At high altitudes, it also suffers from magneto misfiring. (Piper steadfastly refuses to install pressurized magnetos, as Mooney did with its 231, which also uses the TSIO-360.) And finally, the TSIO-360 has had more than its share of broken crankshafts and oil pump drives.

A review of FAA service difficulty reports showed that of the 135 Seneca engine problems listed in the FAA's tally (usually estimated to be about 10 percent of the total number of problems actually experienced in the field), the largest portion (26) were related to electrical system failures — like condensers, capacitors, leads, coils, etc. The second largest group was attributed to cylinder failures and cracks (16). The third stemmed from turbo problems with scrolls, housings, brackets, etc. (9). And the fourth was directed at scarred or damaged pistons (6). Four broken crankshafts were reported, but in 1977 the Piper factory issued a service bulletin calling attention to the fact that there had been 12 engine stoppages due to "technically unexplained" crankshaft fractures. There were two reports of cracked crankcases on the Seneca IIs (out of a fleet of about 1,600 aircraft flying).

Dipstick Mystery

One strange problem that surfaced in connection with the Seneca en-

Seneca Resale Value Chart

gines concerned oil dipstick calibration. Two Seneca II owners had notified us to complain that their dipsticks registered a quart and a half or so too little, which led service personnel to put in too much oil. Four reports of incorrect dipstick calibration were also listed on the FAA's Service Difficulty rundown of Seneca IIs.

Each pilot who contacted us noted he had become involved with Piper and Continental in a heated discussion of the problem, and that they were concerned about engine damage from overloading with oil because of the incorrectly registered dipsticks.

One engine maintenance expert we contacted, however, volunteered that the problem might stem from the fact that the Senecas have different dipsticks for left and right powerplants. This is because the wings have such a pronounced dihedral; and since the dipstick is mounted on the left side on each engine, each has to measure a different oil level.

He speculated that the engines might occasionally come from the factory with the wrong dipsticks installed.

As for whether too much oil could damage the engine or would simply be thrown out of the breather harmlessly, our mechanic pointed out: "Too much oil is no good.

Your crankshaft thrashes around in the oil, and bubbles and aerates it, so the oil pump picks up air and oil rather than pure oil. You can burn up an engine by putting in too much oil, since air is not a very good lubricant."

Mechanic's Nightmare

The judgment of other mechanics and overhaul shops was that the TSIO-360 powerplant was, in general, a nice, smooth running engine. One powerplant instructor at an air university though, insisted that the design posed a problem when things went wrong.

"It's a tough little engine to work on," he said. "It's cramped and nothing fits — it's just a mechanic's nightmare. If it starts giving you trouble, the repair bill looks like the gross national product."

He attributed the electrical accessory problems noted on the Service Difficulty list to the engine being "tightly cowled and tightly baffled, with a lot of heat built up inside."

Some mechanics figured the cylinder and piston problems could be traced to pushing the engine too hard for prolonged periods under turbo boost. For that matter, fleet operators we talked to shared the opinion that the aircraft as a whole was not built ruggedly enough to be pushed too hard in commercial operations, though it seemed to stand up satisfactorily for personal use.

Among idiosyncrasies that turned up in our interviews was one complaint that the alternators put out too little power at low taxi rpms "to do the job," and the comment of one mechanic that it was necessary to reinforce the fiberglass area behind the spinner on the nose cowl because it seemed to have a tendency to crack.

Seneca II engines also are noted for cold-weather starting problems. To tackle this, Piper first issued special starting instructions for pilots, and then came out with an optional cold-weather priming kit for the aircraft.

Resale Value

As might be expected, the resale value curves for the pre- and post-'75 Senecas are quite different. The average '73 Seneca, for example, dropped almost $16,000 the first year whereas a '75 Seneca II could be expected, on the average, to lose only around $13,000. On top of that, where the '73 model bottomed in four years, the '75 model started back up in resale value after only three years.

Modifications

There are two major modifications available for the Seneca. Laminar Flow Systems, Box 8557, St. Thomas, U.S. Virgin Islands 00801 (809) 775-5515, sells an aerodynamic clean-up mod consisting of aileron and flap gap seals, flap track fairings, wing rivet fairings and wheel well fairings. The mod increases speed by 15-20 mph. (Speed gain is less if the airplane is equipped with de-ice boots, which prevents the use of the leading-edge wing rivet fairings.) The LFS mod can be applied to any model Seneca. Cost is $3,000 for the kit. Installation can run another $1,500 or so.

For the Seneca II and III, Turbo-plus, Inc., Gig Harbor, Wash. (800) 742-4202, sells an engine mod kit that includes an intercooler, im-proved induction system, pressurized ignition system and an uprate to the 220-hp standard for the Seneca II. It also sells speedbrakes. Cost for the complete mod is $15,210 installed, although it may be purchased piecemeal.

Owner Comments

We flew our Seneca 2,500 hours in three years with a total cost of $30,000 in maintenance costs. We lost six jugs; three were replaced under warranty, but we paid for the other three. At 1,400 hours, we lost the right engine. I examined it when it was torn down, and there had been detonation. Continental said those engines were overboosted. We ended up rebuilding both, at a cost by Reading Air Service of $14,511. After that our engine maintenance went to nil.

•

We had problems with the dipsticks reading incorrectly. To get the dipstick to read 6 1/4 quarts, you had to put eight quarts in the engine. This could be a real hazard because if you put too much oil in, you can bend the rods.

•

Lost nine jugs in 1,600 hours — average cost, $600 per jug.

Overall utility of my '77 Seneca II is superb. It handles well both on the ground and in the air. Control forces are quite well balanced. I like the way Seneca is off and running in short order, climbing at a solid 1,200 to 1,500 fpm. Landings require slightly more patience.

The not-so-good news includes difficulty maintaining level pitch attitude in cruise configuration. This is especially annoying when accompanied by moderate to strong winds and thermal updrafts. Level pitch trim is particularly elusive at high altitudes. The only other substantial 'handling' complaint is a tendency to yaw in turbulence — a particularly nauseating event for the rear-most passengers.

Also, zero-fuel weight limitation could be a problem for heavy haulers. Seating comfort is quite good with the exception of the rearmost seats (club configuration) which are much to low

Visibility in most directions (with the possible exception of rearward) is very satisfactory. All in all I'm very pleased with this plane's capabilities.

The bad news could be categorized under engine instrumentation and avionics interference, with the latter perhaps related to an alternator or voltage regulator. The most bothersome problem is the sensitivity and continuous discrepancy of engine instrument indications. Uneven surges in manifold pressure needles (even with slow, smooth power applications), and splits in fuel flow indicators are enough to drive even a seasoned pilot up a wall. Continuous engine adjustment and smooth power application seem to be an absolute must.

An incessant 'buzzing' drone on the ADF audio and also the radios (test mode) is currently among the trouble-shooting list items, with alternators and/or voltage regulators as chief suspects. Other irritants include heater malfunction, generator popping off line, voltage spikes (suspect strobe package), faulty operation of optional fuel primer button (for start-up), a precessing DG (suspect bad bearings).

Most of these items are being or have been 'diagnosed' by one or more fixed-base repair shops with limited corrective success. I've gotten fair to good cooperation from the factory on suggestions as to how to solve these glitches, but I'm becoming more impatient with each passing day.

For a new aircraft (375 hours), I've had more than my share of headaches. Were it not for my appreciation for the overall utility of this bird, I'd be driven stark raving mad!

Cessna Skymaster 337

Cessna's most ingenious aircraft, the 337 Skymaster, is one of aviation's greatest paradoxes. As a used-plane, it's both a great buy and a washout. Conceived as the safest twin flying, the 337 is probably one of the biggest used multi bargains to be found, since prices are quite low. But as an investment, the Skymaster is a flop. Values don't level off and eventually rise with inflation; they simply slide down a great toboggan run. And maintenance complaints are fairly high.

Although the recipient of some of Cessna's most intriguing technical innovations — like centerline thrust and pressurization — the Skymaster somehow never made it as a smashing success, for reasons the company often pondered in the past. One popular theory is that so "safe" an airplane loses macho appeal to pilots.

Another theory is simply that the Skymaster doesn't go as fast as multiengines are supposed to. Since the 337 started life as a competitor to the Piper Twin Comanche with a mere 190-mph cruise as an economy twin, it has never been endowed with big enough engines to make it more of a demon speedster, and pull it out of the performance doldroms.

Aside from lackluster speed, the Skymaster suffers also from the lack of a genuine baggage compartment. The rear of the cabin can be devoted either to a fifth and sixth seat, or to baggage. A lower fuselage baggage pod can be added on at the cost of only a modicum of speed, but at the sacrifice of looks.

Centerline Thrust

The Skymaster's major rationale, of course, is elimination of the asymmetrical thrust problems of single-engine operation. Lose an engine on a Skymaster on climbout, and even at low speeds the aircraft won't twist irresistibly to one side or the other at high power settings. On one engine, however, the Skymaster at gross is no zephyr, even at sea level, since it will eke out a climb rate (on the normally aspirated model) of no greater than 235 to 300 fpm on the front engine, and slightly better on the rear one — provided the pilot feathers the right prop and cleans up the aircraft.

The shortage of muscle from just one engine to push the 337 around is impressed upon any pilot who puts the aircraft through its paces with one out, both in the air and on the ground. Lose a fan during taxi,

Skymasters should be the safest twins flying, but NTSB figures disclose a calamitous accident record. U.S. production of the aircraft stopped in 1980.

especially on the grass, and it takes a surprising blast of power on the live engine to keep the Skymaster's bulk moving.

This is not to suggest the Skymaster is a cumbersome, awkward airplane under normal circumstances with both engines operating. Though it takes a ponderous heave to rotate on takeoff, once airborne the aircraft has more facile ailerons than most twins though it possesses the usual heavy Cessna pitch pressures. Most pilots also come to regard the aircraft as a kind of poor-man's STOL, and the airplane is no slouch at getting in and out of tight spaces. Visibility is surprisingly good for a twin, since the wing is set back quite far from the pilot, and there are no engine nacelles out on the wings to obscure an airport on downwind.

Safety

As, theoretically, the safest twin around, the Skymaster received lots of unfavorable publicity and lawsuits a few years back when it was found that pilots were occasionally losing an engine (the rear one, usually) on takeoff roll, and continuing the takeoff attempt with awkward results, not realizing they'd lost a fan, or perhaps not caring.

Early models had a warning light to tell pilots when an engine had failed, activated by torque changes. Proper takeoff technique is to advance the throttle for the rear engine first to make sure everything's working, and then feed in the front engine. A placard mandated by an AD warns pilots not to take off on one engine, if they didn't know.

Another AD required raising the idle speed of the rear engine, so it would be less likely to poop out on takeoff, and pilots were told to taxi mainly by using the rear engine, to keep it warmed up and ready.

A 1979 National Transportation Safety Board study of light twin-engine aircraft accidents showed the Cessna Skymaster had the third worst fatal accident rate of 20 aircraft, after the Beech 18 and the Aero Commander 500, 520 and 560 series. In an attempt to isolate accident causes, we inspected a five-year rundown of accident briefs on the Skymaster from 1973 to 1977.

This examination showed that of the 29 fatal accidents reported during the period the greatest number — seven — were caused by weather related problems. One might reason that perhaps less-experienced pilots tend to migrate toward the Skymaster — supposedly a safe, easy stepup twin. The weather fatalities, however, suggest this is not so since most of the pilots involved had commercial tickets, were instrument rated and had lots of experience, but simply blundered into fog or ice they couldn't handle.

The next three accident categories that generated the highest frequency of fatal crashes did, however, involve the aircraft design. These were: engine failure on takeoff, fuel exhaustion and stall/spins.

Three fatal accidents were caused by loss of power on takeoff and climbout. Two of those involved failure of the rear engine. On one, witnesses had noted the rear engine running during taxi, but it had stopped during the takeoff roll. The aircraft stalled in climbout and then caught fire after impact. The private pilot had 516 hours total, 212 in type.

In another fatal accident, the rear engine failed on takeoff because of a plugged rear fuel pump vapor ejector; the pilot failed to abort and fire broke out after impact. The ATP pilot with 3,570 hours had three hours in type.

In the third fatal, both engines failed on takeoff, followed by a crash and fire. The private pilot had 1,800 hours, 94 in type.

There were two fatal accidents from engine failure because of fuel exhaustion, and two attributed to stall/spins. Most of the stall/spin or mush accidents appear unrelated to any particular aircraft deficiency. Of the two fatals, one occurred during a buzzing incident; the other was attributed to pilot fatigue.

Two nonfatals were related to engine failure. One pilot actually attempted to take off with the rear engine out, and the prop not feathered. He hit the trees. Another pilot stalled after he lost one engine from fuel starvation.

In a surprising number of instances, pilots who lost just one engine were unable to bring the aircraft back to a safe landing, despite the fact that the centerline thrust spared them the usual multi-engine problems of asymmetrical thrust and the traditional stall/spin threat with an engine out.

Skymasters also were plagued with a high rate of nonfatal accidents. Here the greatest toll was

Cost/Performance/Specifications

Model	Year Built	Number Built	Cruise Speed (kts)	Rate of Climb (fpm)	Useful Load (lbs)	S.E. Service Ceiling (ft)	Fuel Std/Opt gals	Engine	TBO (hrs)	Average Retail Price	Overhaul Cost Ea.
336	1964	195	150	1,300	1,580	8,200	93/131	210-hp Cont. IO-360-A	1,500	$16,000	$11,000
337	1965	238	167	1,200	1,565	8,300	93/131	210-hp Cont. IO-360-C/D	1,500	$18,000	$11,000
337A	1966	284	167	1,200	1,585	8,200	93/131	210-hp Cont. IO-360-C/D	1,500	$21,000	$11,000
337B	1967	226	167	1,250	1,685	7,500	93/131	210-hp Cont. IO-360-C/D	1,500	$22,000	$11,000
T-337B	1967	226	196	1,250	1,515	20,000	93/131	210-hp Cont. TSIO-360-A/B	1,400	$22,500	$12,000
337C	1968	207	166	1,200	1,750	6,800	93/131	210-hp Cont. IO-360-C/D	1,500	$22,500	$11,000
T-337C	1968	207	195	1,155	1,705	18,600	93/131	210-hp Cont. TSIO-360-A/B	1,400	$23,000	$12,000
337D	1969	199	166	1,200	1,745	6,800	93/131	210-hp Cont. IO-360-C/D	1,500	$23,000	$11,000
T-337D	1969	199	195	1,185	1,485	16,200	93/131	210-hp Cont. TSIO-360-A/B	1,400	$23,500	$12,000
337E	1970	122	166	1,180	1,820	6,500	93/131	210-hp Cont. IO-360-C	1,500	$23,750	$11,000
T-337E	1970	122	223	1,105	1,780	14,400	93/131	210-hp Cont. TSIO-360-A	1,400	$25,500	$12,000
337F	1971-72	132	166	1,100	1,935	5,100	93/131	210-hp Cont. IO-360-C	1,500	$27,000	$11,000
T-337F	1971	132	194	1,105	1,780	14,400	93/131	210-hp Cont TSIO-360-A	1,400	$28,000	$12,000
337G	1973-74	143	169	1,100	1,517	6,900	90/150	210-hp Cont. IO-360-G	1,500	$31,000	$11,000
T-337G-P	1973-74	194	204	1,250	1,533	18,700	151	225-hp Cont. TSIO-360-C	1,400	$39,000	$12,000
337G II	1975	64	169	1,100	1,517	6,900	90/150	210-hp Cont. IO-360-G	1,500	$34,000	$11,000
T-337G-P	1975	31	204	1,250	1,533	18,700	151	225-hp Cont. TSIO-360-C	1,400	$47,000	$12,000
337G II	1976	76	169	1,100	1,517	6,900	90/150	210-hp Cont. IO-360-G	1,500	$36,000	$11,000
T-337G-P	1976	31	204	1,250	1,533	18,700	151	225-hp Cont. TSIO-360-C	1,400	$54,000	$12,000
337G II	1977	66	169	1,100	1,517	6,900	90/150	210-hp Cont. IO-360-G	1,500	$39,500	$11,000
T-337G-P	1977	34	204	1,250	1,533	18,700	151	225-hp Cont. TSIO-360-C	1,400	$61,000	$12,000
337H II	1978	na	169	950	1,687	6,900	40/150	210-hp Cont. IO-360-G	1,500	$43,500	$11,000
T-337H II	1978	na	200	1,160	1,608	16,500	93/131	210-hp Cont. TSIO-360-H	1,400	$48,500	$12,000
337H II	1979	na	169	940	1,687	6,900	90/150	210-hp Cont. IO-360-GB	1,500	$51,500	$11,000
T-337H II	1979	na	200	1,160	1,608	16,500	93/131	210-hp Cont. TSIO-360-H	1,400	$58,000	$12,000
T-337H-P	1978	na	204	1,120	1,533	18,700	150	225-hp Cont. TSIO-360-C	1,400	$69,000	$12,000
T-337H-P	1979	na	204	1,120	1,533	18,700	150	225-hp Cont. TSIO-360-CB	1,400	$79,000	$12,000
337H II	1980	47	169	940	1,687	6,900	150	210-hp Cont. IO-360-GB	1,500	$61,500	$11,000
T-337H II	1980	30	1,160	1,608	16,500	150		210-hp Cont. TSIO-360-G	1,400	$70,500	$12,000
T-337H-P	1980	14	204	1,120	1,533	18,700	150	225-hp Cont. TSIO-360-CB	1,400	$91,000	$12,000

taken by simple fuel exhaustion — just running completely out of fuel. This happened no less than 13 times. Though Cessna likes to stress the high accuracy of the fuel gauges in the Skymasters, thanks to the capacitance type of measuring system, the location of both fuel gauges on the right side of the instrument panel cannot make fuel monitoring any easier for the pilot in the left seat. The fact that there are only two gauges for four fuel tanks — two mains and two aux tanks, also adds to the complexity of the task, since while any one set of tanks is in use, the pilot cannot see at a glance how much fuel remains in the other tanks.

Skymaster pilots have to switch from main to aux tanks for each engine.

Second biggest cause of nonfatal accidents in Skymasters was hard landings. Eleven of these were called out during the five-year period studied. Most involved propoising, and improper recovery from a bounced landing, often followed by a gear collapse.

Categories

There are four main classes of Skymasters. The aircraft was introduced in 1964 as a fixed-gear twin designated the 336. In 1967 the first turbocharged version was offered, followed in 1973 by the pressurized model. The clamshell door and smaller windows mandated by pressurization were carried over to the entire Skymaster line, except for bigger front-seat side windows for the non-pressurized models.

Note also that the pressurized version does not have a rear baggage door. Unlike most high-wing Cessnas, the Skymasters never had a left-side pilot's door. Entry is from the right front door.

With the pressurized model came a boost in horsepower from 210 each to 225 each. TBO for the powerful engine and the turbo 210 is 1,400 hours vs. 1,500 for the normally aspirated version.

Early models up through the '68 C version had TBOs of only 1,200

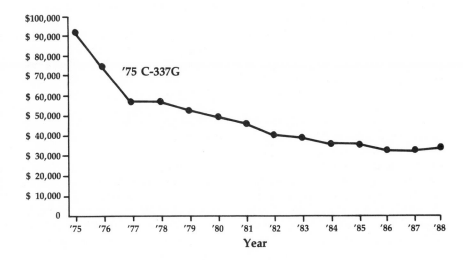

Skymaster 337 Resale Value Chart

'75 C-337G

hours. This went to 1,500 hours with '69 models, thanks to the addition of nickel exhuast valves.

Gross weight on the Skymaster has risen from 4,200 pounds to 4,630 through the years, and to 4,700 pounds on the pressurized version.

Load Carrying

A 1972 model with a 4,630-pound gross and 1,935-pound useful load can handle a pretty good payload for a "light twin." With 150 pounds of optional equipment, the aircraft can heft full optional fuel of 131 gallons along with five adults and about 112 pounds of baggage. Range without reserve at 75 percent works out to about 1,060 sm, at 164 knots.

Maintenance

Skymaster owners report they have the most problems with the electrical system and the brakes. And a nearly universal complaint is that they can't seem to eliminate excess coating of the rear cowl and belly and horizontal stabilizer with oil.

Another dominant gripe among Skymaster owners is that "you can't get parts."

Airworthiness Directives

Aside for the aforementioned ADs

requiring a placard to warn aginst taking off on one engine and raising rear engine idle speeds, among other noteworthy ADs there was an AD requiring inspection of aircraft with over 5,000 hours of service for wing front and rear spar lower cap cracks. And another required checking flap actuator jacks for proper lubrication to forestall inadvertent retraction of flaps. Another AD required installation of a cooling duct for the fuel gauges, to prevent overheating and smoking.

Modifications

There are several STOL mods available for Skymasters from a host of companies. The most elaborate is R/STOL Systems', which installs drooped ailerons, recontoured wing leading edges, stall fences and flap actuated elevator trim springs. This mod also raises takeoff gross weight.

More modest STOL treatment, usually involving cuffing wing leading edges and modifying the wing tips and installation of vortex generators on the fuselage and fairings on the vertical tails is available on Supplemental Type Certificates issued to Horton STOL-Craft in Wellington, Kansas; Mid-America STOL in Wichita, Kansas, and Gus W. Simpson of STOL Aircraft Devices in Dallas, Texas.

A one-piece windshield STC is held by Beryl D'Shannon Aviation Specialties, Inc. in Leesburg, Florida, and an emergency exit door on top of the fuselage is STC'd by Floair, Inc. in Wichita, Kansas.

An electrically driven freon air conditioning system STC is held by JB Systems, Inc. in Longmont, Colorado, and DeVore Aviation in Albuquerque, New Mexico (505) 345-8713, installs recognition lights on the the trailing edge of R/STOL wing tips. Also, a Fiquench fire extinguishing system is approved for the cabin and engine area by Fike Metal Products Corp., Blue Springs, Missouri.

To accommodate wing-mounted weather radar, Renton Aviation in Renton, Wash. has an STC for installation of Bendix RDR 160 radar.

It should be noted that ownership of the above STCs, taken from the FAA's annual summary, may have changed hands in some cases.

Associations

At last word there was no association of Skymaster owners, though O.R. Whitaker (P.O. Box 1950, Liberal, Kansas 67901, (316) 624-2281) issues a newsletter periodically.

Owner Comments

I have owned a 1973 model 337G for about 18 months and have flown it 300 hours. It is roomy and comfortable for two couples, with plenty of baggage space. My wife likes it because it is easy to board and because there is a good view from all seats. The manufacturer didn't cheat any more than normal on owner's manual performance figures, and it comes pretty close to delivering the claimed performance when it is 800 pounds under gross.

I bought a Skymaster because flying terrifies me, and I think it is the safest airplane I possibly could be in — although its accident statistics do not bear this out. I got the opportunity to test its single-engine capabilities much earlier than desired. I had purchased the airplane in Kansas City, and 1:30 into the flight home, while IFR at 10,000 feet in VFR conditions above a solid undercast, I lost the front engine due to failure of the lube oil pump shaft. Flying to the nearest field and setting her down with only the rear engine running was no problem.

The airframe and engines had 800 hours on them at that time and Continental made a fair and reasonable adjustment on a factory-remanufactured engine — one that would make me want to do business with them in the future.

I could not be more pleased with the airplane itself. Unfortunately, the same is not true of the parts availability for the airframe or the Cessna avionics. Example: it recently took over eight weeks to get a replacement for the "ribbon assembly" — a wiring group which passes through the pilot's control column and connects to the autopilot disengage and electric trim switches on the yoke. Airframe parts availability hasn't been any better. Parts frequently must be re-ordered because orders are lost and never heard from and because wrong parts are shipped. It has been a real disappointment to find that a company like Cessna could do such an amateurish job of product support.

If I were to replace the airplane now, it would be a difficult decision as to whether to buy another 337. There is no other airplane I would rather fly in this size and price category. But I don't know whether I would be willing to get back into the service hassle with another 337. ●

Generally my 1968 Skymaster has met or exceeded book figures. We do have later style drooped wingtips, which may account for modest performance improvements.

The only outstanding irritation is the rear engine's oil leaks — not a serious problem, but who likes a greasy rear engine cowl?

Passenger cabin room is excellent. The noise level can largely be controlled if close attention is given to getting the props synchronized.

Lack of baggage area is a pain, and the optional pod would seem to be a satisfactory solution at a nominal loss of speed. (Quoted as two or three mph.) Heater and cabin ventilation is good. Visibility is far superior to other twins.

Parts and backup have given me no problem.

I am currently spending about $40 per hour, which includes engine reserve, 100-hour engine inspection and radio maintenance. A fairly sizable amount is allocated for radios since they are older units. A noteworthy item is insurance cost. We received a better rate than most twins due to the centerline thrust safety factor.

Had one experience where the complete electrical system kicked out due to high load. A complete electrical system shutdown is required to reset alternators. This happened on final, IFR at night, which was disconcerting. I was told, however, that it is not an unusual occurrence on Skymasters.

Prior to the Skymaster I owned a Comanche 250, and had considered buying either a later Comanche or a 210. When I shopped the market, I discovered that Skymasters were a real bargain compared to the high-performance singles. The Skymaster offered good performance, safety and redundancy. It should be pointed out that redundancy goes well beyond just engines; i.e., alternators, voltage regulators, and vacuum systems. This is a tremendous consideration if anyone does much serious IFR flying. Fuel consumption is good for a twin. We usually get 18-19 gph at about 160 knots.

Overall, I think it is a 'super' light twin that didn't make it big because of its unusual appearance and the ego problems of many individuals looking into this class of plane.

Cessna 310

You've talked it over with your accountant (and presumably your psychiatrist), and you've decided that the time has come to trade up: You want to be able to tote a ton of useful load from one Loran chain to the next, at speeds that will have ATC confusing you with heavy iron, and do it with the (alleged) safety of two engines—all for less than the price of a new 172. The choices are few. You can buy a used Baron or Aztec (or possibly an Aero Commander, or a clapped-out Navajo). Or, you can do what more than 5,000 other light-twin buyers have done—and take home a Cessna 310.

As two-engine planes go, the 310 is singularly impressive—in appearance, if in no other category. (Who could fail to notice those Stabila tip tanks?) The George-Lucas-inspired design of the late-model (Roman-nosed) 310R leaves some pilots cold, admittedly. But despite the Baron-with-a-gland-problem appearance, the 310 proves itself a worthy contender in the six-place twin category, combining get-it-done-today performance with surprisingly docile handling, not to mention the load-carrying capacity of a light armored vehicle.

For every Indian head, there's a buffalo, however, and the flip side of aesthetic overachievement (in this case) is mediocre Dutch-roll stability, high V-speeds, and generally unflattering runway handling. (As one owner puts it, "A one-time flight will endear few pilots to the 310.") But what the 310 lacks in cockpit charisma, it makes up for in raw verve: Cob it, and the mother scoots. Topping 174 knots is no problem single-engine ROC is a creditable 330 to

440 fpm (depending on year/model),and the maximum *two-engine* climb rate will have you begging for ear surgery.

Fuel consumption, maintenance, and insurance costs for the 310 are substantial—but the same is true for any six-place twin. Owners point proudly to the 310's beer-hall cabin proportions, extra-tall (and wide) wheel stance, superb cockpit visibility (especially in later models), and logical panel layout as reasons for preferring a 310 to a Baron or Aztec. Another reason: price. In any given model year, 310s tend to underprice Barons by 10 percent (and more).

Model History

As any Sky King fan knows, the 310 (Cessna's first low-wing aircraft, not counting the wartime UC-78 "Bamboo Bomber"—which was *Sky King's* first airplane) began life as a snub-nosed, straight-tailed, tuna-tanked wonder in 1955. Approximately 1,200 tuna-tank models were delivered before Cessna—intent on enhancing the 310's dihedral stability and sex appeal in one bold stroke—introduced the now-familiar slanted tip tanks on the 310G in 1962. Wing lockers (and an underwing exhaust system) appeared two years later with the 'I' model. Total optional fuel was 133 gallons, carried in the tips (50 gals. each) and wing bladders.

The 1971 model had 260-hp engines and a short nose, but no rear window. Current value on the resale market: $40,000.

The 310K-N models (1966-68) were the first to sport double-wide "Vista-view" side windows. Optional fuel capacity increased to 143 gallons, flap speed (white arc) went from 122 to 139 knots, and three-blade props were offered for the first time. With the 1969 'P' model, optional fuel went to 184 gallons; the nose gear geometry was altered slightly; and the IO-470-V engine got changed to the IO-470-VO (the same as before, but with Nimonic valves, richer fuel injection, and piston oil cooling—all for better top-end life). A Turbo 310P model was offered as well, with more powerful TSIO-520-B engines (285-hp, versus the normally aspirated model's 260-hp).

The next big change came in 1972, when Cessna (wanting to rid the 310 of the "tunnel effect" that plagues many long-cabin aircraft) put a rear window in the fuselage of the 310Q. Rear passengers got three extra inches of headroom; the top of the one-piece windshield was extended a full nine inches aft; and the panel eyebrow was lowered. These changes brightened the interior environment indeed. Optional fuel capacity became 207 gallons, and gross weight was boosted to 5,300 pounds (from 5,200 in the 310P). Buyers should note that while all 310s built from 1970 to 1974 are 'Q' models, the rear-window and cabin-brightening mods first appeared in 1972, and apply only to serial number 310Q-0401 and up.

The last, and numerically most abundant, of the 310 models was the 310R, introduced in 1975. With the 310R, 285-hp IO-520 engines (1,400-hr. TBO if turbocharged; 1,700 hours otherwise) became standard, and baggage capacity went to a forklift-busting 950 pounds, thanks to a new 350-lb. cargo hold in the NASA-inspired nose. Max fuel stayed at 207 gals. Gross weight was boosted to 5,500 pounds, but useful load, equipped, remained in the 1,900-pound ballpark—about 200 pounds *less* than full-fuel-and-cargo (never mind pilot/pax).

It should be noted that Cessna made hundreds of minor (but important) changes to the 310 over the years; the forgoing discussion is necessarily cursory, and outlines only the most major changes.

Production of the 310 was terminated in 1981, to make way for the T303 Crusader, a clean-sheet-of-paper design that Cessna felt would better serve the light twin market into the 21st century. Actually, the 310's death was accidental; Cessna had not originally intended the T303 as a 310 replacement. Rather, the original T303 (*nee* "Clipper") was a 180-hp super-light twin aimed at the Duchess/Seminole market. Cessna wisely

decided to withdraw from the "trainer twin" arena at the last minute, however, reconfiguring the T303 with 250-hp turbocharged powerplants. By default, the present Crusader—a lesser airplane than the 310 in almost every performance category—took away the 310's niche. The T303 survives; the 310, alas, is history.

Systems

In contrast to the Aztec, Aerostar, and Navajo, the 310 has no engine-driven hydraulics: Gear and flaps are all-electric, with juice supplied by 50-amp (standard) or 100-amp (optional) alternators on each engine. Cowl flaps are manual (unlike those on most Barons, which are electric). Brakes are Goodyear—which is to say, expensive to repair—and tires are odd-sized (6.50x10 on the mains—same as the Cheyenne), thus costly to replace.

It's perhaps worth noting that ARC 300-series avionics came as standard equipment on 310s (even the later models), although many owners have had King or Collins equipment installed. (Nonetheless, the 310 without an ARC autopilot is rare.) Check the black-box assortment carefully before you buy, and price each plane up or down accordingly.

If the 310 has a serious systems sore-point (and it does), it's the ludicrously labyrinthine fuel system, with its plethora of pumps, pressure switches, valves, vapor

return lines, and underwing drains. (With the 207-gal. system, you can count on draining no fewer than 10 petcocks each morning: One for *each* main tank, aux bladder, 20-gallon locker, crossfeed line, and sump/strainer.) The fuel selectors read "on, off, aux, crossfeed"—simple enough, you say—but thereby hangs an invitation to disaster. Aux fuel can't be crossfed, for example, in a single-engine emergency. Nor can wing-bladder fuel be used in the event of failure of an engine-driven fuel pump, since the boost pumps are *inside the tip tanks*. (Also in the tips are *transfer pumps* to ensure that fuel from the front of the tank can be gotten to the rear—where the pickup line is—in steep descents. These pumps are wired to the landing-light circuit breakers and constitute go/no-go items.)

New 310 owners are often amazed to learn that their wing aux tanks—31 gallons each—are good for no more than 60 minutes' use in cruise (sometimes a lot less). That's because excess fuel is returned by the engine-driven fuel pumps not to the aux tanks (whence it came), but to the *tip tanks*. Accordingly, one must burn 60 to 90 minutes' worth of fuel out of the tips before selecting "aux." Otherwise, return fuel, arriving at already full tip tanks, will be pumped overboard out the vents.

Lockers are another story entirely. Some 310s have but one locker tank, in which case the drill is to burn fuel out of the mains, activate

Cost/Performance/Specifications

Model	Year	Average Retail Priced	Cruise Speed (kts)	Fuel (gals)	Useful Load (lbs)	SE Ceiling (ft)	Engine	TBO (hrs)	Overhaul Cost (each)
310A-B	1955-58	$19,000	178	133	1,740	8,000	240-hp Cont. O-470-M	1,500	$ 9,500
310C-F	1959-61	$21,500	191	133	1,795	7,450	260-hp Cont. IO-470-D	1,500	$10,750
310G-H	1962-63	$23,500	191	133	2,037	7,450	260-hp Cont. IO-470-D	1,500	$10,750
310I-J	1964-65	$26,750	194	133	2,037	6,850	260-hp Cont. IO-470-U	1,500	$10,750
310K-L	1966-67	$30,000	193	143	2,075	6,850	260-hp Cont. IO-470-V	1,500	$10,750
310N	1968	$31,000	193	143	2,030	6,850	260-hp Cont. IO-470-V	1,500	$10,750
310P	1969	$37,000	193	184	2,086	6,850	260-hp Cont. IO-470-VO	1,500	$10,750
310Q	1970-74	$40,000-50,000	192	207	2,086	6,680	260-hp Cont. IO-470-VO	1,500	$10,750
310R	1975-81	$55,000-113,000	194	207	2,047	7,400	285-hp Cont. IO-520-M	1,700	$11,250
T310P	1969	$40,000	226	184	2,108	18,100	285-hp Cont. TSIO-520-B	1,400	$13,000
T310Q	1970-74	$42,000-55,000	225	207	2,208	17,550	285-hp Cont. TSIO-520-B	1,400	$13,000
T310R	1975-81	$60,000-123,000	223	207	2,277	17,200	285-hp Cont. TSIO-520-B	1,400	$13,000

the locker transfer pump (which sends locker fuel to the adjacent tip tank), then crossfeed as necessary to balance the main-tank load. With dual lockers, you simply engage the transfer pumps when the mains have burned down to 30 gallons remaining (or less), and wait for two idiot lights to come on when the lockers are dry. (There are no quantity gauges.)

Obviously, the fellow who designed this system needs to have his bed made, and possibly his straps tightened. The rest of us, meanwhile, would do well to study the handbook carefully before (and after) buying or flying a 310.

Comfort and Handling

Interior comfort is excellent in any model 310 (assuming you can abide the outdoor-patio grade carpets and fade-faster-than-memory seats), although noise levels are high enough to sterilize mice. Pilot and copilot sit miles apart, and rear passengers are pinched neither for leg nor shoulder room (except in the 5th and 6th seats, which are best occupied by Billy Barty types). And thanks to a generous array of baggage compartments (even the short-nosed 310Q can take up to 600 pounds in the lockers and aft cabin), no one is obliged to carry groceries on his—or her—lap.

In terms of handling, the 310 offers typical ''big mutha'' control response, with few or no unpleasant surprises. The ponderous roll response for which the 310 is famous has been overplayed somewhat by the airport-lounge lizards. Roll and yaw damping are poor at lower airspeeds, it's true, due to the concentration of mass in the wings (remember, each tip carries 300 pounds of petrol), and inexperienced pilots tend, as a result, to overcontrol on climbout or approach. The key is to keep a light touch. (One eventually learns to ''husband'' the plane's inertia, rather than fidget constantly with the yoke.) The 310 has a ''wallow'' mode, but so do other aircraft. More than one ATP has observed that ''there's no better training for a future Learjet pilot than a couple hundred hours in a 310.''

Cessna 310 Resale Value Chart

In cruise, the plane is a joy to fly. Stabila-tip models (310G thru R) exhibit little or no adverse yaw, and standard-rate turns can be done with feet flat on the floor. Extended hands-off flight does not result in tumbled gyros. Turbulence, however, produces a nauseous Dutch-rolling which can be quite pronounced at high fuel loadings, even in the post-1969 models with ventral-fin tail stingers. (This is where the $2,160 yaw damper option proves its worth.) Maneuvering speed (Va) is a high 148 knots.

Stalls in the 310 are preceded by mild bucking and shuddering (and steep deck angles, if any power is left on); the break and recovery, however, are straightforward and undramatic. Dirty, the stall comes at 63 KIAS; clean, 75.

Flaps are of the DC-3 (split) variety, producing more drag than lift—which is perhaps just as well, since the 310 is difficult to slow down without chopping power (and TBO). The standard slow-down drill is to squeeze off a couple inches of manifold pressure, then apply 15 degrees of flaps at 160 KIAS or below (139 KIAS in early models); then wait. Initial application of flaps is enough to slow the plane down to gear speed (140 knots), and with the gear down, power can slowly be bled off until—established on final

approach—17 inches of manifold pressure remain.

Landing a 310 with dignity calls for finesse (and, some would argue, retro-rockets). Power is best kept at 17 inches until over the threshold, at which time the throttles can *slowly* be brought back and the elevator trim readjusted. (Yoke forces are high in the flare.) The airspeed decay with power reduction is dramatic, and the plane ''pays off'' quickly. At moderate weights, the best landings seem to come about 9 knots above Vso, with some power still on. (If the stall horn sounds, you're in for a thumper.) At very light loadings, on the other hand, good ''stall horn'' landings are accomplishable with fair regularity. Just don't heave back heartily on the wheel after touchdown, or you're liable to pound the tail into the tarmac.

Performance

The 310 offers nosebleed-on-demand performance and thus is closer to the B55 Baron in all-around pep than to the Aztec. Owners of normally aspirated models typically claim 65-percent cruise speeds of 175 knots (at fuel flows of 22 to 26 gph) or 180 knots at 75 percent (burning 28 to 30 gph), at altitudes to 7,500 feet. Turbo models deliver blistering cruise speeds (up to 222 knots at 16,000 feet, burning 32 to 36 gph, at 75 percent), with top speeds of up to

238 knots—considerably better than the Turbo Aztec F (214 knots max) and dangerously close to Duke territory. Only one non-pressurized piston aircraft in current production is faster than the Turbo 310—viz., the Baron 58TC.

Almost all 310s were ordered with auxiliary fuel, and many have the full 207-gal. complement, which presents interesting possibilities for trip planning. Fill the cabin (six seats), and you can go 690 nm with reserves. Fill the tanks, and you can go 1,400 nm with reserves—although you'll be limited to about 450 pounds in the cabin. Fill the cabin, the tanks, and the baggage bays, and you'll be 1,400 pounds over gross.

On one engine, the normally aspirated 310 climbs 330 to 415 fpm; the turbo models 390 to 440 fpm. (The Aztecs deliver about 100 fpm less.) Single-engine ceiling is 17,000-feet-plus in the turbo models; a Baron-like 6,650 to 8,000 feet otherwise (depending on year-model). The 310s with the highest wing- and power-loadings (and therefore the lowest S.E. performance) are the 310K, L, N, P, and Q.

Safety

A special NTSB study of light twin safety covering the years 1972-76 showed the 310 ranking 10th in fatal accidents—and sixth-worst

Transport-like panel (painted battleship grey in later models) is a 310 trademark. Unfortunately, ARC avionics came standard. The panel shown here is from a 1975 model.

overall—out of 20 twin-engine planes studied. The 310 incurred 2.18 fatal accidents per 100,000 flight hours (versus 2.83 for the Barons and 2.60 for the NTSB's "Apache-Aztec" group, which unfortunately was not broken down further), while the total accident rate for the 310 came out to 9.81 per 100,000 flight hours (against 8.29 for the Barons and 7.54 for the "PA-23"). By comparison, the overall accident rate for general aviation as a whole, at the time of the NTSB's special study, was 9.42.

A more recent (October 1983) FAA computer-search of 310 accident statistics shows a grand total of 694 write-ups in the computer, going back to 1959. Major categories (and the number of incidents pertaining thereto) included: wheels-up landings, 139; gear collapses, 183; gear retractions on ground, 23; collision with ground (controlled), 26; collision with ground (uncontrolled), 28; stall, 31; spin, 1; fire in flight, 5; fire on ground, 6; "systems malfunction," 45.

Finally, an NTSB report analyzing accidents from 1978 to 1982 shows 213 total accidents in the five-year period, of which some 55 crashes—or 26 percent—were fatal. The single largest category of mishap (true to the plane's bag-of-bricks reputation): landing accidents.

Some 45 pilots landed their 310s wheels-up in the five-year period, many for reasons having to do with material failure and/or poor maintenance. Hard landings accounted for another 19 accidents (a surprising number of them non-injury);

gear collapses totaled 26. There was some overlap between "hard landing" and "gear collapse" categories, since NTSB allows more than one line in its type-of-accident description.

Interestingly, as many as a quarter of the wheels-up landings happened in conjunction with engine failure or malfunction (despite the fact that either of a 310's alternators—on either engine—will suffice to power the all-electric gear up or down). A typical scenario has the pilot noticing an engine irregularity, and aborting a departure, just after breaking ground—and also just after selecting "gear-up." The plane subsequently settles onto the runway under complete control, wheels retracted.

In several cases, maintenance personnel apparently forgot to reconnect nose gear doors to actuator arms after performing required inspections of combustion heaters (which in early-model 310s are accessible only through the nose gear well). Jamming of the nose gear in the well—and/or breakage of retract arms—is the frequent result.

Many of the "hard landing" and "gear collapse" accidents involved arrivals in which the plane had accumulated some airframe ice; others happened as pilots unfamiliar with the 310 were being checked out by their instructors. In one case, a pilot making an ice-laden arrival, "dropped hard on all three wheels," after which "the right wing outboard of the engine nacelle buckled downward until the right tip tank struck the runway and was dragged along the ground."

The high number of gear-collapse incidents may be related to several factors, including poor maintenance, poor pilot technique, and outright underdesign of landing gear components in early (particularly pre-1970) 310 models. (Cessna issued numerous landing-gear service bulletins in the late 1960s and early '70s.) An aggravating factor, almost certainly, is the heavy torsional loadings placed on trunnions, struts, and brackets as a result of tip-tank "oversteer"

in taxi. (The inertia of the tanks is felt on the ground, as well as in the air.) Many gear-collapse accidents happen during high-speed turn-offs. *Caveat emptor.*

Engine failure or malfunction was a factor in 35 (or 16 percent) of the reported 1978-1982 Cessna 310 accidents, with fuel contamination, fuel exhaustion, and/or poor maintenance accounting, collectively, for over half the cases.

As light aircraft go, the Cessna 310 has a particularly perverse fuel system. Accordingly, one would expect the 310 to rate high in fuel mismanagement accidents. Not necessarily so, however: Only 13 out of 213 accidents (or a little over six percent of 310 mishaps) involved fuel-system-related brouhahas; and of these, several happened as pilots simply flew their airplanes beyond known endurance limits after exhausting all fuel from all tanks. In addition, fuel selectors were unaccountably found positioned between "aux" and "main" positions in several accidents.

Given the 310's high V-speeds, one might expect a disproportionate rate of stall-spin accidents. But the five-year record shows only eight such mishaps (out of 213 mishaps reported). By comparison, there were almost as many accidents involving marijuana overloads (some half a dozen in all).

Two of 55 fatal 310 accidents involved midair collisions. Another involved wake turbulence as a 310 attempted to land behind a Boeing 737 at Orange County Airport in southern California.

There were no airframe breakups listed in the 1978-1982 printouts.

What kind of pilot crashes a 310? PICs tend to be young (in their early 30s, most commonly)—but not inexperienced: Fully a quarter of all 310 accidents from 1978 to 1982 involved pilots with over 500 hours *in type.* (Only 54 of the reported 213 accidents came at the hands of pilots with less than 100 hours in type.) The vast majority—147 out of 213 (or 69 percent)—of aviators

The $19,000 R/STOL conversion substitutes "back and down" Fowler flaps for the 310's standard split flaps. Result: reduced stall speed, lower Vmc.

involved in 1978-1982 Cessna 310 crashes had more than 1,500 hours in their logbooks; 53 (24 percent of the total) had more than 5,000 hours, while 23 pilots—more than 10 percent—had logged 10,000-hours-plus. One 310 fatal accident involved a 69-year-old commercial pilot with 30,087 logged hours. The crash in question occurred on an IFR air-taxi flight. (The pilot evidently became disoriented during a 400-and-one approach in fog and rain.) "Pilot failed instrument check four days before accident," NTSB noted.

The moral: Don't underestimate the importance of proficiency—and good maintenance—in flying a 310 safely . . . regardless of the amount of time in your logbook.

For all-around single-engine safety, the 310 probably ought to be considered on a par with the Baron. The Aztec bests both planes for Vmc (69 knots vs. 75 for the 310, 81 for the Baron), but the 310 and Baron climb half again faster than the Aztec on one, and you don't have to reach to the ceiling to retrim. The 310 and Aztec both have slow gear retraction times (about 13 seconds, versus the later Barons' four), which can be critical in an emergency. But at least the 310 has all-electric gear, and with an alternator on each engine you can be sure the gear is on its way up as soon as you hit the switch (conveniently and logically located above the upper left side of the power quadrant). Many Aztecs have but one hydraulic pump, on the left en-

gine, and a port-engine failure means pumping the gear up by hand. Barons have fast-retracting electric gear, but the switch is in the wrong place.

The Aztec, Baron, and 310 all have emergency exits in addition to the entry door. In the 310, it's the pilot's side window; in the others, it's a back-seat window.

The 310 has one crashworthiness feature worthy of special note: namely, the tip tanks. Contrary to hangar mythology, aesthetics had little to do with locating the 310's main fuel tanks on the tips of the wings. According to one former Cessna engineer who was there at the time, Cessna felt in 1954 that many post-crash fires might be avoided if fuel were stored in detachable-on-impact external tanks. The 310, as a result, was graced with huge metal tunas, held on with quarter-inch bolts. The wisdom of this decision got an early test, as it turns out: One of the factory's first production prototypes crashed-landed wheels-up in a wheat field. The plane shed its tanks on touchdown; a major fire was averted; and the pilots walked away unscathed (and uncooked). External tanks remained a Cessna-twin trademark for many years thereafter.

Maintenance

Of the 310, Baron, and Aztec, the 310 is the clear winner in terms of the fewest number of Airworthiness Directives. Only eight airframe ADs affect the oldest 310s, and of those only one (on fuel-line inspection) is repetitive (every 50 hours). Turbo models have an additional repetitive-inspection AD of their own, requiring 50- and 100-hour look-sees of exhaust risers, slip-joints, ball joints, etc. (With the installation of Inconel parts, some of the 50-hour items are eliminated or rendered 100-hour items, however.) The Baron 58 has 14 airframe ADs; the Aztec, 24.

Some specific ADs to watch for include 69-14-01, which required installation of transfer pumps in the tip tanks of pre-1969 models; 72-03-07, inspection of main landing gear (the 310Q only); 72-14-08, the 50-hour fuel and oil hose inspection; and 76-04-03 and 78-11-05, requiring modification of ARC autopilot actuators.

A review of FAA Service Difficulty Reports on the 310 series going back six years reveals 1,300 reports covering a multitude of (mostly minor) sins. The single biggest category of complaint: landing gear problems (over 260 reports). Unfortunately, few generalizations can be made, as the reports refer to cracks in numerous locations (trunnions, torque links, rod-ends, brackets) on both main and nose gears, covering all models from 'A' to 'R.' One area that does stand out clearly is the nose gear idler bellcrank, P/N 08421022, which appears to break frequently on 310L-N models. (Also, nose gear drag brace doublers, P/N

081308930, crack on 310R models at upwards of 1,200 hours.) Fortunately, the median breakage time of landing gear components appears to be fairly high in most cases. Be wary of airframes that have racked up thousands of Part 135 hours.

Other problem areas suggested by our SDR printout: aileron bearing seizure in 310Rs; aft spar corrosion (from exhaust gases) in all models up through the 310Q; battery box corrosion (all models); leaking bladder tanks (all models with aux tanks); exhaust mufflers, bellows, and ball joints (turbo models in particular); and defective bearings in Prestolite ALV 9407 alternators (on 310R models).

Crankcase cracking appears to be less a problem with 285-hp 310s than with 285-hp Barons (the Baron 58 in particular). Our SDR listing showed up only 20 instances of crankcase crackage in IO-520-powered 310s in the past six years, versus more than 50 such reports for Barons 58s (IO-520-C) in a little over two years. The Baron fleet is older, on average; but it is also smaller. Thus it appears that the 310, by Baron standards, is relatively crack-immune. (Only four Turbo 310s showed up with cracked cases in our SDR printout.) The flip side of this coin is that the IO-470-powered 310 fleet, considered by many people "crack-proof," isn't. We counted no less than ten IO-470 case cracks in the printout (most at or beyond TBO, however).

Modifications

The 310 was the plane, of course, that rocketed Jack Riley to stardom.

In the early 1960s, Riley—having bought the Rajay turbocharger line from TRW— built up a pair of 290-hp turbosupercharged Lycomings and installed them on a 310D (along with pressurized magnetos, three-blade props, one-piece windshield, pointy radome, and King Faisal control yokes) to create the original Riley Rocket. Many of these 300-mph speedsters are still in service, and they occasionally pop up on the used market in the $29,000-35,000 price range. Most have been through the mill, however, and may be in need of considerable refurbishment. TBO is a short 1,200 hours.

Riley later outdid himself by putting 350-hp Navajo Chieftain engines on a few 1964 and later 310s, thereby creating the Turbostream. This mod is still available (for about $140,000) from Air America of Avoca, Pa., which purchased many of Riley's twin-Cessna STCs some years ago. Air America also does a healthy business installing auxiliary fuel tanks (up to 260 gals). Call Air America at 717/343-1228.

If you have a Turbo 310 or 320 made after 1965, RAM Aircraft Modifications of Waco, Texas (817/752-8381) has a 300-hp upgrade costing $32,500; a 310-hp engine swap which puts intercooled TSIO-520-NBs out front to give 253-knot cruise speeds and 550 fpm single-engine rates of climb ($64,000); and a unique 326-hp conversion that involves special RAM-built TSIO-520-NBR engines, for even more performance ($78,500). RAM does only first-quality work, and its STCs often include many worthwhile minor changes to ignition, cooling baffles, and exhaust systems; we can recommend their work highly.

If you own a 310F through Q (normally aspirated), and you want more power, but you don't want turbochargers, consider the Colemill Executive 600 conversion, which, for $38,500, gets you a pair

Here's the 310 instrument panel, circa 1972. Center console allows plenty of room on panel for avionics. Engine gauges are far from the pilot's eye, however.

of fresh 300-horse Continental IO-520-E engines with three-blade props. This is an excellent mod to have for better single-engine performance. Call Colemill at 615/226-4256.

Finally, R/STOL Systems, of Everett, Wash. (206/355-8702) can give your 310G, Q, or R, or T310P/-Q/R the runway performance (and Vmc) of an Aztec, roughly speaking, by replacing your split flaps with wing-widening Fowlers. The installation takes 15 working days and will set you back one C-bill less than $20,000.

Owner Comments

Since 1978, I have owned two Cessna 310s—a 1969 Turbo 310P with Robertson STOL, a 1973 Turbo 310Q with Colemill conversion. Overall, I think the 310 is an outstanding performer, with straightforward handling, excellent comfort, good parts availability and adequate factory support. Since my airplanes have been based at Crested Butte, Col., 8,850 ft. MSL, and the minimum enroute altitude to Denver is over 16,000 ft., high-altitude performance, especially climb performance, is vital in my operations, In this parameter the 310, especially the Turbo 310, performs admirably; however, at the cost of substantial maintenance expense.

A thorough 100-hour (or annual inspection) on a Turbo 310 by a shop experienced in maintaining turbocharged aircraft (and with all that complex, red-hot turbo exhaust machinery, you certainly want an experienced shop) always cost me at least $4,000.

The cost of properly maintaining the Turbo 310 is what drove me to try the Colemill conversion, which replaces the normally aspirated 260-hp IO-470 Continentals with normally aspirated 300-hp IO-520 Continentals. If you don't have to

In 1975, the 310 got a longer snout. Result: more baggage room up front and better landing characteristics, along with a sleeker look.

have the turbo, I strongly recommend this conversion. At mid-cruise weights, the Colemill will still climb at 500 fpm at 10,000-12,000 ft. MSL, and cuts the hourly maintenance cost of the turbo in half.

A couple of points: We have gotten excellent engine life by (I suppose this applies to any aircraft engine) using light power settings and extreme care on sudden temperature changes by gradual power reductions on descent. We have had no problems with cracking cases on the TSIO-520s. One of our cases is still an old "light case" and is performing very well.

The danger of overboost from cold oil is eliminated by using AeroShell Multigrade. We fly into Truckee, Calif., frequently the coldest weather station in the U.S. Cold starts are easy and we suspect engine wear is considerably reduced.

The 320E and F Models have the heavier gear of the 400 Series. If you can locate a clean 320 in the E or F model it can be an excellent buy.

John A. Linford
Oakland, Calif.

●

Our company has owned and operated Cessna 310s for 12 years—a 1967 "L" model for five years and a 1974 "Q" model with a Colemill

conversion (IO-520-E) for the remainder.

It is my belief that normally aspirated engines in the close-cowled 310 should not be operated at over 65 percent power. The small increase in speed with the increased maintenance and higher fuel burn does not justify going to 75 percent power. Our 310 cruises at altitudes of 5,000 and 12,000 at 187 knots at 27 gph. I have operated the IO-470 and the IO-520 engines to TBO and beyond using 65 percent as a maximum.

Tank management in the 310 was designed by somebody with a sense of humor who hoped to keep the pilot alert on long flights. The improved fuel gauges in the "Q" model are not as accurate or convenient as the gauges in the "L" model. When flying on the aux tanks, approximately 10 gph will be returned to the main tanks.

The wing lockers may be Cessna engineering's greatest claim to fame. Four suitcases, four sets of golf clubs, and all sorts of miscellaneous baggage can be loaded in the locker, very close to the c.g.

The annual inspections of the "Q" model have averaged $2,875. These have been higher than I would have anticipated, but they included some heavy maintenance items: i.e., complete rebushing of landing gear, AD on heater, and corrosion problems on wing flap push rods. The problem with the push rods was simple, but the labor to remove and replace the rods was incredible.

The annual maintenance cost has been just above $7.50 per hour. Approximately one-half of this cost has been in the replacement of vacuum pumps (covered in an earlier issue of *Aviation Consumer*) and three alternators that had to be replaced.

I do not believe that there is any light twin available today that has the speed, good looks, and reasonable price of the Cessna 310.

Art Silverman
McKees Rocks, Pa.

Beech Baron 55, 58, 58P

Beech's Baron is widely regarded as the "class" item among light twins — sort of a twin-engine Bonanza — with lots of performance, superb handling and a reputation for luxury and quality.

More than 5,000 Barons have been built over the past 25 years, ranging from the basic 260-hp 55 model to the pressurized 325-hp 58P. As an investment, the standard Baron has few peers, retaining a high proportion of its original value and, in most cases, appreciating steadily after a few years. For all its popularity and excellent reputation, however, some questions about safety and (in recent models at least) quality control deserve attention from the thoughtful used-Baron buyer.

History

The Baron was introduced in 1961 as an outgrowth of the Model 95 Travel Air series. That first Model 55 Baron had 260-hp Continental engines (up from 180-hp on the Travel Air) and a gross weight nearly 700 pounds higher than the Travel Air's. The 55 was Beech's answer to the very popular Cessna 310, which had been introduced six years previously.

The 1962 and 1963 Barons were called the A55, and offered a sixth seat as an option. The fuselage of the A55 was also 10 inches longer than the straight 55's. In 1964 it became the B55, a designation that lasted until production of the 260-hp Baron was suspended in 1983. In 1966, the gross weight of the B55 was increased from 4,880 to 5,100 pounds (actually, the higher gross weight applied to the last 11 of the 1965 models as well). With the gross weight came another nose extension to accommodate a larger front baggage compartment.

In 1966, the 260-hp B55 was joined by the 285-hp C55, which offered blistering performance (242 mph top speed) and 200 pounds more gross weight. The 1966 and 1967 big-engine Barons were the C55s, evolving to the D55 in 1968 and 1969, and finally to the E55 in 1970. Until the end of their production run in 1982, the 260-hp B55 and the 285-hp E55 remained virtually unchanged.

In 1967, the short-lived 56TC Baron was introduced. It was powered by monstrous turbocharged 380-hp Lycoming engines and a cruise speed of 284 mph was claimed. However, only 94 56TCs were sold over the next five years, and the airplane was discontinued after 1971. Apparently the lack of a large six-place cabin and pressurization doomed the airplane, and single-engine characteristics were reportedly, shall we say, challenging.

Taking up the slack from the unsuccessful 56TC in 1970 was the stretched 58 Baron, which at last provided a full six-seat interior instead of the four-plus-two arrangement of the standard-body Barons. It used the same 285-hp Continental engines as the big-engine 55 Barons, and had virtually the same performance as its short-bodied

Top of the Baron line are the 58s, here stacked up with the TC on top and the pressurized model on the bottom. The 58P has one rear left cabin door instead of double doors on the right side of the fuselage.

stablemate. The 58, with its wide double-door entry and club-car seating, has continued to be a strong seller.

In 1975, Beech introduced the pressurized 58P, with 310-hp engines. These were upgraded to 325 hp in 1979. In addition to the pressurization and bigger engines, the 58P has 100 pounds extra gross weight and a cruise speed that is 22 mph higher than the standard 58 (by the book, at least). A "non-pressurized 58P" was introduced in 1976, called the 58TC. The TC has the same engines as the P model, and got the boost to 325 hp at the same time, in 1979. Production was halted in 1982, however.

Investment Value

Like the Bonanza, the Baron is a real blue-chip in resale value in most cases. For example, a 1970 B55 originally cost $13,000 less than 1970 310, but today is worth $7,000 more. The big-engine E55 also looks good; a 1975 E55 cost $146,000 new and is worth $77,500 today (53 percent). A 1975 310 returns 40 percent, and is worth a fat $22,000 less than the E55 on the used-plane market. The 58 series does even better; a 1975 long-body Baron is now worth 56 percent of its original value.

The pressurized Baron 58P, however, doesn't seem to match the rest of the family in resale value. "The P-Baron has taken a real hit on the used-plane market," one big broker told us. Based on Aircraft Price Digest "Bluebook" retail figures, a 1976 P-Baron is today worth under 50 percent of its original price. For a straight 58 Baron, the figure is about 60 percent. "For the same money that a used 58P costs, you can buy a 421 that's just one year older. And the 421 is full cabin class, a hell of a lot more airplane," explained the dealer.

Another resale loser among the Barons is the ill-fated 56TC. The net value of those big engines over the years has been just about zero; a used 56TC is worth almost exactly the same as an E55 of the same vintage, which had non-turbocharged engines of 100 less horsepower each.

Performance

Here is the Baron's strong suit. The big-engine Barons are faster than any light twin except the Aerostar, and the 260-hp 55, A55 and B55 aren't too far behind. Owners report real-world cruising speeds of about 191 knots for the B55 and 195-200 knots for the E55 and 58 models. The turbocharged versions — 56TC, 58TC and 58P — are of course much faster at high altitude, with max cruise speeds rangin from about 209 knots for the 310-hp 58P and TC to well over 217 knots for the monster 56TC. The 325-hp 58TC and 58P, introduced in 1979, are listed by the books as about 9-13 knots faster than their 310-hp counterparts.

Standard fuel capacity in the small-body 55 Barons is normally 112 gallons (100 gallons usable), which gives a rather marginal endurance

of less than four hours, with no reserve. Many 55s have optional tanks that raise capacity to a more reasonable 142 gallons (136 usable), good for over five hours at moderate cruise power. The 285-hp airplanes burn about five gph more than the 260s, so even the 142-gallon tanks are not exactly generous. The 1973 and later E55s, however, have an optional capacity of 166 gallons, which is satisfactory for most IFR flying.

All the 58 models have standard 166-gallon fuel tanks, and most have optional tanks that raise capacity to 190 gallons. Obviously, a used Baron with long-range tanks is more desirable because of the greater flexibility for ultra-long-range flights with light passenger loads. (But extra tanks can be a mixed blessing from the maintenance standpoint. More on that later.)

Takeoff performance of the Baron is also excellent, particularly in the C, D and E55 models. Even at gross weight, an E55 needs little more than 1,000 feet to clear a 50-foot obstacle on takeoff (under standard conditions, of course). This requires some fairly extreme piloting technique that puts the airplane in the air below Vmc, however. With normal technique, takeoff distances under 2,000 feet are still possible at gross weight in the 55 Barons.

Handling

A major reason for the Baron's popularity and owner loyalty is the aircraft's superb handling qualities. The Baron is responsive and well-harmonized, a delight to fly. "The Baron is a beautiful flying aircraft, and it is just plain fun to handle on the controls," is a typical owner comment. There are no handling idiosyncracies (such as severe pitch-up with flap deployment, as in the Aztec) we're aware of. "Real aviators" like the fact that there are no downsprings or aileron-rudder interconnects in most models of the Baron.

The other side of the "responsive" coin is, of course, sensitivity in turbulent IFR conditions. The same light control forces that win oohs and ahs from pilots demand more attention in the clouds, and a good autopilot is almost a necessity in a Baron flown IFR. One owner reports, "I have had several frightening moments because of its unstable flying characteristics in turbulence."

Like the Bonanza, the Baron is famed for its easy landings (except for the 58P), with a combination of pitch response and landing gear geometry that really boosts the egos of pilots. For many pilots, the way an airplane "feels" can overcome many performance shortcomings; the Baron's handling

Baron 55, 58, 58P Resale Value Chart

qualities have doubtless won over hundreds of piltos who may have been on the verge of buying something else.

Accommodations

The Baron pilot sits high, wide and handsome, with a plush, roomy cockpit and a professional-looking panel thankfully devoid of the plastic found in most other airplanes. Headroom is particularly good.

The 55 Barons are labeled "six-seaters," but the two rear seats are cramped afterthoughts, suitable only for kids or midgets on long flights.

The 58 models have the famous "club car" seating, which puts the back four passengers face to face in the style of the Orient Express. Although lacking Orient-Express roominess, the rear compartment of the 58 is adequate by light aircraft standards, and the fifth and sixth seats at least qualify as small-sized adult repositories.

The 58 models also have a big, wide double-door entrance to the rear compartment, a very nice touch. The 55s have the standard single

right-side pilot's door, which entails a certain amount of clambering for the hindmost travelers.

Baggage capacity is good, with front and rear compartments that allow reasonable balancing and good capacities in most models.

Up front, a couple of items on the panel are worth noting. First, the Baron's throttle quadrant is notorious for its reverse throttle and prop postions: the prop lever is on the left, with the throttle in the middle. An airplane could not be certified that way today, but Beech keeps on building them that way for some reason. Also, the gear and flap levers are reversed from their normal position in other aircraft, which could lead to the sound of

Throw-over wheel, reversed throttles and props, and aileron trim are standard on all the Barons. Only this 58P has the gear (left) and flap (right) levers in the standard position.

crunching metal when the pilot retracts the "flaps" during rollout after landing. (The 58P is an exception.) NTSB figures show many accidents of this type. The single throwover yoke is also an unusual feature, one that sometimes makes multi-engine instruction a tricky business (see "Safety" section for details).

Maintenance Checkpoints

The "Curse of the Cracking Crankcase" has depleted the bank ac-

Cost/Performance/Specifications ――――――――――――

* TIO-540-E1B4   ** IO-520-C   *** IO-520-CB

Model	Year	Number Built	Average Price	Cruise Speed (kts)	Rate Climb (fpm)	Useful Load (lbs)	S/E Ceiling (ft)	Fuel Std/Opt (gals)	Engine	TBO (hours)	Overhaul Cost
56TC	1967-1969	83	$ 44,000	247	2,020	2,340	18,000	142/204	380-hp Lyc.*	1,600	$24,000
A56TC	1970-1971	12	$ 47,000	247	2,020	2,390	18,600	142/204	380-hp Lyc.*	1,600	$24,000
C55	1966-1967	451	$ 44,000	200	1,670	2,225	7,100	112/142	285-hp Cont.**	1,500	$11,250
D55	1968-1969	315	$ 49,500	200	1,670	2,225	7,100	112/142	285-hp Cont.**	1,500	$11,250
E55	1970-1971	82	$ 56,000	195	1,682	2,038	6,000	100/166	285-hp Cont.**	1,500	$11,250
E55	1972-1973	95	$ 64,000	195	1,682	2,038	6,000	100/166	285-hp Cont.**	1,500	$11,250
E55	1974	62	$ 69,000	195	1,682	2,038	6,000	100/166	285-hp Cont.**	1,500	$11,250
E55	1975	62	$ 74,000	195	1,682	2,038	6,000	100/166	285-hp Cont.**	1,500	$11,250
E55	1976	23	$ 80,000	195	1,682	2,038	6,000	100/166	285-hp Cont.**	1,500	$11,250
E55	1977	29	$ 87,000	195	1,682	2,038	6,000	100/166	285-hp Cont.**	1,500	$11,250
E55	1978	28	$ 96,000	195	1,682	2,038	6,000	100/166	285-hp Cont.***	1,500	$11,250
E55	1979	25	$110,000	195	1,682	2,038	6,000	100/166	285-hp Cont.***	1,500	$11,250
E55	1980	12	$126,000	195	1,682	2,038	6,000	100/166	285-hp Cont.***	1,500	$11,250
E55	1981	12	$144,000	195	1,682	2,038	6,000	100/166	285-hp Cont.***	1,500	$11,250
E55	1982	5	$164,000	195	1,682	2,038	6,000	100/166	285-hp Cont.***	1,500	$11,250

Cost/Performance/Specifications

* IO-470-L

Model	Year	Number Built	Average Price	Cruise Speed (kts)	Rate Climb (fpm)	Useful Load (lbs)	S/E Ceiling (ft)	Fuel Std/Opt (gals)	Engine	TBO (hrs)	Overhaul Cost
55	1961	190	$ 30,000	191	1,630	1,920	7,600	112	260-hp Cont.*	1,500	$10,750
A55	1962-1963	309	$ 33,000	181	1,700	1,920	7,600	112	260-hp Cont.*	1,500	$10,750
B55	1964-1965	457	$ 36,500	196	1,670	2,025	7,600	112	260-hp Cont.*	1,500	$10,750
B55	1966-1967	76	$ 41,000	196	1,670	2,025	7,600	112	260-hp Cont.*	1,500	$10,750
B55	1968-1969	244	$ 45,500	196	1,670	2,025	7,600	112	260-hp Cont.*	1,500	$10,750
B55	1970-1971	124	$ 48,500	196	1,670	2,025	7,600	112	260-hp Cont.*	1,500	$10,750
B55	1972-1973	204	$ 55,000	196	1,693	2,025	7,600	100/136	260-hp Cont.*	1,500	$10,750
B55	1974	173	$ 60,000	196	1,693	2,150	6,400	100/136	260-hp Cont.*	1,500	$10,750
B55	1975	123	$ 65,000	196	1,693	2,150	6,400	100/136	260-hp Cont.*	1,500	$10,750
B55	1976	96	$ 70,000	196	1,693	2,150	6,400	100/136	260-hp Cont.*	1,500	$10,750
B55	1977	88	$ 76,000	196	1,693	2,150	6,400	100/136	260-hp Cont.*	1,500	$10,750
B55	1978	88	$ 85,000	196	1,693	2,150	6,400	100/136	260-hp Cont.*	1,500	$10,750
B55	1979	94	$ 92,500	196	1,693	2,150	6,400	100/136	260-hp Cont.*	1,500	$10,750
B55	1980	78	$100,500	196	1,693	2,150	6,400	100/136	260-hp Cont.*	1,500	$10,750
B55	1981	65	$120,500	196	1,693	2,150	6,400	100/136	260-hp Cont.*	1,500	$10,750
B55	1982	35	$132,500	196	1,693	2,150	6,400	100/136	260-hp Cont.*	1,500	$10,750

counts of more than a few 285-hp Baron owners. While crankcase cracks are rarely a safety-of-flight item, they can be expensive maintenance headaches. One operator of a fleet of Barons reports he spent over $70,000 in premature overhauls triggered by case cracks.

As you shop for used Barons, you may hear references to "light cases" and "heavy cases." Pre-1976 airplanes had cases which were particularly prone to cracking. Continental then introduced a beefier case which was supposed to lick the problem. It didn't. An *Aviation Consumer* survey in 1982 showed that, if anything, the "heavy" cases cracked a bit more often — and earlier in the engine's life — than the so-called "light" cases.

There have been so many permutations of IO-520-C crankcases that we can't advise one type as preferable to any other. As far as we can tell, they all are prone to crack. More important than case "heaviness" or "lightness" is heat-treating for stress relief. The crankcases are not heat-treated when they come from the factory, but some owners have their cases heat-treated during overhaul or when cracks are repaired. This ap-

parently reduces internal stress in the metal, dramatically reducing the cracking tendency. "I've heat-treated hundreds of IO-520 cases," one repair shop told us, "and not one of them has cracked that I'm aware of."

The bottom line: carefully check the crankcases of any 285-hp Baron considered for purchase. And count it a plus if the case has been heat-treated.

Despite the epidemic cracking crankcases, the Baron's owner loyalty is striking. One hyperenthusiastic 1974 Baron 58 owner wrote us, "Over a period of five years, my Baron operated flawlessly, with very minor problems, except the usual crankcase crack problems occurred at about 950 hours, necessitating the replacement of both engines at considerable expense . . .".

The other big maintenance headache for Barons is the rubber bladder-type fuel cells. The lifetime of these cells can be as low as three or four years, and 10 years seems to be about the maximum. The tanks of any used Baron should be carefully checked for leakage, and a buyer would be wise to set aside a bladder replacement fund for the

inevitable $3,500-plus wallop and accompanying downtime. Like the man in the cigar commercial says, "We're gonna get you. . .".

Some pre-1964 Barons may still have the so-called "light" cylinders, which proved troublesome and are subject to an AD requiring 20-hour inspections.

Other Baron problems to look out for: crazing windshields, unreliable Goodyear brakes, old B-series autopilots (very difficult to get service anymore), electric cowl flaps on pre-1974 models, 100-amp (Presto-Lite or Crittendon) alternators, and Airborne high-capacity vacuum pumps used for de-ice applications.

Safety

In terms of overall accidents, the Baron ranks about average among light twins. Fatal accident rate was also about in the middle of the pack. From 1972-76, the entire Baron/Travel-Air series scored 2.8 and 8.3, respectively, for fatal and total accident rates. The same group improved to 1.4 and 5.3 in 1977-82, for overall scores of 2.0 and 6.5 for the entire decade.

We decided to separate the 58 and

55 models out of the group to see if there was a difference between the long-body 58s and their smaller forebears. The answer: not much. For the period 1977-82 only, the 58 had a low 1.1 fatal rate, while the 55 was a not-quite-so-low 1.4. The 58 also had a better overall accident rate, 4.5 to 6.4

The Baron's accident rate might have been better without a bunch of stall/spin accidents. An earlier study commissioned by *Aviation Consumer* showed that for the years 1970-74, the Baron had a much higher stall/spin rate than other light twins. In fact, about a quarter of all fatal Baron accidents during that period were stall/spins. Eliminate those, and the Baron's accident rate would improve noticeably.

The Baron stall/spin rate has apparently declined in recent years, however, as more attention has been focused on the subject and Beech has mailed Baron owners

handbook supplements warning of the problem. That may be a big part of the Baron's improved accident rate during the last half of the decade.

A 1974 Army test report on the single-engine stall characteristics of the T-42A, the military version of the Baron, sheds some light on the subject. (The special test came after a series of fatal stall/spin accidents during Army training flights.) The Army test pilot reported that the T-42A would enter a spin within one second after a single-engine stall unless immediate anti-spin action was taken. Even if stall recovery was initiated within one-quarter second after the stall break, said the Army report, a split-S and 1,000-foot altitude loss resulted. The author of the report also criticized the T-42A operator's manual for not warning of the serious consequences of a single-engine stall, and not explaining, for example, that single-engine stall speed was up to 20 knots higher than the

listed stall speed under symmetric power conditions.

Later Baron manual revisions carry blunter warnings in the safety section, however.

Modifications

We know of just one Baron engine conversion, the Colemill "President 600," which replaces the 260-hp engines of the 55, A55, or B55 with 300-hp Continentals. It is reportedly an outstanding performer, with no major problems except the possibility of cracked crankcases in pre-1977 conversions.

Cosmetic mods, such as one-piece windshields and updated side windows are available from Beryl D'Shannon, Jordan, Minn.

We know of no owner's organization for the Baron, although the American Bonanza Society newsletter does occasionally

Cost/Performance/Specifications

* TSIO-520-L ** TSIO-520-WB *** IO-520-C

Model	Year	Number Built	Average Price	Cruise Speed (kts)	Rate Climb (fpm)	Useful Load (lbs)	S/E Ceiling (ft)	Fuel Std/Opt (gals)	Engine	TBO (hours)	Overhaul Cost
58P	1976	85	$105,000	207	1,424	2,115	13,220	190	310-hp Cont.*	1,400	$17,000
58P	1977	36	$120,500	216	1,529	2,115	14,400	166/190	310-hp Cont.*	1,400	$17,000
58P	1978	45	$135,000	214	1,529	2,115	14,400	166/190	310-hp Cont.*	1,400	$17,000
58P	1979	65	$150,500	232	1,481	2,200	13,490	166/190	325-hp Cont.**	1,400	$18,000
58P	1980	80	$165,000	232	1,481	2,200	13,490	166/190	325-hp Cont.**	1,400	$18,000
58P	1981	67	$200,000	232	1,481	2,200	13,490	166/190	325-hp Cont.**	1,400	$18,000
58P	1982	46	$235,000	232	1,481	2,200	13,490	166/190	325-hp Cont.**	1,400	$18,000
58P	1983	20	$280,000	232	1,481	2,200	13,490	166/190	325-hp Cont.**	1,400	$18,000
58P	1984	27	$375,000	232	1,481	2,200	13,490	166/190	325-hp Cont.**	1,400	$18,000
58TC	1976	34	$ 90,000	214	1,461	2,320	14,400	166/190	310-hp Cont.*	1,400	$17,000
58TC	1977	25	$ 98,000	214	1,461	2,320	14,400	166/190	310-hp Cont.*	1,400	$17,000
58TC	1978	24	$110,000	214	1,461	2,320	14,400	166/190	310-hp Cont.*	1,400	$17,000
58TC	1979	24	$112,500	232	1,418	2,412	13,450	166/190	325-hp Cont.**	1,400	$18,000
58TC	1980	23	$140,000	232	1,418	2,412	13,450	166/190	325-hp Cont.**	1,400	$18,000
58TC	1981	12	$162,500	232	1,418	2,412	13,450	166/190	325-hp Cont.**	1,400	$18,000
58TC	1982	4	$190,000	232	1,418	2,412	13,450	166/190	325-hp Cont.**	1,400	$19,000
58	1970-1971	174	$ 64,500	195	1,660	2,147	7,000	136/166	285-hp Cont.***	1,800	$11,250
58	1972-1973	209	$ 76,500	195	1,660	2,147	7,000	166	285-hp Cont.***	1,800	$11,250
58	1974-	139	$ 84,000	195	1,660	2,147	7,000	166	285-hp Cont.***	1,800	$11,250
58	1975	154	$ 92,000	195	1,660	2,147	7,000	166	285-hp Cont.***	1,800	$11,250
58	1976	92	$100,000	195	1,660	2,147	7,000	166	285-hp Cont.***	1,800	$11,250
58	1977	99	$110,000	195	1,660	2,147	7,000	136/194	285-hp Cont.***	1,800	$11,250
58	1978	99	$125,500	195	1,660	2,147	7,000	136/194	285-hp Cont.***	1,800	$11,250
58	1979	106	$140,000	195	1,660	2,147	7,000	136/194	285-hp Cont.***	1,800	$11,250
58	1980	113	$155,000	195	1,660	2,147	7,000	136/194	285-hp Cont.***	1,800	$11,250
58	1981	103	$175,000	195	1,660	2,147	7,000	136/194	285-hp Cont.***	1,800	$11,250
58	1982	57	$195,000	195	1,660	2,147	7,000	136/194	285-hp Cont.***	1,800	$11,250
58	1983	30	$220,000	195	1,660	2,147	7,000	136/194	285-hp Cont.***	1,800	$11,250
58	1984	39	$285,000	195	1,660	2,147	7,000	136/194	285-hp Cont.***	1,800	$11,250

publish material about the Baron. Also, the Barons and Bonanzas have enough in common that ABS membership might well benefit from Baron owners.

Owner Comments

Our company has owned three Barons in the past 12 years, and we hated to part with the first two. We purchased our present one, a 1974 B55, when it was a young demonstrator with about 80 hours. We have flown it 1,100 hours now.

Our '68 B55 performed perfectly for 800 hours when we swapped it for a newer '73 E55. A fine aircraft, but we had the usual problems with cracked cases on the 285 engines, noticeably more engine noise and about six more gallons per hour with only five knots or so more speed. A fine plane, but the B55 is even better.

Now take the B55 — responsive, economical (we use only 24 gallons per hour and cruise at 191 knots), very easy to handle in any type of crosswind, gentle in turbulent air, and the 260 Continentals are quiet. The B55 sits good. You are over the panel with a perfect view. Perhaps the cabin is not as dramatic as the 58 model Baron, but most of our flying is with only one or two passengers or alone.

The B55 is primarily a VFR light twin or mild IFR with no heavy weather. We've had ice a few times and it doesn't carry it very well. The Century 3 autopilot guides the B55 perfectly, and it is a fine night aircraft and good for normal instrument operations — but *not* for rough weather.

I took delivery of my new 1974 Beechcraft Baron 58 at the Beechcraft factory. I operated the aircraft for five years, and even though the aircraft was out of warranty, Beech continued to support certain items that they were not legally bound to support.

When I ultimately sold the aircraft,

Model 58P has depreciated much more than other Barons.

the value had held remarkably strong, even against used pressurized aircraft such as the Cessna 340. My depreciation was a mere 10 percent over a five-year period.

Over a period of five years, the Baron operated in a flawless manner with very minor problems, except the usual crankcase crack problems occurred at about 950 hours total time, necessitating the replacement of both engines at considerable expense. However, the airframe and component parts were all well within tolerances, except for the fuel gauges, which never were right.

It is an extremely efficient form of transportation and consistently flies at 190 knots. Over the five-year period it averaged approximately 30 gallons-per-hour at altitudes 8,000 to 12,000 feet.

●

I own a 1977 Beech Baron 55, which I purchased new in 1977. The aircraft now has 675 hours total time and has been piloted only by myself (4,000 hours) and a friend (1,000) who is also multi-engine and instrument rated.

I have been involved in aviation a long time and I had always felt that owning a Beechcraft would be the ultimate in aircraft ownership, but if this aircraft is an example of current Beech quality and workmanship, I would not recommend a Beech Baron to any friends that are contemplating buying an airplane.

In the first year of operation, I had literally scores of malfunctions,

and spent more than $1,000 just to rent aircraft to ferry me back and forth to the maintenance base after dropping off the Baron for repairs.

In addition, the following have happened to my Baron more recently:

1. 400 hours — the right vacuum pump failed.

2. 450 hours — the left magneto on the right engine failed.

3. 500 hours — the heater motor required replacement.

4. 500 hours –- an oil seal in the right propeller hub failed.

5. 550 hours — left engine failed in flight.

6. 575 hours — new starter on remanufactured Continental engine failed.

7. 600 hours — nose gear door control mechanism failed.

8. The hot props do not work, and the wiring is again protruding from behind the spinner.

9. The yaw damper does not work properly.

The ease of handling in VFR flight makes the plane a delight to fly, but the same lightness of control can be hazardous in hard IFR. I have had several frightening moments because of its unstable flying characteristics in turbulence. I still feel that the Baron has the nicest landing characteristics, the best brakes, the best ground handling and the sleekest looks of any aircraft I have ever flown.

Piper Aerostar

Few aircraft have gone through such such dramatic highs and lows as the much-traveled Aerostar series. Although a hot performer, the aircraft has acquired a disastrous accident record.

As the brainchild of the late Ted Smith, the Aerostar was conceived as a kind of universal paradigm from which would spring all kinds of singles and twins, pistons and jets. Offered to and declined by the parent Rockwell company as a successor to the Aero Commanders (that, in turn, had been designed by Smith), the Aerostar project was then launched by the newly formed Ted Smith Aircraft Co., and the first Model 600 was certificated in 1967.

In one short year the aircraft was sold to, of all companies, American Cement. This relationship lasted a little less than two years before the aircraft was once again sold, this time to Butler Aviation. Shortly afterward, however, with the Aerostar name tainted by scandal and charges that the airframe was subject to corrosion because of improper manufacture, Ted Smith took over the airplane again to remove its scarlet letter and set it on a proper course.

This seemed a *fait accompli* when another uproar broke out in 1978 over the design of the Aerostar fuel system, and a number of double engine failures related to it.

Finally, Piper Aircraft Corp. took over the line and incorporated it as an avant-garde step-up from its aging, stalwart Aztec. This coup gave Piper the satisfaction of having acquired a trio of aircraft built on a common airframe, featuring a choice of normally aspirated, turbocharged and pressurized designs. It also presented Piper with the headache of coming up with a fuel system pilots could comprehend and live with.

The fuel system uproar finally died down by 1980, after FAA Airworthiness Directives required several changes. But in 1982, the Aerostar's stall characteristics came under FAA scrutiny. The result was another AD, this one restricting the center-of-gravity envelope unless the tail was modified to improve stall characteristics.

Piper introduced a couple of souped-up Aerostar versions of its own, but the Great Slump of the 1980s prompted Piper to halt production and put the whole Aerostar line up for sale. As this is written, in 1985, the Aerostar is in limbo, out of production and still on the auction block.

But despite their quirks, the Aerostars were the undisputed speed demons of the light-twin fleet.

Aerostars look fast; they fly fast. This means an astonishing 218 knots/251 mph on a normally aspirated pair of 290-hp Lycomings or 240 knots/277 mph with turbos and pressurization at 24,000 feet. By comparison, the old Aero Commander Shrike with the same normally aspirated engines yields only about 176 knots.

Investment Value

The Aerostar models — all three of them — appear to represent an unusually fine investment value, judging from the figures we obtained from tracking three early models.

After a sharp plunge in resale value in just one year, rather than the three to five in normal patterns, the 1970 normally aspirated 600 and the turbocharged 601 leveled off and began ascending. They did not begin to tail off until the early 1980s, when all aircraft values declined.

The 1974 pressurized 601P we tracked never did take the initial plunge most aircraft betray, but instead bounced up and down, pretty well maintaining its initial value until the early 80s.

Model Evolution

The design has undergone few changes of any significance since its introduction in 1969. In 1973, with the 600A and 601A models, a new so-called "K" crankshaft was incorporated in the Lycoming IO-540 engines. This reduced vibration and boosted the TBO significantly from 1,400 to 2,000 hours on the normally aspirated 600As and from 1,400 to 1,800 hours on the turbocharged models. This came about with serial number 0144 and up.

Non-turbocharged 600A was last built in 1981. It has shorter wings than 601 and 601P, but the engines are more reliable.

Aerostar Resale Value Chart

'74 Aerostar 601P

'70 Aerostar 601

'70 Aerostar 600

Year

The next big modification occurred in 1977 with the addition of 30 more inches in wingspan to the turbo models for better high-altitude performance. At the same time the gross weight was boosted by 300 pounds to 6,000 pounds. This began with serial number 213, designated 601B, and in effect brought the turbocharged model up to the same configuration as the pressurized model. The normally aspirated model kept its lower 5,500-pound gross and shorter wing.

Another significant change affecting all three Aerostars in '77 was a hike in the zero-wing-fuel limitation from 5,400 to 5,900 pounds. This eliminated what many felt was a serious payload shortcoming. Since it was a paperwork engineering exercise on the existing structure, it applied retroactively to the older Aerostars as well.

The year '77 was a good one for improvements in other areas as well. The flap extension speed was raised by 18 knots, making it easier to slow down the aircraft, and a positive down lock was incorporated into the landing gear handle to prevent inadvertent retraction of the nosegear on the ground. There is no squat switch on the gear itself, and in one instance the nosegear collapsed with the handle up and the engines running.

Pilots interested in the turbo-charged Aerostars should note that several evolutionary changes were made. The first models had manual waste gate systems that worked off electric rocker switches. These were replaced on the B models with automatic systems. And in 1978 improved Piper waste gate systems were added, replacing the Rajays, giving much better high-altitude performance right up to 25,000 feet. It also boosted the critical altitude from 16,000 to 23,000 feet. Earlier models are described by pilots as going up to 25 grand when new, but then pooping out at lower altitudes after a few hundred hours' use. Dealers report a booming business on retrofitting these new waste gates to older model Aerostars at about $3,200 a set.

In 1981, Piper introduced the 602P, an improved version of the pressurized 601P. The new model had a Lycoming-designed integral turbocharger installation instead of the add-on Rajay units previously used, along with low-compression pistons. These changes were designed to combat the severe engine detonation problems resulting from the earlier jury-rigged turbo system. While offering much better reliability, the 602P unfortunately couldn't match the all-out performance of the 601P — cruise speed was about 10-15 knots slower.

Shortly after introducing the 602P, Piper dropped the unpressurized

600A and 601B models. In 1984, Piper brought out the 700P, with 350-hp engines, but only a couple of dozen were built before the whole line was folded and put up for sale.

Handling Characteristics

Despite its image as a hot ship, the Aerostar is regarded affectionately by most pilots in terms of handling. Control response is quick and deft; an aileron-rudder link allows almost feet-on-the-floor maneuvering. Pilots rave about engine-out characteristics such as an unusually mild yaw reaction with an engine loss during cruise, and a stall speed set above minimum control speed (Vmc) for added protection. Ted Smith like to boast that the aircraft really didn't need a minimum control speed, but the FAA required it.

Despite all this praise from pilots, however, there have been quite a few fatal Aerostar engine-failure accidents in which the pilot was unable to maintain control after losing an engine.

The takeoff perhaps give fliers the most cause for discussion. The aircraft, which rests on the ground with a negative angle of attack, tends to want to stay earthbound, and the heavy load on the nose-wheel calls for a real heave of the control wheel to get the machine rotated and flying. Some advise a partial easing back on the wheel, at 40 to 50 knots, and holding it there to ease the transition to final rotation.

On final approach the aircraft benignly tends to hold the airspeed determined by power setting, reacting hardly at all to variations in pitch.

In taxi operations, the pilot will have to become accustomed to steering not with the rudder pedals in conventional fashion, but by means of an electric rocker switch on the console beneath the throttle quadrant. It sounds eery, but works quite nicely and actually is great fun and allows unusually sharp manuevering on the ramp.

One complaint that surfaces now and again about the Aerostars is vibration. Some blame it on the engines; some the props. One experienced Aerostar pilot has a theory he says he can prove every time. He maintains the problem is not related in any way to engines or proper, but to an idiosyncracy stemming from the heavier than usual skin gauge used in the wings and fuselage.

According to this theory, the vibration is triggered when the aircraft flies through light turbulence, as when ascending or dropping through a haze layer. This sets up a resonant, tuning fork-like vibration in the structure of the airplane that passes when the disturbance layer is passed.

The high wing loading of the aircraft typically handles normal chop with greater than usual aplomb and no abnormal vibration.

The designer's fondness for electric controls has given rise to the Aerostar moniker as an "electric aircraft." Indeed, the center console is home to a raft of unobtrusive electric switches — not only for steering, but for pitch and rudder trim — and even for turbocharging. A pair of rocker switches on the pre-B models allowed the pilot to close and open the waste gate by electric motor with little nudges of the switches. At least this eliminated the need for another pair of power levers on the throttle quadrant. It does leave the pilot is something of a bind, however, if the electrical system or the switches fail. Similarly, the fuel valve is electrically actuated. If the solenoid fails, the pilot may switch the fuel selector but not realize that the valve itself has failed to respond.

Cabin Comfort

With the constant-section fuselage, none of the up to six riders on the Aerostar can boast of more, or complain of less space, which is quite plentiful, with a small aisle between the seats. Though no conventional club-seating is available, there is a fold-out table arrangement for five seats.

Thanks to the big cabin windows, everybody has lots of light. Thanks to the mid-wing arrangement, though, only the pilots really have a great view of anything except the sky and the wing and engine nacelles. Pilot visibility naturally is fantastic.

The greatest discomfort burden Aerostars have imposed through the years is one of terrible cockpit din, thanks to the droning of the props right outside the window. Pilots report the anguish diminished in stages with later models— especially the pressurized ones—as more and more soundproofing measures were taken.

Baggage

The Aerostars will carry a healthy amount of baggage — up to 240 pounds — but it must be heaved into a chest-high compartment accessible only from the outside rear fuselage. One loading quirk to look out for: the Aerostar is at its most tail-heavy with only a solo pilot aboard. This is because of the aft wing placement, which puts all the passengers ahead of the center of gravity. Unlike virtually all other aircraft, which have the c.g. position at about the pilot's seat, the Aerostar gets progressively nose-heavier as passengers are loaded.

Systems Engineering

Aside from the lack of nose-gear squat switch previously mentioned, which may result in inadvertent, unwanated retraction, the Aerostar lacks another feature in standard configuration that might result in failure to retract when it is most desired — on takeoff with failure of the right engine, housing the single hydraulic pump. An electric hydraulic pump is offered as an important option, however.

The shortcoming on which the most attention has been cast, of course, involves the fuel system. The Aerostars have a 44-gallon fuselage tank and wet wing tanks, each of which holds 66.5 gallons. Though everything is supposed to work automatically, with no need

Cost/Performance/Specifications

Model	Year	Cruise Speed (kts)	Useful Load (lbs)	SE Ceiling (ft)	Fuel (gals)	Engine	TBO (hrs)	Overhaul Cost	Average Price
600	1969-70	224	1,760	6,150	174	290-hp Lyc. IO-540-G1B5	1,400	$14,500	$ 48,000
600A	1973-75	224	1,760	6,150	174	290-hp Lyc. IO-540-K1F5	2,000	$14,500	$ 67,500
600A	1976-78	224	1,760	6,150	174	290-hp Lyc. IO-540-K1F5	2,000	$14,500	$ 87,000
600A	1979	224	1,760	6,150	174	290-hp Lyc. IO-540-K1J5	2,000	$14,500	$ 96,000
600A	1980	224	1,760	6,150	174	290-hp Lyc. IO-540-K1J5	2,000	$14,500	$106,000
600A	1981	224	1,760	6,150	174	290-hp Lyc. IO-540-K1J5	2,000	$14,500	$116,000
601	1969-70	233	1,950	10,800	174	290-hp Lyc. IO-540-P1A5	1,400	$14,500	$ 52,500
601A	1973-76	233	1,950	10,800	174	290-hp Lyc. IO-540-P1A5	1,800	$14,500	$ 75,000
601B	1977-78	233	2,040	9,300	174	290-hp Lyc. IO-540-S1A5	1,800	$14,500	$ 87,000
601B	1979	233	2,040	9,300	174	290-hp Lyc. IO-540-S1A5	1,800	$14,500	$ 97,000
601B	1980	233	2,040	9,300	174	290-hp Lyc. IO-540-S1A5	1,800	$14,500	$107,000
601B	1981	233	2,040	9,300	174	290-hp Lyc. IO-540-S1A5	1,800	$14,500	$117,000
601P	1974-75	230	1,950	9,300	174	290-hp Lyc. IO-540-S1A4	1,800	$14,500	$ 78,500
601P	1976-77	230	1,950	9,300	174	290-hp Lyc. IO-540-S1A5	1,800	$14,500	$ 91,000
601P	1978	230	1,950	9,300	174	290-hp Lyc. IO-540-S1A5	1,800	$14,500	$ 99,000
601P	1979	230	1,950	9,300	174	290-hp Lyc. IO-540-S1A5	1,800	$14,500	$107,500
601P	1980	230	1,950	9,300	174	290-hp Lyc. IO-540-S1A5	1,800	$14,500	$116,000
601P	1980	230	1,950	9,300	174	290-hp Lyc. IO-540-S1A5	1,800	$14,500	$135,000

to switch tanks, it is critical always to have fuel in the fuselage tank. Otherwise, inadvertent unporting of the supply line from either of the wing tanks to its respective engine, in a climb or dive, can result in engine stoppage. Line crews must always be advised to fill the center tank first.

However, in some situations, the fuselage tank does not feed evenly along with both wing tanks, as it should, and depletion of the center tank can trigger a single or a double engine stoppage.

Adding to the confusion was a fuel-monitoring setup that allowed the pilot to read either total fuel in all three tanks or fuel in the left or right wing separately. But he must calculate the amount of fuel in the fuselage tank. The fact that the fuel quantity gauge was located on the very right extreme corner of the instrument panel way out of the pilot's normal scan certainly did not improve the situation.

The first fix to preven inadvertent depletion of the center tank was an Airworthiness Directive mandating a low-fuel warning light for the center tank. Later, a sweeping AD required installation by Dec. 31, 1979 of a new triple fuel gauge showing fuel levels simultaneously in all three tanks. Or owners might install a single gauge showing a continuous readout of the center tank, with provision for switching to readouts on left or right wing tanks separately.

The AD also required a series of checks to insure a good seal of fuel filler caps and reduced the max usable fuel from 174.5 to 165.5 gallons (41.5 gals. in the fuselage tanks and 62 gals. in each wing tank). In addition, an overpressure relief valve

Aft wing placement puts all passengers ahead of the c.g. Aft limit is pushed with pilot only.

was ordered installed in the wing tanks.

The reason for the fuel cap checks was to prevent negative pressures from developing in the wing tanks, restricting fuel flow and causing premature depletion of the fuselage tank.

FAA tests made in connection with the AD also showed that it is rarely possible to fill the wing tanks to their full capacity unless the aircraft is dead level on the ramp and special fueling procedures are used. With normal fueling techniques, discrepancies up to nine gallons were noted. This is because of the configuration of the wing tanks and the lack of dihedral in the wings.

Safety Record

The Aerostar ranks dead last among light twins in safety. According to statistics compiled by *The Aviation Consumer*, it has a fatal accident rate of 4.4 per 100,000 hours — about double that of the typical light twin and more than triple the rate of the Beech Baron, a closely comparable aircraft. Total accident rate is 12.9, again much higher than the average light twin. The Baron's overall rate is 4.9.

Most of the Aerostar's fatal accidents are related to the design of the airplane, in our opinion. Weather played a surprisingly small role in Aerostar accidents, in contrast to most other aircraft. During the period 1978-82, there wasn't a single fatal IFR approach accident in an Aerostar and only about 25 percent of the Aerostar fatals involved weater. (By contrast, 75 percent of the Baron fatals involved weather.)

If weather isn't killing Aerostar pilots, what is? Forty percent of Aerostar fatal accidents followed engine failures of some sort; 35 percent resulted from stalls and/or spins. The pilots in fatal Aerostar crashes, although generally of broad flying experience, tended to have few hours in the Aerostar. Median experience was just 70 hours in type, compared to 300

hours in type for pilots of fatal-crash Barons

Other ADs

Other significant ADs included several in 1970 and '71 involving: installing a kit to prevent failure of the wing flap tracks and jamming the ailerons; inspection of fuel pressure indicators for ruptured diaphragms to prevent fuel discharge into the engine compartment and possible fire; inspection of the cabin door lock pins to prevent possible separation of the door; replacing the main landing gear side brace assemblies to prevent collapse of the gear.

The 1983 anti-stall AD restricted the aft center-of-gravity envelope when flaps are down. The restriction may be lifted if one of two tail modifications is made to improve the stall characteristics. One mod is the Piper factory fix, a moveable ventral fin connected to the rudder. (Its nickname is "the water rudder.") An alternative mod is a set of vortex generators on the vertical tail (along with stall strips and other wing mods) offered by Machen, Inc. in Spokane, Washington, a highly-regarded mod shop that specializes in Aerostars. According to pilots we talked to, the Machen mod is superior; try to find an Aerostar with this mod rather than Piper's.

Maintenance

Owners who reported to us seemed on the whole satisfied with their maintenance experience with the aircraft, and characterized it as average. They described factory backup with the Ted Smith organization as fair to good, but had not had sufficient experience to rate the new Piper management. However, one owner reported that he had misgivings. "My only reservations stem from the Piper takeover . . . and their distribution and service policies," he said. "One of my reasons for purchase of the Aerostar from Ted Smith was to avoid the problems with which I was plagued during my ownership of four different Piper aircraft.''

No significant patterns of maintenance difficulty showed in owner comments, except we received several complaining about wing fuel tank leakage around the rivets.

The average cost of an annual inspection reported to us was $1,700.

As for parts availability, more owners rated it good or average than terrible, under Ted Smith's aegis, at least.

The brouhaha in 1970 over Aerostar corrosion problems was triggered when Butler Aviation International brought suit against American Cement Corp. in seeking to rescind its acquisition of the Aerostar line. The FAA, however, never grounded any Aerostars after inspecting more than 100 of the 130 or so built at that time. The agency said many of the aircraft showed no evidence of corrosion, though others had some, but none serious enough to ground the aircraft.

Summary

In all, then, the Aerostars might well be regarded as the cream of the owner-flown twins in terms of speed, looks and handling. They get much more performance out of 580 or so horsepower than any other airplane in their class.

Up until now the Achilles heels have been the fuel system and stall traits. The FAA-mandated modifications, however, should make the airplane more manageable and safer, provided the pilot knows the aircraft's idiosyncracies and how to cope with them.

Owner Comments

I selected my Model 601P Aerostar after owning a Piper Arrow 180D, an Aztec D and E and a Turbo B-Navajo.

Late-model 601B is the fastest of all the Aerostars, with a blistering 270-mph cruise.

After 350 hours' operating time, I cannot express sufficiently the satisfaction I have received from my Aerostar. No fuel problems have been apparent, and outside of minor waste gate controller adjustment, the aircraft has been free of any problems normally associated with a new aircraft and so evident in the ownership of my previous Piper aircraft.

●

My total maintenance, other than the normal oil filters and grease, has been as follows: brake shoes replacement at 275 hours; main landing gear tires at 275 hours; two ADs on fuselage drain and landing gear scissors; one hydraulic pump failure (warranty).

The interior appointments are outstanding, and the exterior paint has been subjected to severe weather involving heavy rain, snow, ice and hail, but remains in excellent condition.

When comparing all my previously owned aircraft, I find the Aerostar in a class by itself. The workmanship of the aircraft, as well as its performance, put it more in the class of heavy commercial aircraft. The heated windshield installation in the near future will complete my needs for this outstanding aircraft.

The performance data as outlined on the specifications sheets has been, in each case, easily achieved or exceeded.

My only reservations stem from the Piper takeover in May of 1978 and their distribution and service policies. One of my big reasons for purchase of the Aerostar from Ted Smith was to avoid the problem with which I was plagued during my ownership of four different Piper aircraft.''

●

We have owned two 600As and have found both to be fantastic airplanes when compared to their competition.

They are truly the 'sportscars' of the recip aircraft — agile, responsive and fast on less fuel than an Aztec, Turbo 310 or C model Baron. The 600A has a range and performance ahead of any of these.

Like all aircraft, it has drawbacks, such as more than its share of AD notes. It's a little noisier than most of the competition, but a big plus is parts availability. We have bought both while they were damaged, and parts availability is unsurpassed in the industry.

We ordered and received all the parts and repaired the aircraft in less time than it took us to receive a left-hand gas tank for a V35 Beech Bonanza — AOG (three months and two days).

●

We purchased a 1974 600A Aerostar new, early in 1975 and have flown it for 1,100 hours. I am extremely pleased with the Aerostar.

We have been lucky (I am told) with maintenance. We have experienced only two delays for mechanical reasons. One was for magneto problems (cracked magneto block), and one starter failure at a private grass airport.

We have experienced no problems with parts, since we have required few. The plane is a joy to fly. With our normal light loads we always get a true 210 knots from 10-12,000 feet and an average fuel burn of 28 gph. Our complaints are only two: noise level and vibration.

When all is said and done, I believe it is a great plane, and we would again buy the Aerostar today.

Index